THE MAKING O1

The Making of Modern Turkey

Nation and State in Eastern Anatolia,
1913–1950

UĞUR ÜMIT ÜNGÖR

OXFORD
UNIVERSITY PRESS

OXFORD
UNIVERSITY PRESS

Great Clarendon Street, Oxford OX2 6DP

Oxford University Press is a department of the University of Oxford.
It furthers the University's objective of excellence in research, scholarship,
and education by publishing worldwide.

Oxford is a registered trade mark of Oxford University Press
in the UK and in certain other countries

First published 2011
First published in paperback 2012

British Library Cataloguing in Publication Data

Data available

Library of Congress Cataloging in Publication Data

Data available

ISBN 978–0–19–960360–2 (Hbk)
ISBN 978–0–19–965522–9 (Pbk)

Contents

Preface

This book argues that from 1913 to 1950, the Young Turk regime subjected East Anatolia, an ethnically heterogeneous space, to various forms of nationalist population policies aimed at ethnically homogenizing the region. It builds upon the work of other scholars who evolved the thesis that the international system of nation states throughout the past two centuries developed from a pre-national global order of states with culturally heterogeneous territories, into a self-perpetuating system of nation states that produces nationalist homogenization by virtue of various forms of population policies. The book is limited in time and space to addressing population policies in the Young Turk era (1913–50) in Eastern Turkey. It begins with the Young Turk seizure of power in the 1913 coup d'état and ends with the end of Young Turk rule in 1950.[1] It will describe how Eastern Turkey as an ethnically heterogeneous imperial shatter zone was subjected to various forms of nationalist population policies aimed at transforming the region into an ethnically homogeneous space to be included into the Turkish nation state.

How was Eastern Turkey moulded by Young Turk population policies? Why was the Turkish process of nation formation so violent in this region? Why do political elites launch policies to increase homogeneity in their societies? These will be the guiding questions in this book. The focus will be on an account of the implementation of these nationalist population policies in the eastern provinces, in order to discuss the policies in detail. This book argues that the Young Turk nationalist elite launched this process of societal transformation in order to establish and sustain a Turkish nation state. In this process, ethnically heterogeneous borderland regions were subjected to more encompassing and more violent forms of population policies than the core regions. The eastern provinces were one of these special regions. This book highlights the role played by the Young Turks in the identification of the population of the eastern provinces as an object of knowledge, management, and radical change. It details the emergence of a wide range of new technologies of population policies, including physical destruction, deportation, forced assimilation, and memory politics, which converged in an attempt to increase population homogeneity within the nation state. The common

---

[1] A brief note about terminology is in order. In this study, I will follow Zürcher's use of the term 'Young Turk era' to bundle together the Committee of Union and Progress (CUP) (Ittihad ve Terakki Cemiyeti) and its descendant the Republican People's Party (Cumhuriyet Halk Partisi), which ruled the Ottoman Empire and the Turkish Republic in the period 1913–50. This study advances the argument that a strong continuity of population policies can be observed between the CUP era (1913–18) and the Kemalist era (1919–50). Erik-Jan Zürcher, 'The Ottoman Legacy of the Turkish Republic: An Attempt at a New Periodization', in: *Die Welt des Islams* 32 (1992), 237–53. 'Eastern Turkey' will refer to the area east of the line Adana-Giresun, more or less bounded by the former Ottoman provinces of Sivas, Erzurum, Trabzon, Van, Bitlis, Mamuret-ul Aziz, Aleppo, and Diyarbekir—the latter being the main theater of exemplification in this study.

denominator to which these phenomena can be reduced is the main theme of population policies.

The dominant paradigms in the historiography of the great dynastic land empires can be characterized as a nationalist paradigm and a statist paradigm. According to the first paradigm, the phenomenon of nationalism led to the dissolution of the empires. Centrifugal nationalism nibbled at the imperial system for several decades until the empire crumbled into nation states. Due to their relatively early acquaintance with nationalism, the main force behind this nationalist disintegration was often located among minority groups such as Czechs, Serbs, Greeks, and Armenians. In this interpretation, the Young Turks too, were a nationalist movement that reacted to minority nationalisms by pushing for the establishment of a Turkish state in the Ottoman Anatolian heartland. In 1923, they succeeded when a unitary Turkish nation state rose from the ashes of the Ottoman Empire.

Albeit not totally diametrically opposed to this paradigm, the statist paradigm emphasizes the imperial state context, claiming that the imperial political agendas were dominated by retaining what was left of their land and regaining formerly lost territory. Persecutions and deportations are seen as a guarantee to obviate potentially disloyal groups and establish a loyal demographic majority in case of postconflict territorial negotiations. By considering the problem from this angle for the Ottoman case, the persecutions can be seen as the result of calculated plans to preclude external meddling in Ottoman internal affairs by 'abolishing' the minorities. The deportations and massacres were thus born out of the contingencies and exigencies of war and state security, and the Young Turks merely improvised and reacted to these pressures. Most of their decisions and measures ran counter to a purely nationalist program and reveal a much more utilitarian, *Realpolitik* approach. According to the statist paradigm, they were by no means stalwart believers in ideologies of nationalism.

This study will attempt to challenge both of these paradigms by emphasizing that they are not mutually exclusive, and that all of their differences are not completely reconcilable. The relationship between state formation and nation formation, as two disparate but cognate phenomena, needs to be closely scrutinized. Two prior studies of Eastern Turkey have functioned as inspirational sounding boards for this book. Mark Levene argued that once the Western nation-state system had percolated into Ottoman minds, it was only a matter of time before the empire's eastern provinces would become a contested territory for nationalist elites pursuing their own visions of future nation states. When the Young Turks gained the upper hand and launched their policies of ethnic homogenization that engulfed a range of victims, it was the model of the nation state they had in mind.[2] Hans-Lukas Kieser's authoritative study of the eastern provinces describes the origins and manifestations of the coming of nationalism to the region.

---

[2] Mark Levene, 'Creating a Modern "Zone of Genocide": The Impact of Nation- and State-Formation on Eastern Anatolia, 1878–1923', in: *Holocaust and Genocide Studies* 12, no. 3 (1998), 393–433.

Kieser also discusses the homogenizing efforts between 1913 and 1938 and argues that these can be seen as nation-state policies on an imperial scale. Armenians and Kurds became differential victims of these forces in different periods, but for similar reasons.[3] These studies approach the history of Eastern Turkey from a long-term perspective, and both focus on nationalism as a catalyst for violent social change.[4] This book extrapolates from these, and other studies by deepening the notion of nationalist homogenization and demonstrating that the treatment of minorities were integral parts of the Young Turk utopia of the homogeneous nation state.

This book can be located in the field of historical sociology, the comparative, theoretical, and historical study of human societies. It is a combination of process analysis and pattern identification that together forms a sociologically informed history.

Process analysis identifies causal mechanisms of broad scope as well as conditions that affect activation, interaction, and outcomes of those mechanisms. It tries to determine how, why, and under what conditions certain processes (in our case, population policies) have developed. Reconstructing these processes by which societies change engages historical sociologists in looking simultaneously at organizational settings, individual biographies, interpersonal networks, contested bodies of thought, and connections among all of them.[5] From this particular lens, this is not an expressively bottom-up or top-down study, or feminist, subaltern or deconstructivist study. It does not exclusively feature chronologies of decision-making processes in power centres based on primary sources, nor present narratives of the lived experiences of the people based on oral histories. Rather it sets out to trace policies and processes in their relative integration and comprehensiveness.

Pattern identification is the search for recurrent structures and sequences across time and space. This methodology assumes that causally independent, particular historical episodes that may seem unique in fact do not only spring from a common historical source, but also resemble each other as they follow common principles, abstracted from time and place.[6] It is a secondary, more modest aim of this book that its outcomes will serve for future studies focusing more on pattern identification, by comparing how processes of population policies repeat themselves in similar forms in other societies as well. Even though this book is not in execution a comparative study, the history of this particular region is by no means unique from a global perspective. This implicitly comparative approach takes up several critical concepts (state formation, nation formation, mass violence, and population

---

[3] Hans-Lukas Kieser, *Der verpasste Friede: Mission, Ethnie und Staat in den Ostprovinzen der Türkei 1839–1938* (Zürich: Chronos, 2000); id., 'Modernisierung und Gewalt in der Gründungsepoche des türkischen Nationalstaats (1913–1938)', in: *Geschichte in Wissenschaft und Unterricht* 57, no. 3 (2006), 156–67.

[4] See also: Fikret Adanır and Hilmar Kaiser, 'Migration, Deportation, and Nation-Building: The Case of the Ottoman Empire', in: René Leboutte (ed.), *Migrations et migrants dans une perspective historique: permanences et innovations* (Florence: European University Institute, 2000), 273–92.

[5] Norbert Elias, 'Zur Grundlegung einer Theorie sozialer Prozesse', in: *Zeitschrift für Soziologie* 6 (1977), 127–49.

[6] Ton Zwaan, *Civilisering en Decivilisering: Studies over Staatsvorming en Geweld, Nationalisme en Vervolging* (Amsterdam: Boom, 2001), 19–36.

politics), and makes the historical narrative more wieldy by applying geographic and chronological restrictions.

CONCEPTS

In this book, the two concepts of 'population policies' and 'social engineering' are central to my understanding of the techniques of nation formation. Therefore, it is important to unpack these concepts as analytical categories by briefly discussing my working definitions.

In a comparative study, Maria Quine argued that the emergence of the academic discipline of demography sensitized political elites to the composition of the population as a focus of state policy: 'Society became a laboratory and the body a battleground for would-be planners urging politicians to intervene directly in the evolutionary process'. These statesmen shared a belief 'that the state should intervene in the private sphere in order to promote desirable biological and social change'.[7] Milica Zarkovic Bookman introduced a helpful taxonomy of these policies. She distinguishes six strategies of social engineering for their prevalence and relevance. These include: (1) tampering with census numbers; (2) pro- and anti-natalist policies to raise the birth rate relative to that of perceived rival groups; (3) forced assimilation of rival groups into one's own cultural identity; (4) forced population movement to dilute the proportion of undesirable elements in particular areas; (5) boundary alterations to tilt certain subnational units' numerical balances in their own favour, or outright irredentism; and (6) economic and political pressures and incentives to make certain group members feel inclined to leave the country.[8] Homogenization of nation states is thus pursued by means of a range of strategies extending from the least coerced policies such as gradual integration to massively violent ones including genocide. Heather Rae provides a detailed analysis for nationalist homogenization in the modern system of sovereign, identity-based states. She argues that whereas processes of nation-state formation developed autonomously in Western Europe, in many other cases across the globe, political elites actively pursued policies of 'pathological homogenization'.[9] The key point of difference is unintended consequences versus deliberate policy.

Few scholars have understood this difference as well as Zygmunt Bauman. My argument will engage with his thought-provoking description of social engineering: 'Policies meant to bring about a social order conforming to the design of the perfect

---

[7] Maria Sophia Quine, *Population Policies in Twentieth-Century Europe: Fascist Dictatorships and Liberal Democracies* (London: Routledge, 1996), 14–15, 132.

[8] Milica Zarkovic Bookman, *The Demographic Struggle for Power: The Political Economy of Demographic Engineering in the Modern World* (London: Frank Cass, 1997). For a study emphasizing deportation as the main form of demographic engineering, see: John McGarry, '"Demographic Engineering": The State-Directed Movement of Ethnic Groups as a Technique of Conflict Regulation', in: *Ethnic and Racial Studies* 21, no. 4 (1998), 613–38.

[9] Heather Rae, *State Identities and the Homogenisation of Peoples* (Cambridge: Cambridge University Press, 2002).

society'. This perfect society is a garden in which targeted groups are 'weeds' that must be destroyed, 'not so much because of what they are, as because of what the beautiful, orderly garden ought to be'. This is an inclusive as well as exclusive process, based on an ideological utopia (or utopian ideology) aimed at creating perfection.[10] Another definition of social engineering, one that emanates from Soviet studies, is offered by Amir Weiner: 'A comprehensive plan for the transformation and management of society, one that would create a better, purer, and more beautiful community through the removal of unfit human weeds'.[11] Finally, Donald Bloxham offered a recent definition that is concise and pointed. For him, social engineering and population policies are interchangable concepts, 'a series of coercive state measures in pursuit of population homogeneity'.[12] What these definitions have in common are the factors of concentrated political power and radical utopian ideology. In the period under discussion here, a combination of these two fatal elements were present.

SOURCES

In this historical study, other disciplines such as sociology, anthropology, and political science will be raided, and an eclectic mixture of their methods used: theory, oral history, and archival investigation.

The various aspects and consequences of Young Turk population politics are widely documented in official and unofficial documentary collections, private archives, parliamentary proceedings, memoirs, party protocols, missionary collections, consular correspondence, manuscripts, diaries, maps, photo collections, oral histories, and many other sources around the globe. The bulk of these primary sources exist in the states that were involved in one way or the other in Eastern Turkey, most notably the Ottoman Empire, Germany, Austria-Hungary, France, Russia, Italy, Great Britain, Denmark, Persia, and the United States. This corresponds to an enormous corpus of source material that is mostly stored in the official state archives of these countries, in Istanbul, Berlin, Vienna, Paris, Moscow, Rome, London, Copenhagen, Tehran, and Washington. Equally relevant collections are kept in the military archives, of which the Ottoman ones are in Ankara, the German ones in Freiburg, and the Russian ones in Moscow. Considerable parts of these archival collections have been published and all these archives have been opened for research, albeit under differing conditions. Several non-state collections, too, bear importance for the study of this episode and have been partly used. These include the archives of the American Board of Commissioners for Foreign Missions

---

[10] Zygmunt Bauman, *Modernity and the Holocaust* (Oxford: Polity, 1989), 91.

[11] Amir Weiner, 'Nature, Nurture, and Memory in a Socialist Utopia: Delineating the Soviet Socio-Ethnic Body in the Age of Socialism', in: *The American Historical Review* 104 (1999), 1114–55, at 1115; id. (ed.), *Landscaping the Human Garden: Twentieth-Century Population Management in a Comparative Framework* (Stanford, CA: Stanford University Press, 2003).

[12] Donald Bloxham, *Genocide, the World Wars and the Unweaving of Europe* (London: Vallentine Mitchell, 2008), 101.

(ABCFM), the collections of Dominican missionaries in the Bibliothèque du Saulchoir in Paris, and Danish non-governmental materials in the Danish national archives.

A wealth of other sources can be tapped when studying Young Turk population policies. These include for example newspapers, the ones of the armistice era (1918–23) being particularly useful. In these years, the atmosphere of freedom brought veritable torrents of articles on the violence of the population policies. The newspapers that were tolerated by the Young Turk regime are useful insofar as they offer a glimpse of how the regime propagated its ideology to the masses. Official state reports of various committees and inspectorates were published by the regime and by scholars who found these reports during their research.[13] Memoirs of contemporaries are a relatively unreliable but nonetheless indispensable source of places, times, persons, and stories that can show how subjective perceptions of the world by political elites shaped their attitudes and policies. They often contain information lost or censored in the etiquette of official correspondence. There is a large body of memoir literature of Young Turks, various European diplomats involved in Turkey, Armenian survivors of the genocide, and various nationalist activists. Most of these are ridden with apologia. Furthermore, since in this time-frame Eastern Turkey was a peasant society consisting mostly of illiterate villagers, the number of memoirs that detail the lives of these local people can be counted on the fingers of one hand. For this study, one name is indispensible in this regard: Mıgırdiç Margosyan, an Armenian author from Diyarbekir city. With remarkable vitality of style, a good sense of realism, and with a darkly humorous edge, Margosyan has chronicled the aftermath of the genocide and the ebb and flow of the 1940s in at least nine books that proved very useful for this research.[14]

This study also utilized oral history. For the past five years, I have continuously searched and fortunately also found respondents willing to relate their personal experiences or their family narratives. These interviews were semi-structured and taped; in some cases I took notes. While some of these witnesses of the era were unwilling, or unable to speak, and some agreed to speak but wished to remain anonymous, many others were happy to speak, and occasionally even provided me access to their personal documents. My subject position as a 'local outsider', being born in the region but raised abroad, facilitated the research as it gave me the communicative channels to delve deep and then recede at the right times. It also provided me with a sense of immunity from the dense moral and political field in which most of this research is embedded.[15] The quest for the exclusionary practices

---

[13] See e.g. the appendices in: Cemil Koçak, *Umûmî Müfettişlikler (1927–1952)* (Istanbul: İletişim, 2003), 295–330; Mehmet Bayrak (ed.), *Kürtler ve Ulusal-Demokratik Mücadeleleri: Gizli Belgeler—Araştırmalar—Notlar* (Ankara: Özge, 1993); id., *Açık-Gizli/Resmi-Gayriresmi Kürdoloji Belgeleri* (Istanbul: Öz-Ge, 1994).

[14] *Li Ba Me Li Wan Deran* (Istanbul: Avesta, 1999); *Gâvur Mahallesi* (Istanbul: Aras, 2002); *Çengelliiğne* (Istanbul: Belge, 1999); *Biletimiz İstanbul'a Kesildi* (Istanbul: Aras, 2003); *Söyle Margos Nerelisen?* (Istanbul: Aras, 1998); *Kirveme Mektuplar* (Diyarbakır: Lis, 2006); *Tespih Taneleri* (Istanbul: Aras, 2007); *Kürdan* (Istanbul: Aras, 2010); *Zurna* (Istanbul: Avesta, 2009).

[15] Jukka Törrönen, 'The Concept of Subject Position in Empirical Social Research', in: *Journal for the Theory of Social Behaviour* 31, no. 3 (2001), 313–30.

of Young Turk population policies does not only lead to Eastern Turkey, but also to other societies, such as Syria and Armenia. In Europe, the traces of exclusion led me to Diyarbekir Armenians in Amsterdam, Diyarbekir Kurds in Stockholm, Diyarbekir Syriacs in Hannover, and Diyarbekir Bulgarian Turks in Rotterdam.

Fortunately, oral history research on this topic has been conducted by many other scholars as well, and these have been of great help.[16] One name in particular is worthy of mention for the Diyarbekir region: Şeyhmus Diken. In recent years, this Diyarbekir-based researcher published many interviews with elderly Diyarbekir natives, many of whom had lived under the Young Turk regime. These published interviews are a veritable goldmine of information, for example about the destruction of Diyarbekir's Christians, the workings of the dictatorship in the region, the fierce competition between local elites, or the deportations of Diyarbekir's Kurds.[17] This wide range of sources has made possible a multi-dimensional account of Young Turk population policies in Eastern Turkey between 1913 and 1950.

Finally, one fundamental problem with the sources needs to be addressed. Historians understand that significant amounts of source material in dictatorships have been destroyed, censored, culled, purified, or separated into sealed depots. This was as much a process of actively destroying incriminating evidence as it was of latent silencing in the making of sources, the creation of archives, and the narrating by contemporaries.[18] The problem persists *ex post facto* due to the politicization of especially the term 'genocide', due to the identity politics of certain states and lobby groups. Robert Hayden pointed out that 'genocide has been a tool for building a number of nation states that are now honorable members of the world community'.[19] For many of those states, political violence is politically very sensitive. This tautology manifests itself when governments, unhappy about scholars searching for 'skeletons in the closet', deny access to archival collections and libraries, or prohibit them from conducting field work. The opposite is also possible: governments may try to foster or manipulate research by funding politically useful research; by pushing for the establishment of academic chairs at home or abroad; or by offering

---

[16] See: Leyla Neyzi, *İstanbul'da Hatırlamak ve Unutmak: Birey, Bellek ve Aidiyet* (Istanbul: Tarih Vakfı Yurt Yayınları, 1999); id., *'Ben Kimim': Türkiye'de Sözlü Tarih, Kimlik ve Öznellik* (Istanbul: İletişim, 2004). Donald E. Miller and Lorne Touryan-Miller, *Survivors: An Oral History of the Armenian Genocide* (Berkeley: University of California Press, 1993); Kemal Yalçın, *Seninle Güler Yüreğim* (Bochum: CIP, 2003); id., *Sarı Gelin: Sari Gyalin* (Köln: n.p., 2004); Otto Jastrow (ed.), *Die mesopotamisch-arabischen Qəltu-Dialekte* (Wiesbaden: Kommissionsverlag Franz Steiner GmbH, 1981), vol. 2; Susan Meiselas, *Kurdistan in the Shadow of History* (Chicago: University of Chicago Press, 2008); Ahmet Kahraman, *Kürt İsyanları: Tedip ve Tenkil* (Istanbul: Evrensel, 2003).

[17] Şeyhmuş Diken, *Diyarbekir Diyarım, Yitirmişem Yanarım* (Istanbul: İletişim, 2003); id., *Sırrını Surlarına Fısıldayan Şehir, Diyarbakır* (Istanbul: İletişim Yayınları, 2004); *Bajarê Ku Razên Xwe Ji Bircên Xwe Re Dibiline: Diyarbekir* (Diyarbakır: Lis, 2006); id., *Tango ve Diyarbakır* (Diyarbakır: Lis, 2004); id., *İsyan Sürgünleri* (Istanbul: İletişim, 2005); *Amidalılar: Sürgündeki Diyarbekirliler* (Istanbul: İletişim, 2007).

[18] See: Michel-Rolph Trouillot, *Silencing the Past: Power and the Production of History* (Boston: Beacon Press, 2007).

[19] Robert M. Hayden, 'Schindler's Fate: Genocide, Ethnic Cleansing, and Population Transfers', in: *Slavic Review* 55, no. 4 (1996), 727–48, at 732.

scholarships. It is the task of the historian to remain intellectually autonomous and maintain a prudent balance between involvement and detachment.

The Young Turk regime is no exception: there is compelling evidence that a series of serious destructions of source materials occurred. Not only was the scale of these processes of silencing and destruction considerable, but the period and type of documents that were destroyed pertain to key moments in the population policies in the crucial period 1913–50.[20] The construction of nationalist historiographies after 1913 compounded this process (see Chapter 5). These processes of silence and destruction bear consequences for utilizing the documentation as historical evidence, in that informed conjecture and extrapolation need to be added to the historian's conventional methods of analysis. The same vigilance must be observed when using the sources written by the regime's enemies: its victims and opponents. These sources are often obscure and contain strong biases, such as exaggerating the suffering, inflating the number of victims, demonizing the perpetrators, and denying victim collaboration and passivity. Commentary on these sources will be offered in the relevant footnotes.

STRUCTURE AND COMPOSITION

The book is organized into five chapters. Chapter 1, 'Nationalism and population politics in the late Ottoman Empire' will paint a picture of social and economic life in Eastern Turkey, in particular Diyarbekir province. The advent of nationalism to the region will be considered as both an Ottoman domino-effect, and as a function of the European centrifugal spread of nationalism. In order to provide an account of the local people, it will attempt to avoid and deconstruct methodological nationalism by using anthropological research on the region. It will try to circumvent rosy pictures of a pre-nationalist society where brotherhood and peace reigned supreme, as well as deterministic images of a complex society doomed to be the locus of a nationalist struggle or inevitably subjected to colonial rule. This chapter will further attempt to provide an account of how the concepts of nationalism and population policies entered Ottoman society with the result that ultimately, a small group of Turkish nationalists, the Young Turks, theorized a large-scale nationalist transformation of Ottoman society, including the eastern provinces. It will use theoretical and conceptual tools to digest and interpret this projection onto the region's heterogeneous population in an attempt to include the region in the construction of a homogeneous Turkish core state. The chapter will conclude with an analysis of the Ottoman loss of power in the Balkans, and it will argue that this was the trigger

---

[20] This argument is discussed for the Armenian genocide in: Ara Sarafian, 'The Ottoman Archives Debate and the Armenian Genocide', in: *Armenian Forum* 2, no. 1 (1999), 35–44; Vahakn N. Dadrian, 'Ottoman Archives and Denial of the Armenian Genocide', in: Richard G. Hovannisian (ed.), *The Armenian Genocide: History, Politics, Ethics* (New York: St. Martin's Press, 1992), 280–310; Taner Akçam, *'Ermeni Meselesi Hallolunmuştur': Osmanlı Belgelerine Göre Savaş Yıllarında Ermenilere Yönelik Politikalar* (Istanbul: İletişim, 2007), 15–36.

that made possible the progress from idea to act, and enabled the launch of the policies.

Chapters 2 to 5 will closely examine the history of Young Turk population policies in Diyarbekir. Chapter 2 will describe and explain the mass violence that was unleashed against Ottoman Christians in Diyarbekir province during the First World War. The chapter is divided into three parts: first, it will trace the genocidal tendencies of the Young Turks to the crisis of 1914–15 and their entry in the war. Second, it will concentrate on Diyarbekir province and describe the persecution process of Armenians and other Christians in that region. Third, it will analyse how that persecution developed into genocidal destruction by focusing on how local elites in Diyarbekir interpreted, organized, and intensified the destruction of Armenians. The chapter will focus on the close interdependence of victimization and perpetration, the importance of local elites in any genocidal process, and how the genocide can be placed in the broader structure of Young Turk population policies. This approach will attempt to capture the complexity of processes of mass violence.

Chapter 3 will discuss forced migrations, alternatively known as population transfers or simply deportations, as one among the many techniques of social engineering. It will particularly deal with the deportations of untold numbers of Kurds from Eastern to Western Turkey in the course of roughly two decades. The Young Turk dictatorship used forced population transfer as a strategy of 'Turkifying' the country's eastern provinces. Before describing how the Young Turks organized three major phases of deportations, it will trace the aetiology of these policies in the immediate aftermath of the Young Turk seizure of power in 1913. In order to provide a more complete understanding of this process, the chapter will analyse the deportation process as a two-way project of deporting non-Turks away from, and settling Turks into, the eastern provinces, in particular Diyarbekir province. These two vectors of population transfer geared into each other, rendering the deportations a tool of demographic Turkification. The chapter presents a detailed narrative of three phases of Young Turk deportations of Kurds and settlement of Turks in the years 1916, 1925, and 1934. It will draw a systematic comparison between the three phases and emphasize the continuity of population policies in the Young Turk era, without overlooking the subtle differences between the three waves of deportations. Alongside many official texts including justification, laws, logic, and procedures, the chapter will also heavily draw on memoirs and oral histories to portray the experiences of deportees.

Chapter 4 will present those two important patterns of nation formation. Starting from the First World War, the Young Turks acted upon ideas to take the nationalist message 'to the people'. Due to the war and subsequent deconcentration of power, they were not able effectively to devise and carry out grand cultural and educational projects. But after 1923, the regime took the lead in assigning the culture and education offices of the single-party dictatorship to launch ambitious projects of nation formation. This chapter will explore how the party penetrated the eastern provinces using the educational infrastructure of tens of thousands of schools in order to impose the spread of Turkish culture in Eastern

Turkey. Diyarbekir region, special because it was earmarked to become 'a center of Turkish culture in the East', was infused with Turkish culture with particular care. The chapter will also address how high levels of coercion during this process produced high levels of popular resistance towards the government's policies.

Chapter 5 will outline how the Young Turk project of crafting a modern nation state included more than violent policies that affected physically multitudes of human beings. Mentally, the young nation state was still a blank, and needed a national memory. The continuous process of defining and fine-tuning a national identity entailed a parallel process of defining and fine-tuning national memory. This chapter will focus on aspects of Young Turk memory politics, in particular how their memory politics intervened in existing patterns of memory in Diyarbekir. It will also devote attention to how the mass violence of the last Ottoman decade was remembered by the population and the government.

Finally, I will review the main findings and conclusions of this book, and address the problem of the effectiveness of these forms of population policies.

Acknowledgements

In the course of researching and writing this study, I have had the privilege to meet and benefit from a great number of individuals and institutions. My mentioning their names here can only hint at what I owe them. Without the help and support of each one of them, whatever value this study possesses would have been significantly less. Its flaws and shortcomings are wholly mine.

The University of Amsterdam provided an unsurpassed environment in which to study history and sociology. Without the support of the Center for Holocaust and Genocide Studies in Amsterdam I would not have developed my interest in mass violence in the way I have. My colleagues have been most insightful critics, and never failed to challenge me to improve. They have been a great source of ideas, intellectual stimulation, and unstinting encouragement. Ton Zwaan generously shared with me his seemingly boundless knowledge of historical sociology. He never let his enthusiasm for this project waver, and without that support I may not have undertaken this project, let alone completed it. He has been an outstanding mentor and friend, and has supported me in every way. I have learnt a great deal from the experience and guidance of Johannes Houwink ten Cate and Michael Wintle, and I thank them warmly for it. Special thanks goes out to Ahmet Yolcu Taşğın of Dicle University. He has been wonderfully hospitable, graciously taking me on as a newcomer to the region, and sharing with me his expansive and unique knowledge. I would especially like to thank Mehmet Kumaş for going out of his way to support and host me during my research. I thank my good friend Nisan Sarican, whose support and unfailing sense of humor was indispensible during the writing process. I also would like to thank for their assistance the staff of the various archives, institutes, and libraries listed in the bibliography. Most importantly, I have to thank the (partly anonymous) respondents that I interviewed. Their trust in confiding to me some of their most sensitive memories was brave and moving. Finally, I would like to extend my gratitude to Christopher Wheeler, Stephanie Ireland, Claire Hopwood, Michael Burt, and Jenny Townshend of Oxford University Press for their patience and support from the initiation of this project to the final completion of this book.

Among the many people to whom I owe gratitude, the following have supported me and this project in various ways: Nanci Adler, George Aghjayan, Yaman Akbulut, Taner Akçam, Gürdal Aksoy, Ayhan Aktar, Seda Altuğ, Thibaut Angevin, Sabri Atman, Osman Aytar, Yehuda Bauer, Bas von Benda-Beckmann, Fred Beijen, Stephanie Benzaquen, Karel Berkhoff, Jan Bet-Sawoce, Asmêno Bêwayir, Matthias Bjørnlund, Hans Blom, Donald Bloxham, Barbara Boender, Hamit Bozarslan, Martin van Bruinessen, Cathie Carmichael, İsmail Çeliker, Daniele Conversi, Vahakn Dadrian, Hayk Demoyan, Johan van der Dennen, Hrant Dink, Gerhard Eckelstein, Howard Eissenstat, Mas Fopma, David Gaunt, Hervé Georgelin, Robert Gerwarth, Samrad Ghane, Ryan Gingeras, Alexander Goekjian,

Müge Göçek, İlkay Nefin Güçlü, Ido de Haan, Wichert ten Have, Marko Attila Hoare, Peter Holquist, Richard Hovannisian, Theo de Jong, Hilmar Kaiser, Aristotle Kallis, Feyyaz Kerimo, Myroslava Keryk, Raymond Kévorkian, Umut Kibrit, Hans-Lukas Kieser, Teresa Klimowicz, Koen Koch, Cemil Koçak, Paul Koopman, Rober Koptaş, Timuçin Köprülü, Dilek Kurban, Natalya Lazar, Mark Levene, Riikka Loukonen, Etyen Mahçupyan, Marc Mamigonian, Haygan Mardikjan, Eric Markusen, Kay Mastenbroek, Bedross Der Matossian, Mekdes Mezgebu, Bob Moore, Khatchig Mouradian, William Mulligan, Kerem Öktem, David Östlund, Mesut Özcan, Dennis Papazian, Özgür Polat, Mehmet Polatel, Andriy Portnov, Erik van Ree, Erdal Rênas, Michael Reynolds, Nicolai Romashuk, Peter Romijn, Silvia Rottenberg, Ara Sarafian, Dominik Schaller, Jules Schelvis, Jacques Sémelin, Canan Seyfeli, Frédéric Solakian, Ron Suny, Abram de Swaan, Selahattin Tahta, Henry Theriault, Amed Tîgrîs, Samuel Totten, Benjamin Trigona-Harany, Cihan Uğural, Predrag Vitković, Arjan Vlasblom, Anton Weiss-Wendt, Jos Weitenberg, Harry Wes, Altuğ Yılmaz, Müfid Yüksel, Lidija Zelović, Welat Zeydanlıoğlu, and Erik-Jan Zürcher.

Last and far from least, thank you to my extended and nuclear family for their unconditional support: my father Halil Üngör, my mother Gönül Üngör-Turan, and my sister Devran Üngör.

List of Illustrations

List of Maps

List of Abbreviations

ABCFM (or ABC)	American Board of Commissioners for Foreign Missions
AMMU	General Directorate for Tribes and Immigrants (Aşair ve Muhacirîn Müdüriyet-i Umûmiyesi); before 1916 known as İAMM
ASALA	Armenian Secret Army for the Liberation of Armenia
BCA	Başbakanlık Cumhuriyet Arşivi (Republican Archives, Ankara)
BOA	Başbakanlık Osmanlı Arşivi (Ottoman Archives, Istanbul)
CUP	Committee of Union and Progress (İttihad ve Terakki Cemiyeti)
GBA	Gertrude Bell Archives (Robinson Library, University of Newcastle upon Tyne)
İAMM	Directorate for the Settlement of Tribes and Immigrants (İskân-ı Aşair ve Muhacirîn Müdüriyeti)
NARA	National Archives and Records Administration, United States of America
NAUK	National Archives, United Kingdom
PAAA	Politisches Archiv Auswärtiges Amt (German Foreign Office Archives)
PKK	Kurdistan Workers' Party (Partîya Karkerên Kurdistan
RPP	Republican People's Party (Cumhuriyet Halk Partisi)
TBMM ZC	*Türkiye Büyük Millet Meclisi Zabıt Ceridesi*
TRT	Turkish Radio and Television Corporation (Türkiye Radyo Televizyon Kurumu)

Introduction

The world we inhabit is made up of nation states—it is a global nation-state system—and contemporary nation states are involved in a variety of activities that are to do with power, exchange, and communicative relationships that together combine to form a closely knit, complex system of interdependence. This interdependence provides the foundation for the worldwide system of international interaction and remains the key vessel of social and political meaning in the world today. The nation-state system as we currently know it developed through at least three phases: the first saw the emergence of a core nation-state system in Europe, the second saw the internal consolidation and external expansion of that system to the rest of Europe, and the third witnessed its maturation as it spread globally to envelop the entire world.[1] It will be argued that the nationalist homogenization of space was usually an unintended (but directional) process of the first phase, but in many cases a specifically pursued (and coercive) policy during the latter two phases. In this model, the nation-state system is viewed as a relatively autonomous, self-perpetuating system whose dynamics, mechanisms, and logic produce processes of nationalist homogenization, resulting in various forms of population policies as a function of nation formation.

Theories on the emergence of the nation-state system in this first phase have focused on military capacity,[2] internal pacification,[3] the role of wars,[4] and capitalism,[5] as well as other factors. Although these studies diverge in their narrative and explanations, they converge on the same conclusion that in the long term, a new nation-state system developed out of this historical process. The nascence of a

---

[1] This interpretation borrows heavily from James Mayall, *Nationalism and International Society* (Cambridge: Cambridge University Press, 1990); John W. Meyer *et al.*, 'World Society and the Nation State', in: *American Journal of Sociology* 103, no. 1 (1997), 144–81; Dankwart A. Rustow, *A World of Nations: Problems of Political Modernization* (Washington, DC: The Brookings Institution, 1967).

[2] Anthony Giddens, *The Nation State and Violence: A Contemporary Critique of Historical Materialism* (Cambridge: Polity Press, 1985), vol. 2; Michael Mann, *The Sources of Social Power* (Cambridge: Cambridge University Press, 1993), vol. 2: *The Rise of Classes and Nation States, 1760–1914*.

[3] Norbert Elias, *Über den Prozess der Zivilisation: soziogenetische und psychogenetische Untersuchungen* (Basel: Haus zum Falken, 1939); id., 'Processes of State Formation and Nation Building', in: *Transactions of the Seventh World Congress of Sociology, Varna, September 14–19, 1970* (Louvain: International Sociological Association, 1972), vol. 3, 274–84.

[4] Charles Tilly, 'Reflections on the History of European State-Making', in: Charles Tilly (ed.), *The Formation of National States in Western Europe* (Princeton: Princeton University Press, 1975), 3–83; id., 'States and Nationalism in Europe, 1492–1992', in: *Theory and Society* 23, no. 1 (1994), 131–46.

[5] Immanuel Wallerstein, *The Modern World-System* (New York: Academic Press, 1974–81).

nation-state system in Europe can roughly be traced from the Treaty of Westphalia (1648) to the First World War. The Treaty of Westphalia can be seen as marking the historical shift to a new international order in its infancy, in which states formalized recognition of the nation state as the dominant principle of state formation. The structure that developed in Europe was characterized in particular by the consolidation of territorial control, centralization, functional differentiation and coordination of government, the penetration of society by administrative apparatuses, and mutual recognition of state autonomy.[6] In this period, the American Declaration of Independence (1776) and the French Revolution (1789) were two additional watersheds that set the standard for the future development of global processes of state formation. Once the concepts of self-determination and national sovereignty were born, they were destined to play a major role in the development of the nascent nation-state system as it spread to Italy and from there eastwards into the Habsburg, Ottoman, and Russian empires.

The nation state became the political product of the ideology of nationalism *par excellence*. In a nutshell, the term 'nation state' suggests the parallel and simultaneous occurrence of a state and a nation. In other words, 'the doctrine holds that humanity is naturally divided into nations, that nations are known by certain characteristics which can be ascertained, and that the only legitimate type of government is national self-government'.[7] In the ideal nation state, the population consists of the nation and only of the nation, that is, they coincide exactly: every member of the nation is a resident of the nation state, no member of the nation should reside outside it and, most importantly, in principle no non-members of the nation are to reside in the state. Although there are practically no ideal nation states, total, maximum, or sufficient homogeneity remains a prime ideal of the nation state. Even when nationalists include all members of an ethnic group, non-inclusion is *ipso facto* tantamount to exclusion. It is precisely here that the structurally exclusive nature of nationalism lies, even though there are broader sociological ramifications to this phenomenon, for one can argue that all group formation entails exclusion.[8] The concept of nation-state sovereignty was based on two principles: territoriality, and the exclusion of external actors from domestic authority structures. States began to codify activities and norms uniformly over their territory: laws, national standards, cultural policy, and spatial planning.[9] The Westphalia Treaty had 'acknowledged that boundaries drawn around territory circumscribed a single political and legal unit over which the state had sovereignty. The idea of zonal frontiers between core areas of control was rejected and from then, individuals owed allegiance to a specific

---

[6] Jason Farr, 'Point: the Westphalia Legacy and the Modern Nation State', in: *International Social Science Review* 80, no. 3/4 (2005), 156–9; Janice Thompson, 'State Sovereignty in International Relations: Bridging the Gap between Theory and Empirical Research', in: *International Studies Quarterly* 39, no. 2 (1995), 213–34.

[7] Elie Kedourie, *Nationalism* (London: Blackwell, 1994), 1.

[8] Andreas Wimmer, *Nationalist Exclusion and Ethnic Conflict: Shadows of Modernity* (Cambridge: Cambridge University Press, 2002); Daniel Chernilo, *A Social Theory of the Nation State: The Political Forms of Modernity beyond Methodological Nationalism* (London: Routledge, 2007).

[9] Connie L. McNeely, *Constructing the Nation State: International Organization and Prescriptive Action* (Westport, CT: Greenwood Press, 1995), 1–13.

territory which linked them to sovereign control'.[10] Constructing precise boundaries was now of paramount importance as their location would determine

> for millions of people the language and the ideas which children shall be taught at school, ... the kind of money they shall use, the markets in which they must buy and sell; it determines the national culture with which they shall be identified, the army in which they may be compelled to serve, the soil which they may be called upon to defend with their lives.[11]

The characteristics of the new nation state were boundedness in space (territorial unity) and later population (homogeneity), but unboundedness in time (trans-generationality and permanence guaranteed by symbolic national culture and the education system).[12]

The composition of the population had hardly been important in pre-national states. Before the rise of the nation state, 'governments presided over an ordered ethnic diversity, and no one supposed that uniformity was desirable or that assimilation to a common style of life or pattern of culture was either normal or possible'.[13] In this first stage of the nation-state system, if homogenization of the population had emerged, this had been a functional necessity and was not necessarily engineered from above by political elites.[14] According to this interpretation, the economic viability of industrialized societies had required a single national culture: homogeneity was a functional requisite of economic life.[15] According to another perspective, because

> the European states-making process minimised the cultural variation within states and maximised the variation among states within a homogeneous population, ordinary people were more likely to identify with their rulers, communication could run more efficiently, and an innovation that worked well in one segment was likely to work elsewhere as well. People who sensed a common origin, furthermore, were more likely to unite against external threats. Spain, France, and other large states recurrently homogenised by giving religious minorities—especially Muslims and Jews—the choice between conversion and emigration.[16]

---

[10] Ewan W. Anderson, 'Geopolitics: International Boundaries as Fighting Places', in: *Journal of Strategic Studies* 22, no. 2–3 (1999), 125–36, at 127.

[11] S. Whittemore Boggs, *International Boundaries* (New York: Columbia University Press, 1940), 5.

[12] Joep Leerssen, *National Thought in Europe: A Cultural History* (Amsterdam: Amsterdam University Press, 2007), 145–58. The notion of the unity and indivisibility of the nation state has been interpreted in various ways, from power-based explanations of sovereignty to the transfer of religious values: just as God was indivisible according to monotheistic doctrines, now the nation was 'une et indivisible'. Monica Duffy Toft, *The Geography of Ethnic Violence: Identity, Interests, and the Indivisibility of Territory* (Princeton, NJ: Princeton University Press, 2003), 17–33.

[13] William H. McNeill, *Polyethnicity and National Unity in World History* (Toronto: Toronto University Press, 1986), 16.

[14] For a dissenting view, see: Anthony W. Marx, *Faith in Nation: Exclusionary Origins of Nationalism* (New York: Oxford University Press, 2003), 143–64.

[15] Ernest Gellner, *Nations and Nationalism* (Oxford: Blackwell, 1983), 39, 52.

[16] Charles Tilly, *Coercion, Capital, and European States, AD 990–1990* (Cambridge, MA: Blackwell, 1990), 79, 106–7.

Slowly, the contours of modern nationalist homogenization began to emerge. As the principle of sovereignty shifted from dynasties into nations, the structure, formation, and character of populations now came to matter for the functioning of the nation state. Homogenization became an ideal, a model, and a policy.

For centuries after Westphalia, nationalism was still an elite phenomenon, but during the nineteenth century in Europe it spread widely and became popularized among different classes as well as peoples. The system expanded to the world through colonization, imposition, imitation, and domino effects as nationalist elites in multi-ethnic empires and in colonies learned from the European example.[17] Within multi-ethnic empires, ethnic groups were now 'discovered' by competing nationalisms as populations to function as the nation. New nation states were established and, ultimately, state formation came to be limited to one type of group: nations. This process gave birth to the second stage of the nation-state system, when it spread to the rest of Europe and Asia, roughly from the end of the First World War to the end of the Second World War.[18] Between 1918 and 1945, the great multi-ethnic dynastic land empires (Habsburg, Ottoman, and Russian) collapsed and their territories were replaced by new, nationalist orders, and colonial sea empires gained strength. In this era, nationalism was produced by elites and received by populations. The stock of existing ideas and sentiments among various groups interacted with nationalist ideas, rejecting them, displacing older ideas, and re-interpreting them through traditional lenses. Although there was differentiation within the nation-state system, nationalist thought was largely trans-ideological. Leaders across the political spectrum, from Lenin to Woodrow Wilson believed in national self-determination as the basic principle for political legitimacy.[19] This crucial stage marked a dramatic expansion and intensification of the system as both the quantity of states and the quality of their interdependence increased. It saw further integration and weaving together of nation states in institutions such as the Inter-Parliamentary Union, and the League of Nations.[20] Legislative activities within these organizations attempted to lay down requirements and rules of statecraft.[21] This process saw increasing interdependence, isomorphism, and integration between nation states, for example in terms of education, economy, and technology. In this period, more and more nation states engaged in inter-state relations that were increasingly conceived in terms of inter-nation relations, rather than mere inter-state relations.[22]

---

[17] Liah Greenfeld, *Nationalism: Five Roads to Modernity* (Cambridge, MA: Harvard University Press, 1992).

[18] Aviel Roshwald, *Ethnic Nationalism and the Fall of Empires: Central Europe, Russia and the Middle East, 1914–1923* (London: Routledge, 2001).

[19] Antonio Cassese, *Self-Determination of Peoples: A Legal Reappraisal* (Cambridge: Cambridge University Press, 1999), 11–36.

[20] Frederick S. Northedge, *The League of Nations: Its Life and Times, 1920–1946* (Leicester: Leicester University Press, 1986); Michel Marbeau, *La Société des Nations* (Paris: Presses Universitaires de France, 2001).

[21] Cassese, *Self-Determination of Peoples*, 37–162.

[22] Giddens, *The Nation State and Violence*, 255–93.

Territorialization proceeded to play an increasing role in the system. Nationalism is the quintessential set of beliefs that involves the ideological mobilization and appropriation of territory and the struggle for control of land.[23] Rather than an extension of primordial ethnic modes of territorial perception, the dynamics of nationalism warrant the large-scale production and construction of geography and space in terms of the natural property of nations.[24] In this second phase, the nation-state system came to cover most of the space in the world, leaving little room for non-national space. In this process, cartographic knowledge acted as a technology of nationalist world-view through a spatialization of race.[25] The nation state, the product of European nationalism, was a prescriptive and normative idea that projected race onto space, or in the words of George Mosse, 'the linking of the human soul with its natural surroundings'.[26] In other words: certain peoples were believed to *belong* in certain territories. That this was an expressedly global process is attested to by the view that 'one way of studying the naturalization of nationness is to pursue the international; for underlying all the competing nationalisms of the modern era lies a fundamental vision of the global order itself, a vision of the international'. The global order of nation states brought 'the transnational imagining of nation states as a world community or global family'. Spectacles such as the Olympic Games, the Eurovision Song Festival, or the Football World Cup, for example, provide a ceremonial arena 'for nations to take their place at the table (or on the playing fields) of the family of nations'.[27]

The development of nation states in the second era differed considerably from the more gradual and evolutionary formation of Western European states. In this phase the nation state became 'a deliberately erected framework' and 'an artificial, engineered institutional complex, rather than one that has developed spontaneously by accretion'.[28] Consequently, homogenization in this phase was not simply an

---

[23] Robert J. Kaiser, 'Homeland Making and the Territorialization of National Identity', in: Daniele Conversi (ed.), *Ethnonationalism in the Contemporary World: Walker Connor and the Study of Nationalism* (London: Routledge, 2002), 229–47.

[24] Anthony D. Smith & Colin Williams, 'The National Construction of Social Space', in: *Progress in Human Geography* 7, no. 4 (1983), 502–18; Guntram H. Herb, 'National Identity and Territory', in: Guntram H. Herb and David H. Kaplan (eds.), *Nested Identities: Nationalism, Territory, and Scale* (Lanham, MD: Rowman & Littlefield, 1999), 9–30.

[25] Henri Lefebvre, *The Production of Space* (Oxford: Blackwell, 1991, transl. Donald Nicholson-Smith), 111 ff.; Peter J. Taylor and Colin Flint, *Political Geography: World-Economy, Nation State and Locality* (Harlow: Prentice Hall, 2000); Jeremy W. Crampton, 'Maps, Race and Foucault: Eugenics and Territorialization Following World War I', in: Jeremy W. Crampton and Stuart Elden (eds.), *Space, Knowledge and Power: Foucault and Geography* (Aldershot: Ashgate Publishing, 2007), 223–44; Liisa Malkki, 'The Rooting of Peoples and the Territorialization of National Identity among Scholars and Refugees', in: Akhil Gupta and James Ferguson (eds.), *Culture, Power, Place: Explorations in Critical Anthropology* (Durham: Duke University Press, 1997), 52–74.

[26] George Mosse, *Toward the Final Solution: A History of European Racism* (Madison, WI: University of Wisconsin Press, 1985), 202.

[27] Liisa Malkki, 'Citizens of Humanity: Internationalism and the Imagined Community of Nations', *Diaspora* 3, no.1 (1994), 41–68, at 42.

[28] Gianfranco Poggi, *The Development of the Modern State: A Sociological Introduction* (Stanford, CA: Stanford University Press, 1978), 95; Jon G. Wagner, 'The Rise of the State System: 1914–1950', in: Roy R. Andersen, Robert F. Seibert, and Jon G. Wagner (eds.), *Politics and Change in the Middle East: Sources of Conflict and Accommodation* (Englewood Cliffs, NJ: Prentice-Hall, 1982), 74–93.

unintended outcome of contingent, uncontrollable circumstances, or put more precisely: a long-term, unplanned but directional process. States now pro-actively 'worked to homogenize their populations and break down segmentation by imposing common languages, religions, currencies, and legal systems, as well as promoting the construction of connected systems of trade, transportation, and communication'.[29] These processes of homogenization were expressed in phases and shocks of ethnic unmixing, for example when minorities (forcibly or voluntarily) migrated to kin states.[30] For villages, regions, classes, and other groups which stayed in place and continued to identify with their village, region, or class, the organization of a homogeneous national identity 'required an immense effort of symbolization, communication and education, to superimpose these extensive identifications on the preceding identifications of kin and proximity'.[31] This era saw immense reorganizations of populations, ranging from forced assimilation to forced migration and genocide, processes of population policies that brought more homogeneity within nation states and increasing congruence to the nation-state system. Although these processes have been studied as autonomous examples of the aspirations of each nation state, the transnational dimension seems to be unmistakable.[32]

The third phase of the nation-state system saw its maturation as the end of alternative orders (colonialism and Communism) heralded an era of post-colonial and post-Communist-nationalism, roughly from the end of the Second World War up to present times. This era saw the rise of the United Nations, the prime international intergovernmental organization of global scope and universal membership, a complex system that serves as the central site for multilateral diplomacy. The nation-state system now had global coverage and was firmly anchored in its most central international institution.[33] The nation-state system was more than the sum of its parts. The UN both symbolically and actively acted as an engine through which this process of nation-state formation was structurally enforced and reinforced, for example in the establishment of Pakistan and India. In this phase, homogenization was a defining quality of the system.[34] Cultural nationalism, for example, now became territorialized as states sought to impose monocultures on

---

[29] Tilly, *Coercion, Capital, and European States*, 100.

[30] Rogers Brubaker, 'Aftermaths of Empire and the Unmixing of Peoples', in: Karen Barkey and Mark von Hagen (eds.), *After Empire: Multiethnic Societies and Nation-Building: The Soviet Union and the Russian, Ottoman and Habsburg Empires* (Boulder: Westview Press, 1997), 155–80.

[31] Abram de Swaan, 'Widening Circles of Identification: Emotional Concerns in Sociogenetic Perspective', in: *Theory, Culture and Society* 12 (1995), 25–39, at 31; Clifford Geertz, 'The Integrative Revolution: Primordial Sentiments and Civil Politics in the New States', in: id., *The Interpretation of Cultures: Selected Essays* (New York: Basic Books, 1973), 255–310.

[32] For an early study of these processes, see: Stephen P. Ladas, *The Exchange of Minorities: Bulgaria, Greece and Turkey* (New York: Macmillan, 1932). For three excellent discussions at a later point in time, see: Joseph B. Schechtman, *European Population Transfers, 1939–1945* (New York: Oxford University Press, 1946); id., *Postwar Population Transfers in Europe, 1945–1955* (Philadelphia: University of Pennsylvania Press, 1962); id., *Population Transfers in Asia* (New York: Hallsby Press, 1949).

[33] Karen A. Mingst and Margaret P. Karns, *The United Nations in the Twenty-First Century* (Boulder, CO: Westview Press, 2006), 17–52.

[34] Mark Levene, 'The Limits of Tolerance: Nation State Building and What it Means for Minority Groups', in: *Patterns of Prejudice* 34, no. 2 (2000), 19–40; id., *Genocide in the Age of the Nation State* (London: Tauris, 2005), 2 vols.

their populations, and nationalism, initially emancipatory, assumed racial forms.[35] This phase also witnessed the first systematic criticisms of the darker sides of nationalism.[36]

The evolution of the nation-state system from the first to the second phase was not a teleological process that necessarily led to the third stage. Although this 'dynamic of the state system' was drifting in a certain direction (increasing integration as well as increasing homogenization), this process was an unplanned, unintended, and never finished work-in-progress. It has been a blind process, and the nation states of the world, both political elites and populations, have together produced it. The direction of that process is towards more homogenization, although significant trends serve as counterpoints in the process, such as ethnic federalism, transnational migration, and multiple citizenship.

A brief recapitulation of the theory is that the international system of nation states developed from a pre-national global order of states with culturally heterogeneous territories into a self-perpetuating system of nation states which, in continuous interdependence, produces nationalist homogenization by virtue of various forms of population policies. For this book, the conceptual model will function as a backdrop against which the phenomenon of nationalist homogenization in Eastern Turkey will be analysed. This book is a case study of those processes of homogenization. It is the story of a city and a region, the south-eastern province of Diyarbekir. It is a relatively focused regional study that aims to understand the global by concentrating on the local, since it is the region, the city, the village where the consequences of the above macro-sociological processes can best be studied and its implications measured.[37] The focus on a locality rather than an ethnic group implies a rejection of the biases of methodological nationalism that have haunted area studies.[38] This book proceeds beyond these cleavages and studies the locale with its inhabitants, in their interdependence.

---

[35] Leerssen, *National Thought in Europe*, 151.

[36] Walker Connor, 'Nation-Building or Nation-Destroying?' in: *World Politics* 24, no. 3 (1972), 319–55.

[37] For successful applications of the regional method of studying nationalism, see: Mark Mazower, *Salonica: City of Ghosts: Christians, Muslims and Jews 1430–1950* (London: HarperCollins Publishers, 2004); Rogers Brubaker et al., *Nationalist Politics and Everyday Ethnicity in a Transylvanian Town* (Princeton, NJ: Princeton University Press, 2006); Anastasia Karakasidou, *Fields of Wheat, Hills of Blood: Passages to Nationhood in Greek Macedonia, 1870–1990* (Chicago: University of Chicago Press, 1997); Hervé Georgelin, *La fin de Smyrne: du cosmopolitisme aux nationalismes* (Paris: CNRS, 2005).

[38] For a critique, see: Biray Kolluoğlu-Kırlı, 'From Orientalism to Area Studies', in: *Centennial Review* 3, no. 3 (2003), 93–112; Richard Handler, 'On Dialogue and Destructive Analysis: Problems in Narrating Nationalism and Ethnicity', in: *Journal of Anthropological Research* 41, no. 2 (1985), 171–82.

1

Nationalism and Population Politics in the late Ottoman Empire

How did the Turkish nation-formation process develop from the nineteenth into the twentieth century? This chapter will give an account of the eastern provinces, in particular Diyarbekir province, from an anthropological and sociological perspective. It will then address how the process of nation formation in the Ottoman Empire shifted from a relatively inclusive Ottoman patriotism to a relatively exclusive Turkish ethnic nationalism. This shift will be analysed through the prism of processes of identification and disidentification. The chapter will then examine the advent of the notion of population politics. The Young Turk movement's 'discovery of society' and plans for carving out a nation state from the multi-ethnic Ottoman Empire is another prime focus. Finally, the chapter will return to how these ideas of nationalism and population politics, formulated and discussed at top political levels, trickled down to the provincial level, where they became the subject of bitter conflicts.

AN INTRODUCTION TO DIYARBEKIR

At the turn of the twentieth century, the Ottoman Empire straddled three continents and encompassed remarkable diversity among the estimated thirty million people living within its borders (see Map 1). A military-agrarian peasant society with relatively low levels of integration in economy, administration, and culture, the empire allowed for local leaders in disparate regions such as Egypt, Macedonia, the Gulf, or Wallachia to operate with relative autonomy, away from each other and the authority of the Sultan. At the height of its power, the empire contained twenty-nine provinces, organized into districts with district governors, counties with mayors, and communes with directors.

Diyarbekir was a relatively large province (42,100 km^2) locked in between the Euphrates in the west, the Tigris in the east, the Armenian highland in the north, and the Mesopotamian desert in the south (see Map 2). Its continental climate made for mild winters and hot summers. The region became part of the Ottoman Empire during Sultan Süleyman I's campaign against Iraq and Persia in 1534. The city of Diyarbekir became the administrative centre and the headquarters of the sixteenth-century governorship from where large parts of the broader region

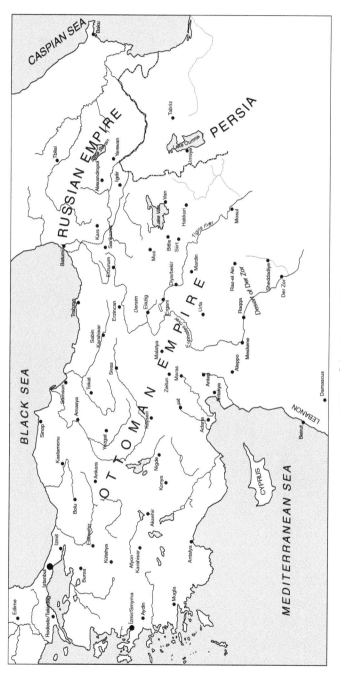

1 Map of the Ottoman Empire

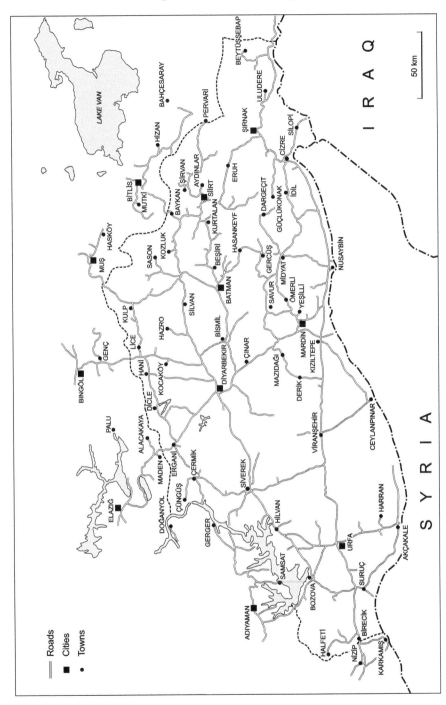

2 Map of the Diyarbekir region

were ruled.[1] Although there were regional variations in the economic conditions of the province, generally it thrived due to its favourable location on the ancient Silk Road.[2] There were copper mines in Maden county, and the border regions with Bitlis province were known for being oil-rich, though no large-scale steps had been taken to exploit either. Like the rest of the empire, Diyarbekir was a pre-industrial region where subsistence farming and cyclic pastoralism were the dominant economic occupations for peasants and nomads in the countryside.[3]

The city of Diyarbekir is a turbot-shaped walled citadel, situated on a basalt plateau nested in a meander of the Tigris river. Within the city walls, the urban structure consists of a square in the centre of town, surrounded by a bazaar and a labyrinth of streets and alleys running criss-cross through the city.[4] The city consisted of several neighbourhoods, and although the city was known to have a Christian neighbourhood and a Muslim neighbourhood, the overlap of ethnicity and settlement was never complete. To a significant degree, historically, the various communities lived in mixed neighbourhoods. Typically, Diyarbekir's houses are closed towards the outside world and have courtyards where social life takes place.[5] Until the 1950s, Diyarbekir lacked a central refuse collection system, waterworks, underground sewerage, and other services.[6] Nevertheless, foreigners travelling to the city were often impressed, and recognized that 'the streets are cleaner than those of many Turkish towns, and the houses better built'.[7] The Ottoman state made its presence felt through the governorship, the Second Army, a court-martial, and one of the largest prisons of the Ottoman Empire. In the nineteenth century

---

[1] Martin van Bruinessen, 'The Ottoman Conquest of Diyarbekir and the Administrative Organisation of the Province in the 16th and 17th Centuries', in: Martin van Bruinessen and Hendrik Boeschoten (eds.), *Evliya Çelebi in Diyarbekir* (Leiden: Brill, 1988), 13–38. Alpay Bizbirlik, *16. Yüzyıl Ortalarında Diyarbekir Beylerbeyliği'nde Vakıflar* (Ankara: Türk Tarih Kurumu, 2002). Nejat Göyünç, 'Diyarbekir Beylerbeyliğinin İlk İdari Taksimatı', in: *Tarih Dergisi* 22 (1969), 23–4.

[2] İbrahim Yılmazçelik, *XIX. Yüzyılın İlk Yarısında Diyarbakır* (Ankara: Türk Tarih Kurumu, 1995); Abdulhalık Bakır, 'Osmanlı Öncesinde Diyarbakır'da Sanayi ve Ticaret', paper presented at the conference *Oğuzlardan Osmanlıya Diyarbakır*, Dicle University, 21 May 2004.

[3] Hellmut Christoff, *Kurden und Armenier: Eine Untersuchung über die Abhängigkeit ihrer Lebensformen und Charakterentwicklung von der Landschaft* (Hamburg: dissertation University of Hamburg, 1935), 19–73.

[4] For descriptions of the city, see: Mehmet Alper, 'Diyarbakır, sa citadelle et ses remparts', in: *Albert Gabriel (1883–1972): Mimar, Arkeolog, Ressam, Gezgin* (Istanbul: Yapı Kredi Yayınları, 2006), 93–109; Albert-Louis Gabriel, *Diyarbakır Surları* (Diyarbakır: Diyarbakır Tanıtma, Kültür ve Yardımlaşma Vakfı, 1993), transl. Kaya Özsezgin; id.; 'Mardin ve Diyarbekir Vilayetlerinde İcra Olunmuş Arkeologya Seyahati Hakkında Rapor', in: *Türk Tarih, Arkeologya ve Etnografya Dergisi* 1 (1933), 134–49; id., *Voyages archéologiques dans la Turquie orientale* (Paris: Institut Français d'Archeologie de Stamboul, 1940).

[5] Gülay Zorer Gedik, 'Climatic Design: An Analysis of the Old Houses of Diyarbakir in the Southeast Region of Turkey', in: *Architectural Science Review* 47, no. 2 (2004), 145–54; Müjgan Şerefhanoğlu Sözena and Gülay Zorer Gedik, 'Evaluation of Traditional Architecture in Terms of Building Physics: Old Diyarbakır houses', in: *Building and Environment* 42, no. 4 (2007), 1810–16. For descriptions of daily life in Diyarbekir in the first half of the twentieth century, see: M. Şefik Korkusuz, *Eski Diyarbekir'de Gündelik Hayat* (Istanbul: Kent, 2007); id., *Bir Zamanlar Diyarbekir: Zamanlar, Mekanlar, İnsanlar* (Istanbul: Yeditepe, 1999).

[6] İbrahim Halil, 'Sıhhat Meseleleri: Şehrimizin Suları', in: *Küçük Mecmua* 8 (24 July 1922), 18–20.

[7] Mark Sykes, *The Caliphs' Last Heritage: A Short History of the Turkish Empire* (London: n.p., 1915), 358.

Diyarbekir's central prison gained infamy throughout the Ottoman Empire as a site where political prisoners such as Bulgarian nationalists were sent to serve harsh sentences for advocating national freedom.[8]

Diyarbekir province boasted a formidable diversity of ethnic and religious groups, small and large, scattered and concentrated, urban and rural. Religious affiliation was decisive in one's identity within Ottoman society, which was organized into the *millet* system, the official macro-organization of religious communities that were partly autonomous in their decision-making.[9] The Ottoman Muslims, later denominated 'Turks', were the majority in most urban areas, for they had been occupying most administrative positions for a long time. Armenians inhabiting the cities made their livings as merchants or craftsmen and in most bazaars the majority of tradesmen were indeed Armenians. Some of these men were quite prosperous, having family members abroad and being active in politics. But the bulk of Diyarbekir Armenians were peasants organized in large extended families (*gerdastans*) in villages, most specifically in the Lice, Silvan, Beşiri, and Palu districts.[10] The Kurdish population of the province, all Muslims, can be divided into several categories: tribal versus non-tribal Kurds, and (semi-) nomadic versus sedentary. The dozens of large and powerful Kurdish tribes in the region were generally commanded by a chieftain (*ağa*), and *de facto* controlled extensive territories. All were able to mobilize thousands, sometimes tens of thousands of mounted warriors, often to combat each other in pursuit of power, honour, and booty. Non-tribal Kurds could be powerless peasants (*kurmanc*) or Kurds from noted clergy families (*meşayih*).[11] It is important to point out that most peasants, irrespective of ethnic or religious background, paid tribute and taxes to Kurdish chieftains and landlords.[12] The mere 1000 Jews of Diyarbekir province owned one small synagogue, and were generally an inconspicuous ethnic group among the

[8] Veselin Sariev, *Diarbekir i Bulgarite: Po Sledite na Zatochenitsite* (Sofia: Khristo Botev, 1996); Tone Kraichov, *Diarbekirski Dnevnik i Spomeni* (Sofia: Izdvo na Otechestveniia front, 1989).

[9] Within the Ottoman Empire the four main *millet*s were the Muslims, Greeks, Armenians, and Jews. Most ethnic groups were categorized under one of these rubrics. Kamel S. Abu Jaber, 'The Millet System in the Nineteenth-Century Ottoman Empire', in: *The Muslim World* 57, no. 3 (1967), 212–23; Macit Kenanoğlu, *Osmanlı Millet Sistemi* (Istanbul: Klasik, 2004); Benjamin Braude, 'Foundation Myths of the Millet System', in: Benjamin Braude and Bernard Lewis (eds.), *Christians and Jews in the Ottoman Empire* (New York: Holmes and Meier, 1982), vol. 1, *The Central Lands*, 69–90; Kemal H. Karpat, 'Millets and Nationality: The Roots of the Incongruity off Nation and State in the Post-Ottoman Era', in: ibid., 141–69; Roderic H. Davison, 'The Millets as Agents of Change in the Nineteenth-Century Ottoman Empire', in: ibid., 319–37; Michael Ursinus, 'Zur Diskussion um "millet" im Osmanischen Reich', in: *Südost-Forschungen* 48 (1989), 195–207.

[10] Raymond H. Kévorkian and Paul B. Paboudjian, *Les Arméniens dans l'Empire ottoman à la veille du génocide* (Paris: Editions d'Art et d'Histoire, 1992), 392.

[11] Paul White, 'Ethnic Differentiation among the Kurds: Kurmanci, Kizilbash and Zaza', in: *Journal of Arabic, Islamic and Middle Eastern Studies* 2, no. 2 (1995), 67–90.

[12] Hamit Bozarslan, 'Remarques sur l'histoire des relations kurdo-arméniennes', in: *The Journal of Kurdish Studies* 1 (1995), 55–76; Martin van Bruinessen, *Agha, Shaikh and State: The Social and Political Structures of Kurdistan* (London: Zed, 1992), chapters 2, 3, and 4. Many communities in Diyarbekir lived under the supremacy of powerful Kurdish tribes, which were relatively autonomous in their affairs. The Ottoman crisis of the late nineteenth century strained the relationship between Kurdish tribes and peasants, a relationship that resembled a type of feudal serfdom. The persistent economic malaise induced the chieftains to levy an extra tax on top of official taxes to sustain their

much larger Christian and Muslim populations. They mainly engaged in small-scale trade and some horticulture.[13] The Yezidis, a monotheist religious group, inhabited villages in the south-eastern regions of the province. Ottoman state discrimination and oppression pushed them into a marginal social status, which caused them to frequently engage in organized brigandry.[14] The Kizilbash were both Turkoman and Kurdish heterodox Shi'ites and inhabited only a few villages in the province, whereas others were semi-nomads.[15] The Zaza, an until recently unexplored ethnic group socially close to the Kurds, were villagers and occupied themselves with agriculture and horticulture. Concentrated in the north and south, the Zaza in Diyarbekir province were and are Muslim, and several important Muslim clerics emanated from them.[16] The Arabs of the province were also named Mahalmi because of the particular dialect they spoke. Most of them lived in Mardin but also in the villages in and around Midyat, though they numbered no more than a few thousand.[17] The Syriacs (alternatively named Assyrians or Arameans), who included all Aramaic-speaking Syrian-Orthodox, Syrian-Protestant, Syrian-Catholic, Nestorian and Chaldean Christians, inhabited many villages, especially those in the south-eastern parts of the province. The mountainous region around Midyat, also known as Tur Abdin, was a Syriac stronghold with dozens of often exclusively Syriac villages.[18] A demographically and politically insignificant group were the Gypsies, who lived in urban centres and were ostracized by most other groups. In the eastern provinces the Gypsies were named Poşa or Kereçi.[19] Finally, there is evidence of the existence of Shemsi communities, although their numbers seem to have shrunk dramatically by the late nineteenth century. These archaic sun-worshippers were most probably the religious offspring of the ancient Zoroastrian religion, and used to worship in several temples all over what became the Ottoman province of Diyarbekir.[20] All in all, the population of Diyarbekir province had a very heterogeneous ethnic and social composition.

---

dominance, threatening neglecters and resisters with violence. The appeals of Armenian nationalists to the Western powers would politicize this situation.

[13] Walther J. Fischel, 'The Jews of Kurdistan a Hundred Years Ago: A Traveler's Record', in: *Jewish Social Studies* 6 (1944), 195–226; Erich Brauer, *The Jews of Kurdistan* (Detroit, MI: Wayne State University Press, 1993); A. Medyalı, *Kürdistanlı Yahudiler* (Ankara: Berhem, 1992), 58.

[14] Ralph H.W. Empson, *The Cult of the Peacock Angel: A Short Account of the Yezidi Tribes of Kurdistan* (London: AMS Press, 1928).

[15] Erdal Gezik, *Dinsel, etnik ve politik sorunlar bağlamında Alevi Kürtler* (Ankara: Kalan, 2000).

[16] Karl Hadank, *Mundarten der Zâzâ, hauptsächlich aus Siwerek und Kor* (Berlin: De Gruyter, 1932).

[17] Hans-Jürgen Sasse, 'Linguistische Analyse des arabischen Dialekts der Mhallamiye in der Provinz Mardin (Südosttürkei)', PhD Thesis, Ludwig-Maximilians University of München, Department of Semitics, 1970.

[18] The Tur Abdin region was particularly famous for its strong tribal cleavages. The two main tribes reigning in Tur Abdin were the Dekşuri and Hevêrkan, the latter originating from the Botan emirate that was violently dismantled in the mid-nineteenth century. Both tribes had hereditary chieftains of Muslim-Kurdish descent and both tribes treated their Muslim and non-Muslim subjects (such as Syriac Christians and Yezidis) alike. Tribal interests and loyalties were superordinated to religious interests and loyalties. The continuous competition between these two tribes often escalated into assassinations and plunder. Hans Hollerweger, *Turabdin* (Linz: Freunde des Tur Abdin, 1999).

[19] Sarkis Seropyan, 'Vatansız tek ulus Çingeneler ve Çingenelerin Ermenileşmişleri Hay-Poşalar', in: *Tarih ve Toplum* 33, no. 202 (2000), 21–5.

[20] Horatio Southgate, *Narrative of a Tour through Armenia, Kurdistan, Persia and Mesopotamia* (London: Bradbury and Evans, 1840), vol. 2, 284–5.

This taxonomy of the ethnic, religious, and cultural composition of Diyarbekir province is not unproblematic. It may well be possible to categorize people based on ethnic markers such as language, culture, religion, class, or political orientation, but by focusing on the differences between people, such overviews of classificatory criteria often risk essentializing and reifying, and often constructing and amplifying the ostensibly objective characteristics.[21] Such biases emanate from a 'tendency to take discrete, sharply differentiated, internally homogeneous and externally bounded groups as basic constituents of social life, chief protagonists of social conflicts, and fundamental units of social analysis … as if they were … unitary collective actors with common purposes'.[22] Besides significant patches of overlap between groups, there were often multiple versions of one identity. The heterogeneity of the ethnic and social composition of the province was further complicated by two additional complexities: the vagueness of identities and the presence of multiple loyalties as tribal cleavages and ethnically mixed villages produced competing loyalties. This complex social reality of overlap, vagueness, and multiplicity withstands simple classifications, and needs to be taken into consideration before any narrative or analysis of the history of this region.

These anthropological subtleties were not peculiar to either Diyarbekir or the Ottoman Empire in general. Sociologically, in peasant societies cultures that seem distinct at first glance are mostly locally organized. Objective differences exist mostly *between* regions separated by natural or administrative borders rather than between groups *within* a region.[23] In other words, people perhaps resembled each other more than they differed. The British officer Mark Sykes wrote about Kurdish villages in a valley where 'side by side with these low Kurds live Armenians, who are much the same as their Moslem neighbours',[24] providing one concrete example:

> The village of Dibneh is inhabited by Armenians, who are independent and wealthy. According to their own account, they are a lonely colony, and have dwelt there from time immemorial. They are identical in physiognomy, habit, and dress with the Tiriki Kurds, by whom they are surrounded, and bear not the slightest resemblance to the ordinary Armenians one meets in the districts of Bitlis, Van, or Diarbekir.[25]

Locality was a tribal matter as well since most tribes lived in one region. Most Kurdish tribes had hereditary Muslim chieftaincy, but they treated their Muslim

---

[21] Alan B. Anderson, 'The Complexity of Ethnic Identities: A Postmodern Reevaluation', in: *Identity: An International Journal of Theory and Research* 1, no. 3 (2001), 209–23; Gerd Baumann, *The Multicultural Riddle: Rethinking National, Ethnic, and Religious Identities* (London: Routledge, 1999), 57–68; Siniša Malešević, *The Sociology of Ethnicity* (London: Sage Publications, 2004); Johan van der Dennen, 'Ethnocentrism and In-Group/Out-Group Differentiation', in: Vernon Reynolds (ed.), *The Sociobiology of Ethnocentrism: Evolutionary Dimensions of Xenophobia, Discrimination, Racism and Nationalism* (Athens: University of Georgia Press, 1987), 1–47.

[22] Rogers Brubaker, 'Ethnicity Without Groups', in: *Archives européennes de sociologie* 43, no. 2 (2002), 163–89, at 164.

[23] See: Teodor Shanin (ed.), *Peasants and Peasant Societies: Selected Readings* (Harmondsworth: Penguin books, 1971).

[24] Sykes, *The Caliphs' Last Heritage*, 357.

[25] Ibid., 361.

and non-Muslim subjects equally.[26] The interests of the tribe or the village always superseded ethno-religious interests and loyalties and produced cultural contact between various groups. For all these reasons, it might be more correct to speak of a distinct culture of the Diyarbekir region rather than co-existing national cultures.

For many of these ethnic communities Diyarbekir province bore more than average importance because of the concentration of pivotal religious sites and presence of the highest clerical authorities. Since religion defined communal boundaries in the Ottoman theocracy, this only added to the portentousness of Diyarbekir. For example, the two main monasteries of the Syriacs, Mor Gabriel and Deyr-ul Zaferan, were located in the Mardin district. These were not only offices of bishops and patriarchs, but in general the heart of Syriac religion, culture, and education in seminaries (*madrashto*s).[27] Diyarbekir city (see Plate 1) harboured the Syrian-Orthodox Virgin Mary Church, the Chaldean church, the Armenian Apostolic church which was one of the largest and most sophisticated churches in the Ottoman Empire, and a Protestant church, while dozens of Armenian villages had churches and schools.[28] For the Muslims of Diyarbekir province the many mosques and seminaries (*medrese*) were important as places of worship, education, and socializing. In a society with very low literacy rates, information circulated mostly by word of mouth, as newspapers were often read out aloud in coffeehouses and bards roamed the countryside updating the people on new developments.

Moreover, influential Islamic orders like the Nakşibendî, Kadirî, Rufaî, and Küfrevî were active all over the province among large Zaza, Arab, but especially Kurdish families. These orders were lodged in large medreses even in small counties, where students were taught religion, languages (Arabic, Persian, Kurdish, Ottoman), and history. Some of these were quite famous for the quality of their education, such as the Red Medrese (Medreseya Sor) of Cizre, the Hatuniye, Zinciriye, and Sitti Radviye medreses of Mardin, and the Mesudiye and Sitrabas medreses of Diyarbekir city.[29] Furthermore, local saints, cults, and shrines (*ziyaret*), visited by people of all religious groups, were scattered all over the province. One example is the Sultan Şeyhmus cult, located at the Şeyhan caves between Diyarbekir and Mardin.

A limited number of Western Europeans lived in the province. Diyarbekir had a French consulate and a British vice-consulate (who were recalled when the Ottoman Empire declared war on France and Britain), and an American Protestant mission. The German government considered the deployment of a vice-consulate because of the possibility that Diyarbekir could become a hub along the Baghdad

---

[26] Martin van Bruinessen, 'Les Kurdes, États et tribus', in: Hosham Dawod (ed.), *Tribus et pouvoirs en terre d'islam* (Paris: Armand Colin, 2004), 145–68.

[27] Gertrude Bell, *The Churches and Monasteries of the Tur Abdin and Neighbouring Districts* (Heidelberg: Carl Winter's Universitätsbuchhandlung, 1913).

[28] Orhan Cezmi Tuncer, *Diyarbakır Kiliseleri* (Diyarbakır: Diyarbakır Büyükşehir Belediyesi Kültür ve Sanat Yayınları, 2002).

[29] Zeynelabidin Zinar, *Xwendina medresê* (Stockholm: Pencînar, 1993); Orhan Cezmi Tuncer, *Diyarbekir Camileri* (Diyarbakır: Diyarbakır Büyükşehir Belediyesi Kültür ve Sanat Yayınları, 1996).

railway, but instead decided to found consulates in Mosul and Aleppo.[30] Several dozen American, German, and French missionaries, both Protestant and Catholic, were active in education and health care in the province, as well as in missionary work. However, due to its rugged and inaccessible terrain like most eastern provinces of the Ottoman Empire, much of the province was *terra incognita* for Western observers. The West also exerted its presence through former Ottoman subjects who had acquired Western passports. Mostly these were Christian notables who had become Russian, French, or British subjects, often to evade high taxes and derive benefit from the political immunity Western citizenship offered in many instances.

It is very difficult to come to grips with the demographics of Diyarbekir province, due to the absence of reliable quantitative data on all the ethnicities inhabiting the province before the war.[31] .Figures from various sources contradict each other, which has hampered academic efforts undertaken to chart the demography of the province. According to the 1913–14 census carried out by the Armenian Patriarchate of Istanbul, the Armenians numbered 106,867 in 249 localities in the province.[32] An Armenian almanac estimated the pre-war number of Armenians at 124,000.[33] Johannes Lepsius (1858–1926), Protestant missionary and director of the Deutsche Orient Mission in the empire, diverged from this calculation:

> Of its total population of 471,500 inhabitants there were 166,000 Christians, namely 105,000 Armenians and 60,000 Syriacs (Nestorians and Chaldeans) and 1000 Greeks. The remaining population is composed of 63,000 Turks, 200,000 Kurds, 27,000 Kizilbash (Shi'ites) and 10,000 Circassians. In addition there are 4,000 Yezidis (so-called devil worshippers) and 1,500 Jews.[34]

Ottoman archival material diverges even further from these numbers as shown in Table 1.

---

[30] *Politisches Archiv Auswärtiges Amt* (German National Archives, Berlin, hereafter cited as *PAAA*), R14078, Notes of Foreign Affairs Undersecretary Zimmermann, 5 March 1913, enclosure no. 2.

[31] The study of early twentieth-century Ottoman demography demands careful scrutiny as it is not only difficult to produce concrete and reliable statistics, but it is also very often a political minefield in which contemporary and present-day partisan scholarship plays a role. See Kemal H. Karpat, *Ottoman Population 1830–1914: Demographic and Social Characteristics* (Madison, WI: University of Wisconsin Press, 1985); Justin McCarthy, *Muslims and Minorities: The Population of Ottoman Anatolia and the End of the Empire* (New York: New York University, 1983); Levon Maraaslian, *Politics and Demography: Armenians, Turks, and Kurds in the Ottoman Empire* (Cambridge, MA: Zoryan Institute, 1991). Also, the Ottoman government often revised its provinces and altered borders. It is possible to interpret this practice of redistricting as an effort to reduce the demographic proportion of Christians to the benefit of Muslims, although no systematic research has been conducted with respect to this subject. Vahakn N. Dadrian, *Warrant for Genocide: Key Elements of the Turko-Armenian Conflict* (New Brunswick, NJ: Transaction, 1999), 139–44.

[32] Kévorkian and Paboudjian, *Les Arméniens dans l'Empire ottoman*, 59.

[33] Theodig, *Mius Merelotzu: Amenoun Daretzoutzu* (Istanbul: n.p., 1921), 261, quoted in: Mesrob K. Krikorian, *Armenians in the Service of the Ottoman Empire 1860–1908* (London: Routledge, 1977), 19, 117 footnote 6.

[34] Johannes Lepsius, *Der Todesgang des Armenischen Volkes: Bericht über das Schicksal des Armenischen Volkes in der Türkei während des Weltkrieges* (Potsdam: Tempelverlag, 1919), 74.

Table 1 Ottoman Demographic Data for Diyarbekir Province, 1913

Ethnicity	Number
Jewish	1954
Protestant	5417
Chaldean	4783
Greek Catholic	113
Greek	1815
Syriac Catholic	3582
Syriac	28,699
Armenian Catholic	9004
Armenian	51,405
Muslim	434,236
Total	**541,203**

Source: Başbakanlık Osmanlı Arşivi (Ottoman Archives, Istanbul, hereafter: BOA), DH. EUM.MTK 74/51, 3 December 1913, enclosure on p.3. Justin McCarthy rectifies another official Ottoman figure of 73,226 to 89,131. Justin McCarthy, *Muslims and Minorities: The Population of Ottoman Anatolia and the End of the Empire* (New York: New York University Press, 1983), 69–70.

According to this demographic classification, Diyarbekir province in 1913 was inhabited by 1954 Jews, 104,818 Christians, and 434,236 Muslims. On the one hand, it is very likely that in Table 1 the demographic balance between Muslims and Christians is skewed to the advantage of the Muslims, and on the other hand there is no mention of marginal social groups such as Yezidis or Kizilbash living in the province. All in all, the provincial statistics clearly contradict each other, and contradictions and vaguenesses such as these apply to Diyarbekir's districts as well.[35] For the bulk of the population it seems reasonable to contend that for approximately one-third it was made up of Christians and two-thirds Muslims.[36]

Social relations within and between these groups remains a topic that is vigorously debated. Essentialistic ideas of homogeneous and hermetically bounded national units in collective action and conflict ('*the* Kurds versus *the* Syriacs' or '*the* Turks against *the* Armenians') are quite ahistorical and need to be critically deconstructed. On the other hand, the same critical gaze needs to be cast over rosy

[35] For example, according to a German consular report, the ethnic distribution in Mardin district was as follows: 27,000 Muslims, 10,000 Armenian Catholics, 10,000 Syriac Christians, 1500 Syriac Catholics, 1400 Protestants, 100 Chaldeans, summing up to a total of 50,000 inhabitants in the entire district. *PAAA*, Botschaft Konstantinopel 170, Aleppo consul Rößler to special ambassador Hohenlohe-Langenburg (Istanbul), 27 September 1915. Conversely, the Armenian Patriarchate calculated the total number of Armenians in Mardin to be 14,547 whereas according to the German consulate they numbered no more than 11,400, assuming that all Protestants were ethnic Armenians. Theodig, *Mius Merelotzu: Amenoun Daretzoutzu* (Istanbul: n.p., 1921), 261, quoted in: Mesrob K. Krikorian, *Armenians in the Service of the Ottoman Empire 1860–1908* (London: Routledge, 1977), 19, 117 footnote 6.

[36] This is confirmed by Lepsius: 'Die christliche Bevölkerung betrug also reichlich 1/3, die muhammedanische 2/3 der Gesamteinwonerschaft des Wilayets.' Lepsius, *Der Todesgang*, 74.

utopian images of an ostensibly peaceful society basking in multi-cultural co-existence in an era when nationalism had not yet poisoned the minds of neighbours.[37] In his travel account of 1895, the British ethnographer Parry wrote about his experiences in Diyarbekir province:

> It is most striking, when one first visits the East, to find a mixed company thoroughly enjoying each other's society, which, when analysed, would be found to contain an Old Syrian or two, a Protestant, half-a-dozen Moslems, and a substantial quota of the Papal varieties. Yet they are all talking together in perfect good-fellowship, smoking each other's cigarettes, and discussing with quite marvellous tact the latest political news.[38]

In Mardin city, for example, serenity ruled when the British traveller and photographer Gertrude Bell visited the citadel town, which she qualified as 'more splendid than any place I have ever seen'. According to her, all the ethno-religious communities peacefully co-existed in perfect harmony.[39] Mark Sykes, who had conducted field work and several studies on the Ottoman Empire, visited Palu in 1913 and wrote that there was no trace of enmity between the local Zazas and Armenians.[40] Sykes also wrote that İbrahim Pasha (d. 1909)[41] of the Mîlan tribe had

> encouraged Christians (Armenians and Chaldaeans) to take refuge in the vicinity of Viranshehr, and established a bazaar in that town, which rapidly increased in size. While other tribes and chiefs plundered and massacred Armenians, Ibrahim protected and encouraged Christians of all denominations. It is estimated that during the great Armenian massacres he saved some 10,000 Armenians from destruction.[42]

The British army major Ely Soane, who was fluent in Kurdish and had traversed the Diyarbekir region in native disguise, commented two years before the First World War that the Diyarbekir Chaldeans 'were on excellent terms with their ferocious neighbours', referring to the Kurdish tribes dwelling north of Diyarbekir city.[43] Benevolent Muslim notables wrote optimistic articles to the effect that in

---

[37] For an introduction to interethnic relations in the nineteenth century, see: Benjamin Braude and Bernard Lewis, 'Introduction', in: Benjamin Braude and Bernard Lewis (eds.), *Christians and Jews in the Ottoman Empire* (New York: Holmes and Meier, 1982), vol. 1, 1–34.

[38] Oswald H. Parry, *Six Months in a Syrian Monastery: Being the Record of a Visit to the Head Quarters of the Syrian Church in Mesopotamia with Some Account of the Yazidis or Devil Worshippers of Mosul and El Jilwah, Their Sacred Book* (London: Horace Cox, 1895), 41.

[39] Gertrude Bell Archives (Robinson Library, University of Newcastle upon Tyne) [hereafter cited as GBA], Gertrude Bell to her mother, 25 April 1911.

[40] Sykes, *The Caliph's Last Heritage*, 366.

[41] İbrahim Pasha was born into the Mîlan tribe in the Urfa area, became chieftain in 1863, and managed to build a reputation for himself by amassing prestige in his tribe. When Sultan Abdulhamid II established the mounted Hamidiye regiments in 1891 he joined them and acquired even more respect from the population. He soon became the single most powerful commander of the Hamidiye regiments in the eastern provinces, boasting fortified headquarters and many thousands of mounted warriors of the 41st, 42nd, and 43rd regiments. When the CUP wrested the 1908 revolution İbrahim repudiated the new cabinet and declared his independence. The Ottoman army was deployed and İbrahim was definitively defeated and forced to flee into the mountains south of Urfa, where he died. M. Wiedemann, 'Ibrahim Paschas Glück und Ende', in: *Asien* 8 (1909), 34–54.

[42] Sykes, *The Caliph's Last Heritage*, 324.

[43] Ely B. Soane, *To Mesopotamia and Kurdistan in Disguise: With Historical Notices of the Kurdish Tribes and the Chaldeans of Kurdistan* (London: J. Murray, 1912), 66.

Diyarbekir Armenians and Kurds had always got along well and that the Ottoman government was to blame for any possible mutual distrust between these two peoples, who had lived in 'eternal brotherhood' (*vifak-ı kadîm*) and even 'consanguinity' (*yekdestî*).[44] According to these views, pre-war interethnic relations were peaceful and the atmosphere was congenial.

The interethnic and interfaith relations in Diyarbekir province in the years before 1914 were in fact not as idyllic as some of these observers portrayed. They were frail due to the prolonged political and economic crisis that afflicted the Ottoman Empire. The gradual crumbling of Ottoman rule in the imperial peripheries throughout the nineteenth century had co-occurred with massacres perpetrated against Muslims in the Balkans and the Caucasus.[45] Among Ottoman Muslims, these events began to lead them to question the loyalty of Christian citizens to the Ottoman state. Moreover, the hundreds of thousands of refugees (primarily Circassians and Chechens from the Caucasus) who poured into the eastern provinces added to the existing tensions between Muslims and Christians. Local authorities often ignored, approved, or abetted encroachments on Armenians by these impoverished refugees.

The Abdulhamid era massacres, which struck Diyarbekir on 1 November 1895, saw massive destruction of human lives and property.[46] Approximately 25,000 Armenians were forcibly converted to Islam across Diyarbekir province, 1100 Armenians were killed in Diyarbekir city and 800 or 900 more in the outlying villages, while 155 women and girls were carried off by Kurdish tribesmen. In Silvan district 7000 Armenians converted and 500 women were carried off. In Palu 3000 and in Siverek 2500 converted to escape being massacred. In Silvan, along with Palu (where 3000 Armenians converted), '7500 are reduced to destitution and 4000 disappeared: killed, died of cold, etc., or escaped elsewhere'.[47] According to another source, 2000 houses and 2500 shops and workshops were burnt down in the province during the 1895 massacres.[48] An unknown percentage of these converts reconverted to their faiths, returned to their villages, reclaimed their possessions, and rebuilt their homes and businesses once the persecution was discontinued.

Still, the memory of the atrocities was very much alive among the population of Diyarbekir. Ely Soane wrote in his travel account,

> it is, among the underworld of western Kurdistan and northern Mesopotamia, a common subject of talk in the cafés how much the Sultan and the Government paid the ruffians of the town to do their dirty work, and how much the Kurdish Aghas presented to the authorities to be allowed to finish unhindered the blood-feuds that

[44] Hüseyin Paşazâde, 'Kürdler ve Ermeniler', in: *Kürd Teavün ve Terakki Gazetesi*, 30 January 1909, 3–6; Mehmed E. Bozarslan (ed.), *Kürd Teavün ve Terakki Gazetesi: Kovara Kurdî-Tirkî 1908–1909* (Uppsala: Deng, 1998), 431–4.

[45] Justin McCarthy, *Death and Exile: The Ethnic Cleansing of Ottoman Muslims, 1821–1922* (Princeton, NJ: The Darwin Press, 1995).

[46] Gustave Meyrier, *Les Massacres de Diarbekir: Correspondance diplomatique du Vice-Consul de France 1894–1896* (Paris: L'Inventaire, 2000).

[47] *Blue Book Turkey*, No. 8 (1896), enclosure in document no. 140, 127.

[48] Kévorkian and Paboudjian, *Les Arméniens*, 398.

existed between themselves and Armenians sheltering in Diyarbekr and the towns of Armenia. A very reign of terror overshadows the apparently peaceful and prosperous town.[49]

The province was beset by various tribal, ethno-religious, and political conflicts. The heavily armed Kurdish tribes of the province frequently engaged in armed combat to overpower each other and spared few lives when they defeated a rival tribe. In the Hazakh district (present-day İdil) Serhan II,[50] chieftain of the Mala Osman dynasty of the Hevêrki tribe, perceived a threat in the person of Khalife Meso of the Mala Meso dynasty of the Şeroxan tribe. In 1913 tribesmen loyal to Serhan carried out a raid against Kîwex village, where Meso, his brother Cercur, and his nephew Kato were living. In the ensuing massacre twenty-four men including young boys and two women were killed. Although Serhan was a Muslim and Meso of Yezidi descent, there were both Yezidis among Serhan's adherents and Muslims among Meso's adherents, thus clearly rendering this a tribal conflict.[51] An unknown number of inhabitants was killed in the Syriac village of B'sorino in 1907 during a punitive campaign by Midyat Kurds who feared that the local chieftains were becoming too influential. The church was burnt down and the houses were destroyed, but inhabitants proclaiming loyalty were allowed to work for the Midyat chieftains.[52]

When Gertrude Bell toured the south-eastern part of Diyarbekir province in the years before the war, she was robbed at night in the village of Khakh.[53] Since the theft was committed in the area ruled practically autonomously by the very powerful Çelebi dynasty of the Hevêrki tribe, their chieftain İsmail was brought in from Mzizah village. İsmail was furious about the breach of cultural norms of hospitality. Having no suspects, he arbitrarily rounded up five men and the mayor of Khakh, a man named Melke, threatening them with incarceration. Soon, it became known that rival tribesmen around chieftain Abdîkê Hemzikê of the semi-nomadic Zakhuran tribe[54] were responsible for the theft.[55] The Çelebi chieftain used the opportunity to settle tribal scores and join forces with local government to assassinate Abdîkê Hemzikê, disperse the Zakhuran, and pillage

---

[49] Ely B. Soane, *To Mesopotamia and Kurdistan in Disguise: With Historical Notices of the Kurdish Tribes and the Chaldeans of Kurdistan* (London: J. Murray, 1912), 65–6.

[50] Serhan II was a notorious Kurdish brigand, whose ruthlessness was only matched by his greed. In the pre-war years his power gained momentum as he succeeded his father as chieftain of the Mala Osman. Fed up with his terror, a group of Tur Abdin Syriacs filed a complaint against him at the Syriac Patriarchate in Istanbul, requesting a parliamentary inquiry and prosecution of Serhan. Contrary to their expectation, the case was neglected and no legal action was undertaken. BOA, DH.MUİ 77–2/15, 9 August 1910.

[51] Ömer Şahin, *Komkujî li hemberi Ezidîyan* (Heidelberg, 2001), unpublished private manuscript.

[52] GBA, diary entry for 17 May 1909.

[53] For details on Khakh village, see: Hollerweger, *Turabdin*, 164–75.

[54] According to tribal myths, the Zakhuran were remnants of a huge tribe commanding a vast area in Northern Mesopotamia, until they split up and formed the two major tribes in the region: Hevêrkan and Dekşurî. Due to their conflicts with the Çelebi core, they sided with Haco Ağa of the Hevêrkan tribe and became active in Kurdish nationalism in the Republican era. Their power crumbled, and in the 1940s they numbered a mere 500 tribesmen. *Aşiretler Raporu* (Istanbul: Kaynak, 2003, second edition), 250.

[55] GBA, diary entries for 24, 25, 26, 27, 28, and 29 May 1909.

their villages, seizing all of their cattle.[56] The uncrowned master of social banditry, however, was Alikê Battê of the Haco dynasty of the Hevêrkan tribe, whose name alone struck fear into the hearts of the locals.[57] Alikê Battê behaved like a warlord in a region he considered to be his dominion, and his propensity for killing was matched only by his lust for pillage. In August 1913, he engaged in a skirmish with gendarmes during an attempt to rob the Ottoman post carriage in Nusaybin. The post was delayed for some time and the brigand escaped into the Tur Abdin mountains.[58] At the end of 1913, Ali and his accomplices were arrested and incarcerated but profited from the general amnesty the government granted soon after.[59] Although they were threatened with re-imprisonment if they continued their brigandage after being released, they resumed their unlawful activities.[60]

Clashes of a tribal nature did not only occur in the Mardin district. The north and east of Diyarbekir province were other peripheral regions with influential Kurdish tribes competing for power. Most specifically, the Xerzan (Garzan) valley in the Beşiri district was torn by tribal warfare. The largest conflict was that between the Reşkotan and Etmankî tribes, which was settled through a victory won by the former.[61] The feud between the Elikan and Pencînaran tribes was another source of violence in the Garzan region.[62] It was provoked by Pencînar chieftain Bişarê Çeto, a loose cannon, who had telegraphically expressed his joy over the 1908 revolution in the hope of being left alone by the government.[63] Together with his equally trigger-happy brother Cemil Çeto they were known for their extortion of Armenian, Kurdish, and Syriac villagers in the region.[64] These two brigands had been

---

[56] This is confirmed by Abdîkê Hemzikê's grandson. Interview conducted with Aslan family (Zakhuran tribe), Midyat (Mardin province), 28 July 2004.

[57] Alikê Battê was relatively young when he became one of the most charismatic and fierce chieftains in Kurdish tribal history. He avenged his uncle Haco II by killing his murderer Cimo with his bare hands. He waged a guerrilla war against the Ottoman government for two decades, only to perish during a skirmish in 1919. For more on Alikê Battê, see: Mustafa Aldur, '1850–1950 yılları arası Turabdin'e Hevêrkan ve Mala Osmên', in: *Özgür Politika*, 15 September 2002; National Archives United Kingdom (London, hereafter cited as NAUK), Foreign Office (FO) 371/107502, 149523, 163688, 3050.

[58] BOA, DH.İD 145–2/38, 13 August 1913.

[59] BOA, DH.EUM.EMN 38/7, 1 December 1913.

[60] BOA, MV 194/22, 8 November 1914.

[61] 'Li Çiyaye Qîre, Delana Paşo, şerê Reşkotiyan û Etmankiyan: Şerê Filîtê Qûto û Mamê Elê Etmankî', in: Salihê Kevirbirî, *Filîtê Qûto: Serpêhatî, Dîrok, Sosyolojî* (İstanbul: Pêrî, 2001), 59–75. In this war Reşkotan chieftain Filîtê Qûto gained a reputation for ferocity and fearlessness as a warrior. His saga was immortalized in a long lamentation (*kilam*) equally named 'Filîtê Qûto' by Kurdish folk singers such as Dengbêj Şakiro, Karapetê Xaço, and Dengbêj Reşo. Salihê Kevirbirî, 'Deng û Awaza Xerzan', in: *Özgür Politika*, 3 January 2000.

[62] 'Şer û kilamak ji herêma Xerzan: Şerê Pencînaran û Elikan', in: ibid., 11–18. This conflict had been raging since the 1890s, when Hamidiye regiments had threatened the Elikan's domination in certain areas around Xerzan. İsmail Beşikçi, *Doğu'da Değişim ve Yapısal Sorunlar (Göçebe Alikan Aşireti)* (Ankara: Sevinç, 1969), 78–9.

[63] Bişarê Çeto and five other chieftains to the editor, Diyarbekir, 28 December 1908, quoted as 'Telgrafât-ı Hususiye', in: *Kürd Teavün ve Terakki Gazetesi*, 9 January 1909, 26. Cf. Bozarslan, *Kürd Teavün ve Terakki Gazetesi*, 302.

[64] BOA, DH.EUM.EMN 38/30, 6 December 1913.

robbing and murdering at will, but legal action was suspended in July 1914 and the Çeto brothers evaded prosecution.[65]

There were also intra-tribal intrigues and power struggles, most notably in the Reman tribe. Its famous female chieftain Perikhan, widow of İbrahim Pasha, had six sons who competed for succession: Mustafa, Said, Emîn, Abdullah, İbrahim, and Ömer.[66] In order to succeed their mother, the sons had to outclass each other in the ability to exert power and express leadership qualities. Of all her sons, Ömer was known for his ferociousness. Before the war, Ömer's campaign of plunder, provocation of government forces, and bravado did not go unnoticed. In the summer of 1914, the government declared him *persona non grata* and ordered him arrested and incarcerated. Ömer escaped prosecution and retreated into the Garzan region.[67] Finally, the Zirkî tribe in Lice had been fighting off the afore-mentioned Mîlan tribe to gain control over parts of the northern region of Diyarbekir province. In order to combat their rivals, the Zirkî chieftain Aziz Sabri had aligned himself with the Ottoman government.[68] These power relations would play a role in the unfolding of events during the First World War.

Ethno-religious conflict was another form of strife. Missionary activity among the various Christian churches was one source of discontent and conflict. When a young Jacobite Syriac dared to convert to Catholicism, one of his fellow villagers reported this and the convert was interned at the Syriac monastery Deyr-ul Zaferan. When he refused to reconvert the monks beat him up and chased him out.[69] This type of violence intended to maintain social closure and reinforce ethno-religious boundaries between groups. Within the Armenian community there was rivalry as well. A Protestant Armenian remembered well that before the war, there were weekly brawls between Catholic and Protestant Armenians in his town. On several occasions even the clergy joined the fighting.[70] In Lice, Syriacs and Armenians squabbled over an old abandoned monastery which both communities aimed to appropriate. The government intervened in the conflict and a compromise was reached.[71] However, the severest conflicts seem to have raged between Muslims and Christians. When Gertrude Bell visited Diyarbekir she noticed that

> the nervous anxiety which is felt by both Christians and Moslems—each believing that the other means to murder him at the first opportunity—is in itself a grave danger and very little is needed at Diarbekr to set them at each other's throats. During the 3 days that I was there tales of outbreaks in different parts of the empire were constantly being

---

[65] BOA, DH.EUM.EMN 89/5, 28 July 1914.

[66] 'Ji birakujiya nava eşîran nimûneyeke sosret: Emînê Perîxanê—Evdilê Birahîm', in: Kevirbirî, *Filîtê Qûto*, 49–58.

[67] BOA, DH.İD 80/5, 8 August 1914.

[68] Şevket Beysanoğlu, *Anıtları ve Kitabeleri ile Diyarbakır Tarihi* (Diyarbakır: Diyarbakır Büyükşehir Belediyesi Kültür ve Sanat Yayınları, 1996), vol. 2: *Akkoyunlular'dan Cumhuriyete Kadar*, 773, footnote 17.

[69] Yves Ternon, *Mardin 1915: Anatomie pathologique d'une destruction* (special issue of the *Revue d'Histoire Arménienne Contemporaine* 4, 2002), 163.

[70] James Sutherland, *The Adventures of an Armenian Boy* (Ann Arbor, MI: The Ann Arbor Press, 1964), 33.

[71] BOA, DH.İD 162–2/51, 16 August 1913.

circulated in the bazaars. I have no means of knowing whether they were true, but after each new story people went home and fingered at their rifles.[72]

These ethnic tensions may well have been conflicts partly based on economic interests, since the labour market was arranged along ethno-religious lines. Therefore many occupations were practically monopolized by one or another group.[73] For example, most merchants in the Diyarbekir bazaar were Armenians and Syriacs, who also worked as cobblers, jewellers, carpenters, millers, stonemasons, and blacksmiths (see Plate 2).

Both groups were also very active in the production of cloth, including the silk for which Diyarbekir was famous. Kurds controlled the livestock trade and most Zazas were woodcutters or skippers on the Tigris. Due to the Abdulhamid era massacres, no love was lost between the Christian and Muslim merchants in the pre-war years. Many Muslim shopkeepers, outnumbered by Christian tradesmen, harboured jealousy and resentment towards their colleagues.[74] This opportunism was reported by the German vice-consul in Mosul, Holstein, as follows:

> In general, the Kurd of the Diyarbekir region does not care much about the politics of a single Kurdish shaikh, he just profits from the opportunity to enrich himself through robbery and pillage and sees in the sometimes therewith connected murder [*Ermordung*] of a couple of Armenians no further crime. Thus a Kurdish wood cutter in Diyarbekir explained to me, upon my question how many Armenians he already had on his conscience, very naively: he could not say it precisely, but it must have surely been around half a dozen.[75]

Possible palliatives and mitigations were dismissed. When Süleyman Bey of the noted Cemilpaşazâde dynasty urged the Muslim market people of Diyarbekir to treat the Armenians with respect and bury the hatchet, he was met with resistance and ridicule, and experienced great frustration.[76] The Armenians, in their turn, boycotted all Muslim-owned shops at Christmas 1908.[77] The Diyarbekir bazaar faced far graver situations when Muslim merchants were simply allowed to seize Christian property during periodic pogroms.

Deeply embedded within the social structure of Diyarbekir were overlapping and competing networks of rich, influential families of Muslim notables who had historically played the role of local power wielders in the city. These were for example the Cizrelizâde and Ekinci families, who lived near the square. The very powerful Pirinççizâde dynasty lived near the Great Mosque, the Ocak family near the Melik Ahmed Mosque, whereas the chieftain of the Cizrelizâde, Mustafa Bey, lived in a large mansion next to the Iskender Pasha Mosque. His neighbours were the powerful Yasinzâde Şevki Bey of the Ekinci family on one side, and the

---

[72] GBA, Gertrude Bell to her mother, 6 June 1909.
[73] Alphons J. Sussnitzki, 'Zur Gliederung wirtschaftlicher Arbeit nach Nationalitäten in der Türkei', in: *Archiv für Wirtschaftsforschung im Orient* 2 (1917), 382–407.
[74] Beysanoğlu, *Diyarbekir Tarihi*, 760–1.
[75] *PAAA*, R14079, Holstein to Bethmann-Hollweg, 22 May 1913.
[76] GBA, diary entry for 30 April 1909.
[77] GBA, diary entry for 9 February 1909.

Iskender Pasha family on the other. Several important Kurdish dynasties such as the Cemilpaşazâde, Hevêdan, Zazazâde, as well as major chieftains from Hazro, Kulp, and Lice had houses in the Ali Pasha neighbourhood. They often commuted between their region of origin and the city. The Cemilpaşazâde were in particular important as pioneers of Kurdish nationalism.[78] To various degrees, all these local elites were connected to each other through multiple familial ties: the Cizrelizâde were in-laws of the Yasinzâde, the Müftüzâde were related to and partly overlapped with the Direkçizâde, several women of the Zazazâde had married into the Gevranizâde family, the Cemilpaşazâde were relatives-in-law of the Azizoğlu, and the powerful Pirinççizâde dynasty was connected to most of these families through marital ties.[79] The ebb and flow of Diyarbekir city's politics was often decisive for provincial politics as well. The competition between these families could rise to boiling point as they engaged in fierce competition over local government. This often resulted in forms of corruption and nepotism, witnessed by the British traveller David Fraser, who argued in 1909 that in Diyarbekir 'misgovernment is at its height, and within its walls there is neither justice for the righteous nor protection for the weak'.[80] Competition within the urban landed notable class coupled with relatively weak central state authority produced these conditions.

The problems in the countryside were equally severe. Ever since the break-up of the Kurdish emirates in the mid-nineteenth century, the Ottoman eastern provinces has remained 'wild' and has never been fully pacified. The absence or very feeble presence of the state's monopoly of violence in rural areas allowed for the existence of quasi-state structures such as tribal regions with their own laws, and the maintenance of many conflicts. Therefore living conditions were relatively insecure, with arbitrary exertion of even mortal violence by certain powerful tribes and state agents.[81] By the turn of the twentieth century, inequalities, injustices, and violence continued to exist at all levels of society because the private use of violence was widespread and was often followed by partial or full impunity. David Fraser witnessed this personally about 'the mountains of south-western Kurdistan, a region where everybody is a robber according to his ability. The aghas of each tribe levy blackmail on all who pass through their country, the little people kill and murder whenever they dare. . . . These people live in such inaccessible places that the Turks have practically no control over them'.[82] The farther away one travelled from Diyarbekir city, the more depacified conditions became. According to Fraser, Diyarbekir province's south-eastern border region was particularly troublesome: 'Here is a sort of no-man's-land, where Arabs and Kurds of different organisations lord it over hapless Christians, Jews, and Yezidis. Robbery and murder are mere

---

[78] Hakan Özoğlu, *Kurdish Notables and the Ottoman State: Evolving Identities, Competing Loyalties, and Shifting Boundaries* (Albany, NY: State University of New York Press, 2004), 103–7.

[79] Şeyhmus Diken, *İsyan Sürgünleri* (Istanbul: İletişim, 2005), 134–5, 204–5, 209.

[80] David Fraser, *The Short Cut to India: The Record of a Journey along the Route of the Baghdad Railway* (Edinburgh: William Blackwood and Sons, 1909), 180–1.

[81] For a study of the monopolization of the means of violence, see: Johan Goudsblom, 'De Monopolisering van Georganiseerd Geweld', in: *Sociologische Gids* 48, no. 4 (2001), 343–59.

[82] Fraser, *The Short Cut to India*, 193–4.

pastimes for those strong enough to indulge in them, and retribution by the law is practically unknown, for the Turk either cannot or does not want to enforce obedience'.[83] These conditions did not contribute to a pacified society but could only have added to an atmosphere of tension, distrust, and sectarianism among the rural inhabitants of the province.

THE ADVENT OF NATIONALISM

In the nineteenth century, the Ottoman Empire went through two interrelated processes: decline and modernization. The empire had reached an apex in the sixteenth and seventeenth century, when it rose from a small principality to become the foremost state in the Mediterranean and Europe. But the empire stagnated and declined slowly as a result of external pressures such as Western imperialism and internal pressures such as nationalist separatism. Due to technological innovations and economic developments, West-European states were able to catch up and by the early nineteenth century had surpassed the Ottoman Empire in economic, military, and political power. Western states penetrated into the Ottoman realm by means of both armies and ideas. One of the most significant Western ideas imported to the Ottoman Empire was undoubtedly nationalism. As it swept through Europe during the nineteenth century, the Ottoman Empire did not remain immune to it and was forced to deal with nationalism both within and beyond its borders. The number of nationalist political parties and uprisings in the empire significantly increased and soon enough became the most important problem determining much of Ottoman politics. Greece was the first country, in 1829, to declare its independence from the Empire. In 1875, Serbia, Montenegro, Bosnia, Wallachia, and Moldova unilaterally declared their independence. Following the Russian-Ottoman war of 1877–8, the Ottomans were forced to grant independence to Serbia, Romania, and Montenegro, and a form of autonomy to Bulgaria. The remaining territories in the Balkans remained under Ottoman control. In 1878, Cyprus was lent to Great Britain in exchange for favours at the Congress of Berlin. Under the cloak of bringing order, Britain also occupied Egypt in 1882. The rest of Ottoman North Africa was lost between 1830 and 1912 in an eastward direction: France occupied Algeria in 1830 and Tunisia in 1881, and Italy invaded Libya in 1912.[84]

By 1900, Ottoman politics was plagued by a crisis so severe that future prospects for the empire seemed gloomy. It tried to catch up to the Western world by passing a series of reforms (in 1839, 1856, and 1863) aimed at adopting Western modes of administration and culture. The reforms had immediate effects such as agricultural and industrial innovations, and brought changes in military, architecture, finance, legislation, institutional organization, and land reform. They

---

[83] Ibid., 205–6.
[84] Cemal Kafadar, 'The Question of Decline', in: *Harvard Middle Eastern and Islamic Review* 4, nos. 1–2 (1997–8), 30–75.

also introduced aspects of European culture such as in clothing and food. The promulgation of a constitution in 1876 brought about a major watershed in Ottoman political history and represented a gradual shift from absolute monarchy to a form of constitutional monarchy. It was Sultan Abdulhamid II who during his reign (1876–1909) formulated a more sustained and coherent Ottoman response to the challenges of Western domination. Under his rule administration, transport, communications, education, and health care were significantly improved. But the reforms did not produce long-lasting results in the long run, as the empire kept on crumbling at its peripheries.[85] They neither halted the rise of centrifugal nationalism nor improved the economy. Nationalism continued unabated, influencing other Ottoman peoples like the falling of dominoes. The more nations broke away from the empire, the more Muslim-dominated Ottoman society became, a process that pointed in a certain homogenizing direction and conjured images of a future in which the empire would simply break up into contiguous nation states.

The most decisive political changes in the empire would emerge from revolutionary activities by a range of people alternately called the Young Ottomans and later Young Turks.

Three phases can be discerned in the development of the Young Turk movement. The first phase may be termed the 'Ottoman patriotic citizenship', roughly running from the 1860s to 1889. The second was the phase of 'Muslim nationalist activism', lasting from approximately 1889 to 1913. The third and final phase was the apex of the Young Turk movement, that of 'Turkish nationalist hegemony', from 1913 to 1950. In the following chapters, this book will concern itself mostly with this third phase of the Young Turk movement. This periodization is rudimentary and serves only to bring some basic structure to what was a highly complex process of ideology and political practice. There was considerable overlap in the periods and actors, as well as some overlap in the three ideologies.[86] The following overview aims to sketch the contours of this tripartite process.

Although it is difficult to pin down a precise date for the first phase of 'Ottoman patriotic citizenship', its beginnings can be placed in the 1860s, and more precisely at around 1865. It was at that time when for the first time organized opposition groups began to formulate liberal criticism in favour of constitutional reform and against the Ottoman sultanate. A group of men established a secret society

---

[85] Selim Deringil, *The Well-Protected Domains: Ideology and the Legitimation of Power in the Ottoman Empire, 1876–1909* (London: Tauris, 1999).

[86] For two contrasting views on the periodization of Turkish nationalism, see: M. Şükrü Hanioğlu, 'Turkism and the Young Turks, 1889–1908', in: Hans-Lukas Kieser (ed.), *Turkey Beyond Nationalism: Towards Post-Nationalist Identities* (London: I.B. Tauris, 2006), 3–19; Erik-Jan Zürcher, 'Young Turks, Ottoman Muslims and Turkish Nationalists: Identity Politics 1908–1938', in: Kemal H. Karpat (ed.), *Ottoman Past and Today's Turkey* (Leiden: Brill, 2000), 150–79, at 173:

a peculiar brand of Ottoman Muslim nationalism, which was to a very high degree reactive. It was defined in a particular and antagonistic relationship between Muslims who had been on the losing side in terms of wealth and power for the best part of a century and Ottoman Christians who had been the winners . . . But the nation for which they demanded this political home was that of the Ottoman Muslims—not that of all of the Ottomans, not only that of the Turks and certainly not that of all the Muslims in the world.

comprised of intellectuals, teachers, and authors who were dissatisfied with the Sultan's reforms and, influenced by the legal writing of Montesquieu, the politics of Rousseau, and the economics of Smith,[87] developed the concept of Ottomanism. This ideology aimed at the creation of an overarching common Ottoman citizenship irrespective of religious or ethnic affiliation. Authors like Nâmık Kemal (1840–88) pioneered the nationalist interpretation of the concepts of 'nation' (*millet*) and 'homeland' (*vatan*) to Ottoman readers. In their search for an Ottoman equivalent to the nationalist movements in Europe, they imitated Young Italy, Young France, and Young Germany, and named their movement *Jeunes Turcs*.[88] Ultimately, Ottomanism failed due to rejection and repression. In the long run, the ideology was rejected by many Muslims and non-Muslims alike. To the latter, it was perceived as a step towards dismantling their traditional privileges. Meanwhile, the Muslims saw it as the elimination of their own superior position. Ottomanism was mainly a literary tradition in that the intellectuals who espoused it rarely went farther than authoring theoretical articles about the need for a conception of Ottoman citizenship. Because of this relative weakness, the Sultans simply exiled and imprisoned the Young Ottomans, depriving them of strength by the last decade of the nineteenth century. Their demise heralded the rise of the second phase of Young Turk opposition, spearheaded by a new generation of nationalist intellectuals who espoused Turkish cultural nationalism.[89]

A century after the French Revolution, in the spring of 1889, five young Ottoman Muslim students founded a secret organization in opposition to the rule of Sultan Abdulhamid II. Their prime aim was to overthrow the Sultan and re-establish the constitution and parliament. Whereas these students convened in the military medical college in Istanbul, many Ottoman oppositionists were living in exile in Western Europe and were to play a decisive role in the movement. In time, after several reorganizations, the diaspora and indigenous movements merged into the Committee of Union and Progress (İttihad ve Terakki Cemiyeti, CUP).[90] Despite Abdulhamid's effective tactics of repression and co-optation, the CUP grew across the empire. The organization branched out into secret cells all over the empire, published articles and books propounding their ideology and striving against the Sultan, accumulated weapons, and especially in the Balkans developed into an activist party defending Ottoman Muslims from Macedonian and Bulgarian nationalist attacks. The CUP also worked with other opposition groups and convened two congresses of opposition to the Ottoman regime, one in 1902 and the other in 1907. Their efforts produced the Constitutional Revolution of July 1908, and launched the Young Turks into the Ottoman parliament and to power

---

[87] Hamit Bozarslan, 'La révolution française et les Jeunes Turcs', in: *Revue de l'Occident Musulman et de la Méditerranée*, nos. 52–3 (1989), 148–62.

[88] For a history of the Young Ottoman movement, see: Şerif Mardin, *The Genesis of Young Ottoman Thought: A Study in the Modernization of Turkish Political Ideas* (Princeton: Princeton University Press, 1962).

[89] David Kushner, *The Rise of Turkish Nationalism, 1876–1908* (London: Frank Cass, 1977), 20ff.

[90] M. Şükrü Hanioğlu, *The Young Turks in Opposition* (Oxford: Oxford University Press, 1995), 71–8.

positions. Ottomans of all denominations marched in the streets under banners bearing the slogan 'Liberté, Egalité, Fraternité' in various languages, and welcomed the age of freedom and democracy.[91] An unprecedented freedom reigned in the press and parliament, where new ideas and methods of government were devised, discussed, and examined. But like many other revolutions, the Young Turk revolution betrayed its initial aspirations and in the third phase of Turkish-nationalist hegemony led to dictatorship, war, and genocide.

Two important aspects of state formation and nation formation need to be considered in describing and explaining this process: political attitudes towards violence, and processes of identification and disidentification.[92]

The second phase in the Young Turk movement was characterized by competition with liberals, Islamist conservatives, and Armenian revolutionaries. Gradually, the Young Turks gained the upper hand and ultimately pushed through a conquest of Ottoman political culture. They owed this victory mostly due to superior force and their recourse to violence. The Young Turk movement was never a pacifistic one, but throughout these three phases a certain radicalization in their use of coercion and violence occurred. The roots of this violence can be traced back, first and foremost, to years of persecution and repression. The Young Turks were deported to the empire's peripheries (such as Libya's south-western desert region), forced to go into exile in Europe for years, and incarcerated in prisons where they met ordinary criminals such as murderers and brigands. If this in itself did not strengthen their resolve and evaporate any hesitation they might have had about using violence, their response was a second important stage that significantly lowered the threshold for violence. This was the Young Turks' turn towards activism, decided upon at the 1902 congress in Paris. Articles published in the Young Turk press argued that 'a nation's salvation depends on the sacrifice it will make and the blood it will shed. Until now no nation has obtained the freedom that is its natural right through printing journals. In fact, theories are tools for preparing the way of evolution. Weapons, however, accelerate this evolution'.[93]

In addition to a more activist stance, from 1905 on the movement began establishing groups of self-sacrificing volunteers (*fedaîs*) based on the tactics of Macedonian and Armenian revolutionaries. Their contacts in prison proved useful as this move caused ordinary criminals to be co-opted by the party.[94] The brutalization of political culture in the Balkans, particularly Macedonia, was indeed considerable and added to the Young Turks' proclivity for using violence. In the second phase of the Young Turk movement, their paramilitaries and hitmen became known for avenging the death of

---

[91] For two detailed histories of the revolution, see: M. Şükrü Hanioğlu, *Preparation for a Revolution: The Young Turks, 1902–1908* (Oxford: Oxford University Press, 2001); Aykut Kansu, *The Revolution of 1908 in Turkey* (Leiden: Brill, 1997).

[92] The twin concepts of identification and disidentification are theorized in: Abram de Swaan, 'Widening Circles of Identification: Emotional Concerns in Sociogenetic Perspective', in: *Theory, Culture and Society* 12, no. 1 (1995), 25–39; id., 'Widening Circles of Disidentification: On the Psycho- and Sociogenesis of the Hatred of Distant Strangers: Reflections on Rwanda', in: *Theory, Culture and Society* 14, no. 2 (1997), 105–22.

[93] Hanioglu, *Preparation*, 221.

[94] Ibid., 217–27.

every Muslim by killing ten Bulgarians in retaliation.[95] From 1906 on, the movement entered a third phase on the path towards violence as countless numbers of young military officers, including some influential ones, joined the Young Turk movement. Young Turk politicians had actively sought this alliance, declaring that 'by propaganda and publications alone a revolution cannot be made. It is therefore necessary to work to ensure the participation of the armed forces in the revolutionary movement'.[96] Ambitious Young Turks could now use the force, discipline, and cohesion of the army to destroy an old social order and initiate a new societal order through 'revolution'. The result was terror, threats, and assassinations. On the eve of the 1908 Revolution, Ottoman political culture was polarized and depacified to the degree that it left little space for negotiation or moderation.[97]

The history of the Young Turk movement can be viewed as a complex process of identifications that went through two important shifts. The movement's transformation from the first phase into the second was a shift from Ottoman nationalism to Muslim nationalism and saw a process of disidentification with non-Muslims. The shift from the second phase of Muslimism to the third phase of Turkish nationalism produced a process of disidentification with non-Turks. These two shifts were crucial for the process of Turkish nation formation. It would be misleading to suggest that from its inception, the Young Turk movement actively steered towards a direction of Turkish nationalism and ethnic unmixing of Ottoman society. First, a demographic Turkification crept into society throughout the nineteenth century as persecution caused large groups of Muslims from the Balkans and the Caucasus to seek asylum in the Anatolian remnant of the empire. Such an external shock to Ottoman society could not have been expected to pass without a disturbance. It brought hundreds of thousands of immigrants over the years and brought tensions caused by distrust and suspicion between people of different backgrounds and interests. Second, Armenians and Greeks already had established political parties closely relating ethnicity with politics although many Armenians and Greeks did not join these parties, but multi-ethnic liberal parties instead. The 1902 Paris conference of the Ottoman opposition had already seen a 'voluntary' ethnic unmixing as the Armenian delegates walked out after a harsh remark about Christian loyalty to the Ottoman state.[98] In time, two scholars remark correctly, 'it did not take long for the non-Turkish parliamentarians to relinquish their support for the CUP and join the liberals'.[99] Ethnic separatism on the part of non-Turks and the rise of Turkish nationalism were two processes that only served to strengthen each other. These processes of disidentification represented the contracting shifts from Ottoman to Muslim to Turkish nationalism. They are richly documented in the sources and examples of this shift are plentiful. The third

---

[95] Ibid., 223.

[96] Bernard Lewis, *The Emergence of Modern Turkey* (Oxford: Oxford University Press, 2002), 202.

[97] George W. Gawrych, 'The Culture and Politics of Violence in Turkish Society, 1903–14', in: *Middle Eastern Studies* 22, no. 3 (1986), 307–30.

[98] Hanioğlu, *The Young Turks in Opposition*, 195.

[99] Feroz Ahmad and Dankwart A. Rustow, 'İkinci Meşrutiyet Döneminde Meclisler, 1908–1918', in: *Güney-Doğu Avrupa Araştırmaları Dergisi*, no. 4–5 (1976), 252.

section of this chapter will illustrate at micro-level how this process developed in Diyarbekir.

To the outer world, at least discursively, the Committee of Union and Progress maintained an image of defender of the pro-Ottomanist principle of 'Unity of Elements' (*İttihad-ı Anasır*).[100] Their understanding of this philosophy of unity was 'for all Ottomans without distinction of race [*bila tefrik-i cins ve mezhep bütün Osmanlılar*]' to unite for the 'peace and safety of the common homeland [*vatan-ı müşterekenin huzur ve selameti*]', while abandoning their 'particular purposes [*mekâsid-i mahsusalar*]'.[101] According to Young Turk journalists, the nations constituting the state had to 'unite around the ideal of Ottomanism, that is a common, indivisible, and strong homeland [(*Osmanlılık yani müşterek gayr-ı kabil-i taksim ve kuvvetli bir vatan fikri etrafında iştirakleri*]'. This would facilitate the spread of 'prosperity and justice in the most distant corners of the country [*memleketin en ücra köşelerine bile refah ve adalet*]'.[102] To Ottoman Christians they would write reassuring messages such as the one sent to a Bulgarian politician: 'This country belongs neither to the Turk, nor to the Bulgarian or Arab. It is the asset and domain of every individual carrying the name Ottoman. . . . Those who think the opposite of this, namely those who try to sever the country into parts and nations, even if they are Turks, are our adversaries, our enemies [*düşmanımızdır*]'.[103] According to one Young Turk writer, 'Turkism' (i.e. Turkish ethnic nationalism) was compatible with Ottomanism, and pursuing the latter would only serve to strengthen the former.[104] Thus, the CUP either denied or downplayed their adherence to Turkish nationalism. But their outward composure of Ottoman unity and progress stood in sharp contrast with their internal discourse of Turkish nationalism. Indeed, it would be misleading to suggest that the CUP merely reacted to ongoing, large-scale processes of unintended and unorganized population unmixing in the late Ottoman Empire. The central committee of the party foresaw a much more pro-active stance on issues of identity politics. Recent scholarly research into the party's internal correspondence clearly reveals a radical and activist Turkish-nationalist core around Dr. Bahaeddin Şakir (1874–1922), Dr. Mehmed Nâzım (1872–1926), Mehmed Talaat (1874–1921), and İsmail Enver (1881–1922), who had given up hope of the ideal of Ottoman unity and citizenship already in the 1900s.[105] Two prominent ideologues of this shift were the sociologist Mehmed Ziyâ Gökalp (1876–1924) and the historian Yusuf Akçura (1876–1935).[106] More than anyone they laid the ideological foundations of the shift from Ottoman patriotism to Turkish nationalism.

---

[100] Hüseyin Cahid, 'Türklük, Müslümanlık, Osmanlılık', in: *Tanin*, 29 September 1908, no. 387.
[101] *Tanin*, 20 February 1910, no. 886.
[102] Hüseyin Cahid, 'İttihad ve Terakki Politikasına Avdet', in: *Tanin*, 6 November 1912, no. 1434.
[103] Cengiz, *Dr. Nazım ve Dr. Bahaeddin Şakir*, 248.
[104] Izzet Ulvi, 'Türklük Duygusu Osmanlilik Fikrine Mani Mi?', in: *Türk Yurdu* 1, no. 16 (June 1912), 269.
[105] Hanioğlu, *Preparation*, 173–81.
[106] François Georgeon, 'Deux leaders du mouvement national: Ziya Gökalp et Yusuf Akçura', in: François Georgeon, *Des ottomans aux turcs: Naissance d'une nation* (Istanbul: Isis, 1995), 55–66.

Mehmed Ziyâ Gökalp was a sociologist, writer, and poet from Diyarbekir.[107] Deeply influenced by contemporary European thought on nationalism, he was most formative in the overhaul of Ottoman Muslim identity and the emergence of Turkish nationalism, and his work was particularly influential in shaping Young Turk ideology. His philosophy was based on a rejection of Ottomanism and Islamism in favour of a unique synthesis of a Muslim Turkish nationalism.[108] This nationalist ideal not only entailed the dismissal of civic interpretations of nationalism but also espoused a collective disidentification with non-Turkish Muslims such as Albanians, Arabs, Kurds, and Persians living in the Ottoman Empire. Gökalp embraced the work of Émile Durkheim, and reinterpreted the French sociologist's thought into a distinct set of ideas that laid the foundations of modern Turkish nationalism. Rather than a rigorous academic exercise, he took elements of Durkheim's theories that he deemed politically useful for Turkish nation formation by selecting and applying quotes and data that seemed to confirm his positions. Gökalp's thought was a blend of ideas. He rejected the individualism of liberal capitalism (without rejecting capitalism itself) and Marxist categories of class struggle. In doing so, he followed Durkheim in believing that society is composed not of individuals, classes, or other interest groups clashing and working for their own good, but of interdependent occupational segments working harmoniously for the public good. This form of 'populism' (*halkçılık*), partly influenced by the Russian Narodnik movement, viewed society as an organic whole and discredited the individual.[109] This approach embodied an axis of tension between scholarship and politics: Gökalp's philosophy was not only a sociological theory of society, but also very clearly an ideological stand: for corporatist nationalism and against liberal democracy. His choice to abandon pure scholarship and engage in politics as well launched him into power as the ideologue of the Young Turk party.[110] As a result, he ended up articulating, underpinning, as well as legitimizing the policies of the Young Turk regime.

A second ideologue who made a coherent attempt at analysing nationalism in the Ottoman Empire was Yusuf Akçura (1876–1935), who was born in the Russian Empire as a Tatar. Akçura founded the journal *Turkish Homeland* (*Türk Yurdu*), which he saw as the major intellectual force behind the development of Turkish

---

[107] Ziyâ Gökalp (1876–1924) was perhaps the most influential intellectual of the CUP era. He was born in Çermik (Diyarbekir) of a Zaza mother and a Turkish father. He studied in Istanbul but was sent back to Diyarbekir because of his support for the constitutional movement. He published countless articles in many journals, founded the CUP branch in Diyarbekir and quickly rose to become a member of the Central Committee of the CUP. After the war he was interned on Malta and began working for the Kemalists. For a political biography, see: Uriel Heyd, *Foundations of Turkish Nationalism: the Life and Teachings of Ziya Gökalp* (Westport, CT: Hyperion Press, 1979).

[108] M. Sait Özervarlı, 'Transferring Traditional Islamic Disciplines into Modern Social Sciences in Late Ottoman Thought: The Attempts of Ziya Gökalp and Mehmed Serafeddin', in: *The Muslim World* 97 (2007), 317–30.

[109] Zafer Toprak, 'Osmanlı Narodnikleri: "Halka Doğru" gidenler', in: *Toplum ve Bilim* 24 (winter 1984), 69–81.

[110] Taha Parla, *The Social and Political Thought of Ziya Gökalp 1876–1924* (Leiden: Brill, 1985), 36; Ziya Gökalp, *Turkish Nationalism and Western Civilization: Selected Essays of Ziya Gökalp* (Westport, CT: Greenwood Press, 1981, transl. Niyazi Berkes).

nationalism. His definition of the Turkish nation was more along ethnic lines and included other Turkish peoples, such as those in the Caucasus and Central Asia.[111] In 1904, Akçura published a seminal article titled 'Three Types of Politics', an assessment of Ottomanism, Muslimism, and Turkism. In this pamphlet Akçura pointed out that the impossibility of forging a nation out of the Ottoman minorities precluded the ideology of Ottomanism from being successful. Akçura then targeted Muslimism and declared it problematic because of the genesis of nationalism among Muslim minorities. (In their turn, the Islamist movement criticized Turkish nationalism since 'Islam does not allow nationalism'.[112]) He pointed out that 'the dominant current in our contemporary history is that of nations', signaling that Turkish nationalism was the only feasible ideology.[113] The major point of contention with his colleague Ziyâ Gökalp was the degree to which Islam was allowed to become a component of Turkish identity. But Gökalp ultimately agreed with Akçura and clearly stated that 'it becomes clear that our nation consists of Turkophone Muslims'.[114] Also, much like Gökalp, Akçura also called for the creation of a 'national economy [*millî iktisad*]' that would sustain a Turkish nation state.

The efforts of Gökalp and Akçura functioned as a catalyst for the shifts from Ottomanism to Muslimism to Turkish nationalism. In a secret speech he gave in Salonica in 1910, the leader of the Young Turk party, Mehmed Talaat Bey, addressed his colleagues in a way that represented a definite departure from Ottomanism:

> You are aware that by the terms of the Constitution equality of Mussulman and Ghiaur [infidel, non-Muslim] was affirmed but you one and all know and feel that this is an unrealizable ideal. The Sheriat [Islamic law], our whole past history and the sentiments of hundreds of thousands of Mussulmans and even the sentiments of the Ghiaurs themselves, who stubbornly resist every attempt to ottomanize them, present an impenetrable barrier to the establishment of real equality. We have made unsuccessful attempts to convert the Ghiaur into a loyal Osmanli and all such efforts must inevitably fail, as long as the small independent States in the Balkan Peninsula remain in a position to propagate ideas of Separatism among the inhabitants of Macedonia. There can therefore be no question of equality, until we have succeeded in our task of ottomanizing the Empire—a long and laborious task, in which I venture to predict that we shall at length succeed after we have at last put an end to the agitation and propaganda of the Balkan States.[115]

For the British Ambassador Gerald Lowther (1858–1916) the picture was much clearer. He wrote a few months later: 'That the Committee have given up any idea of Ottomanizing all the non-Turkish elements by sympathetic and Constitutional ways has long been manifest. To them 'Ottoman' evidently means 'Turk' and their

---

[111] François Georgeon, *Aux origines du nationalisme turc: Yusuf Akçura (1876–1935)* (Paris: ADPF, 1981).
[112] Babanzâde Ahmed Naim, *İslâmda Davayı Kavmiyyet* (Istanbul: Tevsi-i Tıba'at Matbaası, 1332 [1914]), 5ff.
[113] Yusuf Akçura, *Üç Tarz-ı Siyaset* (İstanbul: n.p., 1909).
[114] Ziyâ Gökalp, 'Türkçülük ve Türkiyecilik', in: *Yeni Mecmua* 2–51 (4 July 1918), 482.
[115] Quoted in: Lewis, *The Emergence*, 218.

present policy of 'Ottomanization' is one of pounding the non-Turkish elements in a Turkish mortar'.[116]

On the eve of the First World War, the Young Turks felt logistically and ideologically strong enough to discontinue their denial and understatements of the movement's Turkish nationalist character. After the definitive turn to Turkish nationalism, the Young Turks openly embraced policies that explicitly excluded non-Turks. Two key leaders, the doctors Bahaeddin Şakir and Mehmed Nâzım, wrote to a party branch that the CUP could never be entrusted to 'any enemy of the Turks, Armenian or not [*Türk düşmanı olan ne bir Ermeni'ye ne de bir başkasına*]'. Armenians would only be allowed to join if they pledged total allegiance to the movement's Turkish-nationalist agenda—a rather unlikely scenario. The doctors continued to declare that 'If we take a non-Muslim Ottoman into our committee, it will only be on these conditions. Our committee is a purely Turkish committee [*halis bir Türk cemiyeti*]'.[117] Two years later, in a letter to Zionist leaders, Dr. Nâzım was even more unreserved in expression, leaving nothing implied: 'The Committee of Progress and Union wants centralization and a Turkish monopoly of power. It wants no nationalities in Turkey. It does not want Turkey to become a new Austria-Hungary. It wants a unitary Turkish nation state [*einen einheitlichen türkischen Nationalstaat*], with Turkish schools, a Turkish administration, and a Turkish legal system'.[118] A leading Young Turk could not have been more explicit and unambiguous in describing the party's ideal vision of society.

As a result of inter-state and intra-state pressures, within decades a heterogeneous movement for freedom, equality, constitution, and justice had transformed into a party devoted to ethnic nationalism and prepared to entertain violence. The decline of the Ottoman state as a result of Western imperialism and separatism produced two processes of disidentification among the Ottoman political elite: a shift from Ottoman patriotism to Muslim nationalism, and a shift from Muslim nationalism to Turkish nationalism. On the eve of a devastating series of wars that few saw coming beforehand, nothing could have been deadlier than the combination of hegemonic power and a radical ideology.

THE DISCOVERY OF SOCIETY AND POPULATION POLICIES

For centuries, the Ottomans took for granted that, in the natural order of life, the cultures and languages of state, speech, literature, and religion would vary, from region to region, group to group, city to city, class to class. The Young Turks adhered to an entirely different world-view. They were advocates of the idea of

---

[116] Quoted in: ibid., 219–20.

[117] Dr. Bahaeddin Şakir and Dr. Nâzım to Hayri Efendi, 2 June 1906, in: Yusuf Hikmet Bayur, *Türk İnkılabı Tarihi* (Ankara: Türk Tarih Kurumu, 1991), vol. 2, part 4, 115; Filiz Cengiz, *Dr. Nâzım ve Dr. Bahaeddin Şakir'in Kaleminden İttihad ve Terakki Cemiyeti* (Unpublished MA Thesis, Istanbul University, 1997), 39–40.

[118] Hanioğlu, *Preparation*, 260.

population politics and firmly believed that society needed to be studied with scientific methods and crafted into a homogeneous entity. The emergence of social science gave the Young Turks an intellectual foundation on which they built their ideology of population politics. The main protagonist of this strategy was Ziya Gökalp, and one of the main objects of this policy was the ethnically mixed Ottoman eastern provinces. The moment the CUP seized power, the eastern provinces in particular were subjected to close ethnographic research and prepared for large-scale demographic interventions into civil society. This was accompanied as well as legitimized by a discourse of civilization versus barbarity.

Many Young Turk leaders in Paris were students of August Comte's disciples and deeply influenced by positivism. Their newspaper bore the slogan 'Order and Progress [*İntizam ve Terakki*]' on its masthead.[119] The Young Turks were also in touch with Sorbonne professor David Léon Cahun (1841–1900),[120] whose ideas on Turkish nationality and history had a great effect on the formation of Turkish nationalism. Cahun advanced the argument that centuries of exposure to Islamic and Arabian culture had had a detrimental impact on the Turkish race.[121] In a sense, it was only natural that, in the setting of the late nineteenth-century Ottoman crisis, the academic discipline of sociology developed under severe political pressures and itself became politicized. What was the use of sociology in 'solving' the 'questions' beleaguering Ottoman society? This was a major question occupying the minds of Young Turk sociologists and anthropologists.[122] The birth and rise of Ottoman sociology attests to the pressures under and limits within which science can function in a society in crisis. One scholar who had studied under Young Turk sociology argued that 'it has been more interested in questions concerning what *should be* the ideal Turkish society than in what Turkish society actually *was*'.[123] Studies of society were subservient to the political, military, and economic interests of the Young Turk party. One scholar argued that if their purpose was 'Turkification', by the time the Young Turks assumed hegemony over the state apparatus, 'sociology was used as an intellectual tool to serve this purpose'.[124] In the twilight zone between power and knowledge, it was applied sociology that most interested these sociologists.

---

[119] Z. Fahri Fındıkoğlu, *Auguste Comte ve Ahmet Rıza* (Istanbul: Türkiye Harsî ve İçtimaî Araştırmalar Derneği, 1962); Murtaza Korlaelçi, *Pozitivizmin Türkiye'ye Girişi ve İlk Etkileri* (Istanbul: İnsan, 1986).

[120] Elisabeth-Christine Mülsch, *Zwischen Assimilation und jüdischem Selbstverständnis: David Léon Cahun (1841–1900)* (Bonn: Romanist Verlag, 1987).

[121] Léon Cahun, *Introduction à l'histoire de l'Asie: Turcs et Mongols, des origines à 1405* (Paris: A. Colin et cie, 1896), Part II.

[122] Paul J. Magnarella et al., 'The Development of Turkish Social Anthropology', in: *Current Anthropology* 17, no. 2 (1976), 263–74; Niyazi Berkes, 'Sociology in Turkey', in: *American Journal of Sociology* 42 (1936), 238–46; Zafer Toprak, 'Osmanlı'da Toplumbilimin Doğuşu', in: *Modern Türkiye'de Siyasi Düşünce* (Istanbul: İletişim Yayınları, 2001) vol.1, *Tanzimat ve Meşrutiyet'in Birikimi*, 310–27.

[123] İbrahim Yasa, *Hasanoğlan: Socio-Economic Structure of a Turkish Village* (Ankara: Türkiye ve Orta Doğu Amme İdaresi Enstitüsü, 1957), V–VI.

[124] Recep Şentürk, 'Intellectual Dependency: Late Ottoman Intellectuals between Fiqh and Social Science', in: *Die Welt des Islams* 47, no. 3 (2007), 283–318.

The main Young Turk sociologist-ideologue was undoubtedly Ziyâ Gökalp. The first chair of Sociology was established for him at Istanbul University in 1915. He founded a research institute of sociocultural studies and started a short-lived *Journal of Sociology* (*İçtimaiyat Mecmuası*).[125] Under his supervision, many works by Durkheim, his nephew Mauss, Lévy-Bruhl, and Fauconnet were translated into Ottoman Turkish and the first sociology textbook was introduced. Hence, from the outset sociology in Turkey was dominated by Gökalp's influence. He instrumentalized sociology to grapple with the reality that Ottoman society was not a homogeneous nation state, a reality that frustrated him. He dreamt of a 'monolingual and homogeneous Ottoman nation [*yek-dil ve yek-cihet bir Osmanlı milleti*]'.[126] In his famous poem 'Red Apple' (*Kızılelma*) he fantasized about cultural and linguistic purity, as well as the demographic homogeneity of what he calls a 'new Turkish World'. The poem contains the following passage:

> He said it was important to get to know the East /
> said the people are a garden and we are gardeners [*halk bahçe biz bahçivanız*] /
> trees are not rejuvenated by grafting only /
> first it is necessary to trim the tree.[127]

Gökalp established himself as a pioneer of Young Turk social engineering: the composition of society had to change and the political elite was in charge of doing so. After 1913, he advocated the 'Turkification' of the Ottoman Empire by imposing the Turkish language and culture on all the citizenry and constructing a nascent Turkish nation state.[128]

The production of a Turkish identity was a main focus of Gökalp's job description at the Department of Sociology. In one of his articles, titled 'What is a nation?' (possibly after Renan), Gökalp sketched the contours of his interpretation of criteria for inclusion and exclusion in the nation. First, he dismissed geographic, racial, imperial, and individualist definitions of Turkish nationhood and moved on to argue that

> the science of Sociology demonstrates that national ties lie in upbringing, culture, that is in sentiments ... we want to live in a society where we received these. Only on one condition can we disengage from it and join another society: that condition is to extract the childhood upbringing we received from out of our souls and discard it ... A nation is a cultural group composed of individuals who have received the same upbringing, and are united by a common language. A man will want to live together with people whom he shares an upbringing and language with rather than people with whom he shares blood ... A person will be miserable living in a society whose culture he does not

[125] Recep Şentürk, 'İçtimâiyyât Mecmuâsı', in: *Türkiye Diyanet Vakfı İslam Ansiklopedisi* (Istanbul: Türkiye Diyanet Vakfı, 2000), vol. 21, 448–63.

[126] Şevket Beysanoğlu, *Ziya Gökalp'ın ilk yazı hayatı, 1894–1909: Doğumu'nun 80. yıldönümü münasebetiyle* (Istanbul: Diyarbakırı Tanıtma Derneği, 1956), 95.

[127] Ziya Gökalp, *Kızılelma* (Ankara: Kültür Bakanlığı Yayınları, 1976 [1914], Hikmet Tanyu, ed.). This passage in the poem quite literally reflects Zygmunt Bauman's metaphor of gardening the human landscape.

[128] Hamit Bozarslan, 'M. Ziya Gökalp', in: *Modern Türkiye'de Siyasi Düşünce* (Istanbul: İletişim Yayınları, 2001), vol. 1, *Tanzimat ve Meşrutiyet'in Birikimi*, 314–19.

share. This condition will drive him to suicide, sickness, and insanity.[129] For example, we have many co-religionists who, although they are racially not Turkish, fully possess the Turkish spirit from the perspective of upbringing and culture ... due to the upbringing they have received, they cannot live in any other society and will work for no other ideal than the Turkish one.[130]

The argument for the primacy of nurture over nature in establishing national identity, an idea deeply embedded in Gökalp's thought, prompted corresponding policies by the Young Turk political elites. Social engineering would develop along the lines of the enforced socialization of Turkish culture.

A crucial aspect of Young Turk social science was the creation of ethnographic knowledge on the ethnic structure of Ottoman society. After the 1913 Young Turk coup d'état, CUP research on and interest in the ethnic structure of the Ottoman Empire vastly expanded.[131] The Young Turks were aware that national self-determination or ethnic majoritarianism was becoming the decisive legitimizing principle in the expanding, Europe-led nation-state system. They understood decades of territorial loss to be a result of the fact that Ottoman Muslims could never lay claim to those territories since they never constituted a compact majority in any of them. This nationalist philosophy informed the population politics to be pursued, and the ethnographic research would provide the raw data to work with. The bureaucratic apparatus that was designed for this purpose was the 'Directorate for the Settlement of Tribes and Immigrants' (İskân-ı Aşair ve Muhacirîn Müdüriyeti, İAMM). This organization was established in 1913 and served to advance the sedentarization of the many Turcoman, Kurdish, and Arab tribes, and to provide accommodation for homeless Muslim refugees, expelled from the lost territories.[132] It would later be expanded to constitute four branches, namely Settlement, Intelligence, Transport, and Tribes.[133] For the collection of ethnographic knowledge, the directorate convened a 'Scientific Council', which was to be headed by Ziya Gökalp. The direction to be taken was laid out during the First World War, when Talaat assembled the Young Turk leaders and asserted that 'Anatolia is a closed box for us', arguing that it was first necessary to 'get to know the contents of

---

[129] In 1894, Gökalp attempted suicide but survived. According to one author, Gökalp's mental imbalance was triggered by his identity crisis of being stuck between his Kurdish past and his Turkish future. Rohat, *Ziya Gökalp'ın Büyük Çilesi Kürtler* (Istanbul: Fırat, 1992), 25–37. By the time the CUP had risen to power and his theories had gained a foothold, Gökalp had firmly established his identity as Turkish and Turkish only. Accusations by oppositionists that he was really Kurdish he dismissed with nationalist poetry: 'Even if I was a Kurd, Arab, or Circassian / my first aim would be the Turkish nation!' Fevziye Abdullah Tansel (ed.), *Ziya Gökalp Külliyatı-I: Şiirler ve Halk Masalları (Kızılelma—Yeni Hayat—Altun Işık—Eserleri Dışında Kalan Şiirleri)* (Ankara: Türk Tarih Kurumu Yayınları, 1952), 277. Later he repeated this assertion: 'Even if I found out that my grandfathers came from a Kurdish or Arab region, I would still not have hesitated to conclude that I am a Turk.' Ziya Gökalp, 'Millet Nedir?', in: *Küçük Mecmua* 28 (25 December 1922), 1–6, at 6.

[130] Ziya Gökalp, 'Millet Nedir?', in: *Küçük Mecmua* 28 (25 December 1922), 1–6.

[131] İsmail Görkem, *İttihat ve Terakki'nin Yaptırdığı 'Anadolu'da Gizli Mabetler' Konulu Araştırmalar: Baha Said Bey- Türkiye'de Alevî-Bektaşî, Ahî ve Nusayrî Zümreleri* (Ankara: Kültür Bakanlığı HAGEM Yayınları, 2000), chapter 1, 1–58.

[132] *İkdam*, 29 December 1913 (no. 6052), 3.

[133] Cengiz Orhonlu, *Osmanlı İmparatorluğu'nda Aşiretlerin İskânı* (Istanbul: Eren, 1987), 120.

it' in order to operate on it. After Talaat, party ideologue Gökalp took the floor and declaimed: 'We have made a political revolution . . . But the biggest revolution is the social revolution. The revolutions we can spark in our social body [*içtimaî bünyemiz*], in the field of culture, will be the largest and most productive. This will only work if we get to know the morphological and physiological structure of Turkish society . . . In order to research these structures let us send comrades with scholarly ability to open this box'.[134]

Whereas Gökalp articulated an ideology of population politics and Talaat organized it, junior Young Turk emissaries conducted the field work. A whole host of them descended upon the country to conduct research on the ethnic minorities. These ethnic experts produced dozens of volumes and virtually no group was left unstudied.[135] The following individuals were assigned to study the following groups: Baha Sait Bey for the Kizilbash and Bektashi religious communities, Mehmet Tahir (Olgun) and Hasan Fehmi (Turgal) for the Ahi religious community, Esat Uras for the Armenians, Zekeriya Sertel (a student of Durkheim at the Sorbonne) for the tribes, religious orders, and Alevis. Gökalp himself assumed the task of researching one of the most challenging groups: the Kurds. These men were commissioned by the Young Turk party particularly to travel in the eastern provinces to map these peoples and analyse their political loyalties. The body of knowledge they produced was also a matrix of loyalty and political preference versus ethnicity.[136]

One of the most interesting researchers was a Naci İsmail Pelister (d. 1940), an ethnic Albanian yet an ardent Turkish nationalist, educated in Germany. When the CUP seized power, he began working at the Interior Ministry and published his ethnographic research under his pen name Habil Adem and many other pseudonyms as translator and ghostwriter.[137] Pelister was responsible for researching tribes and Turcomans, but wrote on a range of subjects, including methods of population politics. His first publication as İAMM operative was officially credited to another person named Von P. Gotz, 'an official from the Prussian Ministry of Colonies'. The book was titled *The Settlement of Migrants: the International Method of Assimilation*, and was composed of two parts. The first is a comparative study of methods of assimilating conquered and colonized peoples, with examples drawn from American, British, Dutch, French, German, and Russian history. The second part of the book consists of how to legislate the reception of immigrants in a given society. This part also devotes considerable space to the settlement and integration of immigrants, including examples from immigration societies such as North America, Great Britain, Latin America, and Australia. The author discusses internal and external colonization of a region. External colonization can include the

---

[134] Nejat Birdoğan (ed.), Baha Said Bey, *İttihat ve Terakki'nin Alevilik-Bektaşilik Araştırması* (Istanbul: Berfin, 1995), 8.

[135] For a brief overview of Young Turk ethnographic research, see: Fuat Dündar, 'İttihat ve Terakki'nin Etnisite Araştırmaları', in: *Toplumsal Tarih* XVI, no. 91 (2001), 43–50.

[136] Birdoğan, *İttihat ve Terakki*, 7–8.

[137] Mustafa Şahin and Yaşar Akyol, 'Habil Adem ya da nam-ı diğer Naci İsmail (Pelister) hakkında', in: *Toplumsal Tarih* 2, no. 11 (1994), 6–12.

establishment of a population of settler colonists, the assimilation of indigenous populations, and convincing indigenous populations to accept the settlers. British methods of external colonization are recommended. Internal colonization, on the other hand, can include the deportation of populations from one region to another, importing kin ethnic groups living abroad, and assimilating immigrant labourers. For this type of internal colonization, American methods are recommended. The author concludes the study with a summary of prerequisites for successful colonization: for a process of colonization to yield its fruits, he argues, settlers need to be able to sustain themselves economically, indigenous elites need to be induced to collaborate or face punishment, and the spiritual and cultural life of the indigenous populations needs to be extinguished.[138] The relevance and significance of these studies is manifold: they informed population policies while many of the techniques of internal colonization were carried out throughout the four decades of Young Turk rule, with varying degrees of success.

Ziya Gökalp had researched the Diyarbekir region. After several observations on Kurdish tribes and villages, he argued that 'it is not only man that changes during these affairs of assimilation...but the customs, morals, in other words national culture that changes', and concluded that Kurds would be easy to assimilate since 'Turks and Kurds like each other and resemble each other'.[139] In another article Gökalp argued that those Kurds who were in frequent contact with Arabs were 'doomed to nomadism, tribal life, and reactionism' because 'Arabs are tied to ignorance so tightly that...they have absolutely no talents'. Those Kurds who lived side by side with Turks however, had been 'liberated from feudalism'. Therefore, according to Gökalp, the logical conclusion was that 'neighbourliness with Turks has had a very positive effect on the Kurds'. All in all, he concluded, 'the Kurds' interest is to stay away from the Arabs and live close to the Turks'.[140] This ideological legitimization was complemented with an article entitled, 'Urban Civilization, Village Civilization', in which Gökalp sharply contrasted 'civilized life' in the cities with the 'feudalism' of the villages. Diyarbekir, he lamented, was living in the 'Middle Ages', whereas Turks, 'a nation in love with freedom and equality since time immemorial...settled in the cities from their natural inclinations'. A substantial part of Gökalp's writings was about how population policies towards the eastern provinces should take shape. In one of his articles he set the trend by arguing that when two peoples lived side by side, 'the dominating nation will assimilate the captive nation'. Gökalp named this process 'dénationalisation', and argued that it had proven efficient in the French government's campaign to suppress the use of German in Alsace Lorraine.[141] One of his students went even further and argued that Gökalp's studies were a powerful engine propelling Young Turk population politics: 'Gökalp gave an important report to the Central

---

[138] Von P. Goç, *İskan-ı Muhacirîn: Beynelmilel Usûl-ü Temsil* (Istanbul: Kitabhâne-i Sûdî, 1918, transl. Habil Adem), 7–29, 131–2, 197–204, 237–42.

[139] Ziya Gökalp, 'İstimlâl', in: *Küçük Mecmua* 29 (1 January 1923), 1–6.

[140] Ziya Gökalp, 'Kürtler'in Menfaati', in: *Cumhuriyet*, 20 July 1924, 4.

[141] Ziya Gökalp, 'Şehir Medeniyeti, Köy Medeniyeti', in: *Küçük Mecmua* 30 (10 January 1923), 4–7.

Committee, and later had the question of the minorities researched, in particular the Armenian Question. As a result of this research, deportations of Armenians were carried out'.[142]

The eastern provinces were a special focus in Young Turk ethnographic research. There are few sources on the daily practice of the research, but the existing reports on the encounter between Young Turk idealists and the peasant population reflect a confrontation between diametrically opposed ideas: ethnic nationalism versus religious conservatism. One of the CUP ethnographers went on a fact-finding mission to the eastern provinces and reported a conversation which he saw as characteristic for his travels: 'I am in Erzurum. It is the feast of 10 July. I am speaking to a headman at a construction site. At the right moment, I said, "Father, are you a Turk?" The poor old man seemed annoyed at what he saw as a joke and replied in a begging manner:

"Please don't say such a thing. I am a Muslim".
"But father, aren't the Turks Muslims? Also, haven't the Turks been the ones to protect and kept Islam alive?"
"Sir, when we say Turks we mean the Kizilbash, please, don't say that."'[143]

The son of a missionary who was born and raised in Diyarbekir, after providing an overview of the peoples of the Diyarbekir region, including various Muslims, concluded: '"Turks" no one of these will care to be called'.[144] These interactions indicated that the local Ottoman Muslims did not identify with an abstract sense of Turkish national identity.

Another Young Turk ethnographer conducted his research after the First World War and mapped the various identifications of the population. According to him, the population of Istanbul looked down upon much of the rest of the empire, calling themselves 'city dwellers' and reserving ethnic labels such as Albanian, Arab, Kurd, or Laz for rural people. For much of the rest of the Ottoman Muslim population, their Islamic identity superseded ethnic ones. Moreover, those who did identify with an ethnic group often did so by

voluntarily identifying with a group whose qualities they considered wonderful. This way many originally Turkish youngsters took pride in Albania or with Kurdism. There was nobody who praised himself as being Turkish [*Türklükle mübahat eden tek bir fert yoktu*]. The term Turk seemed to be a shameful one nobody wanted to take upon oneself. In Eastern Anatolia, Turk meant 'Kizilbash', and in Istanbul it meant coarse person or villager.[145]

In a partly autobiographical historical novel, yet another Young Turk intellectual was confronted with Ottoman Muslims denouncing Turkish nationalism and Mustafa Kemal, giving rise to the following exchange:

---

[142] Enver Behnan Şapolyo, *Ziyâ Gökalp: İttihadı Terakki ve Meşrutiyet Tarihi: Ekli ve Fotoğraflı* (Istanbul: İnkılap ve Aka Kitabevleri, 1974), 149.
[143] Fuad Sabit, 'Anadolu Duygularından', in: *Türk Yurdu* 2, no. 28 (11 December 1912), 72.
[144] Talcott Williams, *Turkey: A World Problem of To-day* (New York: Doubleday, Page and Co., 1921), 219.
[145] Hilmi Ziyâ Ülken, *Ziyâ Gökalp* (Istanbul: Kanaat Kitabevi, 1942), 88–9.

'How can one be Turkish and not line up with Kemal Pasha?'

'But we are not Turkish, sir.'

'What are you then?'

'We are Muslims, praise to Allah [*Biz İslamız elhamdulillah*]. The ones you mention live in Haymana.'[146]

The author then went on to formulate a policy to alter these identifications: 'If we are vouchsafed a victory, all we would rescue would be these desolate lands, these rugged hills. Where is the nation? It is not apparent yet, and it will be necessary to remake it over again'.[147] Clearly, to the Young Turks' chagrin, Turkish-speaking Ottoman Muslims did not identify with the concept of 'Turk'.

All in all, the Young Turks produced an enormous (and hegemonic) corpus of knowledge on the eastern provinces. During the First World War, as population politics based on this research was raging in full intensity,[148] the research was evaluated for its empirical and practical value. Young Turk journals praised the fact that 'scientific research' was conducted 'by government force' and had yielded 'abundant results'.[149] Baha Said published the results of his research on ethnic groups in Anatolia in 1918, introducing the Young Turk audience to ethnic groups they had hardly heard of before.[150] The Young Turk tradition of gathering ethnic data on minorities continued well into the 1920s, 1930s, and 1940s. Younger researchers, many of whom were students of Gökalp in Istanbul, now took up the task of developing the methods and theses of their mentors. The establishment of a Young Turk dictatorship in 1913 saw to it that the east became 'a powerless object of power-over-others wielded by the centre'. This meant that the region could 'neither exercise counter-power, to bring about a balance of power, nor exercise pressure to any viable extent . . . the exercise of power is, for all intents and purposes, unilateral and unidirectional'.[151]

This 'lack' of 'Turkishness' in the eastern provinces was a major problem for the Young Turks. The clash between Armenian and Turkish claims on the eastern provinces is symbolized in a discussion between Talaat and prominent Armenian-nationalist leader Karekin Pastermadjian (1872–1923), on the eve of the First World War. The discussion was about the fate of the eastern provinces, and after mutual accusations of nationalism and expressions of suspicion, Pastermadjian inveighed against Talaat:

You are not on the right path any longer. You are dragging the Ottoman Empire towards chaos. With your victories, you imagine yourselves Napoleon and Bismarck.

---

[146] Yakup Kadri Karaosmanoğlu, *Yaban: Millî Roman* (Istanbul: Muallim Ahmet Halit Kitaphanesi, 1932), 110–11.

[147] Karaosmanoğlu, *Yaban*, 139.

[148] Taner Akçam, 'Ermeni Meselesi Hallolunmuştur': Osmanlı Belgelerine Göre Savaş Yıllarında Ermenilere Yönelik Politikalar (Istanbul: İletişim, 2007), 37–77.

[149] 'Aşiretler Hakkında İlmî Tetkikler', in: *Türk Yurdu* 14, no. 193 (1 March 1918), 87.

[150] Baha Said, 'Anadolu'da İçtimâî Zümreler ve Anadolu İçtimâiyatı', in: *Millî Talim ve Terbiye Mecmuası*, no. 5 (August 1918), 18–32.

[151] Majeed R. Jafar, *Under-underdevelopment: A Regional Case Study of the Kurdish Area in Turkey* (Helsinki: Social Policy Association in Finland, 1976), 58.

You don't know where you will take this country but continue your bullheadedness. Proof? Some time ago you told Vramian you would Turkify the Kurds. With what? With which culture? You would not mention these senseless things if you had knowledge about your history. You are forgetting that you have only been on our lands for 500 to 600 years, and that before other nations have passed through these lands: Persians, Romans, Arabs, Byzantines. If they have not been able to assimilate the Kurds, how will you accomplish this? Last summer I went to our three provinces and only saw three bridges in that region: two of them were old Armenian constructions, the third one dates from Tamerlane. I have not seen any traces of your civilization. It is unacceptable that you are so inconsiderate about the important problems of the state. You are insincere in the matter of the reforms. Do you suppose we believe in the economic and political measures you took to be freed of the Armenian question, or the policies you carried out to cleanse the Armenians? Our national consciousness is so mature, we will prevent your purposes from being realized.[152]

This argument is highly relevant as it demonstrates the logic and principles of nationalist population politics of the time.[153] Two years later, the German teacher Martin Niepage, who was stationed in Aleppo and witnessed the genocide, added, 'Where is there any Turkish trade, Turkish handicraft, Turkish manufacture, Turkish art, Turkish science? Even their law, religion and language... have been borrowed from the conquered Arabs'.[154] For the Young Turks these observations were as humiliating as instructive, giving them a sense of what the envisioned Turkish state and society lacked to be truly admitted to the family of nation states. In order to keep a firm hold over the eastern provinces, where the legitimacy of such a Turkish nation state was perceived as dubious at best, the Young Turks were bent on 'proving' that the eastern provinces were 'Turkish', in particular, that their population was Turkish (ethnic majoritarianism), their history was Turkish (national myth-making), and their territory (monuments and architecture) was Turkish.

The genesis of the Young Turk interest in and internal colonization of the Ottoman eastern provinces, developed out of competition with other stakeholders, for they were not the only ones who had visions of the future of the eastern provinces. Tsarist Russia had clear imperialist ambitions in the region.[155] The CUP's fear of a Russian 'invasion'[156] was only matched by its paranoia about Armenian and Kurdish separatism. Armenian, Kurdish, and Assyrian nationalists imagined carving out nation states from the eastern provinces. Both forces, imperialism and separatism, only strengthened the Young Turk desire to ensure and

---

[152] Gaïdz F. Minassian, 'Les relations entre le Comité Union et Progrès et la Fédération Révolutionnaire Arménienne à la veille de la Première Guerre mondiale d'après les sources arméniennes', in: *Revue d'histoire arménienne contemporaine* 1 (1995), 45–99.

[153] The discussion is also fateful in the sense that the Young Turks assaulted precisely those characteristics of the Other that Pastermadjian and Toynbee saw as objective justifications for an expressly *national* existence in the Ottoman territories.

[154] Martin Niepage, *The Horrors of Aleppo* (London: T. Fisher Unwin Ltd., 1917), 20–1.

[155] Michael Reynolds, 'The Ottoman-Russian Struggle for Eastern Anatolia and the Caucasus, 1908–1918: Identity, Ideology and the Geopolitics of World Order.' Unpublished PhD Thesis, Princeton University, 2003), 37–82.

[156] Hüseyin Cahid, 'Devletler ve Şarkî Anadolu', in: *Tanin*, 27 November 1913, no. 1769.

maintain a firm and preferably permanent grip on the region. British policy-makers summarized the difficulty of applying the West European nation-state system to the Ottoman eastern provinces:

> What makes the Armenian national character doubly unfortunate is the geographical and political situation in which the people find themselves. The Armenians of Eastern Asiatic Turkey are for the most part in a minority, or, at best, have but a bare majority; they are dwellers in towns and valleys, and are divided by great belts of sedentary Kurdish mountaineers . . . The example of Bulgaria, where a compact, warlike population was able to drive out a minority by foreign intervention and the incursion of foreign armies, is one that cannot be followed in Eastern Turkey-in-Asia.[157]

Despite the tensions, in the period 1908–12 the fate of the empire was as yet undecided. Everything was still possible. Nationalists, liberals, and conservatives competed in the Ottoman political space, sometimes ferociously. The harsh political atmosphere following the eruption of the Balkan wars would permanently change this fragile equilibrium in favour of nationalists on all sides. Power and ideology were necessary but not sufficient conditions for the catastrophes to come. Severe crisis resulting from war and defeat was the fateful spark which ignited the powder keg.

VIOLENCE, VICTIMIZATION, AND VENGEANCE

On 17 October 1912, Serbia, Montenegro, Greece, and Bulgaria declared war on the Ottoman Empire out of discontent with its rule and the possibilities for territorial expansion. Out-powered, demoralized, unprepared, and poorly equipped, the Ottoman army fought fourteen battles and lost all but one of them. In November, the Bulgarian advance pushed the Ottoman army back to the trenches of Çatalca, 30 kilometres west of Istanbul. There, the onslaught was stopped and the imperial capital remained uncaptured. Warfare continued as two other important Ottoman cities were captured: the old imperial capital of Edirne was besieged and taken by the Bulgarian army, and on 9 November 1912 the Ottoman garrison surrendered the cradle of the Young Turks, Salonica, to the Greek army. The state of war lasted until the Treaty of London was signed on 30 May 1913, which dealt with territorial adjustments arising out of the conclusion of the war.[158] After the cessation of hostilities, the Empire was heavily truncated for good.

Although there were clear distinctions between combatants and non-combatants, as the skirmishes unfolded into total warfare, none of the armies respected this distinction. Atrocities were committed by all sides in the conflict,[159] but contemporary

---

[157] Sykes, *The Caliphs' Last Heritage*, 417, 418.

[158] For an analysis of the Ottoman involvement in the Balkan wars from a military perspective, see: Edward J. Erickson, *Defeat in Detail: The Ottoman Army in the Balkans, 1912–1913* (Westport, CT: Praeger, 2003).

[159] Richard C. Hall, *The Balkan Wars, 1912–1913: Prelude to the First World War* (London: Routledge, 2000), 136–8.

journalists and victims accused the Bulgarian army in particular of systematic mal-treatment of civilian populations.[160] The forces commanded by the Bulgarian generals Ivan Fichev (1860–1931), Vladimir Minchev Vazov (1868–1945), and Radko Dimitriev (1859–1918) committed acts of violence including large-scale destruction and arson of villages, beatings and torture, forced conversions, and indiscriminate mass killing of Ottoman Muslims.[161] Leon Trotski, at that time correspondent for the Russian newspaper *Kievskaya Mysl*, reported that the campaigns of ethnic cleansing and massacre were organized in particular by General Dimitriev, a man 'deeply animated by those features of careerism including careless zeal and moral cynicism'. When his ambition to conquer as much territory as possible as fast as possible was frustrated by stubborn Ottoman defence, he ordered his troops to take prisoners no longer, and to execute all prisoners of war, included the wounded.[162] His forays into the Thracian countryside and the Bulgarian occupation in general spelled persecution and terror, accompanied as it often was by rape of women.[163] The Serbian authori-ties, too, encouraged 'local police officers, secret agents and lawyers, to terrorize the Muslims and to make a calm life for them impossible'.[164] War crimes were another category of mass violence. According to one contemporary account, whenever Bulgar-ian forces captured Ottoman prisoners of war, they would frequently set the Christians free but execute certain numbers of the Muslims among them.[165] Victimized groups who fled to their 'ethnic brethren' with their stories of terror kindled counter-terror against populations associated with their victimizers. Thus, whereas Bulgarian army units ignited the campaigns of terror and ethnic cleansing, the responses of Greek and Ottoman forces against Bulgarian villages were at least as violent.

The territorial erosion of the Ottoman Empire in the Balkans and in the Caucasus during the nineteenth century was a process that produced humiliation and refugee streams.[166] The total and permanent loss of the Balkan peninsula in 1913, however, was a watershed that affected the very existence of the Empire. It is no exaggeration to state that the effect of the Balkan wars on Ottoman society was nothing short of apocalyptic. The loss of many major Ottoman cities, property, human lives, and face was unbearable to a proud Ottoman elite who was dismayed at the helplessness of the imperial army. The shock of the war would have a severe and lasting impact on Ottoman society, culture, and identity. From 1913 on, the hitherto viable umbrella of Ottoman identity was no longer recognized by

---

[160] George F. Kennan, *The Other Balkan Wars: A 1913 Carnegie Endowment Inquiry in Retrospect with a New Introduction and Reflection on the Present Record* (Washington, DC: Carnegie Endowment for International Peace, 1993), 109–35.

[161] Momchil Yonov, 'Bulgarian Military Operations in the Balkan Wars', in: Béla K. Király and Dimitrije Djordjevic (eds.), *East Central European Society and the Balkan Wars* (Boulder, CO: Social Science Monographs, 1987), 63–84.

[162] Leo Trotzki, *Die Balkankriege 1912–13* (Essen: Arbeiterpresse Verlag, 1995, trans. Hannelore Georgi and Harald Schubärth), 296–7.

[163] *Rumeli Mezâlimi ve Bulgar Vahşetleri* (Istanbul: Rumeli Muhâcirîn-i İslâmiyye Cemiyeti, 1913), 49.

[164] Katrin Boeckh, *Von den Balkankriegen zum Ersten Weltkrieg: Kleinstaatenpolitik und ethnische Selbstbestimmung auf dem Balkan* (München: Oldenbourg, 1996), 165, 199.

[165] Ahmed Cevad, *Balkanlarda Akan Kan* (Istanbul: Şamil, n.y.), 118–19.

[166] For an introduction, see: Justin McCarthy, *Death and Exile: The Ethnic Cleansing of Ottoman Muslims, 1821–1922* (Princeton, NJ: The Darwin Press, 1995), 1–22.

hardliners on either side of the political spectrum. The wars had not only accelerated the long-term shift of the empire's demographic composition in favour of Muslims, their loss had also bolstered the myth of the Christian 'stab in the back', the Ottoman equivalent of the German 'Dolchstosslegende', as part of a general discourse of non-Muslim treason and disloyalty. Advocates of this discourse invoked crude generalizations of the conduct of non-Muslim Ottomans during the Balkan wars, against convincing evidence to the contrary.[167]

The most immediate repercussion of the war was the refugee crisis. In the first half of 1913, Istanbul was bursting with hundreds of thousands of refugees.[168] Philanthropic associations such as the 'Association for Muslim Refugees from the Balkans' provided relief for the refugee community, which almost exclusively consisted of Muslims. The stories and trauma these refugees brought to the capital were met with disbelief and rage by the Ottoman press. One commentator on the refugees' fate bewailed how 'our motherland was trampled on by the muddy boots of the poorest enemies. Our coreligionist brothers and compatriots were slaughtered in the thousands like sheep'.[169] The British consul in Salonica witnessed the slow process of forced migration and reported about the refugees:

> The result of the massacre of Muslims at the beginning of the war, of the looting of their goods in the ensuing months, of the settling of Christians in their villages, of their persecution by Christian neighbours, of their torture and beating by Greek troops, has been the creation of a state of terror among the Islamic population. Their one desire is to escape from Macedonia and to be again in a free land.
>   They arrive in Turkey with the memory of their slaughtered friends and relations fresh in their minds, they remember their own sufferings and the persecutions of which they have been victims, and finding themselves without means or resources, encouraged to some extent by their own government, they see no wrong in falling on the Greek Christians of Turkey and meting out to them the same treatment that they themselves have received from the Greek Christians of Macedonia.[170]

The feminist and nationalist author Halide Edib provided an Ottoman Muslim perspective:

> The spectacle of Moslem refugees, men and women and children, fleeing from the fire and sword of the enemy; the slaying of prisoners of war, their mutilation and starvation; atrocities and massacres perpetrated on the civil population—the first of their kind in twentieth century warfare—inflicted wounds far deeper than the defeat itself.[171]

The effect on the Young Turks in particular was formidable as their families were overrepresented among the Balkan refugees. The Young Turk leadership

---

[167] Eyal Ginio, 'Mobilizing the Ottoman Nation during the Balkan Wars (1912–1913): Awakening from the Ottoman Dream', in: *War in History* 12, no. 2 (2005), 156–77.
[168] Ahmet Halaçoğlu, *Balkan Harbi Sırasında Rumeli'den Türk Göçleri (1912–1913)* (Ankara: Türk Tarih Kurumu, 1995).
[169] *Balkan Harbinda neden Munhazim Olduk?* (Istanbul: n.p., 1913), 95.
[170] Quoted in: Mark Mazower, *Salonica, City of Ghosts: Christians, Muslims and Jews, 1430–1950* (London: HarperCollins, 2004), 338–9.
[171] Halide Edib, *Conflict of East and West in Turkey* (Delhi: Jamia Press, 1935), 80.

predominantly originated from three areas: Salonica,[172] the area from Monastir (Bitola) to Ohrid, and the area around Pristina in Kosovo, which were now under Greek and Serbian rule.[173] Young Turk leaders such as Mehmed Talaat, Mustafa Abdülhalik Renda (1881–1957), Mehmet Cavit (1875–1926), and many others now became refugees with their extended families.

One of these refugees was Dr. Mehmed Nazım (1872–1926), who was born and raised in Salonica, had joined the Young Turk movement, and had become director of a hospital in the city. His family had been living in Salonica for generations and ran successful businesses in the city. When Salonica was surrendered in October 1912, he was arrested for being a Turkish nationalist and jailed without due process for eleven months in a cell in Athens. The guards maltreated Dr. Nazım there, claiming that his family had been exterminated, that the Greek flag was waving over Constantinople (obviously not Istanbul), and that it was only a matter of time before Anatolia would be a Greek country as well. Only when the CUP regime requested the release of their brother-in-arms was Nazım transferred to the seaport of İzmir. Exile from his hometown and the sight of his hapless family, including his baby daughter, deeply upset him. Dr. Nazım began writing newspaper articles, exposing and publicizing Bulgarian atrocities against Muslims and calling for vengeance against the remaining Ottoman Christians.[174] The irreversible transformation of a patriotic doctor from Salonica into a rabid, vindictive nationalist symbolized the fate of many others.

Revanchism was cast in the crucible of the Balkan wars. In a letter to his wife, dated 8 May 1913, Enver Pasha wrote, 'If I could tell you of the savagery the enemy has inflicted . . . a stone's throw from Istanbul, you would understand the things that enter the heads of poor Muslims far away. But our anger is strengthening: revenge, revenge, revenge; there is no other word'.[175] In a discussion with one of his confidants, the Pasha was even more outspoken:

> How could a person forget the plains, the meadows, watered with the blood of our forefathers; abandon those places where Turkish raiders had stalled their steeds for a full four hundred years, with our mosques, our tombs, our dervish lodges, our bridges and our castles, to leave them to our slaves, to be driven out of Rumelia to Anatolia: this was beyond a person's endurance. I am prepared to sacrifice gladly the remaining years of my life to take revenge on the Bulgarians, the Greeks and the Montenegrins.[176]

---

[172] Selim İlkin and İlhan Tekeli, 'İttihat ve Terakki Hareketinin Oluşumunda Selanik'in Toplumsal Yapısının Belirleyiciliği', in: Osman Okyar and Halil İnalcık (eds.), *Türkiye'nin Sosyal ve Ekonomik Tarihi (1071–1920): Social and Economic History of Turkey (1071–1920)* (Ankara: Meteksan, 1980), 351–82.

[173] Erik-Jan Zürcher, 'The Young Turks—Children of the Borderlands?', in: *International Journal of Turkish Studies* 9 (2003), 275–86.

[174] Ahmet Eyicil, *İttihad ve Terakki Liderlerinden Doktor Nâzım Bey 1872–1926* (Ankara: Gün, 2004), 130–2, 153.

[175] M. Şükrü Hanioğlu (ed.), *Kendi Mektuplarında Enver Paşa* (Istanbul: Der, 1989), 242.

[176] Hüsamettin Ertürk, *İki Devrin Perde Arkası*, Samih N. Tansu (ed.) (Istanbul: Batur, 1964), 121.

The 1914 opening address of parliament was equally rancorous and emotional: 'Do not forget! Do not forget beloved Salonica, the cradle of the flame of Liberty and Constitutional Government, do not forget green Monastir, Kosovo, İşkodra, Yanya and all of beautiful Rumelia'. The moved deputies exclaimed: 'We shall not forget!'[177]

The emotions of Young Turk elites expelled from their ancestral lands included humiliation, helplessness, anger, loss of dignity, lack of self-confidence, anxiety, embarrassment, shame: a toxic mix that, combined together, contributed to the growth of collective hate and destruction fantasies. Besides these objective effects, the subjective perception of the tragedy in the minds of the Young Turks merits perhaps even more attention. For them, the loss of power and prestige shattered the conventional myth of an Ottoman identity and Islamic superiority. One contemporary commented that for the Young Turks 'it was especially difficult to be forced to live under the rule of their own former subjects after having been the dominant element for hundreds of years'.[178] The fear of being ruled by historical enemies was a theme even before the Balkan wars, when the Young Turk press published widely read articles with a deeply defeatist tone:

> Serbia, Bulgaria, Montenegro, Bosnia-Herzegovina, and Crete were lost. Right now the grand [dear] Rumelia is about to be lost and in one or two years Istanbul will be gone as well. The holy Islam and the esteemed Ottomanism will be moved to Kayseri. Kayseri will become our capital, Mersin our port, Armenia and Kurdistan our neighbours, and Muscovites our masters. We will become their slaves. Oh! Is it not shameful for us! How can the Ottomans who once ruled the world become servants to their own shepherds, slaves, and servants?[179]

After 1913, the Young Turk nightmare indeed came true as many of them became traumatized victims of ethnic cleansing. Their behaviour and political decision-making therefore was based on fear and resentment, and was aimed at securing safety for their families and ultimately, for their nation.

There is some evidence for the claim that the revanchism was not merely an elite affair but was communicated and disseminated into society. In a partly autobiographical novel first published in 1950, noted essayist Ahmet Hamdi Tanpınar (1901–62) expressed this popularization of vengeance in literary non-fiction: 'It was that desperately feverish year in which the Balkan Wars came to an end. We children were immersed in the bitterness of a defeat which we could accept no more than the adults, who had learned to bow their heads with their gaze averted. Every song spoke of strange vengeance marches'.[180] Another contemporary Ottoman author summarized the Balkan drama as follows:

---

[177] Tunaya, *Türkiye'de Siyasal Partiler*, vol. 3, 465.

[178] Bayur, *Türk İnkılabı Tarihi*, Vol. 2, Part III, 250.

[179] Quoted in: Nader Sohrabi, 'Global Waves, Local Actors: What the Young Turks Knew about Other Revolutions and Why it Mattered', in: *Comparative Studies in Society and History* 44, no. 1 (2002), 45–79, 64.

[180] Ahmet Hamdi Tanpınar, *Sahnenin Dışındakiler* (Istanbul: Dergâh, 1973), 54. For an analysis of this novel from the perspectives of historiography and literary theory, see: Erdağ M. Göknar, 'Ottoman Past and Turkish Future: Ambivalence in A. H. Tanpinar's *Those outside the Scene*', in: *The South Atlantic Quarterly* 102, no. 2/3 (2003), 647–61.

The people of the Balkans turned Rumelia into a slaughterhouse for Turks.... The Turks have not forgotten this pain. By retelling the story to students at school, to children at home, to soldiers in the barracks, Turks have awoken a national spirit, a national grudge. They have infected people with a spirit that longs one day to settle accounts for the humiliation and oppression suffered by Turkdom. On maps Rumelia now appears in black. The entire army is urged to avenge its besmirched honor. Soldiers went to training every day singing the song 'In 1328 Turkish honor was sullied, alas. Alas, alas, alas, revenge!' Soldiers returning to their villages would sow more seeds by singing this song.[181]

These were more than just words as a severe crisis raged within Ottoman society. At that time, non-Muslim religious leaders of Eastern Thrace were petitioning the Interior Ministry to complain about the harassment they were constantly enduring from Muslims exacting revenge for their losses. These petitions reported an unprecedented atmosphere of hatred and revenge reigning in Thrace.[182]

Even in Diyarbekir, far away from the direct heat of the Balkan wars, the revanchism could be felt. In the city, national discussions on identity and ideas on population politics had already fuelled competition and conflict between the ethnically organized political factions. Well before the war, Müftüzâde Şeref (Uluğ) had proposed declaring an economic boycott against the 'treacherous Armenians' in order to strengthen Muslim economic power.[183] The Armenians of Diyarbekir, in their turn, were generally anti-Russian and many adhered to the Dashnaktsutiun party, which desired Armenian autonomy. Concretely, its program aimed at more freedom and more decentralization in the Ottoman administration of the eastern provinces, the introduction of Armenian as educational and official language, and an end to injustice, usurpation, and expropriation committed mostly by Kurdish tribes against Armenian peasants.[184] Chief editor of the Armenian newspaper *Azadamart* was Roupen Zartarian, a noted Armenian revolutionary who hailed from Diyarbekir. Kurdish nationalism, though not as organized and settled as its Armenian counterpart, also existed in the province. On 19 September 1908 Müftü Suphî Efendi founded the Diyarbekir office of the 'Kurdish Assistance and Progress Society' (*Kürt Teavün ve Terakki Cemiyeti*) in the city. Prominent members were Dr. Mehmed Şükrü (Sekban), former mayor of Diyarbekir Pirinççizâde Arif, Mirikatibizâde Ahmed Cemil (Asena), Mehmed Tahir, and Halil Hayalî.[185] According to its statutes, it aimed to observe the constitution, pursue the notion of Ottomanism, end tribal warfare, and maintain 'harmony and good relations between their compatriots the Armenians, Nestorians, and other Ottoman subjects'.[186] The Bedirxan dynasty, a remnant of the powerful nineteenth-century

---

[181] Mehmet Cemil Bilsel, *Lozan* (Istanbul: Ahmet İhsan, 1933), Vol. I, 126.
[182] BOA, DH.ŞFR 39/163, Talaat to Edirne, 5 April 1914.
[183] Uluğ, 'Ermeniler', in: *Türk*, no. 110 (21 December 1905), 2.
[184] *PAAA*, Holstein to Bethmann-Hollweg, 22 May 1913. For a history of the Dashnaks, see: Louise Nalbandian, *The Armenian Revolutionary Movement* (Berkeley, CA: University of California Press, 1963), 151–78.
[185] Tunaya, *Türkiye'de Siyasal Partiler*, vol. 1, 430–4.
[186] *Kürt Teavün ve Terakki Cemiyeti Nizamnamesi* (Istanbul: Kasbar, 1324), 1, article 1.

Botan tribal confederation, was involved in explicitly Kurdish-nationalist politics.[187] One opportunistic adherent of Kurdish nationalism was Derwiş Ağa of Çelik village, south of Midyat, who allied himself with the Bedirxans as a means to protest against misrule and corruption by lower Ottoman officials.[188] However, there were also ideologically driven politicians such as Hasan Bey of Cizre, cousin to the nationalist leader Abdulrezzak Bedirxan. Hasan explained to German vice-consul Holstein that he had no doubts that Russia would assist the Kurdish national movement in liberating Kurdistan from the 'Turkish yoke', and establish a Kurdish nation state.[189]

The Committee of Union and Progress had not remained idle in Diyarbekir province either. The first CUP office in Diyarbekir was opened on 23 July 1908 by Ziyâ Gökalp, who after all was a native of the region, and was also its representative in the party's Central Committee.[190] Gökalp began publishing the newspaper *Peyman*, which adopted a relatively modest tone and emphasized co-existence of the various Ottoman subjects.[191] But after the catastrophic defeats of the Balkan wars, the atmosphere changed and interethnic relations became polarized. The CUP dictatorship exerted its influence in this province through a network of mainly urban Kurdish members. The most influential CUP members in Diyarbekir were those related to the wealthy and powerful Pirinççizâde dynasty, who owned large estates in the province, including the rice fields west of Diyarbekir city.[192] One of their kinsmen was deputy Aziz Feyzi (1879–1933), the son of Pirinççizâde Arif, who had adhered to the Kurdish Assistance and Progress Society. According to a German report, Feyzi had undertaken a study trip to Germany in 1911.[193] On behalf of many other Diyarbekir notables, he vehemently protested in the Ottoman parliament against the proposed government plan of expropriating the powerful landowners, and in time Feyzi became a Young Turk hardliner. He had held fierce and hostile discussions with Armenian member of parliament Vartkes Serengulian (1871–1915), in which he accused Vartkes of Armenian separatist designs.[194] He became more and more fanatic in his anti-Armenian sentiments, and reportedly had Ohannes Kazazian, a Catholic Armenian from Mardin and his political rival in the elections, assassinated in 1913.[195] Given his reputation, Aziz Feyzi's assignment

---

[187] Malmîsanij, *Cizira Botanlı Bedirhaniler ve Bedirhani ailesi derneği'nin tutanakları* (Spånga, Sweden: Apec, 1994).

[188] *PAAA*, Holstein to Bethmann-Hollweg, 22 May 1913.

[189] Ibid.

[190] Şevket Beysanoğlu, *Ziyâ Gökalp'ın İlk Yazı Hayatı: 1894–1909* (Istanbul: Diyarbakır'ı Tanıtma Derneği Neşriyatı, 1956), 11–12.

[191] Up until the Balkan wars, Gökalp used to compare Ottoman society to US society, as in both countries many different ethnic groups co-existed under one denomination, Ottoman respectively American. In fact, Gökalp even rejected Turkish ethnic nationalism as it entailed nation-building based on blood bonds, which he considered unreal. Mehmed Mehdî, 'Türklük ve Osmanlılık', in: *Peyman* II, quoted in: ibid., 99–101, 105.

[192] According to one researcher of the period, the Pirinççizâde dynasty owned thirty villages in the vicinity of Diyarbekir city. Malmîsanij, *Kürt Teavün ve Terakki Cemiyeti ve Gazetesi* (Spånga, Sweden: Apec, 1998), 41.

[193] *PAAA*, R14084, Mutius to Bethmann-Hollweg, 14 June 1914.

[194] Tarık Zafer Tunaya, *Türkiye'de Siyasal Partiler* (Istanbul: İletişim, 1997), vol. 1, 600–1.

[195] Jacques Rhétoré, *Les chrétiens aux bêtes! Souvenirs de la guerre sainte proclamée par les Turcs contre les chrétiens en 1915* (unpublished manuscript, Bibliothèque du Saulchoir), 59–60.

to Diyarbekir caused unrest and anxiety among Armenian politicians there.[196] Other CUP sympathizers in Diyarbekir were Pirinççizâde Sıdkı (Tarancı), Yasinzâde Şevki (Ekinci), his brother Yasinzâde Yahya (Ekinci), Müftüzâde Şeref (Uluğ), and others who were less prominent.[197]

The loss of the Balkans in 1913 reverberated throughout Ottoman society, including distant Diyarbekir. As if that had not been traumatic enough, vague talks of and slow but deliberate steps towards a reform plan to 'solve' the Armenian question, by which European 'inspectors' would be appointed to ensure more Armenian and Kurdish autonomy, triggered even more concern and fear among Muslims, including those in Diyarbekir. Right after the signing of the London Treaty, Diyarbekir's governor sent a report to the government that talk of a reform plan was causing turmoil and social unrest among Diyarbekir's ethnic groups. According to the governor, rumours of reform were 'causing much excitement and alarm [*heyecan ve telaş*] among the Islamic population'. Speculative reports in newspapers about the alleged endorsement and possible implementation of a reform plan were 'offending the sentiments and minds of Muslims and were lately giving rise to tumult [*galeyan*]'. The governor argued that the Muslim middle class in Diyarbekir had faith in the government, but could not remain 'indifferent to such a question affecting the life and and future of our homeland [*istikbâl-ı memleketimiz*]'. The Muslims, he concluded his report, would reject such a reform plan and he 'began expressing the possibility that terrible consequences [*fena neticeler*] could emerge from it in the future'.[198]

The final reform plan envisaged the formation of two provinces from six vilayets (Erzurum, Van, Bitlis, Diyarbekir, Mamuret-ul Aziz, and Sivas), and assigned two European inspectors to oversee Armenian affairs. The reform package was signed into law in February 1914. In the spring of 1914, the backlash by Muslims eventuated as expected by the governor. In another report, he mentioned clashes and riots between Muslims and Christians in the bazaar and inner city of Diyarbekir. The Muslims expressed their hatred of Armenians by painting anti-Christian graffiti on walls and insulting Christian symbols such as crucifixes with 'repulsive profanity [*şütumât-ı galîza*]'. The governor concluded that the situation in Diyarbekir was firmly 'unfavourable for Christians', and that Christian communities were 'in complete despair'.[199] Those responsible for the organization of a climate of anti-Armenian hatred were local CUP powerholders. In the summer of 1914, as the European crisis was deepening, the Ottoman civil inspector Mihran Boyadjian was travelling to Diyarbekir and encountered the Young Turk political hardliner

---

[196] Gaïdz F. Minassian, 'Les relations entre le Comité Union et Progrès et la Fédération Révolutionnaire Arménienne à la veille de la Premiere Guerre mondiale d'après les sources arméniennes', in: *Revue d'histoire arménienne contemporaine* 1 (1995), 90, footnote 27.

[197] As argued before, many of these men were related to each other due to the dense network of notable families in Diyarbekir. Thus, Aziz Feyzi was both Ziyâ Gökalp's and Şeref's cousin, and Sıdkı was related to both of them on the maternal and paternal sides. Malmîsanij, *Kürt Teavün*, 41.

[198] BOA, DH.KMS 2–2/5–7, document 7, Diyarbekir governor to Interior Ministry, 26 March 1913.

[199] BOA, DH.SYS 23/4, document 2, Diyarbekir governor to Interior Ministry, May 1914.

Pirinççizâde Aziz Feyzi on the way. Aziz Feyzi openly threatened the Armenians in a bitter condemnation:

> On the road, we often spoke about politics in the car. Feyzi Bey did not fail to slip in, in his conversations, several threats against my coreligionists. 'The Armenians', he repeated, with bitterness, 'have misbehaved towards us in our days of distress during the Balkan Wars. Patriarch Zaven, the Catholicos of Etchmiadzin and Nubar have sought to appeal to foreign intervention; that will cost you dearly my friend, your future is in danger'.[200]

Finally Aziz Feyzi warned: 'You will see now, what it means to demand reforms'.[201] The radicalization of political elites heralded a general deep crisis of interethnic relations in Diyarbekir, which had now reached the threshold between hatred and violence. That threshold was crossed when in August 1914, the grain market of Diyarbekir became the scene of mass plunder as many Muslim merchants joined in seizing the opportunity to loot the stores of Christians and set fire to their shops. Soon it became known that the Young Turk loyalist police chief, Memduh Bey, had 'allowed Kurds and Muslims to pillage Armenian stores [*Kürtlerle müslümanların Ermeni mağazalarını yağma etmelerine müsaade olunduğu*]'.[202] According to Mihran Boyadjian, Memduh Bey had started the fire himself to create opportunities for pillage.[203] Not only was the involvement widespread, but the inaction by local authorities implied tacit approval of the pogrom.

The war and ensuing violence in the Balkans released a wave of nationalist population politics coupling ethnicity to territory. The expansion of the nation-state system onto residual Ottoman lands produced multilateral homogenization campaigns such as forced migration and population exchanges between Bulgaria and the Ottoman Empire. Most of all, the Young Turks' perception that the catastrophe of the Balkans should never be allowed to happen to the remaining territories of the Ottoman Empire, especially the eastern provinces, would give birth to unprecedented forms of population politics and social engineering. One major outcome of these processes was a deep fear, or perhaps a complex, of loss. The fear of losing territory was a persistent phobia of both late Ottoman and Turkish political culture. Some Ottomans foresaw the looming cataclysm. In his 1913 book on the Balkan wars, Aram Andonian wrote with considerable concern that 'the principle of nationality' had spelled disaster in the Balkans and was utterly untenable in the eastern provinces, where most Armenians lived.[204] Andonian had planned to write a second volume to his book. He was never able to do so.

---

[200] Vartkes Yeghiayan (ed.), *British Foreign Office Dossiers on Turkish War Criminals* (Pasadena, CA: AAIC, 1991), 479.

[201] Ibid., 480.

[202] BOA, DH.ŞFR 44/234, Emniyet-i Umûmiye Müdüriyeti (Ali Münif) to Diyarbekir, 13 September 1914.

[203] Yeghiayan (ed.), *British Foreign Office Dossiers*, 480.

[204] Aram Andonian, *Balkan Savaşı* (Istanbul: Aras Yayıncılık, 1999, transl. Zaven Biberian).

DISCUSSION

The Ottoman eastern provinces, much like the rest of the empire, were an ethnically mixed peasant society comprising a diverse array of groups. Diyarbekir province, the focus of this study, was no exception to this rule. Christians, Muslims, and Jews lived side by side for centuries under a fragile equilibrium of political, social, and economic inequality. They were organized in an imperial-monarchical structure in which non-Muslim religious communities were simultaneously privileged and inferior. There was no national economy, no national language, no single national identity, and no common set of symbols of any significance. Despite sectarian divides and group interests, throughout the centuries these peoples were interdependent and continuously collaborated to produce the cultures and economies of Diyarbekir. The advent of nationalism in the nineteenth century, stirred up by the process of Westernization, would have a profound and lasting impact on this societal structure.

By the time the wave of nationalism had swept over south-east Europe and had reached Diyarbekir, it had lost most of its emancipatory principles and egalitarian ideals. The percolation of nationalism into the Ottoman Empire was, in line with the erosion of that empire, a blind process. But by the time nationalism was adopted by various Ottoman groups, it came to signify the glorification of the people as an ethnic or cultural group and fostered ethno-territorial visions of the space they inhabited. Great internal and external pressures, crisis, and war all account for the direction the Turkish nation-formation process would take. The polarization of relations between Muslims and Christians was an important concomitant effect of these forces. Throughout the nineteenth century, as the Empire kept crumbling at its peripheries due to imperialist penetration and minority separatism, Ottoman society went through two shifts of identification and dis-identification. The first process was a shift from Ottoman patriotism to Muslim nationalism, the second one a shift from Muslim nationalism into Turkish nation-alism. These contracting processes of identification and disidentification gave shape to Turkish nationalism as it developed in the period up to the First World War. This process also gave birth to the Young Turk movement, a radical group of nationalists bent on the establishment of a Turkish nation state.

This external and internal dialectic of identification was a dynamic process that shaped Ottoman and Turkish state identity. Scholars of state formation have argued that state identity, embodied in the cultural and ethnic identity of the population, is not meaningful in isolation from the wider world and other states. States may well be unique and variable, but state identity is thoroughly socially constructed, most specifically in the continuing (and often blind) processes of political and social interaction within which states define and redefine themselves and others through their existence.[205] In other words, state identities are not strictly unilateral but subject to interaction with other states. The state's identity as an

---

[205] Liah Greenfeld, *Nationalism: Five Roads to Modernity* (Cambridge: Harvard University Press, 1992), 1–26.

ongoing product of this process is a dialectical synthesis of internal and external definitions of identity, of which territory and population are the prime referents.[206] The continuing losses of territory and ensuing shifts of population imposed upon the Ottoman Empire, defined and redefined Ottoman identity by these two shifts: first, the exclusion of Ottoman Christians and inclusion of Muslims, and, later, the exclusion of Ottoman Muslims and inclusion of Turks. These processes may have brought about large-scale collective othering and disidentification from Christian groups: Muslims were considered to be 'the same' and others (Christians) were 'unlike' them, if only for the Muslims' shared experience of decades of victimization.

The idea that nations or groups are constructed has gained currency among social scientists.[207] But nation-formation processes are processes of construction *and* destruction, inclusion *and* exclusion. To claim that Turkish nationalism was inclusive is apologetic, and to claim that it was exclusive is polemical and moralizing—both arguments miss the central point that processes of inclusion and exclusion co-exist simultaneously in all processes of identity politics. This chapter has argued that exclusion has been a major force, shaping inclusion in the formation of late Ottoman, Muslim, and Turkish nationalism. It has particularly argued that the exclusions from and victimization in the Balkans and Caucasus are what constructed the identity of the late Ottoman Empire and modern Turkey: Turkish national identity was constructed by exclusion and violence. Rather than identity leading in a linear manner to violence, violence had produced identity: as Brubaker argued about the Balkans in the 1990s, 'group crystallization and polarization were the result of violence, not the cause'.[208] Well before people had realized what they were included in, they had been excluded from a society. This may mean that, whereas there might hardly be full consensus among nationalist elites on what the nation is, surely there always will be consensus on what the nation is *not*. Definitions of exclusion can precede those of inclusion and may be more forceful. Whereas the image of the Self may be vague, the image of the Other can be crystal clear.[209] Well before Turkish social engineers crafted the Turkish nation in the 1920s and 1930s, including moulding its ethno-national boundaries, there was full consensus among Ottoman Muslim political elites on the notion that Armenians and others were never to take part in that new group. No matter how much difficulty the Young Turks had in defining what 'Turkishness' was, it took them only a few years to define what Turkishness was *not*.

[206] Rodney B. Hall, *National Collective Identity: Social Constructs and International Systems* (New York: Columbia University Press, 1999).

[207] For an overview of the literature, see: Richard Jenkins, 'Categorization: Identity, Social Process and Epistemology', in: *Current Sociology* 48, no. 3 (2000), 7–25; id., *Social Identity* (London: Routledge, 1996).

[208] Rogers Brubaker, 'Ethnicity Without Groups', in: *Archives européennes de sociologie* 43, no. 2 (2002), 163–89, at 171; James D. Fearon and David D. Laitin, 'Violence and the Social Construction of Ethnic Identity', in: *International Organization* 54, no. 4 (2000), 845–77; Franke Wilmer, *The Social Construction of Man, the State and War: Identity, Conflict, and Violence in Former Yugoslavia* (London: Routledge, 2002), 59–82, 239–69.

[209] Julia Reuter, *Ordnungen des Anderen: Zum Problem des Eigenen in der Soziologie des Fremden* (Bielefeld: Transcript, 2002).

Exclusion was a prime mover behind the creation of the Turkish nation state. Not only did that state consist of hundreds of thousands of people themselves excluded from formerly Ottoman territories beyond the Turkish Republic's control, the political elite itself in its turn began organizing the exclusion of millions of others during and after the establishment of the rump state. The residue was a society of uprooted elites, illiterate peasants, wretched refugees, and peripheral minorities. Exclusion preceded and even defined inclusion. This process set off a dynamic that developed and maintained a fear-based belief system that included negative stereotypes, prejudice, scapegoating—and that ultimately justified violence. Fear became embodied in the Ottoman Muslims' concepts of the Other. These dynamics became systemic in a society as the energy of fear, revenge, and a victim identity became pervasive. How this reality and trope of victimization spiralled into more violence and victimization will be dealt with in the next chapter.

Parallel to this process of identification and disidentification ran the advent of population policy, the exercise of state power aimed at crafting the ideal population within a given territory. This was a shift from monarchical politics to population politics. The Young Turks too, turned their gaze from 'looking up' to the Sultan, to 'looking down' on the population as a source of political legitimacy. From their European education they had apprehended that the modernizing discourse of social knowledge of populations facilitated state intrusions into the ethnic composition of the population, not simply for the sake of greater empirical understanding of the population, but primarily in order to reorganize it. The discovery of society was pioneered by scholars who ventured out to research the population. Young Turk ethnographers and local elites provided the Central Committee with ethnographic knowledge that shaped the very formation of population politics. The ethnographers, who drew inspiration from Western European colonial literature, produced censuses, assisted government commissions charged with delimiting ethnic borders in Turkey, led expeditions to study nomadic tribes, and in the end created a huge amount of ethnographic knowledge about the peoples of the Ottoman Empire.

The complicity of scientists with dictatorial regimes has been the object of many studies focusing on the relationship between power and knowledge. Despite the existence of diverging motives and patterns of the entanglement of science and politics, studies converge on one important aspect: the entanglement of science and politics was as much a top–down affair (the ordering of research with a particular set of results determined beforehand) as a bottom–up one (scholars giving in to temptations of power and utopia and behaving sycophantically to the regime).[210] Whereas social scientists such as Émile Durkheim and Max Weber never stood at the forefront of political decision-making in France and Germany,

---

[210] John Connelly, *Captive University: The Sovietization of East German, Czech, and Polish Higher Education, 1945–1956* (Chapel Hill: The University of North Carolina Press, 2000); Nikolai Krementsov, *Stalinist Science* (Princeton: Princeton University Press, 1997); Mark Walker, *Nazi Science* (New York: Plenum Press, 1995); George Mosse, *Nazi Culture: Intellectual, Cultural, and Social Life in the Third Reich* (New York: Grosset and Dunlap, 1966); Otthein Rammstedt, *Deutsche Soziologie, 1933–1945: Die Normalität einer Anpassung* (Frankfurt am Main: Suhrkamp, 1986); Winfried Schulze and Otto Gerhard Oexle (eds.), *Deutsche Historiker im Nationalsozialismus* (Frankfurt am Main: Fischer Taschenbuch Verlag, 1999); Ingo Haar, *Historiker im Nationalsozialismus: Deutsche Geschichtswissenschaft und der 'Volkstumskampf' im Osten* (Göttingen: Vandenhoeck and Ruprecht, 2000).

the Young Turk sociologist Mehmed Ziya Gökalp was an intimately involved member of the inner circle of power and his ideas were highly influential in the shaping of CUP population politics. He collaborated with an unelected regime and can be considered the brains of Young Turk social engineering. By association, Turkish social science, rooted in Young Turk nationalism, was complicit in the processes of social engineering (including its crimes) launched under its influence.

The disintegration of the Ottoman state, the fragmentation and polarization along ethnic lines of Ottoman society, and subsequent acts of political violence created space in the political landscape for radicals to thrive. When the Young Turks staged a successful coup in January 1913, they proclaimed the dawn of a new era. As they listened to Ottoman society and heard a cacophony of languages, institutions, loyalties, and identifications, they concluded that the status quo was an obstacle to the single tone they sought. The status quo thus became a 'question' or a 'problem'. Young Turk preparations for their rule of Anatolia revealed expectations for the future based on the sociological observations of their experts. On the level of official ideology and propaganda, these expectations gravitated towards the concept of 'Turkification' as outlined, even if only sketchily, in previous Young Turk notions about 'Ottomanization'. In concrete political terms, the importance of 'Turkification' meant focusing on the issue of the non-Turkish demographic structure in the eastern provinces. Any policy tackling this issue would involve much trial and error, for this idea was not explicit, its meaning not self-evident, and often the need to choose priorities and make pragmatic compromises due to the exigencies of international diplomacy forced delays and modifications in the Young Turks' realization of a utopian society. But the ultimate direction was clear. The relatively autonomous spread of the philosophy of population politics and the relatively coincidental explosion of mass violence would prove fatal for the eastern provinces.

The catastrophic losses of the Balkan wars brought about another shock to Young Turk thinking on population policy as the ethnic cleansing of Muslims proved that violence was a politically effective method of state-building and crafting a population. When the issue of the Armenian 'reform plan' was brought to the arena of international politics in 1913, it induced a Pavlovian reflex in the Young Turk mind. The CUP saw Great Power interference in internal politics as yet another humiliating breach of Ottoman sovereignty, a harbinger of the doomsday scenario in which an independent Armenia would be established in the Ottoman eastern provinces. The reform plan was a comprehensive administrative project, including cultural and even linguistic provisions for the eastern provinces. These latter stipulations would partly shape and define Young Turk population policy and social engineering. The Young Turk regime attacked precisely those social characteristics that they felt were threatening Ottoman sovereignty, unity, and homogeneity the most: demography, culture, language, public space. If it were these characteristics of demographic and cultural presence that made the eastern provinces prone to Western intervention and/or the establishment of an Armenian state, then those characteristics needed to be assaulted.

2

Genocide of Christians, 1915–16

This chapter will closely examine the history of the first phase of Young Turk population policies. It will describe and attempt to explain the mass violence that was unleashed against Ottoman Christians in Diyarbekir province during the First World War. The chapter is divided into three parts: first, it will trace the genocidal tendencies of the Young Turks up to the crisis of 1914–15 and their entry into the war.[1] How did the process of persecution begin? Second, it will concentrate on Diyarbekir province and describe the persecution process of Armenians and other Christians in that region. How did the process of persecution develop into genocide? Third, it will analyse how that persecution developed into genocidal destruction by focusing on how local elites in Diyarbekir interpreted, organized, and intensified the destruction of Armenians. How did the behaviour of local elites affect the genocidal process? The conclusions will focus on the close interdependence of victimization and perpetration, the importance of local elites in any genocidal process, and how the genocide can be placed in the broader structure of Young Turk population politics. This approach is designed to capture the complexity of processes of mass violence.

WAR AND PERSECUTION

The assassination of Archduke Franz Ferdinand in Sarajevo on 28 June 1914 stirred up acute international tensions. In the midst of the atmosphere of mounting belligerence, the CUP sought to forge alliances with any of the Great Powers in order to bring the empire out of its diplomatic isolation. Cavid Bey, the pro-British Minister of Finance, had appealed to Britain in 1911, but apart from Winston Churchill, the Foreign Office was not interested.[2] Talaat flirted with Russia on his trip to the Crimea in May, where he spoke to the Russian Foreign Minister Sazonov about a possible alliance. The Russians expressed ambivalence in judgement but in

---

[1] For a recent collection of essays on the Armenian genocide, see: Fatma Müge Göçek, Norman Naimark and Ronald Grigor Suny (eds.), *A Question of Genocide: Armenians and Turks at the End of the Ottoman Empire* (New York: Oxford University Press, 2011). For a narrative account of the Armenian genocide in Diyarbekir, see: Raymond H. Kévorkian, *Le génocide des Arméniens* (Paris: Odile Jacob, 2006), 435–68.

[2] Martin Gilbert, *Winston S. Churchill*, Vol. 3: *1914–1916, The Challenge of War* (Boston: Houghton Mifflin, 1971), 189.

essence were not interested.[3] Cemal Pasha approached France but left empty-handed, lamenting the negotiations with the French as 'a huge disappointment'.[4] On 24 July 1914 a general mobilization was issued by the Ottoman general staff. On 28 July, the same day that Austria-Hungary declared war against Serbia, Enver Pasha proposed a defensive alliance between Imperial Germany and the Ottoman Empire to the German Ambassador Wangenheim. In the next few days Grand Vizier Said Halim, Chairman of the Parliament Halil, Enver, and Talaat launched intensive negotiations with the Germans behind closed doors. Finally, on 2 August, one day after the German declaration of war against Russia, a written agreement was signed between the two states.[5] The discussions were top secret, and even Cemal Pasha had no knowledge of them.[6] Three days later Austria-Hungary joined the Turko-German alliance and completed the Central Powers bloc, whereas Russia, France and Britain united into the Entente Powers. The Ottoman Empire was now officially allied to Germany and on account of the treaty was inevitably obliged in this political constellation to prepare for war. Following the succession of declarations of war in August 1914, the Germans urged Minister of War Enver Pasha to act against Russia. Enver agreed as a sign of goodwill. Without a formal declaration of war, he ordered the Ottoman navy immediately to bomb the Russian shore, destroying oil tanks and sinking fourteen vessels.[7] Though few politicians in Istanbul knew of Enver's attack, the *fait accompli* triggered declarations of war by the Triple Entente powers. From 11 November 1914 on, the Ottoman Empire was officially at war with Russia, France, and Britain.[8]

The First World War was not something that happened incidentally to the Ottoman Empire. Powerful cadres in the CUP's nationalist wing consciously headed in a belligerent direction. By participating in the war it hoped radically to solve the many problems of the Empire. Three days after the outbreak of the war, the Young Turk journalist Hüseyin Cahit Yalçın (1875–1957) published an article entitled, 'The Awaited Day', rejoicing that the war 'had come like a stroke of good fortune upon the Turkish people, who had been sure of their own decline. The day had finally come', he wrote ominously, that 'the Turks would make an historical reckoning with those . . . whom they had been previously unable to do so'. The Turks would exact 'revenge, the horrors of which had not yet been recorded in history'.[9] From the first day of the war, Young Turk dictatorial rule became more repressive towards oppositional groups. Discordant behaviour was dealt with systematically and ruthlessly. On 6 September 1914, Talaat ordered the Ottoman

[3] Sergej D. Sazonov, *Les années fatales: souvenirs de M. S. Sazonov, ancien ministre des Affaires Étrangères de Russie (1910–1916)* (Paris: Payot, 1927), 182.

[4] Cemal Paşa, *Hatıralar: İttihat ve Terakki ve Birinci Dünyâ Savaşı Anıları* (Istanbul: Çağdaş, 1977), 141.

[5] For the eight articles of this treaty, see: Şevket S. Aydemir, *Makedonya'dan Orta Asya'ya Enver Paşa* (Istanbul: Remzi, 1972), Vol. 2 (1908–14), 510.

[6] Cemal, *Hatıralar*, 142–3.

[7] Paul G. Halpern, *A Naval History of World War I* (Annapolis, MD: Naval Institute Press, 1994), 76.

[8] John Keegan, *The First World War* (New York: Vintage, 1998), 217.

[9] *Tanin*, 14 November 1914.

security apparatus to 'follow and observe' closely the local leaderships of Armenian political parties who, according to Talaat, had been engaging in 'agitation and disturbance' against the notion of Ottomanism all along.[10] Another perceived problem were the foreign capitulations, a set of legal concessions under which foreign subjects enjoyed privileges, such as exemption from Ottoman taxes. The CUP regarded the capitulations as humiliating[11] and did not wait long to confront them: all capitulations were unilaterally abrogated on 17 September.[12] The CUP's bold policies not only directly caused the ranks to close, but also led to an indirect form of ethnic unpicking as government functionaries voluntarily left office. On 12 November, Minister of Commerce Süleyman Bustani, a Syriac Protestant, resigned his cabinet portfolio out of protest over what he considered ongoing CUP aggression.[13] This trend of 'Turkification' of Ottoman political culture allowed the CUP to fill these administrative positions with nationalists.

Meanwhile, the mobilization did not go unnoticed in Diyarbekir province. The city streets thronged with soldiers of the Second Army Corps, led by Ahmet İzzet Pasha, which was partly lodged in large mosques such as the Nebii Mosque.[14] On 3 November, the mayor of Diyarbekir held a public speech, explaining the conduct of the war to an exclusively Muslim crowd. Upon hearing that the Russian army was pushing into the provinces of Van and Erzurum, the frantic crowd yelled 'Praise to Mohammed! Death to the Russians and their allies!' The non-Muslims of the city, frightened and cautious because of this outbreak of mass rage, did not leave their homes in the following days.[15] The army began requisitioning goods from the population and drafting men into its ranks. Daniel Thom, a missionary in Mardin, summarized these acts and wrote that 'the Govt. has robbed the city, and the country around, of its men, of its animals, of its money', leaving the people

---

[10] Başbakanlık Osmanlı Arşivi (Ottoman Archives, Istanbul, hereafter: BOA), DH.ŞFR 44/200, Talaat to provinces, 6 September 1914.

[11] In the parliament, CUP members had dubbed the capitulations 'satanic angels'. *Meclisi Mebusan Zabit Ceridesi*, 3rd election period, 4th sitting, 60th session, 1028. In his memoirs Cemal Pasha confessed they wanted to 'tear them apart'. Cemal, *Hatıralar*, 438. The annulment of the capitulations 'was received euphorically as a military success'. Tunaya, *Türkiye'de Siyasal Partiler*, Vol. 3, 420.

[12] 'İmtiyazat-ı Ecnebiyenin (Kapitülasyon) İlgası Hakkında İrade-i seniyye', in: *Takvim-i Vekayi*, no.1938, 17 September 1914. Together with the capitulations, the reform plan for the eastern provinces Russia had designed in 1913 mainly to curb abuses against Christians, was also *de facto* cancelled. Roderic H. Davison, 'The Armenian Crisis, 1912–1914', in: *The American Historical Review* (1947), 481–505.

[13] Feroz Ahmad, 'Unionist Relations with the Greek, Armenian, and Jewish Communities of the Ottoman Empire, 1908–1914', in: Bernard Lewis and Benjamin Braude (eds.), *Christians and Jews in the Ottoman Empire: The Functioning of a Plural Society* (New York: Holmes and Meier Publishers, 1982), Vol. I: *The Central Lands*, 424.

[14] Ali Emîrî, *Osmanlı Vilâyât-ı Şarkiyyesi* (Istanbul: Dâr-ul Hilâfe, 1918), 34.

[15] Ishaq Armalto, *Al-Qousara fi Nakabat an-Nasara* (Beirut: Al-Sharfe Monastery, 1970, 2nd edn.). This detailed chronicle was written in 1919 in Arabic by the Syriac priest Ishaq Armalto and provides a very valuable account of Diyarbekir province before and during the war. The book has recently been translated into Swedish: *De Kristnas Hemska Katastrofer: Osmanernas och Ung-turkarnas Folkmord i norra Mesopotamien 1895 / 1914–1918* (Stockholm: Beth Froso Nsibin, 2005), translated by Ingvar Rydberg. This author has used an unofficial Turkish translation by Turan Karataş (Sweden, 1993), 22.

'pennyless, shops all closed'.[16] Gradually, the Armenian elite of Diyarbekir was targeted and persecuted. Coinciding with his earlier order, on 29 November Talaat ordered the arrest of Thomas Muggerditchian, the former interpreter of the British consulate in Diyarbekir. Muggerditchian was accused of espionage for the Entente Powers and was threatened with a court-martial.[17] He escaped arrest, fled to Egypt and subsequently wrote his memoirs.[18]

From November 1914 on, the CUP began drawing up formations of irregular militia in order to invade Russia and Persia to provoke war. This secret military organization was integrated into an existing 'Special Organization'.[19] (see Plate 3) The cadre of these new guerrilla bands was to be made up of convicts, Kurdish tribesmen and Muslim immigrants, and would be led by the same combatants the CUP had used in the Balkan Wars and in prior political competition. The convicts, named 'savages and criminals' even by CUP officials,[20] were very often Kurdish tribesmen, or local outlaws and bandits who had committed crimes of theft or manslaughter. According to an Ottoman bureaucrat, they were drilled in Istanbul for one week before being deployed in various regions.[21] The entire operation was led by Dr. Bahaeddin Şakir and was kept out of the control of the Ottoman army as much as possible.[22]

On 18 November Talaat personally ordered the drawing up of lists of names of 'those convicts who were able to exert influence on tribes'.[23] A week later, the Special Organization was put together in Diyarbekir. Among the members enlisted in the paramilitary organization were the Zaza brigand Alo,[24] as well as the Chechen social bandit Hamid and his group of loyal warriors. Hamid was recruited by CUP members, who cabled the following notification to the Central Committee in Istanbul:

> The courageous bandit [*eşkiya*] Chechen Hamid, resident of the town of Reşadiye in the Bergama district, has requested help to assist the army with some of his comrads and if allowed, to form a significant corps in Diyarbekir. Since we hope that the aforementioned gentleman is able to serve in this way, their dispatch will benefit the homeland. We would like to request a telegraphic answer on whether their patriotic venture will be necessary or not, and present our compliments, dear brothers.[25]

---

[16] Daniel Thom to William Peet, 16 August 1914, quoted in: Hans-Lukas Kieser, *Der verpasste Friede: Mission, Ethnie und Staat in den Ostprovinzen der Türkei 1839–1938* (Zürich: Chronos, 2000), 336.

[17] BOA, DH.ŞFR 47/243, Talaat to Diyarbekir, 28 November 1914.

[18] Thomas Muggerditchian, *Dikranagerdee Nahankin Tcharteru yev Kurderou Kazanioutounneru* (Cairo: Djihanian, 1919).

[19] A. Mil, 'Umumi Harpte Teşkilâtı Mahsusa', in: *Vakit*, 2 October 1933 up to 18 April 1934, republished as: Arif Cemil (Denker), *I. Dünya Savaşı'nda Teşkilât-ı Mahsusa* (Istanbul: Arba, 1997).

[20] Ibid., 196.

[21] Ahmet Refik (Altınay), *Kafkas Yollarında: İki Komite, İki Kıtal* (Istanbul: Temel, 1998 [1919]), 157.

[22] Denker, *Teşkilât-ı Mahsusa*, 236–8.

[23] BOA, DH.ŞFR 47/70, Talaat to provinces, 18 November 1914.

[24] *Tarihi Muhakeme* (Istanbul: Kitaphane-i Sûdî, 1919), 14.

[25] Quoted from internal CUP correspondence, 23 November 1914, quoted in: Tunaya, *Türkiye'de Siyasal Partiler*, Vol. 3, 349.

During the winter of 1914, the groups began penetrating into Russian and Persian territory to incite the Muslim populations to rise in rebellion and join the Ottoman forces. In this guerrilla war, Special Organization operatives also attacked Armenian villages, plundering, raping, and killing with impunity. Ambassador Wangenheim wrote to the German Chancellor that their anti-Russian actions across the Erzurum border frequently escalated into 'abuses and excesses' (*Übergriffen und Ausschreitungen*) against Armenian villagers in that region.[26]

The war on the eastern front gained momentum when Enver Pasha, driven by ambition, security concerns, and expansionist designs towards the east, attempted to attack the Russian army in Sarikamish on 29 December. Against all military advice from German and Ottoman strategists, Enver insisted on waging an encirclement campaign through the rugged Kars mountains. However, the Russian general Yudenich anticipated the outflanking manoeuvre, outsmarted Enver and delivered a heavy blow to his forces. Enver's attack failed miserably, and as a result the Third Army was effectively wiped out. Of the 90,000 soldiers that engaged in the battle, approximately 78,000 perished, mainly through frost.[27] The CUP leadership was convinced that the disastrous defeat had been caused by 'treacherous Armenian elements'. Retreating Ottoman soldiers took revenge on Ottoman Armenian villagers, massacring many and pillaging their goods. After returning from the front, Enver wrote a letter to the Armenian patriarch of Konya, expressing his respect and admiration for the courage the Armenian soldiers had shown in the Sarikamish battle. He gave the example of sergeant Ohannes who had received a medal for valour,[28] but it may not have been how Enver really felt. In a personal discussion with publisher Hüseyin Cahit, he bitterly blamed the Armenians for the fiasco and proposed their deportation to somewhere they would not cause trouble.[29] The defeat triggered a wave of persecutions, especially in the front line provinces Erzurum, Bitlis, and Van. On 26 December 1914, Talaat ordered 'the dismissal of all Armenian police officers, police chiefs, and government employees, and the deportation of anyone who opposes these measures'.[30] This official notice marked a heightening of CUP suspicion towards Armenian loyalty to the Ottoman state.

---

[26] PAAA, R14085, Wangenheim to Bethmann-Hollweg, 29 December 1914.

[27] Edward J. Erickson, *Ordered to Die: A History of the Ottoman Army in the First World War* (Westport, CT: Greenwood Press, 2000), 51–74. For a detailed account of the Sarikamish disaster, see: Alptekin Müderrisoğlu, *Sarıkamış Dramı* (Istanbul: Kaştaş, 1997), 2 volumes.

[28] Lepsius, *Der Todesgang*, 161–2.

[29] Hüseyin C. Yalçın, *Siyasal Anılar* (Istanbul: Türkiye İş Bankası Kültür Yayınları, 1976), 233.

[30] BOA, DH.ŞFR 48/166, Talaat to the provinces of Erzurum, Bitlis, and Van, 26 December 1914. Talaat Pasha's involvement in the dismissal of Armenian government officials typifies him as a micro-manager. In February he urged local officials to keep him abreast of the developing situation with regards to the Armenian civil servants. BOA, DH.ŞFR 50/3, Talaat to the provinces of Erzurum, Van and Bitlis, 14 February 1915. When he got the impression that the firing wasn't proceeding quickly enough, he personally had police chief Krikor and police officers Armenag, Boghos, and Shahin of the Van police squad removed from their offices and deported to Mosul. BOA, DH.ŞFR 50/179, Talaat to Van province, 6 March 1915. For the official declaration sanctioning the dismissal of all Armenian and Greek police officers, see: BOA, DH.EUM.MEM 80/63, 21 November 1916.

For the population of Diyarbekir city, there was little to celebrate between Christmas and New Year's Eve 1914. The news of Enver's losses reverberated there and had a detrimental effect on the morale of the locals. The war was experienced closely and emotionally, since both Muslims and Christians had been drafted into the army, and many of them had perished in the Sarikamish campaign. The bad news distressed the communities and strained their relationships, sparking suspicion and enmity. The Saint Ephraim church was vandalized and property was stolen, and gendarmes beat up a Syriac village headman.[31] The governor also prohibited the use of all non-Turkish languages in some of the province's institutions, such as the American hospital or the French mission.[32] In February 1915 the government initiated arms searches in Christian houses in Diyarbekir city. During these violent searches the inhabitants were accused of treason and espionage, and hiding guns in secret arms stores. On 18 February twelve young men of the large Syriac village of Qarabash were convicted and sentenced to death under charges of alleged desertion. Four of them were hanged publicly in the central square in Diyarbekir in order to deter potential deserters.[33] When their compatriot villagers protested against the execution, gendarmes clubbed two men to death and dispersed the group.[34]

March also saw the disarming of Armenian soldiers and their recruitment, together with many other Christian men, into labour battalions.[35] The cadre of these battalions were deemed disloyal elements, as an official decree proscribed them 'at all costs' from taking up arms in the regular Ottoman army.[36] The labour battalion conscripts were deployed in road construction under dire circumstances in and around Diyarbekir. Irrespective of weather conditions, every individual, including teenagers, was forced to carry a load of 55 kilograms. They were escorted by two dozen soldiers. Many conscripts in the labour battalions perished of exhaustion, exposure, and maltreatment. On 5 March 1915, a Syriac native of Diyarbekir, Abed Mshiho, was conscripted into a labour battalion numbering 1100 men, and assigned to work on the Diyarbekir-Aleppo road. According to his account, the maltreatment increased every other day, bastinado and other beatings

---

[31] Armalto, *Al-Qousara*, 26, 27.

[32] Ibid., 26.

[33] Abed Mshiho Na'man Qarabashi, *Vergoten Bloed: Verhalen over de Gruweldaden Jegens Christenen in Turkije en over het Leed dat hun in 1895 en in 1914–1918 is Aangedaan* (Glanerbrug, The Netherlands: Bar Hebraeus, 2002, translated by George Toro and Amill Gorgis), 60. This important diary was originally written in Aramaic under the title *Dmo Zlicho* ('Shed Blood') by Na'man Qarabashi, a native of the village of Qarabash. During the war Qarabashi was a theology student at the Syriac monastery Deyr-ul Zaferan. Along with Armalto's account it is one of the very few survivor memoirs. However, his account suffers from victim bias in at least two ways: the myth of extreme cruelty on the part of the perpetrators, and the myth of resistance by the victims. Nevertheless, his account is factually correct and will be utilized, albeit with caution.

[34] Armalto, *Al-Qousara*, 27.

[35] Raymond Kévorkian, 'Receuil de témoignages sur l'extermination des amele tabouri ou bataillons de soldats-ouvriers Arméniens de l'armée Ottomane pendant la première guerre mondiale', in: *Revue d'Histoire Arménienne Contemporaine* 1 (1995), 289–303.

[36] See the official order in: Kâmuran Gürün, *Ermeni Dosyası* (Ankara: Bilgi, 1988), 276.

becoming commonplace, the violence escalating in sporadic murders of individual conscripts by late March.[37]

March 1915 was perhaps the most fateful month for the future development of the Ottoman Empire in general and of Diyarbekir province in particular. The naval attacks upon the Dardanelles straits and the Russian move towards Van cast panic into the hearts and minds of the CUP leaders.[38] This reinforced their established fear of a nightmare scenario in which potential Armenian disloyalty would pave the way for an Allied incursion into Anatolia. This 'wishful suspicion' led to a series of meetings of the Central Committee in Istanbul in mid-March. As a result of these gatherings, Dr. Bahaeddin Şakir was delegated substantial authority to deal with 'the internal enemies'. The Special Organization was reorganized, expanded, and placed under his jurisdiction.[39] The army was given more autonomy on Talaat's orders to 'turn to the Third Army for the application of measures aimed at Armenian actions'.[40] Four days later he imposed total censorship on the Dashnak newspaper *Azadamard* and sent Osman Bedri, police commissioner of Constantinople, to confiscate their presses.[41] This radicalization at the centre metastasized into the periphery as Diyarbekir province saw the appointment of its new governor: Dr. Mehmed Reshid (see Plate 4).

On 25 March 1915 the governor of Diyarbekir, Hamid Bey, was relieved of his duties and replaced by Dr. Mehmed Reshid (Şahingiray). Reshid was born into a Circassian family in Russian Caucasia on 8 February 1873. When the Tsarist government intensified its campaign against the Circassians in 1874, his family fled to the Ottoman Empire. Reshid grew up in Istanbul, where he enrolled in the Military School of Medicine and joined other students to found the kernel of a secret political party that would later adopt the name CUP. In 1897 the Abdulhamid regime exiled him to Tripoli for his politically recalcitrant activities. Having made a career in the army and risen to the rank of major, he wrote a book on the CUP revolution in 1908. However, he was never influential in the CUP core and his power did not match up to that of party bosses Dr. Bahaeddin Şakir or Dr. Nâzım. In 1909 he relinquished his employment in the military and became district governor and mayor in several provinces between 1908 and 1914. During his professional progress Reshid gradually radicalized and scapegoated the Christians as the reason for the Empire's erosion and wretched condition. By 1914 he

---

[37] Qarabashi names nine Armenians who were led away and killed. Qarabashi, *Dmo Zliho*, 62, 64–6.

[38] If the Entente navy were to penetrate the Straits, Talaat promised they would blow up the Aya Sofia and retreat into the Anatolian heartland, from where they planned to resist and repel the Entente. Talaat laughed at Morgenthau's protests by saying that not even six men in the CUP would care about the building. Henry Morgenthau, *Ambassador Morgenthau's Story* (Ann Arbor, MI: Gomidas, 2000), 132.

[39] For a detailed reconstruction of this decision-making process, see: Taner Akçam, *İnsan Hakları ve Ermeni Sorunu: İttihat ve Terakki'den Kurtuluş Savaşı'na* (İstanbul: İmge, 2001), 260–5, especially 264.

[40] BOA, DH.ŞFR 51/15, Talaat to the provinces of Erzurum, Van, and Diyarbekir, 14 March 1915.

[41] Heinrich Vierbücher, *Armenien 1915: Die Abschlachtung eines Kulturvolkes durch die Türken* (Bremen: Donat and Temmen Verlag, 1985 [1930]), 49.

was thoroughly convinced that the Ottoman Christians were abusing their ostensibly privileged positions and therefore were to blame for the Empire's depressed economy. He was delegated the task of secretary-general of the international reform plan for the eastern provinces which was annulled when the CUP engaged in war. In 1915 he became governor of Diyarbekir and in 1916 he was appointed governor of Ankara. When the war was over, he was arrested and incarcerated in Istanbul. With the assistance of his former loyalists, he escaped from prison and lived incognito at various Istanbul addresses. Fed up with being forced to evade the law, and fearing arrest and possible execution, he committed suicide when a police chief tracked him down on 6 February 1919.[42]

When Reshid acceded to the governorship of Diyarbekir province, he brought with him thirty mainly Circassian Special Organization operatives, such as Çerkez Harun, Çerkez Şakir, and Çerkez Aziz.[43] They were joined in Diyarbekir by more troops released from the local prison.[44] This way, Reshid absorbed more effective power than the average Ottoman governor. In his case, it was certainly true that '[i]n the provinces party bosses of one kind or another often exercised substantial control, amounting in some cases,... to virtual autonomy'.[45] Upon arrival in Diyarbekir, Reshid and his men faced a poor rule of law, a serious desertion problem, and an anxious population. The bazaar, for example, was buzzing with rumours that the Russians had invaded Istanbul.[46] The Muslims feared an invasion of Diyarbekir by the Russian army, whose reputation as a valiant fighting corps had preceded its offensive into the south. The Christians were torn between fear and hope: whereas one moderate group (such as the clergy) was terrified that a Russian incursion might trigger reprisals, another, discordant group (such as the nationalists) expressed audacious beliefs that it was possible to defend themselves against the brutal policies of the CUP dictatorship.[47]

The concerns of many young men were of a pragmatic nature. They wanted to avoid the possibility of being conscripted into the Ottoman army and being sent off to an almost certain death, at the front or in the labour battalions. As a result, some had actually gone into hiding in the complex web of rooftops of Khanchepek, a neighbourhood with a large concentration of Armenians. Some of these draft evaders had acquired weapons.[48] Dr. Floyd Smith, an American doctor of the

---

[42] Hans-Lukas Kieser, 'Dr. Mehmed Reshid (1873–1919): A Political Doctor', in: Hans-Lukas Kieser and Dominik J. Schaller (eds.), *Der Völkermord an den Armeniern und die Shoah: The Armenian Genocide and the Shoah* (Zürich: Chronos, 2002), 245–80.

[43] Mehmed Reshid, *Mülâhazât* (Istanbul, 1919), transliterated in: Nejdet Bilgi, *Dr. Mehmed Reshid Şahingiray'ın hayatı ve hâtıraları* (İzmir: Akademi, 1997), 89, footnote 28. According to Abidin Nesimî, son of the then mayor of Lîce, Hüseyin Nesimî, the number of volunteers Reshid employed was 20. Abidin Nesimî, *Yılların İçinden* (Istanbul: Gözlem, 1977), 39.

[44] Yeghiayan, *British Foreign Office Dossiers*, 151.

[45] Alexander L. Macfie, *The End of the Ottoman Empire, 1908–1923* (London: Longman, 1998), 128.

[46] Armalto, *Al-Qousara*, 28.

[47] Ibid., 28.

[48] Mustafa Â. Tütenk, *Mahsûl-i Leyâli-i Hayatım* (Diyarbekir, 1918, unpublished memoirs), fourth notebook titled 'The Armenian Affair in Diyarbekir' (*Diyarbekir'de Ermeni Hâdisesi*), 21–23, quoted in: Beysanoğlu, *Diyarbekir Tarihi*, 787–88.

American Board of Commissioners for Foreign Missions (ABCFM), witnessed that at the end of February, the Armenian bishop Tchilgadian finally 'went upon the roofs and lectured the men, telling them that they were bringing ruin upon themselves and the whole Christian quarter. As a result quite a number surrendered'.[49] Still, there were a number of both Muslim and Christian deserters when Dr. Reshid became governor.

In a post-war booklet titled 'Reflections' (*Mülâhazât*),[50] Reshid defended and sought to legitimize his wartime policies as governor of Diyarbekir. These memoirs, composed of two of his four wartime notebooks (the other two were lost), carry extraordinary importance as they allow a close look at his line of thought when he was appointed governor. From the moment he set foot in Diyarbekir, Reshid found confirmation of his prejudices of a conspiracy of disloyal Christians. He wrote,

> My appointment to Diyarbekir coincided with a very delicate period of the war. Large parts of Van and Bitlis had been invaded by the enemy, deserters were transgressing, pillaging and robbing everywhere. Yezidi and Nestorian uprisings in or at the border of the province required the application of drastic measures. The transgressional, offensive and impudent attitude of the Armenians was seriously endangering the honor of the government.[51]

In his memoirs Reshid especially targeted the Armenians. He accused them of 'high treason' and of 'pursuing the goal of an independent Armenia'.[52] In his paranoia and animosity Reshid ignored the many Muslim deserters, and imagined an army of Armenian deserters whereas they may not have been as numerous and organized as he visualized. He believed that the Armenian draft dodgers on the rooftops were all 'formidably' organized revolutionaries, and that they numbered more than 1000. Moreover, according to Reshid 'there was not a single Armenian in the province who was not participating in this national endeavour'.[53] (see Plate 5)

In order to deal with these perceived problems, Reshid organized a committee for the 'solution of the Armenian question'. This council was named 'Committee of Inquiry' and had a 'Militia Unit' at its disposal.[54] According to a German charity worker the committee, drawn up of a dozen CUP loyalists, was 'a sham committee for the solution of the Armenian question' and served only one purpose: to eliminate the Armenian political parties.[55] It was headed by Colonel Cemilpaşazâde Mustafa Nüzhet Bey, and consisted of deputy Pirinççizâde Aziz Feyzi, postal clerk İbrahim Bedreddin,[56] Majors Rüşdü Bey and Yasinzâde Şevki (Ekinci), his brother

---

[49] *ABCFM* archives, Houghton Library (Harvard University), ABC 16.9.7, reel 716:436, Floyd Smith to James Barton, 18 September 1915.

[50] The booklet was alternately titled 'Persistence' (*Sebat*).

[51] Reshid, *Mülâhazât*, 24.

[52] Ibid., 95, 99.

[53] Ibid., 103, 106.

[54] Süleyman Nazif, 'Doktor Reshid', in: *Hadisat*, 8 February 1919.

[55] PAAA, R14087, director of the Deutscher Hülfsbund für christliches Liebeswerk im Orient (Frankfurt am Main) Friedrich Schuchardt to the Auswärtiges Amt, 21 August 1915, enclosure no. 6.

[56] On 2 September 1914 İbrahim Bedreddin (Bedri for short) became the postal clerk of Diyarbekir province. Previously he had held this office in Basra and Mosul. After the defeat of the Balkan Wars of

Yasinzâde Yahya (Ekinci), representative of the 'Directorate for the Settlement of Tribes and Immigrants' (*İskân-ı Aşâir ve Muhacirîn Müdüriyeti*, henceforth İAMM) and chairman of the Diyarbekir branch of the 'Society for National Defense' Veli Necdet, police chief Memduh Bey, militia commander Şevki Bey, and Müftüzâde Şeref Uluğ, son of the mufti.[57] On orders of Reshid they selected the following civilians and appointed them Captain: Zazazâde Hacı Süleyman (by profession a butcher in the Diyarbekir bazaar), Halil (also a butcher), Cercisağazâde Abdülkerim, Direkçizâde Tahir, and Pirinççizâde Sıdkı (Tarancı). The following volunteers were nominated Lieutenant: Halifezâde Salih (Kalfagil), Ganizâde Servet (Akkaynak), Muhtarzâde Salih, Şeyhzâde Kadri (Demiray), Pirânîzâde Kemal (Önen), Yazıcızâde Kemal, Zaza Alo Efendi, and Hacı Bakır.[58]

At that time a certain Hacı Zeki of Lîce, a radical activist, incited the locals of Mardin to take up arms against the Christians. Zeki convened groups of Muslims at his house in Mardin city where he held inflammatory political speeches, openly calling for pogroms. The moderate district governor of Mardin, Hilmi Bey, was displeased by Zeki's aggressive vilification. Since the outbreak of the war Hilmi had been showing consistent efforts to restrain conflict, and maintain relative stability and moderate rule. He reprehended Zeki and expelled him from Mardin. Zeki then took off to Diyarbekir where he found willing partners among the CUP elite who were just consolidating their rule in the provincial capital.[59] On 6 April 1915 Talaat ordered Reshid to 'appoint a capable, loyal, and devout İttihadist for the vacant position of mayor' in Diyarbekir.[60] Reshid immediately fired the political moderate Cemilpaşazâde Dr. Fuad Bey and replaced him with the anti-Armenian radical Pirinççizâde Sıdkı.[61] Police chief Dersimli Hüseyin Bey was replaced by İAMM boss Veli Necdet, who had previously had occupied the office of provincial secretary.[62] All the key positions in Diyarbekir were now occupied by CUP loyalists.

In Diyarbekir city, Reshid now embarked on a relentless campaign to find and punish deserters. On 1 April he issued a proclamation demanding the surrender of all arms to the police.[63] When this failed to produce the results he had expected, he

---

1912–13, he had coordinated the CUP-sponsored deportation of the Ottoman Greeks of Biga (a town between Çanakkale and Bursa). On 12 September 1915 he was officially appointed district governor of Mardin, which he remained until 11 December 1916. On 24 January 1917 he was assigned to the governorship of Diyarbekir, which he occupied until 24 November 1918. Yeghiayan, *British Foreign Office Dossiers*, 69–70.

[57] A *müftü* (mufti) is a Muslim jurist who is versed in Islamic religious law (the *shari'a*) and provides binding advice on its application.

[58] Beysanoğlu, *Diyarbekir Tarihi*, 793–94; Bilgi, *Dr. Mehmed Reshid*, 26–7. See also: Joseph Naayem, *Shall This Nation Die?* (New York: Chaldean Rescue, 1921), 182–3. Reverend Naayem was a Chaldean priest of Urfa, where he witnessed the killing of his father and the persecution of the Christians. Disguised as a Bedouin Arab, he narrowly escaped with his life.

[59] Armalto, *Al-Qousara*, 29, 34.

[60] BOA, DH.ŞFR 51/220, Talaat to Diyarbekir, 6 April 1915.

[61] Reshid, *Mülâhazât*, 112. Right after the appointment of Sıdkı, a wave of violence swept over the labour battalions as two supervisors came to inspect the workers, yelling 'You're not here to play, come on, I want to see blood on those rocks!' Qarabashi, *Dmo Zliho*, 65.

[62] Yeghiayan, *British Foreign Office Dossiers*, 48.

[63] Floyd Smith to James Barton, 18 September 1915.

brutalized the arms searches from 5 April on. Aided by his gendarme commander, Major Rüşdü, he personally supervised and participated in the warrantless searches of churches and houses.[64] Whereas district governor Hilmi in Mardin visited the Christian clergy to congratulate them on Easter,[65] Reshid's roundups of Armenian men became more and more arbitrary and categorical. As he wrote: 'On a certain day I had the 3 or 4 most important streets in the Armenian neighbourhood barricaded and ordered surprise searches on every single house in the early morning, arresting more than 500 armed deserters'.[66] By 15 April Reshid had already had more than 600 Armenian notables and artisans arrested and put in jail. There he had them tortured to exact confessions on the locations of hidden arms depots. The prisoners were beaten, burnt with hot irons, had their nails pulled out with pliers, and suffered prolonged bastinado.[67] Even so, Reshid was not satisfied with what had been accomplished and wired Istanbul twice to request the deployment of more manpower to assist his force of 300 gendarmes and policemen. The Interior Ministry did not comply with his requests, frustrating and galvanizing him into taking more severe measures.[68]

A peculiar aspect of the operation was the hunt for 'recalcitrant' books and other texts, generally written in non-Ottoman languages. In Young Turk jargon this material was branded 'harmful documents' and needed to be confiscated.[69] As Floyd Smith wrote, 'Books and papers were sure to bring condemnation to a household'.[70] On 22 April Reshid's men went from door to door in the Khanchepek and Fatihpasha neighbourhoods to find books. The Syriac tailor Habib had warned the inhabitants to hide their books, especially books in the French and Armenian languages. The militia also paid a visit to the Armenian bishop Tchilgadian and accused him of hiding arms in secret niches in the large Armenian church of St. Sarkis. They raided his room, took away all his books and documents, and sent them to Reshid for examination. The next day the books were burnt publicly.[71] Vahram Dadrian was a young boy when he was deported with his family

---

[64] Qarabashi, *Dmo Zliho*, 63.

[65] Armalto, *Al-Qousara*, 29.

[66] Reshid, *Mülâhazât*, 105.

[67] Qarabashi, *Dmo Zliho*, 127; Hagop S. Der-Garabedian, *Jail to Jail: Autobiography of a Survivor of the 1915 Armenian Genocide* (New York: iUniverse, 2004), 34; Fa'iz Al-Ghusayn, *Martyred Armenia* (London: C.A. Pearson Ltd., 1917). This source has been discredited in denialist literature, but the level of detail and accuracy Al-Ghusayn provides on Diyarbekir's prison is compelling and corroborates other sources.

[68] Reshid, *Mülâhazât*, 103, 104.

[69] In the First World War, the CUP confiscated and destroyed an unknown but undoubtedly large number of non-Turkish language works. A striking example is the fate of the books at the library of the Armenian school of Sivas. In October 1916 Talaat was disturbed by the idea that the library kept 'important volumes on the condition of the Ottoman Empire in French, German, English, Russian, and Kurdish', and ordered 'the immediate seizure of these books and their dispatch to Istanbul by post.' BOA, DH.ŞFR 69/75, Talaat to Sivas province, 23 October 1916. Five months later, when the books still weren't sent, he repeated his order, requesting the books to be sent 'urgently'. BOA, DH. ŞFR 76/243–14, Talaat to Sivas province, 24 May 1917.

[70] Floyd Smith to James Barton, 18 September 1915.

[71] Armalto, *Al-Qousara*, 29. Patriarch Rahmani, *Les dégâts causés à la nation syrienne: présenté devant la conférence de la paix* (Paris: n.p., 1919).

from Çorum. After many trials and tribulations they arrived in the Syrian desert and met an Armenian man named Pakrad who had just escaped from Diyarbekir. Pakrad related to them that his father Abraham had been caught up in the book searches. A corporal took two of their books and walked out, facing a frantic crowd of Muslims:

> The corporal gestured to the crowd to shut up. 'Listen! Look here. Look what we found in his home', he yelled, lifting a geography book into the air. 'You don't know how to read, so you don't know how dangerous this book is. But I won't have to say much before you can draw your own conclusions. In the hands of our enemies this book is a more terrifying weapon than all the guns and cannons of the army. This book gives the locations of all the cities, villages, rivers, and roads in Turkey. All of them meticulously portrayed. Anybody who goes through this book can find not only the plan of every city, but also the location of every house and whether it belongs to a Christian or a Muslim. They have marked each one with a cross or a crescent, so that one day when they rebel it will be easy for them to tell a Muslim household from the others'. Grumbling from the mob—arms into the air in defiance! 'Oh, oh, oh . . . clobber him, kill him, let him rot, the traitor'. 'Please, calm down. Not so fast', the corporal ordered with authority, 'I haven't finished yet. Look. Here's another book'. He held up another book—a physics text. 'It tells you all you need to know about how to make gun-powder, bullets, and dynamite. These conspirators' homes are filled with books like this. Both the young and the old read these books and learn what to do to destroy our country. But thank God and the Sultan that we have been vigilant and were able to uncover their plot at the last minute. Now it's *we* who will destroy *their* homes and put *their* children to the sword'. The policemen had a hard time clearing a way through the violent crowd. They finally succeeded and, pulling and pushing their victim, they took him off to jail.[72]

Pakrad's father Abraham died in jail, where chances of escape or survival were very slim. As the city prison was now overfilled with prisoners, Reshid ordered the large caravanserai of Diyarbekir evacuated. Every day several dozens of prisoners were locked up and tortured in that khan.[73]

The violent persecutions were not limited to Diyarbekir city. In April a gradual shift occurred from discerning between combatants and non-combatants, to not discerning between them any longer. This momentum is exemplified by the crucial battle of Van, which had very high stakes for all parties. The Van front saw mutual indiscriminate massacring of Muslims by the joint Russo-Armenian forces and of Christians by Ottoman forces.[74] This dynamic between state and minority triggered a process of radicalization, both in geographical scope and in intensity. The anti-Armenian policies at the national level now became more and

---

[72] Vahram Dadrian, *To the Desert: Pages from my Diary* (London: Gomidas Institute, 2003), 64–5.

[73] Qarabashi, *Dmo Zliho*, 82, 128. This famous caravanserai, a large inn providing shelter to travelling businessmen or pilgrims, was also known as 'guest house' (*misafirhane*) or simply 'khan' (*han*) and is presently known as the Deliller Hanı near the Mardin Gate. After restoration in the 1990s, it became the five-star Hotel Kervansaray.

[74] Anahide Ter Minassian, 'Van 1915', in: Richard G. Hovannisian (ed.), *Armenian Van/ Vaspurakan* (Costa Mesa, CA: Mazda, 2000), 209–44.

more categorical as well. Moreover, inspired by the brutalizing war in Persian Azerbaijan and in Transcaucasia, the measures were also gaining 'total' traits: more and more violence was applied. Fear of Allied landings on the western coasts added fuel to the fire. As a result, the CUP began incarcerating dissidents and assailing the Armenian community all over the Ottoman Empire. Beginning on 24 April 1915, the political and cultural elite of the Ottoman Armenian community was targeted for arrest and deportation to the interior. The political prisoners were detained in Ayaş, the intellectual prisoners were sent to the prison of Çankırı. Others were sent to Diyarbekir to be court-martialled.[75] With few exceptions, these men were murdered or tortured to death in the next months. Simultaneously, deportation convoys to the interior were rerouted to Der el-Zor in the Syrian desert. The persecutions soon increased in intensity and were extended to larger parts of the Ottoman Empire.[76] These three factors were conducive to a genocidal process: categorical assaults, geographic expansion, and deadly violence.

In Diyarbekir, Reshid had not distinguished between guilty or innocent Armenians ever since he had arrived. His intensive arms searches of the first three weeks of April had delivered some results for his militia as many arms were found. The scope of armament and the extent of its organization were blown out of proportion and photos were taken of the arms and the culprits.[77] On 27 April Reshid wired an elated telegram to Talaat summarizing and evaluating his work in Diyarbekir:

> For ten days, the pursuit of deserters has been carried out with utmost severity. As a result of yesterday's purges a significant amount of explosives, fifty bombs, lots of ammunition and various arms, and a great deal of dynamite powder was found. 120 leaders and operatives of the villages were taken into custody. Until now, in the city alone more than 1000 deserters of different regions were apprehended, many of whom are party members. Searches and pursuit are continuing.[78]

Having incarcerated the bulk of the political elite of the Diyarbekir Christians, Reshid's militia now targeted their religious leaders. Blanket arrests of priests and monks were carried out and their houses were ransacked. In Mardin, where Reshid's persecutions had not yet started, the news from Diyarbekir nevertheless caused fear. The Armenian Catholic Bishop Ignatius Maloyan had become anxious about the worsening situation and seems to have written a letter to his co-religionists, in case something happened to him. Maloyan urged his parish to

---

[75] Grigoris Balakian, *Le Golgotha arménien: Berlin—Deir es-Zor: Mémoires* (Paris: Le cercle d'écrits caucasiens, 2002), vol. 1, 95–102.

[76] Donald Bloxham, 'The Beginning of the Armenian Catastrophe: Comparative and Contextual Considerations', in: Kieser, *Der Völkermord*, 101–28.

[77] Beysanoğlu, *Diyarbekir Tarihi*, 789. A similar method was applied in Mardin, where Memduh Bey had been sent. Ara Sarafian, 'The Disasters of Mardin during the Persecutions of the Christians, Especially the Armenians, 1915', in: *Haigazian Armenological Review* 18 (1998), 263.

[78] Reshid to Talaat, 27 April 1915, quoted in: Hüsamettin Yıldırım, *Rus-Türk-Ermeni Münasebetleri (1914–1918)* (Ankara: KÖK, 1990), 57.

remain calm and loyal to the government, and wrote, 'Above all, never lose your faith in the Holy Trinity'. The letter was sealed and entrusted to the Syriac Orthodox Bishop Gabriel Tabbuni on the first of May.[79]

While the war was raging in all intensity on the eastern front, the CUP began questioning the loyalty of the Ottoman Armenians even further. On 5 May 1915 Talaat authorized the Third Army to disarm all Armenian gendarmes in Diyarbekir province.[80] This way, even loyal Armenians were categorized as disloyal and treated as such. The next day the Directorate for Employment and Supplies of the Ministry of Economy ordered all its offices to fire their Armenian staff and 'deport those of whom it is necessary to areas where there are no Armenians'.[81] After Reshid had arrested these men in Diyarbekir city, he proceeded to persecute the city's clergy and extend the arrests to the villages. On 9 May he summoned the Chaldean priest Hanna Soha in Mardin to Diyarbekir for interrogation. Upon arrival, the militia publicly maltreated him before killing him in broad daylight in the streets.[82] The absence of constraints in his murder emboldened the militia and triggered a new wave of arrests and violence, this time targeting the surrounding villages as well. The predominantly Christian villages Kabiye, Qarabash, and Qitirbel, all situated on the plain of Diyarbekir, were subjected to brutal arms searches by Yasinzâde Yahya and Pirinççizâde Sıdkı between 10 and 20 May. The village men were tortured with bastinado, and dozens were taken away to the capital, filling the prison and the caravanse-rai.[83] The German charity worker Schuchardt wrote, 'between the 10th and the 30th of May another 1200 of the most notable Armenians and other Christians without distinction of religion were arrested in Diyarbekir province'.[84] Reshid then imposed a death penalty on any Armenian going outside the city walls.[85]

[79] Armalto, *Al-Qousara*, 30.

[80] BOA, DH.ŞFR 52/234, Talaat to Reshid, 5 May 1915.

[81] BOA, DH.ŞFR 52/249, Ministry of the Economy to the provinces of Erzurum, Bitlis, Van, Sivas, Mamuret-ul Aziz, and Diyarbekir, 6 May 1915. Since there were no other educated clerks available, Syriac employees Aziz (son of Yakub) and George Meqdesi Nano of the Diyarbekir office of the Ministry of Economy were allowed to continue their work. The director of this office, Saib Ali Efendi, protected these two secretaries all throughout the war. Armalto, *Al-Qousara*, 33. Most Armenian civil servants had already been fired and replaced by Muslims at that time. Some were still in office at the Ministry of Post. On 23 May this Ministry too took action, and ordered the dismissal of all its Armenian clerks and the transfer of the vacant functions to 'trustworthy Muslims' (*emin ve müslim kimselere*). BOA, DH.ŞFR 53/89, Ministry of Post to the provinces of Diyarbekir, Adana, Sivas, Ankara, Van, and Erzurum, 23 May 1915. For Haleb, see: BOA, DH. ŞFR 53/90. The day after, the Ministry had to deal with the replacement of the Armenian postal clerk responsible for the deliverance of post beween Diyarbekir and Siirt. Although no other qualified employees were available, it warned that the new postal clerk should under no circumstances be an Armenian. BOA, DH.ŞFR 53/97, Ministry of Post to Bitlis, 24 May 1915.

[82] Armalto, *Al-Qousara*, 32.

[83] Qarabashi, *Dmo Zliho*, 81, 86, 92.

[84] PAAA, R14087, director of the Deutscher Hülfsbund für christliches Liebeswerk im Orient (Frankfurt am Main) Friedrich Schuchardt to the Auswärtiges Amt, 21 August 1915, enclosure no. 6.

[85] *National Archives* (United States, Washington, DC, hereafter cited as *NARA*), RG 59, 867.4016/ 77, Morgenthau to Secretary of State, 20 July 1915 (enclosure no.3), in: Ara Sarafian (ed.), *United States Official Records on the Armenian Genocide 1915–1917* (London: Gomidas Institute, 2004), 103.

Diyarbekir had now effectively become an open-air prison as the persecutions also spread into the countryside.[86]

A critical event in Diyarbekir province was the first large massacre involving the integral destruction of entire village populations. On the morning of 20 May 1915 Reshid ordered Yahya and Sıdkı to disarm Qarabash, a village a short distance north-east of Diyarbekir. The village was invaded with fifty men and thoroughly disarmed, seizing even bread knives. Its men incarcerated, its weapons confiscated, Qarabash was now completely emasculated. That same evening Yahya and Sıdkı visited the neighbouring Kurdish villages, inciting them to attack Qarabash and explicitly giving them fiat to plunder. Two days later, on 22 May, the village was invaded by mounted Kurds, who massacred its entire population with daggers, axes, and swords. Its two priests, Paulus and Behnam, were trampled to death under the hooves of the horses. The women were raped, the houses burnt, and valuables seized.[87] The few survivors fled to Diyarbekir city, where some of them were treated by Floyd Smith, who reported the arrival of the Qarabash survivors as follows:

> May 21, 1915, there came to our compound in Diarbekir from the village of Karabash, three hours to the east, three or four wounded and the following day (May 22) over a score of wounded Armenian and Syrian women and children. They, the villagers, told of a night attack by the Kurds three days previous and that the next morning the government had sent gendarmes who refused to allow anyone to come to Diarbekir. Some managed to get away and finally all who could walk or be carried came on the dates mentioned. The wounds were practically all infected and I have classified them as follows: . . .
>
> (c) Wounds made by heavy cutting instruments, probably axes. . . .
>
> 2. Two children about seven and nine years and one woman: attempted decapitations. Deep incised wounds of the nape of the neck (just below the skull), 5–8 inches long and of a depth equal to the thickness of the muscles of this region.[88]

On that same evening, the 160 families of the village of Kabiye were targeted.[89] The terrified villagers, comprised of some remaining men but mostly women,

---

[86] The persecutions were now extended to Mardin city, which was still ruled by Hilmi Bey, who had stalled and resisted anti-Christian persecutions in his district. On 15 May Reshid sent Aziz Feyzi to organize the round-up of the Christian elites of Mardin. During a secret meeting in which tens of Muslim notables participated, a plan was laid out for the crackdown on the Mardin elite. However, this was practically impossible because of Hilmi being in office. Armalto, *Al-Qousara*, 33. Talaat continued micro-managing the national persecution of the Armenian political elite. On 19 May he ordered Henchak leader Paramas court-martialled in the Diyarbekir prison and inquired about the whereabouts of Krikor Nalbandian. BOA, DH.ŞFR 53/58, 19 May 1915, Talaat to Reshid. On the 22nd he requested information on Agnouni, Rupen Zartarian, and their colleagues. BOA, DH.ŞFR 53/74, 22 May 1915, Talaat to Reshid.

[87] Qarabashi, *Dmo Zliho*, 81.

[88] *ABCFM* archives, ABC 16.9.7, vol. 25d, document 485, Floyd Smith to James Barton, 20 September 1919.

[89] In the 1960s, Professor of Semitic Languages Otto Jastrow travelled to Diyarbekir and Beirut to research the local Arabic dialects, but was repeatedly confronted in his interviews with narratives of massacres. He conducted several very valuable interviews with survivors from various villages, uploaded these recordings to an online archive (<http://semarch.uni-hd.de/>) and transcribed them in Aramaic,

children, and the elderly, had taken refuge in the Mor Kiryakos church. Sıdkı had persuaded Ömer, Mustafa, and Emîn, three sons of Perikhan, matriarch of the Raman tribe, to cooperate in the raid. They had brought with them dozens of tribesmen, who combed the village for hemp rope to tie the men together. On orders of Sıdkı the men were tortured with hot iron pins, while women and girls were raped in the church. Within five hours, the militia and the tribesmen had hacked the villagers to death with axes. Many were crammed into haylofts and barns and burnt alive. After the massacre, the Raman brothers loaded two saddle bags of money and gold and carried the goods away.[90] The few survivors escaped to Diyarbekir, where some were killed after all by gendarmes. One survivor stated that she survived the massacre 'between the corpses of her relatives'. When she fled to Diyarbekir city, a Zaza family proposed to take her into their home, but she refused out of fear. Another survivor, a boy, had escaped death by hiding in a vineyard, which was overgrown at that time of the year. He was the only male survivor of the Kabiye massacre.[91]

In April, some Armenians had already sporadically been deported from their native regions, though this was not an empire-wide campaign. The deportation of the entire Armenian people was officially organized from 23 May 1915 on, when Talaat issued orders for the integral deportation of all Armenians to Deir ez-Zor, starting with the north-eastern provinces.[92] That same day he urged the Fourth Army Command to court-martial any Muslim who collaborated with Christians.[93] The Third Army had been put under command of General Mahmud Kâmil Pasha,[94] who had issued a similar order. His orders instructed 'any Muslim who protected an Armenian hanged in front of his house, the burning of his house, his removal from office, and his appearance before a court-martial'.[95] These widespread arrests and persecutions prompted the Entente Powers to announce a joint declaration on 24 May, denouncing CUP policies against the Armenians. The declaration vehemently criticized these 'new crimes of Turkey against humanity

---

Arabic, and German. For the Kabiye massacre, see: Otto Jastrow (ed.), *Die mesopotamisch-arabischen Qltu-Dialekte* (Wiesbaden: Kommissionsverlag Franz Steiner GmbH, 1981), Vol. II, *Volkskundliche Texte in Elf Dialekten*, 309–71.

[90] According to Qarabashi the amount of money stolen was 150 Turkish pounds. Qarabashi, *Dmo Zliho*, 89.

[91] Jastrow, *Die mesopotamisch-arabischen*, 310. Many survivors of the Christian villages of the plain fled to the city but were not received with open arms. Survivors and scared villagers came pouring into the churches. A survivor girl related that upon arrival at the Syriac Mother Mary church, she was chased away at the door by a Syriac Orthodox priest, who cursed at her and would not even give her a morsel of bread. Ibid., 324–5. According to the son of an Armenian survivor from the village of Satıköy, this priest was B'shero Abu Tuma, who had also been forced by Reshid to act as an informer and betray houses where Armenians were hidden. Interview with David Krikorian (aged 75) from Satıköy village (Diyarbekir province), conducted in Turkish in Amsterdam on 16 December 2004.

[92] BOA, DH.ŞFR 53/91, 53/92, and 53/93, Talaat to provinces, 23 May 1915. This is the single instance in which the empire-wide nature of the deportations are reflected in one order at the most central level.

[93] BOA, DH.ŞFR 53/85, Talaat to Cemal, 23 May 1915.

[94] On 12 February 1915 Mahmud Kâmil replaced General Hafız Hakkı, who had died in a spotted typhus epidemic. Erickson, *Ordered to Die*, 104.

[95] *Takvim-i Vekâyi*, no. 3540, 7.

and civilization' and promised 'that they will hold personally responsible... all members of the Ottoman government and those of their agents who are implicated in such massacres'.[96] The CUP leaders, especially Talaat, panicked and attempted to disguise the deportations, requesting permission from the Grand Vizier on 26 May to issue a temporary deportation law. Although the deportations had already begun, the Grand Vizier endorsed Talaat's law on the 29th, rushing the bill through parliament the next day. This was the official legal cover for the deportation of Armenians to the Syrian desert, authorizing the army to proceed with the operation, and delegating its daily implementation to the İAMM.[97]

'BURN, DESTROY, KILL': THE PERSECUTION BECOMES GENOCIDAL

At this stage, moral thresholds were crossed both on the national and provincial level. Talaat had assumed supervision of and therefore responsibility for a very risky operation: the deportation of an entire population. The murderous initiations on the plain of Diyarbekir, too, had crossed a boundary as entire village populations were now targeted for destruction. The relationship between these two developments remains a chicken-and-egg enigma. However, it is possible to reconstruct at least some elements of this momentum. Rafael de Nogales Mendez was a Venezuelan officer in German service, operating in the Ottoman army as a mercenary. In the spring of 1915 he had witnessed the massacres of Christians in Van and Bitlis, committed by Halil Pasha and Tahir Cevdet Bey.[98] He visited Diyarbekir in late June and had the opportunity to speak to Reshid in private. According to Nogales, Talaat had personally ordered Dr. Reshid to unleash hell on Diyarbekir province with a telegram containing a mere three words: 'Burn—Destroy—Kill [*Yak—Vur—Öldür*]'. Although this order was most probably destroyed (assuming it existed at all), there was clearly no instruction for Reshid to desist. Moreover, Reshid admitted himself that he had merely obeyed Talaat's order, who allegedly had confided to him, 'j'assume la responsabilité morale et matérielle'.[99] Reshid interpreted the order as approval of his policy, characterized by American consul Jesse Jackson as a 'reign of terror'.[100]

---

[96] *NAUK*, FO 371/2488/51010, 28 May 1915; *NARA*, RG 59, 867.4016/67, 29 May 1915.

[97] BOA, MV 198/163, 30 May 1915.

[98] Halil (Enver Pasha's uncle) and Cevdet (Enver's brother-in-law) swept through Van and Bitlis after their defeats on Persian territory and in Van. During their retreat, they massacred the Armenian inhabitants of Bitlis, Van, and the plain of Muş. For an eyewitness account, see: Grace Knapp, *The Tragedy of Bitlis* (New York: Fleming H. Revell Co., 1919).

[99] Rafael de Nogales, *Four Years Beneath the Crescent* (London: Sterndale Classics, 2003), 125. This book was first published in Spanish as *Cuatro años bajo la media luna* (Madrid: Editora Internacional, 1924), later published in German as: *Vier Jahre unter dem Halbmond: Erinnerungen aus dem Weltkriege* (Berlin: Verlag von Reimar Hobbing, 1925). See also his: *Memorias del General Rafael de Nogales Méndez* (Caracas: Ediciones Abril, 1974).

[100] *NARA*, RG 59, 867.4016/77, Jackson to Morgenthau, 5 June 1915, in: Sarafian, *United States*, 84.

Content with the results on the Diyarbekir plain and emboldened by Talaat's approval, Reshid had Feyzi conduct arms searches in Mardin on 24 May. These were equally brutal and categorical as those carried out in the previous month in Diyarbekir district. The next day he took it a step further and ordered Hilmi Bey to arrest all Christian notables in Mardin. Hilmi refused by answering he could not think of any reason why he should carry out arrests in his city and openly disobeyed his superior's order. Nevertheless, Feyzi side-stepped bureaucratic protocols and proceeded with the persecutions, backed by a group of Muslim notables and the militia. Together they incarcerated dozens of Christians in Mardin.[101] The persecutions also spread to the northern parts of the province, which were closer to Kharput, capital of Mamuret-ul Aziz province. Reverend Henry Riggs, a missionary in that city, wrote to the American ambassador Morgenthau that the Armenian pastor of Çüngüş (Tchunkoush) had 'died a violent death in prison there'. The same fate had befallen preachers in Hani and Lîce.[102]

For the even worse scenario that was to come, considerable coordination and organization was needed. In May 1915, Reshid summoned Ömer for a secret mission that would bring him riches and earn him an amnesty. Ömer travelled to the governor's office in Diyarbekir, where the terrified urbanites saw him and his entourage enter the city:

> Ömer was of a short stature, darkish, with small-pox scars on his face. He wore a big turban on his head around which hung many coloured silk insignias to show that he was a Kurdish chieftain. He also wore a black short tunic (local made), long breeches, and red shoes ... being armed with a Mauser rifle, two revolvers, a sword, a dagger, a scimitar, and carrying with him an enormous amount of bullets and cartridges.[103]

The recent publication of the family memoir of the Raman tribe has shed light on the division of labour during the genocide. According to the memoirs, Dr. Reshid received them in his office and explained that the Armenians were stabbing the country in the back by helping the Russian army. Aziz Feyzi translated to Kurdish as the governor suggested that he would deliver to the Raman brothers convoys of Armenians, whom they would escort down the Tigris on a raft, ultimately to kill them all. If they agreed, they were entitled to half of the total booty. Absolute secrecy was vital; if he would break silence he would be severely punished. Seduced by the prospect of abundant wealth, the brothers agreed and the plan was set in motion.[104]

By the end of May, the entire Christian elite of Diyarbekir was in prison, where some had already died under torture. Dr. Reshid administered the *coup de grâce* to the elite in the last week of that month. On Sunday 30 May 1915 Major Rüşdü

---

[101] Armalto, *Al-Qousara*, 33.

[102] *NARA*, RG 59, 867.4016/77, Morgenthau to Secretary of State, 25 May 1915, in: Sarafian, *United States*, 35.

[103] Muggerditchian, *Dikranagerdee Nahankin Tcharteru*, pp. 57–8.

[104] The author of the remarkably candid family memoir is Ömer's nephew, who sketches in graphic detail the massacre committed by his uncle. Hüseyin Demirer, *Ha Wer Delal: Emînê Perîxanê'nin Hayatı* (Istanbul: Avesta, 2008), pp. 75–89.

handcuffed 807 notables including Bishop Tchilgadian, and led them through the Tigris Gate. On the shores of the Tigris the men were loaded on seventeen large Tigris rafts under the pretext that they would be deported to Mosul. Militiamen accompanied the notables on the rafts as they sailed one hour downstream to the 'intersection of two rivers' (*serê du avê*), a violent torrent where the Batman creek joins the Tigris, south of Beşiri. This area was the home of the Raman tribe. At this gorge, Major Rüşdü had all rafts moored by the left bank of the river and ordered the Christians to compose reassuring letters to their families in which they were compelled to write that they were safely underway to Mosul. The men were then stripped of their clothes and valuables and massacred by Rüşdü's men near the villages of Shikefta and Bezawan. In carrying out the hands-on killing the militia was assisted by Kurdish tribesmen loyal to Raman chieftain Ömer and his brother Mustafa. All men were slaughtered and dumped in the river, with the exception of Bishop Tchilgadian, who was forced to witness the bloodbath as a form of psychological excruciation before being led back to Diyarbekir.[105] After the massacre, Ömer and Mustafa were invited to Aziz Feyzi's house, where they celebrated their accomplishment. The men were later received at the governorship, where Reshid congratulated them for their bravery and patriotism.[106] Reshid also appealed to the Interior Ministry to have his militia rewarded and awarded medals for their outstanding performances. His wish was granted by the Directorate for General Security, and the militia members received financial benefits and were decorated with medals.[107]

A week later the process was repeated with 674 Christians and thirteen rafts. This time, the murder was supervised by Veli Necdet and fifty militiamen. On arrival at the Raman gorge the victims were robbed of a total of 6000 Turkish pounds and stripped of their clothes. They were killed and thrown in the river as Ömer's tribesmen and the militia lined up on both banks with their guns. Those that managed to swim and rise to the surface were shot dead. Back in Diyarbekir city, the militiamen sold the expensive clothing they had taken from the victims at the market.[108] Among those killed were Onnik Kazazian, a wholesaler from Istanbul who happened to be visiting Diyarbekir, and his friend Artin Kassabian, the former interpreter of the French vice-consulate. Other victims were the noted bankers Khatchadur Dikranian and Tirpandjian.[109] The same fate befell Mihran

---

[105] Qarabashi, *Dmo Zliho*, 128.

[106] *Épisodes des massacres arméniens de Diarbekir: Faits et Documents* (Constantinople: Kéchichian Fr., 1920), 28–30.

[107] BOA, DH.EUM.MEM 67/31, 27 July 1915. Deputies Aziz Feyzi and Zülfü Bey, and militia Major Şevki were decorated with honorary medals for their 'great achievements'. BOA, DH.KMS 43/10, 11 January 1917. According to a British intelligence report, 'Deputy Feyzi was received by the Kaiser and decorated with the Iron Cross'. *Foreign Office* 371/4172/24597, no. 63490, folio 304.

[108] PAAA, R14087, director of the Deutschen Hülfsbundes für christliches Liebeswerk im Orient (Frankfurt am Main) Friedrich Schuchardt to the Auswärtiges Amt, 21 August 1915, enclosure no. 6; Lepsius, *Todesgang*, 75–6.

[109] Report of M. Guys to the French embassy, Istanbul, 24 July 1915, in: Arthur Beylerian (ed.), *Les grandes puissances, l'empire ottoman et les arméniens dans les archives françaises (1914–1918): recueil de documents* (Paris: Université de Paris I, Panthéon-Sorbonne, 1983), 48, document no. 58; Yeghiayan, *British Foreign Office Dossiers*, 48; Krikorian, *Armenians*, 24–5.

Basmadjian, graduate of the Euphrates College in Kharput, Dikran Chakidjian, and Nalband Hagop, all of them Dashnakists, as well as Hagop Hovsepian, the negotiator Stephan Matossian, the former provincial interpreter and secondary school teacher Dikran Ilvanian, member of the municipal council and representative of Singer Missak Shirikdjian, all of them members of the Ramgavar party.[110] To the dismay of Holstein, the German vice-consul at Mosul, a week later the rafts arrived empty. Holstein later found out that the Christian convoys had been 'completely slaughtered' (*sämtlich abgeschlachtet*) and he had witnessed their corpses floating downstream: 'For several days, corpses and human limbs have been floating down the river here'.[111] Several other convoys of Armenian notables followed and were dispatched in a similar way.

Bishop Tchilgadian had been forced to watch how his parishioners were slaughtered. Although Ambassador Wangenheim later reported to Chancellor Bethmann-Hollweg that 'the Armenian Bishop of Diyarbekir is said to have committed suicide out of despair', this was certainly not the case.[112] After the second massacre he was led back to Diyarbekir, where he was ordered to sign a written declaration that the murdered Armenians had died of natural causes.[113] When he refused he was thrown into prison and tortured to death while his wife was raped by several militiamen before being killed.[114] Finally, a large nail was hammered through Tchilgadian's head before he was burnt to ashes in front of the Melek Ahmed mosque by officer Resul Hayri Bey. The other priests and monks were strangled to death with thick ropes. All of this happened on the orders of Pirinççizâde Aziz Feyzi.[115]

After the elimination of the Armenian elite of Diyarbekir, Reshid quickly expanded the violence to genocidal proportions. Having massacred the bulk of the male elite, the rest of the Diyarbekir Armenians were now targeted categorically. On 1 June he had his militia evacuate 1060 Armenian men and women of the Armenian neighbourhood Khanchepek and escort them to the Diyarbekir plain through the Mardin Gate. The people were gathered and a proclamation was read out loud, offering the Armenians their lives in exchange for conversion to Islam. Although the decision was not unanimous, the victims refused, whereupon they were stripped of their clothes and belongings. The militia and local Kurdish villagers then massacred them with rifles, axes, swords, and daggers. Many

---

[110] *Épisodes des massacres*, 22–3.

[111] PAAA, Botschaft Konstantinopel 169, Holstein to Wangenheim, 10 June 1915.

[112] PAAA, Botschaft Konstantinopel 169, Rößler to Wangenheim, 29 June 1915; R14086, Wangenheim to Bethmann-Hollweg, 9 July 1915.

[113] NARA, RG 59, 867.4016/77, Morgenthau to Secretary of State, 20 July 1915 (enclosure no. 3), in: Sarafian, *United States*, 103.

[114] Chilgadian's killing was protracted: his teeth were knocked out, his beard was pulled out, he was forced to squeeze boiling hot eggs in his palms (a common form of torture on the human skin), and his eyes were gorged out. Vierbücher, *Armenien 1915*, 61–2. The account of Chilgadian's death may seem embellished with excessive cruelty but is corroborated in many other sources, such as the German reports, Muggerditchian, Qarabashi, and Armalto.

[115] Dadrian, *To the Desert*, 66; Qarabashi, *Dmo Zliho*, 129; Yeghiayan, *British Foreign Office Dossiers*, 48; *Épisodes des massacres*, 26–8; Interview with David Krikorian.

women were raped, some were sold as slaves to the highest bidders. The corpses were either thrown in wells or trenches, or left on the plain to rot, 'the men on their stomachs, the women on their backs'.[116] It did not take long for Talaat to issue the following deportation order for the Diyarbekir Armenians: 'All Armenians living in villages and towns of the province, will be resettled to Mosul, Urfa and Zor, with no exceptions. Necessary measures will be taken to secure their lives and property during the deportation'.[117] At the same time, the İAMM ordered the 'documentation of the names and places of the Armenian villages, the number of deportees, and the abandoned property and ploughland'.[118]

The İAMM agent for Diyarbekir, Veli Necdet, was charged with implementing Talaat's orders. The remaining Armenians were to be deported to the south, and consisted mainly of women, children, and the elderly. One day after her father was tortured to death by Reshid's militiamen, Aghavni Kassabian, daughter of a noted Armenian merchant, was deported with her family:

> Turkish gendarmes came to our house in the morning and told us that we were going to be put on a deportation march. We were given little time to gather a few things that we could pack on a donkey. We gathered silverware, some clothes, two rugs, a Bible, soap, some family photographs. We packed as much food and water as we could, but we expected to be able to buy food when we needed more. We hid some jewels on our bodies, and each had an allotment of money. . . . By noon we joined a long line of Armenians and were marched down the streets to the Citadel Gardens, where we met up with thousands of Armenians. Some had donkeys, some had ox-drawn carts, and most were on foot carrying packs and small children and infants. The gendarmes began cracking the whip and we began to move in a big mass toward the New Gate from where I could see a long snakish line of Armenians moving around the city walls going south. We were marched out past the Citadel and around the black city walls wavering in the heat. By the end of the day, we were sleeping on the ground somewhere on the flat, hard plateau. The tributaries of the Tigris cut ravines into the limestone ridges, and in their flanks were occasional huts built out of the rock, where Kurds lived. There was nothing but dry ground and sky and limestone ridges. Nothing.[119]

On the fifth day of the deportation, Aghavni's mother had gone delirious and died of exhaustion. On the sixth day, all of their possessions were gone, either consumed or stolen by gendarmes. One night she was raped by a gendarme. Hunger, thirst, murder, and exhaustion had dramatically reduced the number of deportees by the time her convoy had reached the desert. Aghavni herself was abducted by a Kurdish nomad and she bore him two children, before she escaped to the remainder of her extended family in the United States.[120] Those that were

---

[116] Edward W. C. Noel, *Diary of Major E. Noel on Special Duty in Kurdistan* (Basra: n.p., 1919), part 1, 10–11.

[117] BOA, DH.ŞFR 54/87, Talaat to the provinces of Trabzon, Mamuret-ul Aziz, Sivas, Canik, and Diyarbekir, 21 June 1915.

[118] BOA, DH.ŞFR 54/15, İAMM to the provinces of Adana, Haleb, Erzurum, Bitlis, Van, and Diyarbekir, 14 June 1915.

[119] Peter Balakian, *Black Dog of Fate: A Memoir* (New York: BasicBooks, 1997), 217–18.

[120] Ibid., 218–23.

marched further into the desert often did not even make it to Rakka. A German named Greif, living in Aleppo, reported that the convoys of Diyarbekir Armenians were reduced to virtual non-existence in the desert. He wrote that 'many raped female corpses were lying around naked' and added the following detail: 'Many of them had stakes driven in their anus'.[121]

Responses of bystanders such as ordinary Turks and Kurds ranged from collaboration, through shock and sadness, to apathy. This differentiation is exemplified well by the fate of the Armenian and Syriac secretaries and accountants of the Cemilpaşazâde dynasty, who were now rounded up from the family mansion and killed. Some Cemilpaşazâdes, such as militia leader Cemilpaşazâde Mustafa, were collaborating with the Young Turks in the destruction of the Diyarbekir Armenians. Others, such as his brother Cemilpaşazâde Fuad, the liberal mayor of Diyarbekir who had been dismissed by the CUP, 'saved Christians by hiding them in the family haylofts and depots'. The Bahto and Nezo families from the village of Bardizag/Bahçecik were saved this way. Fuad Bey himself died in 1915 of typhoid fever.[122] According to one eyewitness of the Cemilpaşazâde family, 'in that pitiless period, 1.5 million Armenians were killed. I can never forget how my uncle Kasım sat down and cried when they were taken away. Because they were not guilty of anything. They were good and hard-working people. All of them, including those who worked in our mansion, were taken away. The government did it, it was the law. We were unable to protect them'.[123]

By late June 1915, the Young Turk deportation apparatus had already depopulated the Armenian settlements of the north-eastern regions of the Empire. Scores of deportees arrived at Diyarbekir, which was designated by the İAMM as one of the hubs where the Armenians were to be concentrated. From there on they were deported to the south. However, in practice the city was often the final destination for many deportees. Reshid's militiamen and Kurdish villagers robbed and massacred them often before they reached the city gates. At the end of July, a convoy from Kharput arrived in Diyarbekir. An eyewitness summarized their fate as follows:

> Having arrived in Diyarbekir they simply received nothing back, stayed in Diyarbekir for one day and had to continue traveling the next night. That's when young women and girls were abducted by officers and gendarmes. When they left Diyarbekir, the officer who had accompanied them so far came with a couple of gendarmes and sought for himself several pretty young girls and boys, left the rest with 6 to 7 gendarmes, and took off with his loot. On the way to Mardin the gendarmes took from the expellees their few belongings, their little bread and the few remaining jewels.[124]

---

[121] PAAA, R14093, Das Geheime Zivil-Kabinet des Kaisers (Valentini) an den Reichskanzler (Bethmann Hollweg), 10 September 1916, enclosure no. 3.

[122] Interview with Nejat Cemiloğlu conducted by Şeyhmus Diken, published in: Şeyhmus Diken, *İsyan Sürgünleri* (Istanbul: İletişim, 2005), 134–5.

[123] Interview with Esat Cemiloğlu conducted by Şeyhmus Diken, published in: ibid., 154.

[124] PAAA, R14087, Rößler to Bethmann-Hollweg, 3 September 1915, enclosure no. 4 (23 August 1915). Another eyewitness related, 'When we came to Diyarbekir, all our pack animals were led away and one woman and two young girls were dragged off by the gendarmes. For 24 hours we sat in the

Aurora Mardiganian was a little girl when she was deported from Erzurum. On arrival in Diyarbekir she witnessed the slaughter of a convoy and the disposal of their bodies:

> In the meantime the Jews of Diyarbekir had come out from the city, driven by gendarmes, to gather up the bodies of the slain Armenians. They brought carts and donkeys with bags swung across their backs. Into the carts and bags they piled the corpses and took them to the banks of the Tigris, where the Turks made them throw their burdens into the water. This is one of the persecutions the Jews were forced to bear. The Mohammedans did not kill them, but they liked to compel them to do such awful tasks.[125]

Many of those who did manage to slip through the murderous mesh in Diyarbekir either committed suicide or were seized from the convoys and absorbed into Muslim households.[126] The Syriac monk Qarabashi witnessed the deportation of a convoy of several thousands of Armenians heading to Mosul. Between Diyarbekir and Mardin he discovered a naked 10-year-old Armenian girl who had become orphaned in the preceding massacres. Deeply disturbed, Qarabashi fed the emaciated girl bread, cheese, yoghurt, and a pickle. He decided she had to hide in the bushes near the Tigris, for if she was found by militiamen she would certainly be murdered. When he returned the next day to check up on her, she was dead.[127] A couple of days later Qarabashi met three Armenian women in a nearby Kurdish village. The women had been deported from Sivas and Erzincan and were serving as slaves in the household of a Kurd named Sufi Hasan. When one of them became ill, Sufi Hasan took her away and shot her dead.[128] In several instances, local authorities or gendarmes sold entire convoys to Kurdish tribesmen for sums ranging between 500 to 1000 Lira. The tribesmen, aware of the fact that the Armenians had brought along many movable assets, would then strip the clothes from their backs and either leave the deportees to die or kill them outright.[129]

The massacres and deportations quickly spread throughout the province. Whereas the Circassian militiamen were sent to the north of the province, Aziz Feyzi and

---

burning sun in front of the city walls of Diyarbekir. Turks came from the city and took our children away. In the evening we had prepared for decampment when we were attacked by Turks who came from the city. At that time we left all luggage we still had and scattered, to save our lives and our honor. During the night we were attacked by Turks three more times and the girls and young women were dragged off.' PAAA, R14093, Das Geheime Zivil-Kabinet des Kaisers (Valentini) an den Reichskanzler (Bethmann Hollweg), 10 September 1916, enclosure no. 6.

[125] Aurora Mardiganian, *The Auction of Souls* (London: Phoenix Press, 1934), 173–4. This survivor memoir was first published in 1918 under the title *Ravished Armenia: The Story of Aurora Mardiganian, the Christian Girl who Lived Through the Great Massacres* (New York: Kingfield, 1918).

[126] Ara Sarafian, 'The Absorption of Armenian Women and Children into Muslim Households as a Structural Component of the Armenian Genocide', in: Omer Bartov and Phyllis Mack (eds.), *In God's Name: Genocide and Religion in the Twentieth Century* (Oxford: Berghahn, 2001), 209–21; Matthias Bjørnlund, '"A Fate Worse Than Dying": Sexual Violence During the Armenian Genocide', in: Dagmar Herzog (ed.), *Brutality and Desire: War and Sexuality in Europe's Twentieth Century* (London: Palgrave McMillan, 2008), 16–59.

[127] Qarabashi, *Dmo Zliho*, 73–4.

[128] Ibid., 76.

[129] Armalto, *Al-Qousara*, 68.

Memduh Bey were assigned the south. This division of labour may have fluctuated somewhat since Reshid deployed his militia wherever and however he saw fit. Reshid removed the mayor of Çermik, Mehmed Hamdi Bey, for not obeying his orders to destroy the Armenians living in his district.[130] Talaat later approved Reshid's replacement of the mayor of Maden by Dr. Osman Cevdet (Akkaynak).[131] After the dismissal of the mayors the evacuation of the Armenian villages and neighbourhoods of Maden commenced. At first, the thirty-five richest families of Maden were ordered to mobilize for deportation, followed by the rest of the Maden Armenians, many of whom were miners. They were given very little time to prepare, and on the first day of deportation the men were selected and incarcerated in the large caravanserai of Maden. The convoy was then marched off to Urfa via Diyarbekir. In the process, the supervising officer stole 300 pounds from them and stripped them of many private belongings.[132]

The Ergani-Maden district was a station for deportees arriving from Kharput, north of Maden. When a convoy of 1500 people arrived in Ergani after a march of four days, the officer in charge selected the men, ostensibly to work in the mines. All men above the age of 11 were taken away to the caravanserai, where they joined the native Maden Armenians.[133] The bulk of these men were not employed in the mines, but pushed over the edge of the Maden cliff into its deep ravine. This must have happened at least before 7 July, when Mariza Kejejian, a deportee from Kharput, witnessed 'heaps of corpses' (*Leichenhaufen*) on the road between Maden and Ergani.[134] Three months after the massacre, Mary Riggs, a missionary working in Kharput, was allowed to travel south and saw 'unmistakable signs of horrible cruelty'. Riding through the Maden gorge, Riggs looked down the canyon and saw 'countless naked bodies in positions showing how they had been hurled from above'.[135] Four years later, Gertrude Bell (1868–1926) visited the same khan where the Armenian men had been held. A Chaldean carpenter in that khan 'described his escape from Mardin and showed me behind the Khan a deep grave where hundreds of Armenians were buried'.[136]

The genocide struck the adjacent region between Lîce and Piran (renamed Dicle in the Republic) around mid-June. The mayor of Lîce, Hüseyin Nesimi Bey, had

---

[130] This quarrel continued during Reshid's Ankara governorship, when Reshid wired to Hamdi:

The chaos and anarchy in Sungurlu reminds me of your mayorship in Çermik I would prefer to forget. You should have remembered how you were dismissed from there. This telegram bears the quality of last warning. If you continue rule with anarchist administrative customs and harm the government's prestige and honour, your dismissal as in Çermik is as sure as death.

Reshid to Hamdi, 9 December 1916, quoted in: *Tasvir-i Efkâr*, 14 January 1919.

[131] BOA, DH.ŞFR 55-A/186, Talaat to Reshid, 9 September 1915.

[132] PAAA, R14087, Rößler to Bethmann-Hollweg, 3 September 1915, enclosure no. 4 (23 August 1915).

[133] PAAA, R14087, Rößler to Bethmann-Hollweg, 3 September 1915, enclosure no. 4 (23 August 1915).

[134] PAAA, R14093, Das Geheime Zivil-Kabinet des Kaisers (Valentini) an den Reichskanzler (Bethmann-Hollweg), 10 September 1916, enclosure no. 6.

[135] Mary W. Riggs, 'The Treatments of Armenians by Turks in Harpoot' (10 April 1918), in: Barton, *Statements*, 33, Inquiry Document no.III.

[136] *GBA*, diary entry for 21 October 1919.

refused to implement Reshid's orders to persecute the Armenians. When Reshid intensified the violence, he orally communicated an order to Nesimi to murder the Armenians of Lîce. Shocked by this explicit murderous desire, the mayor refused and demanded the order in writing.[137] Reshid ran out of patience, removed him from office and sent Çerkez Harun to murder the disobedient mayor. Nesimi was taken from his home and escorted to Diyarbekir but was shot dead on the way by his company and buried by the roadside.[138] The assassination did not go unnoticed and Reshid was asked about Nesimi's whereabouts,[139] but ignored the request. The question was reiterated a month later in a tone indirectly accusing Reshid of the murder. The Interior Ministry wrote: 'It is contended by the family of the ex-mayor of Lîce, Hüseyin Nesimi Bey, that he was assassinated. Please report whether he was murdered in the line of duty'.[140] Reshid gave an affirmative answer but claimed that a 'notorious Armenian brigand' had put Nesimi to death.[141]

With the elimination of the mayor, Reshid had obviated the most important obstacle to his objective: the destruction of the Armenians in the northern Lîce district. He sent İbrahim Bedreddin to supervise the killings in Lîce. The men were arrested, tied together with rope, led away to a cave named Gohê Gumho, stripped of their belongings, and finally had their throats slit.[142] 'So many ropes were required for the work that a public crier gave orders that the townspeople were to provide a stipulated quantity'. At the same time, the villages around Lîce town were targeted. One by one, the villages were surrounded by the militia and Kurdish tribesmen, either some hours after dark or at daybreak. The village of Henne, a village of 400 Christian families, was invaded and rid of its male population within a day. After the militia had finished the men they returned to the village, where the terrified women had assembled together in houses. They were raped, deported, or left to die in hunger and misery. Similar events took place in the villages of Fûm, Şimşim, Cûm, Tappa and Naghle.[143] The vacant position for mayor in Lîce was occupied by İlyas Nuri Bey, who left the Armenians alone and allowed them some

[137] PAAA, R14087, director of the Deutscher Hülfsbund für christliches Liebeswerk im Orient (Frankfurt am Main) Friedrich Schuchardt to the Auswärtiges Amt, 21 August 1915, enclosure no. 6: 'Der Kaimakam von Litsche hat die durch einen Boten des Walis mündlich überbrachte Ordre die Armenier umzubringen, zurückgewiesen mit dem Bemerken, er wünsche den Auftrag schriftlich zu haben.'

[138] Hüseyin Nesimi's son wrote in his memoirs that his family was very much aware of the fact that Nesimi had been assassinated by Reshid's men. Abidin Nesimi, *Yılların İçinden* (Istanbul: Gözlem, 1977), 39–46.

[139] BOA, DH.ŞFR 56/361, Directorate for Employment to Diyarbekir, 12 October 1915.

[140] BOA, DH.ŞFR 58/46, Directorate for Employment to Diyarbekir, 17 November 1915.

[141] Reshid, *Mülâhazât*, 86–7.

[142] 'Filehên Licê', in: Amed Tigris, *Lîce* (Stockholm: unpublished manuscript, 2005), 40–4.

[143] Naayem, *Shall This Nation Die?*, 199–207. The killings in the neighbouring Piran district were routinely cruel. In that region elderly Kurds remember morbid but vivid anecdotic information from villagers who had participated in the massacres. According to them, the perpetrators would assail the villages and dispatch of their victims by slashing their throats wide open. As they operated with axes, this often lead to decapitations. After the killing was done, the killers saw that the insides of the victims' windpipes were black because of prolonged use of tobacco. Interview conducted with Ş. family (Hani district) in Diyarbekir, 15 July 2004.

respite from the massacres.[144] A number of Christian families converted to Islam to survive the genocidal persecution and indeed managed to live in Lîce for several decades before migrating to Diyarbekir city, Istanbul, or Western Europe.[145]

The example of Lîce was to be a model for other parts of the province. The genocide took on recurrent systematic procedures. Reshid ruthlessly and purposefully eliminated any opposition to the genocide. In July he had his Circassian militiamen Aziz and Şakir assassinate the vice-mayor of Beşiri, Ali Sabit El-Suweydî in a manner similar to Hüseyin Nesimi.[146] After Sabit was eliminated, Reshid's militia and the Raman chieftains razed the Beşiri valley and massacred the Armenians and Syriacs in that region. This time, Talaat personally requested information on the murders of Nesimi and Sabit.[147] However, no form of litigation followed against Reshid, who continued his work with ever more zeal. He dismissed the mayor of Savur, Mehmed Ali Bey, an opportunist who had profiteered from the persecution against the Christians. Allegedly, Mehmed Ali was also involved in a series of gambling and sex scandals, what was worse, in the holy month of Ramadan.[148] The next official to be deposed was İbrahim Hakkı Bey, mayor of Silvan. According to Reshid, he 'distributed Armenian women here and there, stole Armenian property, and exempted Armenians from deportation in exchange for money'.[149] After his dismissal, Reshid appointed Adil Bey, brother of deputy Zülfü Bey, as mayor of Silvan. The militia then cooperated with the local Kurdish chieftain Sadık Bey to carry out the killings in the Silvan district.[150]

An even worse fate befell the mayor of Derik, who had refused to carry out Reshid's genocidal orders, demanding a direct order from Istanbul. The mayor was killed for his opposition to the persecutions of the Christians in his district. Reportedly Reshid personally went to inspect Derik, delegating the persecution to Halil (son of İbrahim Pasha) and Hidayet Bey. This triggered a wave of incarcerations, tortures, and summary executions.[151] Finally, the militia, headed by Tevfik Bey, began massacring the Christians of Derik; they targeted the Yezidis too. A noted Yezidi chieftain was decapitated and several Yezidi families in Derik were forced to convert to Islam.[152] In Derik, the Kurdish chieftains Seyid Ağa and Zülfikar Bey of Khirar village protected the Armenians and Yezidis in the village.[153] Those who could escape made for the caves north-east of Derik, but Reshid sent his loyal militia leader Çerkez Harun to massacre remaining Christians in the district.[154]

---

[144] Reshid, *Mülâhazât*, 84.
[145] Interview conducted with an anonymous Armenian family (Lîce district) in Amsterdam, February 2003.
[146] Reshid, *Mülâhazât*, 83 footnote 20, 89–90.
[147] BOA, DH.ŞFR 54-A/117, Talaat to Reshid, 27 July 1915.
[148] BOA, DH.ŞFR 57/97, Directorate for Employment to Diyarbekir, 24 October 1915.
[149] Reshid, *Mülâhazât*, 83–4, footnote 22.
[150] Interview conducted with Meçin family (Silvan) in Ankara, 19 June 2004.
[151] Armalto, *Al-Qousara*, 81.
[152] Interview conducted with Temel family (Derik) in Bremen, 21 March 2002.
[153] Noel, *Diary of Major E. Noel*, 8.
[154] Jacques Rhétoré, *Les chrétiens aux bêtes! Souvenirs de la guerre sainte proclamée par les Turcs contre les chrétiens en 1915* (unpublished manuscript, Bibliothèque du Saulchoir), 43–4. Rhétoré was a Catholic priest who was in Mardin until 1915. The text has been translated to Italian in: Marco

After these dismissals and political assassinations, the last mayor still resisting the genocidal violence was the mayor of Midyat, Nuri Bey. Reshid first attempted to have Nuri removed by appealing for a legal inquiry about his 'negligence' towards the Armenians. Reshid later claimed that Nuri had not been dealing adequately with an alleged Armenian uprising in Midyat, and wrote that the Armenians were targeting the Muslims with 'the organization of quite a terrible massacre'.[155] Although this was a rather dubious assertion, Reshid still used this pretext to recommend Halil Edib, criminal judge of Mardin, for Nuri's position. However, the Ministry refused twice and stated that there was no need to replace Nuri as he had not acted irresponsibly or incompetently as a mayor.[156] An inquiry was started anyway,[157] but when it did not produce the rapid results Reshid had expected, he resorted to violence once again. Nuri was assassinated and Midyat too was deprived of opposition against the violence.

Another centre of violence was the northern district of Palu. Of the more than 300 villages in Palu, forty-eight contained an Armenian presence. The other villages were mainly inhabited by Kurds and Zazas, and many villages were mixed.[158] According to one survivor, the violence engulfed the Palu villages on a day when the sun was eclipsed (10 August 1915), evoking images of apocalyptic doom among the Armenian villagers.[159] As in other districts of Diyarbekir province, the modus operandi was first to kill the men and then deport the rest. The Armenian male population of Palu town were taken to the bridge over the Murad river, had their throats slashed, and were thrown into the water. Garabed Farshian, an Armenian boy who was orphaned, was taken to a Turkish village and saw that 'there was blood flowing in the river'.[160] A recurrent action in the villages was the requisitioning of rope to tie the men together and lead them away. As Noyemzar Khimatian-Alexanian of Baghin village remembered: 'The soldiers went from house to house asking for rope. After that they took the males, fifteen and older and collected them. They used the rope to tie their hands. The men and teenaged boys were taken to a distant field and stabbed to death'.[161] In another village, the militia rode in and collected all men into the church. The men and the boys came back out with their hands tied behind them. They were taken away to

Impagliazzo (ed.), *Una finestra sul massacro: Documenti inediti sulla strage degli armeni (1915–1916)* (Milano: Guerini, 2000), and recently published in French as: Jacques Rhétoré, *Les chrétiens aux bêtes! Souvenirs de la guerre sainte proclamée par les Turcs contre les chrétiens en 1915* (Paris: Editions du Cerf, 2005).

[155] Reshid, *Mülâhazât*, 85.
[156] BOA, DH.ŞFR 54-A/300, Directorate for Employment to Diyarbekir, 7 August 1915.
[157] BOA, DH.ŞFR 57/167, Directorate for Employment to Diyarbekir, 28 October 1915.
[158] George Aghjayan, 'The Armenian Villages of Palu: History and Demography', paper presented at the conference *UCLA International Conference Series on Historic Armenian Cities and Provinces: Tigranakert/Diarbekir and Edessa/Urfa*, University of California (Los Angeles), 13 November 1999, 2.
[159] Interview with Antanik Baloian, unpublished manuscript titled 'Antanik Baloian's Story', by Nelson Baloian.
[160] Vahé Mamas Kitabdjian (ed.), 'Récit de Garabed Farchian, né à Palou en 1906 ou 1907', reproduced in: Ternon, *Mardin 1915*, 287.
[161] Interview with Noyemzar Khimatian-Alexanian by Linda J.P. Mahdesian.

the banks of the Murad river and butchered with long knives.[162] The militia then carried off pretty women and children for personal use, and did not hesitate to throw babies in the river to drown.[163] Finally, the decimated convoy was deported to the south. Some were able to escape the convoys by bribing officers or villagers, or by giving their children to benevolent local families. For example, the little girl Heranush Gadarian from Habab village was given to an Ottoman corporal and assimilated into his extended family.[164]

The very few Armenian men who were still alive by this time were those working in labour battalions. On 1 April 1915 the Interior Ministry ordered the Third Army to draw up a labour battalion consisting of 4000 men.[165] A week later, the Ministry of War issued another decree, ordering the conscription of more men in order to cope with the shortage. This time, it was authorized to enlist even women into labour battalions.[166] From 27 May on, the practice of 'quittance', ensuring exemption from conscription, was prohibited by Talaat.[167] The battalions became a death trap for the conscripts, as malnutrition, exhaustion and exposure had already begun to decimate their numbers. However, the greatest threat to their physical existence were not these hardships but outright massacres, perpetrated by their Ottoman superiors. On the Palu-Diyarbekir road, Reshid's militiamen massacred 1200 conscripts on 1 June.[168] A week later 160 men working in the labour battalions near Diyarbekir city were taken to the Devil's Gorge (Şeytandere) and battered to death by Sıdkı and Yahya's men. On 5 July the militia murdered another 2000 soldiers near Diyarbekir.[169] By the end of August, the few labour conscripts who still remained alive in the province were serving in battalions near Siverek. Terrified of a similar fate, they inconspicuously dawdled over their work in order to postpone a potential massacre. When that fateful day arrived, a few conscripts resisted by killing a gendarme with a large stone, taking his rifle and shooting two others, including an officer. The desperate men were finally overpowered and massacred.[170] The skirmish was reported to Istanbul, where Talaat interpreted it as 'Armenian men who killed and wounded some of their superiors and Muslims'. He then sent an order to all provinces to 'deal accordingly with this

---

[162] Interview with Katherine Magarian, as 'Voices of New England: Katherine Magarian', in: *Boston Globe*, 19 April 1998, B10.

[163] Interview with Margaret Garabedian DerManuelian by George Aghjayan in Providence, RI, February 1990.

[164] Heranush's story was related to her granddaughter Fethiye Çetin, who attempted to trace her Armenian relatives and found them in the United States. Fethiye Çelik, *Anneannem* (Istanbul: Metis, 2004); for the English translation, see: Idem, *My Grandmother: A Memoir* (London: Verso, 2008).

[165] BOA, DH.ŞFR 51/186, Ali Münif (Directorate for General Administration) to Diyarbekir, 1 April 1915.

[166] BOA, DH.ŞFR 51/231, Ministry of War to Diyarbekir, 8 April 1915.

[167] BOA, DH.ŞFR 53/131, Talaat to Mamuret-ül Aziz, 27 May 1915.

[168] Noel, *Diary of Major E. Noel*, 11.

[169] Qarabashi, *Dmo Zliho*, 70.

[170] Jacob Künzler, *Im Lande des Blutes und der Tränen: Erlebnisse in Mesopotamien während des Weltkrieges (1914–1918)* (Zürich: Chronos, 1999 [1921]), 47–8. Künzler was a Swiss missionary in Urfa during the war and heard about this massacre from a Syriac conscript, who had survived the killing.

issue'.[171] After this event, the fate of the Christian labour battalions was sealed: they were finished off quickly. Even if the work was as yet unfinished, a wave of brutal although selective massacres swept through the provinces. Thousands of conscripts were dispatched mostly with knives and daggers, to save ammunition.[172] Travelling between Urfa and Diyarbekir, a German officer saw an entire labour battalion, laying by the roadside with their throats slit.[173] However, an unknown number of Armenians remained alive in the labour battalions, even after 1915.

The murderous violence against the Christian and especially Armenian population of the Ottoman Empire had long reached genocidal proportions due to its organized, systematic, and categoric nature. While hundreds of thousands of human lives were being destroyed, little was known among the population, especially in the western provinces. Secrecy and censorship were two important regulations to be observed by the organizers of the genocide. Nobody was to speak about the events, and any news of the massacres was to be suppressed. Talaat ordered the Trabzon-based newspaper *Meşveret* closed down because it had published an apologetic explanation of the 'temporary deportation' of the Armenians.[174] The government denied all national and international allegations and tried to counter these with propaganda.[175] For disinformation to be convincing the CUP deemed some sort of visual material necessary. Since Reshid had already displayed piles of guns he had found in Diyarbekir, this formula was reapplied:

> After the gendarmes had killed a number of Armenian men, they put on them turbans and brought Kurdish women to weep and lament over them, saying that the Armenians had killed their men. They also brought a photographer to photograph the bodies and the weeping women, so that at a future time they might be able to convince Europe that it was the Armenians who had attacked the Kurds and killed them, that the Kurdish tribes had risen against them for revenge, and that the Turkish Government had had no part in the matter.[176]

In Istanbul, few people had reliable information of the horrors at their disposal. When Hüseyin Cahit inquired at the prestigious *Cercle d'Orient* about the events, even the Armenian members of the foundation knew nothing about the massacres.[177] Only at a short distance from the club, Talaat was engaged on a daily basis in organizing the dispersion and isolation of the surviving Armenian intelligentsia.

---

[171] BOA, DH.ŞFR 55-A/11, Talaat to provinces, 1 September 1915.

[172] Jacob Künzler, *Dreizig Jahre Dienst am Orient* (Basel: Birkhauser Verlag, 1933), 54.

[173] *Germany, Turkey and Armenia: A Selection of Documentary Evidence Relating to the Armenian Atrocities from German and Other Sources* (London: Keliher, 1917), 80–5.

[174] BOA, DH.ŞFR 54-A/181, Talaat to the provinces of Erzurum, Adana, Bitlis, Urfa, Canik, and Maraş, 29 July 1915.

[175] See for example a book published in 1916 by the Turkish Ministry for Foreign Affairs: *Die Ziele und Taten armenischer Revolutionäre: The Armenian Aspirations and Revolutionary Movements: Aspirations et mouvements révolutionaires arméniens: Ermeni Âmâl ve Harekât-ı İhtilâliyesi, Tesâvir ve Vesâik* (Istanbul: Matbaa-ı Amire, 1332). For the denialist campaign the CUP initiated in 1915, see: Hilmar Kaiser, 'Dall'impero alla repubblica: la continuità del negazionismo turco', in: Marcello Flores (ed.), *Storia, Verità, Giustizia: I crimini del XX secolo* (Milano: Bruno Mondadori, 2001), 89–113.

[176] Al-Ghusayn, *Martyred Armenia*, 42.

[177] Yalçın, *Siyasal Anılar*, 234.

The fate of two Armenian intellectuals indicates both Talaat's and Reshid's direct involvement in their elimination: Vartkes Serengulian (1871–1915), deputy for Erzurum, and Krikor Zohrab (1861–1915), author and deputy for Istanbul. On 12 May 1915 Vartkes dashed to Talaat's house to protest against the mass arrests of the Armenian intelligentsia. Talaat, his personal friend for more than a decade, calmly listened to Vartkes' fulmination, but flatly answered, 'This is a question of the homeland, Vartkes. It does not allow appeals to personal relations and friendships'.[178] Vartkes and Zohrab were arrested in late May.[179] Hüseyin Cahit recalled how he was visited early on a morning by Zohrab's wife, Clara Yazidjian. The nervous woman trembled and sobbed because of Zohrab's arrest, and asked Hüseyin Cahit to implore Talaat to release her husband. Together they went to Talaat's house and woke him up. Mrs. Yazidjian begged Talaat to exempt her husband from deportation but the Interior Minister sat in his pyjamas and heard the woman's story with indifference. He then comforted her that Zohrab was being sent to Diyarbekir for a minor legal affair and that she had nothing to worry about. All pleas were in vain as both Zohrab and Vartkes had been deported. When they reached Adana, Talaat ordered local officials to contact them on 17 June.[180] The pair were deported to Aleppo where they begged Cemal Pasha to intervene and save them from being court-martialled. However, Cemal Pasha's request was rebuffed by Talaat, who insisted they be sent to Diyarbekir. Finally, between Urfa and Diyarbekir the two were murdered by Çerkez Ahmed, on orders of Reshid. Çerkez Ahmed later confessed that he personally shot Vartkes dead with a single bullet to his head and shattered Zohrab's head with a rock.[181] The government spread the story that Zohrab had died of a heart attack. The German journalist Von Tyszka refuted this, claiming that at least Vartkes was 'anyhow in good health' (*jedenfalls kerngesund*) but nevertheless had not arrived in Diyarbekir either.[182]

Alongside these assassinations, witnesses to the explicit killing had to be silenced in order for state secrecy to be tight. The CUP had lost control over some of its Special Organization operatives, who did not fully perform the program as they wished. These loose cannons would for example brag about their genocidal accomplishments, or abuse their licence to kill by shooting people for fun. They had gone out of favour.[183] When the CUP felt it did not require their services any longer, local officials disposed of them by summarily executing them, many of them in the autumn of 1915. For example, Talaat requested the aforementioned Çerkez Ahmed to be sent to Istanbul, as he and his gang would affect security conditions in Urfa.[184] When this did not happen, Talaat issued a

---

[178] Hüseyin Cahit Yalçın, *Tanıdıklarım* (Istanbul: Yapı Kredi, 2002), 49–50.
[179] Beylerian, *Les grandes puissances*, 40.
[180] BOA, DH.ŞFR 54/48, Talaat to Reshid, 17 June 1915.
[181] Refik, *İki Komite, İki Kıtal*, 175–6.
[182] PAAA, R14088, Von Tyszka to Zimmermann, 1 October 1915, enclosure no. 1.
[183] One of the most infamous killers was Çerkez Ahmed, who vaunted himself as follows: 'I served this country. Go and look, I turned the areas around Van into Kaaba soil. You won't find a single Armenian there today. While I'm serving this country, bastards like Talaat are drinking ice-cold beer in Istanbul, and place me under arrest, no, this is damaging my honour!' Refik, *İki Komite, İki Kıtal*, 175.
[184] BOA, DH.ŞFR 55/132, Talaat to Reshid, 21 August 1915.

decree that his 'elimination is required'. Ahmed was deported to Damascus and hanged on Cemal Pasha's order.[185] Yakup Cemil, one of the CUP's most important gangsters, had acquired so much power in the war that he imagined he could get away with practically anything. He went too far when he openly threatened Enver Pasha, whereupon Enver had him arrested and executed in front of a firing squad.[186] The Raman brothers Ömer and Mustafa were killed in September 1915 by Reshid's assistant Çerkez Şakir, who ordered his Circassian militia to murder the tribesmen in their sleep. A peasant who happened to walk by coincidentally saw the violent settlement and was killed as well, in order to silence potential witnesses.[187] Militia member Zaza Alo was first deployed on the Syrian front but deported to Çankırı, where he was later killed in a skirmish with gendarmes.[188] At the same time, Major Rüşdü of the Diyarbekir militia was accused of corruption, embezzlement, and personal enrichment—which was still forbidden, at least officially. He escaped elimination and prosecution owing to protection offered by his superior Reshid, and continued his work in the province.[189]

By autumn 1915, the Christian population of Diyarbekir province was thoroughly dispossessed, deported, and critically reduced in numbers. On 18 September Reshid wired a telegram to Talaat, reporting that 'the number deported from the province amounts to approximately one hundred and twenty thousand'.[190] According to the French missionary Jacques Rhétoré, during the persecutions of 1915–16 a total of 144,185 Christians disappeared, of which 58,000 Gregorian Armenians, 11,500 Catholic Armenians, 10,010 Chaldeans, 3450 Catholic Syriacs, 60,725 Jacobite Syriacs, and 500 Protestants.[191] A higher estimate was calculated by Major Noel, who wrote that the total number of victims was made up of 45,000 Gregorian Armenians, 6000 Catholic Armenians, 7000 Chaldeans, 2000 Catholic Syriacs, 96,000 Jacobite Syriacs, and 1200 Protestants, all in all totalling 157,000 people victimized.[192] Whatever their precise numbers, the Christian population of Diyarbekir province was all but eradicated. Entire villages, neighbourhoods, parishes, and extended families were destroyed or reduced to destitution in the genocidal persecution of 1915.

[185] Refik, *İki Komite, İki Kıtal*, 176–7.
[186] Mustafa R. Esatlı, *İttihat ve Terakki tarihinde esrar perdesi ve Yakup Cemil niçin öldürüldü?* (Istanbul: Hürriyet, 1975).
[187] *Épisodes des massacres*, 30; Demirer, *Ha Wer Delal*, p. 87.
[188] BOA, DH.EUM.AYŞ 24/2, 11 October 1919.
[189] BOA, DH.ŞFR 57/5, Talaat to Karesi province, 14 October 1915.
[190] BOA, DH.EUM, 2.Şb. 68/71, Reshid to Talaat, 18 September 1915.
[191] Rhétoré, *Les chrétiens aux bêtes!*, 241. For specific numbers for Mardin district, see: ibid., 243.
[192] Noel, *Diary of Major E. Noel*, 11. Compared to the demographic data in Chapter 1, these figures demonstrate that between 87 percent and 95 percent of the Christians in Diyarbekir province were destroyed.

CENTRE AND PERIPHERY: WIDENING AND
NARROWING SCOPES OF PERSECUTION

The identities of the organizers and perpetrators of the genocidal persecution in Diyarbekir province have been explored relatively well. There can be little doubt that the local CUP elite collaborated with certain families and tribes to achieve their aim of destroying the Armenian community of the province. On the other hand, little is known regarding the categorical nature of victims targeted. The notion that official CUP policy targeted only the Armenians clearly contradicts the broad diversity of non-Armenian victims, especially in the Mardin district.[193] In other words, how *Armenian* was the genocide supposed to be? The Mardin district can serve as a fitting backdrop for an exploration of this discrepancy because of the district's religious diversity. The evidence, admittedly patchy, supports the argument that Dr. Reshid amplified the anti-Armenian persecution into an anti-Christian persecution, and by the time he was reproached for this policy, it was too late.

Most Christian notables in Diyarbekir city were incarcerated in May. By this time, there had been little persecution in Mardin, the citadel city south of Diyarbekir. As in other provincial towns, Reshid had ordered the mayor, Hilmi Bey, to arrest the Christian notables of the city. Hilmi reportedly answered that the Armenians of Mardin were Arabic-speaking Catholics, and had little in common with the Gregorian Armenians. The mayor also added that they were unarmed and honourable citizens, and that there was no reason at all to arrest any other Christians either.[194] Reshid was not interested in this reply and sent Aziz Feyzi in May to incite Muslim notables to destroy the Mardin Christians. Feyzi toured the region and bribed and persuaded the chieftains of the Deşi, Mışkiye, Kiki, and Helecan tribes. From 15 May on, the scenario of Diyarbekir was repeated in Mardin. Memduh moved into the house of the notable Syriac family Yonan and began organizing the process of persecution. First he arrested dozens of Armenian and Syriac men and tortured them to extract confessions of disloyalty and high treason. In the meantime he extorted large sums of money from the families of the arrested men who offered Memduh financial compensation in exchange for the release of their children.[195]

Reshid sent İbrahim Bedreddin and militiamen Çerkez Şakir and Çerkez Harun to Mardin to organize the physical destruction of the Christian population of Mardin. Together they organized a militia of 500 men and placed them under command of the brothers Nuri and Tahir El Ensari, both of them Sheikhs of the Ensari family.[196] While Hilmi was still in office, the group bypassed standard

---

[193] For detailed studies of the genocidal process in Mardin, see: Yves Ternon, *Mardin 1915: Anatomie pathologique d'une destruction* (special issue of the *Revue d'Histoire Arménienne Contemporaine* 4, 2002); David Gaunt, *Massacres, Resistance, Protectors: Muslim-Christian Relations in Eastern Anatolia During World War I* (Piscatway, NJ: Gorgias, 2006).

[194] Sarafian, 'The Disasters', 263.

[195] Ibid.

[196] Rhétoré, *Les chrétiens aux bêtes!*, 65.

bureaucratic procedures and began arresting Christian notables, such as Anton Gasparian.[197] However, Reshid and his men probably considered the presence of an uncooperative mayor an intransigent obstacle for the organization of a massacre, which was a complex undertaking. Therefore, Reshid attempted to apply his tested method of having the mayor removed, but his appeal only achieved the reinstatement of the equally unwilling official Mehmed Şefik Bey to his old district Mardin. Moreover, Talaat suggested that İbrahim Bedri be 'assigned to a vacant office of district governor'.[198] Having replaced Hilmi by Mehmed Şefik, Reshid did not respect this new constellation either. He ignored Şefik and treated his emissary Bedri as a shadow-official with the authority of a district governor. In Mardin, Bedri was assisted by Halil Edib, who was made a judge on 17 June 1915. Bedri himself officially became district governor only on 12 September.[199] The CUP had not completely taken over the Ottoman bureaucracy, but it was sufficient for the genocidal process to be launched in Mardin.

On 3 June 1915, at eight o'clock in the evening, Mardin was surrounded by Reshid's militiamen, headed by Çerkez Harun. Memduh Bey arrested the Bishop Ignatius Maloyan and his entire Armenian Catholic clergy and locked them up in the Mardin castle, a fortress overlooking the city. Over the next days he arrested hundreds of Christian notables, according to a French eye-witness, 'all taken from various ranks of society, without differences of age, nor of rite, nor of condition'.[200] The men were all taken to prison and severely tortured for a week by judge Halil Edib. On 9 June a group of militiamen arrived from Diyarbekir with dozens of sets of chains and galloped up to the fort. The prisoners were told that they were summoned by Governor Reshid and would be taken to Diyarbekir the next morning. The notables realized at this point they were going to be killed.[201]

The treatment of the Mardin notables was a copy of that of the Diyarbekir notables, who had already been massacred in the Raman gorge by that time. The first convoy, just over 400 Christians of all denominations, left Mardin on 10 June and was marched off to Diyarbekir by Memduh on horseback. After having walked two hours in the burning heat, Memduh took away four notables (Iskender Adem, his son August, Naum Cinanci, and Iskender Hammal) and killed them.[202] Three hours later, the convoy was halted at the Kurdish village Adirshek, near the Sheikhan caves. Memduh Bey gathered the convoy and read their death sentence

---

[197] Armalto, *Al-Qousara*, 40.

[198] BOA, DH.ŞFR 53/291, Talaat to Reshid, 8 June 1915. Hilmi was demoted and assigned to a minor office in the Mosul province. Just as he left for Mosul, Reshid sent out orders for him to be murdered. Hilmi escaped assassination because the mayor that was assigned this task was a personal friend who procrastinated in carrying out the order. In the meantime Hilmi crossed into Mosul province, out of the jurisdiction of the Diyarbekir provincial authorities, and thereby out of Reshid's deadly reach. Sarafian, 'The Disasters', 263.

[199] Suavi Aydın *et al.* (eds.), *Mardin: Aşiret-Cemaat-Devlet* (Istanbul: Tarih Vakfı, 2000), 242. Armalto, *Al-Qousara*, 33.

[200] Hyacinthe Simon, *Mardine: la ville heroïque: Autel et tombeau de l'Arménie (Asie Mineure) durant les massacres de 1915* (Jounieh: Maison Naaman pour la culture, 1991), Naji Naaman (ed.), chapter 3, 17–18.

[201] Rhétoré, *Les chrétiens aux bêtes!*, 70.

[202] Simon, *Mardine: la ville heroïque*, 64.

out loud. He added that conversion to Islam would avert death and gave those who refused conversion one hour to prepare for their deaths. Memduh had barely finished his words when Bishop Maloyan responded he would never convert and preferred to die as a Christian rather than to live as a Muslim. The great majority of the convoy agreed, whereupon Memduh took 100 men, led them away to the Şeyhan caves and had them all murdered and burnt. After this first massacre he returned and took another 100 men off to the Roman castle Zirzawan, where he slaughtered them and threw them in large wells.[203] Those who agreed on conversion were taken away by the Kurdish villagers to their shaikh and became Muslims. Only the next day, the rest of the convoy was marched off further and halted four hours from Diyarbekir. For the last time, Memduh turned to Maloyan and urged him to convert. When he refused, Memduh pulled out his handgun and shot the bishop in the head.[204] He then ordered the firing squad to massacre the rest of the convoy.[205] The work was finished and the perpetrators rode to Diyarbekir and reported their accomplishment to governor Reshid.[206] Two weeks later Talaat asked Reshid about the whereabouts of Maloyan.[207]

The killings in Diyarbekir province had become so explicit that national and international political actors freely began speaking about them. The genocide had definitively broken through the circle of CUP secrecy. Apart from the Catholic clergymen in Mardin, another Western observer of the massacres in Diyarbekir province was the German vice-consul at Mosul, Walter Holstein. On 10 June he wired the German embassy, expressing his abhorrence of the crimes. When Holstein spoke to the governor of Mosul about the killings, the latter responded 'that only the governor of Diyarbekir bears responsibility'.[208] However, Holstein was not content with this evasive reply and dispatched a second, more indignant telegram to the embassy two days later:

> The massacre of Armenians in Diyarbekir province is becoming more and more known here every day and causes a growing unrest among the local population which, with the

---

[203] Rhétoré, *Les chrétiens aux bêtes!*, 78.

[204] Bishop Maloyan was later beatified by the Vatican: *Ciliciae Armenorum seu Mardinen: Beatificationis seu Canonizationis servi Dei Ignatii Choukrallah Maloyan, archiepiscopi mardinensis in opium fidei, uti fertur, interfecti (1915): Positio super vita, martyrio et fama martyrii* (Rome: Tipografia Guerra, 2000).

[205] Armalto, *Al-Qousara*, 47.

[206] PAAA, R14087, director of the Deutscher Hülfsbund für christliches Liebeswerk im Orient (Frankfurt am Main) Friedrich Schuchardt to the Auswärtiges Amt, 21 August 1915, enclosure no. 6: 'In Mardin wurde der Mutessarif auch abgesetzt, da er nicht nach dem Willen des Walis. Von hier hat man einmal 500 und dann wieder 300 der Notabeln aller Konfessionen nach D. bringen lassen. Die ersten 600 sind nie angekommen, von den anderen hat man nichts mehr gehört.'

[207] BOA, DH.ŞFR 54-A/178, Talaat to Reshid, 29 July 1915.

[208] PAAA, Botschaft Konstantinopel 169, Holstein to embassy, 10 June 1915. This telegram contains a footnote which reads: 'Herrn Kap Humann für Enver'. The note refers to Lieutenant Commander and Marine Attaché Hans Humann, a personal friend of Enver Pasha's and a staunch advocate of Ottoman expansion into the Caucasus. According to an intimate observer, Humann had unfettered access to the CUP elite and held 'an outstanding position of extraordinary influence.' Ernst Jäckh, *The Rising Crescent: Turkey Yesterday, Today, and To-morrow* (New York: Farrar and Rinehart, 1944), 119.

foolish unscrupulousness and weakness of the local authorities can easily bring about unforeseen consequences. In the Mardin district . . . the circumstances have grown to a veritable persecution of Christians. It is undoubtedly the government that bears guilt for it.[209]

The well-intentioned message made its way through the German bureaucracy to Talaat and most probably to Reshid too. Talaat seemingly was not moved much by these protests. He listened to the stories about the massacres and replied to an employee at the German Embassy named Dr. Mordtmann, 'that the Porte wants to use the World War, to thoroughly settle scores (*gründlich aufzuräumen*) with its inner enemies—the domestic Christians—without being disturbed by diplomatic intervention from abroad'.[210] What Holstein did not know was that preparations were underway for a second convoy of Christian notables in Mardin, the day after his cable.

In the meantime, the second convoy of Mardin Christians, 266 people of all denominations, was sent off on 14 June. It was led by militia commander Abdul Kadir (a subordinate of Çerkez Şakir) and Tevfik Bey, who had eliminated the Armenians of Derik.[211] As had been done with the first convoy, the group was halted at the Şeyhan caves where they were forced to pay tribute to the Sultan Şeyhmus cult. The men noticed that Kurdish tribesmen, armed with rifles, axes and spades, had surrounded them. The militiamen invited the Christians to descend to the cave to drink from the cold spring water, but those who went never returned. The killings went on during the night and the next day. More than 100 men were killed at the Şeyhan caves, after which the convoy was marched off to Diyarbekir. All of a sudden, the convoy came across three mounted gendarmes approaching at high speed. They reached the convoy and proclaimed that the Sultan had pardoned the non-Armenian Christians from persecution. Their hands were untied and they were allowed to drink water and eat bread. The Armenians were not fed and continued the deportation with their hands tied. The convoy was marched off again and reached Diyarbekir on 16 June, where they were sent to the caravanserai prison.[212]

As in Diyarbekir, after the elimination of the notables, the remaining Christians were sent off to their deaths. These were mainly women, children, and the elderly, although many men were still alive as well. On 2 July, a convoy of 600 men was taken away and slaughtered just outside the city walls. Before sending the victims down the Mardin road to the valley, İbrahim Bedri and Memduh resorted to large-scale extortion. On 13 July, Memduh negotiated with the families of the Christian

[209] PAAA, Botschaft Konstantinopel 169, Holstein to embassy, 13 June 1915.

[210] PAAA, R14086, Wangenheim to Bethmann-Hollweg, 17 June 1915. When Kâmil Bey, a member of parliament for Diyarbekir who opposed the massacres, traveled to Istanbul to complain to Talaat about Reshid and Feyzi's genocidal campaign in Diyarbekir, Talaat threatened to have him assassinated if he didn't quiet down. Yeghiayan, *British Foreign Office Dossiers*, 482.

[211] Rhétoré, *Les chrétiens aux bêtes!*, 83; Simon, *Mardine: la ville heroïque*, 69–70.

[212] Ishak Armalto was one of the survivors of this second convoy. Upon arrival at the caravanserai in Diyarbekir, Armalto and a Joseph Paul Keyip saw three woven baskets (*zembils*) filled with chopped-off human body parts. Armalto, *Al-Qousara*, 52–3, 103.

men still in custody about a considerable ransom, which amounted to several hundreds of Liras per family. The men were sent off and killed on the Diyarbekir road.[213] After the men, their families were targeted. From late June to late October several convoys comprising hundreds of women and children were led away and destroyed. For example, on 10 August, a convoy of 600 women and children were taken through the Mardin plain further south. Some had already died of exhaustion and sunstroke when the convoy was halted in the district of the Kiki tribe. After Kurdish tribesmen had finished selecting women and children they fancied, the 300 remaining victims were massacred with axes and swords. A small batch of survivors was able to flee and hide in the desert caves.[214] Within a month or two, the Christian population of Mardin city had been drastically reduced.

The district of Mardin numbered several substantial villages with large numbers of Christian inhabitants. The largest among these were Eqsor (Gulliye) and Tell Ermen, each harbouring several thousand souls. Tell Ermen had already experienced some persecution and arrests by Memduh's militia, but mass violence was not applied until 1 July. On that day the militia and a large number of Kurdish tribesmen invaded the village, where the terrified villagers had fled to the church. On the orders of the militia commander and with assistance from the village headman Derwiş Bey, the church was attacked and a massacre ensued. The killers did not distinguish between men and women and decapitated many of the victims. Some were drawn and quartered, or hacked to pieces with axes. A little girl who crawled out from under the corpses was battered to death when she refused to convert to Islam. Approximately seventy women were raped in the church before being put to the sword. After the massacre Kurdish women entered the church and used daggers to stab to death any survivors.[215] The bodies were disposed of by being thrown into wells or burnt to ashes.[216] When Rafael de Nogales visited the village a few weeks later, he met a few severely traumatized survivors, and was shocked by 'corpses barely covered with heaps of stone from which emerged here and there a bloody tress or an arm or leg gnawed on by hyenas'.[217] A German navy officer visited Tell Ermen too and saw severed children's hands and women's hair.[218] A week after the massacre, a Major von Mikusch reported to Consul Holstein that he had met the militia, who had 'told about the massacre, beaming with joy' (*freudestrahlend von Massacres erzählt*).[219]

The next day, on 2 July at 8 pm, Memduh Bey ordered the attack on the village of Eqsor (Gulliye), a predominantly Jacobite Syriac agricultural centre on the Mardin plain. The militia was headed by Sergeant Yusuf, son of Nuri Ensari, and

[213] Sarafian, 'The Disasters', 263.

[214] Rhétoré, *Les chrétiens aux bêtes!*, 164–6.

[215] Armalto, *Al-Qousara*, 102–3.

[216] PAAA, R14087, director of the Deutscher Hülfsbund für christliches Liebeswerk im Orient (Frankfurt am Main) Friedrich Schuchardt to the Auswärtiges Amt, 21 August 1915, enclosure no. 5.

[217] Nogales, *Four years*, 171–2.

[218] *Bundesarchiv* (Freiburg), Reichsmarine 40/434, G.B. N. 8289, Engelking to Fleet Command, 11 November 1915, quoted in: Hilmar Kaiser, *At the Crossroads of Der Zor: Death, Survival, and Humanitarian Resistance in Aleppo, 1915–1917* (London: Gomidas, 2002), 84.

[219] PAAA, R14086, Wangenheim to Bethmann-Hollweg, 9 July 1915.

aided by chieftain Mohammed Ağa of the Milli tribe. Kurdish tribesmen of the Deşi, Mişkiye, and Helecan tribes, as well as some Arabs, had come over to Eqsor to participate. The village was invaded and the population was massacred. Children were thrown from roofs and mutilated with axes. Many villagers were crammed together in the house of the village headman Elias Cabbar Hinno, and burnt alive.[220] After the massacre, the village was burnt down, a spectacle visible from Mardin, where the inhabitants looked on in awe. According to Hyacinthe Simon, İbrahim Bedreddin watched the bloodbath too, cheering and applauding:[221]

> During this bloody tragedy a man was seated on the balcony of his terrace, breathing the fresh morning air and gazing at the roseate glow of the fire raging on the plane: it was the governor of Mardin, it was Bedreddin Bey. The barbarians were cutting throats and burning his subjects, he was smoking his cigarette.[222]

Dozens of pretty women were raped and dozens more were carried off. According to survivor Abdulaziz Jacob, Yusuf Ensari had kept at least fifty women in his home in Mardin for serial rape.[223] The mass looting went on for two more days and by the third day the once prosperous village Eqsor had been reduced to a state of complete devastation.[224]

The massacres in Mardin were a major component of the 'reign of terror' that Dr. Reshid pursued all over Diyarbekir province. It is very probable that due to Reshid's fanaticism, the CUP genocide in Diyarbekir exceeded in efficiency, scope, speed, and cruelty any other province of the Ottoman Empire. Reshid's militia murdered without mercy, without distinction, and without consequences. His bloody rule obviously did not go unnoticed, since Vice-Consul Holstein had already denounced the governor's policy. Other international observers were disturbed by his campaign as well. A French report noted about Reshid's treatment of the Christians he imprisoned, 'Il est difficile de décrire ici en détail les souffrances et les tortures que ces malheureux ont subies en prison pendant tout ce temps'.[225] Likewise, Aleppo Consul Jesse Jackson wrote on 28 June that the persecution of the Armenians in his city was intensifying. Jackson informed Ambassador Morgenthau specifically about 'the horrible things taking place in Diarbekir. Just such a reign of terror has begun in this city also'.[226]

Most protests emanated from German officials, stationed in the eastern provinces. Aleppo Consul Walter Rößler wrote about Diyarbekir province that they received 'die schauerlichsten Gerüchte, welche uns ganz an spanische Inquisition

---

[220] Armalto, *Al-Qousara*, 102.

[221] Noel, *Diary of Major E. Noel*, part 1, 11.

[222] Simon, *Mardine: la ville heroique*, 53.

[223] Yeghiayan, *British Foreign Office Dossiers*, 229.

[224] Rhétoré, *Les chrétiens aux bêtes!*, 195–6.

[225] Beylerian, *Les grandes puissances*, 49, document no. 156: 'Note du Département sur les massacres arméniens'.

[226] *NARA, RG 59*, 867.4016/92, Jackson to Morgenthau, 28 June 1915, in: Ara Sarafian (ed.), *United States Official Records on the Armenian Genocide 1915–1917* (London: Gomidas Institute, 2004), 84.

erinnern'.[227] Ambassador Wangenheim forwarded to Berlin the news about 'das Vilajet Diarbekir, in dem die Armenier besonders grausam verfolgt werden sollen'.[228] When Holstein received the news about the Eqsor and Tell Ermen massacres, he wrote an even more indignant telegram to Wangenheim:

> The former district governor of Mardin, briefly here, informed me as follows: the governor of Diyarbekir, Reshid Bey, is raging among the Christians of his province like an insane bloodhound; recently, in Mardin too he had seven hundred Christians (mostly Armenians) including the Armenian bishop gathered during a night by gendarmerie specially dispatched from Diyarbekir, and had them slaughtered like sheep (*wie Hammel abschlachten lassen*) nearby the city. Reshid Bey is continuing his bloody work among the innocents, the number of which, the district governor assured me, now surpasses two thousand. If the government does not immediately take quite vigorous measures against Reshid Bey, the common Muslim population of this local province will launch similar massacres against Christians. The situation from this point of view is becoming more threatening every day. Reshid Bey should immediately be recalled which would document that the government does not condone his infamous acts so that a general uproar here can be allayed.[229]

The insistence pertaining to this message impelled Wangenheim to take a stand about the reports. The next day he replied to Holstein he would convey the content of his message to the Sublime Porte. On 12 July 1915 Wangenheim slightly adjusted the telegram, translated it into French, and sent it to Talaat, who knew French. Wangenheim reproduced the exact wording of 'wie Hammel abschlachten lassen' as 'égorgé comme des moutons'.[230]

After this sequence of written communication, Talaat officially reproached Reshid for 'overdoing' the carnage. Several instances of reprehension are especially significant as they contain intimations of the scope of the massacres. On the same day Talaat received Wangenheim's message about the indiscriminate killings in Diyarbekir province, he dispatched the following telegram to Dr. Reshid:

> Lately it has been reported that massacres have been organized against the Armenians of the province and Christians without distinction of religion, and that recently for example people deported from Diyarbekir together with the Armenians and the Bishop of Mardin and seven hundred persons from other Christian communities have been taken out of town at night and slaughtered like sheep, and that an estimated two thousand people have been massacred until now, and if this is not ended immediately and unconditionally, it has been reported that it is feared the Muslim population of the neighbouring provinces will rise and massacre all Christians. It is absolutely unacceptable for the disciplinary measures and policies procured to the Armenians to include other Christians as this would leave a very bad impression upon public opinion and therefore these types of incidents that especially threaten the lives of all Christians need to be ended immediately, and the truth of the conditions needs to be reported.[231]

---

[227] PAAA, R14086, Rößler to Bethmann-Hollweg, 29 June 1915.
[228] PAAA, R14086, Wangenheim to Bethmann-Hollweg, 9 July 1915.
[229] PAAA, Botschaft Konstantinopel 169, Holstein to Embassy, 10 July 1915.
[230] PAAA, Botschaft Konstantinopel 169, Wangenheim to Talaat, 12 July 1915.
[231] BOA, DH.ŞFR 54/406, Talaat to Reshid, 12 July 1915.

In this important telegram, Talaat not only literally reproduced Holstein's words 'slaughtered like sheep', but also used the euphemism 'disciplinary measures and policies' to endorse what Reshid had been doing correctly so far: destroying the Armenians of Diyarbekir.

In July, Reshid's excesses became notorious among anyone who even came near his province, strewn as it was with corpses. The Governor of Baghdad, Süleyman Nazif (1870–1927), a noted intellectual hailing from Diyarbekir, travelled to his home town in this period. Nazif later wrote that the pungent smell of decaying corpses pervaded the atmosphere and that the bitter stench clogged his nose, making him gag.[232] Nazif had seen only the tip of the iceberg, because most bodies were disposed of in the rivers Euphrates and Tigris. Rößler wrote that the 'floating along of corpses on the Euphrates' had been going on for 25 days, adding: 'The bodies were all tied in the same manner two by two, back to back'.[233] Cemal Pasha, in charge of the Syrian region south of Diyarbekir, reproached Dr. Reshid with an urgent and personal telegram on 14 July, complaining that 'the corpses floating down the Euphrates are probably those of the Armenians killed in the rebellion, these need to be buried on the spot, leave no corpses out in the open'.[234] Two days later Reshid answered Cemal by pointing out that the Euphrates bore little relation to Diyarbekir province, and that the floating corpses were coming from the Erzurum and Mamuret-ul Aziz directions. Reshid noted that burials were exceptional and that 'those who were killed here are either being thrown into deep deserted caves or, as has been the case for the most part, are being burnt'.[235] Faiz El-Ghusayn was a witness to the burning of dead bodies when he entered Diyarbekir province near Karapınar. He saw hundreds of bodies burned to ashes. He also saw that there were many women and children among the dead, consumed by fire.[236] The rumours of Diyarbekir having become an open-air morgue reached Talaat, who ordered Reshid on 3 August to 'bury the deceased lying on the roads, throw their corpses into brooks, lakes, and rivers, and burn their property left behind on the roads'.[237] Alongside these reports, there is photographic evidence that the two men met during the war, possibly because Reshid was summoned to Istanbul.

Reshid did not pay much attention to, let alone seriously consider the wave of negative feedback, and his reputation grew more and more nefarious. The German protests became much more explicit by the end of July. An employee at the German embassy wrote to the German Chancellor Bethmann-Hollweg a most explicit report which read: 'Since the beginning of this month the governor of Diyarbekir, Reshid Bey, has begun the systematic extermination of the Christian population under his jurisdiction, without distinction of race and religion'.[238] As

---

[232] Kocahanoğlu, *İttihat ve Terakki*, 522–3.
[233] PAAA, R14087, Rößler to Bethmann-Hollweg, 27 July 1915.
[234] Cemal to Reshid, 14 July 1915, quoted in: Kocahanoğlu, *İttihat ve Terakki*, 519.
[235] Reshid to Cemal, 16 July 1915, quoted in: ibid., 519.
[236] Al-Ghusayn, *Martyred Armenia*, 20.
[237] Talaat to Reshid, 3 August 1915, quoted in: Kocahanoğlu, *İttihat ve Terakki*, 519.
[238] PAAA, R14086, Hohenlohe-Langenburg to Bethmann-Hollweg, 31 July 1915.

reports of massacres poured into Mosul province, Walter Holstein became increasingly enraged and wrote a bitter telegram to his colleagues in Istanbul:

> Everyone knows that the governor of Diyarbekir ... is the instigator of the terrible crimes committed against the Christians in his province; everyone rightly presumes that we are also aware of the atrocities and they are asking themselves why we allow a notorious mass murderer to remain unpunished and continue to be the governor. It would hardly suffice merely to express our disapproval of the atrocities effectively to counteract the various compromising attitudes towards us. Not until we have forced the Porte ruthlessly to demand that the criminals who are sitting in official positions in Diyarbekir, Mardin, Siirt, etc., account for these allegations and do so as quickly as possible, only then will they drop the suspicions held against us. I read in various German newspapers official Turkish denials of the atrocities committed against the Christians and am surprised at the naivety of the Porte in believing they can obliterate facts about the crimes by Turkish officials by telling blatant lies. Up to now the world has not experienced such atrocities, which have provenly been and are still being committed by officials in Diyarbekir province![239]

This report too was forwarded to Talaat, who began losing his patience, since he was forced to explain Reshid's compromising and embarrassing actions to German officials. Reshid obviously had taken no measures to act according to his instructions a month ago. To clear things up, two days after Holstein's cable, Talaat sent a second telegram admonishing Reshid that the persecution and massacre of all Christians in the province was not permitted. He also urged him to dismantle the militia, that was causing the provincial authorities to be held responsible for the killings.[240] This was still not the end of Talaat's reprimands to his zealous subordinate. It had become clear that Reshid had not only persecuted and murdered non-Armenian Ottoman Christians, but also non-Ottoman Armenians. His indiscriminate slaughter of *ethnic* Armenians without consideration of *political* identity had become a serious problem. One of these was Stepan Katosian, an Armenian-American who had been summarily put to death in the Diyarbekir prison. The execution could have caused a diplomatic incident since the Ottoman Empire was not at war with the United States, in which case it still would have been a legal violation. Talaat therefore asked Reshid for information about Katosian's execution.[241] To ensure that this was the last instance in which Reshid transgressed the rules of the genocide, Talaat ordered the consistent screening of the political identities of Armenians from then on.[242] The purpose of this order was that non-Ottoman Armenians should not be persecuted. For example, an Iranian Armenian named Mıgırdiç Stepanian was allowed to leave for Persia via Mosul.[243]

---

[239] PAAA, Botschaft Konstantinopel 170, Holstein to Embassy, 14 August 1915.

[240] BOA, DH.ŞFR 54-A/248, Talaat to Reshid, 16 August 1915.

[241] BOA, DH.ŞFR 56/131, Talaat to Reshid, 24 September 1915.

[242] BOA, DH.ŞFR 57/50, Talaat to Reshid, 17 October 1915. Talaat later specified the order and requested information on 'Armenian officials employed at consulates of allied and neutral countries'. BOA, DH.ŞFR 70/152, Talaat to provinces, 30 November 1916.

[243] BOA, DH.ŞFR 57/57, Talaat to Reshid, 17 October 1915. Whereas his superordinate Talaat was scolding him continuously, two days later Reshid received an appreciative telegram from his

Apart from specific instructions readjusting Reshid's extreme behaviour, Talaat released several national decrees defining the categories of those to be persecuted and deported. At first, he excluded the Armenian converts to Islam from deportation to the south.[244] Most converts were not persecuted anymore and, provided they kept their silence, were allowed to continue living in their homes. Two weeks later he reincorporated the converts into the deportation program. Talaat's order read that 'some Armenians are converting collectively or individually just to remain in their home towns', and that 'this type of conversion should never be lent credence'. Talaat contended that 'whenever these types of people perceive threats to their interests they will convert as a means of deception'.[245] On 4 August Talaat excluded the Armenian Catholics from deportation, requesting their numbers in the respective provinces.[246] On 15 August the Protestant Armenians were excluded too from deportation to Der ez-Zor. Again, Talaat requested statistical data.[247] Besides these official directions, the general methodology of the genocide consisted of killing the men and deporting those women and children who were not absorbed into Muslim households. This means that in general, Armenian women were not to be subjected to the immediate on-the-spot killing as the men were.[248] Finally, a specific order excluding the Jacobite Syriacs from deportation was issued for those provinces with Syriac communities.[249]

There is contradictory evidence on the precise nature of Reshid's local implementation of Talaat's national instructions. On the one hand, Reshid observed the commands for exclusion of non-Armenian Christians from further genocidal destruction; on the other hand, he disregarded all narrowing of victim categories. According to another interpretation it is conceivable that the series of rebukes compelled him to mitigate the persecution, even though the harm was done. In other words, Reshid discontinued the persecution of the non-Armenian Christian communities when they had already been largely destroyed. These restrictions of time may have added to restrictions of location. It is also possible that this turn of

---

subordinate Halil Edib in Mardin. Edib expressed his praise on the Eid el-Adha, the important Muslim festival involving sacrifice of cattle: 'I congratulate you with your Eid, and kiss your hands that have gained us the six provinces and opened up the gateways to Turkistan and the Caucasus.' Halil Edib to Reshid, 19 October 1915, quoted in: Bilgi, *Dr. Mehmed Reshid*, 29, footnote 73.

[244] BOA, DH.ŞFR 54/100, Talaat to provinces, 22 June 1915.
[245] BOA, DH.ŞFR 54/254, Talaat to provinces, 1 July 1915.
[246] BOA, DH.ŞFR 54-A/252, Talaat to provinces, 4 August 1915.
[247] BOA, DH.ŞFR 55/20, Talaat to provinces, 15 August 1915.
[248] Katharine Derderian, 'Common Fate, Different Experience: Gender-Specific Aspects of the Armenian Genocide, 1915–1917', in: *Holocaust and Genocide Studies* 19, no.1 (2005), 1–25.
[249] BOA, DH.ŞFR 57/112, Talaat to the provinces of Diyarbekir, Bitlis, Haleb, and Urfa, 25 October 1915. A year later, an even more lenient instruction was issued towards the Syriacs, requesting information about their numbers and at the same time allowing them to travel within the country for the sake of trade. BOA, DH.ŞFR 68/98, Mamuret-ul Aziz, Diyarbekir, Bitlis, Musul, and Urfa, 23 September 1916. Although tens of thousands of Syriacs had been massacred by that time, it did save a terrified and traumatized remnant of the Syriac community to live in their native regions. Still, their relative comfort was probably contingent on the appointment of Süleyman Necmi, Reshid's successor in Diyarbekir. The new governor was very merciful compared to Reshid, and permitted the Syriacs a breath before İbrahim Bedreddin became governor of Diyarbekir province and launched a second attack against the Syriacs of Tur Abdin.

events only happened in and around Diyarbekir city, since in Mardin İbrahim Bedreddin, Aziz Feyzi, and Memduh Bey had taken over the district. The most compelling example of selective persecution, steered from above, is the causal link between Holstein's telegram of 12 June and the fate of the second convoy of Mardin notables. In that chain of events Reshid indeed seems to have followed orders and limited the scope of the genocide.

One of the first villages that had been thoroughly destroyed was Kabiye. According to one survivor from that village, a group of survivors from all over the Diyarbekir plain had assembled in Qarabash some time after the massacre, probably around mid-June. Pirinççizâde Sıdkı had drawn up a list of these survivors and had the list read out loud in front of the group. Those with Armenian names were carefully selected from those with Syriac names. Sıdkı declared that the Syriacs were exempted from persecution on orders of the government. When a young man named Dikran was also placed into the Armenian group he protested to Sıdkı, pleading that he was a Syriac Orthodox. Although he had spoken the truth, his protests were futile as he was led away with the rest of the Armenians and butchered.[250] The survivors of the second Mardin convoy had been in prison for a week when Memduh Bey arrived one day and ordered all cells opened. The prisoners were led outside, where Memduh addressed them: 'Those of you who are Syriac, Chaldean, and Protestant, raise your hands and state your names'. The Syriacs, Chaldeans, and Protestants were separated from the Armenians and were allowed to go home.[251] A similar selection was remembered by a Syriac survivor from a labour battalion working on road construction near Akpınar, between Diyarbekir and Mardin. On 17 June Sıdkı reportedly arrived at the road-building site where he separated the Armenians from the other Christians. An Armenian named Migirditch from Qarabash village was moved to the Armenian side but claimed to be a Syriac Orthodox. Though his identity was confirmed by a native of Qarabash, Sıdkı did not believe him and cursed at him: 'Filthy dog, your name is Migirditch and you are supposed to be a Syriac?!' The unfortunate man was then sent off to his death with the other Armenians.[252] A Syriac conscript in a labour battalion working between Urfa and Diyarbekir in mid-August related his tale to the Swiss missionary Jacob Künzler, who reported as follows:

'In the evening', the Syriac recounted, 'a large crowd of well-armed gendarmes had come from the city. They immediately ordered the segregation of the Armenians from the Syriacs. Thereupon the Armenians were tied together and were taken about a quarter of an hour away. Soon one heard many shots . . . It became clear to us, that our Armenian comrades were now being slaughtered . . . When the gendarmes returned to the village, we Syriacs thought that soon it would also be our turn. We were provided with lanterns and had to go towards the place of slaughter . . . We had to throw the murdered Armenians in a deep well. There were several among them, who were still breathing, one could even still walk, he dove into the well voluntarily. When all the

---

[250] Jastrow, *Die mesopotamisch-arabischen*, 327–9.
[251] Armalto, *Al-Qousara*, 54.
[252] Qarabashi, *Dmo Zliho*, 69–70.

dead and half-dead had been dropped down, we had to seal off the well and heap earth and ashes on it'.[253]

These instances of selection of Armenians illustrate that Reshid delegated the implementation of Talaat's orders to Sıdkı. After Talaat's telegrams, some form of selective killing seems to have been applied. By that time, many Syriacs had already been murdered.

These telling examples notwithstanding, there is also evidence that runs counter to Reshid's ostensible pardon to non-Armenian Christians after Talaat's telegrams. The case of the Eqsor massacre shows that orders for differentiation between Christians were simply brushed aside. Reportedly, the executioner of Eqsor, Nuri Ensari, had personally proclaimed the 'amnesty' accorded to the Syriacs, while the predominantly Syriac and Catholic village had just been exterminated and was at that time still being razed.[254] The same treatment befell the Christian women and children, who were supposed to be excluded from immediate massacre as routine. As early as in June, Aleppo Consul Jackson reported about the village of Redwan that 'they even killed little children'.[255] A deportation convoy trudging to Mardin was halted by Reshid's militia at the village of Golikê, where dozens of women were first raped and then killed.[256] There was even a report—though highly suspect—that Reshid himself 'took 800 children, enclosed them in a building and set light to it', burning the children alive.[257]

The few Orthodox or Catholic Greeks were not spared either. The wife of a Catholic Greek citizen of Diyarbekir complained to German vice-consul Rößler she had not heard from her husband Yorgi Obégi ever since he, her daughter, and four of her brothers had gone into hiding with a Muslim colleague in Diyarbekir. It became known that they were found and deported, but shortly outside of Diyarbekir stripped of their valuables and killed. The Greek Orthodox priest of Diyarbekir had disappeared without a trace, and was probably murdered as well. Rößler was informed by an Ottoman officer that the then police chief of Diyarbekir, most probably Memduh Bey, had confessed the murder to him: 'The commissar had told him that he had killed them himself'.[258] In the Silvan district, 425 Greeks out of a total 583 were killed.[259]

---

[253] Künzler, *Im Lande des Blutes und der Tränen*, 47–8.

[254] Yeghiayan, *British Foreign Office Dossiers*, 230.

[255] Jackson to Morgenthau, 8 June 1915, in: Sarafian, *United States*, 60.

[256] Qarabashi, *Dmo Zliho*, 72; There is some propagandistic evidence that Aziz Feyzi became known for his habit of collecting trophies from female victims. On several occasions he reportedly had the militia retrieve a necklace of women's nipples and a rope of women's hair. *Épisodes des massacres*, 50; Yeghiayan, *British Foreign Office Dossiers*, 152.

[257] *Morning Post*, 7 December 1918, quoted in: Vahakn N. Dadrian, 'Children as Victims of Genocide: the Armenian Case', in: *Journal of Genocide Research* 5 (2003), 430, 436 footnote 24. Dr. Reshid's reputation would hardly accord him the benefit of the doubt regarding incidents such as these. This source, however, seems highly dubious and the massacre is not reported in any of the other sources from Diyarbekir province.

[258] PAAA, R14087, Rößler to Bethmann-Hollweg, 3 September 1915, enclosure no. 2. Additionally, Memduh seems to have murdered a Russian and an Englishman. The murdered Englishman was probably Albert Atkinson, a missionary. Talaat later asked Reshid questions on his whereabouts. BOA, DH.ŞFR 56/238, Talaat to Reshid, 30 October 1915.

[259] Noel, *Diary of Major E. Noel*, part 2, 1.

The most compelling evidence supporting the interpretation that Talaat's orders were ignored are the massacres organized in Nusaybin and Cizre. On 16 August 1915 İbrahim Bedri sent militia officer Abdulkadir and chieftain of the Deşi tribe Abdulaziz to Nusaybin.[260] They incarcerated all the Christian men of Nusaybin with no distinction of denomination: Syriac Jacobites, Chaldeans, Protestants, and Armenians. In the middle of the night the men were led away to a desolate canyon, butchered one by one, and thrown into the ravine. Many were decapitated, and each victim was urged to convert to Islam before being killed and hurled down the abyss.[261] Hanna Shouha, the Chaldean priest of Nusaybin, had already been deported to Kharput and died on the road. His wife was violated and killed, his family were sent to Mardin and Diyarbekir and were eliminated either on the road or on arrival. Within two days, the population of Nusaybin dropped from 2000 to 1200, as 800 Christians were destroyed. The Jewish community of 600 persons was left unharmed.[262]

Almost two weeks later Cizre was targeted. On orders of Reshid, deputies Zülfü Bey and Aziz Feyzi had toured the province in April 1915 to organize the genocide. They had also frequented Cizre and had spoken to local Kurdish leaders.[263] On 29 August, Aziz Feyzi led a group of men including the mufti of Cizre Ahmed Hilmi and Raman chieftain Ömer in the attack.[264] All Christian men were arrested and tortured under the pretext that they had arms hidden in secret depots. They were then bound with ropes and chains, and marched out the city, where they were stripped of their belongings and murdered. The naked bodies were dumped downstream in the Tigris, for an obvious reason: the killers did not want the victims' relatives to see the corpses and panic. Two days later the families were placed on *kelek* rafts and sent off, after local Muslims had selected a number of children. Their river journey was short, as their vessels were moored at a Kurdish village shortly downstream. Most women were raped, shot dead, and thrown in the river.[265] The pollution the decaying corpses caused to the Tigris was of such a nature that the population of Mosul was forbidden to drink from the river for a month.[266] In Cizre, the only survivors were four women absorbed in a Muslim household. Three of them were killed after all. The other, Afife Mimarbashi, bribed her kidnapper and fled to Mardin as the only survivor of the Cizre massacre.[267] A total of 4750 Armenians (2500 Gregorians, 1250 Catholics, 1000 Protestants),

---

[260] Rhétoré, *Les chrétiens aux bêtes!*, 220.

[261] Hori Süleyman Hinno, *Farman: Tur'Abdinli Süryanilerin Katliamı 1914–1915* (Athens: n.p., 1993), 30–3.

[262] Armalto, *Al-Qousara*, 97–8. Qarabashi, *Dmo Zliho*, 124–5.

[263] *Épisodes des massacres*, 14; Demirer, *Ha Wer Delal*, p. 75. On his way back to Diyarbekir, Feyzi reportedly visited the Raman district and convinced the brothers Ömer and Mustafa that the time had come to destroy all Christians.

[264] *NAUK*, FO 371/4191, 9 April 1919, reproduced in: Ahmet Mesut (ed.), *İngiliz Belgelerinde Kürdistan 1918–1958* (Istanbul: Doz, 1992), 29. For biographical information on the then Muslim clerics of Cizre, see: Abdullah Yaşın, *Bütün yönleriyle Cizre* (Cizre: n.p., 1983), 147–65.

[265] Armalto, *Al-Qousara*, 89–90.

[266] Jean-Marie Merigoux, *Va a Ninive! Un dialogue avec l'Irak: Mosul et les villages chrétiens, pages d'histoire dominicaine* (Paris: Cerf, 2000), 462.

[267] Sarafian, 'The Disasters', 263.

250 Chaldeans, and 100 Jacobite Syriacs were killed.[268] A week after the mass murder, Holstein reported to his superiors that 'gangs of Kurds, who were recruited for this purpose by Feyzi Bey, deputy for Diyarbekir, with connivance of the local authorities and participation of the army, have massacred the entire Christian population of the town of Cizre (in Diyarbekir province)'.[269]

It is evident that the indiscriminate killings were by no means spontaneous outbursts of popular bloodlust. Neither were they meticulously premeditated and prepared by conspiracy the year before. Talaat's telegraphic reprimands had arrived late, and were not taken into consideration. As the Interior Minister, he was aware of this, as he was continuously being informed of this fact by German officials in Istanbul, who noted 'that the instructions of the Turkish government to the provincial authorities for a large part defeat their purpose as a result of their arbitrariness'.[270] In the summer of 1915, all Christian communities of Diyarbekir were equally hit by the genocide, although the Armenians were often particularly singled out for immediate destruction. As Norman Naimark wrote, 'Protestant and Catholic Armenians could be formally exempted from deportation, even if in practice local authorities made no distinction among the various Christian sects'.[271] Consul Rößler reported that the Ottoman government lost 'control over the elements they had brought into existence'.[272] These 'elements', as Rößler described the genocidal measures, proved particularly ferocious in Diyarbekir province. Major Noel was aware of this, as he incorrectly noted about the Syriacs:

> In Diarbekir itself the Syrian Jacobites were scarcely molested. Of all the Christian communities they know how best to get on with the Turks, and when the massacres were ordered they were officially excluded. In the districts, however, the Government very soon lost control of the passions they had loosed (if they ever wanted to keep them in control), with the result that the Jacobites suffered there as much as anybody else.[273]

Contrary to Rößler's perception, Reshid had a firm control of his murderous infrastructure. Especially in and around Diyarbekir district, most instances of massacre in which the militia engaged were directly ordered by himself. An exploration of the perpetrators involved, the timing, scope, and methodology of the killings clearly reveals Reshid's will propelling them. Due to his personal disposition, Dr. Mehmed Reshid gave a distinct shape to the genocide, configuring the range of victims from the outset, even when his superior tried to modify it.

---

[268] PAAA, Botschaft Konstantinopel 170, Hohenlohe-Langenburg to Auswärtige Amt, 11 September 1915.
[269] PAAA, Botschaft Konstantinopel 170, Holstein to Embassy, 9 September 1915.
[270] PAAA, R14093, 'Aufzeichnung über die Armenierfrage', Berlin, 27 September 1916.
[271] Norman Naimark, *Fires of Hatred: Ethnic Cleansing in Twentieth-Century Europe* (Cambridge, MA: Harvard University Press, 2002), 41–2.
[272] PAAA, R14087, Rößler to Bethmann-Hollweg, 27 July 1915.
[273] Noel, *Diary of Major E. Noel*, part 2, 14.

DISCUSSION

This chapter has addressed the destruction of Ottoman Armenians in Diyarbekir province during the First World War. In 1915, the CUP carried out a systematic campaign of genocidal persecution, the body count of which ran in the hundreds of thousands. This internal policy ran parallel to the external war effort with the Great Powers, especially on the eastern front against Russia. It was no coincidence that most of the direct killing of non-combatant Ottoman Christians occurred in the eastern provinces, where the threat of a Russian invasion backed by 'Armenian insiders' was most immediate in the paranoid minds of the Young Turk dictatorship. However, the deportations and persecutions were mostly autonomous processes and only partly linked to the ebb and flow of the war. The initiation and conduct of the persecutions were generally in the hands of Interior Ministry civil servants, not military personnel of the Ministry of War. The genocide took shape on the distant eastern front as a series of fiats issued after the invasion of Russia and Iran in December 1914. Powerful cadres within the party, government, and army formed a genocidal consensus within the empire during the months of heightened administrative networking, strategic disputes, and factional infighting in the empire's darkest hour.

No single theory or agency guided the implementation of the genocide as ethnographic experts disagreed about ethnic groups' loyalty, Talaat machinated, Reshid thrust ahead, Interior and War Ministry functionaries vacillated, brigands and thugs clashed with intellectual social engineers. But the direction of policy was never in doubt: the Armenians were to be destroyed. The inter-state context only solidified the emergent consensus, especially at a time when no internal danger threatened the elite. If the state of war released the CUP regime from many of the constraints of the past year and a half, and shattered the conventional framework of 'reforms' within which a 'solution' to the 'Armenian question' had been sought, it also reignited the radical factions within the party that had so suddenly surfaced during the devastating Balkan wars. After November 1914 the extremists, with Talaat heading them, were freed from past restraints. When the deportations were launched, their likely outcome was known by the CUP elite. They remembered how Caucasian communities who had been settled in the region earlier had perished in its harsh conditions. Moreover, unlike the pre-war boycotts and persecutions of Ottoman Bulgarians and especially Ottoman Greeks, which had been carried out before the shocked sensibilities of Western observers, the scorching deserts of Northern Syria offered a field of activity at a distance conveniently discreet from direct observation. Defenders of what was called 'resettlement' (*tehcir*) sometimes contend(ed) that the deportation of the entire Armenian population was simply a part of military operations against Armenian revolutionaries. This is not how the Young Turks understood it. Deportation was to continue to the last Anatolian Armenian community, even if the revolutionary parties were quickly neutralized. Deportation was to ensure that Armenian social life of any significance could never arise again, especially in the eastern provinces.

The violence was not only directed against Ottoman Armenians. This chapter has also sought to direct attention to the wartime experiences of other ethnic groups in Diyarbekir province. Diyarbekir was a hub in the maze of deportations, not only of Armenians but also of Kurds (see Chapter 3), and saw some of the most brutal massacres in the summer of 1915. It becomes clear that in the massive destruction process during the First World War, not all perpetrators were Turks and not all victims were Armenians. Certain Kurdish chieftains, Arabs and Circassians also joined in with the mass murder, whereas Yezidis, Syriacs, and Kurds were subjected to persecution as well. In fact, the first villages in Diyarbekir province to suffer wholesale massacres were the Syriac villages on Diyarbekir plain. Then again, certain Kurdish subtribes and several notable families were integrally deported to central and western parts of Anatolia, where a substantial part of them perished from lack of nutrition and contagious diseases. The maelstrom of violence, counter-violence, and multiple victimization arises out of a clear context.

Why were the Armenians and Syriacs destroyed? Finding satisfactory answers to this question requires more than a limited regional focus, but also needs to take into account the victimization of Ottoman Muslims in the years preceding the war. The latter approach may seem paradoxical, but has explanatory value. How does victimization affect a group? Psychological research into groups of people who have been victimized and persecuted demonstrates that they are deeply affected by the violence. Whereas this is undoubtedly true for individual survivors, it may bear relevance for members of the victim group who were not directly affected by the immediate violence. The less affected parts of the group too, by virtue of its identifications with the ethnic, religious, or cultural group, are deeply affected by the persecution and the attempt to eliminate the group they consider themselves members of. Survivors often feel guilt, shame, insecurity, inferiority, and perceive the world as hostile and humans as untrustworthy.[274] Most of all, the violence frustrates their need for security, precludes them from forming positive ties to others, and increases their potential for committing violence themselves. A significant part of the group may come to believe that violence is an effective, indeed necessary tool to protect themselves, as they perceive the world with a warped need for protection and self-defence.[275]

The concept of vengeance is a key in understanding this process. Vengeance can loosely be defined as 'the attempt, at some cost or risk to oneself, to impose suffering upon those who have made one suffer'.[276] In his study of vengeance, Nico Frijda recognizes that the desire for vengeance is one of the most potent

---

[274] Ronnie Janoff-Bulman, 'The Aftermath of Victimization: Rebuilding Shattered Assumptions', in: Charles R. Figley (ed.), *Trauma and its Wake* (New York: Brunner/Mazel, 1985), vol. 1, *The Study and Treatment of Post-Traumatic Stress Disorder*, 15–35; id., *Shattered Assumptions: Towards a New Psychology of Trauma* (New York: Free Press, 1992).

[275] Roy F. Baumeister, *Evil: Inside Human Violence and Cruelty* (New York: Henry Holt, 2001), 128–68.

[276] Jon Elster, 'Norms of Revenge', in: *Ethics* 4 (1990), 862–85, at 862.

of human passions.[277] Vengeance is primarily an emotional state of mind that exists on the individual or collective level, often for a longer period, until it is redeemed. The desire for vengeance can be subsumed under the rubric of moral emotions: 'it is a state of impulse, of involuntary action readiness, generated by an appraisal, often accompanied by bodily excitement, and with every aspect of control precedence: preoccupation, single-minded goal pursuit, neglect of extraneous information, and interference with other activities'. Frijda identifies three main gains of vengeance, first of all the equalization of power. When one group wilfully harms another, the act of harming is a manifestation of the power the offender has, and of the lack of power of the victim to prevent it. This inequality of power is alleviated or annulled by revenge. The restoration of threatened or damaged self-esteem is a second gain achieved by vengeance, a major source of vengeful impulse that gives it much of its emotional force. Revenge can restore some of the damage done to the Self. Finally, vengeance can cause an escape from pain for the avenger. Since pain is not neutralized by inflicting an equal amount of pain but only by taking away its causes (i.e. healing), by inflicting pain upon the offender, the avenger can forget his own unbearable pain: 'The nearest one can come to terminating the pain, perhaps, is to secure the object's total destruction, removing him or her from the face of the earth, erasing him or her from the records of history'.[278] One scholar has argued that this type of disproportional revenge is culturally determined as different cultures have different norms for dealing with suffered harm.[279] All in all, the social functions of vengeance are mainly to restore the power equilibrium between the offender and the offended, and to deter perceived enemies from future offences.

The consequences of these insights for the study of mass violence and genocide are considerable. That studies of genocides often draw a sharp Manichean dividing line between 'perpetrators' and 'victims' and lock these immutable roles at that particular segment in history is perhaps justified.[280] But in many of those same studies, humans' potentially multiple roles in genocidal processes are often overlooked or ignored.[281] Moreover, survivors and victim communities are too often patronized as having drawn universalistic humanist lessons from their victimization and are often expected to forgive and 'reconcile'.[282] Conversely, research on

---

[277] Nico H. Frijda, 'The Lex Talionis: On Vengeance', in: Stephanie H. M. van Goozen, Nanne E. van de Poll and Joseph A. Sergeant (eds.), *Emotions: Essays on Emotion Theory* (Hillsdale, NJ: Erlbaum, 1994), 263–89.

[278] Ibid., at 279.

[279] Alexander L. Hinton, 'A Head for an Eye: Revenge in the Cambodian Genocide', in: *American Ethnologist* 25, no. 3 (1998), 352–77.

[280] For a typical study, see: Raul Hilberg, *Perpetrators, Victims, Bystanders: The Jewish Catastrophe, 1933–1945* (New York: HarperCollins, 1993).

[281] For a critical study, see: Mahmood Mamdani, *When Victims Become Killers: Colonialism, Nativism, and the Genocide in Rwanda* (Princeton, NJ: Princeton University Press, 2001). For survivor testimony of Cambodian 'victim-perpetrators', see: Meng-Try Ea and Sorya Sim, *Victims and Perpetrators?: Testimony of Young Khmer Rouge Comrades* (Phnom Penh: Documentation Center of Cambodia, 2001).

[282] For a critical problematization of these postulates, see: Thomas Brudholm, 'Revisiting Resentments: Jean Améry and the Dark Side of Forgiveness and Reconciliation', in: *Journal of Human Rights* 5 (2006), 7–26.

vengeance has identified how victimization and vengeance are closely related: victimized individuals and groups often feel vindictive (with or without justice), and vice versa, vengeance is almost always justified by calling attention to prior victimization. 'Revenge is involved when thoughts of having suffered at the hands of the object contribute to the force of violence'.[283] Whereas rational-choice approaches to genocide can explain the planning phase and daily conduct of persecutions, for explanations of the forces propelling genocide one has to turn to sociological accounts of how desires of vengeance among victim groups and military elites are capitalized on and propagated to broader segments of society by regimes. Once mobilized, the more such a process of collective vengeful desire escalates, the harder it becomes to reverse that process, especially if it crosses the threshold of violence and thereby becomes relatively autonomous.

In studies of the Armenian genocide and accounts of the killings, the perpetrators, from the organizing elites to the rank-and-file executioners, have too often figured as evil faceless killers, undifferentiated and unexplained. The guerrillas and tribesmen appear in the killing fields of Anatolia ex nihilo and murder people for no apparent reason other than to act out an innate (Turkish or Islamic) cruelty and malignance. This chapter has attempted to challenge this essentialist convention by problematizing the victimization of Ottoman Muslims and Young Turks in the Balkans, and arguing that two years later that victimization served as a motive for collective vengeance against Ottoman Christians. The roots of the Armenian Genocide can partly be traced in the loss of power, territory, war, and 'honor' in the Balkans. Particularly the violent expulsion of Ottoman Muslim civilians was a harbinger of more violence. In 1913, terrified Muslims had fled Rumelia in the hundreds of thousands. The stories and humiliation they brought assured that Muslim-Christian co-existence became all but impossible in the future. The experience also precluded sympathy for the Ottoman Armenians who, two years later, would be persecuted and destroyed. If it is the nationalism and power struggle that explains the motives of the planners of the genocide, then it is the combination of trauma, revenge, and fear of victimization that energized many low-level perpetrators. Ultimately, the self-destructiveness, extreme intensity, and extended duration of the wartime mass murder of Ottoman Christians can for a substantial part be explained by understanding the Young Turk desire for vengeance. This can also help explain why in 1917, when, contrary to the CUP's expectations, the Empire did not collapse, and mass killings diminished somewhat in intensity.

'Revenge', writes Frijda, 'is the social power regulator in a society without central justice'.[284] In the early twentieth century, the notion of justice was poorly anchored in the international system of states. Had some form of justice been delivered to Ottoman Muslims in 1913, there might not have been a vindictive Young Turk dictatorship that launched the later genocide. The idea of the

---

[283] Seymour L. Halleck, 'Vengeance and Victimization', in: *Victimology* 5, no.2 (1980), 99–114; Heather Strang, *Repair or Revenge: Victims and Restorative Justice* (Oxford: Oxford University Press, 2002), 88–130.
[284] Ibid., 270.

Ottoman-Turkish state as victim granted many a necessary moral certainty that enabled mass murder. The perpetrators of the genocide saw themselves 'as the true victims of an ongoing political drama, victims of yesterday who may yet be victims again. That moral certainly explains the easy transition from yesterday's victims to killers the morning after'.[285] This transition from victims to perpetrators is marked by the fact that victims need proof of power or self-efficacy as a function of proof of a sense of Self. In other words, the destruction of the Other was the confirmation of the Self. Thus, as perverted as this sounds, destroying the Armenians was a quasi-therapeutic process for the Young Turks and gave them a renewed sense of power over their Christian subjects. Genocide scholar Jacques Semelin argued that 'the act of massacring is the most spectacular practice which those in power have at their disposal to assert their ascendancy by marking, martyrising and destroying the bodies of those identified as their enemies'.[286] From this subjective moral perspective, the genocide evolved not as a clear evil but rather as the shadow of virtue. Of course, objectively, there was nothing righteous about the mass murder, which was a showcase of humankind at its worst. Cruelty, which is at least a function of power differentials as it is of undiluted hatred and capricious sadism, fed on this process and manifested itself during the killing sessions. A particular form of vengeance that can clarify the direction and level of violence and cruelty is the puzzling phenomenon of what may be called 'dislocated' or 'generalized' vengeance: exacting revenge not on your direct tormentors but on others, either totally unrelated strangers or groups related to your tormentors by identity markers such as language, ethnicity, culture, religion, politics, or indeed gender. Rape of women can be interpreted as an act of 'vengeance toward all women enacted upon the body of one'.[287] Such a mechanism can explain why the Ottoman Armenians had to suffer for crimes the Bulgarian or Greek armies had committed against Ottoman Muslims. This type of vengeance was not motivated by a desire to right the suffered wrong, which, the perpetrators knew, could not be undone anyway.

Did the Young Turks really feel satisfied after having destroyed the Armenians? Although the genocide was deeply repressed and ousted from the memory of Turkish national identity, it always loomed as a public secret, a taboo that never really evanesced. Besides having suffered a trauma of victimization, the Turks had now also developed a trauma of perpetration, two traumas that have become so entangled they are difficult to extricate.[288] The chapter on memory will deal with this problem in detail. Theoretically, the answer to this question would be negative. Psychologists who have worked with avengers argue that 'people who actually commit acts of revenge, such as combat veterans who commit atrocities, do not succeed in getting rid of their post-traumatic symptoms; rather, they seem to

---

[285] Mamdani, *When Victims Become Killers*, 233.
[286] Jacques Semelin, *Purify and Destroy: The Political Uses of Massacre and Genocide* (London: Hurst and Co., 2007), 6.
[287] Susan Jacoby, *Wild Justice: The Evolution of Revenge* (New York: Harper and Row, 1983), 193.
[288] Seyhan Bayraktar and Wolfgang Seibel, 'Das türkische Tätertrauma: Der Massenmord an den Armeniern von 1915 bis 1917 und seine Leugnung', in: Bernhard Giesen and Christoph Schneider (eds.), *Tätertrauma* (Konstanz: UVK, 2004), 381–98.

suffer the most severe and intractable disturbances'.[289] The consummation of revenge does not seem to eliminate stress and pain. Moreover, many scholars agree that most ordinary people dislike committing mass murder and have to be pressured or even coerced to overcome their dislike of murdering. Paradoxically, the realization of vengeful fantasies has to overcome a serious psychological threshold (repulsion of killing), an emotion equally human as the very desire that propels the violence itself. If these emotions clash, then why do avengers go through with their vengeance? This remains an important question to be answered.

Scholars of genocide have argued that local dynamics can influence the course and intensity of the genocidal process. Local political or social elites can expedite and intensify, or delay and resist genocidal destruction steered from above.[290] The Ottoman province Diyarbekir has served as a platform for exemplifying the anti-Armenian policies at the local level, leading us to the dynamics that centre and periphery played in the events of the period. Most of the deportations were micromanaged by Talaat, others by his subordinates. One would need to take a much closer look at Talaat's specific role and the nature of the power he exercised with respect to the persecution of the Ottoman Armenians, which accumulated to full genocidal proportions by the summer of 1915. Even with the extant primary documentation on the secretive nature of the bureaucratically organized destruction of the Armenians, one cannot refrain from seeking to unearth the 'true' intention behind the tens of thousands of telegraphic orders he issued, some of which are deceptive enough to fool the historian. Even so, all such inconsistencies notwithstanding, the sheer magnitude of the campaign leaves not a shred of doubt about the hostile intention of the policy. Talaat's micro-managing qualities and sharp intelligence, coupled with calculating tact and an extraordinary talent for political self-preservation, need more research. Every other step in the radicalization of existing measures was spurred by him, and Reshid's appointment was a vitalizing force underlying the existing program for mass destruction, not a palliative.

It is inconceivable to understand the persecutions without highlighting the dynamics between national policy versus local agency. For this reason, Talaat's relationship with governor Dr. Mehmed Reshid was a question central to this chapter. It is an example of the evolution of CUP policy against proclaimed 'internal enemies', notably the Armenians. No single order to destroy all Armenians has ever been found (and is unlikely ever to be), but when the persecution gained genocidal momentum, between 20 and 30 May 1915, it is highly probable that Talaat wired the doctor-governor one or another euphemistic order to 'act

---

[289] Judith Herman, *Trauma and Recovery* (New York: Basic Books, 1992), 189.

[290] For local studies of genocide, see: Tomislav Dulić, *Utopias of Nation: Local Mass Killing in Bosnia and Hercegovina, 1941–42* (Uppsala: Uppsala University Press, 2005); Dieter Pohl, *Nationalsozialistische Judenverfolgung in Ostgalizien 1941–1944: Organisation und Durchführung eines staatlichen Massenverbrechens* (München: Oldenbourg, 1996); Wendy Lower, *Nazi Empire-Building and the Holocaust in Ukraine* (Chapel Hill: University of North Carolina Press, 2005); Lee Ann Fujii, 'The Power of Local Ties: Mechanisms of Mass Participation During the Rwandan Genocide', paper presented at the annual meeting of the *American Political Science Association*, Philadelphia, 31 August 2006.

ruthlessly'. He certainly did not grant Reshid *carte blanche* to eliminate all Christians, considering future reprimands. The radically anti-Christian Ottoman patriot and Muslim nationalist Dr. Reshid interpreted the order as a licence to kill all Armenians and Syriacs living under his jurisdiction. It is telling that of all the Ottoman governors involved in the violence, none were rebuked for their cruelty and fanaticism as Reshid was—even if the persecutions ran more or less parallel in other provinces. Therefore, Talaat's telegraphic reprehensions unveil a secret in the definition of the scope of the persecutions. The reproval, 'do not destroy the other Christians', was basically synonymous to the speech act, 'do destroy the Armenians', and reveals Talaat's tacit approval of Reshid's anti-Armenian actions. Naturally, Talaat formulated his argument without compromising himself in a written order.

On the local level too, revenge, fear of victimization, and competition between elites played important roles. Dr. Mehmed Reshid, portrayed as a sadistic monster in contemporary sources, was born in the Caucasus but his family had to flee the onslaught of the Tsarist Russian army in the 1860s. Vengeance may well have been a motivating factor in his perception of the world. Circassian families like his, whose parents' generation had been massacred and expelled, had intimate knowledge of Armenian nationalist activism in the Caucasus and, like the Balkan Muslims, were traumatized. The same would have been true for the three dozen Circassian militiamen that Reshid had employed. When the war broke out and the Russian army seemed to be effortlessly conquering its way towards Diyarbekir, it must have been hardly difficult to play into their apocalyptic fear that 'the Russians are coming', and most importantly, that their Armenian neighbours were Russian spies. Competition between urban elites was another factor that contributed to the intensity of the violence. Before the war, the main families in Diyarbekir, mainly Christians and Muslims, were engaged in a fierce struggle for political and economic power. Such a structural factor could easily be abused by the CUP dictatorship for its own ends: collaborate with us and you will be duly rewarded. The Pirinççizâde, Müftüzâde, and Direkçizâde families emerged victorious from this competition by volunteering in the militias, being more ruthless in their competitive efforts, and collaborating with the campaign the CUP regime deemed most salient, the murder of their Armenian neighbours.

3

Deportations of Kurds, 1916–34

This chapter will describe and interpret forced migrations, also known as 'population transfers' or simply 'deportations', as one among the many tactics of social engineering. Deportation, or population transfer, is a distinct aspect of population politics. It can be defined as the forced movement of a large group of people from one region to another by state policy or transnational authorities. Most frequently the victims are selected on the basis of categorical, ascribed identity markers such as ethnicity or religion. The affected population is transferred by force to a distant region often causing substantial harm (including deaths) and the loss of all immovable and often movable property. There is a subtle difference between forced population transfers and ethnic cleansing: the former consists of internal penal transportation whereas the latter is the expulsion of undesired groups beyond national borders. What these policies have in common is the desire for ethnic homogenization of a particular territory and concomitantly, a sense of purification of the nation.

The process of a mass deportation generally passes through four phases. First and foremost, the coerced extraction of the targeted group from their native environment. The victims are rounded up, often by surprise or at very short notice, and severed from their existing social networks. Their possessions are often sequestered by the regime, or sold at below-market prices, or taken with them during the deportation. If this process of extraction is resisted by the targets, government forces will often deploy violent methods, in which case considerable destruction of life and property is caused. Second, the group is transported to its destination, often a distant place to which few of them will ever have been, often under very harsh conditions in cattle cars or on foot. If these conditions are particularly tough, in this phase, too, large numbers of people may die of exposure, exhaustion, or hunger. Third, the group will eventually arrive at their destination and encounter the receiving society, often enduring an initial process of estrangement, adaptation, rejection, or sometimes a modus vivendi with the local population. In this phase, unemployment and famine is often experienced as a result of social ostracism and state neglect. Finally, in those cases in which the regime that deported the group has lost power, it proves possible for at least a part of the victim group to return to its native region, which often produces new problems of reintegration and reparations.[1]

---

[1] See e.g.: Norman M. Naimark, *Fires of Hatred: Ethnic Cleansing in Twentieth-Century Europe* (Cambridge, MA: Harvard University Press, 2001); Benjamin Lieberman, *Terrible Fate: Ethnic Cleansing in the Making of Modern Europe* (Chicago, IL: Dee, 2006); Steven Béla Várdy, T. Hunt

This chapter will deal particularly with the deportations of Kurds from Eastern to Western Turkey in the course of roughly two decades. How did the Young Turk dictatorship use forced population transfer as a strategy of 'Turkifying' the country's eastern provinces? Before describing how the Young Turks organized three major phases of deportations, it will trace the aetiology of these policies in the immediate aftermath of the Young Turk seizure of power in 1913. In order to provide a more complete understanding of this process, the chapter will analyse the deportation process as a two-way project of deporting non-Turks away from, and settling Turks into the eastern provinces, in particular Diyarbekir province. These two vectors of population transfer geared into each other, potentially rendering the deportations an effective tool of demographic Turkification. The chapter aims to present a detailed narrative of three phases of Young Turk deportations of Kurds and settlement of Turks: 1916, 1925, and 1934. It will attempt to draw a systematic comparison between the three phases and emphasize the continuity of population policies in the Young Turk era, without overlooking the subtle differences between the three phases of deportations. Alongside many official texts including justification, laws, and procedures, the chapter will also draw heavily on memoirs and oral histories to portray the experiences of deportees.

1916: PHASE ONE

The Young Turk stance toward the Kurdish population of the Ottoman Empire was of a complex nature. On the one hand, the Kurds were perceived to be Ottoman Muslims, therefore not to be excluded from the new 'national' order. After all, among the first founders of the Committee of Union and Progress there were several Ottoman-Kurdish intellectuals, such as Dr. Abdullah Cevdet (1869–1932)[2] and Dr. İshak Sükûti (1868–1902), the latter being a native of Diyarbekir. Moreover, the doyen of CUP nationalist ideology was Mehmed Ziyâ Gökalp (1876–1924), a Diyarbekir Kurd. In addition to these influential politicians, local CUP elites were often Kurds too. Again, in Diyarbekir province for example, the Pirinççizâde dynasty had exhibited loyalty to CUP policy. In Mardin city, tribal leaders of the Deşi and Kiki tribes used the CUP (and vice versa) to push their agendas. Due to familial ties, ideological conformity, but especially material

Tooley, and Agnes Huszár Várdy (eds.), *Ethnic Cleansing in Twentieth-Century Europe* (New York: Columbia University Press, 2003); Andrew Bell-Falkoff, *Ethnic Cleansing* (New York: St. Martin's Press, 1996); Michael Mann, *The Dark Side of Democracy: Explaining Ethnic Cleansing* (Cambridge: Cambridge University Press, 2005); Akbar S. Ahmed, '"Ethnic Cleansing": A Metaphor for our Time?', in: *Ethnic and Racial Studies* 18, no. 1 (1995), 1–25; Philipp Ther, 'A Century of Forced Migration: The Origins and Consequences of "Ethnic Cleansing"', in: Philipp Ther and Ana Siljak (eds.), *Redrawing Nations: Ethnic Cleansing in East-Central Europe, 1944–1948* (Lanham, MD: Rowman and Littlefield, 2001), 43–72; Anja Kruke (ed.), *Zwangsmigration und Vertreibung: Europa im 20. Jahrhundert* (Bonn: Dietz, 2006); Pieter H. van der Plank, *Etnische Zuivering in Midden-Europa: Natievorming en Staatsburgerschap in de XXe Eeuw* (Leeuwarden: Universitaire Pers Fryslân, 2004).

[2] Mehmet Ş. Hanioğlu, *Bir siyasal düşünür olarak Doktor Abdullah Cevdet ve dönemi* (Istanbul: Üçdal, 1981).

opportunism, many among these Kurdish elites had participated in and profited from the genocidal persecution of the Christians in that province.[3] Other Kurds, however, had resisted the regime. Kurds from the large village of Awina, for example, had been resisting the Young Turk regime since 1913 and more specifically since the First World War. They rescued and sheltered Armenians simply because such acts would put them in a state of confrontation with the regime.[4]

Apart from regional administrative institutions, the relations between the Ottoman army and the Kurds were relatively cordial as well. The army profited from Kurdish manpower which it needed in its war effort against Russia. Diyarbekir Governor Dr. Mehmed Reshid admitted in his memoirs that without the support of the Millî, Mîran, and Karakeçi tribes, generally located in the west of Diyarbekir province, it would not have been possible to provide the necessary resources and requisitions for the Ottoman army.[5] In his memoirs, Commander of the Second Army Ahmed İzzet Pasha detailed some of his efforts to reach out to Kurdish tribal elites. According to İzzet, the stick-strategy had only alienated Kurdish tribesmen from the state, thus not produced the desired results. Therefore he had opted for a carrot-strategy to incorporate the tribes. Interestingly, he also wrote that one of the most successful Ottoman officials who had succeeded in gaining the Kurds' confidence was the district governor of Mardin, İbrahim Bedreddin, who had zealously destroyed the Christian population in that district. Bedreddin had developed strong personal friendships with several influential Kurdish chieftains from the Cizre district.[6]

Taking this bond between the CUP and Kurdish elites into consideration, the CUP seemingly had little to worry about concerning the Kurds. However, this loyalty problem was not as simple as it appeared at first sight. The outbreak of the First World War put considerable pressure on the relations between the Young Turks and the Kurds. The key word was 'trust'. There was fear of collaboration of powerful Kurdish tribes with the advancing Russian army, as well as with Armenian politicians. The CUP also harboured suspicion about Kurdish nationalism and feared the Kurds as a threat to state security in the eastern provinces.[7] The claims were not totally unfounded, for desertion, Kurdo-Armenian alliances, and nationalism all existed. Therefore, the CUP remained vigilant about which Kurdish families and tribes were potentially loyal to the government and which were not. It then pre-emptively distrusted those already suspected of disloyalty as a military precaution, just in case the tribes in question indeed crossed sides and joined the Russians. In that case, if a certain tribe turned out to be disloyal, a threat would

---

[3] *International Institute for Social History* (Amsterdam), Hikmet Kıvılcımlı Papers, inventory no. 56, 'İhtiyat Kuvvet Milliyet (Şark)' (unpublished handwritten manuscript, 1932), 20.

[4] See the family memoir written by a grandson of one of the Awina chieftains: Ramazan Ergin, *Awina ya da Kanın Gizli Tarihi: Reşo Kuri* (Istanbul: Do, 2007).

[5] Mehmed Reşid, *Mülâhazât* (Istanbul: n.p., 1919), transliterated in: Nejdet Bilgi, *Dr. Mehmed Reşid Şahingiray'ın hayatı ve hâtıraları* (İzmir: Akademi, 1997), 82.

[6] Ahmet İzzet Paşa, *Feryadım* (Istanbul: Nehir, 1992), vol. 1, 257.

[7] Harry Stürmer, *Two War Years in Constantinople: Sketches of German and Young Turkish Ethics and Politics* (London: Gomidas, 2004), 7.

have been eliminated; if the tribe was loyal after all, little was lost in the CUP's eyes. Obviously, their actions did not advance Kurdish trust in and loyalty to the CUP either.[8] A concrete example of CUP distrust in local Kurdish elites in Diyarbekir province can be found in the memoirs of Commander of the Second Army, Ahmed İzzet Pasha (1864–1937). The relatively accommodating and liberal İzzet was shocked by an anecdote Mustafa Kemal Pasha (the later Atatürk) had related to him. When Kemal Pasha arrived in Hazro district to explore the region for warfare conditions, he lodged with the local Kurdish notable Hatip Bey.[9] But the mayor of Hazro told Kemal confidentially that the local Kurdish elite was not to be trusted. He suggested that the families needed to be 'exterminated root and branch' as soon as possible.[10]

There are manifold reasons why the CUP engaged in large-scale deportations of Kurds. First, there were direct political reasons, namely to thwart possible alliances between Kurdish tribes and the Russian army. Second, there were economic considerations: many Kurdish tribes were (semi-)nomadic and in order to tax them more effectively, they needed to be sedentarized. Nationalist assimilation was a third concern of the Ottoman Ministry of the Interior. In their efforts to 'nationalize', i.e. 'Turkify', the empire, the Kurds were targeted for cultural and linguistic assimilation, and political absorption into the Turkish nation. The combination between a long-term ideological program and short-term war exigencies drove the CUP to deport hundreds of thousands of Ottoman Kurds. The Directorate for the Settlement of Tribes and Immigrants (İAMM, renamed AMMU in 1916) supervised the deportation of these people. Those Kurds who had fled west from the Russian occupation were incorporated in the deportation program as well.

Altogether, war exigencies, economic considerations, and assimilation policies led Ottoman Kurds to be deported *en masse*. Following the deportation of Armenians, on 2 May 1916 Talaat issued the following order to the governor of Diyarbekir:

> It is absolutely not allowable to send the Kurdish refugees to southern regions such as Urfa or Zor. Because they would either Arabize or preserve their nationality there and remain a useless and harmful element, the intended objective would not be achieved and therefore the deportation and settlement of these refugees needs to be carried out as follows.
>
> - Turkish refugees and the turkified city dwellers need to be deported to the Urfa, Maraş, and Anteb regions and settled there.
>
> - To preclude that the Kurdish refugees continue their tribal life and their nationality wherever they have been deported, the chieftains need to be separated from the common people by all means, and all influential personalities and leaders need to be sent separately to the provinces of Konya and Kastamonu, and to the districts of Niğde and Kayseri.

---

[8] Naci Kutlay, *İttihat Terakki ve Kürtler* (Ankara: Beybûn, 1992), 190–1.
[9] Abdülmelik Fırat, *Fırat Mahzun Akar* (Istanbul: Avesta, 1996), 21.
[10] İzzet, *Feryadım*, 273–4.

- The sick, the elderly, lonely and poor women and children who are unable to travel will be settled and supported in Maden town and Ergani and Behremaz counties, to be dispersed in Turkish villages and among Turks. . . .
- Correspondence will be conducted with the final destinies of the deportations, whereas the method of dispersion, how many deportees have been sent where and when, and settlement measures will all be reported to the Ministry.[11]

The deportation of Kurds had now begun, first of all targeting the Kurds deemed 'disloyal' by the CUP. When a group of mounted Kurds from Ahlat attempted to defect to the Russians, their deportation to Diyarbekir was ordered.[12] Ahmed İzzet Pasha tried to prevent these deportations, suggesting to Talaat that 'tribal cavalry units' should be established instead.[13] His efforts had limited success as the İAMM improvised a makeshift solution. In May, it authorized the temporary settlement of Kurdish chieftains and tribesmen in areas close to the front. This was a local solution between deployment in the war and deportation to the west.[14] Since hundreds of Armenian villages were empty, Kurds perceived as more soundly loyal to the government were to be settled immediately. In Diyarbekir province, Kurds enrolled in the tribal units were settled in the empty Christian villages around Mardin and Midyat.[15] İAMM planners further authorized 280 members of the Zirkî tribe to settle with their families in empty villages in Derik district.[16]

The socio-economic motivations of the deportations were related to the CUP's agricultural policy. Having destroyed hundreds of thousands of (Armenian) peasants, the peasant population of the country needed to be replenished. In 1911, Diyarbekir deputy Aziz Feyzi (see Plate 6) had already suggested the tribes of the eastern provinces be settled, in order to raise the renevue of the land, and to circumvent a possible German imperialist claim on that region.[17] In the 1917 CUP congress an agreement was signed on (re)settling the tribes and redefining the administrative form of the settlements.[18] From then on, one would find specific references to agricultural policy in the deportation orders. On 14 October 1916 the AMMU ordered Kurdish tribesmen from Diyarbekir province deported to central Anatolia via Urfa, specifying that on arrival, the settlers were to be employed in the 'farming industry'. They were to constitute between 5 and 10 percent of the local (Turkish) population.[19] Refugee-deportees who had fled the Russian occupation and had arrived in Diyarbekir province were supposed to work on the land too. The order read that the settlers were to be provided with pack animals and ploughs,

---

[11] BOA, DH.ŞFR 63/172–173, Talaat to Diyarbekir, 2 May 1916.
[12] BOA, DH.ŞFR 57/275, İAMM to Diyarbekir, 3 November 1915.
[13] İzzet, *Feryadım*, 257.
[14] BOA, DH.ŞFR 64/80, İAMM to the provinces of Erzurum, Sivas, Mamuret-ul Aziz, and Mosul, 20 May 1916.
[15] BOA, DH.ŞFR 57/328, İAMM to Bitlis, 7 November 1915.
[16] Fuat Dündar, *İttihat ve Terakki'nin Müslümanları İskân Politikası (1913–1918)* (Istanbul: İletişim, 2002), 143.
[17] *Meclis-i Mebusan Zabıt Ceridesi 1327* (1911), first election period, third sitting, 114th session, 3537.
[18] *Tanin*, 21 September 1917.
[19] BOA, DH.ŞFR 69/8, AMMU to Urfa, 14 October 1916.

in order for them to settle down and 'begin agriculture immediately'.[20] Due to shortages in Diyarbekir, the AMMU ordered seed potatoes to be imported from Elaziz.[21]

Yet most İAMM/AMMU orders reveal that nationalist assimilation was the propelling force behind the deportations. German officials had understood what the CUP was pursuing in the war. A German teacher wrote in September 1916,

> The Young Turks have in mind the European ideal of a unitary nation state [*eines einheitlichen Nationalstaates*]. They fear the Christian nations, the Armenians, Syriacs, Greeks, for their cultural and economic superiority and view their religion as an obstacle to Turkifying them in peaceful ways. Therefore they must be exterminated or forcibly Islamized [*ausgerottet oder zwangsweise islamisiert*]. The non-Turkish Mohammedan races, such as Kurds, Persians, Arabs etc., they hope to Turkify through administrative measures and Turkish school education with reference to the common Mohammedan interest.[22]

When initiating the deportations, Talaat personally paid attention to the efficiency of the Turkification project. In January 1916 he requested specific information on the Kurds living in more than a dozen provinces and districts. Talaat wrote, 'How many Kurdish villages are there, and where? What is their population? Are they preserving their mother tongue and original culture? How is their relationship with Turkish villagers and villages?'[23] In April he checked again, this time asking how and where which convoys were being deported, and whether the Kurdish deportees had begun speaking Turkish.[24] These examples of correspondence indicate the nature of the deportations: they were a large-scale attack on Kurdish culture and language, constituencies that could define the Kurds as a nation and therefore potentially pose a threat.

As in the case of the deportations of Armenians the year before, Diyarbekir city became a hub for deportation. The local İAMM officials were appointed by the İAMM headquarters in Istanbul but were subject to the governors. They enjoyed more rights than other officials as they had clearance to send ciphers without prior authorization.[25] Whereas in 1915 Armenians were concentrated in the city to be deported to the south, in 1916 Kurds were sent off to the west. For the Diyarbekir Kurds, the deportations were a one-way trip out of their native province, as no Kurd was allowed to (re-)enter the province. According to historian Hilmar Kaiser, Diyarbekir became a zone of 'Turkification':

---

[20] BOA, DH.ŞFR 69/235, AMMU to Diyarbekir, 12 November 1916.

[21] BOA, DH.ŞFR 72/180, AMMU to Elaziz, 8 February 1917.

[22] PAAA, R14093, Das Geheime Zivil-Kabinet des Kaisers (Valentini) an den Reichskanzler (Bethmann-Hollweg), 10 September 1916, enclosure no. 3.

[23] BOA, DH.ŞFR 60/140, Talaat to the provinces of Konya, Kastamonu, Ankara, Sivas, Adana, Aydın, Trabzon, and districts of Kayseri, Canik, Eskişehir, Karahisar, Niğde, 26 January 1916.

[24] BOA, DH.ŞFR 62/187, Talaat to Sivas, 16 April 1916; BOA, DH.ŞFR 62/278, Talaat to Adana, 9 April 1916.

[25] BOA, DH.ŞFR 72/222, AMMU to provinces, 13 February 1917.

Besides the 'turkification' of human beings, whole regions or critical localities were targeted as a second major aspect of the government's program. Therefore, whole districts were designated as a 'turkification region'. Consequently, Ottoman officials did not allow Kurdish deportees arriving from the eastern borders areas in the province of Diarbekir . . . to remain there, as Muslims from the Balkans had been earmarked as settlers for these regions.[26]

This strategy for Diyarbekir regulated a segregation of refugee-deportees from Bitlis into ethnic Kurds and ethnic Turks. The Kurdish refugees were not allowed to stay in Diyarbekir but forced to march on westward, whereas the Turkish ones were immediately settled in and around the provincial capital.[27] The official deportation order for Diyarbekir's indigenous Kurds fell on 20 May 1916, eighteen days after Talaat's national guidelines for deportation. The AMMU ordered 'Kurdish tribes to be deported collectively to predetermined settlement areas'.[28] First they were deported to Urfa,[29] but after half a year Urfa became too full and they were rerouted back to Diyarbekir and settled around Siverek.[30] For all Kurdish deportees the general rule was applied that no one was allowed to return to Diyarbekir without prior authorization from the Ministry.[31] The settlements were to be permanent: deportees arriving at their places of destination were ordered to immediately register at the local population registry before being settled.[32]

The conduct of the deportation of Kurdish tribesmen and refugees stood in stark contrast with the Armenian deportation, a year before. The Swiss missionary Jakob Künzler was stationed in Urfa during the war and wrote in his memoirs, 'Among the deportees I also saw many high-ranking Kurdish army officers, who had courageously fought the Russians in the field at the outbreak of the war, and who now bitterly perceived the treatment by the Turks as ingratitude'.[33] Künzler personally witnessed convoys from Palu passing by in Urfa:

> The treatment of these Kurds on their deportation routes differed considerably from that of the Armenians. No harm was done to them on the road, nobody was allowed to torment them. But the most terrible was, that the deportations occurred in the middle of winter. When such a Kurdish convoy arrived in a Turkish village at evening, the inhabitants quickly closed their doors out of fear. That way the paupers had to spend

---

[26] Hilmar Kaiser, 'The Ottoman Government and the End of the Ottoman Social Formation, 1915–1917', paper presented at the conference *Der Völkermord an den Armeniern und die Shoah*, University of Zürich, 7 November 2001, at: <http://www.hist.net/kieser/aghet/Essays/EssayKaiser.html>.

[27] BOA, DH.ŞFR 63/187, İAMM to Urfa, Maraş, Antep, 4 May 1916.

[28] BOA, DH.ŞFR 64/77, İAMM to the provinces of Diyarbekir, Mamuret-ul Aziz, Sivas, Erzurum, Mosul, 20 May 1916.

[29] BOA, DH.ŞFR 69/7, AMMU to Diyarbekir, 14 October 1916.

[30] BOA, DH.ŞFR 74/22, AMMU to Diyarbekir, 3 March 1917.

[31] BOA, DH.ŞFR 63/283, İAMM to Mamuret-ul Aziz, 11 May 1916.

[32] BOA, DH.ŞFR 77/188, İAMM to Niğde, 19 April 1917; BOA, DH.ŞFR 85/262, AMMU to Diyarbekir, 28 March 1918.

[33] Jacob Künzler, *Im Lande des Blutes und der Tränen: Erlebnisse in Mesopotamien während des Weltkrieges (1914–1918)* (Zürich: Chronos, 1999 [1921]), 101.

the winter night under rain and snow outside. The next morning then the villagers had to make mass graves (*Massengräber*) for the frostbitten.[34]

The deportees were often met with xenophobia by many Turkish villagers, who were not familiar with Kurdish tribesmen and therefore feared them. In the cities, the deportees were settled in the deserted Armenian neighbourhoods where they had no means to support themselves. After all, most Kurds were pastoralists and were not versed in agriculture and were often unfamiliar, if not hostile to urban life. The Kurdish poet Cigerxwîn (1903–84) was deported from Mardin to the south of Urfa, where he became an orphan when he lost his parents due to famine.[35] A handful of missionaries and relief organizations tried to help the deportees, appealing to consulates and local Muslim clerics, and providing food and shelter. Even though they left no stone unturned, due to the enormity of the deportation program their efforts were a drop in the ocean.[36]

At that time, inflation was rampant and the black market flourished. Fraudulent CUP officials were massively embezzling funds designated for the population. Among them was Kara Kemal, who was enriching himself under the cloak of 'economic Turkification'. The misappropriations became widespread among a privileged few, creating a stratum living in unrestrained abundance. By the end of the war, the critical press even grumbled of a 'class' of officials who had become very rich and constituted a 'war bourgeoisie' (*harb zengini*).[37] Among local AMMU officials too, corruption was expanding. Talaat considered this utterly unacceptable because it counteracted the deportations and undermined the assimilation program. In November 1916 funds were appropriated for the local AMMU branches: 30,000 Lira were sent to Diyarbekir, 7000 to Siverek, and 7000 to Mardin.[38] When the Ministry found out that the allotments were illegally exhausted by police chief Şeyhzâde Kadri Bey and by the district vice-governor of Mardin, an investigation was ordered.[39] Another corruption scandal was uncovered in Silvan, where the civil servants had neglected their work, causing many refugee-deportees to starve and live under conditions of utter misery.[40] The AMMU headquarters soon found out that it was Silvan's conscription officer Salih Efendi and its mayor Cemilpaşazâde Adil Bey who were in charge of the embezzlements. They had appropriated the daily rations unequally, leaving the deportees 'in an outrageously miserable and wretched state'.[41] Mayor Adil Bey was discharged when the Ministry

---

[34] Ibid., 102.

[35] Cigerxwîn, *Jînenîgariya min* (Spånga, Sweden: APEC, 1995), 55–7. For another account of refugee-deportees, see: Yıldırım Sezen (ed.), *İki Kardeşten Seferberlik Anıları* (Ankara: Kültür Bakanlığı Yayınları, 1999).

[36] Hans-Lukas Kieser, 'Zwischen Ararat und Euphrat: abenländische Missionen im spätosmanischen Kurdistan', in: Hans-Lukas Kieser (ed.), *Kurdistan und Europa: Einblicke in die kurdische Geschichte des 19. und 20. Jahrhunderts* (Zürich: Chronos, 1997), 137.

[37] Refik Halit (Karay), 'Harb Zengini', in: *Yeni Mecmua* 2–42 (2 May 1918), 301–2.

[38] BOA, DH.ŞFR 70/149, İAMM to Diyarbekir, 30 November 1916.

[39] BOA, DH.ŞFR 70/237, Directorate for Employment to Diyarbekir, 12 December 1916.

[40] BOA, DH.ŞFR 69/191, AMMU to Diyarbekir, 5 November 1916.

[41] BOA, DH.ŞFR 71/53, AMMU to Diyarbekir, 21 December 1916.

proved he had been secretly selling sacks of rice, designated for the starving deportees, to the population of Silvan for usurious prices.[42]

At the end of 1917 the culture of embezzlement and moral bankruptcy, combined with economic exhaustion and soaring food prices triggered a national famine that struck the deportees in particular. Locally, prices for bread, meat, sugar, salt, rice, wheat, fat, tea, and coffee quintupled. Even local products of which there had always been surpluses, such as Diyarbekir watermelons and rice, became very scarce.[43] Although the AMMU ordered deportation officials to guard against shortages,[44] only in exceptional situations were the deportations cancelled or postponed. For example, only when an entire convoy from Beşiri became ill was their deportation postponed.[45] As a result of Talaat's insistence on deportation, the AMMU was often unable to provide even a minimal amount of food for the deportees. In Urfa, many Kurdish children died of starvation due to the delayed arrival of the designated amount of flour.[46] In Sivas too, due to negligence 'hundreds of children were wandering around hungry and wretched'.[47] When there was no food at all, deportees ate doves, street cats and dogs, hedgehogs, frogs, moles, snakes, and the organs of slaughtered animals, which would normally be discarded.[48] In some extreme cases the deportees saw no other option than to eat their own relatives who had died on the road.[49] Starvation was but one side of the problem, adequate shelter was another. When an Arab and Kurdish convoy was deported from Diyarbekir westward, nearly the entire convoy froze to death in the desert night. The few remaining survivors were distributed among the local villages.[50]

The deportees often feared that they would be integrally killed like the Armenians. According to popular beliefs, the CUP elite had ostensibly agreed upon first destroying the 'zo' (the Armenians), whereupon they would proceed to annihilate the 'lo' (the Kurds).[51] These fears were most acute in the maverick Dersim district, the south of which had actively opposed the genocide. In July 1915 rumors spread around Dersim that the Ottoman government would destroy the Kurds directly after their anti-Armenian campaign. Talaat immediately ordered counter-propaganda to be disseminated.[52] When the Dersimites were indeed

---

[42] BOA, DH.ŞFR 87/345, Ministry of War (General Directorate for Supplies) to Diyarbekir, 30 May 1918.

[43] Kamal Madhar Ahmad, *Kurdistan During the First World War* (London: Saqi, 1994, transl. Ali Maher Ibrahim), 131–2.

[44] BOA, DH.ŞFR 74/258, AMMU to Diyarbekir, 26 March 1917.

[45] BOA, DH.ŞFR 68/91, Talaat to Diyarbekir, 23 September 1916.

[46] BOA, DH.ŞFR 78/237, AMMU to Urfa, 30 July 1917.

[47] BOA, DH.ŞFR 78/242, AMMU to Sivas, 30 July 1917.

[48] Hasan Hişyar Serdî, *Görüş ve Anılarım 1907–1985* (Istanbul: Med, 1994), 139.

[49] See the memoirs of an ethnically Kurdish officer who had served in the Ottoman army during the First World War: Mehmed E. Zeki, *Kürdistan Tarihi* (Istanbul: Komal, 1977), 168.

[50] BOA, DH.ŞFR 82/180, AMMU to Diyarbekir, 25 December 1917.

[51] The words 'zo' and 'lo' are derogatory expressions in Turkish, referring to the Armenian and Kurdish languages, respectively. Firat Cewerî, *Li Mala Mîr Celadet Alî Bedir-xan* (Stockholm: Nûdem, 1998), 71–5.

[52] BOA, DH.ŞFR 54-A/128, Talaat to the provinces of Mamuret-ul Aziz, Erzurum, Diyarbekir, Bitlis, 25 July 1915.

deported a year later, they sang lamentations, praying to God for survival and accusing the Germans of deporting them.[53] The rumours spread over to other provinces as well, impelling some deportees to attempt escape from the deportation convoys. Kurdish tribesmen from Mardin and Karacadağ apparently overheard that they were to be deported to the interior and tried to seek asylum among the Viranşehir, Beşiri, and Savur tribes. They were tracked down, captured, and deported.[54] But even when they were deported to the western provinces, some deportees still managed to escape. In July 1917 men of the Hasanan tribe were deported from Siverek to Istanbul. Five out of nine deportees escaped from the convoys and were lost without a trace.[55]

On arrival the Kurds were rarely provided with sufficient material to make a living. As the German officer Ludwig Schraudenbach sarcastically wrote,

> The Turks transplanted (*verpflanzten*) at that time thousands of Kurdish families from their mountains to Adana. They would 'engage in agriculture' there. Senior Lieutenant Schalzgruber reported that unfortunately up in the Armenian Taurus the streets were littered with such starved or starving colonizers. A crowd of them was squatting at the Mamouré station as well, their robust bodies in rags, dragging along sacks of fur and carpets, cooking pots put on their verminous heads. Is really anything going to be organized for their reception in Adana? Will they be given land, cattle, and tools? Or will they go to pieces in misery?[56]

The evidence suggests that to various degrees, the last question could be answered affirmatively. The Ottoman directorate for deportation was predominantly interested in whether there were signs of any progress regarding cultural assimilation. When a convoy of Kurds arrived in Konya, the directorate ordered them settled and a report prepared including information on their native region, language, profession, and numbers.[57] Increasing ethno-geographic homogeneity was prioritized over immediate concerns of subsistence.

The deportations caused many Kurdish children to be orphaned. Many of them were already half-orphans as their fathers had died in warfare. Their mothers and aunts tried to protect them from disease, hunger, and violence, thereby often sacrificing themselves. The government ordered the establishment of an orphanage in Urfa to lodge orphans of the Haydaran tribe. The construction of an orphanage in Diyarbekir was not possible due to the 'Turkification' regulations: no Kurdish deportees, not even orphans, were to remain in that province.[58] Only the strongest

---

[53] The deportees lamented: 'German, oh German / Why have you issued a decree on us / May your honour be defiled German / You have brought ruin on our men / May your house burn down German / You have uprooted our men.' (*Alamani Alamani / Te çima mera qenûnek dananî / Ar di mala te kevî Alamanî / Te paşiya mêran mera anî / Mala te bişewite Alamanî / Te kokê mêran mera anî*). Nuri Dersimi, *Dersim ve Kürt Milli Mücadelesine Dair Hatıratım* (Ankara: Öz-Ge, 1992), 80–1.

[54] BOA, DH.ŞFR 69/156, AMMU to Diyarbekir, 1 November 1916.

[55] BOA, DH.ŞFR 78/142, Talaat to Diyarbekir, 16 July 1917.

[56] Ludwig Schraudenbach, *Muharebe: Der erlebte Roman eines deutschen Führers im Osmanischen Heere 1916/17* (Berlin: Drei Masken Verlag, 1924), 459.

[57] BOA, DH.ŞFR 77/45, İAMM to Adana, 6 June 1917.

[58] BOA, DH.ŞFR 69/195, AMMU to Urfa, 5 November 1916.

and luckiest orphans survived the deportations. In Palu, orphans were concentrated and needed to be deported. The AMMU knew their deportation would result in their decimation, but it decided to deport them anyway, adding that they were allowed to be nourished from the Elaziz army depots.[59] The same order was issued for Diyarbekir: the Ministry of War was assigned to provide for widows, orphans, and orphanages.[60] In mid-April 1918, when it had already become clear that an Ottoman defeat in the war was only a matter of time, orphans from Harput, Dersim and Palu were still instructed to march barefoot to Maraş and Elbistan.[61]

The first phase of the Kurdish deportations demands some quantitative data, although it would require a separate study to calculate meticulously how many were deported. According to the Ministry of the Economy the total of all refugee-deportees numbered well over a million.[62] Quantifying the deportations is difficult because many Kurdish tribesmen were deported together with Kurdish refugees from the border provinces Erzurum, Van, and Bitlis. In most accounts, the total number of 700,000 is mentioned,[63] though there are no reliable statistics. According to one researcher, roughly half of these 700,000 deportees died.[64] A concrete example can shed light on the death rate of the deportees. Celadet Ali Bedirxan, a Kurdish intellectual, met a group of Kurdish deportees and asked them how many had survived the death marches. The answer he received shocked him: the leader of the group answered that out of 787 people that were deported from the village, 23 had survived.[65] It is even more difficult to determine precisely how many Diyarbekir Kurds were deported. İAMM/AMMU correspondence surmises some details on the magnitude of the deportations. In October 1916 the number of refugees that had fled the provinces of Bitlis and Van into Diyarbekir was estimated at 200,000.[66] On 17 October 1916 the AMMU ordered the deportation of 15,000 Kurdish refugees to Konya.[67] In November 800 people were deported from Palu to Siverek, an intra-provincial deportation.[68] On 15 July 1917 40,000 Kurds were ordered deported from Diyarbekir to Konya and Antalya.[69] Two weeks later, 40,000 refugees from Mardin were sent off to the east, even though they were infected with contagious diseases and there was a shortage of train carriages.[70] In spite of the deportations further to the west, in April 1920, 35,940 refugee-

[59] BOA, DH.ŞFR 84/169, AMMU to Elaziz, 27 February 1918.

[60] BOA, DH.ŞFR 85/290, Ministry of War (General Directorate for Supplies) to Diyarbekir, 31 March 1918.

[61] BOA, DH.ŞFR 86/46, AMMU to Third Army Commander, 13 April 1918.

[62] BOA, DUİT, 14/28–3, Ministry of Economy memorandum (undated).

[63] Kutlay, *İttihat Terakki*, 272; Soviet Academy of Sciences (ed.), *Yeni ve Yakın Çağda Kürt Siyaset Tarihi* (Istanbul: Pêrî, 1998, transl. M. Aras), 96.

[64] Arshak Safrastian, *Kurds and Kurdistan* (London: Harvill Press, 1948), 76, 81.

[65] Serdî, *Görüş ve Anılarım*, 140.

[66] Justin McCarthy, 'Muslim Refugees in Turkey: The Balkan Wars, World War I, and the Turkish War of Independence', in: *Isis Press and the Institute of Turkish Studies* (Istanbul: Isis, 1993), 96.

[67] BOA, DH.ŞFR 69/35, AMMU to Fourth Army Command, 17 October 1916.

[68] BOA, DH.ŞFR 70/74, AMMU to Mamuret-ul Aziz, 22 November 1916.

[69] BOA, DH.ŞFR 78/128 and 78/129, AMMU to Adana and Diyarbekir, 15 July 1917.

[70] BOA, DH.ŞFR 78/253, AMMU to Diyarbekir, 31 July 1917.

deportees in Diyarbekir still had not been settled.[71] These figures suggest that tens of thousands of Diyarbekir Kurds must have been deported to the western provinces.

Along with deporting Kurds *from* Diyarbekir, the CUP also ordered non-Kurdish Muslims deported *to* that province. This two-track policy would expedite the Turkification process. Most of these settlers were Bosnian Muslims, Bulgarian Turks, and Albanian Muslims who had fled the war and persecutions in the Balkans. Another group of settlers were refugees from Bitlis and Van, the Turkish ones being filtered out for immediate settlement in Diyarbekir. At first the settler-deportees were lodged in the Sincariye seminary, where other poor and miserable Diyarbekirites were temporarily housed as well.[72] These settlers were to be housed in the empty Syriac and Armenian villages, mostly on the Diyarbekir plain. Some were moved north and settled in Palu, others were settled on the Mardin plain. Beginning in the summer of 1915, the settlement policy continued until the end of the war.

The settlers who were deported to Diyarbekir were Muslims who had sought asylum in the Ottoman Empire after the Balkan wars. Many of them had lived in Istanbul in shabby dwellings, impoverished and traumatized. When the war broke out, the CUP activated its plan for ethnic reorganization and the settlers were incorporated in it. The Albanians were but one group to be deported and settled. In June 1915 the İAMM ordered their 'scattered settlement in order for their mother-tongue and national traditions to be extinguished quickly'.[73] The Albanians were to be settled all over the empire, including Diyarbekir province.[74] The Bosnian refugees were to be settled in Diyarbekir as well. On 30 June 1915 the İAMM ordered 181 Bosnian families temporarily residing in Konya deported to Diyarbekir and settled in its 'empty villages'.[75] The next day, the deportation and settlement of ethnic Turks from Bulgaria and Greece was ordered from İAMM headquarters.[76]

In the meantime, the genocidal persecution of the Diyarbekir Christians was raging in full force. While the Armenians and Syriacs were being massacred, the Muslim settlers were on their way. However, preparations were needed in Diyarbekir in order to lodge the settlers successfully. On 17 June 1915 the İAMM headquarters reiterated its request for economic and geographic data on the emptied Armenian villages of Diyarbekir. In order to send settlers to the province, the local capacity to absorb immigrants had to be determined.[77] A week later it ordered educational commodities to be provided for the settlers:

> It is necessary to appropriate the schools of the towns and villages that have been emptied of Armenians to Muslim immigrants to be settled there. However, the present

---

[71] 'Muhacirîn', in: *İleri*, 10 April 1920.
[72] The Sincariye medrese presently serves as the 'Museum of Archaeology and Ethnography' in Diyarbekir city.
[73] BOA, DH.ŞFR 54/216, İAMM to Konya, 28 June 1915.
[74] BOA, DH.ŞFR 54/246, İAMM to Diyarbekir, 6 June 1915.
[75] BOA, DH.ŞFR 54/246, İAMM to Konya, 30 June 1915.
[76] BOA, DH.ŞFR 54/246, İAMM to Diyarbekir, 1 July 1915.
[77] BOA, DH.ŞFR 54/39, İAMM to Diyarbekir, 17 June 1915.

value of the buildings, the amount and value of the educational materials needs to be registered and sent to the department of general recordkeeping.[78]

This national order was a warrant for the seizure of all Ottoman-Armenian schools and their conversion into Ottoman-Turkish schools. School benches, blackboards, book cabinets, and even paper and pens were allocated to the yet-to-arrive settlers. The Commission for Abandoned Properties was assigned to carry out this operation in Diyarbekir.[79]

The CUP intended the deportation and settlement of Albanians, Bosnians, and Turks to be a one-way trip into Diyarbekir province. Whether coming in from the west or east, non-Kurdish settlers were expected to 'Turkify' the province. Turkish refugees from Bayezid and Diyadin (Ararat region) were selected from mixed convoys and directly settled in Silvan. Their livelihood was financed from the 'abandoned property budget'.[80] When non-Kurdish Ottoman refugees arrived in Diyarbekir from Bitlis, they were the only ones who were allowed to be settled in the provincial hinterland. They were Turkophone Ottomans and were therefore earmarked as 'Turks' by the CUP. Only in exceptional situations were the refugees to be sent forth to Urfa, Antep, and Maraş.[81] For example, Talaat personally took care that Muş deputy İlyas Sami and Genç deputy Mehmed Efendi were settled with their families in Diyarbekir city.[82] The AMMU systematically set aside 'abandoned property' for these settlers. In September 1916 it ordered 'abandoned buildings in Diyarbekir assigned to Turkish refugees coming from Van and Bitlis'.[83] The CUP probably considered it very important that the settlers remained in the province, considering that they reiterated this over and over. On 9 November 1916 the AMMU warned provincial authorities 'to prevent by any means that the Turkish settlers in the province be moved to other regions'.[84] Four days later the order was repeated 'with special emphasis'.[85] Even after the Russian army had disintegrated and retreated in 1917 and when the Ottoman army swept all the way into Baku, Turkish refugees in Diyarbekir were not allowed to return to their native regions. The order was repeated in March 1918[86] and in April 1918.[87] The German official Von Lüttichau saw that those settlers who secretly attempted to return to their native regions 'perished by the hundreds on the road back home, because they had no bread'.[88]

The information on the settlements of the Muslim settlers in the districts and towns of Diyarbekir province is sparse. Little field work has been conducted as to

---

[78] BOA, DH.ŞFR 54/101, İAMM to provinces, 22 June 1915.
[79] BOA, DH.ŞFR 54/331, İAMM to Diyarbekir, 7 July 1915.
[80] BOA, DH.ŞFR 59/7, İAMM to Diyarbekir, 14 December 1915.
[81] BOA, DH.ŞFR 61/121, İAMM to Diyarbekir, 26 February 1916.
[82] BOA, DH.ŞFR 61/139, Talaat to Diyarbekir, 28 February 1916.
[83] BOA, DH.ŞFR 67/174, AMMU to Diyarbekir, 3 September 1916.
[84] BOA, DH.ŞFR 69/219, AMMU to Diyarbekir, 9 November 1916.
[85] BOA, DH.ŞFR 69/248, AMMU to Diyarbekir, 13 November 1916.
[86] BOA, DH.ŞFR 85/262, AMMU to Diyarbekir, 28 March 1918.
[87] BOA, DH.ŞFR 86/46, AMMU to Third Army Commander, 13 April 1918.
[88] PAAA, R14104, Karl Axenfeld to Embassy, 18 October 1918.

whether the settlers remained in the designated towns and villages, or if they migrated elsewhere. That they were allotted Armenian property can be established beyond reasonable doubt. Already in December 1915, Vice-Governor İbrahim Bedreddin requested 2000 Turkish Lira for settling the Turks, explicitly on 'abandoned property' (*emval-i metruke*).[89] An Armenian survivor recalled how, in the late summer of 1915, Turks were settled in Palu. Local officials saw to it that the settlers were given the best houses of the deported Armenians.[90] According to a native of Palu, in the Republican period Palu town had a Zaza, a Kurdish, and a Turkish neighbourhood. The latter neighbourhood was populated by 'immigrants' (*muhacir*), most of them Pomacs from Thrace.[91] Three weeks after the Qarabash massacre the İAMM ordered 'the settlement of the immigrants, the confiscation of movables and pack animals, and the reporting of the population settled in emptied Armenian villages'.[92] Colonel Cemilpaşazâde Mustafa took control of Qarabash as Pomacs and Kurds were settled in that village.[93] In Kabiye, all property of the autochtonous Christians was seized and assigned to the settlers: vineyards, watermelon fields, agricultural implements, and the carrier pigeons. The few survivors who dared to return to their village were chased out by the Muslim settlers.[94] Eqsor village, on the Mardin plain, became a command post for the German army in 1917. The Germans demolished the Syriac Catholic church and built houses with its solid stones, settling Kurdish refugees from the Karahisar region in the village.[95] The village of Tell Ermen, the Christian population of which had been integrally massacred in July 1915, was repopulated with Circassians and Chechens. Since the settlers already had ploughs and oxes, all they needed for subsistence farming was seed. The Ministry of War was ordered to provide the requisite seed, distributing 1000 cups of barley and 300 cups of wheat from storage depots to the settlers.[96] When the Chechen population surpassed Tell Ermen's capacity, the construction of a new village for the Chechens was ordered in September 1918.[97] An assessment of the settlement of these communities in Diyarbekir province would produce rather ambivalent results. On the one hand they met with hardship as they had difficulties acclimatizing to the hot Mesopotamian climate, while on the other they were protected and well provided for by the Ottoman government, and later by the Turkish Republic.

---

[89] BCA, 272.74/64.2.5, Diyarbekir vice-governor İbrahim Bedreddin to Interior Ministry, 27 December 1915. This document seems to have strayed into the Republican archives, where it was found.

[90] Vahé Mamas Kitabdjian (ed.), 'Récit de Garabed Farchian, né à Palou en 1906 ou 1907', reproduced in: Yves Ternon, *Mardin 1915: Anatomie pathologique d'une destruction* (special issue of the Revue d'Histoire Arménienne Contemporaine 4, 2002), 288.

[91] Süleyman Yapıcı, *Palu: Tarih-Kültür-İdari ve Sosyal Yapı* (Elazığ: Şark Pazarlama, 2002), 208–11.

[92] BOA, DH.ŞFR 53/242, İAMM to Diyarbekir, 5 June 1915.

[93] Abed Mshiho Na'man Qarabashi, *Dmo Zliho: Vergoten Bloed: Verhalen over de gruweldaden jegens Christenen in Turkije en over het leed dat hun in 1895 en in 1914–1918 is aangedaan* (Glanerbrug, The Netherlands: Bar Hebraeus, 2002, transl. George Toro and Amill Gorgis), 85.

[94] Otto Jastrow (ed.), *Die mesopotamisch-arabischen Qltu-Dialekte* (Wiesbaden: Kommissionsverlag Franz Steiner GmbH, 1981), vol. II, *Volkskundliche Texte in Elf Dialekten*, 346.

[95] Ternon, *Mardin 1915*, 162.

[96] BOA, DH.İUM E-26/9, 27 December 1916.

[97] BOA, DH.ŞFR 91/197, AMMU to Diyarbekir, 22 September 1918.

CUP social engineering came to a halt only with the end of the war. In October 1918 the Ottoman Empire suffered a catastrophic defeat when all of its front lines disintegrated, triggering a sudden implosion of the army. On 30 October 1918 the parties signed a truce that sanctioned unconditional surrender.[98] Paralysed by panic and defeatism, that next night the inner circle of the CUP burnt suitcases full of documents, disbanded the CUP as a political party, and fled on a German submarine to Odessa.[99] The power vacuum was filled by a new cabinet led by the liberal Freedom and Coalition Party, the CUP's sworn enemy. They ruled the Ottoman Empire during the armistice (1918–1923) as long as the Istanbul government wielded sufficient actual power in the imperial heartland.[100] The very day after their rise to power, the liberals immediately began reversing CUP policies: Armenians and Kurds were encouraged to return, orphans were allowed to go back to their families, and most importantly, the Ottoman press broadly exposed and discussed CUP war crimes. But with the resurrection of the CUP in Anatolia this process of reckoning would soon come to an end.

When the CUP dissolved itself in 1918, it continued functioning under other names and succeeded in launching Mustafa Kemal to organize the Anatolian resistance it had planned since 1914. After a transition process many of the CUP's most diligent social engineers ended up working for Mustafa Kemal's Republican People's Party (RPP). The resurrection of Young Turk elites gave rise to the establishment of a modern dictatorship of repressive rule, driven by devotion to the tenets of a Gökalpist ideology, a set of ideas and goals that assumed the mystical character of religious doctrine.[101] As such, the Greco-Turkish and Armeno-Turkish wars (1919–23) were in essence processes of state formation that represented a continuation of ethnic unmixing and exclusion of Ottoman Christians from Anatolia. The subsequent proclamation of a Turkish nation state on 29 October 1923 was more of an intermezzo than a start or an end. Its analytical use for the historiography of the Young Turk era has been convincingly proven shaky, due to compelling continuities in power structure, ideology, cadre, and population policy.[102] No matter how thorough Young Turk social engineering was between 1913 and 1923, it was not the end to ethnic

---

[98] John Keegan, *The First World War* (New York: Vintage, 1998), 415; Erik-Jan Zürcher, 'The Ottoman Empire and the Armistice of Moudros', in: Hugh Cecil and Peter H. Liddle (eds.), *At the Eleventh Hour: Reflections, Hopes, and Anxieties at the Closing of the Great War, 1918* (London: Leo Cooper, 1998), 266–75.

[99] Şevket S. Aydemir, *Makedonya'dan Orta Asya'ya Enver Paşa* (Istanbul: Remzi, 1972), vol. II (1908–14), 497.

[100] Tarık Zafer Tunaya, *Türkiye'de Siyasal Partiler*, vol. 2, *Mütareke Dönemi* (Istanbul: İletişim, 1997), 29–61.

[101] Erik-Jan Zürcher, *The Unionist Factor: The Rôle of the Committee of Union and Progress in the Turkish National Movement 1905–1926* (Leiden: Brill, 1984); Paul Dumont, 'The Origins of Kemalist Ideology', in: Jacob M. Landau (ed.), *Atatürk and the Modernization of Turkey* (Boulder, CO: Westview Press, 1984), 25–44; Sabri M. Akural, 'Ziya Gökalp: The Influence of his Thought on Kemalist Reforms' (unpublished Ph.D. thesis, Indiana University, 1979); M. Şükrü Hanioğlu, 'Garbcilar: Their Attitudes Toward Religion and Their Impact on the Official Ideology of the Turkish Republic', in: *Studia Islamica* 86 (1997), 133–58.

[102] Erik-Jan Zürcher, *Een Geschiedenis van het Moderne Turkije* (Nijmegen: Sun, 1995), 7–8, 271.

homogenization. Untroubled by restraints of any kind, it now continued behind the tightly closed curtains of national sovereignty.[103]

The continuity of discourse and practice of the Kemalist regime in relation to the CUP regime did not take long to manifest itself. Well before Kemalist population politics became well articulated and programmatic, ad hoc and pre-emptive deportations were used to serve the purpose of preventing trouble. Mustafa Kemal, a skilled and opportunist orator who tuned his words to his audience, held speeches and harboured opinions that were often mutually incompatible. In his declarations for foreign consumption, he reiterated time and again that his regime would respect the rights of the minorities, whereas behind closed doors he actively pursued a policy that was manifestly different. His reassuring principle articulated to Kurdish elites that the new Turkey would be a state of Turks and Kurds was disingenuous as well.[104] Already in early 1921, amidst bitter warfare, Mustafa Kemal personally signed a decree ordering 'the deportation of the Milli and Karakeçi tribes from Diyarbekir province to Thrace and their homes given to refugees for settlement'.[105] These policies were harbingers of the future. After his official appropriation of power in 1923, Mustafa Kemal would continue the CUP's policies of persecution and deportation with equal vigour and focus.

1925: PHASE TWO

One aspect of the 1923 establishment of the Turkish Republic was the naturalization of the 'geo-body' of the Turkish nation state: the rectangular shape of the state relocated Diyarbekir province, formerly a centre of economic, political, and cultural activity, to a nation state's periphery. Territoriality and ethnicity were two closely related phenomena in the Young Turk mind and needed to be prioritized in Young Turk population policies and ethnic homogenization. Spatial planning therefore was not only an aspect of 'modernity' but, in the Young Turks' words, had to 'dismember Kurdish territorial unity' (*Kürt arazi vahdetini parçalamak*).[106] The deportation of Kurds away from the eastern provinces and settlement of Turks into the eastern provinces was a prime component of these policies.

The Kemalist abolitions of the sultanate and caliphate in 1923 triggered many different responses throughout Turkey.[107] For Kurdish elites the frontal attack on

---

[103] Donald Bloxham, 'Changing Perceptions of State Violence: Turkey's "Westward" Development through Anglo-Saxon Eyes', in: Richard Littlejohns and Sara Soncini (eds.), *Myths of Europe* (Amsterdam: Rodopi, 2007), 223–34.

[104] Andrew Mango, 'Atatürk and the Kurds', in: Sylvia Kedourie (ed.), *Seventy-Five Years of the Turkish Republic* (London: Routledge, 2000), 1–25; Robert Olson, 'Kurds and Turks: Two Documents Concerning Kurdish Autonomy in 1923 and 1923', in: *Journal of South Asian and Middle Eastern Studies* 15, no. 2 (1991), 20–31.

[105] BCA, 30.18.1.1/2.29.7, decree dated 17 January 1921.

[106] Faik Bulut, *Kürt Sorununa Çözüm Arayışları* (Istanbul: Ozan, 1998), 185–9.

[107] Gavin D. Brockett, 'Collective Action and the Turkish Revolution: Towards a Framework for the Social History of the Atatürk Era, 1923–1938', in: Sylvia Kedourie (ed.), *Turkey Before and After Atatürk: Internal and External Affairs* (London: Frank Cass, 1999), 44–66.

Islam was perceived as an eschatological intrusion into the collective identity of the Kurds, the state, and the fraternity between Muslim groups.[108] A group of Kurdish elites united in a 1924 conference of a clandestine organization called 'Freedom' (*Azadî*) to discuss the Kurdish issue. During the congress, consensus was reached on organizing a widespread, coordinated campaign of resistance in the eastern provinces starting from May 1925.[109] Now, preparations were undertaken for a large-scale resistance movement that would transcend the local and engulf the entire eastern provinces. The ambitious plan was in its planning phase when, remembering Mustafa Kemal's promises to the Kurds, on 1 August 1924 a Kurdish delegation petitioned government officials in Diyarbekir for moderate claims of Kurdish local autonomy.[110] The government ignored their demands, and distrust simmered on for several months until the Kurds ran out of patience. A local grab for power in the small town of Beytüşşebab, east of Diyarbekir, was organized under auspices of Colonel Xalîd Beg Cibranî (1882–1925).[111] The initiative failed and its leaders were arrested. Although at that time the movement was being planned by the Freedom group, the arrest of Colonel Xalîd Beg was the last straw for many. This Kurdish resistance to Young Turk policies was based on a broad spectrum of Kurdish elites: tribesmen, pious clergy, atheist intellectuals, village elders, Hamidiye military, but also ordinary peasants and tribesmen.[112] The leaders of the resistance capitalized on aggravating grievances as Kurdish discontent with twelve years of Young Turk rule now translated into openly violent resistance.

The general revolt erupted prematurely in the Piran district, north of Diyarbekir, on 13 February 1925. During a routine search gendarmes were engaged in a gunbattle with a group loyal to Sheikh Mehmed Said (1865–1925), member of a Zaza family originally from Piran and revered sheikh of the Naqshbandi Sufi order.[113] The gendarmes were fired on and a local outburst quickly spread in the region as Sheikh Said skillfully organized the resistance with the assistance of experienced Kurdish military officers who had served in the Ottoman army during the First World War, as well as powerful chieftains of large tribes. His declaration of war against the regime reveals a complex mix of motives for the resistance:

[108] Hamit Bozarslan, 'Kurdish Nationalism in Turkey: From Tacit Contract to Rebellion (1919–1925)', in: Abbas Vali (ed.), *Essays on the Origins of Kurdish Nationalism* (Costa Mesa, CA: Mazda Publishers, 2003), 163–90.

[109] Martin van Bruinessen, *Agha, Shaikh and State: The Social and Political Structures of Kurdistan* (London: Zed, 1992), 280.

[110] Osman Aydın, *Kürt Ulus Hareketi 1925* (n.p: Weşanên Weqfa Şêx Seid, 1994), 50. NAUK, FO 424/261, 44, no. 63, Henderson to MacDonald, 16 September 1924.

[111] Xalîd Beg was a chieftain of the large Cibran tribe and a graduate of the Military Academy in Istanbul. He had served in the Hamidiye regiments under Sultan Abdulhamid II, served on two fronts in the First World War earning decorations and promotions, and after the First World War spearheaded a Kurdish-nationalist group of officers called *Azadî* (Freedom). Most significantly, he was Sheikh Said's brother-in-law. Cemil Gündoğan, *1924 Beytüşşebap İsyanı ve Şeyh Sait Ayaklanmasına Etkileri* (Istanbul: Komal, 1994).

[112] Robert Olson, *The Emergence of Kurdish Nationalism and the Sheikh Said Rebellion, 1880–1925* (Austin, TX: University of Texas Press, 1989).

[113] See his biographies: Adem Karataş, *Ve Alim ve Mücahid ve Şehid ve Şeyh Said* (Konya: Sena, 1993); İlhami Aras, *Adım Şeyh Said* (Istanbul: İlke, 1992).

For several years we have been able to read in the newspapers and official documents about the oppression, insults, hatred, and enmity that the Turk Republic [*sic*] accords to the Kurdish notables and dynasties. There is a lot of evidence available from authentic sources that they want to subject the Kurdish elite to the same treatment to which they subjected the Armenians and as a matter of fact, this subject was discussed and decided in parliament last year.[114]

Elsewhere Sheikh Said bitterly condemned the Young Turk regime as having 'occupied our country and reduced it to ruins', as a result of which '[n]ever in its history has Kurdistan been in such a state of devastation'. For the sheikh it was 'obvious that the Turks are oppressive and vile towards the Kurds. They do not honour their promises. We must teach them a lesson so the entire world understands their hypocrisy, bloodshed and barbarism'.[115] It seems that the conflict had a pragmatic and an ideological aspect. On the one hand, the Kurds were fed up with Young Turk persecution; on the other hand the secular and Turkish nature of the new regime was despised and fundamentally antithetical to the Islamic and Kurdish nature of the sheikh's identity.[116] According to one of his grandsons, the sheikh considered the Kemalists 'betrayers of Islam' against which resistance was every Muslim's duty.[117]

With surprising military prowess, Sheikh Said's forces, estimated at 15,000 infantry and cavalry, conquered large parts of the eastern countryside.[118] Provincial towns were stormed and state officials, including district governors and public prosecutors, were arrested. By late February, the northern parts of Diyarbekir province were in Said's hands, with one front extending south-west to Siverek and another east to the city of Muş, which they were unable to take. More than 50,000 Turkish soldiers, 'a good half of the Turkish army',[119] were mobilized and the airfield near Harput road, on a patch of confiscated Armenian property, was used for aerial bombardments of the Kurds.[120] Sheikh Said then installed his headquarters in a village just north of Diyarbekir city and personally took the strategic lead of the front. But government forces were anticipating the attack. General Hakkı Mürsel Bakü Pasha (1881–1945) of the Seventh Army, General Mustafa Muğlalı (1882–1951), and General Kâzım İnanç Pasha (1881–1938) of the Third Army were in charge of the defence of Diyarbekir. These experienced

---

[114] Ahmet Süreyya Örgeevren, *Şeyh Sait İsyanı ve Şark İstiklâl Mahkemesi* (Istanbul: Temel, 2002), 31–2.

[115] Aydın, *Kürt Ulus Hareketi 1925*, 154–7.

[116] Mustafa İslamoğlu, *Şeyh Said Ayaklanması* (Istanbul: Denge, 1991).

[117] Kasım Fırat, 'Röportaj', in: *Dava* 8 (1990), 8–16.

[118] For a detailed reconstruction of the military operations from the perspective of the government, see: Reşat Hallı, *Türkiye Cumhuriyeti'nde Ayaklanmalar: 1924–1938* (Ankara: T.C. Genelkurmay Harp Tarihi Baskanlığı Resmî Yayınları, 1972), chapter 3.

[119] NAUK, FO 424/262, 169, no.175/1, Harenc to Lindsay, 2 June 1925.

[120] The army used 12 airplanes in the bombing campaign. Robert Olson, 'The Sheikh Said Rebellion: Its Impact on the Development of the Turkish Air Force', in: *The Journal of Kurdish Studies* 1 (1995), 77–84; idem, 'The Kurdish Rebellions of Sheikh Said (1925), Mt. Ararat (1930), and Dersim (1937–8): Their Impact on the Development of the Turkish Air Force and on Kurdish and Turkish Nationalism', in: *Die Welt des Islams* 40, no. 1 (2000), 67–94.

men were veterans of both Balkan wars, as well as the First World War and the War of Liberation. They declared martial law and a strict curfew for all residents in the city, ordered the city gates to be closed, and sealed off the city hermetically. In the night of 6 to 7 March 1925, Sheikh Said's cavalry of 5000 men laid siege to Diyarbekir. The Kurds attacked the city at all four gates simultaneously but were repelled with machine gun fire and mortar grenades.

Despite both heavy military engagement and shrewd tactics by special operatives to penetrate the city walls, Diyarbekir was an ancient citadel and very difficult to take. From their vantage point in the many towers Turkish officers had an excellent view of the situation on the ground. The fighting went on all night and by the time the Kurds broke contact and retreated the next morning, the grounds around the city were strewn with dead bodies. A second wave of attacks failed as well, and by 11 March the siege was lifted.[121]

In the end, Diyarbekir never fell. When fresh troops arrived from Western Turkey, the pendulum now swung back in favour of the government. On 26 March the Turkish army launched a counter-offensive, shattering the Kurdish forces and causing many to abandon their positions and flee. At this point some Kurdish tribes refused joining the conflict as desertion too became a serious problem. As the resistance collapsed, many fighters saw no other choice than surrendering to government forces. Sheikh Said now realized the battle was lost and retreated, according to one account to regroup in the north-eastern district of Hani, and according to another account to flee to Iran.[122] Said had no other choice than to move east, where he took Silvan, with the Turkish army following him at a distance. There, the sheikh was surrounded by Turkish forces and the Murat river, at that time impassable due to heavy rainfall. When the government succeeded in exploiting intertribal rivalries and mustering in important Kurdish chieftains such as Cemîlê Çeto of the Pencînar tribe and Emînê Perîxanê of the Raman tribe (see Chapter 2), it compounded the difficulties for Sheikh Said. His ranks diluted, his morale sunk, and he was arrested with his companions when attempting to cross a strategically important bridge on the morning of 15 April 1925.[123] Together with the execution of Colonel Xalîd Beg Cibranî,[124] the day before, his capture meant that the Kurdish resistance had been smothered.

When the hostilities began, the government initially announced martial law in the eastern provinces on 21 February 1925 for one month, as all eyes turned to the relatively moderate Prime Minister Ali Fethi Okyar (1880–1943). Okyar addressed parliament on 24 February and declared his government 'determined to take all kinds of measures to protect the Turk Republic [*sic*]' and went on to promise that 'those who prepared and incited this rebellion will be punished with the heaviest measures and with force'.[125]

[121] *Genelkurmay Belgelerinde Kürt İsyanları* (Istanbul: Kaynak, 1992), vol. 1, 163–5.
[122] Nurer Uğurlu, *Kürt milliyetiliği: Kürtler ve Şeyh Sait İsyanı* (Istanbul: Örgün, 2006); Yaşar Kalafat, *Şark Meselesi Işığında Şeyh Sait Olayı, Karakteri, Dönemindeki İç ve Dış Olaylar* (Ankara: Boğaziçi, 1992).
[123] *Genelkurmay Belgelerinde Kürt İsyanları* (Istanbul: Kaynak, 1992), vol. 1, 178–91.
[124] Demir Özlü, *Sokaklarda Bir Avlu* (Istanbul: Dünya, 2004), 43–9, 'Cıbranlı Halit Bey'in Ölümü.'
[125] Behçet Cemal, *Şeyh Sait İsyanı* (Istanbul: Sel, 1955), 46.

The radical wing of the Republican People's Party (RPP) was not satisfied with Okyar's response to the Sheikh Said movement, calling for harsher measures and subjecting Okyar to severe criticism, to which he answered: 'The measures we have taken are sufficient, I will not bathe my hands in blood with unnecessary violence'.[126] But the hardliners were still not satisfied and declaimed provocatively, 'Are you afraid of a handful of Kurds?'[127] The tide would turn with the intervention of Mustafa Kemal, who summoned his loyal subordinate Mustafa İsmet İnönü (1884–1973) from a brief vacation on the Istanbul islands. On arrival in Ankara, Kemal personally picked up İnönü's family at the train station in Ankara and briefed him on the situation, also providing directives as to how to deal with the event.[128] By calling in İnönü, a hardliner, Kemal gave a clear sign to the Okyar government that he was discontented with their approach. On 2 March 1925 the RPP held a meeting demanding the resignation of Okyar, who buckled under the pressure and resigned.[129]

At this point we need to point out that among Sheikh Said's men were many disgruntled Kurdish tribesmen, who considered the Young Turk regime oppressive and therefore illegitimate, and were convinced they could resist it only with violence. The regime did not take their demands seriously but responded with violence and nurtured a discourse that delegitimized the Kurdish movement by baptizing it a 'rebellion'. According to one expert of war, this term 'is usually sought out by insurgents in search of legitimacy, and denied by incumbents who label their opponents "bad guys", bandits, criminals, subversives, or terrorists—and describe the war as banditry, terrorism, delinquent subversion, and other cognate terms.'[130] So too, in Young Turk jargon these Kurds were systematically dehumanized as 'bandits' (*şaki*), 'villains' (*câni*), 'thugs' (*haydut*), or 'bands' (*çete*), to be dealt with only through 'destruction' (*imha*).

The 'rebellion' gave radical Young Turks a pretext to silence all criticism of the press and the opposition.[131] They exploited the incident and endowed it with propagandistic value by fuelling the panic and linking it to larger narrative frameworks about the ostensible innate insubordination of Kurds. Built into their system of domination was the tendency to proclaim its own normalcy. Thus, to acknowledge resistance as a mass phenomenon would have amounted to an acknowledgement of the possibility that something might have been wrong with that system. On 3 March 1925, the day after its inauguration, the İnönü government proclaimed the Law on the Maintenance of Order.[132] It gave the government sweeping authority to wield power as it saw fit. At the same time, the government prolonged

---

[126] Ali Fuat Cebesoy, *Siyasi Hatıralar* (Istanbul: Vatan Neşriyatı, 1957), vol. 1, 144.

[127] Cemal Kutay, *Üç Devirde Bir Adam: Fethi Okyar* (Istanbul: Tercüman, 1980), 369.

[128] İsmet İnönü, *Hatıralar* (Ankara: Bilgi, 1987), vol. 2, 198.

[129] Osman Okyar and Mehmet Seyitdanlıoğlu (ed.), *Fethi Okyar'ın Anıları: Atatürk, Okyar ve Çok Partili Türkiye* (Ankara: Türkiye İş Bankası Kültür Yayınları, 1997), 41.

[130] Stathis N. Kalyvas, *The Logic of Violence in Civil War* (New York: Cambridge University Press, 2006), 17.

[131] Metin Toker, *Şeyh Sait ve İsyanı* (Ankara: Akis, 1968), 127–33.

[132] The law was accompanied by the 'Directive on Censorship to be Applied in the Eastern Region under Martial Law' which silenced all significant publications in the eastern provinces. Mete Tunçay, *Türkiye Cumhuriyetinde Tek Parti Yönetiminin Kurulması 1923–1931* (Ankara: Yurt Yayınları, 1995).

martial law and reinstated the Independence Tribunals, one in Ankara, another in Diyarbekir. These courts had unleashed a campaign of terror during the Greco-Turkish war by executing hundreds of deserters, and now again held unrestricted authority to enforce the law. At the same time, the whole political spectrum ranging from leftist to liberal and conservative opposition was silenced with the closure of their parties and prohibition of newspapers and periodicals.[133] Okyar was removed and assigned to the Turkish embassy in Paris, far away from domestic politics.

The crackdown on (potential) adversaries was so thorough that even provincial Young Turk loyalists were targeted. Pirinççizâde Aziz Feyzi (1879–1933), for example, had been working for the Republican People's Party from day one and during the siege had supported the government from within the city, dropping propaganda leaflets from airplanes.[134] In June 1925 he was accused of having backed the Sheikh Said movement because his brother-in-law was caught up in it. His adversaries were intent upon implying his participation in the 'rebellion' and suggested his appearance before an Independence Tribunal. Feyzi denied the charges, declaring his loyalty to the party and adherence to its ideological principles in a public session. Finally, he was considered more useful alive as a local supporter and sent back to Diyarbekir.[135] Pirinççizâde Sıdkı, notorious mass murderer of 1915, came under suspicion too when one of his friends was charged with supporting Sheikh Said.[136] The conspiracy seemed to be everywhere, and Kemalist paranoia was rampant in the spring of 1925.

This development, the abolition of parliamentary politics and *trias politica*, marked a caesura in which a radical core of men around Mustafa Kemal assumed dictatorial powers in the country. Again, Young Turk radicalism reigned superior. As a result, especially in May 1925, this radicalization at the centre reverberated in the eastern provinces, as a wave of mass violence swept across Diyarbekir province.[137] In a country-wide circular of 25 February 1925, the government had already promised 'severe measures' against the insurgents, though repeatedly declaring the local population to be essentially 'naive, innocent, and patriotic'.[138] The counter-insurgency warfare that followed after the reconquest of Diyarbekir province was total: villages were torched, civilians as well as combatants summarily executed. The killings followed the methods of the destruction of the Armenians, a decade ago in the same region. Upon invading a village, the villagers were routinely disarmed, stripped of their belongings (including gold teeth), and collectively tied by their hands with rope. They were then taken to trenches and cliffs, where they

---

[133] Erik-Jan Zürcher, *Political Opposition in the Early Turkish Republic: The Progressive Republican Party, 1924–1925* (Leiden: Brill, 1991).

[134] Hasan Hişyar Serdî, *Görüş ve Anılarım 1907–1985* (Istanbul: Med, 1994), 226.

[135] NAUK, FO 424/263, 16, no.16, Hoare to Chamberlain, 9 August 1925.

[136] Ahmet Süreyya Örgeevren, *Şeyh Sait İsyanı ve Şark İstiklal Mahkemesi: Vesikalar, Olaylar, Hatıralar* (Istanbul: Temel, 2002), 149.

[137] Hamit Bozarslan, 'Kurdish Nationalism under the Kemalist Republic: Some Hypotheses', in: Mohammed M.A. Ahmed and Michael Gunter (eds.), *The Evolution of Kurdish Nationalism* (Costa Mesa, CA: Mazda, 2007), 36–51.

[138] Interior Ministry to all provinces, 25 February 1925, quoted in: Hasip Koylan, *Kürtler ve Şark İsyanları I: Şeyh Sait İsyanı* (Ankara: T.C. İçişleri Bakanlığı Yayını, 1946), 171.

were executed with machine guns. Another method was cramming people into haylofts and sheds and setting fire to the buildings, burning the people alive.[139]

Two men in particular were the executioners of both clear orders and vague directives from above. Major Ali Haydar (1884–?)[140] was assigned to pacify the north-eastern districts of Pasur (later renamed Kulp), Hazro, and Lice. He inflicted cruelty upon the population to wreck morale and produce quick results in order to receive approval from his superior, General Mürsel Bakü. When his troops were ambushed and decimated in one battle, he abandoned his men and fled to Lice with his four bodyguards. Enraged and frustrated, he unleashed terror in broad daylight in the small town. At his arrival in Lice he randomly arrested seventeen men from the market, took them away to a nearby ditch and had them shot dead one by one. He then moved on to the village of Serdê, a known hotbed of Sheikh Said adherents, and committed a second reprisal massacre. At least fifty-seven unarmed civilians were tied together with rope and mowed down with machine gun fire. The corpses were left to rot in the sun as Ali Haydar's units marched on to the next village. Acts of violence perpetrated by the Major's troops included stoning, beheading, and torture with hot irons and boiling water.[141] The Zirkî tribe of Lice was targeted for supporting Sheikh Said, and their villages (Bamitnî, Barsum, Zara, Matbur and Çaylarbaşı) were destroyed and the inhabitants murdered. The tribe's large mansion and cemetery were levelled, and all livestock was seized, slaughtered, and cooked as provisions for the soldiers. According to survivors, the same units that had destroyed the town's Armenian population a decade ago, had been sent to the Kurdish villages with similar instructions. This unit was known among the population as the 'butcher battalion' (*kasap taburu*).[142] The attack on certain tribes announced that the killings targeted certain categories associated with the enemy: according to official reports, in the Lice district Major Ali Haydar 'had annihilated most of the sheikhs'.[143]

In the north-western districts of Hani, Piran (later renamed Dicle), Palu, and Ergani, Major Ali Barut commanded the army units. Ali Barut became infamous for robbing his victims before killing them. In his districts too, indiscriminate massacres were committed. In the Palu district, they invaded the village of Gülüş-kür and robbed all the houses of their movable property, including cattle. One group of soldiers lashed together and murdered the inhabitants with bayonets, whereas another group burnt the village to the ground. In Erdürük, a large village of more than 100 households, a total of 200 people were crammed into a large stable and burnt alive. According to survivors, the nauseating smell of burnt human flesh lingered in the village for days. Even villages that had never joined Sheikh Said but

---

[139] Zinar Silopî (pseudonym of Cemilpaşazâde Kadri Bey), *Doza Kurdistan: Kürt Milletinin 60 Yıllık Esaretten Kurtuluş Savaşı Hatıraları* (Istanbul: Özge, 2001), 92.

[140] Halil Şimşek, *Geçmişten Günümüze Bingöl ve Doğu Ayaklanmaları* (Ankara: Kültür Bakanlığı, 2001), 85.

[141] Serdî, *Görüş ve Anılarım*, 254–7.

[142] Interview with Nihat Işık conducted by Şeyhmus Diken, published in: Şeyhmus Diken, *İsyan Sürgünleri* (Istanbul: İletişim, 2005), 259–61.

[143] *Genelkurmay Belgelerinde Kürt İsyanları* (Istanbul: Kaynak, 1992), vol. 1, 313.

stayed loyal to the government suffered the same fate. The villagers of Karaman, for example, welcomed the Turkish army with water and buttermilk, but its population was nevertheless massacred and its property seized.[144] As a result of this campaign of carnage, panic and disbelief spread throughout the countryside of northern Diyarbekir. People fled into the hills, caves, and mountain valleys to reach safety; in vain, because army units pursued them into these remote sites as well. According to official army reports, while hunting down a group of survivors on Çotela, a mountain just north of Pasur/Kulp, army units had slaughtered 450 people and burnt 60 villages, rendering the mountain bare of settlement.[145]

The massacres produced innumerable orphans. Hasan Hişyar Serdî (1907–85), secretary to Sheikh Said, was roaming the countryside with a group of Kurdish fighters as the number of orphans they picked up on the way grew more and more. When they entered a village where clearly a massacre had just been committed, a girl, sole survivor of the slaughter, was crying at her dead mother's breast. They took the child with them and delivered the orphans to a large cave where women provided care for survivors.[146] The Kurdish author Yaşar Kemal (1923–) was a toddler when his family fled from Van to Diyarbekir, and was further deported from Diyarbekir to Adana. In his memoirs he related the experiences of the child deportees: 'Children were swarming around, hungry, miserable, and naked.... They were roaming around like flocks'.[147] The Kurdish author and poet Musa Anter (1920–92) was still a child when one day he saw a group of women and children walk into their village. According to Anter, the 'miserable survivors were impoverished and malnourished'. When he ran towards the children to play with them, he marvelled at their language, which was Zazaki and incomprehensible to him. His mother clad and fed the traumatized families and sheltered them in the caves near the village.[148] When the violence halted in the early summer of 1925, the bodycount was considerable. Precise data is lacking, but according to one account, altogether 206 villages had been destroyed, 8758 houses burnt, and 15,200 people killed.[149]

Why were so many civilians killed? One report mentioned that a gendarmerie major who was on short leave from Diyarbekir told a friend that 'he was disgusted with the work he had had to do and that he wanted to be transferred. He had been in the eastern provinces all through the period of tranquilisation and was tired of slaughtering men, women and children'.[150] A British diplomat travelling in the region after the war noted about the killings,

---

[144] Ahmet Kahraman, *Kürt İsyanları: Tedip ve Tenkil* (Istanbul: Evrensel, 2003), 165, 176.
[145] Ibid., 170.
[146] Serdî, *Görüş ve Anılarım*, 246.
[147] Yaşar Kemal, *Yaşar Kemal Kendini Anlatıyor: Alain Bosquet ile Görüşmeler* (Istanbul: Yapı Kredi Yayınları, 1999), 22.
[148] Musa Anter, *Hatıralarım* (Istanbul: Avesta, 1999), 361.
[149] Abdul Rahman Ghassemlou, *Kurdistan and the Kurds* (Prague: Czechoslovak Academy of Sciences, 1965), 52.
[150] NAUK, FO 424/267, 125, no.72, Hoare to Chamberlain, 14 December 1927.

No doubt the repression of the 1925 rising was accomplished with a brutality which was not exceeded in any Armenian massacres. Whole villages were burnt or razed to the ground, and men, women and children killed. Turkish officers have recounted how they were repelled by such proceedings and yet felt obliged to do their duty. No doubt also that whenever there is any further attempt at rebellion it is repressed with an equally heavy hand.[151]

At least two explanations seem to account for the level of violence. First of all, Young Turk officers viewed the population of the eastern provinces as inherently treacherous and anti-Turkish, hence threats to security against which Turkish state and army personnel had to be permanently on guard. Such a colonial attitudinal climate would prove to be highly conducive to the harsh treatment of the civilian population of the east and the committing of atrocities. Second, Young Turk military officers had been in wars since 1911 and were thoroughly brutalized by 1925. The barbarization of warfare, manifesting itself in indiscriminate killings, was a legacy of the previous wars, especially the Balkan wars. These had been ethnic in scope and annihilatory in military ethic: in the Thracian theatres of war, battling the enemy had included massacring enemy civilians and destroying enemy villages. By 1925 this had become a customary practice and distinctions between combatants and non-combatants were hardly made.[152]

That the eastern provinces became a lawless enclave was attested to by the establishment of the Diyarbekir Independence Tribunal, which boiled down to a show trial of the Kurdish elite. The committee assigned to prosecuting Sheikh Said and his colleagues consisted of Young Turk bureaucrats, lawyers, and military officers such as chairman Mazhar Müfit Kansu (1873–1948), prosecutor Ahmet Süreyya Örgeevren (1888–1969), Ali Saip Ursavaş (1887–1939), Avni Doğan (1892–1965), and Lütfi Müfit Özdeş (1874–1940).[153] They arrived in Diyarbekir on 12 April 1925 and were taken to the citadel prison, where the Kurds had been incarcerated. The tone was set very early, when in a private discussion Özdeş told his colleague Örgeevren that the courts had to serve 'a specific national goal' for which it was necessary to 'surpass the law'. Nationalism interfered with and was superimposed on the rule of law. Prosecutor Örgeevren agreed and wired to Prime Minister İnönü about the Kurdish political elite that 'it is a most sacred objective for this spirit to die and be killed. Therefore all harmful persons that could become leaders in Kurdistan should absolutely not be pardoned'.[154] This ominous statement meant that the Kemalists would cast a wide net to rid society, not only of Kurdish intellectuals who indeed posed a threat, but of those who might do so in the future.

---

[151] NAUK, FO 424/272, 116, no.68, Edmonds to Henderson, 21 May 1930, 'Notes on a Tour to Diarbekir, Bitlis and Mush.'

[152] For a set of similar processes, see: George Kassimeris, *The Barbarisation of Warfare* (London: Hurst & Company, 2006).

[153] Ahmet Süreyya Örgeevren, *Şeyh Sait İsyanı ve Şark İstiklâl Mahkemesi* (Istanbul: Temel, 2002), 100–3.

[154] Ergün Aybars, *İstiklâl Mahkemeleri 1920–1923 / 1923–1927* (İzmir: Zeus, 2006), 194, 197.

By that time, blanket arrests of Kurdish elites were taking place. From as far as Istanbul intellectuals and community leaders had been arrested and sent to Diyarbekir (see Plate 7). Among these were thirteen members of the Society for the Advancement of Kurdistan along with dozens of intellectuals, many of whom never resisted the Kemalist regime. The defendants were not represented by defence lawyers, and were severely pressured and maltreated to provide names of Kurdish nationalists, upon which those people were declared co-conspirators and targeted as well. The first men executed were not the active participants of the actual movement but Istanbul's Kurdish elite. Five members of the Society for the Advancement of Kurdistan were brought to Diyarbekir, sentenced to death on 23 May 1925, and executed on 27 May. These included Dr. Fuad Berxo (1887–1925), who was fluent in five languages and had not even been in the region for years.[155] His friend Hizanizâde Kemal Fevzi (1891–1925) from Bitlis was a noted poet and journalist for Kurdish newspapers.[156] The most noted name was Seyid Abdülkadir (1851–1925),[157] chairman of the Society and leading Kurdish-nationalist intellectual. None of these men was affiliated with Sheikh Said, but all were hanged. Taken to the gallows in front of the Great Mosque with his father, Seyid Abdülkadir's son Seyid Mehmed acrimoniously promised a Pandora's box: 'The government has brought calamity on itself'.[158] The hanging of these men set off a long sequence of executions. One eye-witness was a child living in the Mountain Gate district when he saw a long line of gallows 'from the Mountain Gate to the Urfa Gate . . . every morning at wake-up we saw new people dangling from the gibbets'[159] (see Plate 8). Law had become a tool of power as the Diyarbekir trials developed into a travesty of justice. The elaborate set-up of the court only served to lend the proceedings an air of legality. In the end, countless innocent men were executed and walked to the gallows in shock and disbelief. The Diyarbekir court prosecuted a total of 5010 people, of whom 2779 were acquitted and 420 sentenced to the death penalty. The actual number of people put to death was much higher than this figure due to to the many extralegal and summary executions that followed in the months after.[160]

After his arrest, Sheikh Said was taken into custody in the notorious Diyarbekir prison. The reader will remember that only a decade ago the Armenian elite of Diyarbekir city had been incarcerated there (see Chapter 2). As was the case then, within prison walls arbitrary terror reigned. According to one eye witness, 'gendarmes would take Kurdish inmates from the prison to the banks of the Tigris, shoot them, and come back. Then the gendarmes would sell the silk belts of these Zaza young men in prison'.[161] During his trial, the sheikh made a calm impression

---

[155] Mehmet Bayrak (ed.), *Kürtler ve Ulusal-Demokratik Mücadeleleri: Gizli Belgeler-Araştırmalar-Notlar* (Ankara: Özge, 1993), 162–81.
[156] Malmîsanij, *Bitlisli Kemal Fevzi ve Kürt Örgütleri İçindeki Yeri* (Istanbul: Fırat, 1993), 82–7.
[157] İsmail Göldaş, *Kürdistan Teali Cemiyeti* (Istanbul: Doz, 1991), 16–21.
[158] Aybars, *İstiklâl Mahkemeleri*, 202.
[159] Interview with Ali Küçük (an Armenian convert formerly named Markar), conducted by Ahmet Kahraman, published in: Kahraman, *Kürt İsyanları*, 167.
[160] Aybars, *İstiklâl Mahkemeleri*, 228.
[161] Savaş Üstüngel (pseudonym of İsmail Bilen), *Savaş Yolu: Bir Türk Komünistinin Notları* (Sofia: Narodna Prosveta, 1958), 18.

and maintained his resistance to the regime. Although he repeatedly denied even knowing the Cemilpaşazâde brothers (noted Kurdish nationalists who were a thorn in the flesh of the Young Turks), the prosecutors insistently insinuated they had been working together for an independent Kurdistan.[162] In the end nothing the sheikh said mattered. In an interview with the sole remaining pro-government newspaper, prosecutor Örgeevren predicted that 'elements that had incited and created the rebellion' would be 'annihilated root and branch' so that the 'danger in the east' could be neutralized once and for all.[163] The judicial authorities had already determined Said's guilt and the actual trial, retributive rather than correctional, had as its main goal to present the accusation and the verdict to the observing public as an awe-inspiring example to the opposition and a warning to Kurds with defiant ambitions.

On 28 June 1925 Sheikh Said was sentenced to death with forty-seven of his adherents, including his son. One of the sentences was commuted to ten years in prison because the defendant was under 15 years of age.[164] On 29 June 1925, early in the morning Sheikh Said was taken to the Mountain Gate. Before execution he turned to prosecutor Ali Saip Ursavaş, smiled, and spoke his last words: 'I like you. But on Judgement Day we shall settle accounts'. The Sheikh stepped on the stool, the noose around his neck was tightened, and he was hanged. After his death, the others followed, as dozens of spectators watched the mass execution.[165] Said's remains were buried anonymously in a ditch dug below his gallows, to destroy his memory and to prevent the graves from becoming places of pilgrimage. Later, the Diyarbekir city council symbolically erected a statue of Mustafa Kemal Atatürk on the very spot where Sheikh Said had been hanged (see Chapter 5). None of this precluded Said from becoming a legend, many epic poems being written and laments sung in his honour.[166] Up to this day, his descendants are traumatized and vindictive because their (grand)father was executed and his remains had vanished without a trace.[167]

The massive resistance to Young Turk rule served to confirm the government's fears that Kurdish society was a potentially separatist threat that needed to be dealt with urgently. In their eyes, they had once again narrowly escaped losing the eastern provinces. Now, the Young Turk cohort was resolved to obviate once and for all any potential for secession in the eastern provinces. After the political radicalization of March 1925, Mustafa Kemal personally took the lead in arranging population politics in the eastern provinces. For him, the Sheikh Said movement in particular corroborated that Kurdish resistance to the regime depended on the organization by sheikhs and other religious leaders. A general crackdown on religious

---

[162] Örgeevren, *Şeyh Sait İsyanı*, 192, 200.

[163] *Vakit*, 19 June 1925.

[164] For a list of the names of those executed, see: Aybars, *İstiklâl Mahkemeleri*, 213–15.

[165] Ibid., 216. Örgeevren, *Şeyh Sait İsyanı*, 274–80.

[166] Rojvanê Civan, *Şeyh Said İsyanı: 1925 Büyük Kürt Ayaklanması* (n.p.: Özgürlük Yolu, 1990); Yılmaz Odabaşı, *Şeyh Said İsyanı: 1925 Kürt Ayaklanması: Destan* (Istanbul: Zîlan, 1991); Bayrak, *Kürtler*, 407–11.

[167] See articles written by his grandchildren: Kasım Fırat, 'Mazlum Halk Önderi Şeyh Sait', in: *Tevhid* (June 1991), 6–10; Lokman Polat, *Torina Şêx Seîd* (Stockholm: Çapa Yekem, 1993); Abdülmelik Fırat, *Fırat Mahzun Akar* (Istanbul: Avesta, 1996), 120–3.

brotherhoods followed the next summer. The devoted CUP veteran Hasan Tahsin Uzer (1878–1939) wrote a report entitled 'The Function of the Dervish Lodges in Kurdistan', advocating drastic measures to be taken against the Kurds. Most significantly, Uzer drew on his previous experiences as governor in the eastern provinces to lend authority to his argument 'to completely eradicate this social disease'.[168] Mustafa Kemal could hardly ignore these suggestions by his childhood friend from Salonica. On 30 November 1925 Law no. 677 decreed the closure and prohibition of lodges, shrines, and other forms of religious organization. Kemal legitimized this rigorous measure by arguing that 'in the face of the light that enlightenment, science, civilization nowadays radiates, the guidance of this or that sheikh can absolutely not be accepted in a civilized Turkish society'. According to Kemal, 'the Turkish Republic can never be a country of sheikhs, dervishes, disciples, adherents. The truest and most real path is the path of civilization'.[169] These words, spoken after having crushed a sheikh's resistance movement in the eastern provinces, were very soon followed by action.

On 8 September 1925 Mustafa Kemal personally authorized a special council to draft a comprehensive report on 'reforming Eastern Anatolia'. This 'Reform Council for the East' (Şark Islahat Encümeni) was chaired by İsmet İnönü, and major positions were held by military officers and government bureaucrats. The men solicited for writing the policy directives were the same Young Turk officials who had gained experience in this field. CUP members such as Şükrü Kaya (1883–1959), Mahmud Celal Bayar (1883–1986), and Mustafa Abdülhalik Renda (1881–1957), as well as military officers such as Lieutenant-General Kâzım Fikri Özalp (1882–1968), Interior Minister Lieutenant-Colonel Mehmet Cemil Uybadın (1880–1957), and Chief of Staff Marshal Mustafa Fevzi Çakmak (1876–1950).[170] Renda and Uybadın, who had travelled in the region, were assigned to write reports on which 'necessary measures' to take in shaping population politics in the eastern provinces. Their assignment, containing language of 'radical solutions' and 'final solutions', was the crux of Young Turk political thinking on the eastern provinces and foreboded more violence ahead. Although Mustafa Kemal's exhortations for radical measures in the east clarified the general direction state policy was to follow, they were barren of details. On the one hand, these exhortations constituted a *carte blanche* to the various Young Turks descending on the east, indicating that any restraints were now lifted. Ambitious young Kemalists now had to prove themselves capable of living up to the leader's rhetoric. On the other hand, Mustafa Kemal's epideictic oratory was an incitement to social engineers to produce proposals for policies that would concretize his general nationalist pronouncements into specific programs with clearly defined goals. Those who wrote proposals most attuned to Mustafa Kemal's wishes were rewarded with intensified powers to

---

[168] Mehmet Bayrak (ed.), *Açık-Gizli / Resmi-Gayrıresmi Kürdoloji Belgeleri* (Ankara: Özge, 1994), 183–93, at 191.
[169] Nimet Arsan (ed.), *Atatürk'ün Söylev ve Demeçleri* (Ankara: Türk Tarih Kurumu, 1959–1964), vol. II, 215.
[170] Bayrak, *Kürtler*, 481.

launch them. Those who displayed an organizational finesse became the instruments of these comprehensive policies.

Mustafa Abdülhalik Renda wrote his report within a week and presented it in Ankara on 14 September 1925. Renda had traversed the eastern provinces and had 'determined where the Kurds live and how many they are' and 'what language the population uses'. According to Renda, the registered population east of the Euphrates was 1,360,000 of which 993,000 were Kurds, 251,000 Turks and 117,600 Arabs. He charted the ethnic composition of the eastern provinces region by region, lamenting the 'dominant economic and linguistic position of the Kurds' and 'gradual growth of the Kurdish population' in most provinces, including Diyarbekir. Since 'the entire region was full of Kurdish villages and the Kurds were surging into Armenian villages', he rejected the idea of Kurdish-Turkish co-existence and deemed it 'necessary to settle Turks in strategic axes'. In Diyarbekir province, an axis of settlement needed to be carved out from Antep to Diyarbekir over the Urfa road. Moreover, 'it is possible to settle Turkish immigrants on the fertile land . . . of the Armenian villages' and prohibit Kurds from living there. Renda believed that the program of deportation would be easier to implement by building railways and declaring a decade of martial law. Besides using forced population transfer as a method of 'Turkifying' the eastern provinces, he called for forced assimilation and total disarmament 'to make Turks out of the Kurds'.[171]

Simultaneously, Cemil Uybadın wrote his own report and approached the eastern provinces with the same nationalist mindset of social engineering. Uybadın enunciated entire categories of Kurds to be deported: 'overlords, sheikhs, tribal leaders and chieftains, landholders, village elders' and especially 'all supporters of Kurdism', as well as other 'harmful persons'. These categories of people were to be deported to Western Turkey and Eastern Thrace with their families. Then, 'those Turks present in the East need to be supported and supplied and Turkish immigrants from abroad need to be collectively settled and the Agricultural Bank needs to favour the Turks'. Uybadın assessed that it was possible to settle 400,000 households in Diyarbekir province within a year, and to settle 5000 households per year in the future. Turkish immigrants from Romania, Bulgaria, and Serbia were to be settled in the Urfa, Mardin, and Diyarbekir districts to achieve the 'economic and political domination of the Turks'. Kurds who had settled in Armenian villages were to be evicted and the houses were to be given to Turkish immigrants. Moreover, 'the increase in Diyarbekir of Armenians and Syriacs, Chaldeans, Nestorians and other Christians, which always produces inauspicious results, needs to be prohibited and conditions need to be brought about for these harmful elements, who will always be the instruments of the English, as well as Syriacs and Yezidis in the villages, to be expelled from this region'.[172] Their property and

---

[171] Bayrak, *Kürtler*, 452–67.

[172] In the 1920s, Diyarbekir city had become a haven for Armenian genocide survivors, but these new measures completed the expulsions of the Armenian population. Vahé Tachjian, 'Expulsion of the Armenian Survivors of Diyarbekir and Urfa, 1923–1930', in: Richard G. Hovannisian (ed.), *Armenian Tigranakert/Diarbekir and Edessa/Urfa* (Costa Mesa, CA: Mazda, 2006), 519–38.

enterprises would be redistributed to Turks. These measures would 'procure the densification of Turks and extinguish Kurdishness'. Uybadın then made two important suggestions: the East needed to be governed by a 'General Inspector' endowed with 'a colonial method of administration' (*müstemleke tarz-ı idare*). Such a governor would wield extraordinary authority over 'a civil service solely consisting of Westerners and Turks'. Indeed, no state official in the eastern bureaucracy, whether civic, legislative, judicial, or military, would be allowed to be Kurdish; all existing Kurdish civil servants were to be deported away. Disarmament would be ethnically discriminatory as well: whereas the Kurdish population of the eastern provinces was to be totally disarmed, the Turkish settlers would be allowed to bear arms.[173] Uybadın thus explicitly interpreted the 'reform plan' as a form of internal colonization.

Within two weeks after Renda's and Uybadın's reports, the final report of the council was completed and presented to parliament for evaluation. The final report the council signed on 24 September 1925 incorporated many of Renda and Uybadın's suggestions and was nothing short of a radical expansion of existing Young Turk ideology and methods of social engineering. It reflected a staunch belief in the feasibility of crafting a society through large-scale, top-down authoritarian policy, coupled with an ethno-nationalist vision of 'landscaping the human garden' at distance. The report sketched the east's future, recommended patching together the eastern provinces and rejoining them into 'Inspectorates-General' that would exercise authority over an expanded military administration, thereby ruling all of the eastern provinces by martial law for indeterminate time. A total of seven million Turkish Lira would be allocated to help supervise a comprehensive set of measures. The Kurdish political and social elite was to be prevented from reviving as a ruling class once and for all, so that the east would never again become a battlefield. The territory would be cleared of 'persons, families, and their relatives whose residence in the east the government considers inappropriate' through deportation to Western Turkey. East of the Euphrates a policy categorically prohibiting 'the use of all non-Turkish languages' and 'the employment of Kurds in even secondary offices' would be put into vigorous practice. Kurds who had taken up residence in Armenian villages were to be immediately evicted and deported to the western provinces, while Turks were to be settled in those villages.[174]

The government wasted no time in actuating the plan. In the fall of 1925 it drew up lists of Kurds earmarked for deportation and on 10 December 1925 it passed law number 675, vaguely titled 'Law on Migrants, Refugees, and Tribes Who Leave Their Local Settlements Without Permission'. The Interior Ministry and the Ministry of Exchange, Development, and Settlement (charged with all tasks of rebuilding war-torn areas and population management, such as settling exchangees, immigrants, refugees, and the homeless) were assigned with the implementation of the laws.[175] In his memoirs, Prime Minister İnönü wrote that 'the first security

---

[173] Ibid., 467–80.
[174] Ibid., 481–9.
[175] Kemal Arı, *Büyük Mübadele: Türkiye'ye Zorunlu Göç (1923–1925)* (Istanbul: Tarih Vakfı Yurt Yayınları, 2000), 28.

measure was to remove and deport to the West the sheikhs, chieftains and lords of the East'.[176] The list of more than 500 people deported from Diyarbekir contradicts İnönü's assertion and the council's decision that those actually deported necessarily fell within the categories of 'sheikhs, chieftains and lords'. It included a wide range of men drawn from the local elite, from outright atheists like Cemilpaşazâde Ekrem to Sheikh Said's social orbit.

The deportation of oppositionists was a logical measure in itself. But the puzzling fact was that the deportees also included government loyalists such as Ganizâde Dr. Osman Cevdet Akkaynak, Halifezâde Salih, Pirinççizâde Edip and Nedim, Pirinççizâde Bekir Sıdkı, and Cercisağazâde Abdülkerim. These CUP veterans had not only sided with the government during the Sheikh Said crisis, but had even cooperated in the extermination of the local Armenians a decade before. Among these loyal Kurds figured men like noted chieftain Hazrolu Hatip Bey, who had provided Mustafa Kemal with accommodation in his house during the First World War.[177] Another Kurdish notable, Avenalı Kâmil Bey of the Sürgücüzâde tribe, had assembled many armed men to support the government during the siege of Diyarbekir city. To his shock, after the suppression of the siege, he was arrested and sentenced to death. Only an intervention by Pirinççizâde Aziz Feyzi prevented his execution sentence, which was commuted to life in the prison of the northern Black Sea town of Sinop.[178] Now, in the words of Cemilpaşazâde Kadri Bey, 'instead of receiving a reward or at least acclaim . . . those persons who had helped the government . . . became the first victims of the government's operations'.[179] All of these men, more than 500, were deported to İzmir, Aydın, Manisa, Bursa and Antalya, where some were settled on government-allocated property and others were incarcerated in prison.[180]

The disparate backgrounds of the deportees converged into the reality and experience of expropriation and forced migration. Kârerli Mehmet Efendi (1887–1959), a Kurdish intellectual from the northernmost Diyarbekir district, was sentenced to 101 years of imprisonment with hard labour in Afyonkarahisar. Within two days of his conviction he was shackled and deported. Since Diyarbekir had not yet been reached by the railway, he had to walk to the Fevzipaşa station, east of Adana. Mehmet Efendi, suffering from rheumatoid arthritis, was unable to walk that distance and had to rent a cart. After a journey of ten days he arrived in Fevzipaşa, where they were herded into cattle cars and deported to Afyon in a two day journey. On arrival he was locked in solitary confinement to serve his sentence.[181] His

[176] İsmet İnönü, *Hatıralar* (Ankara: Bilgi, 1987), vol. 2, 203.

[177] Abdülmelik Fırat, *Fırat Mahzun Akar* (Istanbul: Avesta, 1996), 21.

[178] Interview with Vahit Altınakar conducted by Şeyhmus Diken, published in: Şeyhmus Diken, *İsyan Sürgünleri* (Istanbul: İletişim, 2005), 233–8.

[179] Silopî, *Doza Kurdistan*, 102. For similar paradoxical targeting of loyalists under Stalinism see: J. Arch Getty and Oleg V. Naumov, *The Road to Terror: Stalin and the Self-Destruction of the Bolsheviks, 1932–1939* (New Haven: Yale University Press, 1999), 276, 538.

[180] Mustafa Âkif Tütenk, 'Diyarbakır İstiklâl Mahkemesinin Kararları ve Sürülen Aileler', in: *Kara-Amid* 2–4 (1956), 342.

[181] Kârerli Mehmet Efendi, *Yazılmayan Tarih ve Anılarım (1915–1958)* (Ankara: Kalan, 2007), 194.

experiences as an individual contrast with those of villagers, who were deported collectively. Feyzullah Koç from the village of Erdürük recalled that a few days after his father had been killed, soldiers came to the village and gave all survivors twenty-four hours to evacuate the village for deportation to the Central Anatolian town Niğde:

> Quickly we packed up. Our relatives helped us. They deported me, my mother, and my sister to Elaziz . . . Our final destination was declared to be Niğde. It was the first time we heard of the name Niğde. We didn't even know where, in what region it was . . . We rented a carriage for 100 Lira. We got on with the clothes and food we could take. We took the road. During the journey we passed through villages, cities, and towns, taking care of our needs, sleeping outside, cooking and eating whatever we brought with us. Everywhere, villages and towns were empty. The Greeks and Armenians had fled and left, leaving behind their houses and shops . . . The bricks in the walls of those beautiful houses were varnished. Clean, whitewashed . . .

After twenty days, the Koç family reached Niğde, where for a long time they were homesick for Diyarbekir. They regretted the fact that the local population treated them as pariahs for years.[182]

Hasan Hişyar Serdî was deported at a time 'when snow covered the surroundings and the waters froze to ice'. His village burnt down, his family murdered, he was taken from prison, shackled by his neck, ankles, and wrists, and deported on foot with eighteen others. After two days they reached the Euphrates and caught up with a group of deportees, consisting mostly of women and children, who had been dispatched earlier. According to Serdî, the convoy was beaten with sticks by the escorting gendarmes and looked 'utterly miserable'. The next day his convoy reached Malatya, where they were locked in prison. Upon arrival the local inmates, many of whom were Kurds from Diyarbekir, received them cordially and sang laments that 'resounded through the market of Malatya'. During roll call the next morning, an officer called for Sheikh Said's soldiers to assemble in the courtyard. Serdî was severely beaten and again, escorted by ten gendarmes, his deportation continued westward. The rest of the deportation was equally harsh as gendarmes frequently whipped and maltreated their captives, and did not allow them to pray. After almost a month of hardship the exhausted men reached the town of Niğde, where Serdî was incarcerated to spend the rest of his life.[183]

The single batch of deportees who were accorded the severest measures were undoubtedly Sheikh Said's family. In his village nobody but women and children remained. The oldest male in the village was one of the sheikh's nephews, the 14-year-old Muhammed. The family's immovable property had already been confiscated by the government when, the day before deportation, gendarmes showed up and carried off his movable property too. His extended family's belongings were sold off on the Piran marketplace and the revenue was distributed

---

[182] Interview with Feyzullah Koç, conducted by Ahmet Kahraman, published in: Kahraman, *Kürt İsyanları*, 182–3.
[183] Serdî, *Görüş ve Anılarım*, 311–30.

among government officials. The night before being deported his family slept in an empty house. When the gendarmes came for the final departure, the women and children were marched off 'barefoot amidst snow and thunderstorms' to Erzurum, where they were registered and sent off to Trabzon. From that port city they were embarked on a boat leaving for Istanbul. In the end, the sheikh's family was deported to Thrace and settled in a small Turkish village.[184]

Whereas the 1925 deportations had been improvised without much forethought or planning, by the spring of 1926 the 'Reform Plan for the East' gradually came into effect. On 31 May 1926 the government passed the 'Settlement Law', authorizing the Interior Ministry to target people 'who do not fall under Turkish culture, those infected with syphilis, persons suffering from leprosy and their families, and those convicted of murder except for political and military crimes, anarchists, spies, gypsies, and those who have been expelled from the country', as well as 'migratory tribes in the country and all nomads' to be 'transported to suitable and available places'. In particular the law prescribed the sedentarization of nomadic tribes.[185] An appendix to the law stipulated that 'Pomaks, Bosniaks, and Tatars are included in Turkish culture'.[186] By trial and error, the Kemalists were refining and elaborating the time-tested method of deportation as a tool of population politics. The ideology informing had evolved since the days of the CUP, but had essentially stayed the same: demographically strengthening 'Turkishness' and demographically diluting the ethnic Others.

One aspect of the deportations had changed noticeably: whereas the CUP had mostly kept them secretive, now both the deportations themselves and their objectives were openly propagated. At this point, the deportations were widely discussed in the regime's inner circle. At a conference, the delegate for Bitlis projected the 'procurance of a critical Turkish majority in the Eastern provinces' and emphasized that this change could only be brought about through a policy of 'resettlement'.[187] Two reasons for this discursive shift were the regime's confidence in its own political legitimacy and sovereignty, and their adoption of an ideology legitimizing the deportations. The man who justified the deportation policies to the outside world was Foreign Minister Tevfik Rüştü Aras (1883–1972), experienced in deportation during the First World War. He stated to the British administrator of Iraq Sir Henry Dobbs (1871–1934) that the regime was 'determined to clear the Kurds out of their valleys, the richest part of Turkey to-day, and to settle Turkish peasants there'. He added that the Kurds 'would be treated as were the Armenians'. Aras underpinned his argument as follows: 'The Kurds would for many generations be incapable of self-government . . . He always said long before the war that Turkey must get rid of the Albanians, Bulgarians and Arabs, and must become more homogeneous'.[188] Although the operative word in this exchange seems to be

---

[184] Ferzende Kaya, *Mezopotamya Sürgünü: Abdülmelik Fırat'ın Yaşamöyküsü* (Istanbul: Alfa, 2005), 33–6.

[185] Naci Kökdemir (ed.), *Eski ve Yeni Toprak, İskan Hükümleri ve Uygulama Klavuzu* (Ankara: n.p., 1952), 25–8.

[186] Kökdemir, *Eski ve Yeni Toprak*, 193.

[187] *Türk Ocakları 1928 Senesi Kurultayı Zabıtları* (Ankara: Türk Ocakları Matbaası, 1929), 417–18.

[188] NAUK, FO 424/265, 50–2, no.46/1, Memorandum by Henry Dobbs, 22 November 1926.

Plate 1 A bird's eye view of Diyarbekir city in 1911.

Plate 2 An Armenian family from Diyarbekir: miniaturist Hovsep and his wife and children.

Plate 3 Special Organization operatives in front of the Ministry of War in Istanbul in 1914.

Plate 4 Dr. Mehmed Reshid (1873–1919).

Plate 5 Young Turk propaganda photo displaying weapons allegedly used by Armenian 'rebels'; Diyarbekir, 27 April 1915.

Plate 6 Pirinççizâde Aziz Feyzi (1879–1933).

Plate 7 Kurdish leaders arrested and taken to Diyarbekir's prison, 1925.

Plate 8 Soldiers marching through Mountain Gate after its demolition, 1920s.

Plate 9 The Cemilpaşazâde family in exile in 1938. The women are widows.

Plate 10 Şükrü Kaya (1883–1959).

Plate 11 The bell tower of Surp Giragos church in Diyarbekir, 1913.

Plate 12 Atatürk, Celal Bayar and Şükrü Kaya on a 1936 tour in the east.

Plate 13 'Abandoned property': the Armenian Surb Stepanos church of Silvan in the 1930s.

Plate 14 The Diyarbekir Music Ensemble, still with two Armenian musicians, 1940.

Plate 15 Kurdish girl named Teti before and after her enrolment in the boarding school.

'homogeneous', Aras' use of the word 'must' merits attention. For the first time the Kemalists explicitly evinced their ideological convictions. This was an amalgam of various philosophies they espoused. First of all, the ideological blend was based on historicism, the ideology that there is an organic succession of developments in society. Widely popular in Europe at that time, it was based on assumptions of historical prediction and historical determinism, bent on identifying patterns and discovering the laws that underlie the evolution of history.[189] Second, the evolving Young Turk conscience adopted a particular interpretation of progressism, a trend of thought which affirms the power of human beings to make, improve and reshape their society, with the aid of scientific knowledge, technology and practical experimentation. In this interpretation, social evolution into one particular direction could be (or had to be) steered from above. Posited as a scientific theory, this notion of social evolution was used to support and justify policies of population control—not unlike European colonialism.[190] Combined together, both these ideological constructs revolved around a specific notion of time that the Kemalists had ethnicized: the past was Ottoman, the future would be Turkish. In other words, Turkish culture would be the pinnacle of social evolution. For the ethnic minorities of Turkey this meant that although they were living in the objective present, in ideological terms they were living in the subjective past. It was now deemed possible and necessary through 'Turkification' to 'push' people forward into time towards the identity of the future.

The laws that Kemalist officials thought governed time were those of social Darwinism. For this too, Aras provided the vindication of the Kemalists' ideological position to British Ambassador George R. Clerk:

> He enunciated his theory of historical philosophy. The pendulum swings between a period of empire of federation and one of independent nations and races; the British Empire alone in history has had the political wisdom to adapt itself to the growth of separatist forces and so to preserve its structure; the pendulum has now reached the maximum of swing towards individual and separate nations and the swing back into groups, if not into empires, is already noticeable. The process is inevitable, but in its course small national units must disappear, or only survive precariously because their absorption by one of their bigger neighbours means war with the others, independent existence for all small nationalities of 1 or 2 millions, e.g, Albania, is henceforth impossible. Thus the Kurds, too, are inevitably doomed, but in their case their cultural level is so low, their mentality so backward, that they cannot be simply assimilated in the general Turkish body politic. Like what his Excellency called 'the Hindus of America', by which presumably he meant the Red Indians, they will die out, economically unfitted for the struggle for life in competition with the more advanced and cultured Turks, who will be settled in the Kurdish districts. After all there are less than 500,000 Kurds in Turkey to-day, of whom as many as can will emigrate into Persia and Iraq, while the rest will simply undergo the elimination of the unfit.[191]

---

[189] Karl R. Popper, *The Poverty of Historicism* (London: Routledge and Kegan Paul, 1957), 3.
[190] Edward L. Schaub, *Progressism: An Essay in Social Philosophy* (Calcutta: University of Calcutta, 1937).
[191] NAUK, FO 424/266, Clerk to Chamberlain, 4 January 1927.

In the press, these opinions were reinforced by senior Young Turks, such as İsmet İnönü, who regularly made statements such as: 'In this country only the Turkish nation has the right to claim ethnic and racial rights. Nobody else has such a right'.[192] This paradigm (known as Kemalism) rationalized the deportation-and-settlement program.

For the Kemalists this was all the justification the regime needed for more deportations to ensue. In the year following the May 1926 law a new wave of deportations was organized by the regime. These were better considered, and targeted elite families such as the Cemilpaşazâde dynasty (see Plate 9). Cemilpaşa-zâde Ekrem Cemil, a prominent Kurdish nationalist, was arrested and sentenced to ten years imprisonment and deported to Kastamonu state prison. He was incarcerated in that prison from September 1925 to May 1928, where he taught the Koran, French and Turkish to forty-four fellow Kurdish deportees. He wanted to teach the inmates Kurdish as well but that was prohibited. Ekrem was then deported to Istanbul and detained for another six months.[193] In total, of the Cemilpaşazâde family, the siblings and cousins Ekrem Cemil, Ahmed Cemil, Mehmed Ferid, Memduh, Muhiddin, Ömer Ali, Bedri and Fikri were deported with their wives and children and settled in the town of Buca near İzmir.[194] The police commissar of İzmir had the men followed and kept under close surveillance.[195]

Other powerful and notable families followed. Members of the Azizoğlu tribe, in particular the family of noted chieftain Hüseyin Azizoğlu (1894–1957),[196] who had been arrested during the 1925 conflict, were deported from their native regions of Silvan and Estel. His daughter Fatma Azizoğlu was 7 years old when gendarmes arrested her family and took them to a nearby mosque, where they waited for further instructions. After a few days, they were taken to a train station on the Berlin-Baghdad railway and herded into cattle cars, which, Azizoğlu recalled, 'smelled of horses, donkeys, and coal'. On the way, they changed wagons once at the Aleppo train station and finally halted in the southern town of Tarsus.[197] Sürgücüzâde tribesmen who had survived the massacres in the east were deported as well. When government officials collected all remaining men, the tribesmen feared they would be killed. Their relief was great when the aim of the operation was announced as deportation to the west. In small groups, the men were taken away by their escorting gendarmes to the Fevzipaşa/Keller train station and deported westward. Of the extended family, one group was sent to Nazilli, another to Aydın, another to Akseki, and so forth. All of these destinations were isolated places.[198]

---

[192] *Milliyet*, 31 Ağustos 1930.
[193] Ekrem Cemil Paşa, *Muhtasar Hayatım* (Brussels: Institute Kurde, 1991), 61, 82.
[194] Malmîsanij, *Diyarbekirli Cemilpaşazâdeler ve Kürt Milliyetçiliği* (Istanbul: Avesta, 2004), 189.
[195] BCA, 272.12/55.137.11, İzmir police commissar to Interior Ministry, 23 October 1927.
[196] For a short biography of Hüseyin Azizoğlu, see: Feqî Hüseyin Sağnıç, *Portreler* (Istanbul: Istanbul Kürt Enstitüsü Yayınları, 2000), 57–61.
[197] Interview with Fatma Azizoğlu conducted by Şeyhmus Diken, published in: Diken, *İsyan Sürgünleri*, 82–4.
[198] Interview with Vahit Altınakar conducted by Şeyhmus Diken, published in: Diken, *İsyan Sürgünleri*, 238–9.

These deportations did not satisfy the Kemalists and were the harbinger of more. Whereas the 1926 law had aimed to deport groups from across the entire country, on 10 June 1927 the Kemalists passed the 'Law Regarding the Transportation of Certain Persons from the Eastern Regions to the Western Provinces'. This enabling law, number 1097, focused on the eastern provinces and decreed the deportation of 1400 persons and their families, and 80 'rebel families' from the 'eastern martial law region' to the western provinces, 'for administrative, military, and societal reasons'. The deportations were to be implemented in August 1927, but those with crops were allowed to stay in their native regions until after harvesting season, in November. Although the law stipulated that the government would cover all the costs of transportation, there is evidence that deportees were forced to pay not only for their own transportation, but for the accompanying gendarmes as well.[199] The deportees were obliged to stay within the boundaries of a specific area of settlement the government had assigned to them. It was strictly prohibited for them to travel beyond that area and especially back to their region of origin. According to article 9, all their immovable property was forfeited to the Turkish government. On arrival in their final destinations in the west, they would be settled on farmland.[200] The Kemalist use of forced relocation was shifting back from pragmatic to ideological reasons. No longer did it aim at retributively pacifying 'insurgent elements', but was developing into a corollary of their ideology of historicism, progressism, and social Darwinism.

The experiences of deportees during this phase of deportations did not differ markedly from those deported before. According to one deportee, gendarmes surrounded the village, assembled a long convoy, and took them to the railway station, where, she remembered, 'they crammed us in the wagon, threw in a sack for us to defecate in, that was it'.[201] Another deportee was a baby when they were deported: 'They loaded my grandmother's family on cattle cars. The wagon was crowded. People could not breathe in the cramped wagon, they traveled one piled up on top of another, hungry and thirsty for days, in the dirty smell'.[202] A British military attaché in Turkey witnessed the August 1927 wave of deportations:

> I saw three separate convoys of Kurds in process of transportation. The first was between Nigde and Develi Kara Hissar. It consisted of three men with about 150 women and children. Their goods and chattels were piled on bullock waggons, most of them were walking, with one or two of the elder women riding on donkeys or in the carts, and they were escorted by ten gendarmes. The second, also on the march, was between Karaman and Konia. It was pointed out to me from the train by a fellow-traveller, and was about 300 strong. Lastly, at Chumrah, near Konia, there was a camp of about 600. I remarked to a station-hand that there were a lot of gipsies about and he corrected me, saying that they were transported Kurds. At Chumrah, also in camp, was

---

[199] Interview with Vahit Altınakar conducted by Şeyhmus Diken, published in: Diken, *İsyan Sürgünleri*, 238–9.
[200] Kökdemir, *Eski ve Yeni Toprak*, 28–30.
[201] Interview conducted in Bursa with Medine Kaya, 23 June 2002.
[202] Kahraman, *Kürt İsyanları*, 343.

about a battalion of infantry and half a company of engineers. They, according to the station-hand, arrived about a fortnight earlier, and were there to guard the Kurds.[203]

On arrival, the deportees faced a new environment, a new culture, and often a new language. One deportee arrived in the central Anatolian town of Kütahya as more deportees kept flowing in. On a given day, he remembered, a trainload of deportees from eastern Diyarbekir arrived in Kütahya. One man walked up to him and asked him: 'Where is this place, are we far from our native regions?' They were in Kütahya but had no clue where Kütahya was.[204] The August deportations were followed by those of November, as projected in the 1927 Law. On 20 November 1927 the government moved a total of ten households (extended families) from the region east of Diyarbekir province to Western Turkey.[205] Despite these ambitious forecasts, much of Kemalist population politics remained on paper: a 1928 scheme to import 60,000 Muslims from the Caucasus to settle among the eastern Kurds never took place.[206] This was a signal of how difficult it was to accomplish a high level of effectiveness in ambitious social engineering policies.

The deportations were not a simple transfer from A to B. During most of 1927 and 1928, the Kemalist regime took measures to settle and provide for the deportees on arrival at their final destination. It ordered all receiving provinces to register the names, sexes, ethnic, or tribal backgrounds, numbers and other characteristics and report these to the Interior Ministry. Furthermore, the receiving provinces were to supply the central government with precise statistics on the ethnic composition of their villages. The report written by the governor of Edirne province is a good example of this policy. It contained lists of deportees and settlers classified by region of origin, date of arrival, and 'race'.[207] Another destination of the Kurdish deportees from Diyarbekir was the town of Polatlı, shortly south of Ankara. Its district governor too, drew up lists of all villages according to household, gender, and 'race'. Table 2 shows the totals in Polatlı district.

Another receiving province was Bolu, whose governor appended district reports written by mayors and district governors. The deportees in that province were settled in villages 'abandoned by Greeks'. A total of 6013 people, around 350 households, had been settled in fourteen villages. The precision of these headcounts would serve to calculate the percentages of Kurds: nowhere they were allowed to comprise more than 5 percent of the local population. In accordance with policy directives, the governor of Bolu had a detailed table prepared, charting 'the places populated by non-Turkish elements'. These people were Kurds, Georgians, Laz, Abkhazians, and Circassians.[208] According to one source, the total number of Kurds moved to Western Turkey between 1920 and 1932 totalled 2774.[209] This

---

[203] NAUK, FO 424/267, 63–4, no.24, Clerk to Chamberlain, 9 August 1927.
[204] Kahraman, *Kürt İsyanları*, 184.
[205] BCA, 272.11/23.120.18, 20 November 1927.
[206] NAUK, FO 371/13090/E129, Clerk (Istanbul) to Chamberlain (London), 9 January 1928.
[207] BCA, 272.12/60.171.3, Edirne governor to Interior Ministry, 11 September 1928.
[208] BCA, 272.12/59.161.6, Bolu governor to Interior Ministry, 12 June 1928. It is important to keep in mind that these settlers also included refugees from the Balkans and the Caucasus.
[209] *İskân Tarihçesi* (Istanbul: Hamit Matbaası, 1932), 137.

Table 2 Ethnic composition in Polatlı district

Ethnicity	Number
Turks	10,838
Bosniaks	312
Kurds	742
Alevis	62
Others	12
Total	14,523

Source: *BCA*, 272.65/6.5.4, Polatlı district governor to Interior Ministry, 12 and 23 March 1927.

seemingly limited number is deceptive: rather than the quantity of deported Kurds, one needs to look at the social classes deported away. It then appears that the deported constituted the top of the pyramid of the eastern Kurds, namely the (surviving) religious, intellectual, and social elites. As long as the Kurdish elites were separated from the general Kurdish population, the policies seemed to pay off, for no nationalist ideas were being propagated to the latter.

Settling the deportees was not always an easy task. Apparently, the settling did not proceed as smoothly as the regime would have it, as some deportees attempted to flee. The governor of Sivas reported to the Interior Ministry his fear that 'Kurdish elements leave their local settlements without permission and flee to their native regions'.[210] Another problem was the resistance of locals against the arrival of unwanted strangers, out of rural conservatism or ethnic xenophobia. In Bolu province, some local residents openly complained about the influx of the Kurdish newcomers. A Turkish war veteran and local official sent a letter to the general staff, listing his grievances: the deportees had been frustrated, violent, and abusive to him and moreover, 'they refused to Turkify'.[211] The complaint reached Chief of Staff Marshal Fevzi Çakmak, who wrote to the Prime Minister's Office that 'it is important to assimilate these foreign-minded crowds of people, who are filling these important and precious Turkish regions, into the Turkish nation'.[212] In other words, the settlement campaign needed more than just the transportation to a place and the allotting of a house; it required a cultural component. Çakmak's advice was valued and acted upon by the regime. In a top secret order issued by the Interior Ministry the year after, settlement directives included the clause that the Kurds who were sent west were to be 'made Turkish in language, tradition, and desire'.[213]

---

[210] BCA, 272.12/60.170.16, Sivas governor Süleyman Sami to Interior Ministry, 29 September 1928.
[211] BCA, 272.12/59.161.6, Mustafa Asım to general staff, 17 July 1928.
[212] BCA, 272.12/59.161.6, Chief of Staff Marshal Fevzi Çakmak to Prime Ministry, 3 March 1928.
[213] Bayrak, *Kürtler*, 509.

The north-western province of Balıkesir was another important destination. In the first half of September 1927, the provincial authorities settled batches of deportees in the province. The governor's report included long lists of deportees from the provinces of Van, Mardin, Muş, Genç, and Diyarbekir. From all regions and neighbourhoods of Diyarbekir, Kurds had been sent to Balıkesir. The margins of the governor's report include notes on specific families, such as, 'Has been settled', or in a sporadic case, 'Has fled'. The deportees were then spread out over dozens of villages in the province, without knowledge of who had been settled where.[214] But in this province too, the local population was not keen for Kurds to settle in their villages. As one deportee from Diyarbekir remembered, 'They dismounted us from the train and took us to a village in Balıkesir. But the villagers didn't want us. 'Piss off!' they yelled. Later they attacked us with stones and sticks. My grandfather was lynched on the village square'. The escorting officials, realizing the difficulty of settling the Kurds in that village, retreated with the families and settled them in another one.[215]

Other deportees faced better circumstances on arrival, for example in the southern districts of Turkey. In November 1927, the governor of Antalya reported that deportees from Diyarbekir had arrived. They would be 'scattered with three to four men, with their families and wives, in the countryside of Antalya'.[216] The Azizoğlu family had been deported to the southern town of Tarsus. Local government officials assigned them, according to Fatma Azizoğlu, 'a lovely house amidst orange orchards'. Living conditions were so good, her father Hüseyin Azizoğlu had even considered relinquishing the idea of a possible future return to Diyarbekir altogether. The locals, mostly Turks and Arabs, often invited them to dinner and shared their resources with them. The family later moved to the nearby town of Mersin and for years entertained cordial relations with the locals.[217]

On 1 January 1928, the Kemalist government established the First Inspectorate-General, centred in Diyarbekir, and appointed Dr. İbrahim Talî Öngören (1875–1952) its first Inspector-General.[218] Öngören was a graduate of the military medical academy and had met Mustafa Kemal during the 1911 Turco-Italian War in Tripolitania. During the First World War, Öngören served as an army doctor in Diyarbekir, where he met Kemal again during the latter's command there in 1916. According to British sources, Öngören had visited Bombay and had studied 'Anglo-Indian administration'.[219] In line with the call for a 'colonial administrative method' recorded in the 1925 Reform Plan, this corroborates the notion that the colonial tendencies embedded in the regime's language and power

---

[214] BCA, 272.11/23.119.34, Balıkesir governor to Interior Ministry, 17 November 1927.
[215] Kahraman, *Kürt İsyanları*, 343.
[216] BCA, 272.11/23.121.1, Antalya governor to Interior Ministry, 28 November 1927.
[217] Interview with Fatma Azizoğlu conducted by Şeyhmus Diken, published in: Diken, *İsyan Sürgünleri*, 82–4.
[218] Dündar Akünal, 'Belge ve Resimlerle Dr. İbrahim Tali Öngören', in: *Tarih ve Toplum* 40 (1987).
[219] NAUK, FO 424/272, 116, no.68, Edmonds to Henderson, 21 May 1930, Notes on a Tour to Diarbekir, Bitlis, and Mush.

structures were to be put into motion for the internal colonization of the eastern provinces. The Inspector was accorded a relatively wide autonomy in decision-making to implement the general policies laid out in the 1925 Reform Plan in the large area under his jurisdiction.[220] The Inspectorate would play a leading role in the organization of the deportation-and-settlement policies. It would track down, arrest, and deport Kurds earmarked for removal, and receive, register, and assign property to Turkish settlers moving in from the west.

In 1928, the regime felt secure enough to proclaim a partial amnesty. With its elites gone, the Kurdish resistance was thought to have collapsed for good. Those left behind were not expected to pose a threat to the regime. When Olaf Rygaard passed the plains of western Diyarbekir in 1928, he noted that the local population was 'even more impoverished in these areas where their dwellings and meagre acres, laboriously tilled little vineyards up in the gorges, had been destroyed and their small sheep and goat flocks had been taken from them when the punitive campaign in 1925 laid waste the area. The fear is still in their blood'.[221] With the revoking of the Law on the Maintenance of Order, in March 1929 some of the deportees were allowed to return to Diyarbekir. Families of the Sürgücüzâde tribe were in exile in the west when the news of amnesty was announced. It took them three days by train to reach their native regions, where they found their house 'miserable and flooded . . . the mice had ripped to shreds all of the furniture'. They barely made it through the harsh winter and tried to pick up agriculture again.[222] Sheikh Said's family too returned to their ruined villages and resumed their lives as best as they could.[223] Most returning deportees recovered whatever was left of their movable and immovable property. This only lasted until 2 June 1929, when the Kemalists passed the Law on the Distribution of Lands to Needy Farmers in the Eastern Regions (no.1505). It authorized the government to confiscate from landowning tribal chieftains and redistribute their estates to 'villagers, tribesmen, nomads, and immigrants'.[224] The wide definition of the law betrayed a deep-seated Young Turk tradition of legalizing population politics *ex post facto*. Passed in the days of ethnic deportations, it amounted to an accelerator of existing practices of expropriating chieftains and landholders. A British traveller wrote in the summer of 1929 that 'one of the main weapons employed was the deportation of rich and powerful Kurdish families. Many of these have since returned under the amnesty, but in the process they have lost all their belongings, and there is not, so I was told, a single wealthy or powerful Kurd in Turkish Kurdistan to-day'.[225] But especially after the

---

[220] For a study of the First Inspectorate-General, see: Cemil Koçak, *Umûmî Müfettişlikler (1927–1952)* (Istanbul: İletişim, 2003), 53–126.

[221] Olaf A. Rygaard, *Mellem Tyrker og Kurder: En Dansk Ingeniørs Oplevelser i Lilleasien* (Copenhagen: Nordisk Forlag, 1935), 107–8.

[222] Interview with Vahit Altınakar conducted by Şeyhmus Diken, published in: Diken, *İsyan Sürgünleri*, 240–1.

[223] Kaya, *Mezopotamya Sürgünü*, 43.

[224] Kökdemir, *Eski ve Yeni Toprak*, 34–5.

[225] NAUK, FO 371/13828/E3538, Clerk (Istanbul) to Henderson (London), 15 July 1929. Enclosure in No.1., 'Notes on a Journey from Angora to Aleppo, Diarbekir, Malatia, Sivas and the Black Sea Coast, June 9–29, 1929'.

third phase of deportations (dealt with in the next section), this law and policy elicited both conservative traditional resistance from landholding chieftains who were dispossessed, and ethnic resistance from eastern Kurds who saw their land being allotted to Turkish settlers.

As in the case of confiscated Armenian property, the property of Kurdish elites was redistributed to Turkish settlers as well. As early as May 1927, the Kemalists prepared the colonization of those villages that were planned to be depopulated according to the 1927 law. The fact that it was possible for settlement plans to predate deportations might conceivably denote that the deportations were but a pretext for clearing out high-quality living quarters for Turkish settlers, although there is no definite evidence for this claim. Whatever its timing, as a receiving province, Diyarbekir needed to be prepared for the influx of Turkish settlers. The vice-governor of Diyarbekir reported to the Interior Ministry that preparations were being made to receive the settlers. Of the seventy-five households of settlers from Yugoslavia, thirty-five households had gone off to various regions and thirty households had still not been settled. The provincial authorities of Diyarbekir settled these refugees from the Macedonian towns of Kumanovo and Veles (Köprülü) in 'empty houses' in the province. According to the governor, since these people had suffered 'destitution and misery' they were compensated with additional immovable and movable property.[226]

These reports suggest that the settlement campaign did not always seem like an easy affair either. British reports were often sceptical about it:

> For the filling of the void made in the Kurdish district by the removal of Kurds, the settlement of immigrants is contemplated. It is hoped that Moslem immigrants may be obtained from Jugoslavia, from the Dobruja, from Bulgaria, from Cyprus and from the Caucasus . . . The experiences of the Moslems who were transplanted into Turkey from Greece are far from encouraging. Peasantry who in the land of the giaour are fairly prosperous and may wear their fezes and say their prayers without loss of esteem are not likely to be anxious to be dumped in the inhospitable regions of Kurdistan in order that they may make a new start in cloth caps.[227]

Travelling through eastern Turkey in the late 1920s, the author Harold Armstrong came across a Turkish migrant on his way to be settled:

> His language was Greek and he could as yet only speak a little broken Turkish with a thick Greek accent, though his ancestors had come from Constantinople. The Turkish and Greek Governments had been exchanging Christians and Moslems, he told me. He had been forcibly rooted up and sent here. He bemoaned his fate. In Crete he was happy and well off. His great-grandfather's father had owned the farm he had inherited, but the Greeks would only have Greeks in Greece. In the village, he said, were refugees from all parts: from Western Thrace, Greece proper, Salonika, Macedonia and even from Cyprus. They had tried to start life again, but they had no capital; the land was not theirs and at any moment they might be moved, so they had patched

---

[226] BCA, 272.12/53.128.7, Diyarbekir vice-governor to Interior Ministry, 25 May 1927.
[227] NAUK, FO 424/266, Clerk to Chamberlain, 12 January 1927.

the houses just sufficiently to live in, and did only just enough work on the land to make it produce. The fruit was beginning to ripen in the gardens and the vineyards; the country was full of foxes and thieves, so that if they did not watch they might be ruined in one night. He was like a child, helpless, lost, pathetic, homeless.[228]

For the Kemalists, the long-term well-being of the settlers was not their primary concern. As long as it increased the demographic ratio of Turks in the eastern provinces, the settlement campaign continued unabated. Time and again, the Interior Ministry wrote to the First Inspector-General's office in Diyarbekir that it had screened individuals and groups of people who wanted to settle in the eastern provinces. The Kurds in these groups were not allowed to settle there, whereas the others were.[229] This practice of barring Kurds' entrance to Diyarbekir province was identical to the 1916 regulations of the CUP. The First Inspectorate-General regulated population movements along ethnic lines: only those of whom it could be 'proven' they were 'Turkish in regards to their blood and language' were allowed to settle and be allotted free land to settle in the east.[230] The 'free land' the Inspectorate-General had in mind was the now empty villages of Armenians and Kurds. One of these was the village of Tcherouk/Çarıklı in the Silvan district.[231] The Armenian inhabitants of the village had been massacred in 1915, and the Kurds who had moved in shortly after had been deported in 1925. Official reports described the village being in a state of 'ruins'. An inventory was set up by construction vice-director Mustafa Hilmi of the Seventh Army Corps, who drew a map and charted a precise list of the village's buildings and fields. Each of these were now numbered and allotted to the settlers when they arrived.[232] After settling in, the Turkish settlers sent a letter to the Inspectorate-General, expressing their gratitude.[233] In this period, 2123 households totalling 8017 people were transferred and settled in the eastern provinces.[234]

Not unlike the deportations of Kurds away from the east, the settlement of Turks into the east was propagated in national discourse and international diplomacy as well. In July 1930 Aras told Clerk that 'it would be necessary to re-people the whole district with Turkish refugees from elsewhere'.[235] An American scholar wrote about the attack on tribal life: 'There were a number of serious Kurd rebellions from 1925 onwards. These have been ruthlessly crushed and tribal autonomy has practically vanished'.[236] American diplomatic sources in 1930

---

[228] Harold Armstrong, *Turkey and Syria Reborn*, 124–5.

[229] DV, 'Gidenler, Mayıs-Haziran-Temmuz-Ağustos 1932', correspondence nr. DV 20133, file nr.1/1010, Interior Ministry to First Inspectorate-General in Diyarbekir, 12 July 1932, quoted in: Çağaptay, *Islam*.

[230] DV, 'Çıkan Şifre 15/6/1933'den 31/7/33'e Tarihine Kadar', correspondence nr. DV-NUM 1/1816/861, file nr.1/1561, Interior Ministry to First Inspectorate-General in Diyarbekir, 2 July 1933, quoted in: Çağaptay, *Islam*.

[231] Raymond Kévorkian, *Les Arméniens*, 392, village no. 80.

[232] BCA, 030.18.01.02/015.49.3, decree dated 5 August 1925.

[233] BCA, 69.454.41, quoted in: Hüseyin Koca, *Yakın Tarihten Günümüze Hükümetlerin Doğu-Güneydoğu Anadolu Politikaları: Umumi Müfettişliklerden Olağanüstü Hal Bölge Valiliğine* (Konya: Mikro, 1998), 335.

[234] Şevket Süreyya Aydemir, *İkinci Adam: 1884–1938* (Istanbul: Remzi, 1967), vol. I, 317.

[235] NAUK, FO 371/14579/E3898, Clerk (Istanbul) to Henderson (London), 21 July 1930.

[236] John Parker and Charles Smith, *Modern Turkey* (London: George Routledge, 1940), 12.

reported a rumour that 'the Turkish authorities plan to exterminate the Kurds and to repopulate Turkish Kurdistan with Turks now resident in Soviet Russia, notably in Azerbaidjan, where they are numerous'.[237] In light of future developments, this report was exaggerated but at the time taken seriously by the Kemalists. In November 1930 Aras spoke at the League of Nations about the 'possibility of a future intense Turkish colonization in order to smother the Kurds in a considerable mass of Turkish population'.[238] The third phase of Young Turk deportations of Kurds would herald the keeping of this promise.

1934: PHASE THREE

The 1930s brought inter-state and intrastate crises to Turkey, a country exporting raw materials to the West. The Great Depression affected the fragile Turkish economy, especially in the economically devastated eastern provinces. As international trade, incomes, tax revenues, prices, and profits declined sharply, Diyarbekir too was hit hard. Impoverished city-dwellers and struggling villagers now faced even greater difficulties to make ends meet. Political developments on the Moscow-Berlin axis spelled an impending European war, and insecurity about the future increased as politicians speculated about which side Turkey would be on. On the level of internal politics, the regime faced a new wave of resistance in the east. This time the Kurdish-nationalist organization 'Independence' (*Xoybûn*) entrenched itself in the Ararat region and forcefully resisted the Kemalist government with demands for autonomy. Again, the Kemalists responded with violence and a local conflagration grew into a guerrilla war quite similar to the Sheikh Said conflict.[239] These two developments combined would ultimately lead to a sharp radicalization of population politics and persecution in the eastern provinces.

The main platform for Kemalist discussions of population politics was parliament. In plenary sessions and closed-door meetings, members of parliament evaluated the previous campaigns of social engineering and discussed the possibilities of new ones. Deputy for Kütahya province and Kemalist ideologue Mustafa Naşit Hakkı Uluğ (1902–77) argued that new strategies for deportations needed to 'exterminate root and branch all of the remaining social institutions from the Middle Ages' so these would 'never blossom again'. Giritli Hasan Ruşeni Barkın (1884–1953), veteran of the CUP's Special Organization and deputy for Samsun, agreed with Uluğ and drew a parallel with Russification and Americanization policies.[240] Elsewhere, Barkın wrote that Turkey's minorities, naming specifically the Laz, Circassians, Persians,

---

[237] NARA, Records of the Department of State Relating to the Internal Affairs of Turkey 1930–1944, SD 867.00/2047. Buxley (Izmir) to the State Department (Washington), 3 October 1930, News of Izmir September 1930.

[238] NAUK, FO 371/14578/E?, Drummond (Geneva) to Cadogan (London), 18 November 1930, 'Note sure un Entretien avec S.E. Tewfik Rouschdy Bey'.

[239] Rohat Alakom, *Hoybûn Örgütü ve Ağrı Ayaklanması* (Istanbul: Avesta, 1998).

[240] *Türkiye Büyük Millet Meclisi Zabıt Ceridesi* (henceforth *TBMM ZC*), vol.23, period IV, session 3 (7 June 1934), 68.

Albanians, Arabs, Kurds, Bosnians, Tatars, and Jews, were 'treacherous citizens' that needed to be 'Turkified with rapid and destructive measures . . . of precise propaganda, unreserved laws, and settlement . . . facilitating their Turkification'. According to him, this would 'salvage' Turkey from the 'plague' of these disloyal groups, who, he argued, needed to be confronted with the following question: 'Are you a Turk? Join us and mingle with us. Are you a stranger? Take off your masks and join the enemy's ranks'.[241]

The main mastermind of the new call to arms was the veteran social engineer Şükrü Kaya (see Plate 10). During discussions in parliament, he explained the need 'to separate the country into west and east', arguing that in the east, it was the government's task to 'render the Turk the master of the soil'.[242] Kaya noted that 'there are approximately two million pure Turks abroad in our near surroundings. It is almost mandatory for them to come to the homeland little by little . . . It is then our obligation to settle them according to the social and economic principles that the science of settlement necessitates'. In his view, nomads were to be sedentarized and 'settled in a civilized and economic manner'.[243] To determine the criteria for the identification and selection of the deportees, Kaya pushed for the use of the term 'race' (*ırk*) instead of 'lineage' (*soy*) which, he believed, meant 'family' rather than 'race'.[244] As discussions continued, Kaya provided a legitimization for new deportations: 'A nation's biggest duty is to annex everybody living within its borders to its own community, to assimilate them. The opposite has been seen with us and has dismembered the homeland. If the Ottomans in their early age had converted the population of the places they went, our Danube borders would still begin at the Danube. We have suffered much from this'.[245] This portentous vindication of nationalist population politics was practically identical to the CUP's discourse that had justified genocide two decades previously. Şükrü Kaya's speech was met with applause and chants of 'Bravo!' in a parliament with a climate strongly hostile to Turkey's ethnic minorities. In later discussions, Çanakkale MP Ziya Gevher Etili threatened the 'traitors' that it would prove necessary to invade their space and 'destroy this serpent in its own nest', adding: 'If it is necessary we will do this. We will send the army and annihilate the treacherous nests'.[246] Deputy for Aydın Dr. Mazhar Germen (1887–1967) identified these 'traitors' as 'the Kurds, who for years have made an art and duty out of committing various betrayals to the Turks' blood and lives . . . and who have played no other role than being a thorn in Turkey's flesh'. Finally, he requested from the government that it 'thoroughly eliminate all of these elements from this region (chants of bravo)', whereupon someone exclaimed: 'They should be deported!'[247]

---

[241] Cemil Koçak, "Ey tarihçi belgen kadar konuş!': Belgesel bir Teşkilatı Mahsusa öyküsü', in: *Tarih ve Toplum: Yeni Yaklaşımlar* 3, no. 243 (2006), 171–214, at 212–14.
[242] *TBMM ZC*, vol. 23, period IV, session 3 (14 June 1934), 139.
[243] *TBMM ZC*, vol. 23, period IV, session 3 (14 June 1934), 141.
[244] *TBMM ZC*, vol. 23, period IV, session 3 (14 June 1934), 145.
[245] *TBMM ZC*, vol. 23, period IV, session 3 (21 June 1934), 249.
[246] *TBMM ZC*, vol. 17, period V, session 45 (7 April 1937), 22.
[247] *TBMM ZC*, vol. 17, period V, session 45 (7 April 1937), 23–4.

And so it happened. During the first half of the 1930s, the Kemalists rapidly expanded and organized new deportation plans. Apart from the setting up of the identification and selection, this wave of deportations also implied major political-administrative decisions: establishing a clear line of command regarding the responsibility for and the implementing of the deportations, as well as determining the criteria for the identification of the deportees. Due to an advanced ethno-territorial vision of Turkey's geography, the new approach also demanded nego-tiated arrangements with various national or local authorities in the western provinces. In the spring of 1932, Young Turk thought on how to solve the Kurdish question in the eastern provinces crystallized and reached an apex with a new 'Settlement Law', which came into force on 14 June 1934 and was published a week later.[248] This law was directly modelled after the previous deportation laws, in particular the 1926 law with the same title. Discussions leading to the drafting of this law were a continuation of the ideological exchanges in parliament and concentrated on the themes of historical justification, language, and how to learn from mistakes and make future population politics more efficient.

The document began with historical visions blaming the Ottoman Empire for neglecting to assimilate the minorities, and continued to prophesy how the new era would herald 'the scientific explanation and dissection of the Turkish sociological corps' that would 'render dominant the Turks as the autochthonous element', ultimately resulting in 'the Turkification of their territory'. The other 'elements', being the minorities, were 'to be distributed household by household in Turkish towns and villages in order to melt and be assimilated'. The Turkish Republic would 'safeguard, consolidate, and homogenize our national body' because 'it was time to pursue and implement a population policy crafted by government hand to develop ... in quality and quantity, population masses suited for our national culture and modern civilization'. The law would further aim at populating sparsely populated areas and sedentarizing nomads and tribes to develop agriculture.[249] Language was an important ethnic marker and selection criterion. 'Population masses whose mother-tongue is not Turkish will be prohibited from gathering, and the existing ones will be scattered ... this way measures will be taken for the unity of culture'. Strict measures would be taken so that nowhere would these non-Turkish peoples constitute more than 10 percent of the general population. In order to 'Turkify' the eastern provinces, in particular the north of Diyarbekir province, the First Inspectorate-General needed to settle at least twice as many Turks as it had settled so far. The Kemalist deportation proposals and decrees contained formulations, provisions, and distinctions directly modelled on the wording of the CUP's previous deportations. Thus the Young Turk jargon of dividing and subdividing settlers into two categories reappeared: those who had come to Turkey of their own volition were called 'immigrants' (*muhacir*), and those

[248] *Resmi Gazete*, no.2733, 21 June 1934.
[249] *TBMM ZC*, vol. 23, period IV, session 3 (7 June 1934), Appendix no. 189, 'I/335 numaralı İskân kanunu lâyihası ve İskân muvakkat encümeni mazbatası' (2 May 1932).

who came 'as a result of exigencies' were called 'refugees' (*mülteci*).[250] The latter category was subdivided into two further categories, those who were needy and those who were not. To the needy free land would be distributed. The Kemalists also wanted to improve their existing techniques of social engineering. From their evaluations of the 1925–7 deportations they concluded that the cadre of civil servants was insufficiently staffed and salaried for the deportation and settlement campaign to be truly effective. Their advice was to expand, within one year, the cadre of trained and experienced experts with the skills required for this specialized area.[251]

In the draft version of the law, the first article captured its essence. It stipulated that the law would operate upon 'the residence and spread of the culturally Turkish population'. The law would be enacted according to 'a program determined by the Cabinet' and under auspices of the Interior Ministry. Article 2 detailed how this would occur. The Cabinet would approve of a map according to which Turkey would be divided into three types of zones: 'Zone number 1: Places where the influx of the population of Turkish culture is wanted; Zone number 2: Places assigned to the transfer and settlement of the population whose pervasion into Turkish culture is wanted; Zone number 3: Places that will be evacuated, and where settlement and residence will be prohibited due to local, sanitary, economic, cultural, political, military and security reasons'. The attraction of Turkish settlers from abroad would be bound by restrictions: 'Those who are not culturally Turkish, anarchists, spies, nomadic gypsies, those who have been evicted from the country will not be taken into Turkey as immigrants. Those who are not from Turkish stock . . . will have to settle in places assigned by the Government and are obliged to stay there . . . those who move elsewhere will be taken back to their initial places of settlement; in case of repetition they will be denaturalized by the Government'.[252]

For the eastern provinces, the second part of the law, titled 'Measures on internal population transfers, culture, and administration', bore at least as much significance. Article 9 stipulated that 'nomads not culturally Turkish will be collectively dispersed and settled in towns that are culturally Turkish', that 'those of whom espionage is sensed . . . and nomads who are not culturally Turkish will be expelled beyond national borders'. These 'nomads' were specified in the next article, which opened a frontal attack on traditional tribal life: 'The law does not accord legal recognition to the tribe . . . all rights based on any decree, document, and decision that have been acknowledged so far are abolished. Tribal chieftaincy, lordship, squirearchy and sheikhdom, and all of these types of organizations based on any document or tradition are abolished'. These people would be deported to 'an appropriate place': non-Turkish tribes in particular would be deported to zone number 2. The article further stated that all property belonging to the aforementioned categories of people would be forfeited to the state, which would redistribute it to

---

[250] *TBMM ZC*, I65, c1, Appendix no. 189, 'İskan kanunu lâyihası muvakkat encümeninin tadili', 28, article 3.
[251] Ibid., 'İskân muvakkat encümeni mazbatası' (27 May 1934).
[252] *TBMM ZC*, vol. 23, period IV, session 3 (7 June 1934), Appendix no. 189, 'I/335 numaralı İskân kanunu lâyihası ve İskân muvakkat encümeni mazbatası' (2 May 1932).

various settlers. Language would serve as a prime selection criterion. The law prohibited 'those whose mother-tongue is not Turkish to assemble in villages and neighbourhoods, and to gather together as workers and artisans'. Moreover, the cabinet was authorized to 'take all kinds of measures based on cultural, military, political, social, and security reasons' against 'those who are not culturally Turkish'. They were never to form more than 10 percent of the local population and were not allowed to establish their own neighbourhoods anywhere.[253]

The third part of the law specified how the country would be sectionalized into the three zones. Article 12 summed up the settlement procedures for zone number 1, which was synonymous with the eastern provinces. In this zone, a range of people would be prohibited from residing, from tribesmen and nomads to 'people who are not culturally Turkish'—both indigenous and former deportees wishing to return. Instead, three categories of people would be allowed to settle in the zone. First, the indigenous Turks, i.e. people from the local villages and towns who were 'racially Turkish', would be allotted land. Second, indigenous Turks who had lived in zone 1 before 1914 but had been forced to leave due to warfare, were encouraged to return and settle in their native lands. Third, 'people who are culturally Turkish' from zone 2 would be transferred and settled in zone 1, 'according to suitable living and climatic conditions'. There, these Turkish settlers would receive a number of benefits, including exemption from various taxes and military service. Military and bureaucratic personnel 'of Turkish race or culture' were especially encouraged to settle in zone 1. Zone 2, roughly speaking the western provinces, would absorb those deported from zones 1 and 3, in particular 'those from zone 1 who are not racially Turkish'. In other words, zone 2 would be the ground on which the eastern deportees would be scattered and settled, according to the regulations for at least ten years.[254] The law further stipulated that all the transfer costs would be covered by the government.

In a later addition to the Settlement Law, the regime laid out with exact precision what constituted the first zone. In zone 1, lands allocated to Turkish settlers would be inaccessible to non-Turks. In the First Inspectorate-General, which included the greater province of Diyarbekir, on both sides of the tracks along the entire network of railroads, from Diyarbekir city east to Tatvan, west to Urfa and north to Elazığ, a strip of twenty kilometres of land would be reserved in which non-Turks would be prohibited from residing. The same regulation was foreseen for the border (a strip of 25 kilometres of land along all eastern borders of Turkey), and all paved roads (a strip of 15 kilometres of land on both sides of the roads in the zone) would be prohibited for non-Turks. Also, a radius of 20 kilometres around Diyarbekir city was an off-limits area for non-Turks. This meant that a large territory in the wider region of Diyarbekir was marked for demographic 'Turkification'.[255] The bureaucratic apparatus for the project was divided into provincial centres, where

[253] Ibid.
[254] *TBMM ZC*, vol. 23, period IV, session 3 (7 June 1934), Appendix no. 189, 'I/335 numaralı İskân kanunu lâyihası ve İskân muvakkat encümeni mazbatası' (2 May 1932).
[255] Kökdemir, *Eski ve Yeni Toprak*, 166–70.

two departments would supervise the deportations and settlements. One department would take care of logistics (sending and receiving people, confiscating and assigning property), one to command the 'cultural front', involving the monitoring of the measures applied, and research on populations, such as the minorities and 'our kin and fellow culture folk abroad'. The second department would be a mobile one for the provinces and the rural areas and would see that the deportation and settlement proceeded smoothly.[256]

The law announced that tribes were a major category to be dissolved, abolished, and 'melted' into the mainstream Turkish population. Their property would be liquidated according to regulations and all leaders, lords, chieftains, and sheikhs were to be 'eliminated' (*tasfiye*), and to preclude new ones from 'sprouting up', their families were to be immediately deported. The comprehensive attack on tribal life and tribal leadership re-targeted Kurdish elites more forcefully. As George Clerk wrote, 'The policy of breaking up the Kurdish tribes, disarming everyone and deporting at any rate the leaders, is still being followed . . . nearly half the entire army is occupied in putting this policy into effect with varying success'.[257] This policy shift was ideologically informed: in the Young Turk interpretation of sociology, Kurds did not manifest nationhood. Therefore it was sufficient to decapitate the nation (i.e. deport their elites) and leave the population (seen as ethnic 'raw material') for mass forced assimilation (see Chapter 4). Thus, two strategies of social engineering were seen as complementary and mutually reinforcing. To this end, the government prepared a detailed, top-secret inventory of Kurdish tribes and published it strictly for internal circulation.[258] These lists, supplemented in the 1970s and republished in book form in 2000, identified for every province dozens of Kurdish tribes classified as 'loyal' or 'disloyal', with details provided on the nature of their relationships with each other.[259] The booklet included ten pages on the tribes of Diyarbekir province and detailed which tribes had stayed loyal to the government and which ones had not.[260] This report would be functional in the process of selecting deportees.

The 1934 Settlement Law read as a typical document of an interwar nation state fortifying its ethnic boundaries through restricting citizenship, expressing a nationalist ideology, and introducing nation formation on an alien population by force. It captures the essence of demographic engineering: the Kemalists sought to increase the relative size and power of the dominant ethnic group, the Turks, at the expense of ethnic minorities. The latter were expected to decrease determinately, and ultimately evaporate into insignificance or disappear sometime in the future.[261]

---

[256] *TBMM ZC*, vol. 23, period IV, session 3 (7 June 1934), Appendix no. 189.
[257] NAUK, FO 424/266, Clerk to Chamberlain, 12 January 1927.
[258] Hıdır Göktaş, *Kürtler-1: İsyan-Tenkil* (Istanbul: Alan Yayıncılık, 1991), 125–7.
[259] *Aşiretler Raporu* (Istanbul: Kaynak, 2000).
[260] Ibid., 92–102.
[261] For two brief discussions, see: Nesim Şeker, 'Demographic Engineering in the Late Ottoman Empire and the Armenians', in: *Middle Eastern Studies* 43, no. 3 (2007), 461–74; Erol Ülker, 'Assimilation of the Muslim Communities in the First Decade of the Turkish Republic (1923–1934)', in: *European Journal of Turkish Studies* (2007), <http://www.ejts.org/document822.html>.

Ethnoterritorialist nationalism, pervading the Kemalists' minds, came to full expression in the division of the country into two ethnicized zones, roughly the Turkish west and the Kurdish east. For Diyarbekir province, this formula maintained, expanded, and systematized important elements of continuity with the CUP's wartime practice of rendering the province a 'Turkification zone' (see Chapter 2).

The Kemalists wasted no time in putting the plan into action. In November 1934, Diyarbekir's second Inspector-General, Ahmet Hilmi Ergeneli, wrote a report on the new deportation and settlement phase. Identifying and selecting the Kurds earmarked for deportation was relatively easy since they had been deported before. However, the mode of settlement of 'our racial brothers' (*ırkdaşlarımız*) in designated places in his district, was not going to be an easy task, he argued: 'A part of the local population does not perceive the settlers warmly'. He indicated that the incoming Turks should be settled in living conditions qualitatively better than their places of origin, in order to satisfy them. Ergeneli called for settling the Turks near the railways, a policy killing two birds with one stone: strategic areas would be populated by a 'reliable population', and the settlers would probably be satisfied by their proximity to the railways. Among the benefits offered to the Turkish settlers were financial rewards and advanced educational opportunities, high-quality housing, children's playgrounds and sports facilities, and others. These were not extended to ethnic and cultural non-Turks. Ergeneli also called for more funds and more consistency in the settlement.[262] These suggestions clearly reveal the discriminatory practices inherent in the Settlement Law. It created a complex pattern of interaction between state and society, in which a regime favoured its kin peoples in a distant geography populated by locals deemed hostile.[263]

The intense correspondence between Ankara and Diyarbekir did not go unnoticed by the population of the east. The promulgation of the law sent a wave of rumours through the eastern provinces, which had the 'effect of causing a great deal of disquietude amongst the thousands of the inhabitants to whom such a law would be applicable'.[264] In Diyarbekir, the Kemalist dictatorship's political paranoia produced a climate of persecution which became contagious along social networks. Tribes and families who were related to central targets of the Settlement Law were summarily included in the deportation plans. Anybody related to the Kurdish elite families of Diyarbekir province, by profession or by marriage, was going to be deported as well. This expanded the number of deportees exponentially. Furthermore, the atmosphere of an omnipresent conspiracy was compounded by the governor of Diyarbekir, who, motivated by a desire to appear diligent in his

---

[262] BCA, 69.457.24, Ergeneli to İnönü, 10 November 1934, quoted in: Koca, *Yakın Tarihten*, 416–20.

[263] The policy of governing a distant land to send settlers in order to shape its demographic similarly as in the homeland is called settler colonialism. For a collection of essays, see: Caroline Elkins and Susan Pedersen (ed.), *Settler Colonialism in the Twentieth Century: Projects, Practices, Legacies* (London: Routledge, 2005).

[264] NAUK, FO 371/17958/E4912, Catton (Mersin) to Loraine (Ankara), 7 July 1934.

superiors' eyes, drew up blanket lists of deportees and unleashed a witch-hunt upon Diyarbekir to produce as many deportees as possible. Most significantly, he urged the residents to turn informer on any Kurdish 'chieftains' and 'lords'.[265] Scores of impoverished citizens coveting their neighbours' property gathered at the governor's office and in the end, the policy of open denunciation inevitably led to a great deal of private settling of old scores. There is evidence that the family most likely responsible for fanning the flames of Kemalist paranoia in Diyarbekir were the pro-government Pirinççizâde. According to one eye-witness, Pirinççizâde members assisted Diyarbekir's chief of police during the selection process of drafting lists of chieftains and tribes, and details on kinship relations between the tribes.[266] Moreover, the Pirinççizâde lobbied the government to deport Kurdish families they saw as their rivals in the Diyarbekir area. If this was true, the Pirinççizâde dynasty had again managed to collaborate with the regime in exchange for power, and most importantly, had again influenced the government's population politics on the local level. These were some of the local mechanisms that underlay and controlled the patterns of population politics in Diyarbekir in the 1930s.

After the first deportation had sent them to Tarsus, in 1928 the Azizoğlu family had returned to their estate in Silvan. In the summer of 1934, Fatma Azizoğlu was sitting on the porch of the family mansion when she suddenly noticed that gendarmes had surrounded the house. She ran inside but before she could tell the family, they heard a loud knock on the door. The commanding officer was standing on the doorstep and asked: 'Where are the men of the house?' The men were out, doing business and working the fields. The officer then read a list of names of people whom he declared would be taken to Diyarbekir city. The family was counted and assembled in the courtyard, and given one hour to gather their personal belongings. The Azizoğlus were loaded onto two trucks and taken away, leaving hundreds of grieving tribesmen behind. When they arrived in Diyarbekir city, their chieftain Hüseyin Azizoğlu, who had been in the city on business, had already been arrested. The whole group was taken to the railway station, locked in a wagon and sent off to Istanbul, escorted by gendarmes. After a few days, they arrived in Istanbul, made a transit to the Thracian city of Kırklareli, and finally ended up in the nearby town of Babaeski.[267] Although the intelligence report on tribes had identified the Azizoğlus as a loyal and obedient family that had not resisted the government, in 1934 they were rounded up again and deported to Thrace. They were not the only ones. The Zirkî tribe in Lice too, had been deported in 1926. Now, as one deportee related, they were rounded up more comprehensively as even the tribe's pro-government families were deported.[268]

---

[265] Interview with Vahit Altınakar conducted by Şeyhmus Diken, published in: Diken, *İsyan Sürgünleri*, 242–3.

[266] Interview with Şahin Cizrelioğlu conducted by Şeyhmus Diken, published in: Diken, *İsyan Sürgünleri*, 213.

[267] Interview with Fatma Azizoğlu conducted by Şeyhmus Diken, published in: Diken, *İsyan Sürgünleri*, 89–94; Interviews conducted with Azizoğlu family in Stockholm, 11 June 2005, and Amsterdam, 20 October 2007.

[268] Interview with Nihat Işık conducted by Şeyhmus Diken, published in: Diken, *İsyan Sürgünleri*, 260.

The Cizrelizâde tribe was deported from their native regions when their chieftain Ahmet Mümtaz Cizrelioğlu, an intellectual educated in law, was arrested in Diyarbekir in the summer of 1934. The Cizrelizâde, at that time living in the eastern border town of Eleşkirt, were rounded up and, without permission to take any belongings, driven to Sivas. From there they were deported by train to Beyşehir in the central province of Konya.[269] Similar experiences were shared by the Sürgücüzâde tribe. On 15 September 1936, Vahit Altınakar (at that time an adolescent of 16) was threshing wheat when he saw a boy from his village running towards him in panic. The boy brought the news that gendarmes had raided the village and told him his mother wanted him to hide under a pile of straw. Only after the gendarmes had left, did he dare to return to the village. His family was gone and the remaining villagers, 'in great anxiety', told him his family had been taken away by gendarmes at gunpoint. Where they had been taken, nobody knew. Vahit decided to go to Diyarbekir city to gauge what was going on and found a huge mass of people at the train station. Spectators were staring at them by the roadside, as susurrant voices murmured: 'They are being deported'. The young Vahit was arrested for having 'escaped' the round-up, held at the Inspectorate-General for several hours, handcuffed, and put in a wagon with the rest of his family. Contrary to the Settlement Law, the Sürgücüzâde had to defray the expenses of the train tickets as they were deported to Kütahya.[270]

After their return to their native villages, Sheikh Said's family had barely recuperated and were trying to make a living when the second deportation struck them in 1934. Again, an extended family largely consisting of women and children was taken from the north-eastern districts of Diyarbekir to Trabzon, where they were boarded on a ship for Istanbul. There, the family was split up and sent to various parts of Thrace. The core of the family ended up in the village of Sergen in Edirne's Vize district. That village was populated by a majority of Turks and a small minority of Albanians.[271] The noted Bukâr dynasty, a family of sufis and sheikhs from Diyarbekir city, were deported as well. They were scattered across the western Anatolian plains to the small towns of Uşak and Kütahya province. The authorities took special care not only that a family was broken up in groups and scattered, but also that none of the various Kurdish families would be deported to the same location. Ignorance of each other's whereabouts upset them and precluded them from contacting each other.[272]

One of the main targets of the Kemalists was undoubtedly the wealthy and influential Cemilpaşazâde dynasty of Diyarbekir. The 1926 deportation campaign had not included the Cemilpaşazâde as much as others, and therefore the local authorities attempted to make a 'clean sweep' and not leave anyone behind this

---

[269] Interview with Şahin Cizrelioğlu conducted by Şeyhmus Diken, published in: Diken, *İsyan Sürgünleri*, 212–14.
[270] Interview with Vahit Altınakar conducted by Şeyhmus Diken, published in: Diken, *İsyan Sürgünleri*, 243–4.
[271] Kaya, *Mezopotamya Sürgünü*, 45–6.
[272] Interview with Mehdiye Çetin-Öngören conducted by Şeyhmus Diken, published in: Diken, *İsyan Sürgünleri*, 25.

time. The family was living in the village of Qarabash when in the middle of the night, a sergeant arrived with ten soldiers. The sergeant read the deportation order out loud, and arrested them. No exceptions were made: their smallest child Felat Cemiloğlu was included in the deportation list and his brother Nejat Cemiloğlu, ill with a high fever, was lifted out his bed, and taken away, leaving behind their house and property as they were. At Diyarbekir central station they were loaded into a cattle car with their relatives. The young man barely survived the train journey, which took him and his family to the northern Black Sea town of Ordu.[273] Other family members were deported to central Anatolia and Thrace. Nejat's cousin Şermin was a young girl in primary school when she was arrested and deported:

It was a rainy, misty, and cold day. The commissioner and two or three officers came. Whatever they ordered, you know, we were able to take two mattresses, three sheets, one kettle, spoons, forks, a portable gas cooker. We had to argue to take a part of our belongings with us. My father was already under arrest. He was not around. We didn't even know where he was. That evening the truck came. We had lots of precious property. Persian rugs, silver, and so forth. They didn't allow us to take any of it . . . They threw us in the truck. Later they brought my father. With my mother and two little children we took the road. We children were not aware of what was going on.[274]

The Cemilpaşazâde were taken to the Fevzipaşa train station in Malatya, where they were locked in wagons and deported to Eskişehir. The father tried to comfort the children by entertaining them and buying toys in towns where the train stopped. This way, the children experienced the deportation as an exciting game. After arrival in Istanbul, the family was deported to the Thracian town of Lüleburgaz.[275] The persecution of the Cemilpaşazâde developed into a witch-hunt: the initial investigation was carried out ostensibly to uncover 'subversive activities', but now it was used to harass and undermine the Cemilpaşazâde simply for being a Kurdish elite family.[276] Fed up with the persecution, some Cemilpaşazâde sought asylum in Syria, which was under French mandate. Among those who fled there were Nazime Cemiloğlu's parents, who were unable to travel back and forth to visit their family members. The moment they attempted it and set foot on Turkish soil in 1932, they were arrested and deported west.[277] Those from the Cemilpaşazâde the regime could not catch were all denaturalized in a sweeping 1933 decree, for 'having fled to Syria'.[278] In 1935, not a single Cemilpaşazâde was left in Diyarbekir province.

The 1934 deportations distinguished themselves by more precision. Besides the transfer of entire categories of humans, the Kemalists also micromanaged the

---

[273] Interview with Nejat Cemiloğlu conducted by Şeyhmus Diken, published in: Diken, *İsyan Sürgünleri*, 131–2.
[274] Interview with Şermin Cemiloğlu conducted by Şeyhmus Diken, published in: Diken, *İsyan Sürgünleri*, 183–6; Malmîsanij, *Diyarbekirli Cemilpaşazâdeler*, 210–13.
[275] Ibid.
[276] See the file of Turkish intelligence on the family: BCA, 030.10/113.771.1 up to and including BCA, 030.10/113.771.9.
[277] Interview with Nazime Cemiloğlu conducted by Şeyhmus Diken, published in: Diken, *İsyan Sürgünleri*, 169, 174.
[278] BCA, 030.18.01.02/40.80.15, decree dated 12 November 1933.

deportation of certain individuals. For example, in November 1935 Kemal Atatürk ordered the deportation of a former Ottoman police officer, who had been living in Syria but desired Turkish citizenship, away from Diyarbekir to Kütahya. His residence in Syria was considered enough justification for deportation.[279] An Armenian tailor living in Diyarbekir was ordered deported because, according to Atatürk's decree, the tailor was 'a staunch enemy of Turks who had converted to Islam in order to escape the deportation and served the Armenian cause with his entire being'. The decree accused him and his sons of travelling to Beirut, Marseille, and Aleppo, where they allegedly were involved in 'pursuing harmful aims'. In this case, travel abroad sufficed for deportation: his family of a dozen women and children was deported to Çorum.[280] In October 1936 the priest of Diyarbekir's Armenian church was ordered deported to Sivas for being 'suspicious' and living in a border province.[281] The mufti of Diyarbekir's northern district of Kulp, son of a Naqshbandi sheikh named Mehmed Emin, reportedly took the locals up the Andok mountain for spiritual retreat. In doing so, he had violated the law and in November 1937 was ordered deported to Aydın with his family.[282] Many other people were deported this way, some for 'reactionary behaviour', others for marrying more than one woman. If the regime sensed anybody's disloyalty, deportation was often the answer.[283]

The deportees who arrived first often witnessed new ones coming immediately after them. One deportee remembered: 'The year was 1938 . . . one day we were strolling around the train station. A train arrived. The doors opened. The people came tumbling out. They were muddled. Many of them were suffering because of lack of air, dirt, hunger and thirst . . . some of them were wailing and yammering. Their dress resembled that of our Diyarbekir people . . . They were a train load. Dirt, disease, hunger, death, there was everything in the train.'[284] Due to strict travel restrictions, few foreigners were able to witness the deportations. The noted Ottomanists Robert Anhegger (1911–2001) and Andreas Tietze (1914–2003) were two of the exceptions. Travelling in central Anatolia in their young years, they witnessed a convoy of deportees arriving in Aydın. Anhegger wrote in his diary that the Kurds were 'simply removed there and distributed over the country. They are then dumped anywhere, without a roof over their head or employment. They do not know a single word of Turkish'.[285] John Frödin, a Swedish geographer, had been permitted to conduct research in Turkey when he witnessed deportees during his travels. He wrote that 'the male population of over 12 years was deported to

---

[279] BCA, 030.18.01.02/59.84.18, decree dated 11 November 1935.
[280] BCA, 030.18.01.02/68.77.9, decree dated 28 September 1936.
[281] BCA, 030.18.01.02/69.85.6, decree dated 26 October 1936.
[282] BCA, 030.18.01.02/79.89.7, decree dated 2 November 1937.
[283] See e.g.: BCA, 030.18.01.02/89.112.15, decree dated 20 November 1939.
[284] Kahraman, *Kürt İsyanları*, 184.
[285] *Internationaal Instituut voor Sociale Geschiedenis* (Amsterdam), Robert Anhegger Papers, 'Die zweite Anatolienreise 5.9.–3.10.1937', 44; Erik-Jan Zürcher, 'The Travel Diaries of Robert Anhegger and Andreas Tietze', in: *Journal of Turkish Studies* 26, no. 1 (2002), 359–69.

concentration camps in Western Turkey'.[286] (In reality, there were never any concentration camps as the deportees were settled in cities, towns, and villages.)

Not unlike eight years before, the authorities of the western provinces where the deportees were sent supplied the Interior Ministry with data. In the autumn and winter of 1934, the governorships of various western provinces sent Ankara long lists of individuals sent to their province. These were ethnically segmented according to family and village. Other necessary information was appended to the communications.[287] The deportees arrived in provinces where local circumstances ranged from favourable through tolerable to dreadful. Şermin Cemiloğlu of the Cemilpaşazâde, for example, grew up in Thrace among Balkan Muslims expelled from Greece, with whom she claimed relations were good.[288] The Sürgücüzâde tribe ended up in a town in Kütahya amidst Bosnians and Albanians, who were themselves migrants. According to Vahit Altınakar, 'if it wasn't for the goodness of those folks, we would have suffered so much wretchedness . . . the Bosnians were so genial and candid, they had nothing but good intentions'.[289] The Bukârs in Kütahya soon realized that there were cultural differences between them and the local Turks. The occasional awkward intercultural moments, however, were more a matter of ignorance than xenophobia. According to Bukâr deportees, the adult population was generally open and cordial, although their children were bullied in school for being different.[290]

The experiences of the Arat family were markedly different. According to Sakine Arat, 'the period of exile was quite difficult. We were different'. The locals would hurl racial epithets at them such as 'Tailed Kurd! Tailed Kurd!', and would mock them for speaking Kurdish.[291] The Azizoğlu, who after the 1926 deportations had fared relatively well in the south, now found themselves amidst a heavily bigoted society in Thrace. According to Fatma Azizoğlu, the Turkish population in the town of Babaeski despised, insulted, and intimidated them to the degree that her father Hüseyin Azizoğlu moved away to Konya without permission. The government quickly tracked him down and ordered him to return to his designated settlement area, but Azizoğlu refused.[292] The Cizrelizâde probably suffered the worst ordeal. Şahin and Mümtaz Cizrelioğlu, always the only Kurds in school, were often bullied, threatened, and assaulted by Turkish children who used racially offensive language. The two brothers were beaten up so often that their mother (who was half Circassian) solicited their Chechen neighbours to gang up on the

---

[286] John Frödin, 'En Resa Genom Östra Turkiet 1936', in: *Ymer*, no. 2–3 (1937), 169–98, at 182–3.

[287] BCA, 272.12/69.190.10, various reports dated 30 December 1934.

[288] Interview with Şermin Cemiloğlu conducted by Şeyhmus Diken, published in: Diken, *İsyan Sürgünleri*, 183–6; Malmîsanij, *Diyarbekirli Cemilpaşazâdeler*, 210–13.

[289] Interview with Vahit Altınakar conducted by Şeyhmus Diken, published in: Diken, *İsyan Sürgünleri*, 246–7.

[290] Interview with Mehdiye Çetin-Öngören conducted by Şeyhmus Diken, published in: Diken, *İsyan Sürgünleri*, 26, 32–3.

[291] Interview with Sakine Arat conducted by Şeyhmus Diken, published in: Diken, *İsyan Sürgünleri*, 52.

[292] Interview with Fatma Azizoğlu conducted by Şeyhmus Diken, published in: Diken, *İsyan Sürgünleri*, 94.

Turks. The call for Caucasian solidarity worked, for from then on, Şahin and Mümtaz stood stronger. At one point they stabbed one of the bullies with a knife, and were left alone for the remainder of their exile.[293] The social reception was not the only climate vexing the Diyarbekir Kurds. Used to the arid climate of the Upper Tigris basin, within days they found themselves on the humid shores of the Anatolian peninsula or the rainy hills of Thrace. Many found the climate unbearable and got sick, such as Sheikh Said's son Abdülhalik and Sheikh Ali Rıza's 18-year-old son, who succumbed to pneumonia.[294] In Ordu province, the Cemilpaşazâde contracted diseases such as malaria. Their request for permission to travel to Istanbul for treatment was granted.[295]

The government monitored the deportation process with great care. In the summer of 1935, most deportees had arrived at their destinations when Mustafa Kemal Atatürk ordered Prime Minister İsmet İnönü to undertake an inspection tour of the eastern provinces. İnönü was to report on how nation formation was developing in a general sense. The Prime Minister toured a large area in the east and south-east of the country and reported that the government's population policies were gradually yielding their fruits. According to İnönü, the government's efforts were sufficient to turn Diyarbekir into a 'strong centre of Turkishness' in the long term. He argued that the army and the Inspectorate-General facilitated the policies, and advised the government to keep their presence intact. He concluded: 'In a well organized East the Republic will be based on a very important foundation. From any viewpoint, such a foundation is necessary for Turkish dominance'.[296] İnönü's report was crucial to the direction that the policy would take. His observations and recommendations were funnelled back into local-level administration for implementation.

On 8 December 1936, Interior Minister Şükrü Kaya convened a conference of all four General Inspectorates in Ankara with the aim of evaluating the progress of the regime's governance of the eastern provinces. The conference, chaired by Kaya, featured First Inspector-General Abidin Özmen, Second Inspector-General General Kâzım Dirik,[297] Third Inspector-General Tahsin Uzer, Fourth Inspector-General General Abdullah Alpdoğan, and gendarme commanders Naci Tınaz and Seyfi Düzgören. This arrangement of persons at the conference clearly showed that veteran Young Turk social engineers were in charge of ruling the East. Over three long days, the inspectors briefed Kaya on how nation formation was proceeding in their districts.[298] Özmen presented his report on Diyarbekir province and promised that the government's measures would obviate the ethnic questions in his area.

---

[293] Interview with Şahin Cizrelioğlu conducted by Şeyhmus Diken, published in: Diken, *İsyan Sürgünleri*, 214–15.

[294] Kaya, *Mezopotamya Sürgünü*, 47.

[295] BCA, 030.18.01.02/97.65.4, decree dated 5 July 1939.

[296] Saygı Öztürk, 'İsmet Paşa'nın Kürt Raporu', *Hürriyet*, 8 September 1992, 7. The entire report was later republished: Saygı Öztürk, *İsmet Paşa'nın Kürt Raporu* (Istanbul: Doğan Kitap, 2007).

[297] Serap Tabak, *Kâzım Dirik Paşa (Askeri, Mülki Hayatı ve Şahsiyeti)* (Çorum: Karam, 2008); K. Doğan Dirik, *Atatürk'ün İzinde Vali Paşa Kâzım Dirik: Bandırma Vapuru'ndan Halkın Kalbine* (Istanbul: Gürer, 2008).

[298] Şükrü Sökmensüer, *Umumî Müfettişler Konferansı'nda Görüşülen ve Dahiliye Vekâleti'ni İlgilendiren İşlere Dair Toplantı Zabıtları ile Rapor ve Hülâsası* (Ankara: Başvekâlet Matbaası, 1936).

However, he also complained that former locals who were now living abroad were collaborating with their friends and family in the region to get back into Turkey and 'disrupt security'. According to Özmen, the border with Syria needed to be sealed off hermetically, and anybody resisting the regime needed to be denaturalized and expelled. He identified these resisters as Kurds, Armenians, Syriacs, and Yezidis living in Syria, who were 'working for the establishment of a greater Armenia and unified Kurdistan'. Their cross-border incitements of ethnic minority elites in Turkey were to be prevented by more gendarme presence in the countryside and a continued deportation and settlement program. Besides these proposals, Özmen also argued that simply continuing the physical removal of people would not solve the Kurdish question durably. In his opinion, long-lasting solutions necessitated propaganda and sustained efforts for forced assimilation, such as linguistic and cultural assaults on the Kurds' identity.[299] These cultural policies will be dealt with in the next chapter.

A second evaluation of the policies implemented up to then was a report presented to the Party's General Secretariat in 1939–40. In this report, Kemalist social engineers reviewed the 1934 Settlement Law and praised it as a productive tool: 'The spirit of the law is assimilation and internal colonization ... to dismember the territorial unity of the Kurds'. Deportations needed to continue to be implemented 'comprehensively' and should 'be elevated to the main politics of the government which will work with full authority to establish and operate a special machinery for internal colonization'. This phrasing clearly suggested that subordinates called on their superiors for stronger measures. They continued to argue that minorities needed to be 'taken to the interior and the villages of these races, wherever they are, need to be scattered ... in places and conditions where this is not possible, Turks need to be settled in their richest and most fertile villages at a rate of at least 50 percent [of the local population]'. The report further iterated that deportation alone was not enough to 'Turkify' the eastern population. It pressed for more realism in dealing with the Kurds, urging their superiors to abandon the self-deceiving discourse of calling the Kurds 'Mountain Turks' or 'Valley Turks', which, they claimed, was a fallacy that only masked the reality of the problem: 'With this propaganda we cannot convince either them or anybody else that they are Turks ... we have to acknowledge and admit that in a large part of the country a foreign element are living in a collective fashion, and to take measures accordingly'. Therefore, the report proposed more radical measures in two fields: 'psychological measures' and 'deportation measures'. The bottom line was that cultural policies were needed to complement the deportation program.[300]

At that time, foreign diplomats recognized that the administrators of the east had been summoned to Ankara, and the Kemalists' preoccupation with ethnic homogeneity was sensed by them very clearly. As a British diplomat wrote,

---

[299] Koca, *Yakın Tarihten*, 452–94.
[300] Reproduced in: Faik Bulut, *Kürt Sorununa Çözüm Arayışları* (Istanbul: Ozan, 1998), 185–9.

In short, Turkey's only policy to-day is to rid itself of extraneous population, without real regard to the eventual results on her population and in the hopes of building up in course of time from the remnants a homogenous Turanian people. Her Arabs, Armenians, Greeks, Jews and, indeed, any people that can, possibly, by tradition, sentiments or blood be linked however remotely to other countries she eyes with the same suspicion as in the past and is determined to supplant and even root out.[301]

Another diplomat reported,

The Kurds of the Eastern provinces, the Arabs of South-Eastern Anatolia, the Moslems from Russia, the territories detached under the Treaty of Lausanne, the Greek islands, Greece, the Balkans and Roumania will be scattered among pure Turkish populations, so that they may lose the characteristics of the countries and districts of their birth, and, in a generation, be Turkish in speech, dress, habits and outlook, undistinguishable from their old-established neighbours.[302]

In the end, the demographic ramifications of the third deportation phase were considerable. According to official sources, the total number of Kurds deported to the west in the 1930s was 25,381 people in 5074 households.[303] Now again, for the third and last time, the voids they left behind were filled by Turkish settlers.

According to the regulations of the 1934 Settlement Law, Diyarbekir was part of zone 1, the zone where 'people who are culturally Turkish' would be transferred from zone 2 (the western provinces) and settled. Inspector-General Abidin Özmen's projections were ambitious. He assured that 'the area would be organized in sections and commissions of expertise such as artisans, administrators, settlement bureaucrats, judges, doctors, engineers, architects, and scientist bureaucrats will be set up and at least 300 houses per year will be constructed'. These commissions would build three to five Turkish villages of 100 houses every year at a cost of 600 lira. When the settlers finally came in, Özmen argued, 'this way our progressive nation can assimilate the backward nation' and establish 'economic dominance in a Turkish centre'.[304] According to official sources, from 1928 to 1938 a total of 1988 migrants were sent to Diyarbekir province. For the year 1938 another 2143 households were expected to settle there. Because the Republican province of Diyarbekir was much smaller than its Ottoman predecessor, to this number needs to be added (parts of) the settlers sent to Elazığ province in the north. There, from 1932 on, a total of 1571 households were sent, totalling 6045 settlers from Yugoslavia, Bulgaria, Greece and some from Syria.[305] As all the settlers were peasants, they were settled in the rural areas.

Of these settlers, twelve households were settled in Kabiye village, fifty in Karabash, 105 in Anbarçayı/Özmen households, five in Şimşim in the Silvan district (all of these were old Syriac and Armenian villages), thirty-four on the banks of the Tigris, seventy-five in Altıok in the Bismil district, thirty-five in

[301] NAUK, FO 424/268/E129.
[302] NAUK, FO 371/17970/E6434.
[303] *Başvekalet Toprak ve İskan İşleri Genel Müdürlüğü Çalışmaları* (Ankara: n.p., 1955), 108–9.
[304] Koca, *Yakın Tarihten*, 495–7.
[305] Hurşit Nazlı, *Elazığ İlinin Coğrafi, Zirai, Ticari, Tarih, Nüfus ve Jeolojik Durumu* (Ankara: Zerbamat Basımevi, 1939), 51.

Harbato in Ergani district, fifteen in Osmaniye city centre. Besides these directed settlements, the government confiscated another 200 houses from Kurds and appropriated them to the settlers. For a large part the resources, considerable in the context of the economic crisis of the 1930s, emanated from the Armenian genocide and the various confiscations from Kurdish elites—some of which were also formerly Armenian goods.[306] According to official sources, this movable property included at least the following additional resources in Diyarbekir: 284 ploughs, 636 oxes, two mares, two donkeys, twenty-two shops, sixty-one drags (large four-horse coaches), 51,975 kilos of seed, 16,407 acres of land, and 68,907 cents in cash.[307]

In official propaganda texts, the settlement of Turks in Diyarbekir province was painted as an unequivocal success. One brochure published by the governorship boasted that it was working hard to 'attract our Turkish brothers from beyond our national borders, settle them in the homeland, and turn them into productive people truly connected to the superior ideal of the nation'.[308] Here, the distinction between the ethnic 'Turkish brothers' versus 'Turkish citizens' is poignant for understanding Young Turk visions on nationalism and citizenship. The local authorities in Diyarbekir did not want to lose face by lagging behind in the settlement of Turks, compared to other provinces. They acclaimed the settlement of the Turks in the same discourse as national directives: 'Three beautiful and brand new villages have been established near Diyarbekir city for our brothers from Bulgaria and Romania... the settlers have now passed into a state of being fully productive people'.[309] Another official wrote in the same vein: 'The attention given to the settlers is considerable. After having provided for their maintenance, farm animals, ploughs, seeds, and land have also been supplied. Their sick are being taken care of by the state. The Bulgarian and Romanian immigrants work hard and have rapidly transformed into productive people'.[310]

But internal correspondence and oral history suggest otherwise. In his 1935 report İnönü remarked in an uneasy tone:

> There have been efforts to settle immigrants from everywhere. A population of about fifteen hundred toil on very fertile and water-rich terrain. There are three groups of immigrants with a gap between them of three to five years... Almost all of them complain to government officials about their condition... The people are needy, destitute, the fields have not yet been productive. The pastureland has been distributed poorly. They are complaining.[311]

The issues vexing the settlers were not always economic. One elderly Turkish settler remembered that even though his parents were allotted plenty of property by the

---

[306] For examples, see: Diken, *İsyan Sürgünleri*, 36, 51, 98, 220, 239.
[307] *Cumhuriyetin 15inci Yılında Diyarbakır* (Diyarbakır: Diyarbakır Matbaası, 1938), 107.
[308] Ibid., 106.
[309] Usman Eti, *Diyarbekir* (Diyarbakır: Diyarbakır Matbaası, 1937), 44.
[310] Nazlı, *Elazığ*, 51.
[311] Saygı Öztürk, 'İsmet Paşa'nın Kürt Raporu', *Hürriyet*, 8 September 1992, 7. In his memoirs İnönü denied the ethnic component of the deportation-and-settlement campaigns, justifying them as a matter of filling a thinly populated area: İsmet İnönü, *Hatıralar* (Ankara: Bilgi, 1987), vol. 2, 270.

government, in his childhood they used to deplore Diyarbekir as 'this accursed place', nostalgically longing for their estate in Thessaloniki.[312] Another family of settlers faced a culture which, in their own words, they 'never understood'. They felt overwhelmed by Diyarbekir's 'cut-throat' economic rivalry and higher levels of everyday violence. They also felt intimidated by their Kurdish neighbours, who envied and despised them for their connectedness and preferential treatment at government offices.[313] The deportations and settlements also sowed the seeds of conflict among local Kurds and Turkish settlers in Diyarbekir province. For these settlers, the climate did not alleviate their lives either, even though the Settlement Law clearly bore a clause that the Turks should be settled 'according to suitable living and climatic conditions'. Although the law had promised to take into consideration the acclimatization of the peasants from the Balkans, who were used to green hills with plenty of precipitation, some became ill in the scorching, arid Tigris valley and some died.[314] Much like the Kurdish deportees in Western Turkey, many Turkish settlers in Eastern Turkey too, often felt alienated and regretted having migrated and being settled.

The settlement campaign continued until the very end of the Young Turk dictatorship. In 1950, on the eve of the Kemalist loss of power, there were still Kurdish deportees in the west who were not allowed to return, and there were still Turkish settlers being sent to Diyarbekir province.[315] Most Kurds who were allowed to return did not need much Kurd to consider the matter. Mehdiye Çetin remembered her father was determined to return as soon as possible. When the news of the amnesty came through, the deportees rushed back to Diyarbekir by train, a journey which took them three days and three nights. Mehdiye saw how 'all of the deportees had poured onto the roads to return'.[316] According to her sister Sakine, on arrival in their village their fellow villagers were delighted and received them well. Surrounding villagers who had profited materially from their deportation, however, feared they might want their property back and therefore resisted their return.[317] When the Azizoğlu family received the news of the amnesty, according to Fatma Azizoğlu, they 'played instruments and organized parties'. But the return was disappointing: their house was in ruins and the Kemalists had turned the large family mansion into a military barracks.[318] Şermin Cemiloğlu of the Cemilpaşazâde claimed she could clearly remember the date of the amnesty: 14 March 1947. On that day, the family was undecided, for

---

[312] Interview conducted in Diyarbekir with Kerim B., 14 August 2007.

[313] Interview conducted in Diyarbekir with A.S., 15 August 2007.

[314] Şevket Beysanoğlu, *Anıtları ve Kitâbeleri ile Diyarbakır Tarihi* (Diyarbakır: Diyarbakır Büyükşehir Belediyesi, Kültür ve Sanat Yayınları, 1996), vol. 3, *Cumhuriyet Dönemi*, 1026–9.

[315] Majeed Jafar, *Under-underdevelopment: A Regional Case Study of the Kurdish Area in Turkey* (Helsinki: Studies of the Social Policy Association in Finland, 1976), 82, footnote 90.

[316] Interview with Mehdiye Çetin-Öngören conducted by Şeyhmus Diken, published in: Diken, *İsyan Sürgünleri*, 33–4.

[317] Interview with Sakine Arat conducted by Şeyhmus Diken, published in: Diken, *İsyan Sürgünleri*, 52.

[318] Interview with Fatma Azizoğlu conducted by Şeyhmus Diken, published in: Diken, *İsyan Sürgünleri*, 98.

once again they would have to migrate and abandon a life they had built. When she returned to Diyarbekir, she felt alienated. 'We felt like strangers when we arrived', she said in an interview.[319] One of the most poignant accounts of the problems surrounding return was that of Şahin Cizrelioğlu of the Cizrelizâde family. He remembered his return as follows:

> The deportees' return aroused indignation in certain circles because the real owners would get their property here back. It sparked competition. The separation into political parties increased this issue. Those in the People's Party found those in the Democratic Party against them . . . Among those in the middle class and in the villages there were people who returned us our lands or handed us small amounts of money and pledged loyalty to us. But in the city, certain circles who were reigning in luxury opposed this. Later, unpleasant incidents happened . . . Those who profited from the void in the period of our absence and claimed to be the owners of Diyarbekir tried to make trouble for us. In fact, they even worked for us to be deported from here again.[320]

Although he did not name any names, Cizrelioğlu undoubtedly thought of the Pirinççizâde and Müftüzâde families. These local families, who had urged the Cizrelizâde's deportation in 1934 and profited from it, were irritated and, out of fear for losing power, urged the local authorities to deport them again. Other families who returned faced similar difficulties. Some deportees simply stayed in their places of exile, either because life was treating them well or in the expectation that if they returned they would be re-deported in a next wave anyway.

But the fourth wave of deportations never came. On 14 May 1950 the first democratic elections in the history of the Turkish Republic were held. The Republican People's Party suffered a crushing defeat with 39.5 percent of the votes, as their rival the Democrat Party took the absolute majority: 52.7 percent. In Diyarbekir, the Democrats won 53.7 percent of registered voters, a sign that the population was discontented with decades of Young Turk rule.[321] The 1950 elections ended the Young Turk regime and their brand of nationalist population politics in Eastern Turkey. A sigh of relief blew through the eastern provinces. However, the Democrat Party was insufficiently 'de-Kemalized' and failed to come to terms with the legacy of Young Turk rule. The crimes were neither discussed nor punished. It did express more tolerance than the Republican People's Party for traditional ways of life and relaxed much of the RPP's anti-Islamic antipathy.[322] In the eastern provinces, this meant that sheikhs and their followers who had survived the Young Turk dictatorship could slowly reopen their seminaries and educate their students. By that time, the human map of Eastern Turkey had been significantly altered.

---

[319] Interview with Şermin Cemiloğlu conducted by Şeyhmus Diken, published in: Diken, *İsyan Sürgünleri*, 190–1.

[320] Interview with Şahin Cizrelioğlu conducted by Şeyhmus Diken, published in: Diken, *İsyan Sürgünleri*, 220–1.

[321] John M. VanderLippe, *The Politics of Turkish Democracy: İsmet İnönü and the Formation of the Multi-Party System, 1938–1950* (Albany, NY: State University of New York Press, 2005), chapters 7 and 9.

[322] Feroz Ahmad, *The Turkish Experiment in Democracy, 1950–1975* (Boulder, CO: Westview Press, 1977), chapters 3 and 4.

DISCUSSION

The scholarship on the deportations of Kurds during Young Turk rule is in its infancy, especially in comparison to deportations in other dictatorships such as Nazi Germany or Russia under Stalinism. One of the first scholars to ever study Young Turk population politics was the Turkish sociologist İsmail Beşikçi, who wrote a trailblazing series of books on Kemalism. His volume on the Young Turk deportations of the Kurds analysed the 1934 Settlement Law and explained the deportations.[323] Beşikçi began his periodization in 1923 and thus ignored the CUP deportations during the First World War and the continuity between these episodes. In other words, in his attempt to criticize Kemalism, Beşikçi used Kemalist assumptions and cast a Kemalist historical gaze. The trap of 'methodological Kemalism' is one of the most common pitfalls that surround scholarship on the Young Turk era. Two other scholars who have studied deportations approached the subject matter similarly, either periodizing from 1923 on, or until 1923.[324] This chapter has attempted to challenge these approaches by looking at the long-term processes of population policy. At this point, we can return to the question that was raised: how did the Young Turk dictatorship use forced population transfer as a strategy of 'Turkifying' the country's eastern provinces?

Three major waves of deportations struck the Kurdish population of the east. The first generation of deportees (1916) suffered perhaps the most amidst the harsh conditions of war and the seasons. The second cohort of Kurds deported right after the establishment of the Republic from 1925 to 1927 did not stay away from their native regions very long and many deportees returned within a year or two. The third deportation was organized after the consolidation of the single-party dictatorship in 1934 and was more sophisticated and categorical. Only when the Young Turks were ousted from power in 1950 were Kurds no longer deported.[325] The deportations show a distinct process of evolution from the first to the last phase. Young Turk social engineers accumulated experience and as they muddled

---

[323] İsmail Beşikçi, *Bilim Yöntemi, Türkiye'deki Uygulama 1: Kürtlerin Mecburi İskânı* (Istanbul: Komal, 1977).

[324] Soner Çağaptay, *Islam, Secularism and Nationalism in Modern Turkey: Who Is a Turk?* (London: Routledge, 2006), chapter 5; and Fuat Dündar, *İttihat ve Terakki'nin Müslümanları İskân Politikası (1913–1918)* (Istanbul: İletişim, 2002), respectively.

[325] Yet a brief caveat is in order about the survival of deportations into the post-1950 era. Avni Doğan, the fourth Inspector-General in Diyarbekir, wrote about the Kurdish 'danger' and the necessity to resume deportations well into the 1960s. Avni Doğan, *Kurtuluş, Kuruluş ve Sonrası* (Istanbul: Dünya, 1964); Koca, *Yakın Tarihten*, 550. According to recently discovered documents on the 1960 military junta, the State Planning Organization established an 'Eastern Task Force' that spurred the leaders to resuscitate Young Turk methods of population politics. The Eastern Task Force toured the region on 8, 10, and 16 February 1961 and presented a report to the junta on 24 March 1961. The report included the following clause: 'In order to transform the structure of the population in the region in favour of the Turks, those who believe they are Kurds need to be transferred outside the region and the excess population of the Black Sea coasts and Turks migrating from abroad need to be settled here.' The cabinet discussed and accepted the report on 18 April, and authorized its implementation by a governmental decree to the Ministries. With the overturn of the junta following the October 1961 elections, the plan was discontinued. *Milliyet*, 22 January 2008.

through, learnt from their prior mistakes and thus sophisticated the craft of deportation. The three phases of deportations exhibit an evolving dialectic: ethno-territorial thinking, the promulgation of a law, the implementation of the deportation, the separation of elites from populace, and the monitoring of the 'output' of the deportation back into the process to regulate the 'input', or keeping track of the deportees' experiences to improve the method.

This evolution towards more sophistication in population policies ran parallel with the biographies of their organizers. In order to support this claim of continuity it is sufficient to cross-reference CUP social engineers with RPP social engineers and accentuate overlap in the composition of the political elites ordering and carrying out the campaigns. It is no coincidence that names such as Mustafa Abdülhalik Renda, Mahmud Celâl Bayar, Kâzım Özalp, İbrahim Tali Öngören, Ali Cenani, and especially Şükrü Kaya appear throughout the 1913–50 era in reports and operative documents regarding population politics (see Plate 12). After 1923, these were the men to be employed in policies of social engineering since they had acquired the requisite know-how and experience in this field during CUP rule. Even though some men were tried and hanged in 1926, most in mid-level positions remained in office and many were even promoted. Moreover, the Kemalist deportation proposals and decrees contained clauses, provisions, and formulations directly modelled on the wording of the CUP deportations. The modus operandi of the deportations, with 'zones of Turkification' and percentage regulations (5% and 10%), bore the unmistakable traces of previous deportation formulas. In some cases the deportees of the 1934 phase were settled close to villages of Kurds who had been deported from the same regions in 1916.[326]

Continuity also existed on the level of the Kurdish resistance. Rather than concomitant effects of the Kemalist abolitions of sultanate and khalifate, resistance was a relatively autonomous process that had been going on since 1913. Many of the tribes and families that resisted the CUP later continued to resist the RPP as well. And vice versa: the deportations themselves were not responses to Kurdish 'uprisings' or 'rebellions' but pro-active, purposeful policy by Young Turk social engineers to which Kurdish elites responded in various ways. Local elites too, remained largely intact and assisted in continuing policies of social engineering. Kurdish collaborators and their families profited from the deportations, became even richer, and are still highly influential in the eastern provinces. However, it also becomes clear from the list of deportees in 1925 that Kemalist notions of Kurdish loyalty could fluctuate: several deportees had sided with the Young Turks but during a severe crisis could paradoxically become targets.

This chapter has argued that the two elements (deporting Kurds away from and settling Turks into the eastern provinces) in Young Turk population policy constituted an indivisible whole where these two parts reinforced each other. This interpretation of interdependency is based on the presence of elements of construction besides the obvious elements of destruction in the policies. The deportations

---

[326] Uğur Ümit Üngör, 'Seeing like a Nation-State: Young Turk Social Engineering in Eastern Turkey, 1913–1950', in: *Journal of Genocide Research*, vol. 10, no. 1 (2008), 15–39.

were *de*structive, not only for the integrity of the tribes and families affected, but for the Diyarbekir region as well. The deportees obviously saw their social ties disrupted, their property confiscated, and their power fractured. But how genocidal were the policies against Kurds between 1913 and 1950? Although thinking in ethnic categories, and the resultant wishful thinking that those ethnic groups disappear, was certainly genocidal in mind, the accompanying violence was too piecemeal to be actually genocidal in practice. The mass executions and persecution of Kurdish elites would qualify as proto-genocidal. Indeed, within a decade, the Young Turk regime had successfully eliminated the social elites of the minorities in the eastern provinces: Armenian elites had been murdered in 1915 and Kurdish elites had been executed, deported, expelled, and isolated in 1925.[327] However, the deportations were also *con*structive. They were part of a plan to reconstruct the Kurds as Turks. The cases of Kurdish elites exemplify the double-edged nature of inclusion and exclusion in nation formation. Their deportation and expropriation was expected to obviate competing loyalties and pave the way for cultural assimilation of the general Kurdish population in the 1930s. Construction was mostly aimed at the Turks. The elimination of Armenians and Kurds left the state an infrastructure of property that was used for the progress of Turkish settler communities. At least on paper, the Young Turks' plans to turn the eastern provinces into Turkish 'Lebensraum' appear obvious. They romanticized the agrarian life of the Turkish peasantry, whom they believed were 'racially pure Turks'. The regime took great care that adequate resources were allocated to the settlers: ploughs, oxen, land, seed, and housing. Bundled together, what seem like two isolated phenomena were part and parcel of a process of nation formation through large-scale social engineering.

Did the deportations 'Turkify' Diyarbekir province? This is hard to assess, for two reasons. If one attempts to enter into the Young Turks' minds and assume their nationalist world-view, then the answer would be negative. In 2009, demographically Diyarbekir still consists of at least three-quarters of Kurds. But if one interprets the question culturally, the answer might differ. For a long time, Turkish culture was the only culture permitted to be produced and consumed. Martin van Bruinessen has argued that by 1960, 'there were quite a few cases of successful assimilation', but adds that this was an urban phenomenon.[328] The mass settlements of Turks into Diyarbekir province did not 'Turkify' the region either. It seems that the settlers' efficacy for 'Turkification' was overestimated by the Young Turks. Many Turks simply left the area after 1950. Decades after the deportations, it seems that most of the Turkish settlers who continued to live in Diyarbekir province themselves became 'Kurdified' rather than 'Turkifying' their Kurdish

---

[327] For a short comparative study of mass murder of elites, see: Antonia Baum *et al.*, 'Review of Mass Homicides of Intelligentsia as a Marker for Genocide', in: *The Forensic Examiner*, 22 September 2007, 34–41.

[328] Martin van Bruinessen, 'Race, Culture, Nation and Identity Politics in Turkey: Some Comments', paper presented at the Annual Turkish Studies Workshop *Continuity and Change: Shifting State Ideologies from Late Ottoman to Early Republican Turkey, 1890–1930*, Department of Near Eastern Studies, Princeton University, 24–26 April 1997, 8–9.

neighbours.[329] Besides the demographic preponderance of the Kurds, ethnic intermarriages and economic ties have undoubtedly contributed to this result. Did the deportations 'Turkify' the Kurdish deportees? Although little systematic longitudinal research has been conducted on the fate of the Kurdish deportees, the available evidence suggests that for most Kurds the deportation project produced limited results. Well into the 1990s, Kurdish communities living in Central Anatolia preserved their tribal and ethnic identities and languages, with the exception of those who moved to the metropoles.[330] Moreover, in the end, neither combined nor in isolation did the three phases of deportations 'solve' any Kurdish 'question'. On the contrary, they were counterproductive, disrupting the local economies and shifting power relations in the East in favour of local families who had stayed aloof during the waves of deportations, especially the Pirinççizâde, Müftüzâde, and Direkçizâde. They had now become even more powerful.

The Young Turk attack on the Kurdish intelligentsia deepened existing grievances and accentuated conflicts across generations. The elites, who initially saw themselves as Muslims or Ottomans, were now constructed, treated, and deported *as Kurds* and as such, made into Kurds. For the deported Kurdish elites, the galvanizing impact of the Kemalists' policies brought frustration and vindictiveness. British diplomats did not fail to record that 'outside Government circles the opinion is freely held that the Kurds were too deeply embittered by the earlier policy of repression for a policy of conciliation to succeed now'.[331] The experiences of the 1930s were remembered and transmitted across time and space to new generations of Kurds. These new generations assimilated these narratives and constructed a paradigm based on their nation's suffering and a longing to return to their homeland, which many had never actually seen. The Azizoğlu family, for example, was deported so often they named one of their children 'Settlement' (*İskân*). The child, İskân Azizoğlu, grew up to become a politician and still carries the legacy of the Young Turk deportations with him. The deportations are still a major political issue—the memory of the massacres and deportations played a major part in the Kurdish-nationalist movement. The deportations had a profound effect on the Kurdish elites of the eastern provinces: most of all they sensitized Diyarbekir's Kurdish elites of their identities, triggering a backlash. The Kurdish-nationalist movement that sprouted from the 1960s on reached an important stage with the establishment of the Kurdistan Worker's Party (PKK). The PKK was spearheaded by many deportee families, and was symbolically established in a village in the Lice district of Diyarbekir province, that had been massacred and deported in 1925.[332] The war that ensued cost 40,000 lives and enormous material and ecological destruction.

---

[329] For a study of settlement issues in Diyarbekir, see: Joost Jongerden, *The Settlement Issue in Turkey and the Kurds: An Analysis of Spatial Policies, Modernity and War* (Leiden: Brill, 2007).

[330] 'Aksaray Kürtleri' and 'Polatlı Kürtleri', in: *Bîrnebûn* 1 (1997), 11–25.

[331] NAUK, FO 424/267, 125, no.72, Hoare to Chamberlain, 14 December 1927.

[332] Yet, some Kurds, such as some individuals of the Azizoğlu and Cemilpaşazâde tribes, remained loyal to the Republican People's Party. This resembles how some victims of Stalin maintained their loyalty to him after returning from the Gulag.

4

Culture and Education
in the Eastern Provinces

The previous chapters gave an account of how, on the Ottoman political spectrum, a hybrid but powerful Turkish-nationalist group seized, monopolized, maintained, and exercised the administrative and executive power of the state to reshape society through coercion and mass violence. The violent expulsion of Balkan Muslims, the genocidal destruction of the Ottoman Armenians and Syriacs, and the massacres and deportations of Kurds can be interpreted as principal vectors of the Turkish process of nation formation. How did the Young Turk regime use culture and education as vehicles of 'Turkification'? So far, not much has been written on how the Young Turks perceived cultural and educational policies as vehicles for assimilation of minorities in Eastern Turkey; this chapter will present these policies as aspects of nation formation and social engineering. Starting from the First World War, the Young Turks acted upon ideas to take the nationalist message 'to the people'. Due to the war and subsequent deconcentration of power, they were not able effectively to devise and carry out grand cultural and educational projects. But after 1923, Mustafa Kemal personally took the lead to assign the culture and education offices of the single-party dictatorship to launch ambitious projects of nation formation. This chapter will explore how the party attempted to penetrate every remote cell in the country using the educational infrastructure of tens of thousands of schools in order to impose Turkish culture in Eastern Turkey. The Diyarbekir region, special because it was targeted to become 'a centre of Turkish culture in the East', was infused with Turkish culture with particular care. The chapter will also address how high levels of coercion during this process produced high levels of popular resistance against government policies.

THE YOUNG TURK CULTURAL REVOLUTION

Young Turk cultural and educational policies are a hotly debated and contested terrain with fierce disagreement on their meaning, intentions, and consequences. The debate ranges from issues such as racism and cultural othering to power relations. One group of scholars argues that Young Turk policies were neither openly racist in content nor particularly successful in practice. According to one of them, 'the interwar Kemalist regime lacked the resources or cadres to establish an effective educational system in this region and inculcate a Turkish identity, myths and language into the local population'.[1] Another expert argues that modernization of the educational system 'was one of the most important and commendable of the Kemalist reforms', one that achieved 'impressive results'.[2] In this beneficial and inclusivist process of 'modernization', another scholar argues, 'an important factor was education, in which the Young Turks achieved their greatest successes'.[3] Turkish cultural and educational policies towards the ethnic minorities in the eastern provinces (such as Kurds) in this tradition is typically explained as 'acculturation', the exchange of cultural features that results when groups come into continuous firsthand contact, leading to cultural change among both groups, but with both groups remaining distinct.[4]

But a second group of scholars criticizes this approach for its alleged Turco-centric bias, regime apologia, and the whitewashing of the symbolic violence inherent in systems of cultural domination. They argue the opposite, namely that Young Turk cultural policies were hegemonic, exclusivist, oppressive, and racist towards non-Turks.[5] One sociologist uses labels such as 'colonization' and 'cultural genocide' to describe Young Turk assimilationist policies in Eastern Turkey.[6] These approaches use post-colonial theory and draw upon Frantz Fanon's accounts of French education in Algeria to explain the feelings of dependency and inadequacy that non-Turkish people experience in a state permeated by Turkish cultural nationalism. They emphasize the loss of native cultural originality and identity, and the imposition of an alien culture. This purportedly engenders an inferiority complex in the minds of minorities, who will try to appropriate and imitate the cultural code of 'Turkish-nationalist cultural colonialism'.[7] In this perspective, the Young Turks colonized the eastern provinces and collectively disempowered the population, subjugated their bodies, and peripheralized their economies. How can we reconcile this sharp contradiction?

This chapter will argue that most Young Turk nationalists treated Turkey's Muslim minorities as assimilable raw ethnic material. They adhered to the epistemological thesis that individual human beings are born with no innate or built-in mental content, in a word, 'blank': not only was their entire resource of knowledge built up gradually from their socialization by the outside world, this socialization could be engineered from above. In other words, their ideologues considered the population fully malleable. In interwar Turkey, integral nationalism triumphed in

---

[1] Dominic Lieven, *Empire: The Russian Empire and its Rivals* (New Haven: Yale University Press, 2002), 357.

[2] Michael Winter, 'The Modernization of Education in Kemalist Turkey', in: Jacob M. Landau (ed.), *Atatürk and the Modernization of Turkey* (Boulder, CO: Westview Press, 1984), 183–94, at 192–3.

[3] Bernard Lewis, *The Emergence of Modern Turkey* (Oxford: Oxford University Press, 2001), 229.

[4] Metin Heper, *The State and Kurds in Turkey: The Question of Assimilation* (London: Palgrave Macmillan, 2007).

[5] Mustafa Çapar, 'Tek Parti Dönemi: Milli Eğitim, Milli Dil ve Türkleştirme Politikaları', in: *Türkiye'de Azınlık Hakları Sorunu: Vatandaşlık ve Demokrasi Eksenli Bir Yaklaşım* (Istanbul: TESEV, 2006), 83–8.

[6] This argument is developed in: İsmail Beşikçi, *International Colony Kurdistan* (London: Parvana, 2004 [1990]).

[7] See e.g.: Welat Zeydanlıoğlu, 'Kemalism's Others: The Reproduction of Orientalism in Turkey' (unpublished Ph.D. thesis, Anglia Ruskin University, 2007).

social and political discourse, and was shared by the collective dictatorship of the party-state. But the regime abandoned its belief in sociological categories above biological ones when it came to the non-Muslims, such as Jews, Greeks, Armenians, and perhaps also Syriacs. Although there were attempts to 'Turkify' these groups, they were generally essentialized in their identifications and considered largely 'unturkifiable'. Moreover, as they were privileged to maintain their own educational infrastructure, the regime had limited means to extend its reach into their schools and spread Turkish nationalism. The rest of the population, consisting of the former Muslim millet, became the object of large-scale educational and cultural policies aimed at 'Turkification'—especially in the culturally diverse and historically multi-ethnic eastern provinces. This was of course a formidable task.

Education

The genesis of Young Turk educational philosophy was rooted in Ziya Gökalp's beliefs that reshaping society was necessary and desirable (see Chapter 1). Throughout the Young Turk era, Gökalp's philosophy informed and guided government policies, even after his death.[8] According to the sociologist, education should be based on the principles of 'Turkism', 'Islamism', and 'Modernism'. The curriculum should include Turkish language, literature, and history, Koran recitation, catechism, the history of Islam and Islamic languages (Arabic and Persian), and mathematics, natural sciences and European languages, as well as handicrafts and gymnastics. In other words, education was to be modern in style, and Turkish in spirit.[9] From his sociological observations, Gökalp drew several conclusions concerning education. He argued, 'since education inculcates culture and culture is national, education must be national'. For him, the difference between plain education and national education meant that primary schooling must include 'Turkish culture'. Also, a major aim of Turkish education must be to develop the youth into 'idealists' with enough 'national character' to be the future guiding elite of the nation.[10] Gökalp's philosophy laid out how education could be utilized as a tool of Turkification and as party ideologue of the CUP, his ideas were in power all throughout the Young Turk era.

Education as nation formation predated Kemalist rule. Although Sultan Abdulhamid's 'School for Tribes' had already tried to affiliate boys from Kurdish tribes with the regime, this policy was not informed by nationalist preoccupations with culture or language.[11] But existing practices changed into new ones as the Young

[8] Ziya Gökalp, *Milli Terbiye ve Maarif Meselesi* (Ankara: Diyarbakırı Tanıtma ve Turizm Derneği Yayınları, 1972).
    [9] Andreas M. Kazamias, *Education and the Quest for Modernity in Turkey* (Chicago: The University of Chicago Press, 1966), 110.
    [10] Gökalp, *Milli Terbiye ve Maarif Meselesi*, 15–16. For Gökalp's statements on education see: Ziya Gökalp, *Turkish Nationalism and Western Civilization: Selected Essays* (New York: Columbia University Press, 1959, transl. and ed. by Niyazi Berkes), 236–43.
    [11] Stephen Duguid, 'The Politics of Unity: Hamidian Policy in Eastern Anatolia', in: *Middle Eastern Studies* 9, nr. 2 (1973), 139–55; Eugene L. Rogan, 'Asiret Mektebi: Abdulhamid II's School for Tribes (1892–1907)', in: *International Journal of Middle East Studies* 28, no. 1 (1996), 83–108;

Turk accession to power heralded the era of coerced, assimilative schooling. The shift from imperial politics to identity politics affected education as the CUP attempted to use education to tie minorities deemed assimilable to Turkey and to bolster its control over the eastern provinces. Kurds and Armenians became the object of this resolve. Before the First World War, the CUP allotted significant funds for schools to be opened near Van and in Kurdish villages.[12] In this phase, the CUP began seeing boarding schools as effective tools to assimilate children into Turkish culture. In 1913 it ordered the Ministry of Education to establish a boarding school in Istanbul that could house dozens of Kurdish children.[13] The same social engineers during the First World War had organized the forced assimilation of Armenian children in schools established for this purpose.

The Young Turk regime not only transformed the existing Ottoman educational system into a decidedly Turkish-nationalist one, but also made serious attempts to reform the system of primary education. In 1913 a new law was passed, aimed at public support of primary schools and better organization of the program of study. The Primary Education Law (*Tedrisat-ı İptidai Kanunu*) of 1913 included compulsory and free six-year education in state schools and the limitation of class size to not more than fifty pupils. The purpose of these schools was stated as preparation for secondary education.[14] Legally, this law remained in effect well after the metamorphosis of the CUP into the RPP. Although it underwent some superficial changes during the war years, it was still fundamentally the same law in the 1930s. One scholar of education in the Young Turk era underlined this continuity: 'The Atatürk Revolution did not radically alter this aspect of Turkish society; rather, it solidified what was already nascent during the pre-republican decades'.[15] One important example of continuity was the fate of the Academy for Civil Service. After a brief eclipse during the First World War, the school reopened in 1918. In 1934 its name was changed to School of Political Sciences, two years later it was moved to Ankara, and in 1950 it was attached to the University of Ankara as its Faculty of Political Sciences.[16]

At the local level, too, attempts were made to modernize and 'Turkify' primary and secondary education. Diyarbekir Young Turks such as Pirinççizâde Aziz Feyzi, saw in the Armenian genocide an opportunity to modernize education in

---

Alişan Akpınar, *Osmanlı Devleti'nde Aşiret Mektebi* (Istanbul: Göçebe, 1997); Bayram Kodaman, *Şark Meselesi Işığı Altında: Sultan Abdülhamid'in Doğu Anadolu Politikası* (Istanbul: Orkun, 1983). For a study of education under Sultan Abdulhamid II, see: Benjamin C. Fortna, *Imperial Classroom: Islam, the State, and Education in the Late Ottoman Empire* (New York: Oxford University Press, 2000).

[12] Michail S. Lazarev, *Kurdskii Vopros (1891–1917)* (Moscow: Akademija Nauk SSSR, 1972), 225–6.

[13] BOA, DH.KMS 20/49, document 2.

[14] Kazamias, *Education*, 83. After 1923 the Kemalists flew over American, Swiss, and German pedagogic experts such as John Dewey (1859–1952), George Kerschensteiner (1854–1932), and Edwin Walter Kemmerer (1875–1945), and requested them for recommendations concerning education in Turkey. Ernest Wolf-Gazo, 'John Dewey in Turkey: An Educational Mission', in: *Journal of American Studies of Turkey* 3 (1996), 15–42.

[15] Kazamias, *Education*, 133.

[16] Türkkaya Ataöv, 'The Faculty of Political Science of Turkey', in: *Middle East Journal* 14, no. 2 (1960), 243–5.

Diyarbekir in a single manœuvre, and continuously pressed for reforms.[17] Interestingly, he also lobbied for a School of Agriculture to be established in Diyarbekir.[18] The educational infrastructure of Diyarbekir Armenians was sequestered by the regime and ordered to be redistributed to Turkish children.[19] These policies, confiscating the schools of the minorities and re-using them for Turkish-nationalist ends, continued from the CUP era into the Republic. The Ministry of Education profited from the sequestration of Armenian property as much as any other state organ. Thus, the Young Turk party offshoot Turkish Teachers' Association (Türkiye Muallimler Birliği), which had 110 centres in the country, requested the Prime Minister's Office that it be allotted 'abandoned property'[20] (see Plate 13). Schools were named after local Young Turk heroes, thus giving birth to schools such as the Ziyâ Gökalp Lycée.

When the fledgling Young Turk movement established its Ministry of Education on 2 May 1920, it had a foundation to build on: the CUP had bequeathed them a nationalist curriculum and cadre of teachers. In July 1921, they convened a Congress on Education in Ankara with the objective of giving 'a national direction to education'.[21] The assemblage of such a conference in the midst of raging warfare symbolized how the Young Turks prioritized education. In the same year they held the First Convention of Education, which lasted a month and culminated in a new law. On 3 March 1924, the same day the Ankara parliament passed a law to abolish the caliphate, the Law for the Unification of Education was passed.[22] It nationalized the education system by subordinating all educational institutions to the Ministry of Education. This included Islamic seminaries and schools formerly administered by private foundations, whose budgets were now integrally transferred to the Ministry. Within a decade, throughout the devastation of war, the Young Turks had assumed a monopoly of schooling over other religious, private, and foreign schools. All children in the country now fell under their educational policies.[23]

For the time being, the Ministry saw as its main responsibility to administer that part of the existing system which was at that particular time under Kemalist military jurisdiction. The Ankara government estimated in 1921 that there were 2345 schools in thirty-nine provinces with 2861 teachers (2384 of whom were male and 477 female). Of these schools, 581 were known to be closed, and only 875 teachers were graduates of pedagogical academies.[24] Efforts to organize the new Ministry of Education branched into four general directorates, each having one

---

[17] *Meclis-i Mebusan Zabıt Ceridesi* (Ankara: Türkiye Büyük Millet Meclisi Basımevi, 1985), election period 1, session 2, vol. 1, 526.

[18] Ibid., 299.

[19] BOABOA, DH.HMŞ 12/25.

[20] BCA, 030.10/140.3.3, Turkish Teachers' Association to Prime Ministry, 4 September 1341.

[21] Yahya Akyüz, 'Atatürk ve 1921 Eğitim Kongresi', in: *Cumhuriyet Döneminde Eğitim* (Istanbul: Milli Eğitim Bakanlığı, 1983), 89.

[22] *Resmi Gazete*, 6 March 1924.

[23] For a lengthy monograph on education in Turkey, see: Osman Ergin, *Türkiye Maarif Tarihi* (Istanbul: Eser, 1977), 5 volumes.

[24] İsmail Hakkı Tonguç, *Eğitim Yolu ile Canlandırılacak Köy* (Istanbul: Remzi Kitabevi, 1947), 259–60.

chairman and two clerks. These four administrative units dealt with primary education, secondary education, statistics, and most importantly, culture. This is where Gökalp's philosophy met Young Turk policy: culture and education were seen to be inextricably intertwined. In addition, there was a three-man Inspectorate and a seven-man Board of Curriculum Development. Collectively, the Ministry was assigned to implement the Kemalist government's educational program.[25] In the face of rampant misery including war, famine, poverty, and epidemics causing sky-high mortality, plus a workforce of demoralized teachers most of whom had not been paid in more than six months, it nevertheless formulated the following strategies: 'Our children's education must be more religious and nationalistic; We must revitalize our schools and cultural institutions according to scientific and modern principles; We must prepare new school books fitting our national spirit, and our historic, geographic and social character'.[26]

The application of nationalist principles and doctrine was at the forefront of Young Turk educational practices. As such, education was the centrepiece of the Republican People's Party's political platform for the 'internal colonization' (*dahili kolonizasyon*) of the eastern provinces. Throughout the Kemalist era, education served two purposes: Turkification and the spread of the regime's propaganda.[27] This was of such importance that Mustafa Kemal personally spearheaded the national campaign for education. In his opening speech to the 1921 Congress on Education, the general outlined his vision for the future of Turkish education:

> Although we are at war and our resources must be spent on the war effort, we should still try to formulate carefully a national educational policy for the post-war period. By this policy I mean a culture fitting for our national and historical character, completely separate from all influences from both the East and the West, and far from influences foreign to our own character.[28]

The aim, according to Kemal, was 'to create a Turkish youth strong enough to battle other nations'.[29] Three years after the Congress, Kemal expounded this approach and dismissed 'religious education' and 'international education' in favour of 'national education'. The latter would be adopted to create 'a new generation in the New Turkish Republic'.[30] In the 1920s and 1930s, Mustafa Kemal launched himself and was presented as the 'Chief Teacher' who would lead the nation into learning. In one classic photograph Kemal is seen wearing a dark suit, pointing at a blackboard to explain the new Latin alphabet to the locals.

---

[25] İlhan Başgöz and Howard E. Wilson, *Educational Problems in Turkey 1920–1940* (Bloomington: Indiana University Press, 1968), 38.

[26] Nevzat Ayas, *Türkiye Cumhuriyeti Milli Eğitimi* (Ankara: Millî Eğitim Basımevi, 1948), 122.

[27] Mete Tunçay, *Türkiye Cumhuriyeti'nde*, 239–40.

[28] *Cumhurbaşkanları, Başbakanlar ve Milli Eğitim Bakanlarının Milli Eğitimle İlgili Söylev ve Demeçleri* (Ankara: Türk Devrim Tarihi Enstitüsü, 1946), vol. 1, 4.

[29] Hasan Ali Yücel, *Milli Eğitimle İlgili Söylev ve Demeçler* (Ankara: T.C. Kültür Bakanlığı Yayınları, 1993), 118.

[30] *Atatürkçülük (Birinci Kitap) Atatürk'ün Görüş ve Direktifleri* (Istanbul: Milli Eğitim Basımevi, 1988), 290.

Whether out of true conviction or political appeasement, in reality Atatürk had trusted followers who supported his enthusiasm and echoed his cries for a nationalist education. İsmet İnönü repeated his superior in a speech about his interpretation of 'national education'. Speaking of Turkish society, he complained that 'the people still do not exhibit the appearance of a monolithic [*mütecanis*] nation'. A new generation needed to be moulded in order for 'the political Turkish nation fully to become a cultural, mental and societal Turkish nation'. According to İnönü, 'foreign cultures need to melt into this monolithic nation ... there can be no other cultures in this nation ... if we are to live, we shall live as a monolithic nation. That is the general aim for the system we call national education'.[31] If this was not clear enough language, Interior Minister Şükrü Kaya particularized this approach in parliament:

> No matter what happens, it is our obligation to immerse those living in our society in the civilization of Turkish society and to have them benefit from the prosperity of civilization. Why should we still speak of the Kurd Mehmet, the Circassian Hasan or the Laz Ali. This would demonstrate the weakness of the dominant element ... *If anybody has any difference inside him, we need to erase that in the schools and in the body politic,* so that man will be as Turkish as me and serve the homeland.[32]

As the message trickled down through the bureaucracy, it seemed to radicalize. Soon lower-level officials of the Ministry of Education personnel were witnessed delivering lectures in which they formulated theories that 'the Turkish school is obliged to transform every Turkish child into an thoroughly useful Turkish citizen who has fully grasped the psychology and ideology of the Republic, the Turkish Nation, and the Turkish Republic'.[33] The ostensible homogeneity and purity of the nation was not a conjunctural but a structural aspect of Young Turk ideology. Well into the Second World War, the Minister of Education called for educational policies that would create 'a Turkish youth in a ... homogeneous nation' (*mütecanis bir millet*), crafted by an elite that would 'govern the country with the exact sciences'.[34] This combination of watchwords represented Young Turk social engineering in its purest form: scientism needed to usher population policies towards the long-term fantasy of total ethnic homogeneity.

How could this policy of homogenization be reconciled with the realities of diversity in the eastern provinces? The reports written by veteran Young Turk social engineers in 1925 provided ample reference to the ends education would aspire in the eastern provinces. Mustafa Abdülhalik Renda pleaded for 'special relevance to be accorded to education ... in order to teach Turkish and revert inclinations to

---

[31] Minister of Education Esat Sagay speaking on 13 December 1931, quoted in: Hasan Ali Yücel, *Türkiye'de Orta Öğretim* (Ankara: T.C. Kültür Bakanlığı Yayınları, 1994), 25.

[32] *Türkiye Büyük Millet Meclisi Zabıt Ceridesi*, vol. 2, session 71 (21 June 1934), 249, emphasis added.

[33] Esat Sagay, 'Son Yapılan Teftiş Neticesi Hakkında Talimat', in: Hasan Ali Yücel, *Türkiye'de Orta Öğretim* (Ankara: T.C. Kültür Bakanlığı Yayınları, 1994), 364–5.

[34] Nuran Dağlı and Belma Aktürk (eds.), *Hükümetler ve Programları, vol. I, 1920–1960* (Ankara: TBMM Basımevi, 1988), 105.

Kurdishness back to Turkishness'. Cemil Uybadın's report stated that 'a strong national organization and educational propaganda will wipe out notions of Kurdishness'.[35]

According to a report by the Republican People's Party, the aim of education was to 'create a unitary people, with a single mother tongue, and a single ideal'. Such a policy had to make sure that minorities would 'feel Turkish . . . and exhibit no loyalty to any other nation', and this had to be 'engraved [*nakşedilmesi*] into their minds'. Policies had to 'melt them into the Turkish nation and have them *forget* their ethnic particularities [*kavmi hususiyetlerini unutdurmak*] . . . never to *remember* their old ethnicity again and fully appropatiate them for Turkishness'.[36] These general plans served as the official planning documents for policy-making dealing with Kurdish issues. Further directives by the Ministry of Education provided more precise criteria for education: 'Students need to be raised with fully republican and nationalist sentiments; Teachers need to pursue the aim of realizing the national ideals and purposes; Teachers need to consider the Turkish Nation as an indivisible whole and . . . work as a cultural agent for its development and progress'.[37] In other words, teachers who were sent to the eastern provinces were commissioned as missionaries of 'Turkishness'. Their duty was to transmit not only knowledge but also ideology and national culture. But in the face of significant cultural difference, the transmission of national culture was a formidable challenge, which many teachers attempted to compensate with zeal. One teacher recalled about his duty in the eastern provinces that 'nationalist sentiments were really excessive'.[38]

Initially, exhortations by top government officials were no more than a cloud of propaganda designed to impress friend and foe, but a glance at the curricula taught to children under Kemalism shows that their ideas were soon translated into reality. The curriculum of the elementary schools included the following subjects: Turkish language, history, geography, civics, natural sciences, mathematics, writing, music (only in urban schools), study of the environment, drawing and manual work, agriculture (only in rural schools), physical education (only in urban schools) and domestic science. The largest single block of time was devoted to Turkish language: 28 percent of the total weekly class periods in the urban, and 30 percent in the rural schools.[39] In practice, the latter figure was even higher in the eastern provinces, where most pupils started school without any significant knowledge of the Turkish language. The curriculum of the secondary schools envisaged performing the tasks of

---

[35] Mehmet Bayrak (ed.), *Kürtler ve Ulusal-Demokratik Mücadeleleri: Gizli Belgeler-Araştırmalar-Notlar* (Ankara: Özge, 1993), 460, 475.

[36] Faik Bulut, *Kürt Sorununa Çözüm Arayışları* (Istanbul: Ozan, 1998), 174, 179–82, 185, italics added. The emphasis on remembrance and oblivion speaks volumes. Identity and memory are closely related, and the Young Turk incursion into Eastern Turkey was profoundly a project of memory: forgetting Armenian and Kurdish pasts and inhabiting Turkish identities and futures.

[37] Nevzad Ayas, *Türkiye Cumhuriyeti Millî Eğitimi: Kuruluşlar ve Tarihçeler* (Ankara: Milli Eğitim Basımevi, 1948), 338–9.

[38] Necdet Sakaoğlu, *Cumhuriyet Dönemi Eğitim Tarihi* (Istanbul: İletişim Cep Üniversitesi, 1993), 95.

[39] *Milli Eğitimle İlgili Kanunlar* (Ankara: Milli Eğitim Basımevi, 1953), 931–52.

developing national consciousness and the feeling of patriotism, protecting the values of Turkish culture and history and following the principles of the reforms, respecting the constitution of the Turkish Republic and its laws, protecting Turkey's natural resources and understanding the importance of science and the scientific method in the development and improvement of life, and improving the ability to read, write, and speak the Turkish language correctly.[40]

These revolutionary plans were most saliently echoed in the curriculum of the lycées, which stated point blank that the lycée needed 'to train a Turk who is committed to the Turkish language, the principles and policies of the Turkish revolution and in general to Turkish ideals'. Being Turkish was thus the most important feature of primary education. 'Turkishness' was not a matter of modesty, as attested to in the aim of the history courses. These were 'to teach the student that our race has been a leader in civilization'.[41]

It is hardly surprising that the set of principles guiding Turkish education in the 1930s was thoroughly nationalist. This, after all, was the characteristic outlook sweeping across the European continent in the interbellum period. What made the Turkish case particularly striking was the totalitarian and militaristic nature of primary and secondary education. Although the Young Turk officers had taken off their uniforms, military ethics were too deeply imbibed to be bothered by liberal ideas on education. In one of his speeches on education Mustafa Kemal declaimed: 'Teachers! The victory won by our army only laid the groundwork for the victory to be won by your army. The real victory will be achieved by you. I and all my friends will follow you with absolute faith and will crush all the obstacles you may come across in your path'.[42] His idea of using army sergeants as village teachers later translated into the idea of the village educators. According to Kemal, 'just as the army is a school, so is the school an army'.[43] During this period military training was added to the curriculum of secondary schools. The textbooks used in these classes were a conjunction of ethnic nationalism and militarism. They addressed the student as follows:

YOU ARE A TURK! You are from the greatest nation on the face of the earth . . . Be aware that, in the eyes of other nations, their first example, support, and advice is your nation, THE GREAT TURKISH NATION.

YOU ARE A TURK! Twelve thousand years ago, when other nations on the planet were living like savages in caves, the civilization your grandfathers established in the heart of your native land CENTRAL ASIA bedazzled everyone. It was your ancestors who brought prosperity and civilization to the world, who brought down horses from mountains like lambs, who mounted them and crossed mountains, leaving other bewildered cave-dwelling nations looking at your nation, THE GREAT TURKISH NATION.

YOU ARE A TURK! You are an unbending, lion-hearted son of the greatest nation that will ever walk the face of the earth! . . . There is no nation that can twist your arm

---

[40] *Orta Okul Proğramı* (Ankara: Türkiye Cumhuriyeti Milli Eğitim Basımevi, 1949), 5–6.

[41] Hasan Ali Yücel, *Türkiye'de Orta Öğretim* (Istanbul: Devlet Basımevi, 1938), 198.

[42] *Cumhurbaşkanları, Başbakanlar ve Milli Eğitim Bakanlarının Milli Eğitimle İlgili Söylev ve Demeçleri*, vol. 1, 7.

[43] Kadri Yaman, *Yurt Müdafaasında Türk Gençliği* (Istanbul: Devlet Basımevi, 1938), 40.

or bow your head. First and foremost, be aware of this and keep your spirit strong and your head up as we will teach you your nation's spotless history. Do not even give in an inch to the enemies of the Turkish homeland and your Turkish character... YOU ARE A TURK![44]

As an ideological paradigm, the Atatürk myth was so dominant it outlived Young Turk rule. In the classroom, Kemal was omnipresent in everything he represented. After his death, İnönü too became a role model in the school. A 1941 textbook boasted: 'İnönü is at the head of the Turkish Nation, İnönü is at the front of the Turkish Nation. We follow him, we do as he orders, we walk the path he points to. He tells us the truth, he makes us walk the right path. We are carrying out our historical and national duties under his command... In order to fulfill his duty for the Turkish Nation every Turk needs to fix his eyes on the Great Chief's, on İnönü's finger'.[45]

This was not hollow rhetoric. The whole system of education was highly centralized and policy-making and school administration were conducted and regulated at the ministerial level.[46] From their desks in Ankara, the Ministry appointed teachers and principals, appropriated money, and sent out its inspectors, who would report any observed irregularities. The tight, top-down bureaucratic control over the schools is typified further by the fact that administration and supervision of the schools were minutely prescribed by regulations issued by the central office.[47] Foreign observers wrote about the stifling government control and regulation of schools: 'It is difficult to imagine a system in which less opportunity is given for individual schools and teachers to exercise initiative, and in which all changes and adjustments must come from a place as remote from the real school situation'.[48] In the classrooms of Kemalist Turkey too, authoritarian culture reigned supreme. Visiting educators from abroad frequently commented on and criticized what was an authoritarian, formal, and rigid classroom atmosphere where no free discussion took place, especially in light of the taboos imposed and maintained by the regime. Teachers controlled and directed most classroom activities, whereas pupils memorized and merely recited what they had 'learned' from their textbooks. Particularly at the level of the lycées, instruction consisted of lectures by the teacher and recitation by the students, who would repeat memorized parts from textbooks in answer to simple, general questions by the teacher.[49] All in all, education in the Young Turk era, authoritarian in form and nationalist in content, served primarily as a vehicle for nation formation. The regime hoped to

---

[44] From the 1934 *Textbook of the Soldier (Askerin Ders Kitabı)*, quoted in: Tanıl Bora, 'Ordu ve Milliyetçilik', in: Ahmet İnsel and Ali Bayramoğlu (eds.), *Bir Zümre, Bir Parti: Türkiye'de Ordu* (Istanbul: Birikim, 2004), 163–78, at 165.

[45] Hasan Ali Yücel, *Milli Eğitimle İlgili Söylev ve Demeçler* (Ankara: T.C. Kültür Bakanlığı Yayınları, 1993), 128–9.

[46] M. Tunç Özelli, 'The Evolution of the Formal Educational System and its Relation to Economic Growth Policies in the First Turkish Republic', in: *International Journal of Middle East Studies* 5, no. 1 (1974), 77–92.

[47] Kazamias, *Education*, 120–1.

[48] Richard E. Maynard, 'The Lise and its Curriculum in the Turkish Educational System' (unpublished Ph.D. dissertation, University of Chicago, 1961), 103.

[49] Kazamias, *Education*, 154–5.

stamp out ethnic differences in the eastern provinces through its vast infrastructure of obligatory education.

Culture

In the Young Turk conscience, education and culture were two sides of the same coin. Not for nothing, in the Kemalist state the 'Cultural Affairs' desk fell under the jurisdiction of the Ministry of Education, and only later was a Ministry of Culture developed. Among the many 'revolutions' Mustafa Kemal presided over, several were related to culture: besides general Turkification in the cultural field, two 1934 laws prescribed European dress (such as the famous top hat), and abolished all titles and appellations, such as religious and tribal ones.[50] For the Young Turk social engineers, their reference point for cultural policies was again Ziya Gökalp. Ever since the ideologue had espoused Turkish nationalism, he argued that the life of the new Turkish nation must be drawn from a rediscovery of the indigenous Turkish culture: its traditions, values, and spirit. Nation formation, according to Gökalp, was the product of the political elite's consciousness of its own distinct culture, which he defined as 'the integrated system of religious, moral, legal, intellectual, aesthetic, linguistic, economic, and technological spheres of life'.[51] By situating culture at the focal point of the nation-formation process, the sociologist set the tone for years of cultural policy.

Ziya Gökalp's philosophy was influential and widely discussed among the Young Turk intelligentsia. The development of Turcology—the study of Turkish languages, history, and culture—in Europe, and the immigration to Turkey of educated Tatars from the Russian Empire had given birth to the establishment of the first Turkish Society in Istanbul in 1908. Its objectives were defined as 'studying the ancient remains, history, languages, literatures, ethnography and ethnology, social conditions and present civilizations of the Turks, and the ancient and modern geography of the Turkish lands'.[52] In 1912 Gökalp joined the editorial board of the society's organ, *Turkish Homeland*, and published many cultural and political articles on the newly discovered Turkishness. Associated with the journal was another club called the Turkish Hearths (*Türk Ocakları*). This organization was established on 25 March 1912 in Istanbul. Its aims were 'to work for the perfection of the Turkish race and language and for the progress of the national education, and the scientific, sociological, and economic level of the Turks'.[53] Through 'social revolution' it intended to rebuild a completely new society based on 'Turkishness' and social scientific principles imported from Europe. The Turkish Hearths quickly spread to other cities and became entwined with the CUP regime. The most obvious link between the two organizations was the person of

---

[50] Law nr. 2596, 'Bazı Kisvelerin Giyilemiyeceğine Dair Kanun', of 3 December 1934, published in: *Düstur*, set 3, vol. 16, 24, and in: *Resmi Gazete*, no. 2879 (13 December 1934).

[51] Gökalp, *Turkish Nationalism*, 245.

[52] Bernard Lewis, *The Emergence of Modern Turkey* (London: Oxford University Press, 1961), 343.

[53] François Georgeon, 'Les Foyers Turcs à l'époque kémaliste (1923–1931)', in: *Turcica* XIV (1982), 168–215.

Gökalp, a prominent member of both. At establishment he was voted into the Committee for Culture with an overwhelming majority of votes. Throughout the First World War, the Hearths generally worked with the CUP on all of its policies, including the persecution of Christian minorities and forced assimilation of Muslim minorities. After Gökalp had consolidated his position in the organization, nation formation as a project to be taken 'to the people' became more pronounced. The Hearths were to induce an 'awakening' of the Turks and approach them 'with the sacrificial dedication and devotion like missionaries'. When Gökalp gave a speech at the Turkish Hearth in Adana on 10 April 1923, he advocated the spread of Turkish culture in the eastern provinces. When Mustafa Kemal spoke to villagers in the same Turkish Hearth and the peasants exhibited a negligible knowledge of Turkish history, Kemal assigned the Hearths with the task of 'introducing the Turks to themselves'.[54]

Discussions on what constituted Turkishness were divided, with the best part of the Hearth cadre siding with Gökalp's culturalist ideas. During the First General Congress in 1924 Hamdullah Suphi (Tanrıöver) posed the question: 'Do you want a Turkishness based on race and blood? Are you going to draw blood and send it to chemists for analysis, they will say it consists of 5% Armenian, 16% Russian, and who knows what percentage Circassian, Albanian, and Turkish blood. You have to choose one of the two paths. Either you accept race, or culture'.[55] The model of biologistic racism was quickly abandoned for that of cultural socialization. However, cultural touchstones presented an equally difficult task in defining a nation. But however hard it was for the members of the Hearths to define what Turkishness really was, and who a Turk really was, consensus was very soon reached on what Turkishness was definitely *not*. According to one researcher, Gökalp would visit the Hearths and infuse his ideas to the youth with particular zeal. During these discussions, his greatest fear was not the threat of alternative nationalisms but the 'menace' of individualism. One of the major conclusions of the 1924 Congress was the outspoken definition of the 'enemies of Turkishness'. These were 'those who support the ideology of Ottomanism, intellectual cosmopolitanists, and internationalists'.[56] Thus, positive definitions were antedated and perhaps even supplanted by negative ones. This was a highly significant development. The incipient definition of Turkishness was based primarily on exclusionary criteria, which were much clearer in the Young Turk mind than the ambivalent and uncertain inclusionary criteria that required more precision and further crafting.

Young Turk support for the Turkish Hearths was incessant. As early as 1924 Mustafa Kemal had declared that 'all of the nation's future hopes are directed towards the Turkish youth who have gathered around the Turkish Hearths'.[57] During the 1927 congress, one delegate proposed to work closely with the government 'since

---

[54] Füsun Üstel, *İmparatorluktan Ulus-Devlete Türk Milliyetçiliği: Türk Ocakları (1912–1931)* (Istanbul: İletişim, 1997), 100, 126, 168.
[55] Ibid., 152–3.
[56] 'Türk Ocakları Kongresi', in: *Hakimiyet-i Milliye*, 30 April 1924, no. 110.
[57] 'Türk Ocakları Kongresi', in: *Hakimiyet-i Milliye*, 30 April 1924, no. 110.

these principles essentially exist in their ideas as well'.[58] The building for the Hearth's central committee was erected in the Cağaloğlu district of European Istanbul on an 'abandoned' Armenian cemetery. It was constructed in 1926 and opened on 21 March 1927 by Prime Minister İsmet İnönü, himself a staunch member of the Turkish Hearths since 1917.[59] Ziyâ Gökalp was buried in the courtyard, which has become a place of pilgrimage for Turkish nationalists ever since. In the interwar era the Ministry of Education supported the Turkish Hearths and more and more overlap appeared in membership lists of the RPP and the Hearths. For example, Justice Minister Mahmut Esat Bozkurt was elected chairman, and Kütahya deputy (later RPP chairman) Recep Peker became vice-chairman. From 1925 to 1926 the Hearths grew from 135 to 217 branches as membership rose to 30,000. By 1930, there were 255 branches of the Hearths in Turkey, a growth which had been registered especially in the eastern provinces. At that point, Mustafa Kemal no longer saw reason to leave the Hearths to operate independently from the party and disbanded them, reorganizing and renaming them the People's Houses (*Halkevleri*).[60] These developments of closer collaboration and more organic links between the Turkish Hearths and the RPP concluded the marriage between the power centre of the single-party state and the ideological nexus of Young Turk nationalism.

The purpose of the People's Houses was 'to bridge the gap between the intelligentsia and people by teaching the former the national culture of the Anatolian masses and the latter the rudiments of civilization and indoctrination of the nationalist secular ideas of the Republican regime'.[61] Whereas İnönü emphasized that 'the People's Houses are not political institutions but social and cultural ones',[62] Şükrü Kaya explained the establishment of the Houses as follows: 'The People's House was established to spread, intensify, and ingrain the principles of the Atatürk revolution among the people. In this regard, one should call them the homes for cultural broadcasting and protection of the revolution'.[63] In other words, while intending to stimulate more national integration of the various social strata in Turkey, the challenge at hand came to be projected as a top-down affair to educate

---

[58] *Türk Ocakları Üçüncü Kurultayı Zabıtları* (İstanbul: Kader, 1927), 196–7.

[59] Üstel, *Türk Ocakları*, 230–1.

[60] Kemal Karpat, 'The People's Houses in Turkey: Establishment and Growth', in: *Middle East Journal* 17 (1963), 55–67.

[61] Arzu Öztürkmen, 'The Role of People's Houses in the Making of National Culture in Turkey', in: *New Perspectives on Turkey* 11 (1994), 159–81; Anıl Çeçen, *Halkevleri: Atatürk'ün Kültür Kurumu* (Ankara: Gündoğan, 1990); Neşe G. Yeşilkaya, *Halkevleri: İdeoloji ve Mimarlık* (Istanbul: İletişim, 1999); Sefa Şimşek, *Bir İdeolojik Seferberlik Deneyimi Halkevleri 1932–1951* (Istanbul: Boğaziçi Üniversitesi Yayınevi, 2002); Şerafettin Zeyrek, *Türkiye'de Halkevleri ve Halkodaları* (Ankara: Anı, 2006); Adem Kara, *Cumhuriyet Döneminde Kalkınmanın Mihenk Taşı: Halkevleri 1932–1951* (Ankara: 24 Saat, 2006); 'The Halkevi: The Turkish People's House', in: *The Scottish Geographical Magazine* 1 (1944), 21–2; Robert Mantran, 'Les "Maisons du Peuple" en Turquie', in: *Revue d'Institut des Belles Lettres Arabes* (1963), 21–8. The concept 'indoctrination' is here literally translated from the Franco-Turkish 'endoktrinasyon'. Indoctrination is distinguished from education by the fact that the indoctrinated person (the student) is expected not to question or critically examine the doctrine they have learned. Based on this definition, it may well be possible to argue that education in the Young Turk era included indoctrinatory aspects.

[62] İsmet İnönü, 'Yeni Halkevlerini Açma Nutku', in: *Ülkü* 5, no. 25 (March 1935), 2.

[63] Şükrü Kaya, 'Halkevlerinin Açılış Konferansı', in: *Ülkü* 11, no. 61 (March 1938), 9.

a population consisting for three quarters of illiterate peasants. In official propaganda texts the People's Houses were 'organizations of mass education and culture, run by the committee of culture of the Republican People's Party'.[64] To this end, the Houses were organized into nine branches covering a whole range of cultural phenomena: language, history and literature; fine arts; dramatic art; sports; social assistance; popular lessons and courses; libraries and publications; museums and exhibitions; village life.[65] Within months, the reach of the Party spread deep into the country, including the provincial peripheries of the east. Under full control of the regime, the number of People's Houses rose from 14 in 1932 to 479 in 1950.[66] The relevance of the People's Houses in the nation-formation process launched by the Young Turks can hardly be overstated. For the first time in history, a uniform canon of culture was being spread all over the country. How the Houses functioned in daily life and how the population perceived these policies will be treated for Diyarbekir province below.

Gökalp's glaring disrespect for anything tribal and Arab and his portrayal of Kurds as noble savages fit for nothing but cultural assimilation was shared by a wide range of Young Turk intellectuals and political leaders. The Turkish Hearths discussions are most noteworthy for their production of a colonial and aggressively assimilationist discourse on the multi-ethnic, predominantly Kurdish eastern provinces. One of its ideologues, Hamdullah Suphi Tanrıöver, wanted the Turkish Hearth emissaries to be sent primarily to 'certain regions where the national culture has not developed yet' and added that regions such as Sivas, Konya, İzmir, and Adana had 'already understood the significance and meaning of Turkishness'. It was not necessary to 'Turkify' these regions.[67] That the eastern provinces were special and therefore needed special treatment was forcefully argued by Mehmet Emin Erişirgil, who emphasized that the Turkish Hearths had a different mission in the eastern provinces: 'The reinforcement of national unity, the spread of Turkish culture, the diffusion of the real and pure Turkish language in the eastern provinces is a vital field of activity for the Hearths'.[68] The differential treatment for the two different regions produced inspection reports for the eastern provinces that included passages such as: 'We considered it a duty to attribute a special significance to the Eastern half of the homeland'. The Central Committee of the Turkish Hearths during their second meeting of the 1927 Congress had agreed that the eastern branches had to work with special care towards Turkification through language schools and 'special conferences'. Only the growing convergence between the Hearths and the RPP could enable this. Tanrıöver declared that the Hearths and the government were in principal 'struggling for the same objective', adding that 'the East is an issue that our government, with its colossal apparatus and various organizations, is handling with great care. We too are concerned with the East and

---

[64] *Public Instruction in the Republic of Turkey* (Ankara: Press Department of the Ministry of the Interior, 1936), 59.

[65] Ibid., 60; *C.H.P. Halkevleri Talimatnamesi* (Ankara: Hâkimiyeti Milliye Matbaası, 1932).

[66] Cevat Dursunoğlu, 'Halkevlerinin 18. Yıldönümü Konuşması', in: *Ülkü* 4, no. 39 (March 1950), 1.

[67] *Türk Ocakları Üçüncü Kurultayı Zabıtları* (Istanbul: Kader, 1927), 255.

[68] Mehmet Emin, 'Türk Ocakları', in: *Hayat* 1, no. 2 (14 April 1927), 381.

we are organized to approach the same issue'.[69] By 1931, the spread of Turkish culture and language in the east had become a priority, and even an obsession.

The key discursive device which the Kemalist centre employed to represent their relationship with the Kurdish periphery was 'civilization' (*medeniyet*). The non-Turkish population of the eastern provinces was looked down upon as primitive and inferior, fit for colonial rule by a Turkish master nation which operated in the name of progress and rationality. They were viewed, moreover, as inherently treacherous and anti-Turkish, and hence as threats to security against which Turkish state and army personnel had to be permanently on guard. In the period after 1931 official discourse acquired a particularly denigrating and racist undertone towards Kurds, among others. *Cumhuriyet*, the mouthpiece of the Kemalist party-state, wrote about Kurds that 'they allow their emotions and brains to be led by simple instincts like ordinary animals and therefore can only think crudely and foolishly . . . there is absolutely no difference between African barbarians and cannibals and these creatures who mix raw meat with cracked wheat and eat it just like that'.[70] In a series of articles, the nationalist journalist Yusuf Mazhar wrote about Kurds,

> Even though they may be more capable than the redskins in the United States, they are—history is my witness—endlessly bloodthirsty and cruel . . . They are completely bereft of positive feelings and civilized manners. For centuries, they have been a plague for our race . . . Under Russian rule they were prohibited to descend from the mountains, where they did not lead humane and civilized lives, therefore these creatures are really not inclined to profit from civilization . . . In my opinion, the dark spirit, crude mental state, and ruthless manners of this Kurdish rabble is impossible to break.[71]

The racist code words and imagery that accompanied nation formation in Eastern Turkey were often exceedingly graphic and contemptuous. The Young Turks consistently emphasized the nonhuman nature of the Kurds, routinely turning to images of 'savages' and 'barbarians' to convey this. They portrayed the Kurds as inherently inferior men and women who had to be understood in terms of primitivism, childishness, and collective mental, intellectual, and emotional deficiency. It is important to recognize at this point that this was a clear departure from pre-existing Ottoman-patriotic or Muslim-nationalist attitudes towards Kurds, both of which had included them in the imagined community. But why did the Young Turks dehumanize the Kurds? First, there were genuine concerns for the repercussions that the (dis)loyalty of the ethnically Kurdish population could have for state security. A second possible explanation could be that such an attitudinal climate was necessary for (and would prove to be highly conducive to) the harsh treatment of the civilian population of the east and the committing of violence against them. These ideas substantiated the belief that the Kurds were a contemptible and treacherous foe who deserved no mercy on the battlefield.

---

[69] *Türk Ocakları 1927 Senesi Kurultayı Zabıtları* (Ankara: n.p., 1928), 122.
[70] *Cumhuriyet*, 13 July 1930, 4.
[71] *Cumhuriyet*, 18, 19, and 20 August 1930, 3.

Philosophizing about the eastern provinces as culturally 'Turkified' territory obviously did not bring about this fantasy. Action plans without teeth were mere blueprints with little impact on the real world; policy-making was needed. The veil on how the culturally distinct peoples would be treated was briefly lifted by Mustafa Kemal in an early speech: 'Nowadays there are citizens and compatriots within the political and sociological Turkish nation who have been subjected to propaganda of Kurdism, Circassianism, and even Lazism and Bosniakism'.[72] Later he elaborated somewhat and called for 'the necessity of struggling against all foreign elements and the full enthusiasm for national thinking when raising our children'. According to Kemal this required 'the indoctrination of the necessity of defending the nation with violence and self-sacrifice against all contrary ideas'.[73] Kemal thus dismissed the reality of ethnic difference and promised harsh action against non-Turkish cultures, but again left the detailed planning of population policies in the eastern provinces to his diligent subordinates. Social engineers such as Mustafa Abdülhalik Renda had clearly stipulated in the first government reports on the eastern provinces that Kurds needed 'to be forced to become Turkish'. Cemil Uybadın was relentless in advocating cultural measures in the east:

> In reality the Eastern territories are under the influence of Kurdism . . . The people are very attached to their language and nationality. The intellectuals are all Kurdish nationalists. We need to work consciously for the destruction of . . . the ideal and movement of Kurdism in the eastern territories and prevent it from effusing into the area west of the Euphrates . . . [The region] has to be turned into a battlefield with a strong organization of education, Hearths, sports, and youth groups, and through the press, schools, theatre, national and general plays the national sentiments of the people and Turkish traditions need to be invigorated.[74]

The martial metaphors suggesting that the eastern provinces were a theatre of war were not idle. Chief of Staff Marshal Fevzi Çakmak personally went on an inspection tour through the eastern provinces and on return to Ankara gave orders to the Turkish Hearths headquarters: 'I want you to strengthen the Hearths in the East'.[75] During the Sheikh Said rebellion İnönü predicted: 'Nationality is our only instrument of adhesion. The other elements are not vested with any power in the face of the Turkish majority. It is our duty to render Turkish everybody in the Turkish homeland, no matter what. We will cut out and throw out the elements that oppose Turks and Turkism'.[76] Moral or practical protests against these ambitious plans were easily dismissed. When during the fifth congress of the Turkish Hearths a delegate argued that coercing people to become Turkish would meet with resistance, delegate Besim Atalay waived the objections away and answered: 'Nations are like organisms. They

---

[72] Nimet Arsan (ed.), *Atatürk'ün Söylev ve Demeçleri* (Ankara: Türk Tarih Kurumu, 1959–1964), vol. II, 72.
[73] *Atatürkçülük (Birinci Kitap) Atatürk'ün Görüş ve Direktifleri* (Istanbul: Milli Eğitim Basımevi, 1988), 296.
[74] Bayrak, *Kürtler*, 462, 468, 475–6.
[75] Üstel, *Türk Ocakları*, 236, footnote 336.
[76] *Vakit*, 27 April 1925, no. 2632.

cannot live if they do not eat. You have to kill, you have to kill in order to live'. Delegates muttered approvingly.[77] These politicians and ideologues believed in the nationalist version of social Darwinism, wherein competition between nations (and not individuals) drives social evolution in human societies.

A major acceleration in the cultural 'Turkification' of the eastern provinces to which the Kemalists aspired developed in 1934. Parliamentary discussions during the drafting of the Settlement Law (see Chapter 3) revolved around the notion of culture. The draft read that the law would operate to 'assimilate those who have stayed distant from Turkish culture'. The government would be vested with 'all types of authority' and would 'melt those who have not set their hearts on the Turkish flag . . . into Turkish culture and tie them more strongly to the homeland'. The objects of the law were 'those from a different language and culture', who were to become the focus of cultural policies to ensure 'that they thoroughly melt into Turkish culture and become dough inside the great Turkishness'.[78] The metaphor of human beings as dough kneaded into shape aptly captures how the political elite saw the population. The kneading would guarantee that within a few generations the 'dough' would have 'risen' and 'baked': it would definitively become 'solid' and homogeneous, never to revert to heterogeneity again. The path from 'dough' to 'bread' was envisioned as a one-way journey. The establishment of the People's Houses across the country and the effectuation of the directives in the 1934 Settlement Law delineated the limitations and circumstances under which local authorities would conduct the mission of cultural 'Turkification' in the east. Again, Diyarbekir would occupy a special place in this process.

THE NATION IN THE PROVINCE: CULTURE AND EDUCATION IN DIYARBEKIR

The main pillar of this policy was regular state-sponsored education, which was also seen as a cultural mission. Government programs stipulated under the paragraph for 'Education' that 'in accordance with the Chief's directives, a cultural centre will be launched in our eastern region'.[79] The 1924 Law for the Unification of Education and the ensuing blanket laicization were frontal attacks on old and established forms of education among the various population groups in Diyarbekir province. These were the seminaries of the Syriacs (*madrashto*) and the Kurds (*medrese*). The Kemalist Ministry of Education set out pro-actively to eradicate these centres of education which it considered 'backward', 'fundamentalist',

---

[77] *Türk Ocakları 1928 Senesi Kurultayı Zabıtları* (Ankara: Türk Ocakları Matbaası, 1929), 123–4, 151–2.

[78] *Türkiye Büyük Millet Meclisi Zabıt Ceridesi*, vol. 23, period IV, session 3 (7 June 1934), Appendix no. 189: 'Esbâbı mucibe lâyihası: İskân muvakkat encümeni mazbatası', 27 May 1934. The draft differs from the final version inasmuch as the draft includes the Young Turks' internal discussions, which were not for public consumption and demonstrate their thinking.

[79] Nuran Dağlı and Belma Aktürk (eds.), *Hükümetler ve Programları, vol. I, 1920–1960* (Ankara: TBMM Basımevi, 1988), 80.

'feudal', and 'reactionary'. One of the official tasks of the Inspectorate-General, based in Diyarbekir city, was indeed to employ 'idealist and strong teachers . . . to educate Kurdish children based on Turkish culture and the principles of assimilation'.[80] This was not entirely new. What was remarkable and recognizable was that education, like other forms of population politics, was a bifurcated process. Besides top-down orders and directives from the Party, local elites often took the initiative to propose suggestions on education in their respective provinces. In the adjacent province of Urfa, for example, a Committee for Enlightenment and Education drafted an educational program on 'the importance and necessity of national education in schools'. The scheme included the following principles:

> to enlighten the people about the saviors and elders of Turkey and their services to the motherland; to persuade people about the sanctity of the Republican regime and its superiority compared to all other forms of government; to inform the people of our national existence and our national enemies by indoctrinating them on what Turkishness and Turkish civilization are; to teach them what to do in order to defeat our enemies.

The committee asked the government to show them 'the paths' that would lead to the overarching objective, 'beginning our national existence strongly from the perspective of national education'.[81] The government did not need this call to arms and very soon schools began mushrooming in the country, including the eastern provinces. Whereas the population doubled between 1927 and 1955, the budget of the Ministry of Education more than quadrupled in the same period.[82]

In Diyarbekir a similar process was happening. Schools had been renamed after (local) Young Turk heroes, such as the Ziya Gökalp Lycée, and the nationalist curriculum was being taught to countless students. Foreign observers did not fail to discern the nationalist and ideological goals embedded in ostensibly 'neutral' education. British diplomats visiting the region observed that 'there was in the Kurdish districts no national feeling worth speaking of, neither Kurdish nor Turkish. Atatürk therefore welcomed the intention of the Minister of Education to run the schools in the east with teachers thoroughly imbued with modern Turkish ideas'.[83] The Inspectorate-General was reported to rely on three factors for carrying out nation formation: 'agriculture, road-building, and education of all kinds, which, in a word, means Turkification'.[84] The Danish engineer Rygaard painted perhaps the most poignant picture about education when touring the region west of Diyarbekir:

---

[80] BCA, 030.10/70.461.1, Report by Inspector-General Abidin Özmen dated 24 August 1937.

[81] BCA 030.10/140.3.3, Urfa Committee on Enlightenment and Education to Prime Ministry, 1 December 1925.

[82] Başgöz and Wilson, *Educational Problems in Turkey*, 233–4. Although nation-building was not the only task of education, the state reports of the Ministry of Education show that it was the main objective.

[83] NAUK, FO 424/268, 85–6, no. 49, Clerk to Chamberlain, 22 June 1927.

[84] NAUK, FO 424/272, 116, no. 68, Edmonds to Henderson, 21 May 1930, 'Notes on a Tour to Diarbekir, Bitlis and Mush.'

The village children are now learning the Latin alphabet and mathematics instead of, as they did previously, the verses of the Koran that were incomprehensible to them. There is a tense relationship between the section and the fanatically nationalist school teacher, who, like the gendarme officer and . . . Turkish government doctor, intensely dislikes the foreigners. If the Turkish youth in Anatolia are to be brought up in the dumbest, most hateful, and excessively self-conscious spirit built on the thinnest of foundations, which these teachers represent, then the outlook for intergroup relations in these areas is very bleak indeed.[85]

Nationalism was not just a matter of primary or secondary education. As part of his plan to 'modernize' Turkey, Atatürk reorganized Istanbul University in 1933 and established several faculties in Ankara during the 1930s. Turkish universities were expected to produce a strong indigenous elite. The Minister of Education, Dr. Reşit Galip, spoke: 'The most essential quality of the new universities is their nationalism and revolutionism. New departments have been established for national history. The ideology of the Turkish Revolution will be made by the university'.[86] The future University of Diyarbekir too, was supposed to produce a 'national elite' on local level.[87] In 1940, the construction of the University of Diyarbekir was proclaimed around the city with speakers. The aim, in accordance with national guidelines, was to build 'a cultural nest to which the nation's intellectuals could wholeheartedly adhere'.[88] This nationalist elite would be equipped with the intellectual tools to carry through Atatürk's ideas. But apart from a hospital that functioned as a Department of Medicine, a university was never established in the Young Turk era. As an offshoot of Ankara University, Diyarbekir's Tigris University (Dicle Üniversitesi) was formally established only in 1966.

From the earliest plans to the day that policy took shape, Diyarbekir was seen as a centre in the eastern provinces from which Turkish culture would radiate. Kemalist propaganda stressed with a vehemence that Diyarbekir would be a 'great centre of Turkish culture'[89] and in accordance with the geo-body of the nation, the organizational structure of the Turkish Hearths consisted of four regions: north, west, south, and east. Diyarbekir was designated the centre of the eastern constituency. In February 1932 thorough preparations were made and great care was taken for the opening of the Diyarbekir People's House, one of the first to be established. Recep Peker, chairman of the Republican People's Party, instructed İbrahim Tali Öngören, First Inspector-General in Diyarbekir city, to organize an opening ceremony, assign leadership, and announce the establishment of the House throughout town. If newspapers were not available, declarations were to be printed and hung on walls in public places such as mosques and city walls. The party also

---

[85]   Olaf A. Rygaard, *Mellem Tyrker og Kurder: En Dansk Ingeniørs Oplevelser i Lilleasien* (Copenhagen: Nordisk Forlag, 1935), 70.

[86]   Cavit Binbaşıoğlu, *Türkiye'de Eğitim Bilimleri Tarihi* (Istanbul: Milli Eğitim Bakanlığı Yayınları, 1995), 231.

[87]   'The New University in Turkey', in: *School and Society* 39, no. 994 (January 1934), 45.

[88]   BCA, 490.01/1006.882.1, RPP People's Houses Inspector Kemal Güngör to RPP People's Houses Bureau Directorate, 8 October 1943.

[89]   *Cumhuriyetin 15inci yılında Diyarbakır* (Diyarbakır: Diyarbakır Matbaası, 1938), 20.

dictated a precise program for the opening ceremony. After a recital of the national anthem, an oath would be taken to the Republic and an opening speech would be delivered.[90] Tali reported the opening of the Diyarbekir People's House on 23 February 1932. At that point it was lodged in the Turkish Hearth building, using its equipment, but it was soon to be moved to the former governor's residence.[91] The early months of the People's House were marked by teething troubles such as organizing the presidency, selecting committee members, and logistics. By the time Interior Minister Şükrü Kaya visited the eastern provinces for inspection, he noted that all People's Houses were up and functioning properly, including the Diyarbekir one.[92]

After consolidation, the Diyarbekir People's House began working towards the construction of a canon of Turkish culture tailor-made for the province. The Kemalists' desire was for culture, obviously always Turkish, to include a strong local component. The correspondence between the Diyarbekir People's House and the Interior Ministry provides a vivid insight into the activities of the House. The first inspection report dated from 1935 and registered that in the past two years the House had worked hard. In the branch for Language, History, and Literature 'special importance was accorded to language and culture works' in the city and in the villages. In the villages it had organized courses in Turkish language and 'knowledge of the fatherland'. Also, the branch was praised for having 'collected more than 500 pieces of poetry, songs, and folklore, and launched initiatives to write the history of Diyarbekir'. The Sports section had established a shooting range and a hunting club, for which the Gendarmerie had provided help, as well as a football club named 'Turkish Sports' (*Türkspor*) with two teams, and a tennis club named 'Grey Wolf' (*Bozkurt*). The Art section had established an orchestra, which so far had performed nine concerts. The Social Aid section had been very active: it had bought clothes for 200 orphans, provided support for 100 widows, sent out doctors and veterinaries to villages, vaccinated 700 children against smallpox, distributed quinine and aspirin, opened an eye clinic in the People's House building, and most of these services were provided free of charge. Section 8 (Museum and Exhibition) had 'compiled a photo album of old historical photos of Diyarbekir'. The last section (Villages) had ventured into the countryside 'to spread Turkish' and 'assign villagers who speak Turkish as teachers to those who did not'. Plans were pending for the construction of a cinema, and the furnishing of a central heating and a comprehensive electricity system.[93]

The Diyarbekir People's House cadre consisted of CUP veterans. The chairman of the House was Tahsin Çubukçu and the mayor of Diyarbekir was Şeref Uluğ. The Inspector-General's function was circumscribed as being 'the spiritual and

---

[90] BCA, 490.01/937.637.01, RPP General Secretary Recep Peker to First Inspector-General İbrahim Tali, 12 and 14 January 1932.

[91] BCA, 490.01/937.637.01, First Inspector-General İbrahim Tali to RPP General Secretary Recep Peker, 29 January 1932.

[92] BCA, 030.10/117.817.2, Şükrü Kaya to İsmet İnönü, 2 October 1932.

[93] BCA, 490.01/1005.880.3, People's House Inspector Alaettin Tekmen to RPP General Secretary Recep Peker, 28 August 1935.

physical patron of all the People's Houses in the area of the Inspectorate-General'. He had assigned a 'young and active idealist friend' by the name of Osman Eti to the party's 'daily affairs'.[94] Diyarbekir's deputies for the Grand National Assembly in Ankara were former CUP operatives and sympathizers Veli Necdet Süngütay, General Kâzım Sevüktekin, Zeki Mesun Alsan, Zülfü Tiğrel, and Rüştü Bekit. A professional breakdown from January 1941 of the thirty-seven members of the People's House showed sixteen teachers, eight civil servants, four merchants, three doctors, one retired military official, one pharmacist, one dentist, one lawyer, one photographer, and one publisher. This list of names conveys a strong sense of continuity of Diyarbekir's local elites from the CUP era into the RPP era. Of the 35,000 inhabitants of Diyarbekir, 958 people had officially enlisted, of which 194 were women and the rest men.[95]

Other visitors frequented the House without being full members. The financial expenses of the House indicated how seriously the cultural revolution was taken. For the entire campaign the People's House had spent 4145 Turkish Lira in 1932, which had more than doubled to 9318 lira in 1933. In 1934 the budget had grown to 15,320 Lira and halfway through 1935 it was already 21,941 Lira.[96] In 1941 the budget exceeded 50,000 Lira, half of which was provided by the provincial authorities and the other half by various admission fees.[97]

The Houses were involved in a broad spectrum of nationalist policies. Local officials reported that they had drawn up lists of villages with non-Turkish names and had 'requested the appropriate offices for these names to be changed'. House members had also published books on 'Diyarbekir folklore' and the advent of the railways, and plans were on the way to write a history of Diyarbekir (see Chapter 5). Particularly striking was that the villages where folkloric dances, expressions, and other cultural phenomena had been 'collected' were, exclusively the few Turkoman villages in the vicinity. The People's House generally operated in the city, but in 1935 attempts were made to take the message to eight villages on the Diyarbekir plain.[98] The objectification of ordinary peasants' dress, habits, and lives as 'folklore' was a projection of the RPP regime that saw in peasants a 'pure Turkish' society, uncorrupted by city life. Nationalism, folklorization and ruralism were three dimensions of a cultural policy that propelled the idealization of peasant life yet never developed into agrarian utopia.[99] Rather, the objective was to discover and unearth 'the rich folkloric treasure' that the Turks possessed. The ultimate aim of this undertaking was to establish a 'Folklore and Ethnography Museum' and

---

[94] BCA, 490.01/996.850.1, Şükrü Kaya to First Inspectorate-General, 26 April 1938, appendix 1937 Diyarbekir People's House Evaluation.
[95] BCA, 490.01/996.850.1, RPP General Secretariat to Fourth Bureau, 3 January 1941.
[96] BCA, 490.01/1005.880.3, People's House Inspector Alaettin Tekmen to RPP General Secretary Recep Peker, 28 August 1935.
[97] BCA, 490.01/996.850.1, RPP General Secretariat to Fourth Bureau, 3 January 1941.
[98] BCA, 490.01/1005.880.2, Report evaluating the 'Language and History' sections of all the People's Houses in 1935.
[99] M. Asım Karaömerlioğlu, 'The People's Houses and the Cult of the Peasant in Turkey', in: *Middle Eastern Studies* 34, no. 4 (1998), 67–91.

publish books on the local 'folklore' of Diyarbekir.[100] In the same year, a compilation of Diyarbekir's 'folklore' was published by the People's House.[101] Subsequent
books published across the country mapped the various 'regional folkloric traditions'
that together integrated into an exclusively national canon that bore two features: it
was Turkish and thus devoid of any ethnic or alternative cultural connotations,
and confined to the borders of the nation state.[102] The folklorist Ferruh Arsunar
(1908–65) cruised the country, collecting music and folkloric traditions as the cultural
assets for the national canon. Diyarbekir became an object of cultural attribution,
reification, and sacralization.[103] Thus Turkish songs were sprouting from regions
where Turkish was hardly known or spoken, let alone sung. The new national
repertoire was published in the form of a booklet, titled *Diyarbekir Folk Songs*
(*Diyarbekir Halk Türküleri*) in 1937. It contained eight songs, making up
the backbone of a growing canon in exclusively Turkish 'folk music'.[104]

In the course of 1937, a radicalization developed in Kemalist nation formation.
The predominantly Kurdish and discordant region of Dersim had been opposing
the structures of the Turkish nation state in their area. When in the summer of
1937 a violent incident occurred between villagers and gendarmes, the tribal
resistance crossed a threshold and escalated into violence against state officials.
The ensuing clashes between several Kurdish tribes and Turkish gendarmes developed into a guerrilla war that lasted for almost a year and ended in large-scale
massacres and deportations of Dersim Kurds in the summer of 1938.[105] To the
Kemalists this was a sign that the policy of assimilation in the eastern provinces
needed to be accelerated, especially in the villages. Frustration and impatience
about the absence of immediate results of the 'Turkification' in which they had
so passionately invested turned to radicalization. A new chairman was assigned to
the Diyarbekir People's House, the young doctor and anthropologist Bedri Noyan
(1912–97). He had published on folklore and was one of the young social scientists
who had travelled into the Anatolian heartland to 'discover' and provide the
government with ethnographic data on the minorities. His books, wrought with
Turkish nationalism, produced a condescending discourse towards Kurdish sheikhs
in particular and prescribed how Islamic culture needed to be understood.[106] In the

---

[100] BCA, 490.01/1006.882.1, RPP People's Houses Inspector Kemal Güngör to RPP People's
Houses Bureau Directorate, 8 October 1943. Scholars of nationalism have analysed these practices of
attempting to root the nation as the 'invention of tradition'. See: Eric Hobsbawm, 'Mass-Producing
Traditions: Europe, 1870–1914', in: Eric Hobsbawm and Terence Ranger, *The Invention of Tradition*
(Cambridge: Cambridge University Press, 1992), 263–308.
[101] Şevket Beysanoğlu, *Diyarbakır Folkloru* (Diyarbakır: Diyarbakır Matbaası, 1943).
[102] Cenab Ozankan, *Türk Millî Oyunları: Ağrı Bölgesi, Balıkesir, Bursa, Çorum, Diyarbakır, Ege
Bölgesi, Elâzığ, Erzurum, Gazi Antep, Hatay, Kars, Kastamonu, Konya, Malatya, Rize, Seyhan Bölgesi,
Sivas, Trabzon, Urfa* (Istanbul: Sucuoğlu Matbaası, 1955). For a discussion of folklore as nationalist
practice in Turkey, see: Arzu Öztürkmen, *Türkiye'de Folklor ve Milliyetçilik* (Istanbul: İletişim, 1998).
[103] Cahit Beğenç, *Diyarbekir ve Raman* (Ankara: Ulus, 1949), 33. For one of Arsunar's collections,
see: Ferruh Arsunar, *Türk Anadolu Halk Türküleri* (Ankara: Başnur, 1965).
[104] *Diyarbekir Halk Türküleri* (Istanbul: Numune Matbaası, 1937).
[105] Hans-Lukas Kieser, *Der verpasste Friede: Mission, Ethnie und Staat in den Ostprovinzen der
Türkei 1839–1938* (Zürich: Chronos, 2000), 408–12.
[106] See his multi-volume book on Anatolian Shi'ites: Bedri Noyan, *Bütün Yönleriyle Bektâşilik ve
Alevîlik* (Ankara: Ardıç, 1998–2006). For comments on sheikhs as 'ignorant reactionaries' and 'traitors
of the motherland', see vol. VI, 703–9.

course of 1937, the premises of the People's House were expanded as well: instead of two scattered buildings a single large one was constructed just outside the city walls. The new director was counselled to 'work systematically' in order to be more productive.[107] In July 1937 the new Inspector-General reported with content: 'These fruitful institutions of culture and national ideal in the East will be one notch more productive and useful'.[108]

In order to gauge how this improvement of cultural assimilation was to be developed, the government sent a special envoy to inspect the countryside. In the autumn of 1940, People's Houses Inspector Kemal Güngör travelled through south-eastern Turkey and wrote a lengthy report on the cultural state of affairs in the region. The inspector noted about the provincial towns of Diyarbekir that for the majority of the people Turkish was a second or even third language. Güngör expressed strong disapproval that across the countryside people spoke Kurdish and Arabic 'in their houses, at the market, in the coffeehouse, and even in the People's Houses'. He solicited their superiors to take measures that would 'eradicate the deplorable influence of these cultures and render our national culture and mother tongue dominant in their stead'. According to Güngör this would require a higher level of organization in the countryside of Diyarbekir, stretching eastwards. That way, he argued, chances were much higher to 'spread our national language here and remove the foreign influence' and 'render worthwhile services to our national unity and integrity, as well as our mission for a national culture'. After all, he concluded, it was imperative to 'spread our national culture and revolution into these corners of the motherland because these areas need it . . . most of all from a cultural and social perspective'.[109] Thus, radicalization on the one hand implied geographical expansion and on the other hand resulted in a shift from urban politics to rural politics.[110] To realize their goals, the government developed the concept of the People's Rooms, the rural equivalent of the People's Houses. Starting from 1940, the Rooms quickly spread into the districts of Diyarbekir's countryside, as narrated by an American observer:

> Like on an expedition to Africa, a large convoy consisting of many members, intellectuals, and politicians arrived in the village by car and by bus. Among them were doctors, dentists, poets, Pedagogy students and People's House orators. They were equipped with an amount of canned food that would have sufficed for a convoy out to discover an unknown continent. After the flag was hoisted and speeches were given, the sick in the village were examined and treated. The rural experts in the convoy took many interesting pictures of the village and the villagers.[111]

---

[107] BCA, 490.01/1006.882.1, RPP People's Houses Inspector Kemal Güngör to RPP People's Houses Bureau Directorate, 8 October 1943.

[108] BCA, 490.01/996.850.1, RPP General Secretariat to First Inspector-General Abidin Özmen, 22 July 1937.

[109] BCA, 490.01/1006.882.1, RPP People's Houses Inspector Kemal Güngör to RPP General Secretariat, 10 November 1940.

[110] As every niche of society now had to be 'Turkified', even prisons, enclaves normally placed outside the confines of society, were subjected to the nation formation process. According to one report in the city prison of Diyarbekir a reading room was opened for the convicts to learn Turkish. BCA, 490.01/996.850.1, Dr. Münir Soykam to RPP General Secretariat, 15 August 1941.

[111] Fay Kirby, 'The Village Institute Movement in Turkey: An Educational Mobilization for Social Change' (unpublished Ph.D. dissertation, Teachers' College, Columbia University, New York, 1960), 71.

Rituals such as these represented nation formation in the province. The villagers were now confronted with new symbols they should adhere to. Kemal Güngör also noted that one effective medium to reach the people in the countryside was the radio. He wrote: 'I am convinced that sending radios to the villages will prove more effective than many other measures'. The special inspector was irritated that especially in the villages, he had witnessed Kurdish songs being sung by children who did not speak Turkish.[112] The radio, 'a most important instrument of enlightenment in our age', would reach into the homes of people living 'far from the centre' and spread Turkish language and culture among those who would tune in to Ankara radio. Güngör's final recommendations included supplying the Diyarbekir People's House with speakers strong enough to reach an audience in the streets, and sending as many radios as possible to the villages.[113] After approval from Ankara, the People's House immediately began implementing these principles as People's Rooms mushroomed in every district of Diyarbekir.

The first People's Room established in the province was that of Bismil, a small town 40 kilometres east of Diyarbekir city. Initially, setting up a People's Room in this town was a plan advanced tentatively to test public reaction. Its convenient proximity to the provincial capital was advantageous because it made the Room easy to observe for the Diyarbekir elite. According to reports by the founding officials, at establishment most people in town spoke Turkish. In the villages, on the other hand, everybody spoke Kurdish, with the exception of seven villages close to the town. Out of a total population of 2612 inhabitants, 224 children were enjoying primary education as the process of appointing teachers and building schools continued. Since by January 1941 there was still no radio, the chairman of the Room ordered some.[114] By the end of that year the People's Room was reported to be modest but functioning. Visitors reportedly came to listen to the radio and celebrate national holidays.[115] The People's Room was kept under tight surveillance, and when an inspector found out that citizens had used the Room to organize a lottery, he immediately took measures and had the culprits arrested.[116] The nation, after all, was no joke and its activities were expected to be taken very seriously. Since the overall response of Bismil's population had been positive towards the activities of the Room, this trial and the formula were declared a success and the decision was taken to expand the enterprise into other areas.

The difference in nation formation manifested itself in those districts where few people spoke Turkish and even fewer identified with the nation state. The small, provincial, county or district town acted as tiny capital for the surrounding villages and was typically a sleepy place, periodically awakened when the brief bustle of the weekly market or Friday call to prayer broke the quiet. Yet it was through these towns

[112] BCA, 490.01/1006.882.1, RPP People's Houses Inspector Kemal Güngör to RPP General Secretariat, 10 November 1940.
[113] BCA, 490.01/996.850.1, RPP General Secretariat to Fourth Bureau, 3 January 1941.
[114] BCA, 490.01/996.850.1, Dr. Münir Soykam to RPP General Secretariat, 27 January 1941.
[115] BCA, 490.01/996.850.1, Dr. Münir Soykam to RPP General Secretariat, 2 December 1941.
[116] BCA, 490.01/996.850.1, RPP General Secretary Dr. Ahmet Fikri Tuzer to Bismil People's House, 19 January 1942.

that Young Turk ideology and the changes it suggested were transmitted to the surrounding countryside. In such a social microcosm, political processes functioned according to the principles of centre and periphery, very much like a colonial situation. The provincial towns were under the trusteeship of Ankara, which ruled them from afar by sending them its civil servants, its newspapers, its garrisons. It was in these towns where the cultural mission of 'Turkification', that Turkish Hearth and People's House members propagated, was most challenging and immediate.

With only 50 percent of its children in school, a quarter of the men and only a tenth of the women being able to speak Turkish, the north-western district of Ergani was such a region. According to official reports, of the 3253 town-dwellers and 18,015 villagers, 'most speak in the Zaza language, others in Kurdish'.[117] The People's Room in Ergani was a makeshift one, with newly planted trees, a newly constructed road, and a loosely arranged library—of which reports boasted it did 'not include any prohibited books'. The Room was run by local Kemalists such as the town's schoolteacher, Şükrü Tanili, who, according to the Diyarbekir People's House journal, would 'lecture on the topic of the Turkish revolution in front of hundreds of excited locals'. The town doctor, Şevki Kılıççı, in his turn lectured on venereal diseases, which reportedly left a 'deep impression' on the people. Anniversaries of the Republic and the establishment of the People's Houses were celebrated with feasts involving 'the decoration of the whole town with the party and national flags'. The ceremonies would routinely be opened with the national anthem as schoolchildren would read nationalist poems and sing nationalist songs. At 3:00 PM the radio was turned on as Prime Minister Refik Saydam delivered a 'great and valuable lecture'. Finally, the local chairman closed the celebration by declaring that everybody needed to work 'day and night' to preserve the legacy of 'the Eternal Chief Atatürk'.[118] Through repetition the national anthem, principles of national defence, and patriotism in general were instilled.[119]

In 1941, Çermik, the adjacent district more to the west of the province, had a population of 3360 people living in the town and 26,627 living in the villages. In the city, one-fifth of the girls and half of the boys were reported to be in school. In the fourteen villages, 237 of 279 boys and only seventy-three girls were in school. Again, the use of languages was closely monitored. Reports noted that whereas Turkish was understood by most townsfolk, only in ten villages were there people who spoke Turkish: 'the rest speaks in the Zaza and Kurmanci languages'. Officials had taught thirty people Turkish in one month of intensive teaching. The people had been taught how to use the radio and how to use the library, which numbered 278 volumes of books and magazines. The People's House headquarters in Diyarbekir ordered that once every two weeks, the young people should assemble in the square in front of the People's Room and 'dance national dances and sing national songs'. Moreover, teachers needed to make 'the youth sing marches with one voice' and inculcate 'national morals'. People's Room officials needed to 'take great care to

[117] BCA, 490.01/996.850.1, Dr. Münir Soykam to RPP General Secretariat, 30 April 1941.
[118] Münip Gültekin, 'Ergani Halkevi Çalışmaları', in: *Karacadağ* III, no. 25, 20 February 1940.
[119] BCA, 490.01/996.850.1, Dr. Münir Soykam to RPP General Secretariat, 30 April 1941.

eliminate the languages of these citizens . . . while conducting language and literature research in the villages of these people, who are racially Turks'. Therefore it was pivotal 'especially in this region to teach them how to read and write Turkish'.[120] The highbrow discussions on cultural 'Turkification' of the 1930s had trickled down into actual policies on the ground a decade later.

Relatively small in comparison to the other district towns of Diyarbekir, Piran (later renamed Dicle) was situated only fifty kilometres north of the provincial capital and was populated by 25,359 people. Here, as in most towns, most men were able to speak Turkish but only few women were. In the villages of Piran 'only those who have completed their military service can speak Turkish'. Half of the locals spoke Kurmanci, the other half spoke Zazaki.[121] It is noteworthy that the report mentions the existence of 285 Armenian Catholics in the district.[122] The People's Room was 'functioning well' with 130 books and journals stored in its library. In 1940 twelve people were taught to read and write Turkish. Once in every fifteen days the youth was assembled in the Room to 'sing national songs (especially our national marches with one voice all together)'. The inspector further wrote to Ankara that 'although this is the place where Sheikh Said's rebellion erupted, the people whom I have met are loyal to the government'. According to the inspector, the only things the town needed was a district governor and a capable gendarmerie officer.[123] In the far north-eastern district of Kulp, a dilapidated town of only 671 inhabitants, twenty-eight girls and seventy-seven boys were going to school. Here, too, many in the town were reported to understand Turkish, but in the villages everyone spoke Kurmanci. The report put the proportion of the Turkish-speaking population at only 2 percent, perhaps the lowest in the entire province. Of all the social problems in the district, inspector Soykam identified the crucial challenge to be the spread of the Turkish language among the local Kurds. This process had been lagging behind because of corruption. The local district governor had been using the People's Room radio for his personal ends and literature sent to the People's Room was known to be in his private possession. Every time the district governor was asked for commentary he happened to be 'organizing the census in the countryside'. In general the Kulp People's Room was very modest.[124]

More serious problems were registered in the eastern district of Silvan. Of all the inspection reports, the Silvan People's Room was the thickest file, for 'Turkification' was not progressing fast enough according to the Party's wishes. The 1940

---

[120] BCA, 490.01/996.850.1, Dr. Münir Soykam to RPP General Secretariat, 29 April 1941.

[121] The majority of the Kurds in Turkey speak Kurmanci, a minority the related language Zazaki; due to intermarriage, historically, some people spoke both. Both languages were historically mostly spoken rather than written. Even though many Kurdish men traditionally spoke or understood Turkish, it was never a marker of ethnic identity, much like Russian in the Caucasus.

[122] It is quite possible that at this time 285 Armenians were living in Piran district. According to an account of an Armenian man from the region, one large extended family of Armenians had survived the genocide under Sheikh Said's protection. Interview conducted with Dikran E. in Hilversum (the Netherlands), 29 May 2005.

[123] BCA, 490.01/996.850.1, Dr. Münir Soykam to RPP General Secretariat, 31 May 1941, and Dr. Münir Soykam's inspection report synopsis, 27 May 1941.

[124] BCA, 490.01/996.850.1, Dr. Münir Soykam to RPP General Secretariat, 22 May 1941.

census stated that the town's population of 2930 included mostly Kurds, but also seventy-three Armenians and Syriacs. Again it was emphasized that most of the men spoke Turkish but only a fraction of the women and children did. In the 160 villages of the district, the report noted that all of these spoke Kurmanci. The Silvan People's Room was housed in the former Armenian church, which needed repairs, but since there were no ownership documents, it was left in dilapidation when the Room moved.[125] Discontent over the Silvan People's Room was rooted in their dysfunctional performance: apparently, the 'level of work was zero', members had 'wasted time gossiping', the logbook had been used as a visitor's book, the radio was broken with no attempts made at repairing it, and the record-keeping was described as 'a disgrace'. But what outraged the leadership most of all was the fact that the Turkish language courses were poorly taught.[126] Another one of the problems the People's House headquarters in Diyarbekir faced was transportation. The road from Diyarbekir to Silvan was not up to par, and during heavy rainfall a considerable detour became necessary. Officials did not find the functioning up to standard and 'wanted these shortcomings eliminated immediately'.[127] Inspector-General Abidin Özmen dismissed the Silvan People's House director and assigned the district governor as the new one, 'totally removing any discord' and streamlining the organization. Among the measures taken were the increase of members, the opening of branches, the convening of more meetings, and greater care for record-keeping.[128] From then on conditions improved: the library began functioning anew, newspapers and journals were being read, and very soon all was 'as intended'.[129]

In the northern district of Lice there were flaws as well. Its People's Room could not function ideally due to the fact that the building was not sufficient to provide for it. The Room was housed on the bottom floor of the municipal building, which was in need of repairs. Therefore, not enough sessions for activities could be organized. With its population of 6160, a total of 85 percent of Lice's men and 60 percent of its women could understand Turkish, though few children spoke it. In the villages practically nobody spoke Turkish but Zazaki, which was portrayed as 'a mix between Asiatic Turkish and coarse Persian'. The radio was listened to and the library owned 437 books, journals and newspapers, though no proper shelves existed for them. Here too, the reports were ubiquitously positive about the people's stance on the government's policies of nation formation. 'All of them', Soykam wrote to Ankara, 'reported their gratitude and indebtedness to the Republican government and our elders...and said they were always at their

---

[125] BCA, 490.01/996.850.1, Şükrü Kaya to First Inspectorate-General, 26 April 1938, appendix 1937 Diyarbekir People's House Evaluation.

[126] BCA, 490.01/996.850.1, First Inspector-General Abidin Özmen to RPP General Secretariat, 9 May 1938.

[127] BCA, 490.01/996.850.1, RPP General Secretariat to First Inspector-General Abidin Özmen, 30 April 1938.

[128] BCA, 490.01/996.850.1, RPP General Secretary Dr. Tuzer to Silvan People's House, 17 June 1941.

[129] BCA, 490.01/996.850.1, Dr. Münir Soykam to RPP General Secretariat, 31 May 1941.

command'.[130] Suggestions for improvement of the Lice People's House ranged from involving more women in the library activities to offering villagers the opportunity to have letters and petitions written for them, for free.[131]

The inspection report for the People's Room of Hani is noteworthy for including an important example of popular resistance against Turkish nation formation. Hani, a town of 2475 inhabitants, boasted dozens of shops, two mosques, and three bakeries. For a small Kurdish town it was remarkable that 95 percent of the men and 70 percent of the women and children understood Turkish. Most people were reported to speak Zaza, although Kurmanci was widely spoken as well. On 'national days and whenever ordered', many activities were organized. Although the radio was temporarily out of order, and the doctor was in military service, the library was up and functioning with 106 books, newspapers and journals, and a reading table. There was special surveillance and vigilance regarding Hani since many locals had joined Sheikh Said in 1925. One of the resisters was Ömer Boran, son of Sheikh Salih Bey, who had been one of Sheikh Said's supporters and advisors. Because his father had been executed in the summer of 1925, Boran was under continuous scrutiny by local government officials. According to inspector Soykam, the man 'assumed a negative attitude toward the Republican government and the People's Room . . . because his father had been rightfully hanged'. The local teacher was Mehmet Güzel, a friend of Ömer Boran and brother-in-law of another sheikh who had been executed in 1925, Sheikh Sıddık from the village of Güzelşeyh. Mehmet Güzel's family had been deported to the western province of Kütahya, and therefore he too had been resisting the government. The children of the three executed sheikhs (Sheikh Salih, Sheikh Mustafa, and Sheikh Seyfullah) were in touch with each other and bore a grudge against the government. Moreover, they had befriended local gendarme officers and were pitting them against District Governor Mustafa Çetin, who had been awarded a medal during the violent suppression of the 1925 rebellion in the region. Münir Soykam immediately took action and had both Güzel and Boran deported, and the gendarme officers assigned somewhere else. He then assembled the locals in the People's Room and gave a speech about the 'blessings of the Republic' and the People's Rooms. He emphasized that the government existed to 'educate and integrate' them, and warned that anyone who resisted the government would meet with severe measures.[132] The state's response to organized dissent and frustration followed the same pattern everywhere: imposition, silencing, dispersion, and in the worst case incarceration.

The considerable efforts the government expended on cultural policies can count as evidence for how seriously it took the cultural program in the east. But the Kemalists essentialized culture. Rather than a continuously changing and socially learned process of shared interpretations and intangible symbols, culture was viewed as a vehicle for Turkification and a carrier or embodiment of Turkishness.

---

[130] BCA, 490.01/996.850.1, Dr. Münir Soykam to RPP General Secretariat, 11 May 1941.
[131] BCA, 490.01/996.850.1, Dr. Münir Soykam to RPP General Secretariat, 9 May 1941.
[132] BCA, 490.01/996.850.1, Dr. Münir Soykam to RPP General Secretariat, 12 May 1941.

This reification of culture in the Kemalist single-party state is exemplified in the 1934 law prescribing European and prohibiting indigenous dress. The law not only prohibited sheikhs from wearing their traditional clothes, but also discouraged ordinary villagers from wearing their traditional baggy pants (*şalwar*) and headgear (*puşi*), suitable for the climate, in favour of the corduroy pants and top hat. In the Kemalist mind, the traditional Diyarbekir headdress was associated with Kurdish ethnicity and therefore potentially dangerous. Indeed, Kurdish nationalists had flaunted traditional dress as a symbol of Kurdishness in Diyarbekir city.[133] The Kemalists kept an eye on these developments and made sure nobody appropriated the dress as symbols of Kurdish culture. In later policies the approach to 'Kurdish' dress was softened and the clothes were relegated to 'local folklore'.[134] A seemingly banal phenomenon as dress could become a battleground for national hegemony.[135]

A major component of Kemalist cultural policies in the east was music. Şükrü Kaya had proudly declared that 'music is an element of national upbringing'.[136] But what type of music was it acceptable to listen to? The musical heritage of the past was a reminder of an embarrassing age and therefore, far from harmless. After all, Ottoman music confronted the Turkish nationalists with its offensively conspicuous multi-cultural Ottoman past, during which Armenian composers, Albanian instrumentalists, and Greek singers played music in the Ottoman language. The Ministry of Culture therefore ignored Ottoman music and replaced the musical canons with European music or 'Turkish Folk Music' (*Türk Halk Müziği*), an aggregate of many Turkish-language songs collected in the countryside. An official propaganda booklet boasted in 1936,

> Turkey has now abandoned oriental music, under the influence of which she had remained for centuries. The lurid and monotonous music of the Arabs and Persians, which could no longer satisfy our country, was doomed to disappear, sooner or later. At the head of this movement, which is sure to have a positive influence on the development of our own national music, is Atatürk himself. That is why the

---

[133] Ekrem Cemil Paşa, *Muhtasar Hayatım* (Brussels: Kurdish Institute, 1991), 36–7.

[134] *Diyarbekire Bir Bakış* (Diyarbakır: Diyarbekir Basımevi, 1935), 2.

[135] Dress was but one example of how national hegemony was achieved through cultural policies; film was another. Although the government saw in film a powerful propaganda tool, the Ministry of Culture issued clear regulations on its use. During Young Turk rule, all films produced and viewed in Turkey needed to comply with ten constraints and requirements, according to which films were not to: offend national sentiments and harm the national ideal; oppose the Republican regime and suggest other forms of government; suggest ideas against the military and weaken sentiments for National Defence; weaken the notion of family; weaken the morals of the student; stimulate religious feelings whether negatively or positively; contain lewd scenes or shots of debauchery; contain occurrences of murder and suicide; contain scenes of mass violence or cruelty, even against animals; weaken discipline in the student. Esat Sagay, 'Son Yapılan Teftiş Neticesi Hakkında Talimat', in: Hasan Ali Yücel, *Türkiye'de Orta Öğretim* (Ankara: T.C. Kültür Bakanlığı Yayınları, 1994), 373–4. The Diyarbekir People's House lacked many resources to screen films. Therefore, Interior Minister Şükrü Kaya ordered more 'moral and cultural' films to be sent to Diyarbekir and suggested the House staff repeat the screening of the two available government propaganda films. BCA, 490.01/996.850.1, Şükrü Kaya to First Inspectorate-General, 26 April 1938, appendix 'Diyarbekir People's House Evaluation of 1937'.

[136] Ekrem Ergüven (ed.), *Şükrü Kaya: Sözleri—Yazıları 1927–1937* (Istanbul: Cumhuriyet Matbaası, 1937), 157.

dominating spirit in the Normal School of Music, ever since its foundation, has been one of modern and European character, based on western technique... The Normal School of Music of Ankara is an advanced temple of Occidental Music in Asia Minor.[137]

This was not mere propaganda but a nation-wide policy. British observers reported from Diyarbekir that every Friday 'a military band discoursed Western music to... the entire population'. But conservative urbanites refused to listen to the Western music, especially on the holy Friday, reserved for religious observance.[138]

For the regime, the indigenous music of the eastern provinces was equally problematic due to its manifestly multi-cultural character. This was perhaps even more dangerous to the Kemalists. Kurdish, Syriac, Zaza, and Arabic music could raise awareness among Kurds and Arabs of their ethnicity and therefore needed to be banned. Turkish Hearths members had discussed the role of music for nation formation in the east. When during its 1927 congress the floor was opened for submitting proposals, Mardin delegate Dr. Cevdet Şakir had proposed that 'the customs bureau needs to take great care that gramophone records and written music imported to the Eastern provinces are not in Arabic and Kurdish', and even proposed a law to be adopted for such a prohibition.[139] Such a law was never passed because it was never considered necessary explicitly to pronounce the prohibition of non-Turkish culture and music—this was self-evident under Young Turk rule. Indeed, from then on, the government prohibited entry of many records with Kurdish and Arabic music at a time when gramophones were penetrating the eastern cities.[140]

In a peasant society, oral traditions sung by bards (*dengbêj* in Kurdish) were naturally more widespread than record players. Upon realizing that Kurdish oral culture was continuing to produce Kurdish music in the interbellum period, the Kemalists even banned this tradition. Seîdê Axayê Cizrawî, a famous troubadour in the eastern Diyarbekir region, would tour the province and sing Kurdish songs (often laments on recent history) during clandestine nightly storytelling sessions (*şevbuhêrk* in Kurdish) of notable Kurdish chieftains. On one occasion he sang the following lament about the 1925 massacres in Diyarbekir province:

> The land of the Kurds is fertile and blessed /
> It is all minerals, silver, and gold /
> What can we do, nowadays it's in the hand of others /
> Ah alas alas /
> They killed us and threw us in the rivers /
> There are no more lion-hearted valiants left among us.

---

[137] *Public Instruction in the Republic of Turkey* (Ankara: Press Department of the Ministry of the Interior, 1936), 39–40.
[138] NAUK, FO 424/271, 28, no. 10, Clerk to Henderson, 11 July 1929, 'Notes from a Journey from Angora to Aleppo, Diarbekir, Malatia, Sivas and the Black Sea Coast, June 9–29, 1929'.
[139] *Türk Ocakları 1927 Senesi Kurultayı Zabıtları* (Ankara: n.p., 1928), 353.
[140] NAUK, FO 424/271, 28, no. 10, Clerk to Henderson, 11 July 1929, 'Notes from a Journey from Angora to Aleppo, Diarbekir, Malatia, Sivas and the Black Sea Coast, June 9–29, 1929'.

When local government officials found out that Cizrawî was singing this lament they ordered his arrest but he escaped and fled to the Syrian border town of Qamishli.[141]

Parallel to a ban on all non-Turkish music, in Diyarbekir efforts were underway to build a local canon of Turkish music. This was difficult since most musicians in the province were surviving Armenians and Syriacs who had played in various formations in the city. The young musician Celal Güzelses (1900–59) was assigned by the Diyarbekir People's House to 'research the regional folklore'. In 1938 he published his results, a compilation of songs from Diyarbekir.[142] What was interesting is that in his repertoire, Turkish-language songs had been improbably traced to Kurdophone villages. Indeed, of the untold number of songs Güzelses had collected, he had kept the melodies but had translated their texts into Turkish. In 1943 he faced difficulties in attempting to establish a Diyarbekir Music Ensemble (Diyarbakır Musiki Cemiyeti) due to lack of musicians. The interwar expulsions that had rid the province of most of its last Christians had also dealt a fatal blow to musical life in the region. Whereas in the mid-1940s two out of the ten musicians of the Diyarbekir Music Ensemble were still Armenians (a violinist and a percussionist; see Plate 14), in 1948 there was not a single Armenian musician left.[143] The government's policies were as counterproductive as its aims incompatible: on the one hand it expelled Armenian musicians to Syria, while on the other hand it spurred the People's House to perform more musical works. Musical activity stagnated to the degree that the People's House director complained to the Party that it needed a violinist, 'preferably a graduate of the conservatory', to play in its orchestra.[144] It took years before the Ensemble could function at a modicum of activity. Only in early 1945 could the director report that 'the Folk Music Ensemble is continuing its productive activities. It has drawn great attention and praise for its weekly concerts in our House and during its trips to surrounding districts'. In accordance with instructions from the Ministry, the Ensemble had also widely played 'national songs'.[145]

How did the population perceive and receive these educational and cultural policies? Some scholars of peasant societies have argued that peasants are often suspicious towards education imposed by the state. Education is often perceived as 'a foreign element, coming from the outside. It limits the family's rearing influence, tears the child from the harmonious system of work and life and introduces into its consciousness patterns which are dissonant with, and values foreign to or

---

[141] Salihê Kevirbirî, *Bir Çığlığın Yüzyılı: Karapetê Xaço* (Istanbul: Sî, 2002), 59.

[142] Celal Güzelses, *Diyarbakır Halk Türküleri* (Istanbul: n.p., 1938). Reportedly, Güzelses was summoned to Dolmabahçe Palace by Atatürk and had his skull measured for ascertaining his race profile. He turned out to be soundly Turkish. Şeyhmus Diken, *Sırrını Surlarına Fısıldayan Şehir: Diyarbakır* (Istanbul: İletişim Yayınları, 2003).

[143] Compare the two photographs published in: Şeyhmus Diken, *Diyarbakır Diyarım, Yitirmişem Yanarım* (Istanbul: İletişim, 2003), 183, 250.

[144] BCA, 490.01/832.283.01, Diyarbekir People's House Director Çubukçu to RPP General Secretariat, 28 September 1937.

[145] BCA, 490.01/1036.986.01, Diyarbekir People's House Director Reşid İskenderoğlu to RPP General Secretariat, 9 February 1945.

impossible of realization within that system: hence the resistance confronted by the school in rural areas'.[146] A frequently quoted rhetorical question among peasant families in the countryside is: 'So you study, and then what?' (*Okuyup da ne olacaksın?*). For many villagers, it was much more important to have their children continue working on the farm. Conversely, if one takes the People's House reports at face value, nation formation was an unequivocal success in Diyarbekir province. Both postulates, of total rejection and of total success, lack sufficient evidence to allow the conclusion that nation formation towards eastern peasants failed or succeeded as a result of social engineering in the Young Turk era. Careful analysis is required to assess the full implication of the material at hand.

The official correspondence was openly celebratory. If one is to believe the account of the general evaluation of all People's Rooms in Diyarbekir province, the policies yielded nothing but approval by the population. According to the 1941 progress report, 'in these days when the whole world is plunged into fire, blood, death, tears and pain', the people ostensibly felt gratitude because of their 'fortunate lives' and because they could 'sleep well at night, knowing that their elders were working for the happiness of the nation'.[147] Some foreign allies of the regime, too, portrayed a happy population enjoying free government education. The Swiss anthropologist Eugène Pittard (1867–1962), who had become a cultural advisor to Mustafa Kemal, lavished superlatives on the Kemalist educational campaign: 'I went from Ankara to Diyarbakır, from Sivas to Konya. I stopped in every village and town; I witnessed the zeal that the entire population felt and the enthusiasm of young and old was impressive. I gave lessons to a young man in Diyarbakır. This young fellow walked two hours a day to meet with me'.[148] In these accounts, the educational policies of the Young Turk regime were nothing but successful.

However, the fate of the government's enthusiastic radio policies aptly demonstrates that Young Turk high-modernist social engineering achieved only limited success. According to official statistics of 1963, out of 663 villages in Diyarbekir province 323 had radios in public possession and 965 households owned radios that ran on batteries.[149] This meant that many people listened to public broadcasts in the Turkish language. But when Turkish journalist Nedim Gürsel was touring the south-eastern region in 1962, he found locals listening not to the state's broadcasting company TRT (Türkiye Radyo Televizyon Kurumu) but to Radio Teheran and, to his horror, Radio Yerevan. When admonishing the villagers to tune to TRT, the Kurds burst into laughter and tuned to Ankara's frequency. The radio muttered a dull crackle,

---

[146] Bogusław Gałęski, 'Sociological Problems of the Occupation of Farmers', in: Teodor Shanin (ed.), *Peasants and Peasant Societies* (Harmondsworth: Penguin, 1971), 180–201, at 195.

[147] BCA, 490.01/996.850.1, Dr. Münir Soykam to RPP General Secretariat, 30 April 1941. This was obviously propaganda since the strict wartime censorship was observed with even more vehemence in the eastern provinces. Interviews conducted with elderly peasants confirm that they knew next to nothing about the brutality of the Second World War.

[148] Eugène Pittard, 'Atatürk'ün Hatırasını Tazim', in: *Belleten* 3, no. 10 (April 1939), 175.

[149] Mustafa E. Erkal, *Bölgeler Arası Dengesizlik ve Doğu Kalkınması* (Istanbul: Şamil, 1972), 196–7.

intermittently emitting vague sounds.[150] The authorities were distraught by this situation and attempted to scramble the signal of Radio Yerevan and send more radios to the border regions. In its broadcasting policies too, the regime regarded Diyarbekir as a missionary centre from where 'Turkishness' would radiate. In the words of a Young Turk official: 'For the Eastern Anatolian region, TRT Diyarbakır bears vital importance'.[151] In Diyarbekir, Radio Yerevan was a very popular radio channel, particularly because it broadcast music in Kurdish. As one Kurd reminisced about his adolescence, 'I vividly remember my father laying on the couch and listening to Radio Yerevan. He would hold the small radio close to his ear, finger on the button, ready to switch it off in the face of spying eyes. My mother would be terrified then, cursing around: "Is he listening to those damn Kurds again?" But as long as Radio Yerevan kept broadcasting, my father kept on listening'.[152]

Evidence of resistance against education is even more compelling.[153] Observers of education in the Young Turk era have frequently commented on the villagers' lack of appreciation for an extended period of schooling or for any schooling at all. First of all, the academic year of state education was discordant with the peasants' temporal regime: 'The village schools open in Autumn and continue until the end of Spring. These two seasons are periods in which the children are especially needed for work in the villages. Starting from an early age there is always work for a village boy to do. That is why they work for their families rather than attend school'.[154] One researcher who had travelled to the countryside argued that most peasants had scoffed at the intangible results of modern education. 'According to such families, the boys will sooner or later learn to read and write in the army, and the girls need not know at all...most of the village families are not yet aware of the meaning of education. To them, gardening, digging a ground toilet, ploughing a field are activities which have nothing in common with education'.[155] Another writer well acquainted with the countryside noted that 'village children have little motivation to go into town to school. It is not within the village pattern of behaviour for them to do so. Normally, the village child graduates from a primary school in his or a neighboring village and then reverts to the traditional pattern of village life. In village eyes, he is "educated". That is enough'.[156] A particularly revealing example of rural obduracy lies in the answer given to an official who had asked the inhabitants of a village in the east what they wanted from the government. Without hesitation the villagers replied: 'Sir, take

[150] Necmi Onur, *Şark Cephesinde Yeni Birşey Yok* (Istanbul: Belge, 1972), 290–1.

[151] Erkal, *Bölgeler Arası Dengesizlik*, 196.

[152] Interview conducted with M.Ü. in Istanbul, 19 June 2004.

[153] Not wanting education has to be distinguished from not being able to enjoy education. Village school children often found it difficult to avail themselves of opportunities for a secondary school education. Many such children lived in very isolated villages away from towns or cities, often without means of transportation to and from places with secondary schools. Leaving the village to study in the city presented the peasant child with insurmountable obstacles. Due to widespread poverty only very few could afford the luxury of sending their child(ren) to school.

[154] Emin M. Soysal, 'Köy Muallimi ve Köy', in: *Dönüm* 20 (1934), 23.

[155] İbrahim Yasa, *Hasanoğlan: Socio-Economic Structure of a Turkish Village* (Ankara: Public Administration for Turkey and the Middle East, Yeni Matbaa, 1957), 145.

[156] Andreas M. Kazamias, *Education and the Quest for Modernity in Turkey* (Chicago: The University of Chicago Press, 1966), 173.

this school away from our village, and we will ask nothing of you. Because of it, our cows go astray, and our work does not progress'.[157]

Problems also stemmed from the clash between the secular nationalist values of the teachers, and the pious and conservative outlook of the peasants. An official from the Ministry of Education complained,

> The teacher sent by the Ministry to the villages looks down on the villagers. He does not like village children. Moreover, he [the villager] wears clothes that are objectionable to the theoretical knowledge that the teacher gives him. The imam of the village, on the other hand, taught the Koran, *İlmihal*, and *Muhammediye* [sacred literature] to the village children, led the villagers in prayer at the village mosque five times each day, went to weddings and funerals and visited the sick where he performed his ritual of chasing away evil spirits by blowing on the patient. The imam had a small house, a garden and a field given to him by the villagers. At harvest time each year, the villagers set aside a share of their produce to be given to the imam. Also, if the imam did not work his field, the villagers worked it for him. They paid the imam at births and weddings, for the night worship during Ramadan, and they gave him alms during the *Bayram*s [religious feasts]. Since the imam also settled disputes among the villagers, he was held in higher esteem than the teachers.[158]

Similar processes occurred in Diyarbekir province. An idealistic teacher who was sent to a village west of Diyarbekir wrote in his memoirs that villagers resisted the message of secular education. Most villagers did not speak a word of Turkish whereas the teacher did not speak a word of Kurdish. Most of all, they despised his atheism and venerated the imam. Disillusioned and bitter, the teacher finished his mandatory duty and left, never to return. Village life carried on as usual.[159]

How ethnically non-Turkish children in the eastern provinces perceived this style of education is difficult to gauge.[160] Many people who were educated in the Young Turk era have passed away. Şahin Cizrelioğlu of the noted Cizrelizâde family, remembered in an interview that on the morning of 9 November 1938 (Atatürk's death), he was sitting in class when the teacher walked in and ordered the children to cry. When the young Şahin responded, 'But Sir, my eyes won't fill with tears', the teacher told him to rub saliva on his cheekbones.[161] An insight into these experiences of education is provided by the noted Kurdish author Mehmed Uzun (1953–2007), a native of a village west of Diyarbekir city. Uzun's account of his first day in school is so vivid one is justified in quoting him at length:

> The first lesson goes back to 1960, the year I was seven. On a hot, clear day at the end of summer, the very day on which, dressed in new clothes from head to foot, I was

---

[157] Maynard, *The Lise*, 63.
[158] Kâzım Nâmi Duru, 'Köy mü, kasaba mı?', in: *Anadolu Terbiye Mecmuası* 2 (1922), 4.
[159] Kazım Cömert, *Çiğdemler Çıkarsa Eğer* (Istanbul: Aydınlar Matbaacılık, 1992).
[160] Without presenting any credible evidence, one researcher argues that Turkish state education for Kurdish children inevitably led to trauma and identity crisis. Rohat, *Kürdistan'da Eğitim Süreçleri* (Diyarbakır: Dilan, 1992), 46–50.
[161] Interview with Şahin Cizrelioğlu conducted by Şeyhmus Diken, published in: Şeyhmus Diken, *İsyan Sürgünleri* (Istanbul: İletişim, 2005), 213.

beginning grammar school, I received a violent slap in the face in the guise of a lesson on the importance of language and words. I had been born and raised in the shelter of a Kurdish tribe. My family possessed no books except for the Koran, which hung on the wall, and had neither a radio nor a television set. In this enormous house, its garden planted with some pomegranate trees and an equal number of peach trees, the garden where roses bloomed, there was nothing besides my father's *bilur* [shepherd's pipe], the stories and legends told by my grandfather, and the beautiful *stran*s [traditional songs] that my grandmother sang in the Zaza dialect of Kurdish. It was a universe forged in the feelings, ideas, norms, and values of the Kurdish language. I was seven years old and loved this universe that I was part of. But from the first hour of the first day that I set foot in school I was instructed by a slap in the face, ineradicably engraved in my memory, that my universe was meaningless, useless, primitive, and taboo, and that I had to leave it. While I was joining the ranks of my classmates in the yard of the grammar school, which was named after the poet Ibrahim Rafet, the teacher, who came from central Anatolia and was fulfilling his civil service, called me to order by a violent slap because I was speaking with a classmate in my maternal tongue. 'It is forbidden to speak Kurdish!'[162]

Another Kurdish man from the northern Lice, who later became a teacher himself, argued that the children's treatment depended on how nationalist their teacher was. His primary school teacher, a fervent nationalist, would frequently beat the children 'for even whispering a single word in Kurdish'.[163] One anthropologist documented the most radical example of linguistic oppression: an old Kurdish man had his tongue cut out by the army for speaking Kurdish.[164] Another scholar, a musicologist researching the Kurdish oral tradition, once met a man named Seyidxan Boyacı, a bard singing traditional songs and laments in Diyarbekir. Boyacı was once threatened by the authorities that if he sang inside the city walls his tongue would be cut out.[165] Examples such as these possibly suggest that cultural and educational policies could not and did not achieve the desired ends in the east on a short term. But the Young Turk legacy outlived the Young Turks themselves, for their curricula and methods remained in effect after the end of Young Turk rule in 1950.

THE BOARDING SCHOOL FOR KURDISH GIRLS

The policy of 'Turkification' through schooling manifested itself in the eastern provinces most identifiably in the boarding schools. The 1925 Kemalist reports on

---

[162] Mehmed Uzun, 'Diyarbakir: the Slap in the Face', in: *International Journal of Kurdish Studies* 1, no. 1 (January 2003).

[163] Interview conducted with Amed Tîgrîs in Stockholm, 18 May 2005.

[164] Christopher Houston, 'Creating a Diaspora within a Country: Kurds in Turkey', in: Melvin Ember, Carol R. Ember and Ian Skoggard (eds.), *Encyclopedia of Diasporas: Immigrant and Refugee Cultures Around the World* (New York: Kluwer Academic, 2004), vol. 2, 403–14.

[165] Interview conducted with Seyidxan Boyacı by Emrah Kanısıcak in the summer of 2007, available at: <http://sazny.blogspot.com/2008/05/nightingale-of-amed-new-edit.html> (accessed 6 November 2008).

'Reform in the East' had vaguely sketched that the policy of assimilation would be carried out through boarding schools. In regions where Kurds and Arabs lived, Turkish Hearths and schools needed to be opened and 'most importantly, all sacrifices need to be endured to establish girls' schools and ensure that the girls enroll... By opening boarding schools, the region can be saved from getting involved with Kurdism... and girls' schools can induce women to speak Turkish'.[166] These ideas would materialize when during the interwar campaigns, the Turkish military elite understood that assimilating the Kurds could not only be a matter of destroying and dispersing the armed resistance. Education was rediscovered as a complementary and vital method of social assimilation. The Chief of Staff solicited the government for the foundation of an educational institute that could accelerate the 'Turkification' process.[167] Precise plans for the establishment of boarding schools in the east were formulated by Interior Minister Şükrü Kaya. On 4 June 1937, Kaya sent the Ministry of Culture a top-secret circular about the boarding schools:

> Boarding schools for girls and boys need to be opened and girls and boys from the age of five need to be brought into these schools for education and upbringing. These boys and girls need to be married to each other and settled dispersedly on property inherited from their parents where they can establish a Turkish Nest so that Turkish Culture can be thoroughly implanted [in the region]... Therefore... it is necessary and essential that small children be placed in this type of boarding schools.[168]

According to Kaya, girls in particular needed to be placed in the schools since mothers were seen as the carriers of the Kurdish culture that needed to be exorcised from their minds. This order had come from Atatürk himself, who had expressed determination to pursue a policy leaving no place for mothers to raise their children with languages other than Turkish. The aim was to drive a cultural wedge between generations in order for Kurds to become 'future Turks'. The road to the nation was as coercive as it was gendered: women were seen as carriers of national reproductivity, vessels of national identity, and transmitters of culture.

The first boarding school in the eastern provinces was established in Elazığ in 1937.[169] Although it mostly aimed at schoolgirls from the Dersim district, it also drew students from the regions north of Diyarbekir.[170] There were pupils from Çermik, Ergani, and Palu—the latter being a district of Elazığ province by that time. A relatively young and idealistic teacher from Istanbul named Sıdıka Avar was appointed as director. Avar's private archive and its distillate, her memoirs, offer a rare and valuable

---

[166] Bayrak, *Kürtler*, 487.

[167] Nuriye D. Hekimoğlu, 'Kız Enstitüsü Niçin Açıldı', in: *Altan: Elaziz Halkevi Dergisi* 33–34–35 (January 1938), 32–3.

[168] Şükrü Kaya to Ministry of Culture, 4 June 1937, reproduced in: Nurşen Mazıcı, *Celal Bayar: Başbakanlık Dönemi 1937–1939* (Istanbul: Der, 1996), 233, appended document no. 3.

[169] For a study of Avar's school, see: Sevim Yeşil, 'Unfolding Republican Patriarchy: The Case of Young Kurdish Women at the Girls' Vocational Boarding School in Elazığ' (unpublished MA thesis, Middle East Technic University, Department of Gender and Women's Studies, 2003).

[170] See Abidin Özmen's report in: Cemil Koçak, *Umûmî Müfettişlikler (1927–1952)* (Istanbul: İletişim, 2003), 101 ff.

source of insight into the official perspective on educational policies in the east, and into how the Kemalist policy-makers organized the transformation process of the children from 'primitive Kurds' to 'civilized Turks'.[171] From the authorities' point of view, this 'civilization process' required a twofold assault on Kurdish children's identities. On the one hand, the school needed to strip away all outward signs of the children's identification with tribal and rural life, that is to say, their 'savage' ways. On the other hand, the children needed to be instructed in the principles, values, ideas, and behaviours of Turkish 'civilization'. These twin processes—the tearing down of the old selves versus the building of new ones—were to be carried out simultaneously. As the 'savage' Kurdish selves gave way, so the 'civilized' Turkish selves would emerge.

From the moment of her assignment Avar began travelling in the countryside on horseback, searching for girls to enroll in her boarding school. On arrival in a village, she would approach the locals and explain to those who understood Turkish what her objective was. In some villages she was received cordially, in others with outright hostility. After taking girls from a village, each one was photographed on arrival. These 'before the school' photos would later be contrasted with the 'after the school' photos to demonstrate the transition to 'civilization'. The girls would be put in quarantaine for two weeks and only then began attending classes. The curriculum in the boarding school was obviously nationalist and patriarchal. A standard program for the Kurdish village girls was three years and provided training with a special curriculum at elementary school level. Forty-four hours of class were taught in a week, and clear priority was given to Turkish language classes. Other classes were civics and math, but also child-care, housekeeping, cooking, embroidery, and sewing, which, Avar argued, were 'indispensable for a housewife'.[172]

The levels of coercion in enrolling children varied from relative voluntariness to legalized abduction, especially in the case of young orphans who had lost their families in the massacres of 1925 and 1938. Those coerced into attending school were probably more bitter than those who went voluntarily and with their parents' blessing. Children who had visited the city before must have found it easier than those taken directly from the village. Because different Kurdish tribes had been exposed to the Ottoman and Turkish states with varying intensity and experience, it was to be expected that those children coming from cultures where there had been sustained contact with Ottoman and Turkish officials would find both the idea and necessity of schooling more comprehensible than those to whom the boarding school was the first taste of education. Regardless of these varying circumstances, leaving for boarding school was generally an awkward and painful affair. Many naive and hesitant villagers fostered prejudices towards Avar's school. They suspected that their daughters would be taken away to the highly despised and distrusted city to be 'turned into communists' or 'given away to English officers'. It was feared that the girls who came back would 'neither remember their own parents nor speak their own language anymore'.[173]

[171] Sıdıka Avar, *Dağ Çiçeklerim (Anılar)* (Ankara: Öğretmen, 1986).
[172] Yeşil, *Unfolding Republican Patriarchy*, 96–8.
[173] Ibid., 234.

The often traumatic nature of being taken to the boarding school is evidenced by the example of an orphan girl named Xezal. In August 1938 Avar received a phone call from the General Inspectorate headquarters. The army had found children of 'those who had been mass-executed' roaming around the mountains. The Inspectorate ordered Avar to receive the children, not to educate them, but to make them work in the school. According to the authorities the orphans were children of 'dishonourable insurgents' and therefore did not deserve to be educated. Xezal was one of these girls who had lost their family in the 1938 massacre. She was malnourished, dressed in rags, and life in the mountains had brutalized her. When Avar first approached her, the terrified girl slapped the morsel of bread from Avar's hand and resisted being taken to the school. When Avar contained her by force and took her to school, she stripped her of her clothes and found a festering wound in her shoulder, most likely from a ricochet gunshot. It took Avar a long time to calm down the hysterical Xezal, who kept screaming in Kurdish. The girl finally went to sleep, but when her bed was found empty during dormitory inspection, Avar found the trembling girl under her bed, rolled up in her blanket. It took her weeks to get used to her new environment and she never really reconciled herself with her fate or, for that matter, with the new Turkish name that was assigned to her.[174] This example, however, was not typical of girls' experiences in the boarding school. Some of the girls prospered in the school, but a common theme that recurs is that most of them felt alienated from their families, and in a sense, from their earlier selves.

Despite these difficulties, for Kemalist philanthropists the journey of Kurdish children to the boarding school was that first step out of the darkness of 'savagery' into the light of 'civilization'. The official discourse was euphoric in the example of Avar's boarding school. One major official explained at length that the objective of the school would be 'speaking in the national language' for students who would be 'told that they are Turks in their feelings and in their lifestyles'. These students would be raised 'as conscious citizens and educated mothers committed to the revolution, the national ideal, the country', then to be sent back to their villages. There, they were expected to 'indoctrinate [*aşılamak*] their children to protect and maintain . . . the works of civilization brought by the Republic to their region', for 'only in this manner, the civilization brought by the Republic will not remain as a veneer that disappears at the slightest strain, but will leave profound traces in the deepest corners of the public spirit that cannot be rubbed out by any force'.[175] The veteran Young Turk journalist Ahmed Emin Yalman called Avar a 'first degree Turkish-nationalist raider [*akıncı*]' who had promoted 'cultural unity in our eastern provinces' by introducing 'Turkish civilization' in that region. A secondary school teacher wrote a letter to Avar, praising her for 'elevating the children to the level of civilized people by teaching them our language'.[176] The observations of the mayor of the small town of Karlıova are at least as thought-provoking:

---

[174] Ibid., 87–90.
[175] Nuriye D. Hekimoğlu, 'Kız Enstitüsü Niçin Açıldı', in: *Altan: Elaziz Halkevi Dergisi* 33–34–35 (January 1938), 32–3.
[176] Muzaffer B. to Sıdıka Avar, 18 April 1955, quoted in: ibid., 341.

You know the story of how in America a cow enters [a factory] at one end and a sausage exits at the other. Here in Elazığ we possess such a factory for 'civilized people'. In the Girls' Institute, the most primitive and savage young girls are taken in from all villages . . . Madame director gathers children like Janissaries . . . Yes indeed, squalid, ragged, savage-natured, stubborn and ill-tempered children with no language skills are going to school now. It is difficult to believe that the jovial, civilized child that offers you coffee two, three years later and speaks fluent Turkish is the same girl.[177]

This equation of 'civilization' with 'Turkishness' was expressed by Avar herself as well. In one of her annual reports to the Ministry of Education she wrote that her school was engaged in a 'war for the sake of Turkishness' in which she claimed to be facing 'a populace that does not welcome us with good will but always perceives us with suspicion and hesitation . . . and therefore needs to be indoctrinated with the Turkish ideal'.[178]

The boarding school, especially in the eastern provinces, was the institutional manifestation of the government's determination to restructure completely the Kurds' minds and personalities. To understand how it functioned in this regard one must attempt to understand how Kurdish students actually came to know and experience it. And this effort must necessarily begin at that point in time when Kurdish youth left behind the familiar world of tribal and rural ways for the unfamiliar world of the state's school. The girls' immediate physical transformation included the cutting of hair, the changing of dress, and the changing of names (see Plate 15). The first transformation, the cropping of their hair, was a *rite de passage* which symbolized their initiation into 'modernity' and 'civilization'. For many Kurdish village girls long hair was traditionally seen as a symbol of beauty and femininity, and the cutting of it was perceived as humiliating. The girls felt it made them look boyish.[179] Although the short-hair policy was rooted in considerations of controlling the problem of head lice, the reason went deeper than cleanliness. At the heart of the policy was the belief that the children's long hair was symbolic of 'savagism', and removing it was central to their new identification with 'civilization'. The changing of dress was another policy that stripped the children of their past culture. The traditional baggy trousers (*şalwar*) worn in the villages were prohibited in favour of school uniforms.[180] Since the Kemalists saw in Kurdish given names symbols of Kurdish ethnicity, many students' names were forcibly changed on arrival. Many of the orphan girls snatched from the countryside had their names changed.[181] As another graduate remembered, 'When I arrived at the school, my Kurdish name was changed into a Turkish one. But I never forgot it: Delale'.[182]

---

[177] Ibid., 233, quoted from his book: *Köyden Haber* (Istanbul: Varlık, 1950).
[178] Ibid., 255.
[179] Yeşil, *Unfolding Republican Patriarchy*, 111–14.
[180] Avar, *Dağ Çiçeklerim*, 389.
[181] Yeşil, *Unfolding Republican Patriarchy*, 121–2. Aziz Baran, 'You Must Give a Kurdish Baby a Turkish Name', in: *Kurdish Times* 1, no. 1 (1986), 12–15.
[182] Interview conducted with Şemsiye Gezici (born 1936), in Bursa, 15 June 2002.

Finally, and most importantly, the assault on Kurdish ethnic identity diverged into the absolute prohibition of speaking Kurmancî and Zazaki on the one hand, and the practising of Islam on the other. Fatma Demir, according to Avar one of her favourite students,[183] remembered the total ban on the Kurdish language well: 'Some of my friends spoke Kurdish among themselves because they did not understand Turkish yet and they were punished severely. They were not given dinner, they were beaten on the palms of their hands with a ruler, and had to stand on one foot for a long time'.[184] Another girl responded, 'We would never speak in Kurdish among ourselves. None of us. Who can dare to speak in Kurdish? There is no such possibility. There were watchmen and others'. Speaking Kurdish or bad Turkish entailed corporal punishment, as one girl remembered: 'We did not like the Turkish language classes because our former teacher was scolding us, beating us with a ruler'. Religion was another factor. It was no surprise that the Kemalist state, a secular dictatorship, prohibited all expressions of any religion in the schools. Students bitterly remembered the prohibition of the prayer, the veil,[185] and various fasting episodes, important pillars of Islamic faith. Avar defended the measures with the argument that praying was 'unscientific' and fasting bad for 'a healthy brain'.[186]

Throughout the years, the boarding school operated under strict control of the General Inspectorate and by proxy, the army. Their official visits to the boarding school are worthy of mention as they clearly demonstrate how the authorities considered the children as objects of their ideas for social engineering. Avar's account of the visit by Bingöl Governor Mehmet Rıfat Şahinbaş is revealing:

> The governor asked, 'Are these the Kurdish girls?' The expression on the faces of the children immediately changed from affection into malice. 'These are the Turkish girls of Tunceli, sir'. The governor continued, 'You have seen how your fathers and grandfathers have paid with their lives for having rebelled'. I wanted to interrupt him and said, 'Please sir, not the fathers of these children, they are honourable...' 'What do you mean? Aren't they all Kurds? If you behave like this...' Although I tried to interrupt him again he continued, 'The government is very strong. It will destroy all of you!'[187]

The governor then stepped out to inspect the other classes. When Avar came back into the class, the girls were all crying and asking questions such as: 'Why do they blame us like that? Why do they insult us by calling us Kurds? Why do they view the Kurds as lower than trash? I thought you said we were all Turks?' Prime Minister İsmet İnönü's visit in early September 1944 disclosed what the highest echelons in the dictatorship expected from the boarding school. İnönü was curious about whether it had produced any 'results', and inspected a girl by the name of Elmas. After a brief conversation with the girl in Turkish, İnönü expressed his

---

[183] Avar, *Dağ Çiçeklerim*, 203–6.
[184] Interview conducted with Fatma Demir (1925–2007), in Istanbul, 10 June 2002.
[185] See: 'Kemalism: The Civilizing Mission', in: Nilüfer Göle, *The Forbidden Modern: Civilization and Veiling* (Ann Arbor, MI: University of Michigan Press, 1996), 57–82.
[186] Quoted in: Yeşil, *Unfolding Republican Patriarchy*, 115–16, 118, 132–3.
[187] Avar, *Dağ Çiçeklerim*, 197–8.

satisfaction and grabbed her wrist, pulled her hand up and addressed the people: 'This hand will not hold a weapon or a sword, it will hold a pen and a needle!'[188]

A final account was the visit by Inspector-General General Abdullah Alpdoğan, which stirred up much excitement among the boarding school staff. Everything had to be perfect, as the general was known for his brusque manner. Alpdoğan marched into a class and saluted the children in military fashion, whereupon the children rose as a phalanx and exclaimed, 'Thank you!' When the general asked Avar which class he was facing, Avar answered that it was the third grade. Alpdoğan snubbed, 'Incorrect, you have to report properly'. When Avar asked what that meant, the general answered she had to recite the grade, the number of students present, the number of students absent, the name of the class, and the topic. Avar declaimed: 'Third grade, thirteen present, none absent, sir! The class is Turkish, the topic is 23 April, sir!' In Alpdoğan's honour the children had to sing nationalist songs and military marches. One of these was: 'Turkish children, Turkish children / Eyes ahead, heads high / Tomorrow's life is the nation's horizon / Everything is yours, Turkish children'.[189] The general's visit seemed an exception, but it was the rule. The boarding school environment was not only authoritarian, but militaristic. The school was organized like a military training camp, ostensibly because of the sheer organizational problems created by having to house, feed, teach, and, most significantly, control many children. Good health, neatness, politeness, the ability to concentrate, self-confidence, and patriotism were also attributed to military regimen. But there were deeper reasons for the military atmosphere, reasons related to Kemalist perceptions of the 'wildness' of Kurdish children. Kurdish children, it was argued, were products of cultures devoid of order, discipline, and self-constraint, all prized values in 'Turkish civilization'.[190]

Like other examples of Young Turk social engineering, the boarding school was closed after the Kemalists were ousted from power in 1950. In the end, all discourse they produced on the boarding school, whether Avar's memoirs, official inspections, or newspaper articles, was celebratory. The lived experiences of the girls was silenced and their afterlife as women was sanitized of anything perceived as negative. The discrepancy of discourse versus reality surfaces when comparing Avar's published memoirs with her unedited notes. Indeed, she mentions that many girls fled, many relished being back in their villages, and several girls committed suicide. But the most telling example of these silences built into the official narrative is the case of Anik Ö. (her last name is not disclosed in the memoirs). According to Avar's memoirs, Anik was a girl from a surviving Armenian family that had blended in with local Kurds. She was beautiful, 'with dark eyebrows, long wavy hair, a round face beaming with joy, and a charming giggle'. As a student Anik was successful; when she graduated she returned to her village, where

---

[188] Ibid., 124.
[189] Ibid., 56.
[190] Zeynep Türkyılmaz, 'The Republican Civilizing Mission: The Case of Mountain Flowers in Dersim/Tunceli (1937–1950)', paper presented at the annual conference of the Middle East Studies Association, Washington, DC, 24 November 2002.

conflicts arose because her newly acquired values clashed with existing rural and tribal values. According to Avar's official version, the girl had hanged herself on a tree in her village because her 'struggle to bring civilization to their villages had met with resistance from the villagers'. In Avar's words, the 'little heroine' was a 'victim of the onslaught of civilization'. But from her raw memoirs evidence arises that Anik had plunged into a severe identity crisis: time and again, she came into conflict with her family over cultural practices. Years of nationalist indoctrination had perverted her sense of self: was she Armenian, or Kurdish, or Turkish?[191]

The boarding school represented the Kemalist belief that the school's capacity to accomplish the transformation from 'savage Kurds' to 'civilized Turks' would determine the long-term fate of the Kurds, for if the doctrine of historical progress and the story of Turkish civilization taught anything, it was the incompatibility of 'Turkish civilization' and 'Kurdish savagism'. The assault on cultural identity was not seen as a racist and colonial practice but as a *mission civilisatrice*—like all colonial and nationalist civilizing offensives. This idea was so enduring that, in her preface to her mother's edited memoirs of 1986, Avar's daughter could argue that her late mother had been a member of 'the Turkish army of education' that had ventured to 'enlighten the east'.[192] In an effort to eradicate all traces of tribal identity and culture, the Kemalists presumed that the school would break up persisting associations with Kurdish cultural and tribal life. Forced education through boarding schools indeed caused considerable damage to the structure and function of Kurdish tribes in the eastern provinces. But interviews with the students, now in their seventies, disclose the co-existence of opposing attitudes in the women's world-views and identities. On the one hand, they seem to identify with Turkish national identity and believe in Kemalist ideology, even though the Kurdish language (which was still spoken in their families) is an embarassing reminder of their 'uncivilized' pasts. Even some orphans whose families were murdered, or children who were often beaten and maltreated for speaking Kurdish, decades later remain loyal to their tormentors.[193] But for many others the boarding school was the first place where they realized they were Kurds. For them, the chief consequence of attending the boarding school was an enlarged sense of Kurdish-ness. This fundamental ambivalence is compounded by the fact that many children of the boarders suffer from persisting identity uncertainties: although they were never taught Kurdish, they were still perceived as Kurds. Ironically, the very institution designed to extinguish Kurdish identity altogether may well have in fact contributed to its persistence in the form of pan-Kurdish consciousness and nationalism at the turn of the millenium. Only extensive further research would test the veracity of this hypothesis.

---

[191] Avar, *Dağ Çiçeklerim*, 111–13, 281, 373; cf. Sıdıka Avar Private Archive (unpublished and uncatalogued), second notebook, 177–9.

[192] Ibid., 15.

[193] For examples, see Yeşil, *Unfolding Republican Patriarchy*, 115. This may be typical of victims' behaviour: Judith Lewis Herman, *Trauma and Recovery: The Aftermath of Violence from Domestic Abuse to Political Terror* (New York: BasicBooks, 1997), 180.

DISCUSSION

One of the key elements of the vision of the new Turkey was that it was an indivisible unity. The Turkish citizen ought to bear no marks in the public sphere of his or her difference from the others in the national community. Although this meant that in principle difference was confined to the private sphere of the home, episodically rather than structurally, it too was often raided by social engineers, strongly resolved on eradicating difference. The new Turkey sought to create a nation in which no cultural and linguistic divisions would exist, with a single national culture that was open and accessible to all who were willing to adopt it. But in principle, within the Turkish nation and national imagery there was no recognized place for ethnic diversity or regional difference. The dismantling of the ancient regime from 1913 on guaranteed that never again would there be any question of individuals or groups getting special treatment, rights, or concessions according to their culture. Rather than a minimum of Turkish culture, minorities were expected to acquire fully Turkish national culture and assimilate into national society. Space for negotiating ways to be integrated into the nation was thin, and with considerable ethnic difference in the eastern provinces, this was a formidable task. Still, Young Turk nation builders sought to invent a nation with a single identity, one that was culturally homogeneous, admitted no sub-groups or categories of citizenship, but would instead be made up of universal citizens all equal to one another. While the universalist, assimilationist values did manage to integrate many minorities into the nation, difference persisted in the eastern provinces and simmered on, until it was politically mobilized in the late 1960s.

The relationship between education and nationalism has been researched fairly thoroughly.[194] Education plays a critical role in the establishment and consolidation of nations. Indeed, 'education is the most important means of consolidating national unity and passing it on to later generations'.[195] In the era under discussion in this chapter, education embodied 'an ideal of undivided one-ness' and, much as in the French case, 'a programme for creating a single, undifferentiated culture for all citizens'.[196] Paradoxically, this was at the same time an espousal of egalitarian principles and a mistrust of cultural difference. Partly for this reason, education is a contested borderland between the public responsibilities of the state and the private concerns of parents, since the identity of new generations is constructed in transactions which occur at and across this boundary. It is in these transactions that a balance between private and public socialization is struck, and the future of communities shaped.

---

[194] For an overview of the literature, see: Susanne Wiborg, 'Political and Cultural Nationalism in Education', in: *Comparative Education* 36, no. 2 (2000), 235–43.
[195] Abram de Swaan, *Human Societies: An Introduction* (Cambridge: Polity, 2005), 126.
[196] Joep Leerssen, *National Thought in Europe: A Cultural History* (Amsterdam: Amsterdam University Press, 2007), 140.

So how do we resolve the conflict between those who argue that Young Turk education must be interpreted as ordinary forms of state formation, and those who insist that they are colonial forms of cultural domination? Is this an issue incapable of resolution? Not quite. The false opposition implicit in this polemics must be seen as part of the problem rather than a genuine concern for finding an answer to the problem. Here, violence and intentions seem to be key notions in conceptualizing and understanding the issue, for there is a clear axis of tension between heavily violent and less coerced cultural policies. There is an ontological difference between the cultural and linguistic policies of dictatorial regimes and those of relatively moderate states. In a continuum of population policies, contemporary democracies would figure at one end with considerable space for negotiation and low levels of coercion. Gliding towards more coercion, nineteenth-century educational policies in southern France would figure next, before colonial policies towards Native Americans and Aboriginals (such as boarding schools). The overtly destructive policies of occupational regimes such as Nazi Germany in Eastern Europe would figure firmly at the other extreme of the continuum.[197] The problem of intentions revolves partly around the tension between contingency versus conspiracy: cultural change can be the unintended historical product of two groups that make contact, or the manipulation of a group's future through pro-active cultural policies, respectively. The Young Turks adhered to the latter theory.

Colonialism is associated with the seizing of land and the imposition of an alien dominant culture by force. It would perhaps stretch the definition of colonialism to apply it to Young Turk population policies in Eastern Turkey and label these forms of internal colonization.[198] After all, the Young Turks did also attempt to redistribute land to landless peasants and sedentarize nomads. But some aspects of their policies do bear the imprint of colonialism, if only for the fact they were literally worded that way by Young Turk leaders. Although much more research would be needed on different regions to draw wider conclusions, Young Turk population policies in Eastern Turkey can perhaps be placed in the realm of the colonial. The policies were professedly intolerant of local cultures, were resolved to impose a single hegemonic culture, but left the door open for assimilation. Most importantly, they were accompanied by large-scale campaigns of violence against those who refused to be subdued. The violence cannot be bracketed off and analysed separately, for it was part and parcel of the same logic of subduing populations perceived to be different. There is a sense of fate here. After the massively violent suppression of Kurdish dissent in the 1920s and 1930s, cultural policies could hardly have been soft-handed. Terminology such as 'extermination of cultures' and 'eradication of languages' perceived as alien and inferior, fundamentally were coupled to the large-scale violence against civilian populations.

---

[197] For a comparative, theoretical argument, see: Robert van Krieken, 'Reshaping Civilization: Liberalism between Assimilation and Cultural Genocide', in: *Amsterdams Sociologisch Tijdschrift* 29, no. 2 (2002), 215–47.

[198] The arguments are made in: Michael Hechter, *Internal Colonialism: The Celtic Fringe in British National Development, 1536–1966* (London: Routledge and Kegan Paul, 1975); Elia T. Zureik, *The Palestinians in Israel: A Study in Internal Colonialism* (London: Routledge and Kegan Paul, 1979).

One important clue to the colonial nature of Young Turk culture and education is indeed its diction. Intimately connected to the ideology of excising 'backwardness' was the Kemalists' world-view. According to one specialist, one of the key concepts of Kemalist ideology was the notion of 'civilization' (*medeniyet*).[199] This concept, Eissenstat argues, 'was fundamentally designed to act as an inclusionary (if aggressively assimilationist) rather than exclusionary discourse'.[200] The opposite of civilization was Eastern Turkey, which, they declaimed, was living in the Middle Ages. The Young Turks' apprehension of this conception of 'civilization' is characterized by Ussama Makdisi as 'Ottoman orientalism', which, in the case of the Young Turks, featured a complex of attitudes produced by exposure to an amalgam of modern European ideas, 'that implicitly and explicitly acknowledged "the West" to be the home of progress and "the East", writ large, to be a present theater of backwardness'.[201] Interwoven throughout much of their writings was the belief that Turkish is the language of civilization, administrative rationalism, and cultural enlightenment—and that the non-Turkish peoples operated on a lower cultural plane. Nation formation in the Young Turk era was therefore also a civilizing mission, comparable in discourse and practice to the European colonial ones.[202]

Moreover, educational policies in the eastern provinces were not regarded primarily as intellectual enrichment of the population, but as a vehicle for forcible assimilation of a population perceived as alien. Top-level government officials declared innumerable times that Muslim minorities in the east needed to be 'Turkified' through education. The fundamental difference between education and indoctrination here is that the pupils were never expected to question or examine critically the doctrine they were taught, especially when it came to political and historical matters (see next chapter). The space for critical self-evaluation and sceptical scrutiny of the ideas transmitted by Young Turk teachers was very limited. The totalitarian ambition of the regime manifested itself most explicitly in the field of cultural and educational policies. For almost three decades, Ministry of Education and Ministry of Culture officials closely monitored attendance at schools, films, plays, exhibits, and rallies, examined library circulation, and reported on book sales. Parallel duties were carried out by the same ministries, as well as police and gendarmerie, to ensure that no non-Turkish culture was produced visibly and distributed in the eastern provinces.

But the totalitarian nature of the Kemalist dictatorship is symbolized perhaps nowhere more clearly than in the boarding school for Kurdish children. The Ministry of Education held the children in its powerfully assimilationist embrace, designed to

---

[199] Erik-Jan Zürcher, 'The Core Terminology of Kemalism: Mefkûre, Millî, Muasir, Medenî', in: François Georgeon (ed.), *Les mots de politique de l'Empire Ottoman a la Turquie kemaliste* (Paris: EHESS, 2000), 55–64.

[200] Howard Eissenstat, 'Metaphors of Race and Discourse of Nation: Racial Theory and the Beginnings of Nationalism in the Turkish Republic', in: Paul Spickard (ed.), *Race and Nation: Ethnic Systems in the Modern World* (New York: Routledge, 2005), 239–56.

[201] Ussama Makdisi, 'Ottoman Orientalism', in: *American Historical Review* 107 (2002), 768–96.

[202] Jürgen Osterhammel, '"The Great Work of Uplifting Mankind": Zivilisierungsmissionen und Moderne', in: Boris Barth and Jürgen Osterhammel (eds.), *Zivilisierungsmissionen* (Konstanz: UVK Verlagsgesellschaft, 2005), 363–425.

carry out the mission of 'Turkification' as a classical example of a 'total institution'.[203] But the children started their education in Turkish at the age of 7 to 12, too late to socialize children from scratch. Psychologists have argued that by that age, a child will have passed 'the capacity for full cultural acquisition' of one single national culture.[204] Sociologists, too, emphasize that 'identities which are established this early in life— selfhood, human-ness, gender, and . . . kinship and ethnicity—are primary iden- tities, more robust and resilient to change in later life than other identities'.[205] Partly for this reason, the boarding school experience for many initially was a traumatic, and on the long term an alienating experience. At the time, the practice was presented as promoting the welfare of individual Kurdish children, because Kurdish cultural identity was seen as an insurmountable obstacle to the capacity to take a 'normal' part in 'modern' Turkish social life. As such, contemporary officials maintained that the overall effect was beneficial, and that the intentions were good.

Inasmuch as the Young Turks allowed difference and cultural initiatives in the civil society, these were only tolerated if they served 'Turkishness' as defined by the regime. Whether in Kurdish, Arabic, Syrian-Aramaic, Laz, Zaza, Circassian, or any other non-Turkish language, no texts were published, no music was played and sold, no plays were performed, and no programs broadcast in the public space. The prohibition of non-Turkish culture in the public space may have been rigorous, but ordinary people, surrounded by omnipresent 'Turkishness', created within its strictures space to live their lives, and non-Turkish culture could function invisibly, that is, not visible in the public domain. One expert has argued that by 1960, 'there were quite a few cases of successful assimilation', but adds that this was an urban phenomenon.[206] But decades after the end of Young Turk rule, millions of peasants living in the countryside continued speaking their own languages until a new wave of nation formation prohibited the private use of

---

[203] Erving Goffman identified the following characteristics of total institutions: 'First, all aspects of life (eating, sleeping, playing, working, learning) are conducted in the same place and under the same single authority. Second, each phase of a member's daily activity is carried out in the immediate company of a large batch of others, all of whom are treated alike and required to do the same thing together. Third, all phases of the day's activities are tightly scheduled, with one activity leading at a prearranged time into the next, the whole circle of activities being composed from above through a system of explicit, formal rules and a body of officials. Finally, the contents of the various enforced activities are brought together as parts of a single, overall, rational plan purportedly designed to fulfill the official aims of the institution.' By Goffman's definition, examples of total institutions include concentration camps, mental hospitals, army barracks, plantations, prisons, and work camps. Erving Goffman, 'The Characteristics of Total Institutions', in: Amitai Etzioni (ed.), *Complex Organizations: A Sociological Reader* (New York: Holt, Rinehart, and Winston, 1961), 313–14.
[204] For a general discussion of language acquisition by children, see: Victoria Fromkin *et al.* 'The Development of Language in Genie: A Case of Language Acquisition Beyond the Critical Point', *Brain and Language* 1 (1974), 81–107. For a criticism of this approach, see: David Singleton, *The Age Factor in Second Language Acquisition: A Critical Look at the Critical Period Hypothesis* (Clevedon: Multilingual Matters, 1995).
[205] Richard Jenkins, *Social Identity* (London: Routledge, 1996), 21.
[206] Martin van Bruinessen, 'Race, Culture, Nation and Identity Politics in Turkey: Some Comments', paper presented at the Annual Turkish Studies Workshop *Continuity and Change: Shifting State Ideologies from Late Ottoman to Early Republican Turkey, 1890–1930*, Department of Near Eastern Studies, Princeton University, 24–26 April 1997, 8–9.

Kurdish.[207] Urbanization, as a result of labour migration from the 1960s on, or the destruction of villages during the war between the Kurdistan Workers' Party (PKK) and the Turkish army (1984–97), contributed more to the spread of Turkish language and culture among these people than the massive campaigns of nation formation in the Young Turk era ever did. (This, however, is beyond the scope of this study.)

Therefore, one can perhaps argue that Young Turk nation formation in the eastern provinces largely failed, not because it was Turkish, but because it was totalitarian and violent. The high levels of coercion behind the educational and cultural policies were violent forms of political expression the regime deployed in order to retain its sovereignty over the region and the population. It was the culture of prohibitions, impositions, coercion, and violence that deeply upset many people. For many, too much violence had been at the foundation of Turkish nation formation to be truly attractive. That violence backfired when culture and education became a critical point of contention for the Turkish Republic after the Second World War. Disgruntled Kurdish nationalists saw in decades of Kemalist educational policies 'cultural genocide'[208] or 'linguistic genocide',[209] and demanded that the Kurdish language be taught in the eastern provinces. Many Kurdish nationalists who fled Turkey in the 1970s and 1980s and now live in diaspora in their turn categorically refuse to speak Turkish, and raise their children only in Kurdish. But Kurdish resistance towards Turkish education went much farther when in the late 1980s the PKK fatefully declared teachers 'agents of cultural genocide in Kurdistan'. From then on, the organization began murdering teachers, often symbolically on 'National Teachers' Day' (24 November). Between 1987 and 1997 the organization assassinated an estimated 138 teachers and 153 Ministry of Education officials, of which at least thirty-three in Diyarbekir province.[210] One of the most notorious killings occurred in the village of Hantepe in central Diyarbekir. On the night of 30 September 1996, two PKK militants raided the teacher's house in the village and kidnapped four teachers, including one who was a 19-year-old female. The teachers were taken away, made to kneel down at a nearby ditch, and shot in the back of the head.[211]

Identity is a matter of self-conviction or perhaps self-hypnosis. For those who were not convinced, either from experiences with discrimination or memories of mass violence, education was a difficult ordeal. But once a Kurd had convinced himself that he was Turkish, he found himself backed by the state's powerful educational infrastructure that confirmed the identity every day and left little insecurity for the person. The Self was continuously reinforced by the nation

---

[207] Hamit Bozarslan, *La question kurde: états et minorités au Moyen-Orient* (Paris: Presses de Sciences Po, 1997), 84.

[208] Haydar Işık, 'Kürtlerin sonu', in: *Yeni Özgür Politika*, 30 November 2006. See also: Abdullah Öcalan, *Kürt Sorununda Demokratik Çözüm Bildirgesi* (Istanbul: Mem, 1999), 36.

[209] Tove Skutnabb-Kangas, *Linguistic Genocide in Education or Worldwide Diversity and Human Rights?* (Mahwah, NJ: Erlbaum, 2000), 320–7.

[210] *Zaman*, 2 October 1996.

[211] *Diyarbakır Olay*, 1 October 2007.

state. One expert portrayed this as a zero-sum identity game in which Kurds could only join the Turkish nation if they cancelled, postponed, repressed, or forgot their Kurdishness.[212] The word 'forgot' could not have been phrased better since identity is closely related to memory. That 'identity work' was related to 'memory work' even the Young Turks had understood: Kurds had to 'forget' their Kurdishness to become Turkish. The Young Turk regime would sustain this autohypnosis by a body of knowledge in the form of myths and symbolization, a prime function of another vector of Young Turk nation formation. That phenomenon was the politics of memory, and the subject of the next chapter.

[212] Mesut Yeğen, *Devlet Söyleminde Kürt Sorunu* (Istanbul: İletişim, 2003), 120.

5

The Calm after the Storm:
The Politics of Memory

> If the Party could thrust its hand into the past and say of this or that event, *it never happened*—that, surely, should be more terrifying than mere torture and death.[1]

In the previous chapters we have explored how Young Turk elites moulded the population of the eastern provinces through a wide range of population policies, involving mass destruction, deportation, settlement, and the politics of cultural assimilation. But the Young Turk grand project of crafting a modern nation state included more than these policies that affected multitudes of human beings physically. Mentally, the young nation state was still blank and needed a memory. The continuous process of defining and fine-tuning a national identity entailed a parallel process for a national memory. This chapter will focus on aspects of Young Turk memory politics. How did their memory politics intervene in existing patterns of memory in the eastern provinces, in particular Diyarbekir? And how was the mass violence of the last Ottoman decade remembered by the population and the government?

SILENCING THE VIOLENCE:
THE ORGANIZATION OF OBLIVION

After so much violence in the Ottoman territories, it was only logical that hundreds of thousands of people were physically wounded and psychologically traumatized. Demobilized soldiers came home with frightening stories of mass death, entire neighbourhoods having been emptied, families having lost their male populations, widows begging by the roadside, miserable orphans roaming the streets naked. War, genocide, famine, flight, and displacement had thoroughly scarred the memory of all participants and witnesses. Despite the self-healing ability of families and communities, the violence had caused severe and lasting damage to the psychological development of the region and society at large. How did the Young Turk regime deal with this legacy of violence? In 1937 Şükrü Kaya addressed parliament on the question of the violence of bygone days: 'If we do not want to return to those bitter memories and relive that painful life . . . in any event the Turkish nation has to be

---

[1] George Orwell, *Nineteen Eighty-Four* (London: Secker & Warburg, 1949), 35.

Turkist and Nationalist'. The speech was followed by a long applause and chants of 'Bravo! Live long!'[2]

One good illustration of the vicissitudes of Young Turk memory politics was the representation of the Greco-Turkish war. Speaking in March 1922, Mustafa Kemal denounced the 'atrocities' of the 'Greek princes and generals, who take particular pleasure in having women raped'. The general continued to decry these acts of 'destruction and aggression' that he considered 'irreconcilable with humanity' and most of all, 'impossible to cover up and deny'.[3] However, after the establishment of the Republic, the tide turned and the accusatory tone of moral indignation was dropped. The 1930s saw a diplomatic rapprochement between Turkey and Greece as relations improved with the signing of several agreements and conventions. By the time the Greek Premier Panagis Tsaldaris (1868–1936) visited Turkey in September 1933, the same Mustafa Kemal now spoke of the Greeks as 'esteemed guests' with whom the contact had been 'amicable and cordial'.[4] Throughout the interbellum period, the Turkish and Greek nations were portrayed as having co-existed perennially in mutual respect and eternal peace.[5] Friendly inter-state relations in the service of Turkey's acceptance and stabilization into the nation-state system had gained precedence over old grief, without any serious process of closure or reconciliation in between.

Lacking statehood, the Armenians and Syriacs were not accorded the same treatment as Greece. They were either deeply traumatized survivors living in wretched refugee camps or terrified individuals keeping a low profile in ruined villages.[6] The Kemalist regime continued on all fronts the preceding Young Turk policies of effacing physical traces of Armenian existence: churches were defaced and buildings rid of their Armenian inscriptions.[7] Although the Armenians were gone, in a sense they were still deemed too visible. In Diyarbekir city, a landmark event that marked the decay of Armenian existence was the collapse of the church, Surp Giragos (See Plate 11).[8] Another important stage was the razing of the local Armenian cemeteries. One of the men mainly responsible for the destruction of Armenians, Müftüzâde Şeref Uluğ, who had become mayor after 1923, ordered the

---

[2] Ekrem Ergüven (ed.), *Şükrü Kaya: Sözleri—Yazıları 1927–1937* (Istanbul: Cumhuriyet Matbaası, 1937), 236.

[3] Nimet Arsan (ed.), *Atatürk'ün Söylev ve Demeçleri* (Ankara: Türk Tarih Kurumu, 1959–64), vol. I, 241.

[4] *Cumhuriyet*, 6 and 9 September 1933; Arı İnan, *Düşünceleriyle Atatürk* (Ankara: Türk Tarih Kurumu, 1991), 162.

[5] For a study of Turkish-Greek rapprochement after 1923, see: Damla Demirözü, *Savaştan Barışa Giden Yol: Atatürk-Venizelos Dönemi Türkiye-Yunanistan İlişkileri* (Istanbul: İletişim, 2007).

[6] Thomas H. Greenshields, 'The Settlement of Armenian Refugees in Syria and Lebanon, 1915–39', in: John I. Clarke and Howard Bowen-Jones (eds.), *Change and Development in the Middle East* (London: Methuen & Co., 1981), 233–41.

[7] Anush Hovannisian, 'Turkey: A Cultural Genocide', in: Levon Chorbajian and George Shirinian (eds.), *Studies in Comparative Genocide* (New York: St. Martin's Press, 1998), 147–56. This was not different in Diyarbekir's districts. For the example of Ergani, see: Müslüm Üzülmez, *Çayönü'nden Ergani'ye Uzun Bir Yürüyüş* (Istanbul: n.p., 2005), chapter 4.

[8] In the 1960s the roof collapsed into the deserted building and in subsequent decades the structure was stripped of its assets and neglected into dilapidation. For a website commemorating Surp Giragos, see: <http://www.surpgiragos.com>

erasure of one of the city's last vanishing Armenian landmarks two decades after the genocide.[9] That this was not merely a function of 'urban modernization' but a conscious expunction of the Other's memory appeared from the fact that not only on the west side (where 'modernization' was carried out) but also on the east side of town, Armenian cemeteries were either willfully neglected, simply flattened, or used for paving stones in floors or roads. No Armenian ever had a say in this process, since most deportees and survivors were illiterate peasants living under cover or in Syria.

For the same reason the Diyarbekir Armenians had no chance of writing and publishing their memories. Thus, the production of memory among them did not take off until decades later or until later generations. The killing and displacement brought by Young Turk rule created an archipelago of nuggets of memory spread across the world.[10] Well before groups of survivors could formulate narratives about what had happened, a master narrative was being constructed by the perpetrators. In one of his speeches in parliament in 1937 Şükrü Kaya asserted that

> it has been the livelihood of certain politicians to foster the notion that there is an eternal enmity between Turks and Armenians... Turks and Armenians, forced to pursue their true and natural interests, again instinctively felt friendliness towards each other. This is the truth of the matter... From our perspective the cordiality expressed by the Armenian nation towards us has not diminished.[11]

Such an assessment of Turkish-Armenian relations in the wake of the genocide was to be expected only from a political elite pursuing a distinct memory-related agenda. Ever since its rise to power, the Kemalist dictatorship continued the CUP policy of suppressing all information on the 1915 genocide. The 1931 Press Law served as a catch-all for any texts the regime considered as dissent. When the regime caught wind of the memoirs of Karabet Gapikyan, subtitled *What We Saw During the Deportation from Sivas to Aleppo* (Boston: Hairenik, 1924), the book was prohibited from entering Turkey for 'containing very harmful writings'.[12] Marie Sarrafian Banker, a graduate of the İzmir American College, had written her memoirs in 1936.[13] Her book too was prohibited from entering the country. All existing copies were ordered, confiscated, and destroyed for containing 'harmful texts'.[14] When Armen Anoosh, an Armenian survivor living in Aleppo, in 1922 wrote his memoirs entitled, *The History of a Ruined City: Urfa*, the volume was denied entry and existing copies that had found their way into the country were ordered confiscated.[15]

---

[9] Bedri Günkut, *Diyarbekir Tarihi* (Diyarbakır: Diyarbekir Halkevi, 1937), 150–1.

[10] For similar process of dislocated memory, see: Pamela Ballinger, *History in Exile: Memory and Identity at the Borders of the Balkans* (Princeton, NJ: Princeton University Press, 2003); Lubomyr Y. Luciuk, *Searching For Place: Ukrainian Displaced Persons, Canada, and the Migration of Memory* (Toronto: University of Toronto Press, 2000).

[11] *Türkiye Büyük Millet Meclisi Zabıt Ceridesi*, vol. 17, period V, session 45 (1937), 7 April 1937, 26.

[12] BCA, 030.18.01.02/46.49.5, Prime Ministry decree, 10 June 1934.

[13] Marie Sarrafian Banker, *My Beloved Armenia: A Thrilling Testimony* (Chicago: The Bible Institute Colportage Association, 1936).

[14] BCA, 030.18.01.02/79.82.14, Prime Ministry decree, 28 September 1937.

[15] BCA, 030.18.01.02/118.98.20, Prime Ministry decree, 10 February 1949.

At times the policy extended beyond the prohibition of genocide memoirs and included 'normal' history books. This contradicted the ideas of some of those who had contributed to the development of those histories. A few days before he committed suicide in 1919, Dr. Mehmed Reshid spoke with a leading Young Turk and answered the question whether he feared 'historical responsibility' as follows: 'Let other nations write about me whatever history they want, I couldn't care less'.[16] Most other Young Turks, however, did care. When Turkish customs intercepted Arshak Alboyajian's two-volume classic *History of Kayseri*, sent from Syria to Istanbul by surface mail, it was ordered confiscated, destroyed, and prohibited.[17] An Armenian-language book published in Cairo in 1940 on the small town of Bahçecik was prohibited simply for the fact that it produced a history of a region which fell under Turkish national jurisdiction.[18] What is striking about these prohibitions is that they generally limited themselves to the Turkish Republic. For the regime it did not matter much that Armenians wrote and circulated memoirs among themselves—just as long as memory was produced and consumed within an Armenian milieu and did not trickle back into Turkey. One of the exceptions to this rule was the September 1935 incident between the United States and Turkey over plans by Metro-Goldwyn-Mayer to film Franz Werfel's novel *The Forty Days of Musa Dagh*. After strong diplomatic pressure from the Turkish embassy the idea was abandoned.[19] The regime had already officially prohibited the book itself in January 1935.[20] The same fate befell Paul du Véou's less fictional book on the Musa Dagh Armenians on the eve of the Turkish annexation of Hatay province.[21] That book, too, was blacklisted and barred from entry to the country.[22] The Young Turk dictatorship feared these narratives might enter local history and memory, of which, as we shall see later, they claimed a strict monopoly.

Whereas and perhaps because the official position of the political elite was one of amnesia and denial, there is scant information available on how the remaining population felt in the years and decades after the destruction of their Armenian neighbours. Regional life was too disturbed to return to normal and people undoubtedly felt something was permanently lost. Whether the genocide was remembered, and how, is a question with which it is difficult to engage. The British official Harold Armstrong travelled through the southern provinces of Turkey and met an imam in a village, whose eyes became 'hard and dangerous' when speaking of Armenians. The imam responded, 'If one came back I would kill him with my own hands', adding that he personally had led the villagers in the

---

[16] Mithat Şükrü Bleda, *İmparatorluğun Çöküşü* (İstanbul: Remzi, 1979), 59.
[17] BCA, 030.18.01/127.95.11, Prime Ministry decree, 31 December 1951.
[18] BCA, 030.18.01.02/95.60.3, Prime Ministry decree, 10 July 1941.
[19] Donald Bloxham, *The Great Game of Genocide: Imperialism, Nationalism, and the Destruction of the Ottoman Armenians* (Oxford: Oxford University Press, 2005), 204.
[20] BCA, 030.18.01.02/51.3.2, Prime Ministry decree, 13 January 1935.
[21] Paul du Véou, *Chrétiens en péril au Moussadagh! Enquête au Sandjak d'Alexandrette* (Paris: Baudinière, 1939).
[22] BCA, 030.18.01.02/90.12.7, Prime Ministry decree, 25 January 1940.

destruction of the Armenians, cutting off the conversation: 'Let us talk of other things'.[23] The Danish engineer Olaf Rygaard toured the eastern provinces in 1929 and asked local Turks about what had happened to the Armenians. A group of Turks sitting in a coffeehouse pointed at a spot where Armenians had been massacred in August 1915. 'While laughing coarsely they remind each other about how they then tried to find out how many victims a single rifle bullet could penetrate'.[24] Similar experiences were observed by Patrick Kinross, who during a trip to Turkey visited a village and asked the same thorny question about what had happened to the local Armenians. The villagers laughed and pointed downwards: 'The Armenians are under the ground!'[25] Although many were aware that they were living in the historical landscape of Ottoman Armenians and many others also asserted that life had been better when their Armenian compatriots were around, the genocide was often followed by a general apathy and indifference among the bystander communities.

Even less leeway was afforded to Kurds who had been deported by the regimes. The 1934 Settlement Law had clearly prohibited memorialization of the past by dictating that 'especially the nomads and tribesmen deported to the interior will have to cut off completely all their ties to the past and will have to affix all their goals to the future generations they will raise'.[26] They were not allowed to commemorate their dead or visit their graves, if any of these existed. Sheikh Said's remains had been dumped in a mass grave near the Mountain Gate for the particular reason of thwarting memorialization. Many others had shared his fate. To most surviving family members, who were pious Muslims, this was a breach of Islamic burial customs. In their memoirs they claim to have felt humiliated and shocked at the way their leaders had been treated.[27] After the repression, under the Young Turk regime a curtain of silence descended on key moments of the near past. Local officials from the northern district of Hani reported to Ankara,

> This is a town where Sheikh Said's movement convened for decisions, and the children and close relatives of those who were sentenced to various punishments after the movement live here. This is a place where we need to work to make them forget their feelings of resentment and agony [*kırgınlık ve iztirab duygularını unutdurmak*] . . . district governors, gendarmes, and teachers need to operate on the new generation with great care.[28]

Everything that could remind the people of the violence was banned. One of Sheikh Said's lectures, recorded on gramophone record, was prohibited from entrance into the country for containing 'words harmful to the nation'. All existing

---

[23] Harold Armstrong, *Turkey and Syria Reborn: A Record of Two Years of Travel* (London: J. Lane, 1930), 145.

[24] Olaf A. Rygaard, *Mellem Tyrker og Kurder: En Dansk Ingeniørs Oplevelser i Lilleasien* (Copenhagen: Nordisk Forlag, 1935), 165.

[25] Patrick Kinross, *Within the Taurus: A Journey in Asiatic Turkey* (London: n.p., 1954), 74.

[26] *Türkiye Büyük Millet Meclisi Zabıt Ceridesi*, vol. 23, period IV, session 3 (1934), Appendix no.189: 'I/335 numaralı İskân kanunu lâyihası ve İskân muvakkat encümeni mazbatası' (2 May 1932).

[27] See e.g. the memoirs of Sheikh Said's grandson: Abdülmelik Fırat, *Fırat Mahzun Akar* (Istanbul: Avesta, 1996).

[28] BCA, 490.01/996.850.1, Dr. Münir Soykam to RPP General Secretariat, 12 May 1941.

copies were ordered to be collected and destroyed.[29] The survivors themselves were silenced, for writing memoirs was anathema. Even when the violence was remembered and commemorated in the privacy of their homes, it took place under conditions of great fear.[30] A largely illiterate peasant society with strong tribal structures, such as Eastern Turkey, depended on bards who kept the oral tradition of storytelling alive and passed down narratives of the events from one generation to the next. These troubadours and bards were persecuted for singing laments for the dead Kurdish elites during clandestine nightly storytelling sessions (see Chapter 4). Some saw no other choice than to flee to Syria.[31]

An exemplary story of how the regime dealt with the memorialization of murdered family members was the case of a local Justice Ministry official in the Ergani district. The man, a Kurd by the name of Feyzi Artıkoğlu, reportedly spoke to the townsmen about the grave of a local leader named Şevki, who was killed in 1925 by the Turkish army. He had pointed out the grave and impelled the locals to put cobblestones on it to commemorate his death. Those who did not remember whose grave it was, he rebuked: 'You idiot, how can you forget Şevki, go place a stone'. According to the report written by local officials, a small pile of stones had been heaped up on the grave in memory of the dead. Artıkoğlu would assemble people at the mosque after Friday prayers, walk them to the grave, and pray in memory of Sheikh Said and his men. Government officials strongly disapproved of this practice which 'perpetuated devoutness and the kurdist mentality'. Feyzi Artıkoğlu was censured as 'a Mardinite fluent in arabic, kurdish, and zazaki ... whose employment as a civil servant can absolutely not be permitted here from the perspective of our national ideal and revolution'. His deportation to the western provinces was considered 'urgent'. In the correspondence, the party official who received this letter heavily underscored this text with the handwritten note: 'Needs to be reported to the Ministry of Justice'.[32] Not much later Artıkoğlu was arrested and deported west for producing a memorial narrative that deviated from the official one.

All in all, violence was repressed and ousted from public memory. The massive disruption of the first decades of the twentieth century was disposed of through silence, amnesia, and repression, instead of reflection, discussion, processing, and memorialization. The striking aspect of this process was that the violence that was repressed was not only that in which Young Turks had been perpetrators, but also that in which they had been victims. A whole century of Muslim victimization in the Caucasus and in the Balkans, in particular during the twin Balkan wars, was dismissed and forgotten in favour of 'looking towards the future' and amicable inter-state relations with Greece, Bulgaria, Serbia, and the Soviet Union. Ottoman minorities who were targeted in this victimization, such as Armenians, Kurds, Syriacs, and Arabs, did not have a chance of healing their wounds or memorializing

[29] BCA, 030.18.01.02/71.8.6, Prime Ministry decree, 28 January 1937.
[30] Şeyhmus Diken, *İsyan Sürgünleri* (Istanbul: İletişim, 2005), *passim*.
[31] Salihê Kevirbirî, *Bir Çığlığın Yüzyılı: Karapetê Xaço* (Istanbul: Sî, 2002), 59–60.
[32] BCA, 490.01/996.850.1, Dr. Münir Soykam to RPP General Secretariat, 30 April 1941.

their losses. The new memory of the nation did not permit cracks, nuances, shades, subtleties, or any difference for that matter. Like the new identity, it was total, absolute, and unitary.

DAMNATIO MEMORIAE: DESTRUCTION AND CONSTRUCTION OF MEMORY

Besides locating and delimiting the nation in space, the Young Turks also devised and developed ideas of delimiting the nation in time. In other words, the question of '*where* the nation was' needed to be supplemented with the question of '*when* the nation was'. They argued that the Turkish nation had just been born, its father being Atatürk and its mother the fertile lands of Anatolia. As early as 1922 Mustafa Kemal had emphatically proclaimed, 'The new Turkey has absolutely no relation with the old Turkey. The Ottoman state has gone down in history. Now, a new Turkey is born'.[33] As true millennialists, the Kemalists saw 1923 as the 'Year Zero' and rejected all prior history, culture, and tradition of the Ottoman Empire.[34] This way, periodization of the nation defined inclusion and exclusion into it: the 'new Turkey' was not foreseen to be a state and society for anyone interested in Islamic history. By defining the confines of Turkish history, they attempted to cut off the population's gaze beyond their political era and launched themselves as the origin of the nation. By monopolizing memory the regime had monopolized identity. As an official 1938 booklet on Diyarbekir read, 'In this beautiful country, which we inherited in a wretched and miserable condition from Ottoman rule, today everywhere the lights of civilized life are shining . . . free from the legacy of yesterday's dark mentality'.[35] 1923 represented a *Year Zero* when darkness gave way to light. In 1928, the temporal boundaries of the nation would be carved out in a most radical way.

On 9 August 1928 Mustafa Kemal publicly presented the new Turkish alphabet after many months of discussion on the possible Romanization of the centuries-old Ottoman-Turkish script.[36] From 1 November 1928 on, the latter was officially changed in favour of Latin characters as part of a general reconfiguration of the Turkish language. The Latin alphabet was supposed to bring Turkey closer to 'modern European civilization'—ignoring the fact that no 'European' country bordering Turkey used that alphabet. To the Young Turk modernists, the Arabic alphabet was a strong dimension of Ottoman culture and a constant reminder of Turkey's fundamentally non-European past. But the Eurocentric and Orientalist view that Arabic was the very antithesis of Western thought pervaded the minds of the modernizers. They thus developed a discourse discrediting Ottoman and

---

[33] Arsan (ed.), *Atatürk'ün Söylev ve Demeçleri*, vol. III, 50–1.
[34] Mustafa Kemal explicitly declared 1923 to be 'the First National Year'. Ibid., vol. I, 240.
[35] *Cumhuriyetin 15inci yılında Diyarbakır* (Diyarbakır: Diyarbakır Matbaası, 1938), 21–2.
[36] 'Mustafa Kemal Pasha's Address on Launching the New Characters', in: Lutfy Levonian (ed.), *The Turkish Press 1925–1932* (Athens: School of Religion, 1932), 90–1.

favouring its abolition, arguing that the alphabet was 'difficult to learn' and 'unfit for the Turkish language'.[37] These concerns were obviously not simply linguistic: the attack on the Arabic alphabet was a thinly disguised symbolic attack on the Islamic Ottoman past. The change of alphabet was part of a wider Turkish-nationalist cultural revolution, but in its intent and public manifestations it was a quintessential act of memory politics.

Radical Young Turk thinkers advocated the alphabet change by maintaining they had 'no time to listen to such objections that insistently point out to us the risk which our culture and traditions may run. The foremost thing in our minds is the present and the future. Let those who are fond of the past, remain in the past'.[38] Dissenting voices were ignored and silenced, and before the opposition knew it, they saw themselves facing a *fait accompli* with the government announcing that the reforms would be put on the fast track. Foreign observers did not misperceive the impact the alphabet change had on the collective memory of society. The Danish scholar Johannes Østrup noted, 'For the generation that is growing up now all the Turkish literature that was printed before 1929 will be like a closed book, only accessible to philological specialists'. A Turkish writer with whom he once spoke about the alphabet change answered his reservations about the far-reaching consequences of the reform: 'We don't worry about such things; for us, the history of our people begins with the War of Liberation and the establishment of the Republic, and what lies before that is ordinary world history without national value'. But Østrup was not convinced and concluded, 'One cannot run from one's own past'.[39]

How successful was this ambitious project, in particular in the peasant society that was Eastern Turkey? When Şükrü Kaya went on an inspection tour to the east he reported to Kemal Atatürk that the new Turkish alphabet did not seem to be in use among the people. Kaya deplored that 'most intellectuals among the people conduct all their business with the Arabic alphabet' and urged for 'new signs and directives' from Mustafa Kemal.[40] However, the dictator did not have to adjust his policy since time was on his side. Textually, society was being blanked, as the persistence of the policy began to yield its fruits so quickly that 'by the time of Atatürk's death (1938), many a school child could not remember any life but that of the Republic'.[41] What these school children did and did not 'remember' was both experienced and constructed memory. They were too young personally to remember Ottoman times, and educated in such a way that they were oblivious to the wider Ottoman past. Indeed, already a generation after the change, scholars wrote that

---

[37] Geoffrey Lewis, *The Turkish Language Reform: A Catastrophic Success* (Oxford: Oxford University Press, 1999).

[38] 'Some Extracts from the Address of Mustafa Şekip Bey, Professor of Psychology in the University of Constantinople', in: Levonian, *The Turkish Press*, 87.

[39] Johannes Østrup, *Det Nye Tyrki* (Copenhagen: n.p., 1931), 180.

[40] BCA, 030.10/12.73.4, Şükrü Kaya to Mustafa Kemal, 22 June 1929.

[41] Lewis V. Thomas and Richard N. Frye, *The United States and Turkey and Iran* (Cambridge, MA: Harvard University Press, 1951), 86.

no Turk under thirty-six or thirty-seven can ordinarily read anything published in his own language before 1928. Very few older works have been transliterated into the new letters. To teach or use the old letters is (or was) technically illegal. Actually they are still widely used by the older generation, but the younger generation has had its principal bridge to its own cultural past burnt for it . . . Atatürk would have rejoiced at this, for he was out to kill the past.[42]

Within just a few years it was as if the Arabic script had never been used. But for the regime the slate was still not clean enough.

During their rule, the Young Turks outlawed, confiscated, and destroyed innumerable books, manuscripts, and other texts in non-Turkish languages. Similar to the reorganization of the population through exclusion and inclusion of people, the reorganization of memory required an exclusion and inclusion of the cognitive process of remembering. Having entered the age of information, the Young Turks acknowledged the power of knowledge and realized that certain bodies of knowledge had to be produced and others had to be destroyed.[43] Concordant with national guidelines, the destruction and construction of memory involved the 'reorganization' of existing bodies of knowledge in the peripheries. Besides continuing the CUP practice of confiscating and destroying Armenian libraries and collections, the Kemalists attacked and banned all texts that were either non-Turkish or 'non-Turkifiable'—i.e. unfit to be cast retrospectively as 'Turkish', as they defined it. This policy continued unabated and was pursued relentlessly. During the sixth Turkish Hearths congress in 1928, Hasan Reşit Tankut presented an account of his work as 'Eastern Inspector', which meant the conduct of 'ethnographic research' in the eastern provinces, including Diyarbekir. He was emphatic in pointing out that he had 'confiscated many books written in foreign languages'. This included minority languages as Kurmanci, Zazaki, Syrian Aramaic, Arabic, and especially Armenian.[44] During those same tours through the eastern provinces, in autumn 1940 Tankut passed through Bitlis, home town of the sixteenth-century Kurdish chronicler Sharaf Khan, and reported with content that his book the *Sharafname*[45] was not read anymore among Kurds: 'I believe that the pages of the Sharafname and its Kurdish sagas are not read any more or are read with less excitement than before'.[46] Tankut's attack on Sharaf Khan's classic was matched by practical intervention in the field: during the 1920s and 1930s the dictatorship confiscated and destroyed copies of the book. For the sake of intelligence, the Hearths gathered lists of other books on Armenians and Kurds as well.[47]

---

[42] Ibid., 82.

[43] Cf. A.Oğuz İçimsoy and İsmail E. Erünsal, 'The Legacy of the Ottoman Library in the Libraries of the Turkish Republic', in: *Libri* 58, no. 1 (2008), 47–57.

[44] 'Türk Ocakları Altıncı Kurultayı', in: *Türk Yurdu* 4/24, no. 29/223, May 1930, 85.

[45] Sharaf al-Dîn Bitlîsî, *The Sharafnâma: Or the History of the Kurdish Nation, 1597*, transl. and ed. Mehrdad R. Izady (Costa Mesa, CA: Mazda, 2005).

[46] BCA, 490.01/1015.916.4, Hasan Reşit Tankut to RPP General Secretariat, 16 October 1940.

[47] Füsun Üstel, *İmparatorluktan Ulus-Devlete Türk Milliyetçiliği: Türk Ocakları (1912–1931)* (Istanbul: İletişim, 1997), 215, 333, 394.

Among the hundreds of books prohibited and confiscated by the regime figured: Kamuran Ali Bedir-Khan and Herbert Örtel, *Der Adler von Kurdistan* (Potsdam: Ludwig Doggenreiter, 1937); Sureyya Bedir Khan, *The Case of Kurdistan Against Turkey* (Philadelphia: The Kurdish Independence League, 1928); Cigerxwîn, *Dîwana Yekem: Prîsk û Pêtî* (Damascus: n.p., 1945); a 1932 booklet on the Circassian alphabet published in Syria; Abdulaziz Yamulki, *Kürdistan ve Kürt İhtilalleri* (Baghdad: n.p., 1946); Kamiran Alî Bedir-xan, *Xwendina Kurdî* (Damascus: Çapxana Tereqi, 1938), and many others.[48] These books were literary, linguistic, and historical studies, as well as outright nationalist pamphlets. What they had in common was their language, often Kurdish and Armenian, and topic, often Kurds and Armenians. Besides these books, all Armenian and Kurdish-language periodicals were individually identified and categorically banned.

As in the case of nation formation, the destruction of memory always went hand in hand with the construction of it. The change of alphabet and the destruction of unwanted texts represented a radical departure from all existing schools of thought. On the emerging *tabula rasa* the building blocks could now be constructed. An aspect of central importance of the alphabet change was that the Young Turk regime became the sole custodian of the past. After the reform, newspapers and journals needed financial support from the government to sustain their press run, and so critical newspapers were deprived of those pivotal subsidies and thus were reduced to impoverishment and bankruptcy.[49] This conveniently silenced the intellectual opposition and 'gave the state a chance to control the whole process of publishing all writings as well as transcriptions of existing ones'.[50] Besides teaching the population history at various levels of mass education, the dictatorship had now monopolized the means of and access to knowledge production in Turkey. It could now pursue its memorial agenda more directly. This agenda consisted of a mix between remembrance and oblivion, because for Kemalism history consisted of a series of erasures, emendations and amalgamations. The new Turkey was manifestly and consciously a state of memory.[51] Whatever the past was, its depiction depended on how the nationalist elites felt in the 1920s and 1930s. Their subjective experience of the past and perception of contemporary realities produced an archaeology of knowledge possibly quite similar to that of other totalitarian dictatorships in the European 1930s. Now, the time was ripe to write and rewrite history.

There was a clear prehistory of 1930s Kemalist history rewriting for reasons other than intellectual ones.[52] The CUP issued a decree for the establishment of a

---

[48] See the various decrees from the file: BCA, 030.18.01.02.

[49] Henry E. Allen, *The Turkish Transformation: A Study in Social and Religious Development* (New York: Greenwood Press, 1968), 126.

[50] Yılmaz Çolak, 'Language Policy and Official Ideology in Early Republican Turkey', in: *Middle Eastern Studies* 40, no. 6 (2004), 67–91 at 73.

[51] For a collection of articles dealing with this, see: Esra Özyürek (ed.), *The Politics of Public Memory in Turkey* (Syracuse, NY: Syracuse University Press, 2006).

[52] 'History-Writing in the Late Ottoman/Early Republican Era', in: Ebru Boyar, *Ottomans, Turks and the Balkans: Empire Lost, Relations Altered* (London: Tauris Academic Studies, 2007), 9–28.

committee, assigned to 'write brochures *to prove the historical existence of the Turks and the immigrants in Syria, Iraq, Aleppo, and Eastern Thrace, and to collect information on the Kurdish element*'.[53] This sudden interest in historiography emanated as the underpinnings of an early archaeology of the Turkish nation— 'proving' not the contemporary but the historical existence of 'Turks' would accord a level of surety to entitlement and political legitimacy over the region. The level of prioritization of writing history was characterized by the fact that in times of pressing military concerns (as early as October 1920), the first Kemalist government program read that the government should 'make intellectuals produce works of history, literature, and sociology that will augment our national spirit'.[54] Writing history was now a priority and predominantly a matter of serving politics. In the next three decades, the consolidating dictatorship would lay the foundations of a hegemonic canon of official history that would last and persist up to today. This 'mythistory'[55] comprises an enormous number of books and articles and still constitutes the backbone of the Turkish national narrative.[56]

Mustafa Kemal's personal role in rewriting history was considerable. The general was a fervent reader of history books,[57] and during his rule personally directed and interfered in the historiography. After the climax of the Greco-Turkish war, Mustafa Kemal gave a grand speech on Ottoman and Islamic history in order to delegitimize and abolish the sultanate. In the speech heavily influenced by CUP mythistory, Mustafa Kemal laid out a template for a narrative of the Turkish nation, tracing its roots from Genghis Khan to the Seljuks and ending with the last Ottoman Sultan.[58] The speech epitomized the victory of national sovereignty over monarchical sovereignty as Kemal highlighted the nation as the only legitimate site for securing state identity and political power. Later he would add to this furious diatribe against the House of Osman: 'From now on, the nation will read in its history books the legends of sultans and padishahs, of these tyrants and usurpers'.[59] By providing a narrative of the nation, Mustafa Kemal also drew an official version of history. In 1927, he would do this again in a thirty-six-hour speech delivered personally to the Turkish Grand National Assembly. The 'Speech' (*Nutuk*) covered the events between 1919 and 1923 and in essence represented an

---

[53] *BOA*, MV 213/30, 26 November 1918, emphasis added.

[54] Nuran Dağlı and Belma Aktürk (eds.) *Hükümetler ve Programları, vol. I, 1920–1960* (Ankara: TBMM Basımevi, 1988), 4.

[55] There is a huge and growing body of literature on the crucial role that historical myths play in the construction of communal identities. The task of historiography is to illuminate these fictions and explain how they shape human societies. Joseph Mali, *Mythistory: The Making of a Modern Historiography* (Chicago: University of Chicago Press, 2003), 1–35.

[56] According to estimates, during their rule the Kemalist dictatorship published between 1.5 and three million books. Uluğ İğdemir, 'Halkevleri Üzerine', in: *Yılların İçinden* (Ankara, 1976), 237; Hasan Taner, 'Halkevlerinin Kitaplık Çalışmaları', in: *Ülkü* 2, no. 15 (March 1948), 12.

[57] Leman Şenalp, 'Atatürk'ün kütüphanesi', in: *Türk Kütüphaneciliği* 16, no. 2 (2002), 171–8; id., 'Atatürk'ün Tarih Bilgisi', in: *Uluslararası İkinci Atatürk Sempozyumu* (Ankara: Atatürk Araştırma Merkezi Yayınları, 1991), vol. 2, 717–27.

[58] Arsan (ed.), *Atatürk'ün Söylev ve Demeçleri*, vol. I, 269–80.

[59] *Cumhurbaşkanları, Başbakanlar ve Milli Eğitim Bakanlarının Milli Eğitimle İlgili Söylev ve Demeçleri* (Ankara: Milli Eğitim Basımevi, 1946), vol. 1, 9.

official version of the War of Independence.[60] Since Kemal believed that the new Turkey should not be mired in the past, from the late 1920s on he ordered a thorough rewriting of history, arranged to suit his ideological parameters and nationalist imagination.

Others had opinions about history as well. İsmet İnönü wrote about previous cultures that they were 'erased root and branch by the Republic'. In order to create the new Turkey, the long-time Prime Minister noted that 'it was not only necessary to eradicate centuries-old traditions, beliefs, and customs, *but to efface the memory as well*'.[61] These general directives were received and acted upon at various levels by loyal subordinates such as Şükrü Kaya. During one of his monologues in parliament, Kaya boasted,

> Again it was proven by a Turk, with the Turks' hands and the Turks' blood, that the outcome of history is not inevitable and predestined. We have changed the course of history . . . [applause] They tried to eliminate the Turks from this geography and erase them from the future of history . . . In our opinion every nation makes its own history[62]

Kaya's exhortations could not have better characterized the relationship between power and the production of historical narratives. According to them, those who held power held the unforfeitable right to write history as they pleased. It would not take long before this attitude crystallized into the first concrete steps towards the (re)writing of history. As with most other intellectual and cultural pursuits under Young Turk totalitarianism, this would not be a multi-centred and democratic affair but a strictly top-down managed operation with minimum dissent. After a preparation period, Mustafa Kemal instituted the Association for the Study of Turkish History (*Türk Tarihi Tetkik Cemiyeti*) in the summer of 1930. The association employed veteran Young Turks as well as younger historians educated under CUP rule and would play a leading role in the construction of a hegemonic paradigm of Turkish historiography.[63] In the early 1930s, the Association was ordered to produce history books on the Turks. The first product was a 605-page volume entitled *Outlines of Turkish History* (*Türk Tarihinin Ana Hatları*) and reflected the very ontology of nationalist mythistory.[64] Many other volumes with similar content followed.[65] These books chiefly traced the roots of the Turkish nation to prehistoric times, ascribed Turkishness to the Hittites, Sumerians, Akkadians, Kelts, Irish, Mongols, Russians, and Chinese, argued that 'Turks' had spread 'civilization' across the globe, and in general transcendentalized the nation.

---

[60] Hülya Adak, 'National Myths and Self-Na(rra)tions: Mustafa Kemal's *Nutuk* and Halide Edib's *Memoirs* and *The Turkish Ordeal*', in: *South Atlantic Quarterly* 102, no. 2/3 (2003), 509–27.

[61] İsmet İnönü, *Hatıralar* (Ankara: Bilgi, 1987), vol. 2, 272; emphasis added.

[62] *Türkiye Büyük Millet Meclisi Zabıt Ceridesi*, vol. 16, period V, meeting 2 (1937), 59.

[63] Étienne Copeaux, *Espaces et temps de la nation turque: analyse d'une historiographie nationaliste 1931–1993* (Paris: CNRS Éditions, 1997), 190–6.

[64] Afet İnan *et al.*, *Türk Tarihinin Ana Hatları* (Istanbul: Devlet Matbaası, 1930).

[65] For a treatment of the hegemonic canon of Turkish-nationalist mythistory, see: Büşra Ersanlı, *İktidar ve Tarih: Türkiye'de 'Resmi Tarih' Tezinin Oluşumu (1929–1937)* (Istanbul: İletişim, 2003), 114–38; id., 'History Textbooks as Reflections of the Political Self: Turkey (1930s and 1990s) and Uzbekistan (1990s)', in: *International Journal of Middle East Studies* 34, no. 2 (2002), 337–50.

Perfectly consistent with the current *Zeitgeist*, racism was one of the driving ideologies behind the production of these official histories. Textbooks offered to secondary school students contained passages arguing that 'the Turkish race was the race which has preserved its character the most' and that Turks possessed 'eternally superior distinct biological qualities'.[66] Mustafa Kemal closely followed these works and convened the first 'Turkish Historical Congress' in Ankara between 2 and 11 July 1932. The dictator personally attended the conference from beginning to the very end, on a balcony elevated above the participants. One of the speakers was Assistant Professor of Anthropology Dr. Şevket Aziz (Kansu) of Istanbul University's Department of Medicine, who delivered a speech entitled, 'The Anthropology of the Turks'. His lecture, frequently interrupted with loud rounds of applause, included charts of skull measurements of various 'races' and pseudohistorical arguments for the racial superiority of the Turks. Aziz finished by turning to Mustafa Kemal and perorating: 'O Hero, noble and great, strong-willed great man, I salute you with sincerity in the name of Turkish science and Turkish intellectuals'.[67] The thunderous applause that followed captured the essence of mythistory produced under the Young Turk dictatorship: by deploying racist tropes of Turkish superiority against prevalent racist ideas in Europe that Turks were inferior, the regime was fighting fire with fire. For them, there was nothing ironic about the idea that in their phantasmagoria of battling Europe they had become fundamentally European. In addition, many contemporary European observers saw nothing problematic in this campaign and even offered rhetorical strategies of apologia. As two British authors wrote, 'In so far as the "new history" helps the modern Turks to break with the immediate decadent past it no doubt has a beneficial effect . . . Unlike the Nazi racial theories the Turkish study of the past has not yet reached sacrosanct conclusions'.[68]

Whereas the early history books ignored late Ottoman and Republican history in favour of Antiquity and the Middle Ages, when a history of the Republic was written, the narrative was an elaborate replica of Mustafa Kemal's famous 1927 speech.[69] The foundations of the myths and memories of the Turkish nation had been laid for decades to come. But these exercises involved more than the construction of the national narrative. In dismissing and sanitizing the Ottoman past, the Young Turk intelligentsia directly silenced the histories of the Ottoman peoples, many of whom were still existing in Turkey. Circassians, Kurds, Syriacs, Arabs, Armenians, Greeks, and others remained unmentioned in the historiography and thus were obliterated from the theatres of memory. RPP party officials did not fail to emphasize this by denying that Kurds had a history.[70] Just as society had been cleared of 'non-Turkish elements', at this point so was history. Nationalist intellectuals such as İshak Refet (Işıtman) could state during the Turkish Hearths

---

[66] *Ortamektep İçin Tarih* (Istanbul: Devlet Basımevi, 1936), 20–1.

[67] Şevket Aziz, 'Türklerin Antropolojisi', in: *Birinci Türk Tarih Kongresi: Konferanslar Münakaşalar* (Istanbul: T.C. Maarif Vekaleti, 1932), 271–8.

[68] John Parker and Charles Smith, *Modern Turkey* (London: Routledge, 1940), 166.

[69] *Tarih IV: Türkiye Cumhuriyeti* (Istanbul: Devlet Basımevi, 1931).

[70] İsmail Beşikçi, *Türk Tarih Tezi ve Kürt Sorunu: Güneş-Dil Teorisi* (Istanbul: Komal, 1977), 219–37.

conferences that 'the Kurds have no history'.[71] Lieutenant-Colonel Kadri Perk, who served in the 1925 campaigns, was at least as emphatic: 'I have established through historical research that there is no race called Kurds; as for Armenians, they only came here as a result of migration and...quickly disappeared. I know the intricacies of writing history'.[72] Colonel Nuri Bey of the General Staff told a British military attaché that 'Kurds are of very mixed and doubtful national origin and have no national unity'. According to him, the Kurds' historical roots were 'very doubtful' and since Kurdish 'bears a strong resemblance to the Turkish dialects spoken in parts of Anatolia, such as the lower slopes of Erçiş Dağ', the Kurds 'derive largely from the Seljuk Turks, who preceded the Ottoman invasion'.[73] Whenever Kurds were mentioned in less radical terms, they still were the stepchildren of history. Writing about the Diyarbekir Kurds during the Ottoman-Safavid wars of the sixteenth century, one author contended that 'many kurdish chieftains in this region changed sides during dangerous times in the war...opened fire on our army and in this way stabbed the Turkish army in the back. Throughout history these traitors have exhibited no merits other than banditry'.[74] Which ethnic group had a history and which one did not was dictated by the hegemonic canons of nationalist historiography.

It is perhaps surprising to discover that Kemalist eagerness for historiography was only thinly disguised as memory and identity politics. After all, in order to mete out a new identity for society, a new memory needed to be meted out first. The writing of new histories would serve this purpose, and the regime did not make a particular effort to cloak this. One of the main contributors to the new nationalist historiography acknowledged that the creation of a new version of history would 'quickly cause this society, consisting of Turks, to gain an identity'.[75] That people already had identities did not matter. These could be changed, starting with the root of identity: surnames. The 1934 Surname Law, which enforced the adoption and registration of hereditary surnames in Turkish, was manifestly a project of memory politics. By strictly prohibiting all non-Turkish (i.e. Arabic, Persian, Slavic, Syriac, Greek, Armenian) suffixes and prevalent names such as 'Son of a Kurd' (Kürtoğlu) or 'Son of an Albanian' (Arnavutoğlu),[76] the law attempted not only to make identities 'legible'[77] but also cut off their ties with the past. It also prescribed which surnames to assume.[78] Where 'Turkification' needed to be pursued at a more

---

[71] *Türk Ocakları Üçüncü Kurultayı Zabıtları* (Istanbul: Kader, 1927), 225.

[72] Kadri Perk, *Cenupdoğu Anadolu'nun Eski Zamanları* (Istanbul: İnkılap, 1934), 71.

[73] *NAUK*, FO 371/15369/E68, Clerk to Henderson, 5 January 1931, Interview between Major O'Leary and Nury Bey, 22 December 1930, 'Some Observations on Kurdistan by Colonel Nuri Bey, General Staff.'

[74] Günkut, *Diyarbekir Tarihi*, 116.

[75] Afet İnan, *Tarih İlminin Dinamik Karakteri* (Ankara: Ankara Üniversitesi, 1956), 7; emphasis added.

[76] 'Soy Adı Nizamnamesi', in: *Resmi Gazete*, no. 2805 (20 December 1934).

[77] Jeremy Mathias, James C. Scott and John Tehranian, 'Naming Like a State: The Production of Legal Identities Proper to States: The Case of the Permanent Family Surname', in: *Comparative Studies in Society and History* 44, no. 1 (2002), 4–44.

[78] Ahmet Yıldız, *Ne Mutlu Türküm Diyebilene: Türk Ulusal Kimliğinin Etno-Seküler Sınırları (1919–1938)* (Istanbul: İletişim, 2001), 236.

aggressive pace and intensity, such as in cosmopolitan Istanbul or in the eastern provinces, last names including the term 'Turk' (*Türk*) or even 'Pure Turk' (*Öztürk*) were imposed on non-Turks.[79] In the eastern provinces, where people often bore a complex combination of personal names and the names of their tribes, households and extended families, this form of identity politics was generally experienced as intrusion into the private sphere.

These national memory and identity politics percolated into the fibres of society at an inexorable pace. The message radiated from Ankara to the nation and became institutionalized in local government, society, culture, education, media, academe, and intellectual life. For every region in Turkey, local historians educated in the Young Turk spirit or Ankara-based official historians assigned to write regional histories began gearing the new memory to local conditions. As was the case on the national level, local practices also consisted of two components: the construction of memory, and the destruction of memory.

MEMORY POLITICS IN DIYARBEKIR

The People's Houses were partly responsible for publishing these books, for their periodicals were seen as suitable mouthpieces of official historiography.[80] The canon of local history was written by the same local elites that had collaborated with the previous Young Turk regime. In Diyarbekir these were the Pirinççizâde and Müftüzâde families. As discussed in Chapter 1, it was none other than Ziya Gökalp who had initiated the study of Diyarbekir in the service of nationalist memory politics. Here too, there was a prehistory of CUP history-writing. More comprehensive studies of history were ordered by the Republican People's Party in the late 1920s and especially the early 1930s. When it was Diyarbekir's turn, the General Secretariat ordered the People's House to 'conduct scientific research in this region that is rich from the perspective of Turkish History and Archeology'. It allotted funds to this end and sparked off a decade of Young Turk historiography.[81]

One of the first texts written by the Republican People's Party on Diyarbekir was a 1935 booklet titled *A Glance at Diyarbekir*. A city like Diyarbekir, with its rich ethnic heterogeneity and diverse architecture, embarassed the Young Turk intelligentsia, who were continuously seeking to write 'Turkishness' into history and society for particular reasons. The conclusion of *A Glance at Diyarbekir*, summarized in the last paragraphs, provided insight into the historical culture of the Young Turks:

---

[79] Meltem Türköz, 'Surname Narratives and the State-Society Boundary: Memories of Turkey's Family Name Law of 1934', in: *Middle Eastern Studies* 43, no. 6 (2007), 893–908, at 903; Beşikçi, *Türk Tarih Tezi*, 219.

[80] İlhan Başgöz and Howard E. Wilson, *Educational Problems in Turkey 1920–1940* (Bloomington: Indiana University Press, 1968), 155.

[81] BCA, 490.01/996.850.1, RPP General Secretariat to Fourth Bureau, 3 January 1941.

The city of Amid [Diyarbekir] is not a city founded by the Assyrians, nor of the Iranians, Arabs or Greeks. It was founded in 2000 BC by Turkish Hittites who migrated westwards from Central Asia, and although in time it suffered invasions by the Assyrians, Persians and Romans, it never lost its Turkishness, national existence and language, and is a city that has always stayed Turkish.[82]

Through the lens of this particular foundational myth, the origin of Turkish culture was located so early in history that it was lost in the mists of not real but mythic time, which symbolized the timelessness of the nation. The booklet set the tone for much of Young Turk official historiography on Diyarbekir. The first proper history book was the ambitious three-volume *The History of Diyarbekir*, published in 1936 by the party press.[83] It was the local equivalent of the national histories provided by the Association for the Study of Turkish History. The first two volumes expounded on pre-Ottoman history in the same way that national histories had: Diyarbekir was established by the Hittites, the Hittites were Turks, ergo Diyarbekir was Turkish. A second history book was published by Usman Eti, who argued that 'Diyarbekir, the foundation of which was laid by Turks, is Turkish and nothing but Turkish from its smallest pebble to the largest tower, and today just like yesterday is a cultural center of the east and a sacred nest of Turkishness'.[84] History books were written about the districts of Diyarbekir or provincial towns as well. The publication of the book *History of Silvan*,[85] of which 2000 copies were printed, was reported as 'the grateful fruit of a labor and effort to present the place of Silvan in Turkish history'. Local officials requested the Party to purchase 1000 copies to 'distribute to all People's Houses and Rooms'.[86]

Probably the most significant and exemplary book on Diyarbekir history was written by regime propagandist Bedri Günkut, entitled *The History of Diyarbekir* and published by the Diyarbekir People's House. In his study Günkut ascribed a universal Turkishness to all the regions of Diyarbekir province, harking back to the Assyrian era. But unlike the previous books, Günkut's study went to far greater lengths to identify the 'Turkishness' and erase all non-Turkish cultures from Diyarbekir history. His book is worth examining in some detail. The second chapter was titled 'History', and 'began' history with the Sumerian era: 'The Turkish nation, which was living the world's most civilized life even in Prehistory, fled westwards 9 to 10,000 years ago due to natural and inescapable reasons and undoubtedly also passed through Mesopotamia and the vicinity of Diyarbekir'.[87] Günkut went on to state that 'the nation first to have eked out a civilized existence in the Diyarbekir area is the Turkish nation'. He did not deviate from the party line when portraying the myths of origin: 'Despite temporary invasions and destructions by the Assyrian, Persian, Greek, and Roman regimes, the great Turkish race

---

[82] *Diyarbekire Bir Bakış* (Diyarbekir: Diyarbekir Basımevi, 1935), 24–30.
[83] Basri Konyar, *Diyarbekir Tarihi* (Ankara: Ulus Basımevi, 1936).
[84] Usman Eti, *Diyarbekir* (Diyarbakır: Diyarbekir Matbaası, 1937), 55.
[85] Süleyman Savcı, *Silvan Tarihi* (Diyarbakır: CHP Diyarbakır Halkevi Neşriyatı no. 13, 1949).
[86] BCA, 490.01/902.525.1, RPP Regional Inspector of Diyarbakır Fırat to RPP General Secretariat, 18 February 1949.
[87] Bedri Günkut, *Diyarbekir Tarihi* (Diyarbakır: Diyarbekir Halkevi, 1937), 26.

has always lived in this country'.[88] Under the title, 'Stories about the foundation of this city', Günkut reviewed nine historical narratives about the 'origins' of the city: the Akkadian, Persian, Assyrian, Arab, Parthian, Greek, Armenian, Hittite, and Turkish theses. The author evaluated all the myths and dismissed, with increasing severity, disapproval, and contempt, one by one, the first eight theories. For example, according to Günkut, 'the claim that Amid was founded by arabs can be nothing else than a lie, a ludicrous fabrication by arabs and arabophiles'. Out of disdain the names of non-Turkish ethnic groups were consciously and consistently written not with capital but with small letter: the literature spoke not of Kurds, Arabs, and Armenians, but of kurds, arabs, and armenians. As a grand finale Günkut repeated the regime's mantra: 'Diyarbekir city has never lost its Turkishness, its National Existence and has always remained Turkish'.[89]

With its obviously varied architecture, Diyarbekir needed symbolization and discourse for retrospective 'Turkification' of its cityscape as well. Whereas public space in the city was contested in the Ottoman Empire, the Young Turks now held hegemony over it. Nationalist historians such as Günkut went on to deny that any other culture than the Turkish one had ever contributed to Diyarbekir's architectural heritage. Writing about the Behram Pasha mosque, he denied: 'Nowadays whether in or on the building there is no single trace of persian and arab work', accusing anybody claiming 'that Behram Pasha was an arab' of 'fabricating this from scratch'. The author then explored the architectural history of the Great Mosque, an Orthodox church which was converted to a mosque following the Muslim capture of Diyarbekir in 639 AD. He attacked Ottoman historians, observers, and travellers such as Evliya Çelebi for noting that the minaret had been a bell tower, concluding, 'In short, no matter how one interprets this, it is not likely but absolutely certain that this mosque was built by the Turks'.[90] Although Günkut simply ignored the Syrian Orthodox and Chaldean churches and Jewish synagogues of Diyarbekir, his depiction of the Armenian heritage was most radical: 'Above all, I can state with absolute certainty that nowhere in the entire city there is even a single trace of armenianness to be found'.[91]

After skipping six centuries of Ottoman history, Günkut leaped straight to the first decades of the twentieth century. His historical portrayal of the Young Turk era of violence is most striking. In a region in which more than 100,000 Armenians were destroyed, this author pioneered the denial of the genocide: 'In the Great War, this region was saved from Russian invasions and Armenian massacres and arson'. With the Sheikh Said rebellion only a decade past, Günkut's narrative on the 1925 violence was more elaborate. The Kurdish insurgency was almost exclusively attributed to conspiracies from outside: Sheikh Said was not part of the Kurdish

---

[88] Ibid., 27.
[89] Ibid., 45.
[90] Ibid., 122, 133–5, 141.
[91] Ibid., 156. This discourse of total denial of anything Armenian was reproduced in Kemalist texts on the districts of Diyarbekir as well. One author wrote that Armenian existence in Ergani 'had not had the slightest significance'. Muhtar Körükçü, 'Ergani'nin Zülküf Dağı', in: *Karacadağ* VII, no. 85–6 (December/January 1945–6).

intelligentsia or elite but 'an extremely ignorant fanatic . . . who became the tool of foreigners . . . with several other uncultured vagabonds'. The narrative then took a turn towards disinformation as Günkut argued that the Kurds had 'committed bloodcurdling atrocious acts in Lice and Silvan', where they had purportedly 'monstrously dismembered young Turkish patriots'.[92] In this remarkable reversal of the historical account, all violence in Diyarbekir had been committed by Armenians and Kurds against Turks. Misrepresentation could only be called so if there was a body of knowledge to counteract it. Whatever counter-narratives were being produced in Syria in Armenian, Kurdish, or Arabic, the regime did not allow them to compete for consumption by the population of Diyarbekir. Especially when it came to the violence, the dictatorship held hegemony over memory politics and debates about the past.

The canon of official literature was as much about dictating the past as projecting the future. Early in the book, Günkut prognosticated about Diyarbekir, 'Every traitor should know that Diyarbekir city, every molecule of which came into being from the flesh and bones of pure Turks, and its soil, which was watered by the very clean blood of the Turks, will always remain Turkish just like all other cities of the Turks'.[93] More than a hundred pages later the message was repeated. Not only was it certain that there were 'not hundreds but thousands of documents in the city proving that Diyarbekir is a Turkish city', but these 'documents' would serve to 'illustrate that, just as it has been the case so far, from now on Diyarbekir will always remain a Turkish city *at all points in time*'.[94] The transcendentality in this future vision was as explicit as it was exclusionary. At a time when Armenians and Syriacs were being expelled to Syria at rapid pace, this narrative of the nation, created and perpetuated in Ankara, acted to shape politics: there was no place anymore for non-Turkish cultures in Diyarbekir. As minorities were being driven out of the country, they were literally being driven out of history and memory as well.

A final dimension of the magnum opus, *The History of Diyarbekir*, was its narrative of the Diyarbekir economy. Although that had been multi-ethnic for centuries, now even the economy was whitewashed as always having been 'Turkish'. The disappearance of silk weavers, miners, carpenters, blacksmiths, jewellers, and many other craftsmen was explained as follows:

> Once upon a time, especially before the Great War, these crafts had developed to a high level. The recession that had struck all countries also made itself felt here. As in all Turkish cities, during the political crisis that continued briefly after the war, the locals here too were preoccupied with the struggle for Turkish independence, as a result of which the crafts stagnated even further. But the National War and revolutions that our Great Leader Atatürk created gave birth to the growth of various crafts in Diyarbekir. Nowadays, the aforementioned crafts are developing beyond the pre-war level.[95]

---

[92] Günkut, *Diyarbekir Tarihi*, 144–5.   [93] Ibid., 37–45.
[94] Ibid., 158–9; emphasis added.   [95] Ibid., 17.

In this account, the crafts, devoid of agency, had declined during the war due to unknown forces, and most of all, the anonymous craftsmen had disappeared. Not surprisingly, nowhere in this narrative is there a reference to the CUP's devastating policies of 'Turkification' of the economy by violent expropriation of Christians.

Another propagandist, Hasan Reşit Tankut, offered an answer to this enigma: 'The Turks were the first people to find mines and bring them into production'. According to him, these first Turks, 'of a beautiful race . . . with light skins, eyes, and hair', had brought these crafts from Central Asia to the Diyarbekir region in 5000 BC.[96] According to Tankut, Qitirbil, one of the villages on the Diyarbekir plain where the genocidal killings were initiated in 1915, was Turkish 'from days immemorial . . . because in that region minerals were plenty and the Turks were skillful miners . . . When these miner Turks came to this region they named it after the nearby copper mines'.[97] It is most likely that this myth of mining captured in Tankut's and Günkut's narratives contributed to the production of a new discourse on the very name 'Diyarbekir' in the mid-1930s (see below).

There was nothing hyperbolic or paradoxical to the authors that in these theories, 'Turks' had founded Diyarbekir in an ancient past, but still had to conquer it at a later time; 'Turks' had founded a 'superior civilization' there, but still had to 'civilize' the city in the 1930s. Constructing the myths and memories of the nation did not meet much resistance from an intellectually and politically emasculated Diyarbekir. After all, the population now consisted of barely educated peasants, a few indifferent or self-serving elites, and acquiescent collaborators. Counter-narratives were written in cities such as Paris, Cairo, Boston, Aleppo, Los Angeles. For two generations of local citizens and scholars growing up under the Young Turk regime in Diyarbekir, these Kemalist books represented the cornerstones of modern history. They were widely distributed and read by younger generations with no recollections of the times that were recorded and represented in the official histories. The books by the 1930s *école* of official historians still constitute the canon of Diyarbekir histories. They laid the foundation of a body of knowledge which generations of students would tap into.

Even during the first years of the Republic, the local Young Turk elites attempted to carve out a local niche for the national canon of books. In May 1926 the Diyarbekir Turkish Hearth proposed that the government establish a 'national library' in the city. The chairman, Arif Mehmet, reported to the Ankara government that the Diyarbekir Turkish Hearth was 'renowned for struggling for the erasure of traces of foreign cultures in Diyarbekir, which has historically and ethnographically been a completely Turkish city'. In order to continue this mission, the government was petitioned for support to establish a library for the Turkish 'national and civilized existence'. This would in its turn 'spread national sentiments and the principles of republicanism and populism'. In his letter, the chairman asked the government to send Turkish-language books on sociology, history, science,

---

[96] Hasan Reşit Tankut, *Diyarbakır Adı Üzerinde Toponomik bir Tetkik* (Ankara: Ulus Basımevi, 1937), 3.
[97] Ibid., 4–5.

education, and literature.[98] As discussed in the previous chapter, the Chairman of Section 1 of Diyarbekir's People's House (Language, History, Literature) was the mayor, former militia leader Müftüzâde Şeref Uluğ. At least two members of the Pirinççizade family were involved in the section on Villages.[99] In addition, during the Turkish Hearths conferences of the 1920s the representative for Diyarbekir was the former militia leader Pirinççizâde Sıdkı.[100] These men were assigned to publish a local journal titled *Karacadağ*, which followed the Ankara-based journal *Ülkü* by translating the national Turkish narrative to local conditions.[101] Ceding authority to the local génocidaires for writing local historiography naturally solidified the existing culture of denial and systemic exclusions in the construction of the 'national' body of knowledge.

One of the major actions of these local Young Turks was to appropriate the very rich library established in 1764 by the Ottoman official Sarı Abdurrahman Pasha. This library was situated adjacent to the Great Mosque.[102] From the late 1920s on, the library became the object of nationalist politics by Culture Ministry officials as its then content of books in Ottoman Turkish, Arabic, and Persian was assessed for its usefulness and suitability as a resource for 'Turkishness'. Eventually that would define its level of retention. To reflect this change, in 1932 the library was renamed National Library by local Young Turks and General Cevat Şakir (Çobanlı) (1871–1938).[103] In this process it was reconstituted and filled with post-1928 books, journals, and newspapers. In 1939 the library was united with the People's House library, now numbering a total of 7000 volumes, and placed under the aegis of Müftüzâde Şeref Uluğ. Two years later, the Party sent cultural inspector Kemal Güngör to evaluate the library's old collection. Güngör found the old collection, which he characterized as 'invaluable', stored in a depot in an uncatalogued, unread, unused and neglected state. He reported widespread negligence and made a list of the 5856 volumes.[104] The fate of these two libraries in Diyarbekir symbolized the transition from Ottoman to Turkish, a cultural rupture engineered from above.

The construction of new libraries did not suffice for consumption by the public. The Party continuously examined circulation, even in the smallest of the libraries. As one contemporary observer wrote,

---

[98] BCA, 30.10.0.0/117.816.13, Chairman of the Diyarbekir Turkish Hearth Arif Mehmet to Interior Ministry, 4 May 1926.

[99] BCA, 490.01/984.814.2, Diyarbekir People's House Director Çubukçu to RPP General Secretariat, 23 December 1935.

[100] *Türk Ocakları 1928 Senesi Kurultayı Zabıtları* (Ankara: n.p., 1930), 2–3.

[101] Both journals were published by the respective People's Houses. *Ülkü* was published from 1933 to 1950, *Karacadağ* from 1933 to 1946.

[102] Günkut, *Diyarbekir Tarihi*, 125.

[103] Usman Eti, *Diyarbekir* (Diyarbekir: Diyarbakır Matbaası, 1937), 41. General Çobanlı had been put in charge of destroying the 1924 Nestorian 'rebellion', a military campaign which escalated into the wholesale destruction of Nestorian villages in the Hakkari region.

[104] BCA, 490.01/1045.1015.2, People's House Inspector Kemal Güngör to RPP General Secretariat, 26 December 1940.

The House libraries were also major cultural assets. This was particularly so once the change had been made from the Arabic to Latin script. Book collections in Arabic soon became antiquated. In provincial towns, that were often without any other library, the People's Houses made printed materials available to thousands of people. Books were selected and purchased by the Party's central offices. In 1943, 55,147 books were acquired and distributed by the RPP. And the House in Ankara alone managed to accumulate a library of 40,000 volumes over the years that the program had been in effect.[105]

In the summer of 1935, the Library and Publishing section of the Diyarbekir People's House was reported of boasting a library of almost 1000 books. According to the report 'no less than 10 readers' could be found in the reading room every day.[106] Annual evaluation reports sent directly to the Party summed up how many people had been reading the new canon: from 1 January 1935 to 15 December 1935 a total of 2580 people had visited the reading room and had read from the 1500 books the library possessed.[107] The 1941 evaluation of the province's People's Houses was no less glowing: the province harboured five libraries (Diyarbekir, Silvan, Ergani, Lice, and Çermik), numbering a total of 22,000 books. But the Party monitored more than how many people were reading the approved, new literature. It also kept its eye on the old, prohibited literature. Not infrequent the reports were signed with the note: 'There are no prohibited books in the library catalogue'.[108] Perhaps the most poignant illustration of Young Turk memory policies in Diyarbekir is represented in the last sentence of a report sent by the Director of the Ergani People's House, who reported to his superiors in Ankara, 'It is a great honour to report that our library . . . does not contain any books written in foreign languages or in the old letters'.[109] Indeed, by the time the Second World War broke out, monolingualism had become an entrenched literary culture and a source of pride in modern Turkey. In 1942 the poet Cahit Sıtkı Tarancı, based in Diyarbekir, wrote to his friend in Istanbul, 'The People's House here does not receive any other journal than *Ülkü*'.[110] Young Turk cultural policies aimed to produce a continuous process of cultural homogenization.

The politics of memory consists of more than the production of narratives and maintenance of libraries. Constructing museums, holding public commemorations, and erecting sculptures were also part of the broad ambit of the regime's practices of memorialization. The 1941 evaluation of the People's House suggested the thousands of old books of Diyarbekir, now obsolete and useless due to the change of alphabet, be sent to the National Museum in Ankara. The regime was disinterested in having

[105] Başgöz and Wilson, *Educational Problems in Turkey*, 151. For numbers of books distributed, see: *Cumhuriyet Halk Partisi Halkevleri ve Halkodaları* (Ankara: Ulus, 1945), 13.

[106] BCA, 490.01/1005.880.3, People's House Inspector Alaettin Tekmen to RPP General Secretary Recep Peker, 28 August 1935.

[107] BCA, 490.01/984.814.2, Diyarbekir People's House Director Çubukçu to RPP General Secretariat, 23 December 1935.

[108] BCA, 490.01/996.850.1, RPP General Secretariat to Fourth Bureau, 3 January 1941.

[109] BCA, 490.01/1036.986.01, Ergani People's House Director Dr. Şevki Kılıççı to RPP General Secretariat, 8 February 1945.

[110] Cahit Sıtkı Tarancı to Ziya Osman Saba, 19 February 1942, quoted in: Ziya Osman Saba, 'Cahit'le Günlerimiz', in: Cahit Sıtkı Tarancı, *Ziya'ya Mektuplar 1930–1946* (Istanbul: Varlık, 1957), 98.

these books read, so perfectly legible cultural assets now became museum pieces.[111]
The suggestion was accepted and implemented a decade later, when a comprehensive
reorganization of the People's Houses libraries was carried out by the General Directorate of Old Works and Museums of the Ministry of National Education. The old
books were collected in the national museum in the city and in Ankara.[112] Like all
nation states, Young Turkey also engaged in large-scale commemorative events. The
'great days' of the Republic were routinely commemorated in grandeur: 23 April
('National Independence Day'), 19 May ('Day of Atatürk'), 30 August ('Day of
Victory'), 29 October ('Day of the Republic'). To this a special day was added for
commemorating Atatürk's special ties with Diyarbekir: on 5 April 1926 the Young
Turks in city hall proclaimed the dictator 'honorary compatriot' of Diyarbekir city in
honour of Kemal's 5 April 1917 visit to the city. From then on, 5 April would be
celebrated in Diyarbekir as 'Atatürk Day'.[113]

Occasional commemorations were about specific historical events. In July 1943
the People's House hosted several lectures in Diyarbekir about the history of the
Bosporus. The lectures always finished with the words: 'The straits are Turkish and
will remain Turkish for eternity'.[114] To commemorate the twentieth anniversary of
the 'Lausanne victory' on 24 July 1943 a group of People's House members
convened in the institution's garden. The chairman of the House, Dr. Bedri
Noyan, then gave a long speech on the Sevrès and Lausanne treaties, advocating
the latter's 'greatness as a victory'. This speech was delivered 'in a language that the
people would understand really well' and was followed by an evening celebration.[115] The evidence suggests that commemorations like this were not mere local
initiatives of goodwill, but were often intended to keep local memory in line with
what politicians in Ankara were propagating.

Mustafa Kemal Atatürk was the central focus of public manifestations of memory. Sculptures of him spread across the country in a matter of years and well before
his death adorned every main square in the country. Diyarbekir was no exception.
In the case of memorializing Atatürk too, bottom-up initiatives that fit into the
strategic framework of the decision makers in the political centre were undertaken.
In March 1935, the local Young Turk elite in Diyarbekir, under the auspices of
mayor Müftüzâde Şeref Uluğ, proposed the erection of a statue of Kemal Atatürk in
the main square of Diyarbekir. They pointed out their willingness to spend 20,000
TL on this statue but could not decide whether 'the statue should represent General
Mustafa Kemal Pasha who saved Diyarbekir from a Russian invasion during the
Great War, or the revolutionary Atatürk'. They also asked 'which one among the
Turkish artists comes highly recommended'.[116] The Party did not make its

---

[111] BCA, 490.01/996.850.1, RPP General Secretariat to Fourth Bureau, 3 January 1941.
[112] BCA, 490.01/1045.1015.2, Minister of National Education to RPP General Secretariat, 5 July
1951.
[113] Günkut, *Diyarbekir Tarihi*, 148–9.
[114] *Diyarbakır*, 21 July 1943.
[115] *Diyarbakır*, 30 July 1943.
[116] BCA, 490.01/2013.9.1, Diyarbekir Mayor to RPP General Secretary Recep Peker, 28 March
1935.

disciples wait long for a one-line answer: 'It is appropriate to be constructed as the revolutionary Atatürk'.[117] The locals now went to work. Sketches were drawn, the statue's location in the city was discussed, and a sculptor by the name of Arif Hikmet was recruited for the job. Finally the Diyarbekir elite decided on having the statue erected on a 'large and modern sculpture square' at the entrance of Diyarbekir's Mountain Gate, at that time the object of 'urban modernization'. Since nothing was too good for Mustafa Kemal, financial obstacles were dismissed and 25,000 TL was allotted for the project, scheduled for completion in the spring of 1936.[118] The project was finished and a large Atatürk sculpture arose on the left side of the boulevard leading from the Mountain Gate to the barracks. Symbolically, Atatürk the omniscient was overseeing all entry into and exit from the city.[119] In the provincial towns of Diyarbekir the procedure seems to have been more top-down. The erection of the Atatürk statue in Ergani, for example, was directly ordered by Atatürk's loyal Interior Minister Şükrü Kaya.[120]

TOPONYMICAL CHANGES

Though geography and memory are two seemingly unrelated phenomena, in nationalist thought they are closely linked. Nation-formation processes entail the nationalization of territory, co-occurring with the changing of place-names.[121] The attack on non-Turkish memory implied as a necessary accompaniment an attack on the memory of the space in which the non-Turkish peoples lived.[122] To the Young Turks, non-Turkish place-names were constant obnoxious reminders of the region's diverse past (and present) and therefore needed to be tackled through large-scale Turkification of place-names. Enforcing new place-names would symbolically express Turkish nationalism in the face of the existing vista of multi-ethnic diversity. Both the Committee of Union and Progress and the Republican People's Party attempted to Turkify the political landscape of Turkey by forcibly changing place-names. What seemed like (and has been studied as) an isolated and relatively innocent undertaking was an inextricable part of the broader, long-term campaign to 'Turkify' every corner of the eastern provinces.[123]

---

[117] BCA, 490.01/2013.9.1, RPP General Secretary Recep Peker to Diyarbekir Municipality, 8 June 1935.

[118] *Diyarbekire Bir Bakış* (Diyarbakır: Diyarbekir Basımevi, 1935), 4–5.

[119] Konyar, *Diyarbekir Tarihi*, 266.

[120] BCA, 490.01/2013.9.1, Interior Minister Şükrü Kaya to Diyarbekir Vice-Governor Kâzım Demirer, 26 July 1937.

[121] See e.g.: Saul B. Cohen and Nurit Kliot, 'Place-Names in Israel's Ideological Struggle over the Administered Territories', in: *Annals of the Association of American Geographers* 82, no. 4 (1992), 653–80.

[122] Kerem Öktem, 'Incorporating the Time and Space of the Ethnic "Other": Nationalism and Space in Southeast Turkey in the Nineteenth and Twentieth Centuries', in: *Nations and Nationalism*, vol. 10, no. 4 (2004), 559–78.

[123] Kerem Öktem, 'The Nation's Imprint: Demographic Engineering and the Change of Toponymes in Republican Turkey', in: *European Journal of Turkish Studies*, no. 7 (2008), at: <http://www.ejts.org/document2243.html>.

When the British diplomat Mark Sykes travelled through Diyarbekir before the First World War he noted that 'the whole country between Palu and Diarbekir is singularly poor in nomenclature, mountains, rivers, torrents, and even villages being equally unconnected with any definite designation. One bunch of villages will have one name, and the people, whether Christian or Moslem, dwelling therein are known by that name, even as are the rivers passing the villages, the valleys in which they lie, and the mountains which overlook them'.[124] This would change. During the First World War, the CUP issued orders for place-names of provinces, cities, towns, villages, rivers, forests, and mountains 'that have no relation with Turkishness to be changed', excising specifically Armenian, Greek, and Bulgarian names and appending a list of acceptable names with the order.[125] All throughout the war detailed reports came pouring in from the provinces on the local state of affairs regarding toponymics. When the renaming campaign caused considerable confusion for the army, it was suspended and postponed to the end of the war, even though the collection of information continued.[126] However, the Turkification of place-names was not a strictly top-down affair. The CUP's Turkish Hearths frequently took the initiative to have village and neighbourhood names changed, even during the deportation and destruction of those communities after whom the villages were named. Thus, during and after the killing and deportation of local Armenians, physical traces that reminded of the Armenians were often effaced.[127] Destruction of the community was immediately followed by the destruction of their memory.

In this campaign too, there are continuities to be found between the first and the second Young Turk era. During the Independence War, furious parliamentarians persistently launched thunderous verbal demands for place-names to be changed. As one fulminated, 'As someone living in this country I refuse to carry the name of a nation that has wanted to attack our honour, existence, and presence like dogs'.[128] Although in principle these types of motions were endorsed by all, the government considered it unwise to act impulsively in the heat of the war and generally shelved their execution until after the war. Postponement did not mean cancellation: from the 1920s place-names were changed systematically, starting with some of the most conspicuous examples of Armenian, Greek, and Bulgarian symbolism.[129] But the campaign did not only affect Christian place-names. With the promulgation of the Republic the political climate in Turkey was so conducive to silencing minorities that non-Turkish Muslim cultures too were silenced and relegated to invisibility in the public sphere. Thus, the term 'Lazistan', named after the ethnic Laz of the eastern Black Sea region, disappeared from maps and public discourse. Nationalist journals published articles arguing that 'in no part of Anatolia is there a place called

---

[124] Sykes, *The Caliphs' Last Heritage*, 363.
[125] *BOA*, İUM 48/28, document 1, Talaat to Elaziz province, 12 January 1916.
[126] *BOA*, İUM 48/28, document 37.
[127] Necdet Sakaoğlu, *Kuruluşundan günümüze kadar 'çeşm-i cihan' Amasra: coğrafî, içtimâî ve turistik özellikleri ile 35 asırlık tarihi ve tarih eserleri* (Istanbul: Latin, 1966), 186–7.
[128] *Türkiye Büyük Millet Meclisi Zabıt Ceridesi*, vol. 11, period 1, 100.
[129] Murat Koraltürk, 'Milliyetçi bir Refleks: Yer Adlarının Türkleştirilmesi', in: *Toplumsal Tarih* 19, no. 117 (2003), 98–9.

Kurdistan. Anatolia is only Anatolia, Anatolia is strictly a Turkish land. Anatolia is a unitary body and no fragment can be separated. Kurdistan is a fabricated, imagined part in the map of Anatolia. Naming a part of Anatolia after this name is a threat to the unity of Anatolia'.[130] Although the Kurdish-nationalist intelligentsia had protested against this form of toponymical erasure ever since the CUP had initiated it, the regime insisted and stretched the term 'Anatolia' all the way to Turkey's eastern borders.[131] This campaign had international ramifications as well. When the regime discovered that *Der Grosse Weltatlas* contained the terms 'Kurdistan' and 'Armenia' within Turkish national borders[132] it had all copies of the German-language atlas confiscated and destroyed, and further entry of the book into Turkey prohibited.[133] For the same reason the French map *L'asie mineure*, published by Girard et Barrère, and the *Atlas Mondial* published by Jean Dolfus, were prohibited and ordered destroyed.[134] The message was clear: drawing maps of the future or the past was unacceptable, and the renaming campaign was to continue until the very last hamlet.

The non-Turkish names were changed into various Turkish ones, including the names of leading Young Turks. Several places were renamed after Talaat ('Talat-paşa') and Mustafa Kemal ('Kemalpaşa' and 'Mustafakemalpaşa'). In addition to *re*naming, leading Young Turks were imprinted on the landscape when constructions were named after them. One example was the concrete bridge over the Euphrates, constructed in 1932. On the order of Mustafa Kemal, on completion the bridge was named after Prime Minister İsmet İnönü.[135] The train station of Surek near Erzincan was named Cebesoy (after Ali Fuat Cebesoy),[136] and the town of Saray in Van province was changed into Kâzımpaşa (after one of the four generals named Kâzım).[137] Right after the 1938 massacre of Dersim the town of Pulur was renamed Fevziçakmak, after Chief of Staff General Fevzi Çakmak, key person responsible for the killings.[138] From the 1930s on, the Turkification became more categorical and systematic. The 1936 Law for Provincial Rule stipulated in its first article that within the borders of the Turkish Republic all place-names were to be changed into Turkish ones.[139] Thus the name 'Elaziz' was felt to be too

[130] A.M. (Ziyaeddin Fahri Fındıkoğlu), 'Ayın İzleri', in: *Anadolu Mecmuası* 9–11 (May 1925), 390–1.

[131] Mehmet Bayrak (ed.), *Kürtler ve Ulusal-Demokratik Mücadeleleri: Gizli Belgeler-Araştırmalar-Notlar* (Ankara: Özge, 1993), 497.

[132] *Der Grosse Weltatlas: Bearbeitet und mit der Hand gestochen in der kartographischen Anstalt des Bibliographischen Instituts, mit Bemerkungen zu den Karten von Dr. Edgar Lehmann und einem Register mit etwa 80.000 Namen. 6., vermehrte und verbesserte Auflage* (Leipzig: Bibliographisches Instiut AG, 1939).

[133] BCA, 030.18.01.02/88.83.20, Prime Ministry decree, 3 September 1939.

[134] BCA, 030.18.01.02/90.31.7, Prime Ministry decree, 3 April 1940; 030.18.01.02/123.70.2, Prime Ministry decree, 4 September 1950.

[135] BCA, 030.10/155.90.8, General İzzettin Çalışlar to Prime Minister İsmet İnönü, 5 October 1932.

[136] BCA, 030.11.1.0/173.2.6, Interior Ministry decree, undated.

[137] BCA, 030.18.1.02/26.13.10, Council of Ministers decree, 2 March 1932.

[138] BCA, 030.11.1.0/87.52.20, Interior Ministry decree, 10 June 1939.

[139] *Türkiye Büyük Millet Meclisi Zabıt Ceridesi*, vol. 12, period V, session 1 (1936), 14.

Table 3 Toponymical changes in the eastern provinces by 1967

	Number of villages	Names changed	Percentage
Adıyaman	354	220	65
Ağrı	564	362	65
Antep	596	284	48
Bingöl	319	247	80
Bitlis	278	229	86
Diyarbakır	698	461	68
Elazığ	595	396	68
Erzincan	580	352	63
Erzurum	1054	650	63
Gümüşhane	508	342	68
Hakkari	147	111	80
Kars	790	401	52
Malatya	512	219	44
Mardin	726	652	91
Muş	381	286	77
Siirt	515	420	84
Trabzon	566	401	72
Tunceli	453	288	68
Urfa	710	394	57
Van	580	426	75

Source: Zeyrek, 2006.

Arabic and changed into 'Elazığ'.[140] The same was in store for the border town of Reyhaniye, 'Turkified' into Reyhanlı immediately after the Turkish annexation of 1939.[141] Mapavri in the eastern Black Sea region was regarded to be too Laz-sounding and was changed into Çaybaşı.[142] Armenian names bore the brunt of the renaming fervour. When the regime found out that the name of Bingöl's provincial capital, Çabakçur, meant 'cold water' in Armenian, it was changed into Bingöl.[143]

It was clear that the eastern half of Turkey, with its thousands of Armenian, Syriac, Kurdish, and Arab villages, was more affected by these nationalist memory politics. Compared to the western provinces, more names were changed in the eastern provinces than in any other region, as shown in Table 3. In the eastern provinces, 7141 village names were changed out of a total of 10,926, averaging up to 69 percent. For the western provinces, this number was only 21 percent.[144] In a province like Mardin, almost all place-names were changed into Turkish ones. All other place-names were deemed sufficiently Turkish and remained unchanged.

---

[140] BCA, 030.18.1.02/80.100.14, Council of Ministers decree, 10 December 1937.
[141] BCA, 030.11.1.0/161.11.6, Interior Ministry decree, 2 June 1943.
[142] BCA, 030.11.1.0/104.9.1, Interior Ministry decree, 20 January 1944.
[143] BCA, 030.11.1.0/107.85.14, Interior Ministry decree, 13 December 1944.
[144] Şerafettin Zeyrek, 'Türkiye'de Köy Adlarını Değiştirme Politikası', in: *Çukurova Üniversitesi Eğitim Fakültesi Dergisi* 1, no. 31 (2006), 86–95.

As with the other eastern provinces, Diyarbekir was thoroughly affected by the changing of place-names. In an effort to cut off ties to the Ottoman past and de-Islamize it, the name of the province and the city was changed from Diyarbekir to Diyarbakır. As we saw in Chapter 4, the discourse legitimizing this change was formulated by authors such as Bedri Günkut and Hasan Reşit Tankut, but the final decision was made by the highest authority. During his tour of the northern Diyarbekir region, on 17 November 1937 Atatürk ordered one of his clerks to wire Ankara and ask, 'Are there any studies of the etymology of the name Diyarbekir? In reality, this city needs to be known as Diyarbakır, which means land of copper, and from now on it will be known by this name. The Turkish Language Society and the Turkish Historical Society are ordered to collaborate and conduct historical and linguistic research on this matter'. Whereas Diyar*bekir* ('The Land of Bekir' after the first caliph Abū Bakr) symbolized the Islamic past, Diyar*bakır* ('bakır' is Turkish for copper) would from then on symbolize its secular Turkish future. The morning after Atatürk's order, a committee of Young Turk intellectuals convened and discussed the Leader's proposal. Although a few hard-liners proposed changing the name into the more Turkish-sounding *Bakıreli*, soon consensus was reached over the issue that Atatürk's proposal should be considered. Thus, the committee agreed on providing the pseudo-academic support for his thesis and the change became reality.[145] The final order was signed on 2 December 1937 by Mustafa Kemal, Celal Bayar, Kâzım Özalp, Şükrü Kaya, and others. From 10 December 1937 on, Diyar*bekir* was officially known as Diyar*bakır*.[146]

Together with this, names of streets and neighbourhoods were changed from those of Ottoman sultans into Young Turk politicians and military officers. Mail addressed to the old names was not delivered and sent back, causing dysfunctions, delays, and confusion even in official communications, and travellers often got lost and had to resort to the gendarmerie or locals for support. We have seen how many of the Diyarbekir villages became objects of renaming: Kabiye became Bağıvar, Aynetu became Güvercinlik, Karakilise became Dökmetaş, Matrani became Kuş-lukbağı, Şemami became Yenievler, Qitirbil became Eğlence, and countless others. Regional names denoting tribes or tribal confederations such as Botan, Pervari or Mutki were purely Turkish names, according to the new doctrine.[147] To the town of Ergani the term 'Maden' (Turkish for 'mine') was added to stress its industrial function: Ergani Maden.[148] Even the name of the Tigris ('Dicle') was Turkified: according to official texts the name emanated from the 'Akkadian Turks' who had given the river this name. Those who did not believe this were urged to look it up 'in the first volume of the Great History Book that the Turkish Historical Associa-tion had published'.[149] Geography was thus stripped of its Ottoman, Armenian,

---

[145] 'Diyarbakır adı üzerine çalışmalar', in: *Türk Dili*, no. 29/30 (June 1938), 69–87.
[146] BCA, 030.18.01.02/80.99.17, Council of Ministers decree, 10 December 1937; *Resmi Gazete*, no. 3789, 18 December 1937, Cabinet decree no. 7789.
[147] For a list of villages in Diyarbekir province including renamed ones, see the 1973 almanac: *Diyarbakır İl Yıllığı* (Ankara: Türkiye Cumhuriyeti İçişleri Bakanlığı Diyarbakır Valiliği, 1973), 71–116.
[148] BCA, 030.10/8.1111.6, TBMM decree, 4 February 1926.
[149] Bedri Günkut, *Diyarbekir Tarihi* (Diyarbakır: Diyarbekir Halkevi, 1937), 6–7.

and Kurdish connotations. Mardin province was thoroughly 'de-Arabized' through renaming: all names including the term 'Tel' (Arabic for 'hill') were changed into either its Turkish equivalent ('Tepe') or another name was made up.[150] Regime propagandists wrote that the name 'Mardin' itself was not, as Syriac authors had written, a Syrian Aramaic word, but 'a name and land that has been Turkish and of the Turks all throughout history'.[151]

Within years the onomastics of the eastern provinces changed, and it continued to change. At least on paper the map had become unrecognizable. The government rationalized it through nationalism and normality: since the constitution decreed that the official language was Turkish, it seemed logical for the regime to assume that villagers had the right to understand what the name of their village meant. Naturally, the constitution had ignored the fact that millions of people did not speak Turkish. Many villagers in the east used to know why their village was named in a certain way and now did not anymore. The question was not so much that place-names were changing, but that the state was imposing this on a population who had never asked for any such thing. Though in time the population found ways to cope with the renaming phenomenon, for example by using the old names among themselves and the new names when dealing with government employees, it never quite understood why the government had changed all those names. It did not empathize with the Young Turks' obsession with the Turkishness of the names. After all, what was in a name? No matter how ambitious this campaign was, continuing deep into the 1980s, it did not produce the results the Kemalists had hoped for. The more the state pushed for Turkish names to be adopted, the more the tightly knit, rich local cultures persisted in using the 'old' or 'real' names, up to today. This aspect of nation formation was not as effective in the short term as expected.

DISCUSSION

This chapter has discussed the politics of memory pursued by the Young Turks during their single-party dictatorship. In meting out a new identity for the country, they also needed to mete out a new memory for it. During the 1920s and especially the 1930s the Young Turk treatment of the past ranged from the organization of oblivion regarding the traumatic past to the construction of an official narrative that included heroic and eternalized images of the nation. All throughout the country, but particularly for the eastern provinces, orders were given to write new local histories. These official textbooks, nationalist canons, and city histories not only imposed broad silences on critical historical issues, they also banished all ethnic minorities from (regional) history. However, memory is obdurate and the narra-

---

[150] BCA, 030.11.1.0/190.6.2, Interior Ministry decree, 3 March 1947; BCA, 030.18.1.01/20.38.13, Council of Ministers decree, 7 June 1931.
[151] Hasan Reşit Tankut, *Diyarbakır Adı Üzerinde Toponomik bir Tetkik* (Ankara: Ulus Basımevi, 1937), 13.

tives which locals kept in their minds diverged considerably from the narratives they were fed by the official books. Anybody who wanted to learn about the history of Diyarbekir in 1950 had at least two bodies of knowledge at his or her disposal: the libraries constructed by the Young Turkist regimes, and the oral tradition nested in extended families in the city and the countryside. These two corpora of information continued to co-exist for years and decades, but from the 1960s on the latter came under duress from urbanization and increasing levels of education among the uneducated strata of eastern peasants. Nowadays private memory co-exists and at times openly clashes with official public memory. What will come of this collision and competition between loci of memories remains to be seen, but it seems that the oral tradition and its social memory is being documented at a rapid pace after a period of fading away.

The significance of the Young Turk hegemony in memory politics is difficult to assess. Although the eastern provinces were a peasant society where illiteracy figures were as high as 80 percent, the official texts were not only the *first* ones the population would read, they were often the *only* ones available to the population. The organization of a hegemonic canon through exclusion and inclusion aimed at the formation of a *closed circuit of knowledge*. This act precluded the possibilities of a participatory memory and identity formation in the eastern provinces. The regime warded off both external penetration and internal criticism of their belief system by banning and destroying texts on a scale perhaps only matched by the Soviet dictatorship. 'Turkishness' was measured by the level of exposure to that body of knowledge. For example, subsequent studies of cities and regions were to quote the 'classics' of Young Turk historiography in order to be 'scientific' enough to be allowed to be published. The regime did not realize that its blunt-instrument memory policies would foster a cultural impoverishment for the population of Turkey. Up to today, the number of Turks who can read texts written in the Ottoman language (i.e. published before 1928) is limited to historians, theologians, and hobbyists, and is therefore negligible. The regime had refuted Henry Ford's famous adagium that 'history is bunk': history was paramount in the construction of a national memory and a national identity. The 'historical myopia' they pro-duced not only had consequences for the hundreds of thousands of Ottoman-language books that now languish in antiquarian bookstores across the country, but also for the image of history in society. Nowadays, Turkey's historical culture is relatively thin and shallow. The lack of photographic documentation only aggra-vates the textual scarcity problem to the extent that few people nowadays can actually imagine Ottoman society. For them, the past is a different country.[152]

To vindicate their claim that the eastern provinces had eternally been Turkish, the Young Turks left a formidable imprint of memory in the region. From large

---

[152] The racial and historical theories reviewed in this chapter should not be waved away as typical interwar nationalist myth-making whose influence waned after the Young Turks lost power. Their legacy continues to inspire younger generations of Turks. During a recent conference on the history of Diyarbekir, one scholar suggested that the name 'Siverek' (a local town) was possibly of Armenian etymological background. The man was brought up short and severely censured by the panel chair for having brought that up. *Tarihte Siverek Sempozyumu*, Siverek, Diyarbakır, 13–14 October 2001.

cities to small towns, across the geography of the eastern provinces place-names bear the names of Young Turk officers, politicians, brigands, many of whom were implicated in the destruction of Ottoman Armenians. In Diyarbekir, buildings such as Ziya Gökalp High School, the Cahit Sıtkı Tarancı Museum, and other highly visible monuments celebrating prominent Young Turks eclipse the decrepitude of the Armenian church Surp Giragos, the Cemilpaşazâde mansion, and the Pirinççizâde flour factory—silent voices of the violence. The most powerful symbol of the multifaceted silences imposed on the mass violence of the Young Turk era must be the strongly fortified citadel in the north-eastern corner of Diyarbekir city. Many urbanites and neighbouring peasants revere this ancient redoubt as one of the most important historical monuments of their country. The stronghold—what remains of it—stands on a small elevation overlooking a meander in the Tigris river. It is impressive if only because of its position: both the Ottoman Empire and the Turkish Republic built their state apparatus in the compound to instill a long-lasting deference. Anyone who comes here, enticed by one or another historical narrative, is at least vaguely familiar with Diyarbekir's record of violence, and assumes history to be dormant within these dark, crumbling walls. The compound shelters the governorship, the provincial court, and most notably the infamous Diyarbekir prison. The latter building might be considered as the single most evocative landmark of mass violence in Diyarbekir: in it, Bulgarian revolutionaries were incarcerated in the late nineteenth century, Armenian elites were tortured and murdered in 1915, Sheikh Said and his men were sentenced and executed in 1925, various left-wing activists and Kurdish nationalists were kept and subjected to torture during the junta regime following the 1980 military coup, and PKK members were tortured and frequently killed in the 1990s. Up to the year 2000 it housed the security forces of the Turkish war machine including gendarmerie intelligence operatives and special counter-guerrilla militias. This sad account of Diyarbekir's central prison reflects the city's century of violence, during which none of the violence was ever mentioned in any way at any of the sites. In the summer of 2007, the area had been cleared of security forces and was being converted by the Ministry of Culture and Tourism to an open-air 'Atatürk Museum'. The future of the past remains silent.[153]

The Turkish Republic's memory politics towards the Armenian genocide was and is characterized by denial. But, not unlike the genocide itself, this too was part of a larger campaign, namely to exorcise all violence from the memory of society. This imposition of collective amnesia on Turkish society was a double-edged sword. It is still unclear why the Young Turks never commemorated the massive tragedy of their expulsion from the Balkans but chose to move on and look towards the future. Here too, silences were imposed on society: no sane Turk living in the 1930s would have dared to call Mustafa Kemal a refugee, which, technically, he was. There is little nostalgic tourism to the lost territories, and Turkish nationalism in principle excludes territories beyond the borders of the Republic. The Turkish

---

[153] For a theoretical argument on memory and architecture, see: Robert Bevan, *The Destruction of Memory: Architecture at War* (London: Reaktion Books, 2006), 7–60.

treatment of the past became problematic after two developments: on the one hand, the intensification and globalization of Armenian attempts to draw international attention to and memorialize the genocide after the 1960s, and on the other hand, the upsurge of the practice and study of memory roughly in the same era. Both developments deeply polarized the positions and sharpened the tools and mechanisms of official state denial: the narratives became more sophisticated, the image control campaigns better organized, and the domestic surveillance of dissent more aggressive. But why do many Turks share the official viewpoint of the Turkish government?

Three partly overlapping explanations can be offered to this problem. First, the hegemony and imposition of the official Turkish memory to Turkish society has been thorough in the long term. As argued in this chapter, since 1923 the genocide has been ignored under strict censorship, giving birth to several generations of Turks incognizant of any reliable knowledge about 1915. It was in the Young Turk era, most specifically in the 1930s, when the seeds of 'Turkish denial' were sown. For many Turks this is often an 'honest' denial borne out of genuine ignorance. The aforementioned 'closed circuit of knowledge' creates in Turkish minds (i.e. people educated in Turkish state schools and consuming post-1928 Turkish texts) a frame of reference which does not include the mass violence of that era. Second, besides 'genuine ignorance', obstacles to autodidacticism have played a role. In the interbellum period the dictatorship silenced historians, refused entry of foreign books into the country, and systematically censored, removed and destroyed a large corpus of existing texts about the deportations from libraries. Finally, the number of Turks that can speak, read, or write Armenian can probably be counted on the fingers of one hand. Most Turks have never met Armenians and heard their stories, partly because in large cities the various ethnic groups keep to themselves and the Turkish-Syrian border remains very rigid. These three processes cause normal Turks to lapse into cognitive dissonance when confronted with the history of the mass violence.

Ernest Renan famously wrote that nations are bound together not by what they choose to remember, but by what they choose to forget.[154] Denial is a vector of this process of forgetting.[155] The memory of the Armenian genocide is a case in point: being Turkish consists of denying and 'forgetting' the genocide, and being Armenian includes forgetting realities and nuances such as centuries of Turkish-Armenian co-existence, and 'good Turks' who rescued Armenians and resisted the genocide.[156] Thus, in essence, the Armenian-Turkish conflict can be interpreted

---

[154] Ernest Renan, 'What is a Nation?', in Geoff Eley and Ronald Grigor Suny, *Becoming National: A Reader* (Oxford: Oxford University Press, 1996), 41–55, especially 52–4.

[155] For two comparative studies on denials of history, see: Tony Taylor, *Denial: History Betrayed* (Melbourne: Melbourne University Publishing, 2009); Stanley Cohen, *States of Denial: Knowing about Atrocities and Suffering* (Oxford: Polity, 2001). See also: Mirko Grmek, 'Un memoricide', in: *Le Figaro*, 19 December 1991.

[156] For two studies of the instrumentalization of the memory of the Armenian genocide see: Natasha May Azarian, 'The Seeds of Memory: Narrative Renditions of the Armenian Genocide Across Generations' (unpublished Ph.D. thesis, University of California, Berkeley, 2007); Robert

as a conflict of memory: Armenians wish to remember a history that Turks would like to forget. This would not have been a problem if memory was not a core component of identity. Therefore, loss of memory entails a loss of identity, something fundamentally problematic for many people.[157] Since these constructed memories are a primal component of group identity, both Armenians and Turks experience any deviation from that memory as a direct attack on their very identity. Turks who express a sincere, agnostic interest in history are accused of having a dubious (read: Armenian) ethnic background. Then, according to the paradigm of nationalism, any deviation from the official memory automatically implies a deviation from the identity, which in its turn disturbs social closure in the group. A conflict of absolutely exclusive memories has expanded to a conflict of absolutely exclusive identities. The 'revenge of memory' appeared in the 1970s when Kurdish and Armenian nationalists began committing acts of political violence against their historical enemy, 'the Turks'. The Turkish wall of silence precluded traumatized survivor communities from really coping with the violence. During the Nagorno-Karabakh war the Armenian army sang songs about the remote Sason region, whereas Kurdish PKK members memorialized the violence committed against their ancestors. This resembled the fate of Ottoman Muslims in the 1910s: traumatized refugees took revenge years later on a population not identical but associated with their tormentors. The violence also propelled a process of social closure: intra-ethnic conflicts (intra-Kurdish or intra-Armenian) were forgotten to the benefit of a supposedly unitary memory and identity.

The Young Turks assumed that society, and mankind itself, is completely malleable, that no crumbs of memories remain after shock and trauma, and that people will forget. They themselves had tried to bury the unpleasant memories that would come to haunt Turkey decades later. They could not have known at the time that their policies were based on sociological miscalculations. The memory of the violence in Eastern Turkey exists explicitly in the absence of grandparents or entire segments of many Kurdish families, not to mention the entire Ottoman Armenian community. Physically it exists in the many mass graves in the region, of which recently one was discovered by Kurdish villagers in the south-east of Mardin province. When diaspora Armenians called for forensic research, the grave was promptly effaced by the Turkish army and gendarme forces.[158] The international dimension in this scandal was unmistakable. According to one specialist, the 'explosion' or 'revenge' of memory after the Second World War created a new moral standard, which he calls a 'neo-Enlightenment morality' or 'public morality' in international relations.[159] But in the formation of this transnational 'universal

---

Owen Krikorian, 'The Re-appropriation of the Past: History and Politics in Soviet Armenia, 1988–1991' (unpublished Ph.D. thesis, Harvard University, 2003).

[157] This may be even more so for those thousands of Armenian converts living in Eastern Anatolia as Turks, Arabs or Kurds, as well as for Armenian-Turkish mixed marriages. For hints of identity-related questions, see: Ayşe Gül Altınay and Fethiye Çetin, *Torunlar* (Istanbul: Metis, 2009).

[158] Ayşe Günaysu, 'Toplu mezar Ermeni ve Süryanilere ait', in: *Özgür Gündem*, 7 November 2006.

[159] Elazar Barkan, *The Guilt of Nations: Restitution and Negotiating Historical Injustices* (New York: W.W. Norton, 2000), XXVIII.

global memory', of which the Holocaust has become a core constituent, diametrically opposed nationalist memories are competing for inclusion of their own
version of historical events in this canon. Whereas Armenian lobbyists deem the
memory of the genocide a qualified candidate for incorporation, Turkish lobbyists
and the Turkish government are crampedly trying to fend off any memorialization
of the genocide. Denial by states other than the perpetrator society is generally
motivated by immediate inter-state strategic concerns. Whereas Turkish state
officials travel to Yad Vashem and pay homage to the memory of the Shoah,
Iranian state officials fly to Yerevan and do so for the Armenian genocide. The
level of tolerance the totalitarian Syrian regime accorded Armenians to commemorate the genocide in the desert was directly commensurate with Turkish threats to
that regime for supporting the Kurdish nationalists. In international politics too,
memory and power were and are much more closely related than memory and
ethics.

Conclusion

This book has argued that from 1913 to 1950, the Young Turk regime subjected Eastern Turkey, an ethnically heterogeneous area, to various forms of nationalist population policies aimed at ethnically homogenizing the region and including it in the Turkish nation state. It has highlighted the role played by the Young Turks in the identification of the population of the eastern provinces as an object of knowledge, management, and radical change. It has detailed the emergence of a wide range of new technologies of population policies, including physical destruction, deportation, forced assimilation, and memory control, which all converged to increase ethnic and cultural homogeneity within the nation state. It also provides evidence for the thesis that a clear continuity can be observed in population policies between the first Young Turk regime of 1913–18 (the Committee of Union and Progress), and the second of 1919–50 (the Republican People's Party). This section reviews the main conclusions of this study in a brief recapitulation. Rather than repeating each chapter's discussion, it will draw together the main strands and threads of the arguments and move towards a synthesis.

At the outset, the question was raised of how Eastern Turkey was moulded by Young Turk population policies. To provide answers to this question, four forms of population policies were analysed in the subsequent chapters: genocide, deportations, assimilation, and memory politics. In order to integrate those separate but interconnected chapters, a general, introductory framework was laid. It explained how the ideas of nationalism and population policies gained currency among new upcoming classes of Ottoman Muslim military officers, intellectuals, bureaucrats, and experts, divided by profession but united in ethnic nationalism. The ideology of population policies was the common source from which the various policies were derived. It illustrated how the spread of nationalism and population policies reached the Ottoman Empire and deeply influenced its political elite. Of paramount importance was the emergence of the Young Turk party in the late nineteenth century, a nationalist revolutionary movement that engaged in a power struggle with its liberal, religious, and monarchist competitors as well as with ethnic minority parties. In 1908 the party succeeded in overthrowing the Sultan and moving into the corridors of power. Although the movement had propagated freedom, equality, and brotherhood, like so many revolutions the Young Turk revolution too betrayed its initial ideals and the principles of liberal rule: constitutional monarchy and individual freedom quickly perished. The movement grew in power, emerged victorious in the 1913 coup d'état, and installed a dictatorship with totalitarian ambitions that never shunned the use of violence against its opponents and parts of its own population. The Young Turks were convinced that the only way the Ottoman state could survive was as a nation state. They embraced the idea of a Turkish nation state, partly for ideological reasons, but to a large extent also for pragmatic political reasons: the nation-state formula provided an almost absolute protection from foreign interference in the name of national sovereignty. In the face of the wide vista of social heterogeneity in Ottoman society, this meant that a profound ethnic homogenization needed to be organized. In this process, the eastern provinces came to hold a special place (and for this reason are worthy of special attention in this book). The east differed in terms of geopolitical position, economic development, and ethnic composition far from the utopian ideal of the Young Turk vision. As a result, it became a particularly violent crossroads in the evolution from empire to nation state.

The first set of population policies launched were forced assimilation and expulsion, but the outbreak of the First World War radicalized these policies into physical destruction. The genocide of the Armenians developed from this radicalization. But reducing the Armenian genocide to 'mere' mass murder would downplay its complexity. The genocide consisted of a set of overlapping processes that geared into each other and together produced an intended and coherent process of destruction. These processes were mass executions, deportations, forced assimilation, destruction of material culture, and the construction of an artificially created famine region. Nor would it be correct to reduce the Armenian genocide to a 'mere' destructive process. The genocide heralded the coming of a new era and stipulated the parameters of a formative Turkish nation state, or an empire with a dominant Sunni Turkish core and a marginalized periphery. The destruction of Ottoman Armenians represented the first stage in the organization of inclusion and exclusion in the eastern provinces. More precisely, inclusion in the nation was defined by exclusion. As the Armenians were deported, the residual population became a vague Turkish-Ottoman-Muslim in-group. By excluding the Armenians from a certain region the Young Turks delineated a tentative ethno-territorial conception of the new society they envisioned. In other words, they not only defined the social location of the nation but also its territorial location: the motherland was those territories where the excluded were no longer living. Turkey *was* where Armenians were *not*. This was not a precise geometric border, but a provisional ethnic space. This shaping of such a future was a very important aim and outcome of the genocide, and precluded potential future ethno-majoritarianist claims by minorities. The many ethnically formatted demographic directives towards maximums (such as 5% and 10% of the total population) exemplify this, and were the result of the import of those ideas of population policies from other parts of Europe. It was not a total coincidence that the Turkish-Syrian border was established alongside several large villages that were more or less successfully 'Turkified' during the war. This interpretation suggests that the Armenian genocide not only influenced but shaped the contours of the Turkish process of nation formation.

These policies affected the city of Diyarbekir as much as they did its population. Everything in the city that reminded the visitor of its multi-ethnic past needed to be effaced in favour of a 'purely Turkish city'. This was a Europe-wide phenomenon, and the modern history of Diyarbekir does not differ markedly from Salonica's, Wrocław's, or Lviv's in this respect.[1] Total war and genocide swept away a multi-ethnic past representing an imperial order, replacing it with the order of the nation state. Whereas one or more of the victimized minorities were integrally destroyed through genocide, others were expelled to neighbouring kin states or deported in other ways. In all cases, the city itself radically changed as a result of the persecutions. Cemeteries were levelled, gravestones used for road construction, old writings effaced, and victimized groups expelled from history books. This violent metamorphosis was part of a totalitarian policy to reforge the whole of society, including urban space. Social engineers across Europe planned the future of the Other's city, and legitimized its 'restructuring' and nationalist appropriation.

Deportations of Kurds away from and the settlements of Turks into the eastern provinces formed another vector of population policies. Three major waves of deportations struck the Kurdish population of the east. The first generation of deportees suffered perhaps the most amidst the harsh conditions of the First World War and the seasons. The second cohort, deported right after the establishment of the Republic from 1925 to 1927, did not stay away from their native regions very long and many deportees returned within a year or two. The third deportation was organized after the consolidation of the single-party dictatorship in 1934 and was more sophisticated and categorical. Only when the Young Turks were ousted from power in 1950 were Kurds no longer deported. The deportations displayed a distinct process of evolution from the first to the last phase. Young Turk social engineers accumulated experience and as they muddled through, learnt from their prior mistakes and thus sophisticated and perfected the craft of deportation. The three phases of deportations exhibit an evolving dialectic: ethno-territorial thinking, the promulgation of a law, the implementation of the deportation, the separation of elites from populace, and the monitoring of the 'output' of the deportation back into the process to regulate the 'input', i.e. keeping track of the deportees' experiences to improve the method. The Young Turk regime, as it consolidated its power base, sharpened its tools of population policies and developed a distinct finesse in organizing them. The regime became increasingly agile in fine-tuning the various frequencies of population policies in mutual harmony, and its retrospective evaluations were veritable educational experiences.

The type of education they foresaw for the population of the eastern provinces was markedly different. We have seen what happens when schools are put in the service of a political ideology. The chapter on education detailed the tireless diligence with which Young Turk educators infused their ideology into every aspect of the educational infrastructure, from history to geography, and from literature to gymnastics. The dictatorship's particular understanding of teaching (the cultivation of skills, trades and professions, as well as mental, moral, and aesthetic

---

[1] Mark Mazower, *Salonica: City of Ghosts: Christians, Muslims and Jews 1430–1950* (London: HarperCollins Publishers, 2004), 275–428; Norman Davies and Roger Moorhouse, *Microcosm: Portrait of a Central European City* (London: Cape, 2002); Delphine Bechtel, 'Lemberg/Lwów/Lvov/Lviv: Identities of a "City of Uncertain Boundaries"', in: *Diogenes*, no. 210 (2006), 62–71.

development) sought to do three things: naturalize the nation state and the place of the eastern provinces in it, craft through propaganda new generations loyal to the party, and 'Turkify' the non-Turkish population culturally. To this end, the regime constructed hegemonic canons of culture and language, practising culture beyond which was prohibited and punishable. These canons were embedded in and widely disseminated through the school textbook. Education played a very important part under the Young Turk regime in trying to cultivate a loyal following for the nation, Atatürk, and the Young Turk party. The Young Turk leadership appreciated the difficulty of indoctrinating the older generation and were all the more determined to mould the new generation along Young Turk lines, reasoning that he who controls the youth, controls the future. Thus, the regime hoped that education would create new generations of loyal young men and women by the time they reached adulthood. The schools were to play a critical part in setting this process in motion. Indoctrination and the use of propaganda were to sow the seeds of nationalism in Young Turkey's education system and with the passage of time, educational material more and more came to resemble propaganda. Young Turk education was also gendered, or perhaps even sexist: the idealization of motherhood for girls and martialism for boys was a regular theme, as well as rural life. Girls and boys were taught that they had clear roles in Turkish society: boys would go on to be soldiers and fight for the nation, and it was girls' duty to become mothers and produce the next generation of soldiers. Most importantly, schools were also to achieve the 'Turkification' of children from non-Turkish backgrounds, such as Kurds, Arabs, Circassians, and others, so as to assimilate them into the Turkish nation. Ministry of Education officials repeatedly asserted that education in the east would markedly differ from that in the west. These decisions taken and measures adopted and implemented by the Young Turks constituted a frontal attack on existing forms of culture and education in the eastern region. The multiple assaults on cultural identities were informed by racism and colonial attitudes but masked as a civilizing mission.

Finally, the Young Turk regime, by meting out a new identity for the country, also meted out a new memory for it. From 1913 on, the Young Turk treatment of the past ranged from the organization of oblivion regarding the traumatic past, construction of an official narrative that included heroic and eternalized images of the nation. All throughout the country, but particularly for the eastern provinces, orders were given to write new local histories. These official textbooks, nationalist canons, and city histories not only imposed broad silences on critical historical issues, they also banished all ethnic minorities out of (regional) histories. To vindicate their claim that the eastern provinces had eternally been Turkish, the Young Turks left a formidable imprint of memory in the region. From large cities to small towns, across the geography of the eastern provinces, places bear the names of Young Turk officers, politicians, and myths. The Young Turk era left a troublesome legacy in terms of memory. Although the era itself is over, all its politicians, military officers, and intellectuals mentioned in this book having passed away, their legacy remains problematic, not least for Eastern Turkey. The main political challenges for the Turkish Republic still lie in Eastern Turkey and are symbolized by two seemingly irrelevant strips of frontier: the closed border with the Republic of Armenia, and the severely militarized strip with Iraq, or the Kurdistan Regional Government. Both of these governments represent ethnic groups excluded from the eastern territories in the Young Turk era, Armenians by destruction and Kurds by deportation and persecution. The legacy of the Young Turk era continues to bedevil the relations between these groups.[2]

The relative autonomy of ideas is particularly relevant when studying the effects of the official memory constructed by the Young Turks. The seeds that the Young Turks planted into society had a lasting influence. Although they are no longer in power, their ideas are still very much alive. A system that had been ingrained for generations could not be easily undone by a simple regime change at the top level. The Young Turks created a moral and cultural gaze, firmly anchored in modern Turkish identity, the horizon of which is limited to the Turkish nation state. These are purposefully created spheres of language, geography, and knowledge which function as closed circuits and whose contours are meant to function as cognitive barriers. Current generations of townsmen in Diyarbekir have little or no knowledge of their Armenian compatriots living in Syria because maps present Syria as socially empty space; because it is difficult to get a visa to travel to Syria; because Armenians are enemies; and because travel to Syria is discouraged with the argument that Turkey itself offers plenty of opportunity for tourism. Diyarbekir's youth interested in their region's history have no access to pre-1928 texts in Ottoman Turkish, let alone in any other relevant languages. The libraries in Diyarbekir barely offer anything substantial and realistic that cannot be subsumed under the rubric of memory politics and nationalist narrative left by Young Turk librarians. Therefore, the racial and historical theories of Chapter 5 should not be waved away as typical interwar nationalist myth-making, whose influence waned after the Young Turks lost power. They still stand firm as hegemonic corpora of historical knowledge and narrative produced by the Young Turk regime.

The coherence in these chapters revolves around the ontology of nationalist population policies. It was the paradigm of ethnic majoritarianism that served as a framework for the political legitimacy shaping Young Turk population policies. The logic and laws of those policies followed an ethno-territorial line of thought. There was a mutual dependence between these various forms of population policy: Young Turk social engineers had divided the population of the eastern provinces into elites and populace. Deportation of the elite was one aspect of Young Turk social engineering; it would be complemented by the concurrent policy of assimilation of ordinary people. Genocide and expulsion of undesirable peoples such as Armenians and Syriacs was inherent and implicit in this process of destruction and construction. This co-existence can perhaps be called 'creative destruction': it constitutes inclusion and construction, but it also amounts to destruction and exclusion. Young Turk rule was at once formative and annihilatory.

---

[2] Uğur Ümit Üngör, 'Recalling the Appalling: Mass Violence in Eastern Turkey in the Twentieth Century', in: Nanci Adler, Selma Leydesdorff and Leyla Neyzi (eds.), *Memories of Mass Repression* (Piscataway, NJ: Transaction, 2008), 175–98.

The systematic sorting of peoples, based on qualitative as well as quantitative criteria, was one of the cornerstones of these policies of measuring the value of human lives in terms of ethnicity. When it came to the 'restructuring' of the eastern provinces, racism and modernization were not conflicting processes but complementary ones. Modernization of the state's technological and administrative infrastructure ensured that population policies could be conducted on a larger scale and more systematically than ever before. The deportees were dispatched westward on foot during the First World War, but by train in the interbellum period. As ideology merged with modern scientific rationalism, a series of vague and improvised schemes developed into concrete programmes. These policies accompanied bureaucratic professionalization, a key prerequisite for the organization of the population policies. Modern were its methods, such as the division of labour, the cataloguing, marginalizing, dispossessing, isolating, and compartmentalizing of victims. But no less modern were the ideologies invoked by Young Turk social engineers to justify their beliefs of fundamentally changing the social and ethnic composition of the eastern provinces. This included the ethnic segmentation and hierarchization of eastern society, the nationalist moral universe, and the tabula rasa scenario of the eastern provinces—all of which excited the imagination of territorial planners and social engineers. For the Young Turks, population policies, violent or not, were a quest for a respectable, 'scientific' (thus legitimate) persecution of minorities. Herein lies the major distinction between persecution and social engineering—disorganized versus organized violence. Persecution appeared not as a clear evil but rather as the shadow of virtue. Just as there was no contradiction between modernization and ethnic nationalism, there was no ambiguity in the co-existence of civilization and barbarism. As civilized life continued and flourished in the pacified streets of Ankara, hermetic compartments of mass killing were constructed in the valleys and plateaus of Diyarbekir.[3]

The paradox lies elsewhere, namely in the relationship between the systematization of population policies and the relatively weak output resulting from them. The policies the Young Turks launched with great fervour were less successful than they had hoped them to be. How can these apparently paradoxical developments be reconciled? In other words, how effective were these forms of population policies? Armenian and Kurdish nationalists hasten to explain the dichotomy as a function of stubborn resistance by brave men and women defending their ethnicity or homeland. But more plausible possible explanations need to be sought elsewhere. However, fully measuring the effectiveness of any policy is not only difficult, but

---

[3] For discussions of this dialectic of civilization and barbarism see: Norbert Elias, *Studien über die Deutschen: Machtkämpfe und Habitusentwicklung im 19. und 20. Jahrhundert* (Frankfurt am Main: Suhrkamp, 1989), 391–516; Bernard Wasserstein, *Barbarism and Civilization: A History of Europe in Our Time* (Oxford: Oxford University Press, 2007), 793; Robert van Krieken, 'The Barbarism of Civilization: Cultural Genocide and the "Stolen Generations"', in: *British Journal of Sociology* 50, no. 2 (1999), 297–316; Abram de Swaan, 'Dyscivilization, Mass Extermination and the State', in: *Theory, Culture and Society* 18, no. 2–3 (2001), 265–76; Peter Imbusch, *Moderne und Gewalt: zivilisationstheoretische Perspektiven auf das 20. Jahrhundert* (Wiesbaden: Verlag für Sozialwissenschaften, 2005); Frank Bajohr (ed.), *Zivilisation und Barbarei: die widersprüchlichen Potentiale der Moderne: Detlev Peukert zum Gedenken* (Hamburg: Christians, 1991).

is also beyond the scope of this book, for it would require in-depth research on the post-Young Turk era. Therefore, the following comments are meant to be indicative rather than authoritative.

First of all, severely coercive policies launched by a political elite on a society can hardly be measured statically as absolute 'successes' versus 'failures'. A more 'process' approach posits that the homogenizing processes launched by the Young Turk regime faced other processes that resisted and counterbalanced the homogenizing forces, much like kinetic friction or musical counterpoints. A concise answer to this question would be that the policies did not deliver the immediate results the organizers had hoped for, and when they did so, partially produced long-term concomitant processes either aggravating the initial problems or counterbalancing them. The destruction of the Armenians, for example, was pursued as a definitive 'solution' to the Armenian 'question', but years later reemerged as a new Armenian question still frustrating Turkish politics. The deportations of Kurds and settlements of Turks did not 'Turkify' the Diyarbekir region, since many Kurds moved back and many Turks moved away when the regime was voted out of office. The effectiveness of the policies of cultural and educational 'Turkification' hardly affected the population either: the city already spoke Turkish and conservative peasants and nomadic pastoralists in the countryside cared little for modern education. Finally, the politics of memory faced the same consequences as it continued to co-exist for years with the local oral tradition, and lately has come under pressure. All in all, the effectiveness of Young Turk population policies is debatable at best.

Four important processes need to be taken into account when considering the question of effectiveness: the nature of the Young Turk dictatorship, the unrealistic goals formulated by the regime, the resilience of peasant societies, and the counter-productivity of violence.

First of all, the Young Turk dictatorship was no monolithic moloch in perfect inner harmony. There was considerable rivalry and intrigue within the dictatorship, most notably between the army and the Interior Ministry. Bureaucrats at all levels competed to satisfy their superiors (including Talaat and Atatürk), and to draw attention to their solutions to the lingering ethnic 'questions' of the eastern provinces. In addition to rivalry, method and ideology was contested at times. Considerable dissent between political hawks and ethnic philanthropists bickering over whether integrally to deport or forcibly to assimilate the victims interrupted or retarded more efficient implementation. Although the regime appeared to have organized the population into a disciplinary unity and could ostensibly mobilize its resources to achieve goals swiftly, unacknowledged political conflicts beneath the surface and repression of public debate had heavy costs, with some achievements such as nation formation more a matter of propaganda than effectiveness. Due to these processes, at the very root, the stage of policy formulation and implementation, a degree of inefficacy existed.

The problem of inefficiency touches upon the closely related issue of totalitarianism. In this book, the use of the term 'totalitarian' in characterizing the regime and its policies has been a deliberate and conscious choice. Although this is not the place to discuss at length how models of totalitarianism apply to the Young Turk regime (a major controversy in Turkish history), a caveat is in order. Totalitarian dictatorships can be defined by domination by a single, like-minded governing elite of all (or virtually all) organized political, economic, social and cultural activities in a country. There are five prime pillars of totalitarianism: first, an official ideology of exclusive and comprehensive claim based upon radical rejection of some aspects of the past and chiliastic claims for the future; second, a centralized, unitary movement claiming classless equality but organized hierarchically as a single, monopolistic party under authoritarian leadership; third, the co-optation, suppression, or often destruction of opposition, the suppression not only of all forms of dissent but also of plurality of thought and opinion in general, including independent private organizations (such as religious orders); fourth, control of the means of communication and the mass media and their use for disseminating propaganda to inculcate the principles of the official ideology; and finally, the bureaucratic direction, via state control or socialization, of the economy and social relations. Totalitarianism constitutes an assault on the 'public sphere', and it is here that totalitarian states differ from traditional dictatorships: they build hegemony with respect to the broader ('total') scope of human behaviour.[4] All five of these facets apply to the Young Turk regime in various ways, but it is the realm of power relations that bears relevance for gauging the effectiveness of Young Turk population policies.

As Hannah Arendt pointed out in *The Origins of Totalitarianism*, in totalitarian dictatorships efficiency is so subordinated to control that the state often spends 50 percent to 75 percent of its resources and energies enforcing control of one sort or another on its citizens.[5] Studies of Stalinist totalitarianism expose that

> no aspect of human life remained outside the presumed competence of the authorities, no autonomous organizations were allowed to exist, and fear governed the life of all, from the lowliest peasant to members of the Politburo. But of course that did not mean that this political system functioned like a well-oiled machine, that one man alone, namely Stalin, made all the decisions. On the contrary: totalitarian societies are never efficient. In this totalitarian society, properly constituted institutions were emasculated, and decisions were made in a haphazard fashion . . . It is a mistake to think that totalitarianism implies efficiency, that in such a system all orders are carried out as intended. In fact, the world has never known an efficient totalitarian regime.[6]

In Turkey, too, control did not mean that the apparatus functioned well. The Young Turk regime between 1913 and 1950 faced an underdeveloped country with a poorly functioning governmental machinery and, despite having filled its ranks with loyal Young Turks, an ill-educated, venal bureaucracy lacking in public spirit. The country had no well-developed communication and transportation systems (key for efficient control), which only increased local power and bred

    [4] Karl D. Bracher, 'Totalitarianism', in: Philip P. Wiener (ed.), *Dictionary of the History of Ideas* (New York: Charles Scribner's Sons, 1973–4), vol. 4, 406–11.
    [5] Hannah Arendt, *The Origins of Totalitarianism* (London: Harcourt Brace, 1973), 419.
    [6] Peter Kenez, *A History of the Soviet Union from the Beginning to the End* (Cambridge: Cambridge University Press, 2006), 110, 174.

confusion. True total control over society was only utopian, but this did not mean the regime was not totalitarian. In other words, rather than a social reality, totalitarianism is a political ambition by a dictatorial elite and has to be analysed as such.

Still, opinions on the nature of the Young Turk regime differ radically. Popular myths uphold the metahistorical idea that Atatürk established democracy in Turkey, and that the post-war Young Turk regime was a modern parliamentarian democracy. But some scholars reject the comparison between the Young Turk regime and interwar European fascism and totalitarianism.[7] Zürcher, on the other hand, writes that the Young Turk party had 'totalitarian tendencies', and continues to argue that what made it totalitarian was 'the extreme nationalism, with its attendant development of a legitimizing historical mythology and racist rhetoric, the authoritarian character of the regime and its efforts to establish a complete totalitarian monopoly for its party of the political, social and cultural scene, the personality cult that developed around . . . Atatürk and İnönü . . . and the emphasis on national unity and solidarity with its attendant denial of class conflicts'.[8] To this might be added the violent treatment of ethnic minorities. Despite these pointed insights, the field still lacks sophisticated, nuanced, and comparative studies of the nature of the Young Turk regime.

This book has attempted to take the debate a step further. Considering the Young Turk regime's monist urge to gain mastery over social processes and human destinies, its ambition to monopolize power at the centre, destroy or silence opposition, commit mass violence against its own citizens, develop a radical ideology and a personality cult around a single leader, and extinguish non-Turkish cultural life in the public sphere of the eastern provinces, the regime perhaps may be classified as a nationalist, colonial, totalitarian, and violent dictatorship. The local approach may provide a tentative solution for the effectiveness paradox. According to one sociological study, occupational and colonial regimes can only be efficient when they enjoy local support from indigenous collaborators.[9] Chapter 2 has argued that the local Ottoman Muslim elite of Diyarbekir collaborated with the Young Turk regime in return for power, significantly expediting and amplifying the destruction process. This may explain why the Armenian genocide was, in the words of one expert, a 'completely successful genocide in its own nationalist terms',[10] but the anti-Kurdish campaigns were not as effective, for by that time the local elites were themselves targeted by the regime.

A second obstacle that hindered the effectiveness of Young Turk population policies was their unrealistic expectations and goals. The Young Turks' sociological imagination of what identity was played an important role in this process. The

[7] Zafer Toprak, 'Bir Hayal Ürünü: "İttihatçıların Türkleştirme Politikası"', in: *Toplumsal Tarih* 146 (2006), 14–22; Interview with Zafer Toprak, *Taraf*, 10 November 2008.

[8] Erik-Jan Zürcher, *Turkey: A Modern History* (London: I.B. Tauris, 2004), 186.

[9] Cornelis J. Lammers, *Vreemde Overheersing: Bezetten en Bezetting in Sociologisch Perspectief* (Amsterdam: Bakker, 2005).

[10] Donald Bloxham, *The Great Game of Genocide: Imperialism, Nationalism, and the Destruction of the Ottoman Armenians* (Oxford: Oxford University Press, 2005), 110.

Young Turks saw social identity as an axis of two diametrically opposed poles, with 'Kurdishness' at one extreme, and 'Turkishness' at the other. Cultural change along this axis was seen as zero-sum game: the more one became Kurdish, the less one would become Turkish. Their understanding of sociology was of such a nature they did not grasp that the identity always involves criteria of sameness and difference, and most of all is a process of perennial change. But in order to construct a monolithic Turkish identity that would exhibit characteristics of pure sameness, they considered the annihilation of those perceived differences necessary for the sustenance of the sameness.[11] One scholar summarized this fallacy as follows:

> The myth of inevitable conformity suggests that the outward spread of cultural influences from the center will make communities on the periphery less like their former selves—indeed, will dissipate their distinctive cultures—and will turn them, instead, into small-scale versions of the center itself. These culturally imperialistic influences will move outwards along the tracks of the mass media, of mass information, of spreading infrastructure, of mass production, national marketing and consumerism, ushering in a monolithic urban culture which will transform behaviour . . . that people can have their culture stripped away, leaving them quite void, then to be refilled by some imported superculture . . . in other words, that people are somehow passive in relation to culture: they receive it, transmit it, express it, but do not create it.[12]

By locating an essentialized conception of culture at the core of Turkish identity, the regime contributed to an essentialization, reification, and politicization of culture. But social identity is rather a variational process of multiple, co-existing layers and frames which people invoke whenever useful and necessary.[13] Therefore it was no surprise that imposing a Turkish national identity on Kurdish tribesmen and villagers overnight was not realistic for myriad reasons, most prominently because such a process only smeared a layer of unlikely identifications on existing identifications, or more precisely, provided the villagers with a relatively weak identity frame to draw from. So the new Turkish identifications were only used when travelling to the city and dealing with the state's administrative organs or to western Turkey and communicating with non-Kurds. Turning peasants into Frenchmen may have been easier than turning Kurds into Turks.

One important corollary that arises from this is a third reason for inefficacy, the relative resilience of peasant societies, especially pastoralist highlanders.[14] Peasant societies may be vulnerable, but kinship ties are relatively obdurate. For national identifications to trump regional ones in peasant societies requires an immense process of symbolization, and several generations to pass. In the words of one

[11] Alexander L. Hinton, 'The Dark Side of Modernity: Toward an Anthropology of Genocide', in: Alexander L. Hinton (ed.), *Annihilating Difference: The Anthropology of Genocide* (Berkeley: University of California Press, 2002), 1–40, at 12.

[12] Anthony P. Cohen, *The Symbolic Construction of Community* (London: Tavistock, 1985), 36.

[13] Richard Jenkins, *Social Identity* (London: Routledge, 2008), 95–107, 111–20.

[14] On the resistance of mountain regions to 'the establishment of the state' and 'dominant languages', see: Fernand Braudel, *The Mediterranean and the Mediterranean World in the Age of Philip II* (New York: Harper & Row, 1976), vol. I, 38–41.

scholar, 'The corollary idea is that peasants become national citizens only when they abandon their identity as peasants: a local sense of place and a local identity centered on the village or valley must be superseded and replaced by a sense of belonging to a more extended territory or nation'.[15] An indicator of the resilience of the rural nature of Turkish society is the number of regional associations, organizations based on the locale—often a city, provincial town, or village. According to a study of these associations conducted in Istanbul in 1989, of all seven regions of Turkey, the eastern and south-eastern regions far outweighed the other ones in the number of regional associations.[16] One scholar who studied the lives of these 'urban villagers' added,

> The village is a paramount feature in the lives of these migrants and has proved to be an organizing principle of behavior. A close sense of identity with the village of origin and its inhabitants is a pervasive element among most migrants. Concordantly, certain associated forces that are stabilizing in effect operate the lives of these peasants. These stabilizing forces flow from village social life and interaction, and reciprocally, enhance village solidarity even in an urban center some 900 miles away.[17]

These local identifications remain significant for the easterners even in diasporas. One can meet Diyarbekir Armenians in Amsterdam, Diyarbekir Kurds in Stockholm, Diyarbekir Syriacs in Hanover, and Diyarbekir Bulgaro-Turks in Paris. When interviewed, ethnicity or religion mattered for some of them, Turkish citizenship mattered for none, but the locale mattered for all. Their offspring, however, are going through a different process. From the 1960s on, the long-term effects of comprehensive waves of urbanization and migration coupled with the emergence of new interacting generations accomplished more in the field of nation formation than Young Turk coercion ever did.[18] The relative resilience of ethno-familial ties in peasant societies seems to have caused a considerable setback in the efficacy of Young Turk social engineering.

Perhaps the most salient dimension of resistance, failure, and friction is the inevitable counter-productivity of mass violence. By launching these types of severely coercive policies the Young Turks exposed to the population their ideological motives for pursuing those policies, causing a serious backlash by many among the persecuted and victimized peoples who were traumatized by them. The

---

[15] Peter Sahlins, *Boundaries: The Making of France and Spain in the Pyrenees* (Berkeley: University of California Press, 1989), 8.

[16] Harald Schüler, *Türkiye'de Sosyal Demokrasi: Particilik, Hemşehrilik, Alevilik* (Istanbul: İletişim, 1999), 210. There are good reasons to presume that this number has grown considerably after the civil war of the 1990s emptied the eastern countryside and sent millions of villagers to the western metropoles. TESEV, *Overcoming a Legacy of Mistrust: Towards Reconciliation between the State and the Displaced* (Istanbul: Turkish Economic and Social Studies Foundation, 2006), 26–7.

[17] Peter Suzuki, 'Peasants Without Plows: Some Anatolians in Istanbul', in: *Rural Sociology* 31, no. 4 (1966), 428–38, at 432; Günter Seufert, 'Between Religion and Ethnicity: A Kurdish-Alevi Tribe in Globalizing Istanbul', in: Ayşe Öncü and Petra Weyland (eds.), *Space, Culture and Power: New Identities in Globalizing Cities* (London: Zed, 1997), 157–76.

[18] For a discussion of these processes see: Arjun Appadurai, *Modernity at Large: Cultural Dimensions of Globalization* (Minneapolis: University of Minnesota Press, 1997), chapter 9, 'The Production of Locality', 178–99.

memories of the mass violence were unresolved, not dealt with, and unsettled. One scholar noted that the most important Ottoman legacy relates to issues stemming from requited and unrequited nationalism: 'Armenian nationalism, Kurdish nationalism were thwarted... Memories of bloody engagements with the Ottoman Turks, and cries of genocide, coupled with feelings of inadequacy that accompany the failure to achieve nationhood, poisoned and continue to poison the relationships between Armenians and Turks, and Kurds and Turks'.[19] The Young Turks saw an east where a Turkish majority needed to be established by force. But by treating the territory as if it was on the verge of secession (as Greece, Bulgaria, Montenegro, Macedonia, or Albania had been), the Young Turks significantly contributed to the production of a nationalist politicization of the Kurdish-inhabited territories.

It took a few decades for the revenge of the past to erupt. The backfiring of Armenian and Kurdish traumas was a process that developed as new generations were confronted by and discovered their bloody pasts and responded to them, ranging from internal discussions to non-violent protests, and later into political violence. On 20 January 1975, a group of Lebanese Armenians founded the Armenian Secret Army for the Liberation of Armenia (ASALA) in Beirut. The ASALA began carrying out assassinations of Turkish diplomats around the world. Three years later, on 27 October 1978, the Kurdistan Worker's Party (PKK) was founded by a group of Kurdish students and activists. In its initial phase, the PKK also began assassinating Turkish state officials and Kurdish 'collaborators' in the east. For the Turkish authorities, these acts of violence were perceived as sudden outbreaks from a clear blue sky. But they were not: Armenian and Kurdish-nationalist political violence was a desperate attempt to make their political cases and historical grievances heard to the international audience. It did not take long for the two organizations to find each other, united in combating their common enemy, launching coordinated attacks on Turkish consulates. Although there were clear differences between the two organizations, one pivotal theme united them, besides leftist ideology and territorial claims on the eastern provinces: their allegations of violence suffered by their peoples under the Young Turk regime.[20] ASALA's spearhead was its demand for genocide recognition, and the PKK too accused the Turkish state of genocide against the Kurds. These traumas continue to linger, as Turkish governments have persistently tried to deflect responsibility for discussing and coming to terms with this difficult past. This knot of inextricable traumatic memories remains tightly tied.

Ultimately, when it came to the state's policies and the population's responses, the types of population policies recounted in this book to a large extent failed, not because they were Turkish but primarily because they were of a violent nature. The

---

[19] Norman Itzkowitz, 'The Problem of Perceptions', in: L. Carl Brown (ed.), *Imperial Legacy: The Ottoman Imprint on the Balkans and the Middle East* (New York: Columbia University Press, 1997), 30–8, at 35–6.

[20] Khachig Tölölyan, 'Terrorism in Modern Armenian Political Culture', in: *Terrorism and Political Violence* 4, no. 2 (1992), 8–22; Nur Bilge Criss, 'The Nature of PKK Terrorism in Turkey', in: *Studies in Conflict and Terrorism* 18, no. 1 (1995), 17–38.

population of the eastern provinces resisted, not because it differed ethnically, but primarily because it was a peasant society with a strong sense of ethnicity and kinship ties.

This book has set out to develop the theoretical argument that homogenization in the nascent European nation-state system was an unintended but directional process (a blind process), but as it spread out into the rest of the world, it became intended and directional, imposed and organized by political elites seeking to build nation states. These political elites that emerged, first from the ashes of the great multi-ethnic dynastic land empires and later during the process of European decolonization, saw the nation state as a template, the protector of their own culture, the opponent of cultural imperialism, and the basis of collective self-reliance. Although throughout time this theory has proven reliable and true, it overlooks the effectiveness aspect of nation formation. In building the nation state, nationalist elites' designs were often confronted with ethnic realities on the ground. Ethnic groups, with or without organized nationalist leadership, often contested the nation state's rule over their people and territory. In some nation states, these disputes were mediated and the claims of minorities accommodated; in others, a combination of government intransigence and minority resistance escalated political disputes into violent conflicts.[21] In the latter cases, the nation formation process failed. The theory of the expanding nation-state system, therefore, needs to take into account the reality that the expansion process functions under two restrictions: popular consent, and the infeasibility of absolute homogeneity.

Homogenizing forces remain an important feature of societies where nation formation has been problematic and painful. One important question remains unanswered: given these restrictions, why do political elites launch policies to increase homogeneity in their societies? Surely, there can never be such a thing as objective homogeneity, not even in cultural or ethnic terms, no matter how much nationalist elites would wish it so?[22] For this reason, it might be more fruitful to conceptualize this problem in terms of homogenizing processes versus dehomogenizing processes. At the dawn of the twenty-first century, there is an axis of tension between these two types of processes. In Europe, the interwar ideal of a pure homogeneous nation state has given way to principles of consociationalism and co-existence of regional cultures. Processes of heterogenization also seem to be pioneered in Europe: whereas the once persecuted Hungarian minority in Slovakia now enjoys its own schools and media, the Muslim minority in Western India still lives under threats of violent persecution. Now, as the European Union presses for educational reform and instruction in autochthonous languages and cultures in Turkey and elsewhere, the topic is now more current than ever.[23]

---

[21] Donald L. Horowitz, *Ethnic Groups in Conflict* (Berkeley, CA: University of California Press, 2000), ch. 6.

[22] Walker Connor, 'Illusions of Homogeneity: Myths of Hemispheric, Continental, Regional, and State Unity', in: id., *Ethnonationalism: The Quest for Understanding* (Princeton: Princeton University Press, 1993), 118–43.

[23] European Parliament, Resolution 1519, 28th Sitting (4 October 2006), 'The Cultural Situation of the Kurds.'

Genocide, deportations, and forced migration destroyed historical regions and emptied multi-cultural cities, clearing the way for modern nation states. The mass murder and displacement of elites uprooted traditions and precluded alternative futures. The transformations in the societies affected by this whirlwind of population policies was of an ontological character. Countries such as Turkey, Greece, or Syria were profoundly shaped by phenomena such as forced migration. The elites organizing these processes did not work with a limited set of assumptions but a broad-brush model of human societies gravitating around the concept of the blank slate, the notion that society is fully malleable through the conditioning or crafting of its individuals. But as one researcher has pointed out, 'the Blank Slate had, and has, a dark side. The vacuum that it posited in human nature was eagerly filled by totalitarian regimes, and it did nothing to prevent their genocides. It perverts education, childrearing, and the arts into forms of social engineering . . . It is an anti-life, anti-human theoretical abstraction'.[24] Authoritarian and violent social engineering seems to be a self-defeating, perhaps self-destructive process launched by political elites that use violence as a routine technique of statecraft. These elites underestimate the fact that the consequences of mass violence are irreversible, especially if no concentrated effort at developing forms of justice are employed.

---

[24] Steven Pinker, *The Blank Slate: The Modern Denial of Human Nature* (London: Allen Lane, 2002), 421.

Bibliography

PRIMARY SOURCES

Archives

American Board of Commissioners for Foreign Missions, Houghton Library, Harvard University, Cambridge, MA

ABC 16.7: Mission to the Armenians
ABC 16.8: Syrian, Assyrian, and Nestorian missions
ABC 16.9: Mission to Turkey
ABC 16.10: Near East Mission: archives from mission stations
ABC 76: Personal papers
ABC 78: Picture collection

Başbakanlık Osmanlı Arşivi, Ottoman Archives, Istanbul

Dahiliye Nezâreti

- Emniyet-i Umumiye Müdüriyeti (DH.EUM)
- Hukuk Müşavirliği Kalemi (DH.HMŞ)
- Kalem-i Mahsûs Müdüriyeti (DH.KMS)
- Mebânî-i Emîriye ve Hapishâneler Müdüriyet-i (DH.MB.HPS)
- Muhaberât-ı Umumiye İdaresi (DH.MUİ)
- İdarî Kısım (DH.İD)
- İdâre-i Umumiye (DH.İUM)
- Siyasî Kısım (DH.SYS)
- Şifre Kalemi (DH.ŞFR)
- Dosya Usulü İrade Tasnif (DUİT)

Hariciye Nezareti

- Hukuk Müşavirliği İstişare Odası (HR.HMŞ.İSO)
- Hariciye Siyasi Fon (HR.SYS)

Bab-ı Alî Evrak Odası

- Hariciye Müteferrikası

Meclis-i Vükelâ Mazbataları

Başbakanlık Cumhuriyet Arşivi, Republican Archives, Ankara

030.01	Başbakanlık Özel Kalem Müdürlüğü Evrakı Kataloğu
030.10	Başbakanlık Muamelât Genel Müdürlüğü Evrakı Kataloğu
030.11	Müşterek Kararnameler Kataloğu
030.18	Bakanlar Kurulu Kararları Kataloğu
030.18	Bakanlar Kurulu Karar Ekleri
230	Bayındırlık Bakanlığı Kataloğu
272.1	Toprak İskân Genel Müdürlüğü Kataloğu

490.01   Cumhuriyet Halk Partisi Evrakı Kataloğu
130.16.13.02   Muhtelit Mübadele Komisyonu Tasfiye Talepnameleri Kataloğu

Gertrude Bell papers, Robinson Library, University of Newcastle

Letters
Diaries
Photographs

Hikmet Kıvılcımlı papers, International Institute for Social History, Amsterdam.

Inventory no.56: Manuscripts

Jacques Rhétoré papers, Bibliothèque du Saulchoir, Paris

Manuscripts

Ministry of the Interior Archive, Ankara

Personnel file of Şükrü Kaya
    National Archives, United States National Archives, Washington
Record group 59 (State Department)

National Library, Ankara

Manuscripts section
Maps section

Politisches Archiv Auswärtiges Amt, German National Archives, Berlin

Record group R14078–R14106
Botschaft Konstantinopel, files 168–174

National Archives United Kingdom, Kew, London

Foreign Office files FO 371 and 424

Sıdıka Avar papers (unpublished and uncatalogued, in author's private collection)

Unpublished manuscripts
Photographs

Turkish Grand National Assembly Library, Ankara

Republican People's Party collection

PUBLISHED PRIMARY SOURCES

Akçam, Taner and Vahakn N. Dadrian (eds.), *Tehcir ve Taktil Divan-ı Harb-i Örfi Zabıtları: İttihad ve Terakki'nin Yargılanması 1919–1922* (Istanbul: İstanbul Bilgi Üniversitesi Yayınları, 2008).
Armenians in Ottoman documents (1915–1920) (Ankara: Turkish Republic Prime Ministry General Directorate of the State Archives, Directorate of Ottoman Archives, 1995).

Arsan, Nimet (ed.), *Atatürk'ün Söylev ve Demeçleri* (Ankara: Türk Tarih Kurumu, 1959–64).

Arşiv Belgelerine Göre Kafkaslar'da ve Anadolu'da Ermeni Mezâlimi (Ankara: Devlet Arşivleri Genel Müdürlüğü Yayınları, 1995), 4 volumes.

Aşiretler Raporu (İstanbul: Kaynak, 2003).

Atatürkçülük (Birinci Kitap) Atatürk'ün Görüş ve Direktifleri (İstanbul: Milli Eğitim Basımevi, 1988).

Atatürk'ün Söylev ve Demeçleri (İstanbul: Türk İnkılâp Tarihi Enstitüsü Yayınları, 1945).

Atatürk'ün Bütün Eserleri (İstanbul: Kaynak, 1998–2009), 15 volumes.

Barton, James (ed.), *Statements of American Missionaries on the Destruction of Christian Communities in Ottoman Turkey, 1915–1917* (Ann Arbor, MI: Gomidas Institute, 1998).

Başvekalet Toprak ve İskan İşleri Genel Müdürlüğü Çalışmaları (Ankara: n.p., 1955).

Bayrak, Mehmet (ed.), *Kürtler ve Ulusal-Demokratik Mücadeleleri: Gizli Belgeler-Araştırmalar-Notlar* (Ankara: Özge, 1993).

—— (ed.), *Açık-Gizli/Resmi-Gayriresmi Kürdoloji Belgeleri* (İstanbul: Öz-Ge, 1994).

Beylerian, Arthur (ed.), *Les grandes puissances, l'empire ottoman et les arméniens dans les archives françaises (1914–1918): recueil de documents* (Paris: Université de Paris I, Panthéon-Sorbonne, 1983).

Blair, Susan K. (ed.), *The Slaughterhouse Province: An American Diplomat's Report on the Armenian Genocide, 1915–1917* (New Rochelle, NY: Caratzas, 1989).

Blue Book Turkey, No.8 (1896).

Bozarslan, Mehmed E. (ed.), *Kürd Teavün ve Terakki Gazetesi: Kovara Kurdî-Tirkî 1908–1909* (Uppsala: Deng, 1998).

C.H.P. Halkevleri Talimatnamesi (Ankara: Hâkimiyeti Milliye Matbaası, 1932).

Ciliciae Armenorum seu Mardinen: Beatificationis seu Canonizationis servi Dei Ignatii Choukrallah Maloyan, archiepiscopi mardinensis in opium fidei, uti fertur, interfecti (1915): Positio super vita, martyrio et fama martyrii (Rome: Tipografia Guerra, 2000).

Cumhurbaşkanları, Başbakanlar ve Millî Eğitim Bakanlarının Millî Eğitimle İlgili Söylev ve Demeçleri (Ankara: Türk Devrim Tarihi Enstitüsü, 1946).

Cumhuriyet Halk Partisi Halkevleri ve Halkodaları (Ankara: Ulus, 1945).

Dağlı, Nuran and Belma Aktürk (eds.) *Hükümetler ve Programları, vol. I, 1920–1960* (Ankara: TBMM Basımevi, 1988).

Der Grosse Weltatlas: Bearbeitet und mit der Hand gestochen in der kartographischen Anstalt des Bibliographischen Instituts, mit Bemerkungen zu den Karten von Dr. Edgar Lehmann und einem Register mit etwa 80.000 Namen. 6., vermehrte und verbesserte Auflage. (Leipzig: Bibliographisches Institut AG, 1939).

Die Ziele und Taten armenischer Revolutionäre—The Armenian Aspirations and Revolutionary Movements—Aspirations et mouvements révolutionaires arméniens—Ermeni Âmâl ve Harekât-ı İhtilâliyesi, Tesâvir ve Vesâik (İstanbul: Matbaa-ı Amire, 1332).

Diyarbakır İl Yıllığı (Ankara: Türkiye Cumhuriyeti İçişleri Bakanlığı Diyarbakır Valiliği, 1973).

Documents on Ottoman Armenians (Ankara: Prime Ministry, Directorate General of Press and Information, 1982–6).

Düstur (1923–50).

Épisodes des massacres arméniens de Diarbekir: Faits et Documents (Constantinople: Kéchichian Fr., 1920).

Ergüven, Ekrem (ed.), *Şükrü Kaya: Sözleri—Yazıları 1927–1937* (İstanbul: Cumhuriyet Matbaası, 1937).

European Parliament Resolution 1519, 'The Cultural Situation of the Kurds', 28th Sitting (4 October 2006).

Genelkurmay Belgelerinde Kürt İsyanları (İstanbul: Kaynak, 1992).

Germany, Turkey and Armenia: A Selection of Documentary Evidence Relating to the Armenian Atrocities from German and Other Sources (London: Keliher, 1917).

Gooch, George P. and Harold W. V. Temperley (eds.), *British Documents on the Origins of the War 1898–1914* (London: Printed and published by His Majesty's Stationery Office, 1926–38), 11 volumes.

Gust, Wolfgang (ed.), *Der Völkermord an den Armeniern 1915/16: Dokumente aus dem Politischen Archiv des deutschen Auswärtigen Amts* (Hamburg: Zu Klampen, 2005).

Hanioğlu, M. Şükrü (ed.), *Kendi Mektuplarında Enver Paşa* (Istanbul: Der, 1989).

Impagliazzo, Marco (ed.) (2000), *Una finestra sul massacro: Documenti inediti sulla strage degli armeni (1915–1916)* (Milano: Guerini, 2000).

İskân Tarihçesi (Istanbul: Hamit Matbaası, 1932).

Kaiser, Hilmar (ed.), *Eberhard Count Wolffskeel Von Reichenberg, Zeitoun, Mousa Dagh, Ourfa: Letters on the Armenian Genocide* (London: Gomidas Institute, 2004).

La Verité sur le mouvement révolutionnaire arménien et les mesures gouvernementales (Istanbul: Imprimerie Tanine, 1916).

Madajczyk, Czesław (ed.), *Vom Generalplan Ost zum Generalsiedlungsplan: Dokumente* (München: Saur, 1994).

Meclis-i Ayan Zabıt Ceridesi (1908–18).

Meclis-i Mebusan Zabıt Ceridesi (1908–18).

Mesut, Ahmet (ed.), *İngiliz Belgelerinde Kürdistan 1918–1958* (Istanbul: Doz, 1992).

Milli Eğitimle İlgili Kanunlar (Ankara: Milli Eğitim Basımevi, 1953).

Noel, Edward W.C., *Diary of Major E. Noel on Special Duty in Kurdistan* (Basra: n.p., 1919).

Ohandjanian, Artem (ed.), *Österreich-Armenien, 1872–1936: Faksimilesammlung Diplomatischer Aktenstücke* (Wenen: Ohandjanian Verlag, 1995), 12 volumes.

Orta Okul Proğramı (Ankara: Türkiye Cumhuriyeti Milli Eğitim Basımevi, 1949).

Ortamektep İçin Tarih (Istanbul: Devlet Basımevi, 1936).

Osmanlı Belgelerinde Ermeniler (1915–1920) (Ankara: T.C. Başbakanlık Devlet Arşivleri Genel Müdürlüğü, 1994).

Patriarch Rahmani, *Les dégâts causés à la nation syrienne: présenté devant la conférence de la paix* (Paris: n.p., 1919).

Public Instruction in the Republic of Turkey (Ankara: Press Department of the Ministry of the Interior, 1936).

Said Halim ve Mehmed Talât Paşalar kabinelerinin Divan-ı Âli'ye sevkleri hakkında Divaniye mebusu Fuad Bey merhum tarafından verilen takrir üzerine berây-ı tahkikat kur'a isâbet eden Beşinci Şube tarafından icrâ olunan tahkikat ve zabt edilen ifâdatı muhtevidir (Istanbul: n.p., 1918).

Sarafian, Ara (ed.), *The Treatment of Armenians in the Ottoman Empire 1915–16: Documents Presented to Viscount Grey of Fallodon by Viscount Bryce* (London: Gomidas Institute, 2005).

—— (ed.), *United States Diplomacy on the Bosphorus: The Diaries of Ambassador Morgenthau, 1913–1916* (London: Gomidas Institute, 2004).

—— (ed.), *United States Official Records on the Armenian Genocide 1915–1917* (London: Gomidas Institute, 2004).

—— (ed.), *British Parliamentary Debates on the Armenian Genocide 1915–1918* (London: Gomidas Institute, 2003).

——, 'The Disasters of Mardin during the Persecutions of the Christians, Especially the Armenians, 1915', in: *Haigazian Armenological Review* 18 (1998).

Sökmensüer, Şükrü, *Umumî Müffetişler Konferansı'nda Görüşülen ve Dahiliye Vekâleti'ni İlgilendiren İşlere Dair Toplantı Zabıtları ile Rapor ve Hülâsası* (Ankara: Başvekâlet Matbaası, 1936).

Şimşir, Bilâl N. (ed.), *İngiliz belgeleriyle Türkiye'de 'Kürt sorunu' (1924–1938): Şeyh Sait, Ağrı, ve Dersim ayaklanmaları* (Ankara: Türk Tarih Kurumu, 1991).

Tarih IV: Türkiye Cumhuriyeti (Istanbul: Devlet Basımevi, 1931).

Tarihi Muhakeme (Istanbul: Kitaphane-i Sûdî, 1919).

Toynbee, Arnold (ed.), *The Treatment of Armenians in the Ottoman Empire 1915–16: Documents Presented to Viscount Grey of Fallodon, Secretary of State for Foreign Affairs* (London: Hodder and Stoughton, 1916).

Treaty of Peace with Turkey: signed at Sèvres, August 10, 1920 (London: His Majesty's Stationery Office, 1920).

Türk Ocakları 1929 Senesi Kurultayı Zabıtları (Ankara: n.p., 1930).

Türk Ocakları 1928 Senesi Kurultayı Zabıtları (Ankara: Türk Ocakları Matbaası, 1929).

Türk Ocakları 1927 Senesi Kurultayı Zabıtları (Ankara: n.p., 1928).

Türk Ocakları Üçüncü Kurultayı Zabıtları (Istanbul: Kader, 1927).

Türkiye Büyük Millet Meclisi Zabıt Ceridesi (1919–50).

Yeghiayan, Vartkes (ed.), *British Foreign Office Dossiers on Turkish War Criminals* (Pasadena, CA: AAIC, 1991).

Yıldız, Hasan (ed.), *Fransız Belgeleriyle Sevr- Lozan- Musul Üçgeninde Kürdistan* (Istanbul: Doz, 2005).

SECONDARY SOURCES

'Diyarbakır adı üzerine çalışmalar', in: *Türk Dili*, no. 29/30 (June 1938), 69–87.

'The Halkevi: The Turkish People's House', in: *The Scottish geographical magazine* 1 (1944), 21–2.

'The New University in Turkey', in: *School and Society* 39, no. 994 (January 1934), 45.

Abu Jaber, Kamel S., 'The Millet System in the Nineteenth-century Ottoman Empire', in: *The Muslim World* 57, nr. 3 (1967), 212–23.

Adak, Hülya, 'National Myths and Self-Na(rra)tions: Mustafa Kemal's *Nutuk* and Halide Edib's *Memoirs* and *The Turkish Ordeal*', in: *South Atlantic Quarterly* 102, no. 2/3 (2003), 509–27.

Adanır, Fikret and Hilmar Kaiser, 'Migration, Deportation, and Nation-Building: The Case of the Ottoman Empire', in: René Leboutte (ed.), *Migrations et migrants dans une perspective historique: permanences et innovations* (Florence: European University Institute, 2000), 273–92.

Aghjayan, George, 'The Armenian Villages of Palu: History and Demography', paper presented at the conference UCLA International Conference Series on Historic Armenian Cities and Provinces: Tigranakert/Diarbekir and Edessa/Urfa, University of California (Los Angeles), 13 November 1999.

Ahmad, Feroz and Dankwart A. Rustow, 'İkinci Meşrutiyet Döneminde Meclisler, 1908–1918', in: *Güney-Doğu Avrupa Araştırmaları Dergisi*, no. 4–5 (1976).

—— *The Turkish Experiment in Democracy, 1950–1975* (Boulder, CO: Westview Press, 1977).

Ahmad, Kamal Madhar, *Kurdistan During the First World War* (London: Saqi, 1994, transl. Ali Maher Ibrahim).

Ahmed Cevad, *Balkanlarda Akan Kan* (Istanbul: Şamil, n.y.).

Ahmed Naim, Babanzâde, *İslâmda Davayı Kavmiyyet* (Istanbul: Tevsi-i Tıba'at Matbaası, 1332 [1914]).

Ahmed, Akbar S., ' "Ethnic Cleansing": A Metaphor for our Time?', in: *Ethnic and Racial Studies* 18, no. 1 (1995), 1–25.

Ahmet İzzet Paşa, *Feryadım* (Istanbul: Nehir, 1992).

Akçam, Taner, *'Ermeni Meselesi Hallolunmuştur': Osmanlı Belgelerine Göre Savaş Yıllarında Ermenilere Yönelik Politikalar* (Istanbul: İletişim, 2007).

—— *İnsan Hakları ve Ermeni Sorunu: İttihat ve Terakki'den Kurtuluş Savaşı'na* (Istanbul: İmge, 2001).

Akçura, Yusuf, *Üç Tarz-ı Siyaset* (İstanbul: n.p., 1909).

Akpınar, Alişan, *Osmanlı Devleti'nde Aşiret Mektebi* (Istanbul: Göçebe, 1997).

Akünal, Dündar, 'Belge ve Resimlerle Dr. İbrahim Tali Öngören', in: *Tarih ve Toplum* 40 (1987).

Akural, Sabri M., 'Ziya Gökalp: The Influence of his Thought on Kemalist Reforms' (unpublished Ph.D. thesis, Indiana University, 1979).

Akyüz, Yahya, 'Atatürk ve 1921 Eğitim Kongresi', in: *Cumhuriyet Döneminde Eğitim* (Istanbul: Milli Eğitim Bakanlığı, 1983).

Alakom, Rohat, *Hoybûn Örgütü ve Ağrı Ayaklanması* (Istanbul: Avesta, 1998).

Aldur, Mustafa, '1850–1950 yılları arası Turabdin'e Hevêrkan ve Mala Osmên', in: *Özgür Politika*, 15 September 2002.

Al-Ghusayn, Fa'iz, *Martyred Armenia* (London: C.A. Pearson Ltd., 1917).

Ali Emîrî, *Osmanlı Vilâyât-ı Şarkîyyesi* (Istanbul: Dâr-ul Hilâfe, 1918).

Allen, Henry E., *The Turkish Transformation: A Study in Social and Religious Development* (New York: Greenwood Press, 1968).

Alper, Mehmet, 'Diyarbakır, sa citadelle et ses remparts', in: *Albert Gabriel (1883–1972): Mimar, Arkeolog, Ressam, Gezgin* (Istanbul: Yapı Kredi Yayınları, 2006), 93–109.

Altınay, Ahmet Refik, *Kafkas Yollarında: İki Komite, İki Kıtal* (Istanbul: Temel, 1998 [1919]).

Altınay, Ayşe Gül and Fethiye Çetin, *Torunlar* (Istanbul: Metis, 2009).

Anderson, Alan B., 'The Complexity of Ethnic Identities: A Postmodern Reevaluation', in: *Identity: An International Journal of Theory and Research* 1, no. 3 (2001), 209–23.

Anderson, Ewan W., 'Geopolitics: International Boundaries as Fighting Places', in: *Journal of Strategic Studies* 22, no. 2–3 (1999), 125–36.

Andonian, Aram, *Balkan Savaşı* (Istanbul: Aras Yayıncılık, 1999, transl. Zaven Biberian).

Anter, Musa, *Hatıralarım* (Istanbul: Avesta, 1999).

Appadurai, Arjun, *Modernity at Large: Cultural Dimensions of Globalization* (Minneapolis: University of Minnesota Press, 1997).

Arendt, Hannah, *The Origins of Totalitarianism* (London: Harcourt Brace, 1973).

Arı, Kemal, *Büyük Mübadele: Türkiye'ye Zorunlu Göç (1923–1925)* (Istanbul: Tarih Vakfı Yurt Yayınları, 2000).

Armalto, Ishaq, *Al-Qousara fi Nakabat an-Nasara* (Beirut: Al-Sharfe Monastery, 1970, 2nd edition).

—— *De Kristnas Hemska Katastrofer: Osmanernas och Ung-turkarnas Folkmord i norra Mesopotamien 1895/1914–1918* (Stockholm: Beth Froso Nsibin, 2005, transl. Ingvar Rydberg).

Armstrong, Harold, *Turkey and Syria Reborn: A Record of Two Years of Travel* (London: J. Lane, 1930).

Arsunar, Ferruh, *Türk Anadolu Halk Türküleri* (Ankara: Başnur, 1965).

Ataöv, Türkkaya, 'The Faculty of Political Science of Turkey', in: *Middle East Journal* 14, no. 2 (1960), 243–5.

Avar, Sıdıka, *Dağ Çiçeklerim (Anılar)* (Ankara: Öğretmen, 1986).

Ayas, Nevzad, *Türkiye Cumhuriyeti Millî Eğitimi: Kuruluşlar ve Tarihçeler* (Ankara: Milli Eğitim Basımevi, 1948).

—— *Türkiye Cumhuriyeti Millî Eğitimi* (Ankara: Millî Eğitim Basımevi, 1948).

Aybars, Ergün, *İstiklâl Mahkemeleri 1920–1923/1923–1927* (İzmir: Zeus, 2006).

Aydemir, Şevket Süreyya, *Makedonya'dan Orta Asya'ya Enver Paşa* (Istanbul: Remzi, 1972), vol. 2 (1908–14).

—— *İkinci Adam: 1884–1938* (Istanbul: Remzi, 1967).

Aydın, Osman, *Kürt Ulus Hareketi 1925* (n.p: Weşanên Weqfa Şêx Seid, 1994).

Aydın, Suavi, *et al.* (eds.), *Mardin: Aşiret-Cemaat-Devlet* (Istanbul: Tarih Vakfı, 2000).

Azarian, Natasha May, 'The Seeds of Memory: Narrative Renditions of the Armenian Genocide Across Generations' (unpublished Ph.D. thesis, University of California, Berkeley, 2007).

Aziz, Şevket, 'Türklerin Antropolojisi', in: *Birinci Türk Tarih Kongresi: Konferanslar Münakaşalar* (Istanbul: T.C. Maarif Vekaleti, 1932), 271–8.

Bajohr, Frank (ed.), *Zivilisation und Barbarei: die widersprüchlichen Potentiale der Moderne: Detlev Peukert zum Gedenken* (Hamburg: Christians, 1991).

Bakır, Abdulhalık, 'Osmanlı Öncesinde Diyarbakır'da Sanayi ve Ticaret', paper presented at the conference Oğuzlardan Osmanlıya Diyarbakır, Dicle University, 21 May 2004.

Balakian, Grigoris, *Le Golgotha arménien: Berlin–Deir es-Zor. Mémoires* (Paris: Le cercle d'écrits caucasiens, 2002).

Balakian, Peter, *Black Dog of Fate: A Memoir* (New York: BasicBooks, 1997).

Balkan Harbında neden Munhazim Olduk? (Istanbul: n.p., 1913).

Ballinger, Pamela, *History in Exile: Memory and Identity at the Borders of the Balkans* (Princeton, NJ: Princeton University Press, 2003).

Baran, Aziz, 'You Must Give a Kurdish Baby a Turkish Name', in: *Kurdish Times* 1, no. 1 (1986), 12–15.

Barkan, Elazar, *The Guilt of Nations: Restitution and Negotiating Historical Injustices* (New York: W.W. Norton, 2000).

Başgöz, İlhan and Howard E. Wilson, *Educational Problems in Turkey 1920–1940* (Bloomington: Indiana University Press, 1968).

Baum, Antonia, *et al.*, 'Review of Mass Homicides of Intelligentsia as a Marker for Genocide', in: *The Forensic Examiner*, 22 September 2007, 34–41.

Bauman, Zygmunt, *Modernity and the Holocaust* (Oxford: Polity, 1989).

Baumann, Gerd, *The Multicultural Riddle: Rethinking National, Ethnic, and Religious Identities* (London: Routledge, 1999).

Baumeister, Roy F., *Evil: Inside Human Violence and Cruelty* (New York: Henry Holt, 2001).

Bayraktar, Seyhan and Wolfgang Seibel, 'Das türkische Tätertrauma: Der Massenmord an den Armeniern von 1915 bis 1917 und seine Leugnung', in: Bernhard Giesen and Christoph Schneider (eds.), *Tätertrauma* (Konstanz: UVK, 2004), 381–98.

Bayur, Yusuf Hikmet, *Türk İnkılabı Tarihi* (Ankara: Türk Tarih Kurumu, 1991).

Bechtel, Delphine, 'Lemberg/Lwów/Lvov/Lviv: Identities of a "City of Uncertain Boundaries"', in: *Diogenes*, no. 210 (2006), 62–71.

Beğenç, Cahit, *Diyarbakır ve Raman* (Ankara: Ulus, 1949).

Béla Várdy, Steven, T. Hunt Tooley, and Agnes Huszár Várdy (eds.), *Ethnic Cleansing in Twentieth-Century Europe* (New York: Columbia University Press, 2003).

Bell, Gertrude, *The Churches and Monasteries of the Tur Abdin and Neighbouring Districts* (Heidelberg: Carl Winter's Universitätsbuchhandlung, 1913).

Bell-Falkoff, Andrew, *Ethnic Cleansing* (New York: St. Martin's Press, 1996).

Berkes, Niyazi, 'Sociology in Turkey', in: *American Journal of Sociology* 42 (1936), 238–46.

Beşikçi, İsmail, *Bilim Yöntemi, Türkiye'deki Uygulama 1: Kürtlerin Mecburi İskânı* (Istanbul: Komal, 1977).

—— *Doğu'da Değişim ve Yapısal Sorunlar (Göçebe Alikan Aşireti)* (Ankara: Sevinç, 1969).

—— *International Colony Kurdistan* (London: Parvana, 2004 [1990]).

—— *Türk Tarih Tezi ve Kürt Sorunu: Güneş-Dil Teorisi* (Istanbul: Komal, 1977).

Bevan, Robert, *The Destruction of Memory: Architecture at War* (London: Reaktion Books, 2006).

Beysanoğlu, Şevket, *Anıtları ve Kitabeleri ile Diyarbakır Tarihi* (Diyarbakır: Diyarbakır Büyükşehir Belediyesi Kültür ve Sanat Yayınları, 1996).

—— *Diyarbakır Folkloru* (Diyarbakır: Diyarbakır Matbaası, 1943).

—— *Ziya Gökalp'ın ilk yazı hayatı, 1894–1909: Doğumu'nun 80. yıldönümü münasebetiyle* (Istanbul: Diyarbakırı Tanıtma Derneği, 1956).

Bilgi, Nejdet, *Dr. Mehmed Reshid Şahingiray'ın hayatı ve hâtıraları* (İzmir: Akademi, 1997).

Bilsel, Mehmet Cemil, *Lozan* (Istanbul: Ahmet İhsan, 1933).

Binbaşıoğlu, Cavit, *Türkiye'de Eğitim Bilimleri Tarihi* (Istanbul: Milli Eğitim Bakanlığı Yayınları, 1995).

Birdoğan, Nejat (ed.), Baha Said Bey, *İttihat ve Terakki'nin Alevilik-Bektaşilik Araştırması* (Istanbul: Berfin, 1995).

Bitlîsî, Sharaf al-Dîn, *The Sharafnâma: Or the History of the Kurdish Nation, 1597* (Costa Mesa, CA: Mazda, 2005, transl. and ed. Mehrdad R. Izady).

Bizbirlik, Alpay, *16. Yüzyıl Ortalarında Diyarbekir Beylerbeyliği'nde Vakıflar* (Ankara: Türk Tarih Kurumu, 2002).

Bjørnlund, Matthias, '"A Fate Worse Than Dying": Sexual Violence During the Armenian Genocide', in: Dagmar Herzog (ed.), *Brutality and Desire: War and Sexuality in Europe's Twentieth Century* (London: Palgrave McMillan, 2008), 16–59.

Bleda, Mithat Şükrü, *İmparatorluğun Çöküşü* (İstanbul: Remzi, 1979).

Bloxham, Donald, 'Changing Perceptions of State Violence: Turkey's "Westward" Development through Anglo-Saxon Eyes', in: Richard Littlejohns and Sara Soncini (eds.), *Myths of Europe* (Amsterdam: Rodopi, 2007), 223–34.

—— 'The Beginning of the Armenian Catastrophe: Comparative and Contextual Considerations', in: Hans-Lukas Kieser and Dominik J. Schaller (eds.), *Der Völkermord an den Armeniern und die Shoah: The Armenian Genocide and the Shoah* (Zürich: Chronos, 2002), 101–28.

—— *Genocide, the World Wars and the Unweaving of Europe* (London: Vallentine Mitchell, 2008).

—— *The Great Game of Genocide: Imperialism, Nationalism, and the Destruction of the Ottoman Armenians* (Oxford: Oxford University Press, 2005).

Boeckh, Katrin, *Von den Balkankriegen zum Ersten Weltkrieg: Kleinstaatenpolitik und ethnische Selbstbestimmung auf dem Balkan* (München: Oldenbourg, 1996).

Boeder, André, *Door het Oog van de Naald: Het Verhaal van Aurora, een Armeens Meisje* (Houten: Den Hertog, 2003).

Boggs, S. Whittemore, *International Boundaries* (New York: Columbia University Press, 1940).

Bora, Tanıl, 'Ordu ve Milliyetçilik', in: Ahmet İnsel and Ali Bayramoğlu (eds.), *Bir Zümre, Bir Parti: Türkiye'de Ordu* (Istanbul: Birikim, 2004), 163–78.

Boyar, Ebru, *Ottomans, Turks and the Balkans: Empire Lost, Relations Altered* (London: Tauris Academic Studies, 2007).

Bozarslan, Hamit, 'Kurdish Nationalism under the Kemalist Republic: Some Hypotheses', in: Mohammed M.A. Ahmed and Michael Gunter (eds.), *The Evolution of Kurdish Nationalism* (Costa Mesa, CA: Mazda, 2007), 36–51.

—— 'La révolution française et les Jeunes Turcs', in: *Revue de l'Occident Musulman et de la Méditerranée*, no. 52–3 (1989), 148–62.

—— 'M. Ziya Gökalp', in: *Modern Türkiye'de Siyasi Düşünce* (Istanbul: İletişim Yayınları, 2001), vol. 1, *Tanzimat ve Meşrutiyet'in Birikimi*, 314–19.

—— 'Remarques sur l'histoire des relations kurdo-arméniennes', in: *The Journal of Kurdish Studies* 1 (1995), 55–76.

—— *La question kurde: états et minorités au Moyen-Orient* (Paris: Presses de Sciences Po, 1997).

Bracher, Karl D., 'Totalitarianism', in: Philip P. Wiener (ed.), *Dictionary of the History of Ideas* (New York: Charles Scribner's Sons, 1973–4), vol. 4, 406–11.

Braude, Benjamin and Bernard Lewis, 'Introduction', in: Benjamin Braude and Bernard Lewis (eds.), *Christians and Jews in the Ottoman Empire* (New York: Holmes and Meier, 1982), vol. 1, 1–34.

—— 'Foundation Myths of the Millet System', in: Benjamin Braude and Bernard Lewis (eds.), *Christians and Jews in the Ottoman Empire* (New York: Holmes and Meier, 1982), vol. 1, *The Central Lands*, 69–90.

Braudel, Fernand, *The Mediterranean and the Mediterranean World in the Age of Philip II* (New York: Harper and Row, 1976).

Brauer, Erich, *The Jews of Kurdistan* (Detroit, MI: Wayne State University Press, 1993).

Brockett, Gavin D., 'Collective Action and the Turkish Revolution: Towards a Framework for the Social History of the Atatürk Era, 1923–1938', in: Sylvia Kedourie (ed.), *Turkey Before and After Atatürk: Internal and External Affairs* (London: Frank Cass, 1999), 44–66.

Brubaker, Rogers *et al.*, *Nationalist Politics and Everyday Ethnicity in a Transylvanian Town* (Princeton, NJ: Princeton University Press, 2006).

—— 'Aftermaths of Empire and the Unmixing of Peoples', in: Karen Barkey and Mark von Hagen (eds.), *After Empire: Multiethnic Societies and Nation-Building: The Soviet Union and the Russian, Ottoman and Habsburg Empires* (Boulder: Westview Press, 1997), 155–80.

—— 'Ethnicity Without Groups', in: *Archives européennes de sociologie* 43, no. 2 (2002), 163–89.

Brudholm, Thomas, 'Revisiting Resentments: Jean Améry and the Dark Side of Forgiveness and Reconciliation', in: *Journal of Human Rights* 5 (2006), 7–26.

Bulut, Faik, *Kürt Sorununa Çözüm Arayışları* (Istanbul: Ozan, 1998).

Çağaptay, Soner, *Islam, Secularism and Nationalism in Modern Turkey: Who is a Turk?* (Abingdon: Routledge, 2006).

Cahid, Hüseyin, 'Devletler ve Şarkî Anadolu', in: *Tanin*, 27 November 1913, no. 1769.

Cahun, Léon, *Introduction à l'histoire de l'Asie: Turcs et Mongols, des origines à 1405* (Paris: A. Colin et cie, 1896).

Çapar, Mustafa, 'Tek Parti Dönemi: Milli Eğitim, Milli Dil ve Türkleştirme Politikaları', in: *Türkiye'de Azınlık Hakları Sorunu: Vatandaşlık ve Demokrasi Eksenli Bir Yaklaşım* (Istanbul: TESEV, 2006).

Cassese, Antonio, *Self-Determination of Peoples: A Legal Reappraisal* (Cambridge: Cambridge University Press, 1999).

Cebesoy, Ali Fuat, *Siyasi Hatıralar* (Istanbul: Vatan Neşriyatı, 1957).

Çeçen, Anıl, *Halkevleri: Atatürk'ün Kültür Kurumu* (Ankara: Gündoğan, 1990).

Cemal Paşa, *Hatıralar: İttihat ve Terakki ve Birinci Dünyâ Savaşı Anıları* (Istanbul: Çağdaş, 1977).

Cemal, Behçet, *Şeyh Sait İsyanı* (Istanbul: Sel, 1955).

Cengiz Orhonlu, *Osmanlı İmparatorluğu'nda Aşiretlerin İskânı* (Istanbul: Eren, 1987).

Cengiz, Filiz, 'Dr. Nazım ve Dr. Bahaeddin Şakir'in Kaleminden İttihad ve Terakki Cemiyeti' (Unpublished MA Thesis, Istanbul University, 1997).

Çetin, Fethiye, *Anneannem: Anlatı* (Istanbul: Metis, 2004).

—— *My Grandmother: A Memoir* (London: Verso, 2008).

Cewerî, Firat, *Li Mala Mîr Celadet Alî Bedir-xan* (Stockholm: Nûdem, 1998).

Chernilo, Daniel, *A Social Theory of the Nation state: The Political Forms of Modernity beyond Methodological Nationalism* (London: Routledge, 2007).

Christoff, Hellmut, *Kurden und Armenier: Eine Untersuchung über die Abhängigkeit ihrer Lebensformen und Charakterentwicklung von der Landschaft* (Hamburg: dissertation University of Hamburg, 1935).

Cigerxwîn, *Jînenigariya min* (Spånga, Sweden: APEC, 1995).

Civan, Rojvanê, *Şeyh Said İsyanı: 1925 Büyük Kürt Ayaklanması* (n.p.: Özgürlük Yolu, 1990).

Cohen, Anthony P., *The Symbolic Construction of Community* (London: Tavistock, 1985).

Cohen, Saul B. and Nurit Kliot, 'Place-Names in Israel's Ideological Struggle over the Administered Territories', in: *Annals of the Association of American Geographers* 82, no. 4 (1992), 653–80.

Cohen, Stanley, *States of Denial: Knowing about Atrocities and Suffering* (Oxford: Polity, 2001).

Çolak, Yılmaz, 'Language Policy and Official Ideology in Early Republican Turkey', in: *Middle Eastern Studies* 40, no. 6 (2004), 67–91.

Cömert, Kazım, *Çiğdemler Çıkarsa Eğer* (Istanbul: Aydınlar Matbaacılık, 1992).

Connelly, John, *Captive University: The Sovietization of East German, Czech, and Polish Higher Education, 1945–1956* (Chapel Hill: The University of North Carolina Press, 2000).

Connor, Walker, 'Illusions of Homogeneity: Myths of Hemispheric, Continental, Regional, and State Unity', in: id., *Ethnonationalism: The Quest for Understanding* (Princeton: Princeton University Press, 1993), 118–43.

—— 'Nation-Building or Nation-Destroying?' in: *World Politics* 24, no. 3 (1972), 319–55.

Copeaux, Étienne, *Espaces et temps de la nation turque: analyse d'une historiographie nationaliste 1931–1993* (Paris: CNRS Éditions, 1997).

Crampton, Jeremy W., 'Maps, Race and Foucault: Eugenics and Territorialization Following World War I', in: Jeremy W. Crampton and Stuart Elden (eds.), *Space, Knowledge and Power: Foucault and Geography* (Aldershot: Ashgate Publishing, 2007), 223–44.

Criss, Nur Bilge, 'The Nature of PKK Terrorism in Turkey', in: *Studies in Conflict and Terrorism* 18, no. 1 (1995), 17–38.

Cumhuriyetin 15inci yılında Diyarbakır (Diyarbakır: Diyarbakır Matbaası, 1938).

Dadrian, Vahakn N., 'Children as Victims of Genocide: the Armenian Case', in: *Journal of Genocide Research* 5 (2003), 421–39.

—— 'Ottoman Archives and Denial of the Armenian Genocide', in: Richard G. Hovannisian (ed.), *The Armenian Genocide; History, Politics, Ethics* (New York: St. Martin's Press, 1992), 280–310.

Dadrian, Vahakn N., *Warrant for Genocide: Key Elements of the Turko-Armenian Conflict* (New Brunswick, NJ: Transaction, 1999).

Dadrian, Vahram, *To the Desert: Pages from my Diary* (London: Gomidas Institute, 2003).

Dağlı, Nuran and Belma Aktürk (eds.), *Hükümetler ve Programları, vol. I, 1920–1960* (Ankara: TBMM Basımevi, 1988).

Davies, Norman and Roger Moorhouse, *Microcosm: Portrait of a Central European City* (London: Cape, 2002).

Davison, Roderic H., 'The Armenian Crisis, 1912–1914', in: *The American Historical Review* (1947), 481–505.

—— 'The Millets as Agents of Change in the Nineteenth-Century Ottoman Empire', in: Benjamin Braude and Bernard Lewis (eds.), *Christians and Jews in the Ottoman Empire* (New York: Holmes and Meier, 1982), vol. 1, *The Central Lands*, 319–37.

De Nogales, Rafael, *Cuatro años bajo la media luna* (Madrid: Editora Internacional, 1924).

—— *Four Years Beneath the Crescent* (London: Sterndale Classics, 2003).

—— *Memorias del General Rafael de Nogales Méndez* (Caracas: Ediciones Abril, 1974).

—— *Vier Jahre unter dem Halbmond: Erinnerungen aus dem Weltkriege* (Berlin: Verlag von Reimar Hobbing, 1925).

De Swaan, Abram, 'Dyscivilization, Mass Extermination and the State', in: *Theory, Culture and Society* 18, no. 2–3 (2001), 265–76.

—— 'Widening Circles of Disidentification: On the Psycho- and Sociogenesis of the Hatred of Distant Strangers—Reflections on Rwanda', in: *Theory, Culture and Society* 14, no. 2 (1997), 105–22.

—— 'Widening Circles of Identification: Emotional Concerns in Sociogenetic Perspective', in: *Theory, Culture and Society* 12 (1995), 25–39.

—— *Human Societies: An Introduction* (Cambridge: Polity, 2005).

Demirer, Hüseyin, *Ha Wer Delal: Eminê Perîxanê'nin Hayatı* (Istanbul: Avesta, 2008).

Demirözü, Damla, *Savaştan Barışa Giden Yol: Atatürk-Venizelos Dönemi Türkiye-Yunanistan İlişkileri* (Istanbul: İletişim, 2007).

Denker, Arif Cemil, *I. Dünya Savaşı'nda Teşkilât-ı Mahsusa* (Istanbul: Arba, 1997).

Derderian, Katharine, 'Common Fate, Different Experience: Gender-Specific Aspects of the Armenian Genocide, 1915–1917', in: *Holocaust and Genocide Studies* 19, no. 1 (2005), 1–25.

Der-Garabedian, Hagop S., *Jail to Jail: Autobiography of a Survivor of the 1915 Armenian Genocide* (New York: iUniverse, 2004).

Deringil, Selim, *The Well-Protected Domains: Ideology and the Legitimation of Power in the Ottoman Empire, 1876–1909* (London: Tauris, 1999).

Dersimi, Nuri, *Dersim ve Kürt Milli Mücadelesine Dair Hatıratım* (Ankara: Öz-Ge, 1992).

Diken, Şeyhmus, *Amidalılar: Sürgündeki Diyarbekirliler* (Istanbul: İletişim, 2007).

—— *Bajarê Ku Razên Xwe Ji Bircên Xwe Re Dibiline: Diyarbekir* (Diyarbakır: Lis, 2006).

—— *Diyarbekir Diyarım, Yitirmişem Yanarım* (Istanbul: İletişim, 2003).

—— *İsyan Sürgünleri* (Istanbul: İletişim, 2005).

—— *Sırrını Surlarına Fısıldayan Şehir, Diyarbakır* (Istanbul: İletişim, 2004).

—— *Tango ve Diyarbakır* (Diyarbakır: Lis, 2004).

Dirik, K. Doğan, *Atatürk'ün İzinde Vali Paşa Kâzım Dirik: Bandırma Vapuru'ndan Halkın Kalbine* (Istanbul: Gürer, 2008).

Diyarbekir Halk Türküleri (Istanbul: Numune Matbaası, 1937).

Diyarbekire Bir Bakış (Diyarbakır: Diyarbekir Basımevi, 1935).

Doğan, Avni, *Kurtuluş, Kuruluş ve Sonrası* (Istanbul: Dünya, 1964).

Du Véou, Paul, *Chrétiens en péril au Moussadagh!: Enquête au Sandjak d'Alexandrette* (Paris: Baudinière, 1939).

Duguid, Stephen, 'The Politics of Unity: Hamidian Policy in Eastern Anatolia', in: *Middle Eastern Studies* 9, nr. 2 (1973), 139–55.

Dulić, Tomislav, *Utopias of nation: local mass killing in Bosnia and Hercegovina, 1941–42* (Uppsala: Uppsala University Press, 2005).

Dumont, Paul, 'The Origins of Kemalist Ideology', in: Jacob M. Landau (ed.), *Atatürk and the Modernization of Turkey* (Boulder, CO: Westview Press, 1984), 25–44.

Dündar, Fuat, 'İttihat ve Terakki'nin Etnisite Araştırmaları', in: *Toplumsal Tarih* XVI, no. 91 (2001), 43–50.

—— *İttihat ve Terakki'nin Müslümanları İskân Politikası (1913–1918)* (Istanbul: İletişim, 2002).

—— *Modern Türkiye'nin Şifresi: İttihat ve Terakki'nin Etnisite Mühendisliği (1913–1918)* (Istanbul: İletişim, 2008).

Dursunoğlu, Cevat, 'Halkevlerinin 18. Yıldönümü Konuşması', in: *Ülkü* 4, no. 39 (March 1950), 1.

Duru, Kâzım Nâmi, 'Köy mü, kasaba mı?', in: *Anadolu Terbiye Mecmuası* 2 (1922), 4.

Ea, Meng-Try and Sorya Sim, *Victims and Perpetrators?: Testimony of Young Khmer Rouge Comrades* (Phnom Penh: Documentation Center of Cambodia, 2001).

Edib, Halide, *Conflict of East and West in Turkey* (Delhi: Jamia Press, 1935).

Eissenstat, Howard, 'Metaphors of Race and Discourse of Nation: Racial Theory and the Beginnings of Nationalism in the Turkish Republic', in: Paul Spickard (ed.), *Race and Nation: Ethnic Systems in the Modern World* (New York: Routledge, 2005), 239–56.

Ekrem Cemil Paşa, *Muhtasar Hayatım* (Brussels: Institute Kurde, 1991).

Elias, Norbert, 'Processes of State Formation and Nation Building', in: *Transactions of the Seventh World Congress of Sociology, Varna, September 14–19, 1970* (Louvain: International Sociological Association, 1972), vol. 3, 274–84.

—— 'Zur Grundlegung einer Theorie sozialer Prozesse', in: *Zeitschrift für Soziologie* 6 (1977), 127–49.

—— *Studien über die Deutschen: Machtkämpfe und Habitusentwicklung im 19. und 20. Jahrhundert* (Frankfurt am Main: Suhrkamp, 1989).

—— *Über den Prozess der Zivilisation: soziogenetische und psychogenetische Untersuchungen* (Basel: Haus zum Falken, 1939).

Elkins, Caroline and Susan Pedersen (ed.), *Settler Colonialism in the Twentieth Century: Projects, Practices, Legacies* (London: Routledge, 2005).

Elster, Jon, 'Norms of Revenge', in: *Ethics* 4 (1990), 862–85.

Emin, Mehmet, 'Türk Ocakları', in: *Hayat* 1, no. 2 (14 April 1927), 381.

Empson, Ralph H.W., *The Cult of the Peacock Angel: A Short Account of the Yezidi Tribes of Kurdistan* (London: AMS Press, 1928).

Ergin, Osman, *Türkiye Maarif Tarihi* (Istanbul: Eser, 1977).

Ergin, Ramazan, *Awina ya da Kanın Gizli Tarihi: Reşo Kuri* (Istanbul: Do, 2007).

Erickson, Edward J., *Defeat in Detail: The Ottoman Army in the Balkans, 1912–1913* (Westport, CT: Praeger, 2003).

—— *Ordered to Die: A History of the Ottoman Army in the First World War* (Westport, CT: Greenwood Press, 2000).

Erkal, Mustafa E., *Bölgeler Arası Dengesizlik ve Doğu Kalkınması* (Istanbul: Şamil, 1972).

Ersanlı, Büşra, 'History Textbooks as Reflections of the Political Self: Turkey (1930s and 1990s) and Uzbekistan (1990s)', in: *International Journal of Middle East Studies* 34, no. 2 (2002), 337–50.

Ersanlı, Büşra, *İktidar ve Tarih: Türkiye'de 'Resmi Tarih' Tezinin Oluşumu (1929–1937)* (Istanbul: İletişim, 2003).

Ertürk, Hüsamettin, *İki Devrin Perde Arkası*, Samih N. Tansu (ed.) (Istanbul: Batur, 1964).

Esatlı, Mustafa R., *İttihat ve Terakki tarihinde esrar perdesi ve Yakup Cemil niçin öldürüldü?* (Istanbul: Hürriyet, 1975).

Eti, Usman, *Diyarbekir* (Diyarbakır: Diyarbekir Matbaası, 1937).

Eyicil, Ahmet, *İttihad ve Terakki Liderlerinden Doktor Nâzım Bey 1872–1926* (Ankara: Gün, 2004).

Farr, Jason, 'Point: the Westphalia Legacy and the Modern Nation State', in: *International Social Science Review* 80, no. 3/4 (2005), 156–9.

Fearon, James D. and David D. Laitin, 'Violence and the Social Construction of Ethnic Identity', in: *International Organization* 54, no. 4 (2000), 845–77.

Fındıkoğlu, Ziyaeddin Fahri, *Auguste Comte ve Ahmet Rıza* (Istanbul: Türkiye Harsî ve İçtimaî Araştırmalar Derneği, 1962).

—— 'Ayın İzleri', in: *Anadolu Mecmuası* 9–11 (May 1925), 390–1.

Fırat, Abdülmelik, *Fırat Mahzun Akar* (Istanbul: Avesta, 1996).

Fırat, Kasım, 'Mazlum Halk Önderi Şeyh Sait', in: *Tevhid* (June 1991), 6–10.

—— 'Röportaj', in: *Dava* 8 (1990), 8–16.

Fischel, Walther J., 'The Jews of Kurdistan a hundred years ago: A traveler's record', in: *Jewish Social Studies* 6 (1944), 195–226.

Fortna, Benjamin C., *Imperial Classroom: Islam, the State, and Education in the Late Ottoman Empire* (New York: Oxford University Press, 2000).

Fraser, David, *The Short Cut to India: The Record of a Journey along the Route of the Baghdad Railway* (Edinburgh: William Blackwood and Sons, 1909).

Frijda, Nico H., 'The Lex Talionis: On Vengeance', in: Stephanie H. M. van Goozen, Nanne E. van de Poll and Joseph A. Sergeant (eds.), *Emotions: Essays on Emotion Theory* (Hillsdale, NJ: Erlbaum, 1994), 263–89.

Frödin, John, 'En Resa Genom Östra Turkiet 1936', in: *Ymer*, no. 2–3 (1937), 169–98.

Fromkin, Victoria, *et al.*, 'The Development of Language in Genie: a Case of Language Acquisition Beyond the Critical Point', *Brain and Language* 1 (1974), 81–107.

Fujii, Lee Ann, 'The Power of Local Ties: Mechanisms of Mass Participation During the Rwandan Genocide', paper presented at the annual meeting of the *American Political Science Association*, Philadelphia, 31 August 2006.

Gabriel, Albert, *Diyarbakır surları* (Diyarbakır: Diyarbakır Tanıtma, Kültür ve Yardımlaşma Vakfı, 1993, transl. Kaya Özsezgin).

—— *Voyages archéologiques dans la Turquie orientale* (Paris: Institut français d'archeologie de Stamboul, 1940).

—— 'Mardin ve Diyarbekir vilayetlerinde icra olunmuş arkeologya seyahati hakkında rapor', in: *Türk Tarih, Arkeologya ve Etnografya Dergisi* 1 (1933), 134–49.

Gałęski, Bogusław, 'Sociological Problems of the Occupation of Farmers', in: Teodor Shanin (ed.), *Peasants and Peasant Societies* (Harmondsworth: Penguin, 1971), 180–201.

Gaunt, David, *Massacres, Resistance, Protectors: Muslim-Christian Relations in Eastern Anatolia during World War I* (Piscataway, NJ: Gorgias Press, 2006).

Gawrych, George W., 'The Culture and Politics of Violence in Turkish Society, 1903–14', in: *Middle Eastern Studies* 22, no. 3 (1986), 307–30.

Gedik, Gülay Zorer, 'Climatic Design: An Analysis of the Old Houses of Diyarbakir in the Southeast Region of Turkey', in: *Architectural Science Review* 47, no. 2 (2004), 145–54.

Geertz, Clifford, 'The Integrative Revolution: Primordial Sentiments and Civil Politics in the New States', in: id., *The Interpretation of Cultures: Selected Essays* (New York, NY: Basic Books, 1973), 255–310.

Gellner, Ernest, *Nations and Nationalism* (Oxford: Blackwell, 1983).

Georgelin, Hervé, *La fin de Smyrne: du cosmopolitisme aux nationalismes* (Paris: CNRS, 2005).

Georgeon, François, 'Deux leaders du mouvement national: Ziya Gökalp et Yusuf Akçura', in: François Georgeon, *Des ottomans aux turcs: Naissance d'une nation* (Istanbul: Isis, 1995), 55–66.

—— 'Les Foyers Turcs à l'époque kémaliste (1923–1931)', in: *Turcica* XIV (1982), 168–215.

—— *Aux origines du nationalisme turc: Yusuf Akçura (1876–1935)* (Paris: ADPF, 1981).

Getty, J. Arch and Oleg V. Naumov, *The Road to Terror: Stalin and the Self-Destruction of the Bolsheviks, 1932–1939* (New Haven: Yale University Press, 1999).

Gezik, Erdal, *Dinsel, etnik ve politik sorunlar bağlamında Alevi Kürtler* (Ankara: Kalan, 2000).

Ghassemlou, Abdul Rahman, *Kurdistan and the Kurds* (Prague: Czechoslovak Academy of Sciences, 1965).

Giddens, Anthony, *The Nation State and Violence: Volume 2 of A Contemporary Critique of Historical Materialism* (Cambridge: Polity Press, 1985).

Gilbert, Martin, *Winston S. Churchill*, vol. 3: *1914–1916, The Challenge of War* (Boston: Houghton Mifflin, 1971).

Ginio, Eyal, 'Mobilizing the Ottoman Nation during the Balkan Wars (1912–1913): Awakening from the Ottoman Dream', in: *War in History* 12, no. 2 (2005), 156–77.

Göçek, Fatma Müge, Norman Naimark and Ronald Grigor Suny (eds.), *A Question of Genocide: Armenians and Turks at the End of the Ottoman Empire* (New York: Oxford University Press, 2011).

Goffman, Erving, 'The Characteristics of Total Institutions', in: Amitai Etzioni (ed.), *Complex Organizations: A Sociological Reader* (New York: Holt, Rinehart, and Winston, 1961), 312–38.

Gökalp, Ziyâ, 'İstimlâl', in: *Küçük Mecmua* 29 (1 January 1923), 1–6.

—— 'Millet Nedir?', in: *Küçük Mecmua* 28 (25 December 1922), 1–6.

—— 'Şehir Medeniyeti, Köy Medeniyeti', in: *Küçük Mecmua* 30 (10 January 1923), 4–7.

—— 'Türkçülük ve Türkiyecilik', in: *Yeni Mecmua* 2–51 (4 July 1918), 482.

—— *Kızılelma* (Ankara: Kültür Bakanlığı Yayınları, 1976 [1914], Hikmet Tanyu, ed.).

—— *Milli Terbiye ve Maarif Meselesi* (Ankara: Diyarbakırı Tanıtma ve Turizm Derneği Yayınları, 1972).

—— *Turkish Nationalism and Western Civilization: Selected Essays of Ziya Gökalp* (Westport, CT: Greenwood Press, 1981, transl. Niyazi Berkes).

Göknar, Erdağ M., 'Ottoman Past and Turkish Future: Ambivalence in A. H. Tanpinar's *Those outside the Scene*', in: *The South Atlantic Quarterly* 102, no. 2/3 (2003), 647–61.

Göktaş, Hıdır, *Kürtler-1: İsyan-Tenkil* (Istanbul: Alan Yayıncılık, 1991).

Göldaş, İsmail, *Kürdistan Teali Cemiyeti* (Istanbul: Doz, 1991).

Göle, Nilüfer, *The Forbidden Modern: Civilization and Veiling* (Ann Arbor, MI: University of Michigan Press, 1996).

Görkem, İsmail, *İttihat ve Terakkî'nin Yaptırdığı 'Anadolu'da Gizli Mabetler' Konulu Araştırmalar: Baha Said Bey- Türkiye'de Alevî-Bektaşî, Ahî ve Nusayrî Zümreleri* (Ankara: Kültür Bakanlığı HAGEM Yayınları, 2000).

Goudsblom, Johan, 'De monopolisering van georganiseerd geweld', in: *Sociologische Gids* 48, no. 4 (2001), 343–59.

Göyünç, Nejat, 'Diyarbekir Beylerbeyliğinin İlk İdari Taksimatı', in: *Tarih Dergisi* 22 (1969), 23–4.

Greenfeld, Liah, *Nationalism: Five Roads to Modernity* (Cambridge, MA: Harvard University Press, 1992).

Greenshields, Thomas H., 'The Settlement of Armenian Refugees in Syria and Lebanon, 1915–39', in: John I. Clarke and Howard Bowen-Jones (eds.), *Change and Development in the Middle East* (London: Methuen and Co., 1981), 233–41.

Grmek, Mirko, 'Un memoricide', in: *Le Figaro*, 19 December 1991.

Gültekin, Münip, 'Ergani Halkevi Çalışmaları', in: *Karacadağ* III, no. 25, 20 February 1940.

Günaysu, Ayşe, 'Toplu mezar Ermeni ve Süryanilere ait', in: *Özgür Gündem*, 7 November 2006.

Gündoğan, Cemil, *1924 Beytüşşebap İsyanı ve Şeyh Sait Ayaklanmasına Etkileri* (Istanbul: Komal, 1994).

Günkut, Bedri, *Diyarbekir Tarihi* (Diyarbakır: Diyarbekir Halkevi, 1937).

Gürün, Kâmuran, *Ermeni Dosyası* (Ankara: Bilgi, 1988).

Güzelses, Celal, *Diyarbakır Halk Türküleri* (Istanbul: n.p., 1938).

Haar, Ingo, *Historiker im Nationalsozialismus: Deutsche Geschichtswissenschaft und der 'Volkstumskampf' im Osten* (Göttingen: Vandenhoeck and Ruprecht, 2000).

Hadank, Karl, *Mundarten der Zâzâ, hauptsächlich aus Siwerek und Kor* (Berlin: De Gruyter, 1932).

Halaçoğlu, Ahmet, *Balkan Harbi Sırasında Rumeli'den Türk Göçleri (1912–1913)* (Ankara: Türk Tarih Kurumu, 1995).

Hall, Richard C., *The Balkan Wars, 1912–1913: Prelude to the First World War* (London: Routledge, 2000).

Hall, Rodney B., *National Collective Identity: Social Constructs and International Systems* (New York: Columbia University Press, 1999).

Halleck, Seymour L., 'Vengeance and Victimization', in: *Victimology* 5, no. 2 (1980), 99–114.

Hallı, Reşat, *Türkiye Cumhuriyeti'nde Ayaklanmalar: 1924–1938* (Ankara: T.C. Genelkurmay Harp Tarihi Başkanlığı Resmî Yayınları, 1972).

Halpern, Paul G., *A Naval History of World War I* (Annapolis, MD: Naval Institute Press, 1994).

Handler, Richard, 'On Dialogue and Destructive Analysis: Problems in Narrating Nationalism and Ethnicity', in: *Journal of Anthropological Research* 41, no. 2 (1985), 171–82.

Hanioğlu, M. Şükrü, 'Garbcilar: Their Attitudes Toward Religion and Their Impact on the Official Ideology of the Turkish Republic', in: *Studia Islamica* 86 (1997), 133–58.

—— 'Turkism and the Young Turks, 1889–1908', in: Hans-Lukas Kieser (ed.), *Turkey Beyond Nationalism: Towards Post-Nationalist Identities* (London: I.B. Tauris, 2006), 3–19.

—— *Preparation for a Revolution: the Young Turks, 1902–1908* (Oxford: Oxford University Press, 2001).

—— *The Young Turks in Opposition* (Oxford: Oxford University Press, 1995).

—— *Bir siyasal düşünür olarak Doktor Abdullah Cevdet ve dönemi* (Istanbul: Üçdal, 1981).

Hayden, Robert M., 'Schindler's Fate: Genocide, Ethnic Cleansing, and Population Transfers', in: *Slavic Review* 55, no. 4 (1996), 727–48.

Hechter, Michael, *Internal Colonialism: The Celtic Fringe in British National Development, 1536–1966* (London: Routledge and Kegan Paul, 1975).

Hekimoğlu, Nuriye D., 'Kız Enstitüsü Niçin Açıldı', in: *Altan: Elaziz Halkevi Dergisi* 33–34–35 (January 1938), 32–33.

Heper, Metin, *The State and Kurds in Turkey: The Question of Assimilation* (London: Palgrave Macmillan, 2007).

Herb, Guntram H., 'National Identity and Territory', in: Guntram H. Herb and David H. Kaplan (eds.), *Nested Identities: Nationalism, Territory, and Scale* (Lanham, MD: Rowman and Littlefield, 1999), 9–30.

Herman, Judith, *Trauma and Recovery* (New York: Basic Books, 1992).

Heyd, Uriel, *Foundations of Turkish Nationalism: the Life and Teachings of Ziya Gökalp* (Westport, CT: Hyperion Press, 1979).

Hilberg, Raul, *Perpetrators, Victims, Bystanders: The Jewish Catastrophe, 1933–1945* (New York: HarperCollins, 1993).

Hinno, Hori Süleyman, *Farman: Tur'Abdinli Süryanilerin Katliamı 1914–1915* (Athens: n.p., 1993).

Hinton, Alexander L., 'A Head for an Eye: Revenge in the Cambodian Genocide', in: *American Ethnologist* 25, no. 3 (1998), 352–77.

—— 'The Dark Side of Modernity: Toward an Anthropology of Genocide', in: Alexander L. Hinton (ed.), *Annihilating Difference: The Anthropology of Genocide* (Berkeley: University of California Press, 2002), 1–40.

Hobsbawm, Eric, 'Mass-Producing Traditions: Europe, 1870–1914', in: Eric Hobsbawm and Terence Ranger, *The Invention of Tradition* (Cambridge: Cambridge University Press, 1992), 263–308.

Hollerweger, Hans, *Turabdin* (Linz: Freunde des Tur Abdin, 1999).

Horowitz, Donald L., *Ethnic Groups in Conflict* (Berkeley, CA: University of California Press, 2000).

Houston, Christopher, 'Creating a Diaspora within a Country: Kurds in Turkey', in: Melvin Ember, Carol R. Ember and Ian Skoggard (eds.), *Encyclopedia of Diasporas: Immigrant and Refugee Cultures Around the World* (New York: Kluwer Academic, 2004), vol. 2, 403–14.

Hovannisian, Anush, 'Turkey: A Cultural Genocide', in: Levon Chorbajian and George Shirinian (eds.), *Studies in Comparative Genocide* (New York: St. Martin's Press, 1998), 147–56. <http://www.surpgiragos.com>.

İbrahim Halil, 'Sıhhat Meseleleri: Şehrimizin Suları', in: *Küçük Mecmua* 8 (24 July 1922), 18–20.

İçimsoy, A.Oğuz and İsmail E. Erünsal, 'The Legacy of the Ottoman Library in the Libraries of the Turkish Republic', in: *Libri* 58, no. 1 (2008), 47–57.

İğdemir, Uluğ, 'Halkevleri Üzerine', in: *Yılların İçinden* (Ankara, 1976), 237.

İlkin, Selim and İlhan Tekeli, 'İttihat ve Terakki Hareketinin Oluşumunda Selanik'in Toplumsal Yapısının Belirleyiciliği', in: Osman Okyar and Halil İnalcık (eds.), *Türkiye'nin Sosyal ve Ekonomik Tarihi (1071–1920): Social and Economic History of Turkey (1071–1920)* (Ankara: Meteksan, 1980), 351–82.

Imbusch, Peter, *Moderne und Gewalt: zivilisationstheoretische Perspektiven auf das 20. Jahrhundert* (Wiesbaden: Verlag für Sozialwissenschaften, 2005).

Impagliazzo, Marco (ed.), *Una finestra sul massacro: Documenti inediti sulla strage degli armeni (1915–1916)* (Milano: Guerini, 2000).

İnan, Afet, *et al.*, *Türk Tarihinin Ana Hatları* (Istanbul: Devlet Matbaası, 1930).

—— *Tarih İlminin Dinamik Karakteri* (Ankara: Ankara Üniversitesi, 1956).

İnan, Arı, *Düşünceleriyle Atatürk* (Ankara: Türk Tarih Kurumu, 1991).

İnönü, İsmet, 'Yeni Halkevlerini Açma Nutku', in: *Ülkü* 5, no. 25 (March 1935), 2.

—— *Hatıralar* (Ankara: Bilgi, 1987).

Işık, Haydar, 'Kürtlerin sonu', in: *Yeni Özgür Politika*, 30 November 2006.

İslamoğlu, Mustafa, *Şeyh Said Ayaklanması* (Istanbul: Denge, 1991).

Itzkowitz, Norman, 'The Problem of Perceptions', in: L. Carl Brown (ed.), *Imperial Legacy: the Ottoman Imprint on the Balkans and the Middle East* (New York: Columbia University Press, 1997), 30–8.

Jäckh, Ernst, *The Rising Crescent: Turkey Yesterday, Today, and To-morrow* (New York: Farrar and Rinehart, 1944).

Jacoby, Susan, *Wild Justice: The Evolution of Revenge* (New York: Harper and Row, 1983).

Jafar, Majeed R., *Under-underdevelopment: a regional case study of the Kurdish area in Turkey* (Helsinki: Social Policy Association in Finland, 1976).

Janoff-Bulman, Ronnie, 'The aftermath of victimization: Rebuilding shattered assumptions', in: Charles R. Figley (ed.), *Trauma and its Wake* (New York: Brunner/Mazel, 1985), vol. 1, *The Study and Treatment of Post-traumatic Stress Disorder*, 15–35.

—— *Shattered Assumptions: Towards a New Psychology of Trauma* (New York: Free Press, 1992).

Jastrow, Otto (ed.), *Die mesopotamisch-arabischen Qltu-Dialekte* (Wiesbaden: Kommissionsverlag Franz Steiner GmbH, 1981).

Jenkins, Richard, 'Categorization: Identity, Social Process and Epistemology', in: *Current Sociology* 48, no. 3 (2000), 7–25.

—— *Social Identity* (London: Routledge, 1996).

Jongerden, Joost, *The Settlement Issue in Turkey and the Kurds: An Analysis of Spatial Policies, Modernity and War* (Leiden: Brill, 2007).

Kafadar, Cemal, 'The Question of Decline', in: *Harvard Middle Eastern and Islamic Review* 4, no. 1–2 (1997–8), 30–75.

Kahraman, Ahmet, *Kürt İsyanları: Tedip ve Tenkil* (Istanbul: Evrensel, 2003).

Kaiser, Hilmar, 'Dall'impero alla repubblica: la continuità del negazionismo turco', in: Marcello Flores (ed.), *Storia, Verità, Giustizia: I crimini del XX secolo* (Milano: Bruno Mondadori, 2001), 89–113.

—— 'The Ottoman Government and the End of the Ottoman Social Formation, 1915–1917', paper presented at the conference *Der Völkermord an den Armeniern und die Shoah*, University of Zürich, 7 November 2001, at: <http://www.hist.net/kieser/aghet/Essays/EssayKaiser.html>.

—— *At the Crossroads of Der Zor: Death, Survival, and Humanitarian Resistance in Aleppo, 1915–1917* (London: Gomidas, 2002).

Kaiser, Robert J., 'Homeland Making and the Territorialization of National Identity', in: Daniele Conversi (ed.), *Ethnonationalism in the Contemporary World: Walker Connor and the Study of Nationalism* (London: Routledge, 2002), 229–47.

Kalyvas, Stathis N., *The Logic of Violence in Civil War* (New York: Cambridge University Press, 2006).

Kansu, Aykut, *The Revolution of 1908 in Turkey* (Leiden: Brill, 1997).

Kara, Adem, *Cumhuriyet Döneminde Kalkınmanın Mihenk Taşı: Halkevleri 1932–1951* (Ankara: 24 Saat, 2006).

Karakasidou, Anastasia, *Fields of Wheat, Hills of Blood: Passages to Nationhood in Greek Macedonia, 1870–1990* (Chicago: University of Chicago Press, 1997).

Karaömerlioğlu, M. Asım, 'The People's Houses and the Cult of the Peasant in Turkey', in: *Middle Eastern Studies* 34, no. 4 (1998), 67–91.

Karaosmanoğlu, Yakup Kadri, *Yaban: Milli Roman* (Istanbul: Muallim Ahmet Halit Kitaphanesi, 1932).

Karataş, Adem, *Ve alim ve mücahid ve şehid ve Şeyh Said* (Konya: Sena, 1993); İlhami Aras, *Adım Şeyh Said* (Istanbul: İlke, 1992).

Karay, Refik Halit, 'Harb Zengini', in: *Yeni Mecmua* 2–42 (2 May 1918), 301–2.

Karpat, Kemal H., 'Millets and Nationality: The Roots of the Incongruity off Nation and State in the Post-Ottoman Era', in: Benjamin Braude and Bernard Lewis (eds.), *Christians and Jews in the Ottoman Empire* (New York: Holmes and Meier, 1982), vol. 1, *The Central Lands*, 141–69.

—— *Ottoman Population 1830–1914: Demographic and Social Characteristics* (Madison, WI: University of Wisconsin Press, 1985).

—— 'The People's Houses in Turkey: Establishment and Growth', in: *Middle East Journal* 17 (1963), 55–67.

Kassimeris, George, *The Barbarisation of Warfare* (London: Hurst and Company, 2006).

Kaya, Ferzende, *Mezopotamya Sürgünü: Abdülmelik Fırat'ın Yaşamöyküsü* (Istanbul: Alfa, 2005).

Kaya, Şükrü, 'Halkevlerinin Açılış Konferansı', in: *Ülkü* 11, no. 61 (March 1938), 9.

Kazamias, Andreas M., *Education and the Quest for Modernity in Turkey* (Chicago: The University of Chicago Press, 1966).

Kedourie, Elie, *Nationalism* (London: Blackwell, 1994).

Keegan, John, *The First World War* (New York: Vintage, 1998).

Kemal, Yaşar, *Yaşar Kemal Kendini Anlatıyor: Alain Bosquet ile Görüşmeler* (Istanbul: Yapı Kredi Yayınları, 1999).

Kenanoğlu, Macit, *Osmanlı Millet Sistemi* (Istanbul: Klasik, 2004).

Kenez, Peter, *A History of the Soviet Union from the Beginning to the End* (Cambridge: Cambridge University Press, 2006).

Kennan, George F., *The Other Balkan Wars: A 1913 Carnegie Endowment Inquiry in Retrospect with a New Introduction and Reflection on the Present Record* (Washington, DC: Carnegie Endowment for International Peace, 1993).

Kevirbirî, Salihê, 'Deng û Awaza Xerzan', in: *Özgür Politika*, 3 January 2000.

—— *Bir Çığlığın Yüzyılı: Karapetê Xaço* (Istanbul: Sî, 2002).

—— *Filîtê Quto: Serpêhatî, Dîrok, Sosyolojî* (Istanbul: Pêrî, 2001).

Kévorkian, Raymond H. and Paul B. Paboudjian, *Les Arméniens dans l'Empire ottoman à la veille du génocide* (Paris: Editions d'Art et d'Histoire, 1992).

—— *Le génocide des Arméniens* (Paris: Odile Jacob, 2006).

—— 'Receuil de témoignages sur l'extermination des amele tabouri ou bataillons de soldats-ouvriers Arméniens de l'armée Ottomane pendant la première guerre mondiale', in: *Revue d'Histoire Arménienne Contemporaine* 1 (1995), 289–303.

Kieser, Hans-Lukas, 'Modernisierung und Gewalt in der Gründungsepoche des türkischen Nationalstaats (1913–1938)', in: *Geschichte in Wissenschaft und Unterricht* 57, no. 3 (2006), 156–67.

—— 'Zwischen Ararat und Euphrat: abenländische Missionen im spätosmanischen Kurdistan', in: Hans-Lukas Kieser (ed.), *Kurdistan und Europa: Einblicke in die kurdische Geschichte des 19. und 20. Jahrhunderts* (Zürich: Chronos, 1997).

—— *Der verpasste Friede: Mission, Ethnie und Staat in den Ostprovinzen der Türkei 1839–1938* (Zürich: Chronos, 2000).

Kinross, Patrick, *Within the Taurus: a journey in Asiatic Turkey* (London: n.p., 1954).

Kirby, Fay, *The Village Institute Movement in Turkey: An Educational Mobilization for Social Change* (unpublished Ph.D. dissertation, Teachers' College, Columbia University, New York, 1960).

Knapp, Grace, *The Tragedy of Bitlis* (New York: Fleming H. Revell Co., 1919).

Koca, Hüseyin, *Yakın Tarihten Günümüze Hükümetlerin Doğu-Güneydoğu Anadolu Politikaları: Umumi Müfettişliklerden Olağanüstü Hal Bölge Valiliğine* (Konya: Mikro, 1998).

Koçak, Cemil, "Ey tarihçi belgen kadar konuş!': Belgesel bir Teşkilatı Mahsusa öyküsü', in: *Tarih ve Toplum: Yeni Yaklaşımlar* 3, no. 243 (2006), 171–214.

—— *Umûmî Müfettişlikler (1927–1952)* (Istanbul: İletişim, 2003).

Kodaman, Bayram, *Şark Meselesi Işığı Altında: Sultan Abdülhamid'in Doğu Anadolu Politikası* (Istanbul: Orkun, 1983).

Kökdemir, Naci (ed.), *Eski ve Yeni Toprak, İskan Hükümleri ve Uygulama Klavuzu* (Ankara: n.p., 1952).

Kolluoğlu-Kırlı, Biray, 'From Orientalism to Area Studies', in: *Centennial Review* 3, no. 3 (2003), 93–112.

Konyar, Basri, *Diyarbekir Tarihi* (Ankara: Ulus Basımevi, 1936).

Koraltürk, Murat, 'Milliyetçi bir Refleks: Yer Adlarının Türkleştirilmesi', in: *Toplumsal Tarih* 19, no. 117 (2003), 98–9.

Korkusuz, M. Şefik, *Bir zamanlar Diyarbekir: zamanlar, mekanlar, insanlar* (Istanbul: Yeditepe, 1999).

—— *Eski Diyarbekir'de Gündelik Hayat* (Istanbul: Kent, 2007).

Korlaelçi, Murtaza, *Pozitivizmin Türkiye'ye Girişi ve İlk Etkileri* (Istanbul: İnsan, 1986).

Körükçü, Muhtar, 'Ergani'nin Zülküf Dağı', in: *Karacadağ* VII, no. 85–6 (December/January 1945–6).

Körüklü, Muhtar, *Köyden Haber* (Istanbul: Varlık, 1950).

Koylan, Hasip, *Kürtler ve Şark İsyanları I: Şeyh Sait İsyanı* (Ankara: T.C. İçişleri Bakanlığı Yayını, 1946).

Kraichov, Tone, *Diarbekirski Dnevnik i Spomeni* (Sofia: Izdvo na Otechestveniia front, 1989).

Krementsov, Nikolai, *Stalinist Science* (Princeton: Princeton University Press, 1997).

Krikorian, Mesrob K., *Armenians in the Service of the Ottoman Empire 1860–1908* (London: Routledge, 1977).

Krikorian, Robert Owen, 'The Re-appropriation of the Past: History and Politics in Soviet Armenia, 1988–1991' (unpublished Ph.D. thesis, Harvard University, 2003).

Kruke, Anja (ed.), *Zwangsmigration und Vertreibung: Europa im 20. Jahrhundert* (Bonn: Dietz, 2006).

Künzler, Jacob, *Dreizig Jahre Dienst am Orient* (Basel: Birkhauser Verlag, 1933).

—— *Im Lande des Blutes und der Tränen: Erlebnisse in Mesopotamien während des Weltkrieges (1914–1918)* (Zürich: Chronos, 1999 [1921]).

Kürt Teavün ve Terakki Cemiyeti Nizamnamesi (Istanbul: Kasbar, 1324).

Kushner, David, *The Rise of Turkish Nationalism, 1876–1908* (London: Frank Cass, 1977).

Kutay, Cemal, *Üç Devirde Bir Adam: Fethi Okyar* (Istanbul: Tercüman, 1980).

Kutlay, Naci, *İttihat Terakki ve Kürtler* (Ankara: Beybûn, 1992).

Ladas, Stephen P., *The Exchange of Minorities: Bulgaria, Greece and Turkey* (New York: Macmillan, 1932).

Lammers, Cornelis J., *Vreemde Overheersing: Bezetten en Bezetting in Sociologisch Perspectief* (Amsterdam: Bakker, 2005).

Lazarev, Michail S., *Kurdskii Vopros (1891–1917)* (Moscow: Akademija Nauk SSSR, 1972).

Leerssen, Joep, *National Thought in Europe: A Cultural History* (Amsterdam: Amsterdam University Press, 2007).

Lefebvre, Henri, *The Production of Space* (Oxford: Blackwell, 1991, transl. Donald Nicholson-Smith).

Lepsius, Johannes, *Der Todesgang des Armenischen Volkes: Bericht über das Schicksal des Armenischen Volkes in der Türkei während des Weltkrieges* (Potsdam: Tempelverlag, 1919).

Levene, Mark, 'Creating a Modern "Zone of Genocide": The Impact of Nation- and State-Formation on Eastern Anatolia, 1878–1923', in: *Holocaust and Genocide Studies* 12, no. 3 (1998), 393–433.

—— 'The Limits of Tolerance: Nation State Building and What it Means for Minority Groups', in: *Patterns of Prejudice* 34, no. 2 (2000), 19–40.

—— *Genocide in the Age of the Nation State* (London: Tauris, 2005).

Levonian, Lutfy (ed.), *The Turkish Press 1925–1932* (Athens: School of Religion, 1932).

Lewis Herman, Judith, *Trauma and Recovery: The Aftermath of Violence from Domestic Abuse to Political Terror* (New York: BasicBooks, 1997).

Lewis, Bernard, *The Emergence of Modern Turkey* (Oxford: Oxford University Press, 2002).

Lewis, Geoffrey, *The Turkish Language Reform: A Catastrophic Success* (Oxford: Oxford University Press, 1999).

Lieberman, Benjamin, *Terrible Fate: Ethnic Cleansing in the Making of Modern Europe* (Chicago, IL: Dee, 2006).

Lieven, Dominic, *Empire: The Russian Empire and its Rivals* (New Haven: Yale University Press, 2002).

Lower, Wendy, *Nazi empire-building and the Holocaust in Ukraine* (Chapel Hill: University of North Carolina Press, 2005).

Luciuk, Lubomyr Y., *Searching For Place: Ukrainian Displaced Persons, Canada, and the Migration of Memory* (Toronto: University of Toronto Press, 2000).

Macfie, Alexander L., *The End of the Ottoman Empire, 1908–1923* (London: Longman, 1998).

Magnarella, Paul J., *et al.*, 'The Development of Turkish Social Anthropology', in: *Current Anthropology* 17, no. 2 (1976), 263–74.

Makdisi, Ussama, 'Ottoman Orientalism', in: *American Historical Review* 107 (2002), 768–96.

Malešević, Siniša, *The Sociology of Ethnicity* (London: Sage Publications, 2004).

Mali, Joseph, *Mythistory: The Making of a Modern Historiography* (Chicago: University of Chicago Press, 2003).

Malkki, Liisa, 'Citizens of Humanity: Internationalism and the Imagined Community of Nations', *Diaspora* 3, no. 1 (1994), 41–68.

—— 'The Rooting of Peoples and the Territorialization of National Identity among Scholars and Refugees', in: Akhil Gupta and James Ferguson (eds.), *Culture, Power, Place: Explorations in Critical Anthropology* (Durham: Duke University Press, 1997), 52–74.

Malmîsanij, *Bitlisli Kemal Fevzi ve Kürt Örgütleri İçindeki Yeri* (Istanbul: Fırat, 1993).

—— *Cızira Botanlı Bedirhaniler ve Bedirhani ailesi derneği'nin tutanakları* (Spånga, Sweden: Apec, 1994).

—— *Diyarbekirli Cemilpaşazâdeler ve Kürt Milliyetçiliği* (Istanbul: Avesta, 2004).

—— *Kürt Teavün ve Terakki Cemiyeti ve Gazetesi* (Spånga, Sweden: Apec, 1998).

Mamdani, Mahmood, *When Victims Become Killers: Colonialism, Nativism, and the Genocide in Rwanda* (Princeton, NJ: Princeton University Press, 2001).

Mango, Andrew, 'Atatürk and the Kurds', in: Sylvia Kedourie (ed.), *Seventy-Five Years of the Turkish Republic* (London: Routledge, 2000), 1–25.

Mann, Michael, *The Dark Side of Democracy: Explaining Ethnic Cleansing* (Cambridge: Cambridge University Press, 2005).

—— *The Sources of Social Power* (Cambridge: Cambridge University Press, 1993), vol. 2: *The Rise of Classes and Nation States, 1760–1914*.

Mantran, Robert, 'Les "Maisons du Peuple" en Turquie', in: *Revue d'Institut des Belles Lettres Arabes* (1963), 21–8.

Marashlian, Levon, *Politics and Demography: Armenians, Turks, and Kurds in the Ottoman Empire* (Cambridge, MA: Zoryan Institute, 1991).

Marbeau, Michel, *La Société des Nations* (Paris: Presses Universitaires de France, 2001).

Mardiganian, Aurora, *Ravished Armenia: The Story of Aurora Mardiganian, the Christian Girl who Lived Through the Great Massacres* (New York: Kingfield, 1918).

—— *The Auction of Souls* (London: Phoenix Press, 1934).

Mardin, Şerif, *The Genesis of Young Ottoman Thought: A Study in the Modernization of Turkish Political Ideas* (Princeton: Princeton University Press, 1962).

Margosyan, Mıgırdiç, *Biletimiz İstanbul'a kesildi* (Istanbul: Aras, 2003).

—— *Çengelliiğne* (Istanbul: Belge, 1999).

—— *Gâvur Mahallesi* (Istanbul: Aras, 2002).

—— *Li Ba Me Li Wan Deran* (Istanbul: Avesta, 1999).

—— *Kirveme Mektuplar* (Diyarbakır: Lis, 2006).

—— *Söyle Margos nerelisin?* (Istanbul: Aras, 1998).

—— *Tespih Taneleri* (Istanbul: Aras, 2007).

—— *Zurna* (Istanbul: Avesta, 2009).

—— *Kürdan* (Istanbul: Aras, 2010).

Marx, Anthony W., *Faith in Nation: Exclusionary Origins of Nationalism* (New York: Oxford University Press, 2003).

Mathias, Jeremy, James C. Scott and John Tehranian, 'Naming Like a State: The Production of Legal Identities Proper to States: The Case of the Permanent Family Surname', in: *Comparative Studies in Society and History* 44, no. 1 (2002), 4–44.

Mayall, James, *Nationalism and international society* (Cambridge: Cambridge University Press, 1990).

Maynard, Richard E., 'The Lise and its Curriculum in the Turkish Educational System' (Ph.D. dissertation, University of Chicago, 1961).

Mazıcı, Nurşen, *Celal Bayar: Başbakanlık Dönemi 1937–1939* (Istanbul: Der, 1996).

Mazower, Mark, *Salonica: City of Ghosts: Christians, Muslims and Jews 1430–1950* (London: HarperCollins Publishers, 2004).

McCarthy, Justin, 'Muslim Refugees in Turkey: The Balkan Wars, World War I, and the Turkish War of Independence', in: *Isis Press and the Institute of Turkish Studies* (Istanbul: Isis, 1993).

—— *Death and Exile: The Ethnic Cleansing of Ottoman Muslims, 1821–1922* (Princeton, NJ: The Darwin Press, 1995).

—— *Muslims and Minorities: The Population of Ottoman Anatolia and the End of the Empire* (New York: New York University, 1983).

McGarry, John, '"Demographic Engineering": The State-Directed Movement of Ethnic Groups as a Technique of Conflict Regulation', in: *Ethnic and Racial Studies* 21, no. 4 (1998), 613–38.

McNeely, Connie L., *Constructing the Nation state: International Organization and Prescriptive Action* (Westport, CT: Greenwood Press, 1995).

McNeill, William H., *Polyethnicity and National Unity in World History* (Toronto: Toronto University Press, 1986).

Medyalı, A., *Kürdistanlı Yahudiler* (Ankara: Berhem, 1992).

Mehmet Efendi, Kârerli, *Yazılmayan Tarih ve Anılarım (1915–1958)* (Ankara: Kalan, 2007).

Meiselas, Susan, *Kurdistan in the Shadow of History* (Chicago: University of Chicago Press, 2008, 2nd edn.).

Merigoux, Jean-Marie, *Va a Ninive! Un dialogue avec l'Irak: Mosul et les villages chrétiens, pages d'histoire dominicaine* (Paris: Cerf, 2000).

Meyer John W., *et al.*, 'World Society and the Nation state', in: *American Journal of Sociology* 103, no. 1 (1997), 144–81.

Meyrier, Gustave, *Les Massacres de Diarbekir: Correspondance diplomatique du Vice-Consul de France 1894–1896* (Paris: L'Inventaire, 2000).

Miller, Donald E. and Lorne Touryan-Miller, *Survivors: An Oral History of the Armenian Genocide* (Berkeley: University of California Press, 1993).

Minassian, Gaïdz F., 'Les relations entre le Comité Union et Progrès et la Fédération Révolutionnaire Arménienne à la veille de la Premiere Guerre mondiale d'après les sources arméniennes', in: *Revue d'histoire arménienne contemporaine* 1 (1995), 45–99.

Mingst, Karen A. and Margaret P. Karns, *The United Nations in the Twenty-First Century* (Boulder, CO: Westview Press, 2006).

Morgenthau, Henry, *Ambassador Morgenthau's Story* (Ann Arbor, MI: Gomidas, 2000).

Mosse, George, *Nazi Culture: Intellectual, Cultural, and Social Life in the Third Reich* (New York: Grosset and Dunlap, 1966).

——— *Toward the Final Solution: A History of European Racism* (Madison, WI: University of Wisconsin Press, 1985).

Müderrisoğlu, Alptekin, *Sarıkamış Dramı* (Istanbul: Kaştaş, 1997).

Mugurditchian, Thomas, *Dikranagerdee Nahankee Tcharteru, Aganadesee Badmoutiun* (Cairo: Djihanian, 1919).

Mülsch, Elisabeth-Christine, *Zwischen Assimilation und jüdischem Selbstverständnis: David Léon Cahun (1841–1900)* (Bonn: Romanist. Verlag, 1987).

Naayem, Joseph, *Shall This Nation Die?* (New York: Chaldean Rescue, 1921).

Naimark, Norman M., *Fires of Hatred: Ethnic Cleansing in Twentieth-Century Europe* (Cambridge, MA: Harvard University Press, 2001).

Nalbandian, Louise, *The Armenian Revolutionary Movement* (Berkeley, CA: University of California Press, 1963).

Nazif, Süleyman, 'Doktor Reshid', in: *Hadisat*, 8 February 1919.

Nazlı, Hurşit, *Elazığ ilinin coğrafi, zirai, ticari, tarih, nufus ve jeolojik durumu* (Ankara: Zerbamat Basımevi, 1939).

Nesimî, Abidin, *Yılların İçinden* (Istanbul: Gözlem, 1977).

Neyzi, Leyla, *'Ben Kimim': Türkiye'de Sözlü Tarih, Kimlik ve Öznellik* (Istanbul: İletişim, 2004).

——— *İstanbul'da Hatırlamak ve Unutmak: Birey, Bellek ve Aidiyet* (Istanbul: Tarih Vakfı Yurt Yayınları, 1999).

Niepage, Martin, *The Horrors of Aleppo* (London: T. Fisher Unwin Ltd., 1917).

Northedge, Frederick S., *The League of Nations: Its Life and Times, 1920–1946* (Leicester: Leicester University Press, 1986).

Noyan, Bedri, *Bütün Yönleriyle Bektâşîlik ve Alevîlik* (Ankara: Ardıç, 1998–2006).

Öcalan, Abdullah, *Kürt Sorununda Demokratik Çözüm Bildirgesi* (Istanbul: Mem, 1999).

Odabaşı, Yılmaz, *Şeyh Said İsyanı: 1925 Kürt Ayaklanması: Destan* (Istanbul: Zilan, 1991).

Öktem, Kerem, 'Incorporating the Time and Space of the Ethnic "Other": Nationalism and Space in Southeast Turkey in the Nineteenth and Twentieth Centuries', in: *Nations and Nationalism* 10, no. 4 (2004), 559–78.

—— 'The Nation's Imprint: Demographic Engineering and the Change of Toponymes in Republican Turkey', in: *European Journal of Turkish Studies*, no. 7 (2008), at: <http://www.ejts.org/document2243.html>.

Okyar, Osman and Mehmet Seyitdanlıoğlu (ed.), *Fethi Okyar'ın Anıları: Atatürk, Okyar ve Çok Partili Türkiye* (Ankara: Türkiye İş Bankası Kültür Yayınları, 1997).

Olson, Robert, 'Kurds and Turks: Two Documents Concerning Kurdish Autonomy in 1923 and 1923', in: *Journal of South Asian and Middle Eastern Studies* 15, no. 2 (1991), 20–31.

—— 'The Kurdish Rebellions of Sheikh Said (1925), Mt. Ararat (1930), and Dersim (1937–8): Their Impact on the Development of the Turkish Air Force and on Kurdish and Turkish Nationalism', in: *Die Welt des Islams* 40, no. 1 (2000), 67–94.

—— 'The Sheikh Said Rebellion: Its Impact on the Development of the Turkish Air Force', in: *The Journal of Kurdish Studies* 1 (1995), 77–84.

—— *The Emergence of Kurdish Nationalism and the Sheikh Said Rebellion, 1880–1925* (Austin, TX: University of Texas Press, 1989).

Onur, Necmi, *Şark Cephesinde Yeni Birsey Yok* (Istanbul: Belge, 1972).

Örgeevren, Ahmet Süreyya, *Şeyh Sait İsyanı ve Şark İstiklal Mahkemesi: Vesikalar, Olaylar, Hatıralar* (Istanbul: Temel, 2002).

Orwell, George, *Nineteen Eighty-Four* (London: Secker and Warburg, 1949).

Osterhammel, Jürgen, '"The Great Work of Uplifting Mankind": Zivilisierungsmissionen und Moderne', in: Boris Barth and Jürgen Osterhammel (eds.), *Zivilisierungsmissionen* (Konstanz: UVK Verlagsgesellschaft, 2005), 363–425.

Østrup, Johannes, *Det Nye Tyrki* (Copenhagen: n.p., 1931).

Ozankan, Cenab, *Türk Millî Oyunları: Ağrı Bölgesi, Balıkesir, Bursa, Çorum, Diyarbakır, Ege Bölgesi, Elâzığ, Erzurum, Gazi Antep, Hatay, Kars, Kastamonu, Konya, Malatya, Rize, Seyhan Bölgesi, Sivas, Trabzon, Urfa* (Istanbul: Sucuoğlu Matbaası, 1955).

Özelli, M. Tunç, 'The Evolution of the Formal Educational System and its Relation to Economic Growth Policies in the First Turkish Republic', in: *International Journal of Middle East Studies* 5, no. 1 (1974), 77–92.

Özervarlı, M. Sait, 'Transferring Traditional Islamic Disciplines into Modern Social Sciences in Late Ottoman Thought: The Attempts of Ziya Gökalp and Mehmed Serafeddin', in: *The Muslim World* 97 (2007), 317–30.

Özlü, Demir, *Sokaklarda Bir Avlu* (Istanbul: Dünya, 2004).

Özoğlu, Hakan, *Kurdish Notables and the Ottoman State: Evolving Identities, Competing Loyalties, and Shifting Boundaries* (Albany, NY: State University of New York Press, 2004).

Öztürk, Saygı, *İsmet Paşa'nın Kürt Raporu* (Istanbul: Doğan Kitap, 2007).

Öztürkmen, Arzu, 'The Role of People's Houses in the Making of National Culture in Turkey', in: *New Perspectives on Turkey* 11 (1994), 159–81.

—— *Türkiye'de Folklor ve Milliyetçilik* (Istanbul: İletişim, 1998).

Özyürek, Esra (ed.), *The Politics of Public Memory in Turkey* (Syracuse, NY: Syracuse University Press, 2006).

Parker, John and Charles Smith, *Modern Turkey* (London: Routledge, 1940).

Parla, Taha, *The Social and Political Thought of Ziya Gökalp 1876–1924* (Leiden: Brill, 1985).

Parry, Oswald H., *Six Months in a Syrian Monastery: Being the Record of a Visit to the Head Quarters of the Syrian Church in Mesopotamia With Some Account of the Yazidis or Devil Worshippers of Mosul and El Jilwah, Their Sacred Book* (London: Horace Cox, 1895).

Paşazâde, Hüseyin, 'Kürdler ve Ermeniler', in: *Kürd Teavün ve Terakki Gazetesi*, 30 January 1909, 3–6.

Pekesen, Berna, 'The Exodus of Armenians from the Sanjak of Alexandretta in the 1930s', in: Hans-Lukas Kieser (ed.), *Turkey Beyond Nationalism: Towards Post-Nationalist Identities* (London: I.B. Tauris, 2006), 57–73.

Perk, Kadri, *Cenupdoğu Anadolu'nun Eski Zamanları* (Istanbul: İnkılap, 1934).

Pinker, Steven, *The Blank Slate: The Modern Denial of Human Nature* (London: Allen Lane, 2002).

Pittard, Eugène, 'Atatürk'ün Hatırasını Tazim', in: *Belleten* 3, no. 10 (April 1939), 175.

Poggi, Gianfranco, *The Development of the Modern State: A Sociological Introduction* (Stanford, CA: Stanford University Press, 1978).

Pohl, Dieter, *Nationalsozialistische Judenverfolgung in Ostgalizien 1941–1944: Organisation und Durchführung eines staatlichen Massenverbrechens* (München: Oldenbourg, 1996).

Polat, Lokman, *Torina Şêx Seîd* (Stockholm: Çapa Yekem, 1993).

Popper, Karl R., *The Poverty of Historicism* (London: Routledge and Kegan Paul, 1957).

Qarabashi, Abed Mshiho Na'man, *Dmo Zliho: Vergoten Bloed. Verhalen over de Gruweldaden Jegens Christenen in Turkije en over het Leed dat hun in 1895 en in 1914–1918 is Aangedaan* (Glanerbrug: Bar Hebraeus, 2002, transl. George Toro and Amill Gorgis).

Quine, Maria Sophia, *Population Policies in Twentieth-Century Europe: Fascist Dictatorships and Liberal Democracies* (London: Routledge, 1996).

Rae, Heather, *State Identities and the Homogenisation of Peoples* (Cambridge: Cambridge University Press, 2002).

Rammstedt, Otthein, *Deutsche Soziologie, 1933–1945: Die Normalität einer Anpassung* (Frankfurt am Main: Suhrkamp, 1986).

Renan, Ernest, 'What is a Nation?', in Geoff Eley and Ronald Grigor Suny, *Becoming National: A Reader* (Oxford: Oxford University Press, 1996), 41–55.

Reuter, Julia, *Ordnungen des Anderen: Zum Problem des Eigenen in der Soziologie des Fremden* (Bielefeld: Transcript, 2002).

Reynolds, Michael, 'The Ottoman-Russian Struggle for Eastern Anatolia and the Caucasus, 1908–1918: Identity, Ideology and the Geopolitics of World Order' (Unpublished Ph.D. thesis, Princeton University, 2003).

Rhétoré, Jacques, 'Les chrétiens aux bêtes! Souvenirs de la guerre sainte proclamée par les Turcs contre les chrétiens en 1915' (Unpublished manuscript, Bibliothèque du Saulchoir).

Rogan, Eugene L., 'Asiret Mektebi: Abdulhamid II's School for Tribes (1892–1907)', in: *International Journal of Middle East Studies* 28, no. 1 (1996), 83–108.

Rohat, *Kürdistan'da Eğitim Süreçleri* (Diyarbakır: Dilan, 1992).

——*Ziya Gökalp'ın Büyük Çilesi Kürtler* (Istanbul: Fırat, 1992).

Roshwald, Aviel, *Ethnic Nationalism and the Fall of Empires: Central Europe, Russia and the Middle East, 1914–1923* (London: Routledge, 2001).

Rumeli Mezâlimi ve Bulgar Vahşetleri (Istanbul: Rumeli Muhâcirîn-i İslâmiyye Cemiyeti, 1913).

Rustow, Dankwart A., *A World of Nations: Problems of Political Modernization* (Washington, DC: The Brookings Institution, 1967).

Rygaard, Olaf A., *Mellem Tyrker og Kurder: En Dansk Ingeniørs Oplevelser i Lilleasien* (Copenhagen: Nordisk Forlag, 1935).

Saba, Ziya Osman, 'Cahit'le Günlerimiz', in: Cahit Sıtkı Tarancı, *Ziya'ya Mektuplar 1930–1946* (Istanbul: Varlık, 1957).

Sabit, Fuad, 'Anadolu Duygularından', in: *Türk Yurdu* 2, no. 28 (11 December 1912), 72.

Safrastian, Arshak, *Kurds and Kurdistan* (London: Harvill Press, 1948).

Sagay, Esat, 'Son Yapılan Teftiş Neticesi Hakkında Talimat', in: Hasan Ali Yücel, *Türkiye'de Orta Öğretim* (Ankara: T.C. Kültür Bakanlığı Yayınları, 1994), 364–5.

Sağnıç, Feqi Hüseyin, *Portreler* (Istanbul: Istanbul Kürt Enstitüsü Yayınları, 2000).

Şahin, Mustafa and Yaşar Akyol, 'Habil Adem ya da nam-ı diğer Naci İsmail (Pelister) hakkında', in: *Toplumsal Tarih* 2, no. 11 (1994), 6–12.

Şahin, Ömer, 'Komkujî li hemberî Ezidîyan' (Heidelberg, 2001), unpublished private manuscript.

Sahlins, Peter, *Boundaries: The Making of France and Spain in the Pyrenees* (Berkeley: University of California Press, 1989).

Said, Baha, 'Anadolu'da İçtimâî Zümreler ve Anadolu İçtimâiyatı', in: *Millî Talim ve Terbiye Mecmuası*, no. 5 (August 1918), 18–32.

Sakaoğlu, Necdet, *Cumhuriyet Dönemi Eğitim Tarihi* (Istanbul: İletişim Cep Üniversitesi, 1993).

——*Kuruluşundan günümüze kadar 'çeşm-i cihan' Amasra: coğrafî, içtimâî ve turistik özellikleri ile 35 asırlık tarihi ve tarih eserleri* (Istanbul: Latin, 1966).

Şapolyo, Enver Behnan, *Ziyâ Gökalp: İttihadı Terakki ve Meşrutiyet Tarihi: Ekli ve Fotoğraflı* (Istanbul: İnkılap ve Aka Kitabevleri, 1974).

Sarafian, Ara, 'The Absorption of Armenian Women and Children into Muslim Households as a Structural Component of the Armenian Genocide', in: Omer Bartov and Phyllis Mack (eds.), *In God's Name: Genocide and Religion in the Twentieth Century* (Oxford: Berghahn, 2001), 209–21.

—— 'The Ottoman Archives Debate and the Armenian Genocide', in: *Armenian Forum* 2, no. 1 (1999), 35–44.

Sariev, Veselin, *Diarbekir i Bulgarite: Po Sledite na Zatochenitsite* (Sofia: Khristo Botev, 1996).

Sarrafian Banker, Marie, *My Beloved Armenia: A Thrilling Testimony* (Chicago: The Bible Institute Colportage Association, 1936).

Sasse, Hans-Jürgen, 'Linguistische Analyse des arabischen Dialekts der Mhallamiye in der Provinz Mardin (Südosttürkei)' (Ph.D. Thesis, Ludwig-Maximilians University of München, Department of Semitics, 1970).

Savcı, Süleyman, *Silvan Tarihi* (Diyarbakır: CHP Diyarbakır Halkevi Neşriyatı, 1949).

Sazonov, Sergej D., *Les années fatales: souvenirs de M. S. Sazonov, ancien ministre des Affaires Étrangères de Russie (1910–1916)* (Paris: Payot, 1927).

Schaub, Edward L., *Progressism: An Essay in Social Philosophy* (Calcutta: University of Calcutta, 1937).

Schechtman, Joseph B., *European Population Transfers, 1939–1945* (New York: Oxford University Press, 1946).

—— *Population Transfers in Asia* (New York: Hallsby Press, 1949).

—— *Postwar Population Transfers in Europe, 1945–1955* (Philadelphia: University of Pennsylvania Press, 1962).

Schraudenbach, Ludwig, *Muharebe: Der erlebte Roman eines deutschen Führers im Osmanischen Heere 1916/17* (Berlin: Drei Masken Verlag, 1924).

Schulze, Winfried and Otto Gerhard Oexle (eds.), *Deutsche Historiker im Nationalsozialismus* (Frankfurt am Main: Fischer Taschenbuch Verlag, 1999).

Schüler, Harald, *Türkiye'de Sosyal Demokrasi: Particilik, Hemşehrilik, Alevilik* (Istanbul: İletişim, 1999).

Scott, James C., *Seeing Like a State: How Certain Schemes to Improve the Human Condition Have Failed* (New Haven: Yale University Press, 1998).

Şeker, Nesim, 'Demographic Engineering in the Late Ottoman Empire and the Armenians', in: *Middle Eastern Studies* 43, no. 3 (2007), 461–74.

Semelin, Jacques, *Purify and Destroy: The Political Uses of Massacre and Genocide* (London: Hurst and Co., 2007).

Şenalp, Leman, 'Atatürk'ün kütüphanesi', in: *Türk Kütüphaneciliği* 16, no. 2 (2002), 171–8.

—— 'Atatürk'ün Tarih Bilgisi', in: *Uluslararası İkinci Atatürk Sempozyumu* (Ankara: Atatürk Araştırma Merkezi Yayınları, 1991), vol. 2, 717–27.

Şentürk, Recep, 'İçtimâiyyât Mecmuâsı', in: *Türkiye Diyanet Vakfı İslam Ansiklopedisi* (Istanbul: Türkiye Diyanet Vakfı, 2000), vol. 21, 448–63.

—— 'Intellectual Dependency: Late Ottoman Intellectuals between Fiqh and Social Science', in: *Die Welt des Islams* 47, no. 3 (2007), 283–318.

Serdî, Hasan Hişyar, *Görüş ve Anılarım 1907–1985* (Istanbul: Med, 1994).

Şerefhanoğlu Sözena, Müjgan and Gülay Zorer Gedik, 'Evaluation of Traditional Architecture in Terms of Building Physics: Old Diyarbakır houses', in: *Building and Environment* 42, no. 4 (2007), 1810–16.

Seropyan, Sarkis, 'Vatansız tek ulus Çingeneler ve Çingenelerin Ermenileşmişleri Hay-Poşalar', in: *Tarih ve Toplum* 33, no. 202 (2000), 21–5.

Seufert, Günter, 'Between Religion and Ethnicity: A Kurdish-Alevi Tribe in Globalizing Istanbul', in: Ayşe Öncü and Petra Weyland (eds.), *Space, Culture and Power: New Identities in Globalizing Cities* (London: Zed, 1997), 157–76.

Sezen, Yıldırım (ed.), *İki Kardeşten Seferberlik Anıları* (Ankara: Kültür Bakanlığı Yayınları, 1999).

Shanin, Teodor (ed.), *Peasants and peasant societies: selected readings* (Harmondsworth: Penguin books, 1971).

Silopî, Zinar, *Doza Kurdistan: Kürt Milletinin 60 Yıllık Esaretten Kurtuluş Savaşı Hatıraları* (Istanbul: Özge, 2001).

Simon, Hyacinthe, *Mardine: la ville heroïque: Autel et tombeau de l'Arménie (Asie Mineure) durant les massacres de 1915* (Jounieh: Maison Naaman pour la culture, 1991, ed. Naji Naaman ed.).

Şimşek, Halil, *Geçmişten günümüze Bingöl ve Doğu ayaklanmaları* (Ankara: Kültür Bakanlığı, 2001).

Şimşek, Sefa, *Bir İdeolojik Seferberlik Deneyimi Halkevleri 1932–1951* (Istanbul: Boğaziçi Üniversitesi Yayınevi, 2002).

Singleton, David, *The Age Factor in Second Language Acquisition: A Critical Look at the Critical Period Hypothesis* (Clevedon: Multilingual Matters, 1995).

Skutnabb-Kangas, Tove, *Linguistic Genocide in Education or Worldwide Diversity and Human Rights?* (Mahwah, NJ: Erlbaum, 2000).

Smith, Anthony D. and Colin Williams, 'The National Construction of Social Space', in: *Progress in Human Geography* 7, no. 4 (1983), 502–18.

Soane, Ely B., *To Mesopotamia and Kurdistan in Disguise: With Historical Notices of the Kurdish Tribes and the Chaldeans of Kurdistan* (London: J. Murray, 1912).

Sohrabi, Nader, 'Global Waves, Local Actors: What the Young Turks Knew about Other Revolutions and Why it Mattered', in: *Comparative Studies in Society and History* 44, no. 1 (2002), 45–79.

Southgate, Horatio, *Narrative of a Tour through Armenia, Kurdistan, Persia and Mesopotamia* (London: Bradbury and Evans, 1840).

Soviet Academy of Sciences (ed.), *Yeni ve Yakın Çağda Kürt Siyaset Tarihi* (Istanbul: Pêrî, 1998, transl. M. Aras).

Soysal, Emin M., 'Köy Muallimi ve Köy', in: *Dönüm* 20 (1934), 23.

Strang, Heather, *Repair or Revenge: Victims and Restorative Justice* (Oxford: Oxford University Press, 2002).

Stürmer, Harry, *Two War Years in Constantinople: Sketches of German and Young Turkish Ethics and Politics* (London: Gomidas Institute, 2004 [1917]).

Sussnitzki, Alphons J., 'Zur Gliederung wirtschaftlicher Arbeit nach Nationalitäten in der Türkei', in: *Archiv für Wirtschaftsforschung im Orient* 2 (1917), 382–407.

Sutherland, James, *The Adventures of an Armenian Boy* (Ann Arbor, MI: The Ann Arbor Press, 1964).

Suzuki, Peter, 'Peasants Without Plows: Some Anatolians in Istanbul', in: *Rural Sociology* 31, no. 4 (1966), 428–38.

Sykes, Mark, *The Caliphs' Last Heritage: A Short History of the Turkish Empire* (London: n.p., 1915).

Tabak, Serap, *Kâzım Dirik Paşa (Askeri, Mülki Hayatı ve Şahsiyeti)* (Çorum: Karam, 2008).

Tachjian, Vahé, 'Expulsion of the Armenian Survivors of Diyarbekir and Urfa, 1923–1930', in: Richard G. Hovannisian (ed.), *Armenian Tigranakert/Diarbekir and Edessa/Urfa* (Costa Mesa, CA: Mazda, 2006), 519–38.

Tankut, Hasan Reşit, *Diyarbakır adı üzerinde toponomik bir tetkik* (Ankara: Ulus Basımevi, 1937).

Tanpınar, Ahmet Hamdi, *Sahnenin Dışındakiler* (Istanbul: Dergâh, 1973).

Tansel, Fevziye Abdullah (ed.), *Ziya Gökalp Külliyatı-I: Şiirler ve Halk Masalları (Kızılelma-Yeni Hayat-Altun Işık-Eserleri Dışında Kalan Şiirleri)* (Ankara: Türk Tarih Kurumu Yayınları, 1952).

Taylor, Peter J. and Colin Flint, *Political Geography: World-Economy, Nation State and Locality* (Harlow: Prentice Hall, 2000).

Taylor, Tony, *Denial: History Betrayed* (Melbourne: Melbourne University Publishing, 2009).

Ter Minassian, Anahide, 'Van 1915', in: Richard G. Hovannisian (ed.), *Armenian Van/Vaspurakan* (Costa Mesa, CA: Mazda, 2000), 209–44.

Ternon, Yves, *Mardin 1915: Anatomie pathologique d'une destruction* (Special Issue of the *Revue d'Histoire Arménienne Contemporaine* 4, 2002).

TESEV, *Overcoming a Legacy of Mistrust: Towards Reconciliation between the State and the Displaced* (Istanbul: Turkish Economic and Social Studies Foundation, 2006).

Ther, Philipp, 'A Century of Forced Migration: The Origins and Consequences of "Ethnic Cleansing"', in: Philipp Ther and Ana Siljak (eds.), *Redrawing Nations: Ethnic Cleansing in East-Central Europe, 1944–1948* (Lanham, MD: Rowman and Littlefield, 2001), 43–72.

Thomas, Lewis V. and Richard N. Frye, *The United States and Turkey and Iran* (Cambridge, MA: Harvard University Press, 1951).

Thompson, Janice, 'State Sovereignty in International Relations: Bridging the Gap between Theory and Empirical Research', in: *International Studies Quarterly* 39, no. 2 (1995), 213–34.

Tigris, Amed, 'Lîce' (Stockholm: unpublished manuscript, 2005).

Tilly, Charles, *The Formation of National States in Western Europe* (Princeton: Princeton University Press, 1975).

—— 'States and Nationalism in Europe, 1492–1992', in: *Theory and Society* 23, no. 1 (1994), 131–46.

—— *Coercion, Capital, and European States, A.D. 990–1992* (Oxford: Blackwell, 1990).

Toft, Monica Duffy, *The Geography of Ethnic Violence: Identity, Interests, and the Indivisibility of Territory* (Princeton, NJ: Princeton University Press, 2003).

Toker, Metin, *Şeyh Sait ve İsyanı* (Ankara: Akis, 1968).

Tölölyan, Khachig, 'Terrorism in Modern Armenian Political Culture', in: *Terrorism and Political Violence* 4, no. 2 (1992), 8–22.

Tonguç, İsmail Hakkı, *Eğitim Yolu ile Canlandırılacak Köy* (Istanbul: Remzi Kitabevi, 1947).

Toprak, Zafer, 'Bir Hayal Ürünü: "İttihatçıların Türkleştirme Politikası"', in: *Toplumsal Tarih* 146 (2006), 14–22.

—— 'Osmanlı Narodnikleri: "Halka Doğru" gidenler', in: *Toplum ve Bilim* 24 (Winter 1984), 69–81.

—— 'Osmanlı'da Toplumbilimin Doğuşu', in: *Modern Türkiye'de Siyasi Düşünce* (Istanbul: İletişim Yayınları, 2001), vol. 1, *Tanzimat ve Meşrutiyet'in Birikimi*, 310–27.

Törrönen, Jukka, 'The Concept of Subject Position in Empirical Social Research', in: *Journal for the Theory of Social Behaviour* 31, no. 3 (2001), 313–30.

Trotzki, Leo, *Die Balkankriege 1912–13* (Essen: Arbeiterpresse Verlag, 1995, transl. Hannelore Georgi and Harald Schubärth).

Trouillot, Michel-Rolph, *Silencing the Past: Power and the Production of History* (Boston: Beacon Press, 2007).

Tunaya, Tarık Zafer, *Türkiye'de Siyasal Partiler* (Istanbul: İletişim, 1997).

Tunçay, Mete, *Türkiye Cumhuriyetinde Tek Parti Yönetiminin Kurulması 1923–1931* (Ankara: Yurt Yayınları, 1995).

Tuncer, Orhan Cezmi, *Diyarbakır Kiliseleri* (Diyarbakır: Diyarbakır Büyükşehir Belediyesi Kültür ve Sanat Yayınları, 2002).

—— *Diyarbekir Camileri* (Diyarbakır: Diyarbakır Büyükşehir Belediyesi Kültür ve Sanat Yayınları, 1996).

Türköz, Meltem, 'Surname Narratives and the State-Society Boundary: Memories of Turkey's Family Name Law of 1934', in: *Middle Eastern Studies* 43, no. 6 (2007), 893–908.

Türkyılmaz, Zeynep, 'The Republican Civilizing Mission: The Case of Mountain Flowers in Dersim/Tunceli (1937–1950)', paper presented at the annual conference of the Middle East Studies Association, Washington, DC, 24 November 2002.

Tütenk, Mustafa Âkif, 'Diyarbakır İstiklâl Mahkemesinin Kararları ve Sürülen Aileler', in: *Kara-Amid* 2–4 (1956).

Uğurlu, Nurer, *Kürt milliyeçiliği: Kürtler ve Şeyh Sait İsyanı* (Istanbul: Örgün, 2006); Yaşar Kalafat, *Şark Meselesi Işığında Şeyh Sait Olayı, Karakteri, Dönemindeki İç ve Dış Olaylar* (Ankara: Boğaziçi, 1992).

Uluğ, 'Ermeniler', in: *Türk*, no. 110 (21 December 1905), 2.

Ursinus, Michael, 'Zur Diskussion um "millet" im Osmanischen Reich', in: *Südost-Forschungen* 48 (1989), 195–207.

Uzun, Mehmed, 'Diyarbakir: the Slap in the Face', in: *International Journal of Kurdish Studies* 1, no. 1 (January 2003).

Ülken, Hilmi Ziyâ, *Ziyâ Gökalp* (Istanbul: Kanaat Kitabevi, 1942).

Ülker, Erol, 'Assimilation of the Muslim communities in the first decade of the Turkish Republic (1923–1934)', in: *European Journal of Turkish Studies* (2007), <http://www.ejts.org/document822.html>.

Üngör, Uğur Ümit, 'Seeing like a Nation-State: Young Turk Social Engineering in Eastern Turkey, 1913–1950', in: *Journal of Genocide Research* 10, no. 1 (2008), 15–39.

—— 'Recalling the Appalling: Mass Violence in Eastern Turkey in the Twentieth Century', in: Nanci Adler, Selma Leydesdorff and Leyla Neyzi (eds.), *Memories of Mass Repression* (Piscataway, NJ: Transaction, 2008), 175–98.

Üstel, Füsun, *İmparatorluktan Ulus-Devlete Türk Milliyetciliği: Türk Ocakları (1912–1931)* (Istanbul: İletişim, 1997).

Üstüngel, Savaş (pseudonym of İsmail Bilen), *Savaş Yolu: Bir Türk Komünistinin Notları* (Sofia: Narodna Prosveta, 1958).

Üzülmez, Müslüm, *Çayönü'nden Ergani'ye Uzun Bir Yürüyüş* (Istanbul: n.p., 2005).

Van Bruinessen, Martin, 'Les Kurdes, États et tribus', in: Hosham Dawod (ed.), *Tribus et pouvoirs en terre d'islam* (Paris: Armand Colin, 2004), 145–68.

—— 'Race, Culture, Nation and Identity Politics in Turkey: Some Comments', paper presented at the Annual Turkish Studies Workshop Continuity and Change: Shifting State Ideologies from Late Ottoman to Early Republican Turkey, 1890–1930, Department of Near Eastern Studies, Princeton University, 24–26 April 1997, 8–9.

—— 'The Ottoman Conquest of Diyarbekir and the Administrative Organisation of the Province in the 16th and 17th Centuries', in: Martin van Bruinessen and Hendrik Boeschoten (eds.), *Evliya Çelebi in Diyarbekir* (Leiden: Brill, 1988), 13–38.

—— *Agha, Shaikh and State: The Social and Political Structures of Kurdistan* (London: Zed, 1992).

Van der Dennen, Johan, 'Ethnocentrism and In-group/Out-group Differentiation', in: Vernon Reynolds (ed.), *The Sociobiology of Ethnocentrism: Evolutionary Dimensions of Xenophobia, Discrimination, Racism and Nationalism* (Athens: University of Georgia Press, 1987), 1–47.

Van der Plank, Pieter H., *Etnische Zuivering in Midden-Europa: Natievorming en Staatsburgerschap in de XXe Eeuw* (Leeuwarden: Universitaire Pers Fryslân, 2004).

Van Krieken, Robert, 'Reshaping Civilization: Liberalism between Assimilation and Cultural Genocide', in: *Amsterdams Sociologisch Tijdschrift* 29, no. 2 (2002), 215–47.

—— 'The Barbarism of Civilization: Cultural Genocide and the "Stolen Generations"', in: *British Journal of Sociology* 50, no. 2 (1999), 297–315.

VanderLippe, John M., *The Politics of Turkish Democracy: İsmet İnönü and the Formation of the Multi-Party System, 1938–1950* (Albany, NY: State University of New York Press, 2005).

Vierbücher, Heinrich, *Armenien 1915: Die Abschlachtung eines Kulturvolkes durch die Türken* (Bremen: Donat and Temmen Verlag, 1985 [1930]).

Von P. Goç, *İskan-ı Muhacirîn: Beynelmilel Usûl-ü Temsil* (Istanbul: Kitabhâne-i Sûdî, 1918, transl. Habil Adem).

Wagner, Jon G., 'The Rise of the State System: 1914–1950', in: Roy R. Andersen, Robert F. Seibert and Jon G. Wagner (eds.), *Politics and Change in the Middle East: Sources of Conflict and Accommodation* (Englewood Cliffs, NJ: Prentice-Hall, 1982), 74–93.

Walker, Mark, *Nazi Science* (New York: Plenum Press, 1995).

Wallerstein, Immanuel, *The Modern World-System* (New York: Academic Press, 1974–81).

Wasserstein, Bernard, *Barbarism and Civilization: A History of Europe in Our Time* (Oxford: Oxford University Press, 2007).

Weiner, Amir (ed.), *Landscaping the Human Garden: Twentieth-Century Population Management in a Comparative Framework* (Stanford, CA: Stanford University Press, 2003).

—— 'Nature, Nurture, and Memory in a Socialist Utopia: Delineating the Soviet Socio-Ethnic Body in the Age of Socialism', in: *The American Historical Review* 104 (1999), 1114–55.

White, Paul, 'Ethnic Differentiation among the Kurds: Kurmanci, Kizilbash and Zaza', in: *Journal of Arabic, Islamic and Middle Eastern Studies* 2, no. 2 (1995), 67–90.

Wiborg, Susanne, 'Political and Cultural Nationalism in Education', in: *Comparative Education* 36, no. 2 (2000), 235–43.

Wiedemann, M., 'Ibrahim Paschas Glück und Ende', in: *Asien* 8 (1909), 34–54.

Williams, Talcott, *Turkey: A World Problem of To-day* (New York: Doubleday, Page and Co., 1921).

Wilmer, Franke, *The Social Construction of Man, the State and War: Identity, Conflict, and Violence in Former Yugoslavia* (London: Routledge, 2002).

Wimmer, Andreas, *Nationalist Exclusion and Ethnic Conflict: Shadows of Modernity* (Cambridge: Cambridge University Press, 2002).

Winter, Michael, 'The Modernization of Education in Kemalist Turkey', in: Jacob M. Landau (ed.), *Atatürk and the Modernization of Turkey* (Boulder, CO: Westview Press, 1984), 183–94.

Wolf-Gazo, Ernest, 'John Dewey in Turkey: An Educational Mission', in: *Journal of American Studies of Turkey* 3 (1996), 15–42.

Yalçın, Hüseyin Cahit, *Siyasal Anılar* (Istanbul: Türkiye İş Bankası Kültür Yayınları, 1976).

—— *Tanıdıklarım* (Istanbul: Yapı Kredi, 2002).

Yalçın, Kemal, *Sarı Gelin: Sari Gyalin* (Köln: n.p., 2004).

—— *Seninle güler yüreğim* (Bochum: CIP, 2003).

Yaman, Kadri, *Yurt Müdafaasında Türk Gençliği* (Istanbul: Devlet Basımevi, 1938).

Yapıcı, Süleyman, *Palu: Tarih-Kültür-İdari ve Sosyal Yapı* (Elazığ: Şark Pazarlama, 2002).

Yasa, İbrahim, *Hasanoğlan: Socio-Economic Structure of a Turkish Village* (Ankara: Türkiye ve Orta Doğu Amme İdaresi Enstitüsü, 1957).

Yaşın, Abdullah, *Bütün yönleriyle Cizre* (Cizre: n.p., 1983).

Yeğen, Mesut, *Devlet Söyleminde Kürt Sorunu* (Istanbul: İletişim, 2003).

Yeşil, Sevim, 'Unfolding Republican Patriarchy: The Case of Young Kurdish Women at the Girls' Vocational Boarding School in Elazığ' (unpublished MA thesis, Middle East Technic University, Department of Gender and Women's Studies, 2003).

Yeşilkaya, Neşe G., *Halkevleri: İdeoloji ve Mimarlık* (Istanbul: İletişim, 1999).

Yıldırım, Hüsamettin, *Rus-Türk-Ermeni Münasebetleri (1914–1918)* (Ankara: KÖK, 1990).

Yıldız, Ahmet, *Ne Mutlu Türküm Diyebilene: Türk Ulusal Kimliğinin Etno-Seküler Sınırları (1919–1938)* (Istanbul: İletişim, 2001).

Yılmazçelik, İbrahim, *XIX. Yüzyılın İlk Yarısında Diyarbakır* (Ankara: Türk Tarih Kurumu, 1995).

Yonov, Momchil, 'Bulgarian Military Operations in the Balkan Wars', in: Béla K. Király and Dimitrije Djordjevic (eds.), *East Central European society and the Balkan wars* (Boulder, CO: Social Science Monographs, 1987), 63–84.

Yücel, Hasan Ali, *Milli Eğitimle İlgili Söylev ve Demeçler* (Ankara: T.C. Kültür Bakanlığı Yayınları, 1993).

—— *Türkiye'de Orta Öğretim* (Ankara: T.C. Kültür Bakanlığı Yayınları, 1994).

Zarkovic Bookman, Milica, *The Demographic Struggle for Power: The Political Economy of Demographic Engineering in the Modern World* (London: Frank Cass, 1997).

Zeki, Mehmed E., *Kürdistan Tarihi* (Istanbul: Komal, 1977).

Zeydanlıoğlu, Welat, 'Kemalism's Others: The Reproduction of Orientalism in Turkey' (unpublished Ph.D. thesis, Anglia Ruskin University, 2007).

Zeyrek, Şerafettin, 'Türkiye'de Köy Adlarını Değiştirme Politikası', in: *Çukurova Üniversitesi Eğitim Fakültesi Dergisi* 1, no. 31 (2006), 86–95.

—— *Türkiye'de Halkevleri ve Halkodaları* (Ankara: Anı, 2006).

Zinar, Zeynelabidin, *Xwendina medresê* (Stockholm: Pencînar, 1993).

Zürcher, Erik-Jan (ed.), 'The Core Terminology of Kemalism: Mefkûre, Millî, Muasir, Medenî', in: François Georgeon (ed.), *Les mots de politique de l'Empire Ottoman a la Turquie kemaliste* (Paris: EHESS, 2000), 55–64.

—— 'The Ottoman Empire and the Armistice of Moudros', in: Hugh Cecil and Peter H. Liddle (eds.), *At the Eleventh Hour: Reflections, Hopes, and Anxieties at the Closing of the Great War, 1918* (London: Leo Cooper, 1998), 266–75.

—— 'The Ottoman Legacy of the Turkish Republic: An Attempt at a New Periodization', in: *Die Welt des Islams* 32 (1992), 237–53.

—— 'The Young Turks—Children of the Borderlands?', in: *International Journal of Turkish Studies* 9 (2003), 275–86.

—— 'Young Turks, Ottoman Muslims and Turkish Nationalists: Identity Politics 1908–1938', in: Kemal H. Karpat (ed.), *Ottoman Past and Today's Turkey* (Leiden: Brill, 2000), 150–79.

—— *Een Geschiedenis van het Moderne Turkije* (Nijmegen: Sun, 1995).

—— *Political Opposition in the Early Turkish Republic: The Progressive Republican Party, 1924–1925* (Leiden: Brill, 1991).

—— *The Unionist Factor: The Rôle of the Committee of Union and Progress in the Turkish National Movement 1905–1926* (Leiden: Brill, 1984).

—— *Turkey: A Modern History* (London: I.B. Tauris, 2004).

Zureik, Elia T., *The Palestinians in Israel: A Study in Internal Colonialism* (London: Routledge and Kegan Paul, 1979).

Zwaan, Ton, *Civilisering en Decivilisering: Studies over Staatsvorming en Geweld, Nationalisme en Vervolging* (Amsterdam: Boom, 2001).

NEWSPAPERS AND JOURNALS

Bîrnebûn
Cumhuriyet
Diyarbakır
Diyarbakır Olay
Diyarbekir
Hadisat
Hakimiyet-i Milliye
Hayat
İkdam
İleri
Jin
Karacadağ
Kürd Teavün ve Terakki Gazetesi
Millî Gazete
Milliyet
Özgür Gündem
Peyman
Resmi Gazete

Takvim-i Vekayi
Tanin
Taraf
Tasvir-i Efkâr
Türk Dili
Türk Yurdu
Ülkü
Vakit
Yeni Istanbul
Yeni Özgür Politika
Zaman

Oral history (from author's private collection)
Aslan family (Zakhuran tribe), Midyat, 28 July 2004.
Ş. family (Hani district), Diyarbekir, 15 July 2004.
Anonymous Armenian family (Lice district), Amsterdam, February 2003.
Meçin family (Silvan district), Ankara, 19 June 2004.
Temel family (Derik district), Bremen, 21 March 2002.
Meryem Krikorian (Satıköy village), Amsterdam, 16 December 2004.
M.Ş., Diyarbekir city, August 2004.
S. family, Amsterdam, 15–16 October 2005.
D.E. (Piran/Dicle district), Amsterdam, May 2005.
A.T., Diyarbekir, July 2004.
Kenan Y., Berlin, 14 January 2005.
Amed Tîgrîs, Stockholm, 12 and 18 May 2005.
Yolcu T., Diyarbekir, 2 July 2005.
Azizoğlu family, Stockholm, 11 June 2005, and Amsterdam, 20 October 2007.
Kerim B. Diyarbekir, 14 August 2007.
A.S., Diyarbekir, 15 August 2007.
Dikran E., Hilversum (the Netherlands), 29 May 2005.
M.Ü., Istanbul, 19 June 2004.
Şemsiye Gezici, Bursa, 15 June 2002.
Fatma Demir (1925–2007), Istanbul, 10 June 2002.

Other interviews
Interview with Antanik Baloian, unpublished manuscript titled 'Antanik Baloian's Story',
by Nelson Baloian.
Interview with Noyemzar Khimatian-Alexanian, by Linda J. P. Mahdesian.
Interview with Katherine Magarian, as 'Voices of New England: Katherine Magarian', in:
Boston Globe, 19 April 1998, B10.
Interview with Margaret Garabedian DerManuelian, by George Aghjayan in Providence,
RI, February 1990.
Interview with Seyidxan Boyacı by Emrah Kanısıcak in the summer of 2007, available at:
<http://sazny.blogspot.com/2008/05/nightingale-of-amed-new-edit.html>.

Index

Printed in the USA/Agawam, MA
August 5, 2020

759308.031